# Sustainable Economic Development and the European Green Deal

Costinela Fortea

# Sustainable Economic Development and the European Green Deal

## Creating Energy Efficiency, Industrial Innovation, and Inclusive Growth

palgrave
macmillan

Costinela Fortea
Business Administration
University Dunarea de Jos of Galati
Galati, Romania

ISBN 978-3-032-10325-3 ISBN 978-3-032-10326-0 (eBook)
https://doi.org/10.1007/978-3-032-10326-0



This Palgrave Macmillan imprint is published by the registered company Springer Nature Switzerland AG.
The registered company address is: Gewerbestrasse 11, 6330 Cham, Switzerland

# Preface

The present volume was born out of the conviction that sustainable development represents not only a global imperative, but also a scientific and political challenge of unprecedented complexity. The contemporary world is experiencing profound transformations, driven by the dual pressures of climate change and technological innovation, while being simultaneously marked by recurrent crises of an economic, social and geopolitical nature. Against this background, the question of how societies can secure economic growth while preserving natural resources and ensuring social equity has become one of the most pressing of our time.

The European Green Deal and the 2030 Agenda for Sustainable Development have established ambitious goals and benchmarks that reconfigure the logic of economic policy. Clean energy, decent work and resilient industrial systems emerge not as isolated objectives, but as deeply interconnected pillars of a broader architecture of sustainability. This book is situated at the intersection of these three essential dimensions—energy, economy and industry—seeking to provide both theoretical grounding and empirical evidence capable of supporting coherent policies at national and European levels.

The originality of this work lies in its integrative perspective: it combines conceptual clarifications with advanced econometric modelling and comparative efficiency analysis, applied systematically to the case of Romania in relation to the EU. By moving from the global and theoretical frameworks to sectoral analyses, from statistical indicators to regression and panel data models, and from diagnostics to policy recommendations, the volume aspires to offer not only a descriptive assessment but also prescriptive insights for decision-makers.

Equally important, the book addresses a dual readership. For scholars, it provides a comprehensive analytical framework, synthesizing international literature and proposing new models of sustainability. For policymakers and practitioners, it offers concrete strategies, grounded in empirical evidence, that may guide the transition towards a greener, more inclusive and more resilient economy.

The structure of the volume reflects this dual ambition. The first chapters revisit the global foundations of sustainable development and critically synthesize the main economic models addressing energy, labour and industry. The subsequent sections apply this knowledge to the European and Romanian contexts, modelling energy sustainability (Chaps. 3–7), economic sustainability through the lens of growth and decent work (Chaps. 8–12), and industrial sustainability with a focus on innovation and infrastructure (Chaps. 13–17). Each part concludes with policy-oriented solutions, thus closing the circle between theory, evidence and practice.

Ultimately, this book is not only an academic contribution but also a call to action. Sustainable development requires coherent strategies, continuous monitoring, and the courage to align short-term policies with long-term visions. By integrating conceptual analysis, empirical modelling and strategic recommendations, the volume seeks to illuminate possible pathways for Romania and the EU in their pursuit of a sustainable and equitable future.

Galati, Romania — Costinela Fortea

# Contents

# About the Author

**Costinela Fortea** has a PhD in Economics and is an assistant teacher in the Department of Business Administration of the Dunărea de Jos University of Galati, Romania. She is a member of prestigious academic organizations such as the European Regional Science Association and the Regional Science Association International. Subjects taught include economics, private finance and public finance. She obtained both a bachelor's degree and a master's degree, both in Finance, at the Faculty of Economics and Business Administration of the Dunărea de Jos University of Galati.

She is an author with an extensive portfolio of papers published in internationally recognized journals. Her works address topical issues such as energy economics, economic development, taxation, public finance, financial and economic analysis, and environmental economics, contributing to the understanding of the economic and financial mechanisms that influence both national developments and international economic dynamics. She also frequently participates in international conferences and is involved in interdisciplinary research projects, both national and international.

She successfully combines academic research, teaching activity and active participation in interdisciplinary projects and international collaborations, contributing to the development of knowledge in the fields of energy economics, taxation, sustainable economic development and financial analysis. Her professional profiles on the ResearchGate, ORCID (https://orcid.org/0000-0003-1482-8450) and Google Scholar (https://scholar.google.ro/citations?user=-nEtvw0AAAAJ&hl=ro&oi=ao) platforms provide details of her scholarly activity and relevant contributions.

# List of Figures

# List of Tables

# Introduction

In recent decades, debates on sustainable development have become a central feature of the international academic, political and economic agenda, shaping a normative and analytical framework aimed at harmonizing economic progress with social equity and environmental protection. The United Nations 2030 Agenda and the European Green Deal are fundamental milestones in this direction, providing a set of integrated goals through which the world's states are called upon to ensure the transition to a sustainable growth model. However, the implementation of these goals at the national and regional levels reveals a variety of structural challenges, generated both by differences in institutional and economic capacity and by the multiple pressures associated with climate change, health crises and geopolitical tensions.

The novelty of this work lies in its integrated approach to the trinity of clean energy, decent work and economic growth, and industry, innovation and infrastructure, as reflected in Sustainable Development Goals 7, 8 and 9. Through this perspective, the book proposes a complex methodological framework for analysis, combining established theoretical models with advanced empirical tools (linear regressions, panel data models, DEA efficiency analysis) to quantify Romania's performance in the European context and identify optimal strategies for sustainable transition. This methodological option contributes to the literature by articulating functional models of energy, economic and industrial sustainability, capable of capturing both the quantitative dimensions of the phenomenon and its strategic implications for public policy.

The motivation for this chapter stems from the urgent need to respond to major dilemmas: how can an emerging economy such as Romania's accelerate its convergence with mature European economies while maintaining a balance between competitiveness, social inclusion and the protection of natural resources? In addition, the current context—marked by the European energy crisis, the impact of the pandemic and the destabilizing effects of armed conflicts—highlights the relevance of a multidimensional analysis that provides practical answers and scientific foundations for decision-makers.

The overall aim of the book is to build a solid analytical framework for assessing Romania's sustainable economic development in relation to the EU Member States, through the lens of the integration of SDGs 7, 8 and 9, and to design public policy solutions tailored to national specificities and the requirements of the European green transition. In this regard, the research aims not only to take stock of existing progress and gaps but also to provide operational tools for shaping coherent and feasible sustainable development strategies.

In particular, the chapter addresses research objectives structured on three fundamental levels. The first level focuses on clean and affordable energy (SDG7), including the identification of sustainable development stages (O1), the analysis of theoretical models in the literature (O2), evaluating Romania's performance using specific indicators (O3), constructing regression and panel data models to determine energy sustainability (O4–O5), analysing efficiency through DEA (O6), formulating the energy sustainability function (O7) and designing policies and strategies adapted to the Romanian context (O8–O9). The second level is dedicated to economic growth and decent work (SDG8), through the estimation of econometric sustainability models (O10–O12), comparative analysis of Romania's efficiency (O13), definition of the economic sustainability function (O14) and formulation of sustainable economic policies and strategies (O15–O16). The third level investigates industry, innovation and infrastructure (SDG9) by applying linear and panel data models to research and development expenditure (O17–O19), comparing Romania's industrial efficiency with that of Europe (O20), defining the industrial sustainability function (O21) and developing policies and strategies to strengthen industrial sustainability (O22–O23).

Overall, the book is part of an academic and practical effort to provide an analytical map of sustainability in the economy, capitalizing on the convergence between theory, methodology and policy practice. Thus, its main contribution lies in demonstrating that sustainability should not be seen merely as a normative requirement imposed by international bodies, but as a sine qua non condition for long-term economic and social resilience.

The book begins with an introductory section, in which Chap. 1 outlines the theoretical and normative framework for sustainable development. The focus is on the conceptual definition of sustainability and how the Sustainable Development Goals shape public policies and economic strategies at the global level. This section establishes the intellectual infrastructure necessary for the subsequent approach, discussing the difficult balance between economic growth, social equity and environmental protection, as well as the mechanisms for monitoring and standardizing progress. Complementing this, Chap. 2 brings to the fore a critical analysis of existing economic models, providing an overview of the methodological tools applied in the fields of clean energy, decent work and innovative industry. Convergences but also fragmentation in the literature are observed here, identified through meta-analyses and syntheses that justify the need for more refined empirical constructs tailored to the specific European and Romanian context.

On this basis, the book enters the applied dimension of sustainable energy. Chapters 3–7 are dedicated to SDG7 and offer a gradual transition from strategies and indicators (Chap. 3) to econometric constructions (Chap. 4), panel models (Chap. 5), then to comparative efficiency analyses using DEA (Chap. 6) and, finally, to public policy recommendations (Chap. 7). This sequence is not random: first, the empirical and institutional benchmarks of the energy transition are established, then models are calibrated to measure the causal relationships between energy policies and economic and environmental performance, so that the results can ultimately be translated into a set of strategic solutions. This first empirical part demonstrates that the energy transition is not just a technical issue, but a systemic process that requires coherent policies, sustained investment and the correction of regional asymmetries.

The second major section, devoted to SDG8, is covered in Chaps. 8–12 and addresses the complexity of the relationship between economic growth and decent work. The analysis begins with an assessment of economic and labour market strategies and indicators, with a focus on digitalization, job quality and labour mobility. Subsequently, the statistical and econometric models in Chaps. 9 and 10 highlight the drivers of economic resilience, threshold effects and the mechanisms through which employment policies influence long-term sustainability. This approach is reinforced by efficiency comparisons (Chap. 11), where Romania is compared to other EU Member States, highlighting both strengths and structural vulnerabilities. The section concludes with the formulation of applicable solutions (Chap. 12), which aim to reduce territorial and wage disparities, increase the quality of human capital and adapt the labour market to new technological requirements. Overall, the analysis of this thematic block highlights the interdependence between economic and social sustainability, showing that inclusion and equity in the labour market are sine qua non conditions for genuine sustainable development.

The last empirical section of the volume is devoted to SDG9 and is covered in Chaps. 13–17. Here, industrial and infrastructure development strategies are explored in the context of the green transition and digitalization. Chapter 13 provides the strategic framework, while Chap. 14 introduces economic models that measure the impact of infrastructure and innovation on economic and environmental performance. An important step is taken in Chap. 15, where research and development expenditure is analysed using a panel model, highlighting its contribution to industrial sustainability. The comparative DEA assessment in Chap. 16 highlights the relative efficiency of Romanian and European industrial sectors, and Chap. 17 proposes concrete directions for strengthening industrial resilience and harmonizing economic and environmental objectives. This part of the chapter emphasizes that innovation and infrastructure are not only drivers of economic competitiveness but also essential elements for an industrial transition compatible with climate and social imperatives.

The entire book concludes with a section of conclusions that integrates the results of the three dimensions—energy, economy and industry—into a coherent framework of sustainability functions and strategies.

CHAPTER 1

# Approaches to Sustainable Development Through the Lens of Specific Global Goals

## Introduction

Sustainable development is a theoretical framework used in practice to ensure that people's needs can be met without limiting future populations' access to resources (United Nations, 1987). Thus, sustainable development, by means of 17 indicators, addresses the major problems facing today's society. The crisis situations are based on the trend of depletion of natural resources, deterioration and pollution of environmental factors and damage to life support systems (Rendtorff, 2019). Currently, all these factors have been compounded by the frequency of climate change and the outbreak of multiple military conflicts across the globe, the economic crisis and the health crisis. This complex of uncertainties has forced the signatory states of the 2015 Paris Agreement on climate change to adopt measures to alleviate social pressures, moving them away from the goals set out in the 2030 Agenda for Sustainable Development. Under these circumstances, a reorientation towards sustainable development principles (social inclusion, clean energy, responsible consumption, guaranteed access to public services) is needed in order to ensure economic progress on a sustainable basis (Dousa, 2019).

In the current context, global society is facing multiple crises that threaten economic sustainability as well as social and ecological balance. Among the most pressing problems are environmental degradation, excessive pollution, climate change, unsustainable economic growth and social



C. Fortea, *Sustainable Economic Development and the European Green Deal*, https://doi.org/10.1007/978-3-032-10326-0_1

inequalities. According to research, (Hu et al., 2024; Xu & Zhao, 2023) the negative effects of these phenomena are exacerbated by the accelerating depletion of natural resources, leading to the destabilization of ecosystems and a reduction in their ability to sustain life. A key factor in the intensification of these crises is climate change, mainly driven by human activities which increase greenhouse gas emissions. Rising global temperatures, extreme weather events and rising sea and ocean levels are just some of the immediate consequences of global warming. These impacts are strongly felt in sectors of the economy such as agriculture, industry and urban infrastructure, creating additional challenges in achieving the Sustainable Development Goals (Adom, 2024). In addition to environmental issues, the global geopolitical context has deteriorated in recent years, marked by outbreaks of military conflicts and major humanitarian crises (Hook & Marcantonio, 2023). Wars and political instability are causing massive migration, destabilizing local economies and aggravating social inequalities. At the same time, recent economic and health crises, such as the COVID-19 pandemic, have highlighted the structural vulnerabilities of global economies, putting additional pressure on countries in their efforts to maintain a trajectory towards sustainability (Bhattacharya & Bose, 2023).

An important role in this process is played by technological innovation and digitalization, which can facilitate the transition to a more efficient and greener economic model. For example, the use of artificial intelligence and green technologies can help optimize energy consumption and reduce industrial pollution. International cooperation is also essential to implement effective solutions globally, through the exchange of best practices and the creation of strategic partnerships between states, international organizations and the private sector.

## Main Directions for Sustainable Development as Reflected in the Sustainable Development Strategy

The Sustainable Development Strategy, as presented in the OECD Newsletter, is based on the principles of harmonious economic development, integrating social, environmental and economic aspects with the judicious use of natural capital elements (OECD, 2001). According to the World Commission on Environment and Development, the Brundtland

Report defined sustainable development as "development that meets the needs of the present without compromising the ability of future generations to meet their own needs" (United Nations, 1987). According to the report, there is an accumulation of global threats to population growth, particularly in geo-climatically affected countries where environmental management is poor, with high infant mortality rates due to hunger and large disparities between rich and poor populations. At the same time, environmental challenges after Underdal A. (Underdal, 2010) tend to affect the planet in the long term, as every year we face the desertification of productive areas, an aspect also observed in Romania, in the Bărăgan Plain (Vrînceanu et al., 2012). Forest destruction due to vegetation fires, according to the authors Dale V.H. and others, contributes to climate damage (Dale et al., 2001), and extreme weather events also affect agricultural production with an impact on food security, as shown in the 2016 Food and Agriculture Organization of the United Nations report (Gitz et al., 2016). Other issues raised in the Brundtland Report include the increase in greenhouse effects as carbon dioxide is released into the atmosphere with impacts on rising sea and ocean levels that can lead to catastrophic flooding of coastal areas and short-circuiting of national economies in the coastal zone.

These concerns have generated active measures in the field of sustainable development, which have been adopted by the United Nations institution, at a global level on the basis of successive agendas for sustainable development; thus in 1992 at the "Earth Summit" held in Rio de Janeiro, several treaties and conventions were adopted by the 170 participating states, which aimed to reduce methane and carbon dioxide emissions to prevent climate change (European Parliament, 2011), species conservation to protect biological diversity and stop massive deforestation (Najam, 2005). On this occasion, a plan to support sustainable development called Agenda 21 was launched (Dahl, 2014).

In 2002, a Sustainable Development Summit was held in Johannesburg, focusing on building partnerships for the implementation of the Millennium Development Goals (MDGs) (Najam, 2005). Following the Summit, all 193 UN (United Nations) Member States committed themselves to implement by 2015 measures to achieve the 8 MDG goals: eradicate poverty and hunger in the world; promote universal primary education; promote gender equality and empower women; reduce child mortality; reduce maternal mortality; combat diseases such as HIV, AIDS, malaria, etc.; ensure environmental sustainability; and develop a global partnership for sustainable development. A global stocktaking of this approach showed that the achievement of the goals has been uneven, with new commitments needed to improve social conditions for women and children and to fight poverty, hunger and disease (Ki-moon & Secretary-General, 2015).

In 2012, 20 years after the Rio de Janeiro Conference, the "United Nations Conference on Sustainable Development" was held to reconcile the Sustainable Development Goals. The conference took place in Rio de Janeiro and was attended by all UN Member States and had a global impact, bringing to public attention the need to integrate economic and environmental development, raising urgent issues of environmental protection and sound socio-economic development. The conference established the Global Green Agenda and the Climate Change Agreement was signed (European Commission, 2019).

In 2015, the United Nations General Assembly set 17 Sustainable Development Goals (SDGs) as a blueprint for achieving a "sustainable future for all", which are included in the UN resolution called Agenda 2030 (Yigit, 2021).

## Objectives on Sustainable Improvement of Quality of Life from an Economic Perspective

Sustainable Development Goal 1 (SDG1)—end poverty in all its forms everywhere—is a global United Nations commitment to eradicate poverty in all its forms by 2030. This goal aims to ensure access to basic resources, including food, drinking water, health services and education, for all people, regardless of where they live or their social status. By implementing this goal, communities around the world could enjoy a more equitable and prosperous life. This goal is an essential pillar of the United Nations Sustainable Development Agenda, recognizing that poverty is one of the greatest challenges of the modern world. By eradicating poverty, it creates an enabling environment for sustainable development, in which everyone can reach his or her full potential and contribute to the collective prosperity of society.

With regard to Sustainable Development Goal 1, the sustainable development targets are based on the premise that most of the world's people live below the poverty line, i.e. 85% of the world's population has an average daily basket of less than $30, of which 66% have a basket of less than $10 a day and 10% have a basket of $2.15 a day (Roser & Esteban, 2022).

In this context, the international extreme poverty line is low, limited to 10% of the global population. The main indicator that measures poverty is the level of consumption and monetized income, so people at high risk of poverty face hunger, lack of access to education, poor health and lack of access to lighting at night (Moatsos & Lazopoulos, 2021). In these circumstances, improving overall health and education become poverty eradication goals. Under the goals of the 2030 Agenda eradicating extreme poverty means increasing the middle class and overall well-being of the population (United Nations, 2015). Compared to the targets proposed at previous Summits, the 2030 Agenda is expected to reduce the number of people living in extreme poverty from 730 million in 2015 to 500 million by 2030. According to Fig. 1.1, the most affected areas of the world in terms of extreme poverty are currently in Sub-Saharan Africa, North Africa and South Asia (Olaoye et al., 2021). These targets require Sub-Saharan Africa and North Africa to develop economically, just as the economies of China and India have developed in the past and contributed to reducing global inequality, for East Asia (1990) and South Asia (2000) (Roser & Esteban, 2022).

Sustainable Development Goal 2 (SDG2)—eradicate hunger—aims to ensure food security (Arora & Mishra, 2022; Yang et al., 2020) and the promotion of balanced nutrition, against the background of sustainable

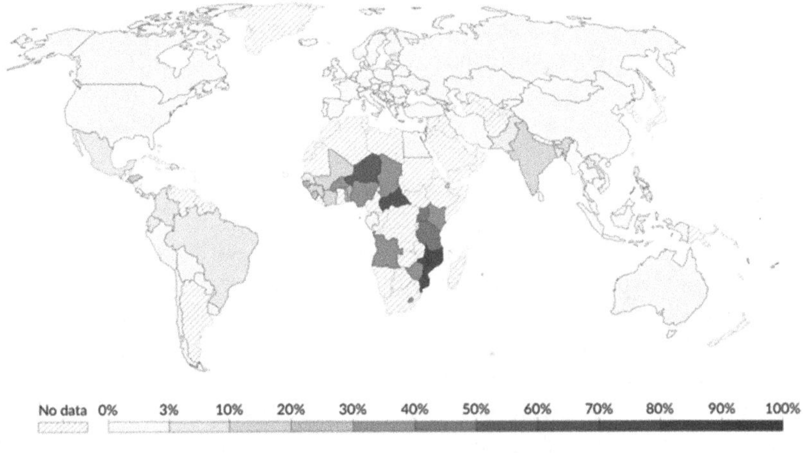


**Fig. 1.1** Share of population below the extreme poverty line in 2022. Source: Our World in Data (Our World in Data team, 2023d)

farm improvement (El Bilali et al., 2021; Knez et al., 2024). Although significant progress has been made in eradicating malnutrition in the wake of climate shocks, locust crisis, or pandemics, population vulnerability has increased and the issue of food accessibility for the entire global population has been brought back into question (Mason-D'Croz et al., 2019; United Nations, 2024). Thus, the UN's goal to stop undernutrition is linked to rethinking food consumption (Hansen et al., 2022). This objective aims both to reduce the number of undernourished people and to promote sustainable and environmentally friendly food production. The implementation of this objective aims to increase global food security and reduce inequalities in access to quality food. It is also important to take climate change and natural resource protection issues into account in the development of sustainable agriculture (A. Saleem et al., 2024).

According to the report by Our World in Data team (2023c), the majority of the undernourished population is found in countries in Saharan Africa (Democratic Republic of Congo, Chad, Somalia, Madagascar) but also in Asia (North Korea) and the Middle East (Iraq, Yemen, Afghanistan). Other countries with a prevalence of undernourished population are found in South America (Venezuela, Ecuador and Bolivia), Central America (Honduras, Belize, Mexico, Nicaragua), or Oceania, Papua New Guinea, Indonesia, Philippines (Fig. 1.2). In terms of food security, the most affected countries are in Africa (Niger, Sierra Leone, Cameroon, Egypt, Kenya, Tanzania, Ghana, Mozambique, South Africa and Namibia), Oceania (Philippines), Central America (Honduras and Mexico), Asia (Cambodia, Mongolia, Afghanistan, Bangladesh, Tajikistan).

Under Goal 2 as a sustainable development target, the United Nations has proposed doubling small producers' productivity and incomes. For this target, indicators have been set for monitoring the volume of production and income of the agricultural factor (Hansen et al., 2022; Maheshwari et al., 2024).

Sustainable Development Goal 3 (SDG3)—health and well-being—starts from the premise of the need to increase life expectancy and reduce child and maternal ***mortality*** (F. R. da Silva et al., 2024; González-Pier et al., 2016). Access to water is therefore essential to reduce infectious diseases such as tuberculosis, malaria, polio and HIV/AIDS. This objective aims to ensure a healthy life and promote well-being for all people, regardless of age or social status. Achieving this goal requires strengthening health systems, improving access to quality health services and promoting healthy lifestyles among the population (World Health

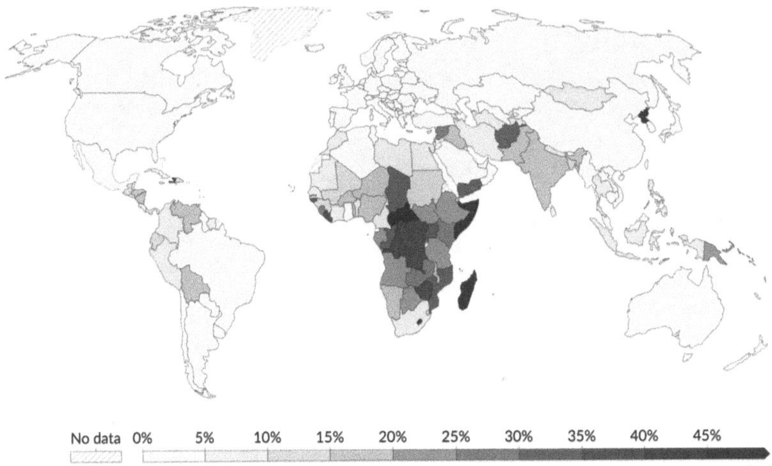


**Fig. 1.2** Share of undernourished population in total global population in 2021. Source: Our World in Data (Our World in Data team, 2023c)

Organization, 2024). It is also important to pay more attention to disease prevention, educating people about good hygiene and healthy nutrition and combating inequalities in access to health services (Chamut et al., 2024).

At a global level, maternal mortality rates, i.e. the number of women dying as a result of pregnancy, is a problem, particularly for countries in Central Saharan Africa and the Middle East. Although considerable progress has been made since 2000 in countries such as Sierra Leone, Eritrea, Guinea-Bissau, Ethiopia or Burundi, there were still at least three countries in the world in 2017 (South Sudan, Chad and Sierra Leone) with a maternal mortality rate of over 1000 women per 100,000 live births (Ritchie & Mispy, 2022). This comes amid a shortage of trained personnel to assist women during pregnancy, labour and the post-partum period, with the biggest problems in Somalia, South Sudan, Chad, Ethiopia and Eritrea.

According to the report (Our World in Data team, 2023g) infant mortality rate for children under 5 years of age is decreasing, with the highest number of such incidents in 2021 in Central Saharan Africa (countries such as Nigeria, Chad, Somalia, Central African Republic, Sierra Leone) as shown in Fig. 1.3. In these countries, the infant mortality rate exceeds 100

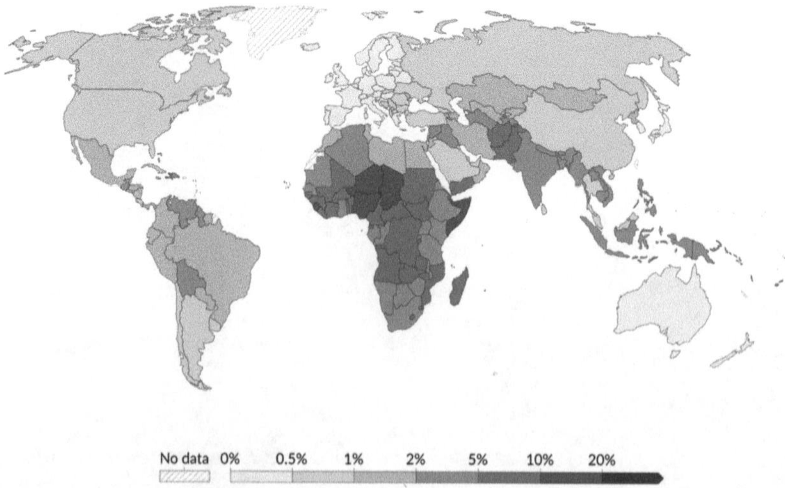


**Fig. 1.3** Global child mortality rate in 2021. Source: Our World in Data (Our World in Data team, 2023g)

per 1000 live births (Micah et al., 2020). In countries such as the above, the neonatal mortality rate is also high, exceeding 35 babies per 1000 live births, joined by countries such as Lesotho and Pakistan with neonatal mortality rates of over 400 babies per 1000 live births.

Other issues contributing to the challenges of ensuring healthy lives are the incidence of infectious diseases: HIV infections above 1 per 1000 people in Africa; tuberculosis above 100 per 100,000 people in Africa, South-East Asia, South America and Antarctica; malaria above 100 per 1000 people in Africa and Oceania; hepatitis B above 2.5% per 100,000 people (proportion of children with active infection) in Africa and the Middle East (Ritchie & Mispy, 2022). Mortality rates attributed to chronic diseases above 25% in Africa, Middle East and Mongolia; above 20% in Asia and Oceania; and above 15% in South and Central America. Mortality attributed to air pollution (Halkos & Argyropoulou, 2022) in 2021 is over 250 people per 100,000 inhabitants in Africa and the Middle East and over 50 people per 100,000 inhabitants in Asia, Oceania and South America.

## Sustainable Economic and Technological Development Objectives

Sustainable Development Goal 8 (SDG8)—decent work and growth—promotes inclusive and sustainable growth and decent work for all (Hendriks & Babu, 2024; Rai et al., 2019), given that about half of the world's population still lives on about $2 a day (Our World in Data team, 2023n). Unequal access to decent work fosters poverty, which is a target of economic policies to remedy and guarantee welfare for all (Coulibaly & Yogo, 2020).

This goal is a global commitment to promote fair, safe and decent work opportunities for all workers, regardless of gender, age or socio-economic status (Hughes & Eduarda-Duarte, 2024). It also implies the promotion of sustainable and inclusive economic growth that provides stable and well-paid jobs, thus contributing to the reduction of poverty and social inequality. By achieving this goal, communities can benefit from higher living standards and economies can become more competitive and more resilient to global change (Anukwonke et al., 2022). Promoting decent work and sustainable economic growth can also help improve the quality of life for all members of a society.

For the development of economic policies, for Sustainable Development Goal 8, the most important achievements are in terms of increasing Gross Domestic Product per capita (Rai et al., 2019). At the global level, the growth rate of GDP per capita has been directly influenced by economic crises, so that in 1989 global society was predominant, with the exception of some countries in South America and the Middle East, and some countries in Africa, in the economic boom period, with the global economy growing at an average rate of 3–5% per year, as shown in Fig. 1.4.

This led to a deep crisis with negative growth in the former communist bloc countries of up to −12.16% in the case of Romania, −7.37% in the case of Poland and −7.53% in Bulgaria (Our World in Data team, 2023n). The situation is shown in Fig. 1.5.

In 1994, another crisis hit Mexico's economy, which suffered a 7.83% downturn, after the Mexican economy had previously experienced a period of accelerated growth with controlled exchange rate stabilization (Sosa & Ortiz, 2015). The change of President Carlos Salinari de Gortarie brought a change in monetary policy, with the exchange rate allowed to fluctuate freely and the national currency devalued by 80% against the dollar in just one week. These elements of monetary policy reflect the vulnerability of

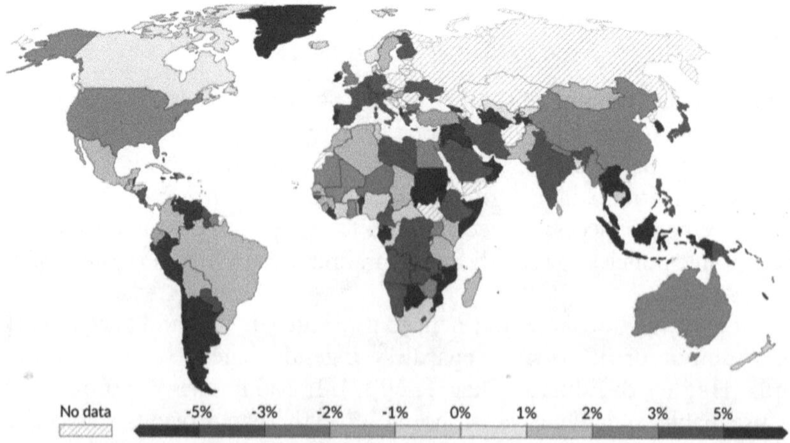


**Fig. 1.4** GDP per capita growth at global level in 1989. Source: Our World in Data (Our World in Data team, 2023n)

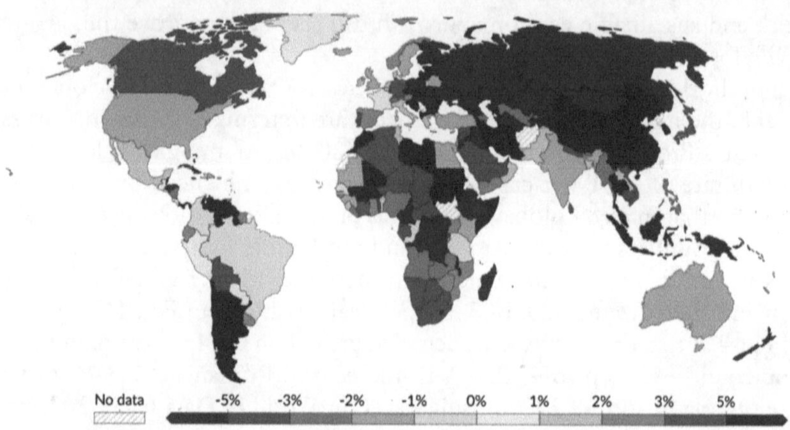


**Fig. 1.5** GDP per capita growth at global level in 1991. Source: Our World in Data (Our World in Data team, 2023n)

an economy in a financial boom, which according to crisis theory accumulates volatility risk with repercussions on medium-term sustainable development. Most affected monetary policy indicator (Mann et al., 2004) being the balance of payments and the budget deficit (Fig. 1.6).

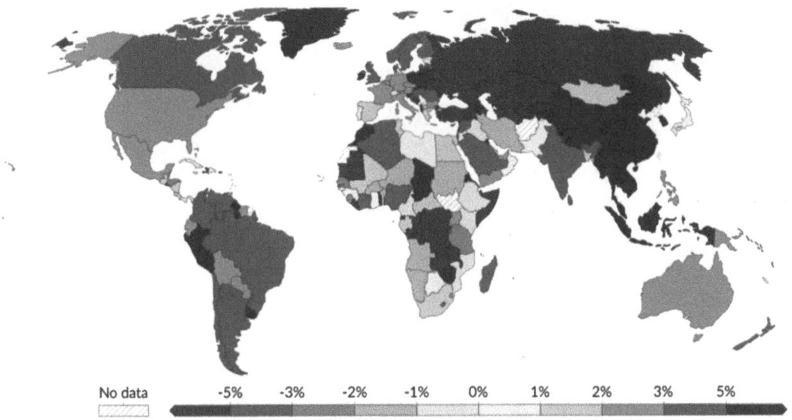


**Fig. 1.6** GDP per capita growth at global level in 1994. Source: Our World in Data (Our World in Data team, 2023n)

The year 1998 brings another major crisis to the fore—the Russian financial crisis (K. Saleem, 2009) (Fig. 1.7). Russia, as an exporting country, felt the effect of falling prices and went into default. The Russian government experienced a period of severe financial instability when the cost of borrowing to finance the budget deficit through bonds reached extremely high levels (Akata, 2023). This crisis highlighted the importance of macroeconomic stability, prudent fiscal policy and structural reforms in maintaining investor confidence and financial stability in a globalized economy.

Since the year 2000, the global economy has entered a period of recovery and rebalancing, with significant growth, particularly in Asia and South America, where economic growth has been above 10% per year (Onishi, 1986) (China 13.64% in 2007, Russia 8.7% in 2007, Kazakhstan 9.54% in 2006, Mongolia 7.18% in 2006, etc.). In 2008, economic growth slowed down, with China and Mongolia remaining economies growing at around 10% per year, joined by Romania with 11.14% growth per year (Ritchie & Mispy, 2022) (the largest in Europe) as shown in Fig. 1.8.

The financial crisis in America was triggered by the collapse of Lehman Brothers in 2009 (Beccar-Varela et al., 2017). The crisis spread rapidly to Europe and then globally, affecting mainly the economies of Europe, Mexico, Argentina, Argentina, Russia, Japan and some African countries.

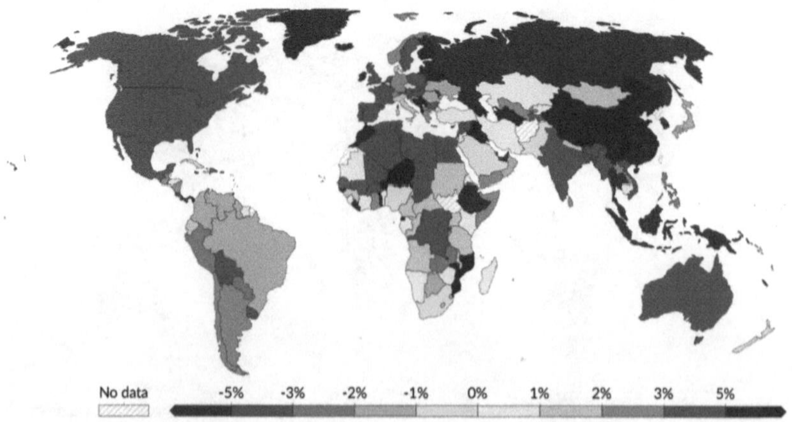


**Fig. 1.7** GDP per capita growth at global level in 1998. Source: Our World in Data (Our World in Data team, 2023n)

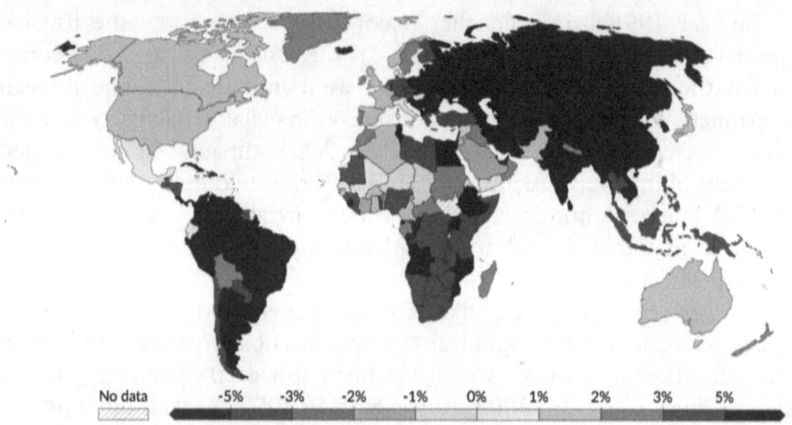


**Fig. 1.8** GDP per capita growth at global level in 2007. Source: Our World in Data (Our World in Data team, 2023n)

During this period (2009), China's economy remains on an upward trend with a growth of 8.86%. This (2009 crisis) has highlighted the vulnerability of the global economy's dependence on the US dollar and fossil fuel-based energy sources (Ma et al., 2023). The crisis resulted in a paradigm shift and a global orientation towards the green economy in the economic recovery that followed (Fig. 1.9).

After a period of about 5 years, during which the economy recovered from the economic crisis of 2009, in 2015 Russia is once again going through a period of financial crisis amid the volatility of the national currency and the lack of investor confidence in the Russian economy (Rodionov et al., 2015). This crisis emerged due to a significant decline in oil prices compared to 2014 and the international economic sanctions imposed on Russia following the conflict with Ukraine, which resulted in the annexation of Crimea. During this period, the Russian stock market experienced a substantial downturn, reflected in a sharp drop in the RTS index, a free-float capitalization-weighted index of major Russian stocks traded on the Moscow Exchange and calculated in US dollars (Garicano et al., 2022).

After 2015, the global economy recovered for the most part, with the exception of African countries that experienced economic downturns (Chad −5.93%, Yemen −7.35%, Congo −6.81%) until the pandemic hit and the entire global economy went into economic recession (Our World in Data team, 2023n). Subsequent to the pandemic, the war in Ukraine aggravated the energy crisis in Europe, further worsening economic conditions in the EU Member States and favouring the onset of consumer price increases and inflation (Fig. 1.10).

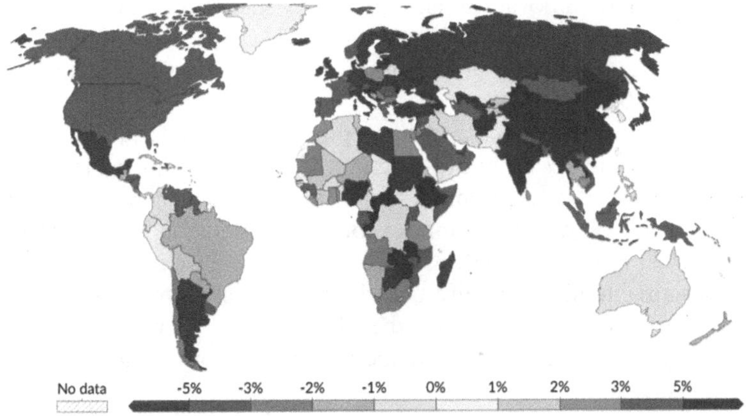


**Fig. 1.9** GDP per capita growth at global level in 2009. Source: Our World in Data (Our World in Data team, 2023n)

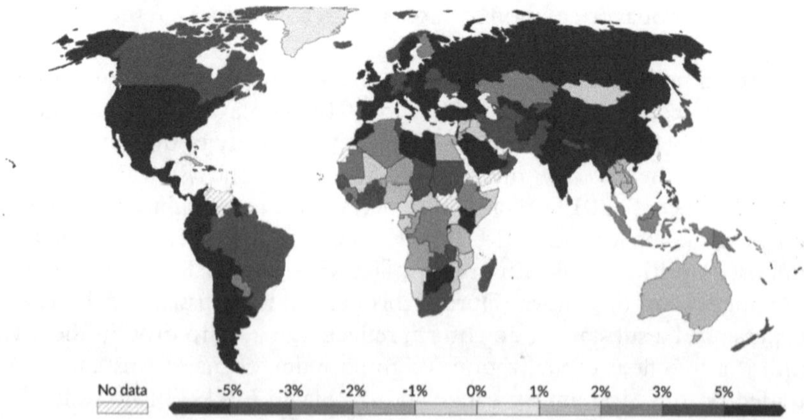


**Fig. 1.10** Global GDP per capita growth in 2021. Source: Our World in Data (Our World in Data team, 2023n)

In the context of this global picture, under the Goal on promoting growth and employment inclusion, the global economy has seen a decline in informal employment, facing rising unemployment and gender disparities, and the material footprint has seen an inflection point since 2019 due to the COVID-19 pandemic. Sustainable Development Goal 9 (SDG9)—industry, innovation and infrastructure—aims to build resilient infrastructure, stimulate innovation and promote sustainable industrialization, targeting investments in infrastructure such as transport, irrigation systems, energy industry, information and communication technology (Ulbrych, 2020).

By investing in research and development as well as facilitating access to quality technologies and infrastructure, Objective 9 aims to increase sustainable growth of economies, improve access to energy and efficient transportation and support innovation in the industrial sector (Mondejar et al., 2021). At the same time, promoting the development of modern and sustainable infrastructure contributes to making communities more resilient to climate change and other threats. Implementing this objective brings significant economic and social benefits, both locally and globally (Kufeoglu, 2022).

At the global level, passenger and freight flows follow the needs of the population and goods-producing entities and are generally quite intense with peaks of representation on developed countries. At the opposite pole are countries in Africa and Central America whose transportation flows are lower than in the rest of the world (Our World in Data team, 2023a). China leads the world together with India in the number of passengers carried by rail, and in air freight, China shares supremacy with the United States, with over 20 billion tonnes per kilometre in China and 40 billion tonnes per kilometre in the United States (Liengpunsakul, 2021).

Socially inclusive industrialization highlights that the level of value added of output to GDP is higher, above 20% in South East Asian countries (China 26.18%, Myanmar 24.76%, Thailand 25.24%) with a peak of value added of output to GDP in 2020, respectively, Puerto Rico 48.24% in 2021 (Our World in Data team, 2023a).

R&D expenditure as a share of GDP has grown steadily in recent years as shown in Fig. 1.11, reflecting the increased commitment to promoting innovation and technology. This growth has also been supported by private sector investment, which has contributed significantly to the development and deployment of new technologies.

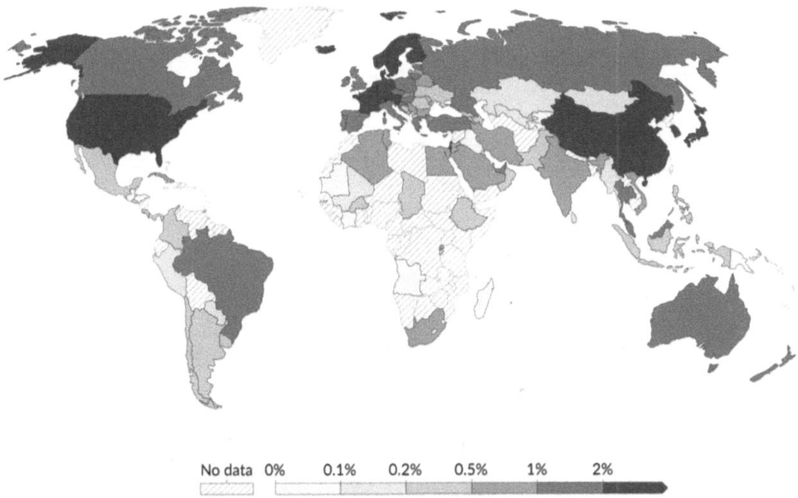


**Fig. 1.11** R&D expenditure as a share of global GDP in 2021. Source: Our World in Data (Our World in Data team, 2023a)

## Sustainable Social Development Objectives

Sustainable Development Goal 11 (SDG11)—sustainable cities and communities—aims to make cities inclusive, safe and resilient from a sustainable ***perspective*** (Yang et al., 2020) on the premise that the development and prosperity of communities must take into account the sustainable use of resources and the reduction of poverty and pollution (Hansson et al., 2019). The world's urban population is growing, but in poor areas of the world such as Africa and South Asia there are many urban agglomerations in slums, as shown in Fig. 1.12 (Abubakar & Aina, 2019).

This objective relates to inclusive and sustainable urbanization, ensuring access to safe housing and adequate services, accessible transport systems, protecting the cultural heritage of cities, reducing the negative effects of natural disasters and reducing the environmental impact of cities (Yang et al., 2020).

Sustainable Development Goal 16 (SDG16)—peace, justice and effective institutions—aims to promote just, peaceful and inclusive ***societies*** (Calvo et al., 2019). The most important measures are aimed at reducing violence, protecting children from exploitation of trafficking and influence, promoting the rule of law and access to justice, fighting organized

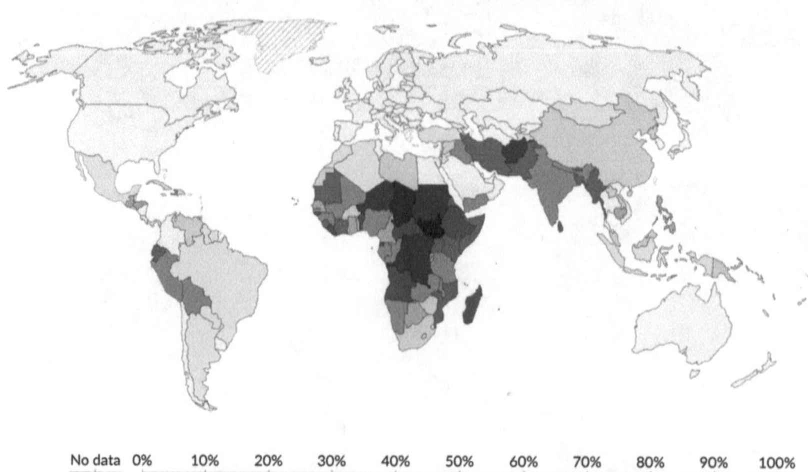


**Fig. 1.12** Population dynamics of people living in urban peripheries worldwide in 2020. Source: Our World in Data (Our World in Data team, 2023l)

crime, reducing corruption and developing effective accountable and transparent institutions (Eurostat, 2022). The situation is shown in Fig. 1.13.

Other approaches aim to ensure inclusive and responsive decision-making, strengthen participation in global governance and provide universal legal identity.

Sustainable Development Goal 17 (SDG17)—partnerships for achieving the goals—aims to revitalize inclusive global partnerships for sustainable development based on principles and values, a shared vision and common objectives such as mobilizing resources to improve revenue collection, engaging in relief and development, supporting developing countries, fostering knowledge sharing and cooperation for access to science, technology and innovation, and strengthening global macroeconomic stability (Lamichhane et al., 2021). Annual global consumer price inflation in 2021 is shown in Fig. 1.14.

The year 2021 was marked by a significant increase in global inflation, driven by multiple factors, including supply chain disruptions and energy price increases. This has put pressure on households around the world, highlighting the need for effective economic policies to manage the impact

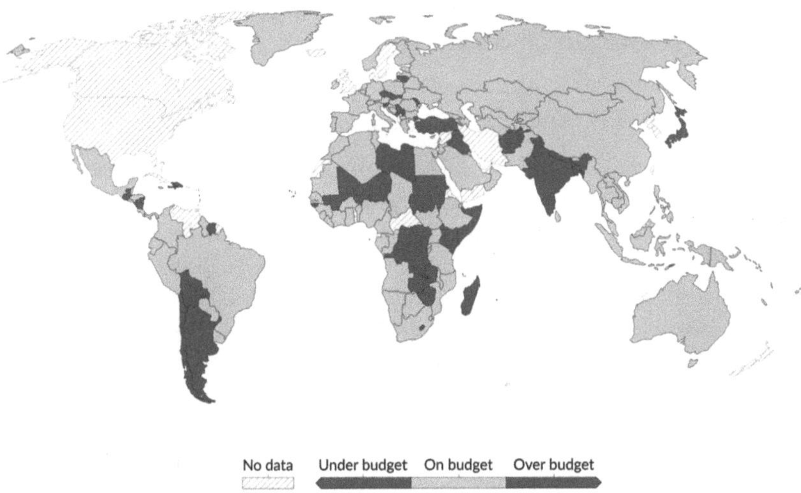


**Fig. 1.13** Share of primary government expenditure in the initial budget in 2021. Source: Our World in Data (Our World in Data team, 2023m)

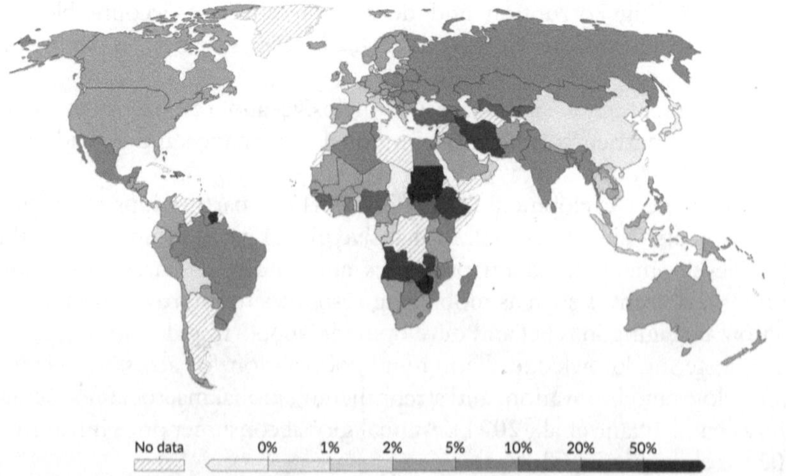


**Fig. 1.14** Annual consumer price inflation in 2021. Source: Our World in Data (Our World in Data team, 2023o)

of inflation and support economic recovery (International Monetary Fund, 2022). Goal 17 acts as a binding link for all sustainable development policies as it sets out the basic instruments for promoting sustainable development principles (Biermann et al., 2022).

## Sustainable Social Equality Objectives

Sustainable Development Goal 4 (SDG4) is quality education, under which inclusive education and lifelong learning are sought and ***promoted*** (Eurostat, 2022). To date, considerable success has been achieved in worldwide literacy and gender equality in access to primary education. While this success has been global, it is nevertheless differentiated by level of education across the globe (Heleta & Bagus, 2021). Quality education is the key to building an educated generation capable of contributing to the social and economic progress of a country. Quality education is not just a fundamental right, but an investment in a nation's future. By providing quality education, social and economic inequalities are reduced, and young people can have equal opportunities to reach their full potential (Farquharson et al., 2024). Investing in quality education is thus essential for sustainable development and building a better society for all.

According to Fig. 1.15, in Central Saharan African countries such as Morocco, Senegal, Niger etc., the share of primary school pupils does not exceed 20% of the school-age population, and for most African countries there are no school enrolment figures reported (Our World in Data team, 2023h). The same problems arise for primary school pupils achieving proficiency in mathematics or reading. In secondary education, the lowest shares in reading or mathematics are found in African and Central American countries, although many of these countries do not provide relevant statistics in this area, leading to the conclusion that the minimum share of 20% may be lower in some countries. In terms of net enrolment ratios in primary education, the lowest ratios are in Yemen, Bhutan and Chad in 2021, with less than 1.3% of children enrolled in organized learning, and low shares in all African countries, some countries in Oceania (Myanmar, Timor) or South America (Paraguay). Turkey and other Arab countries such as Kazakhstan, Jordan and Yemen are also experiencing difficulties (Our World in Data team, 2023h). Equal access to further education, as measured by gross enrolment ratios in tertiary education in 2021, is deficient (less than 10% of the population of the corresponding age

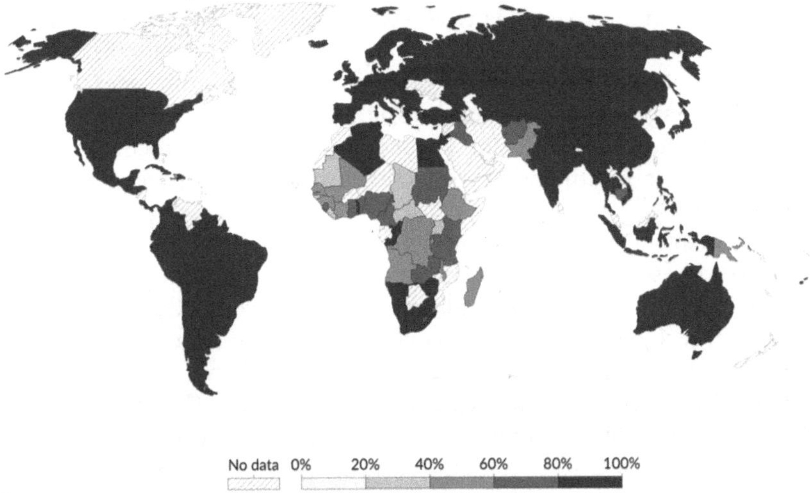


**Fig. 1.15** Share of pupils in early primary education achieving a minimum reading proficiency in 2021. Source: Our World in Data (Our World in Data team, 2023h)

group) in Central Saharan Africa and the Middle East (Afghanistan, Pakistan and Turkmenistan), but also in countries such as Malawi or Haiti. Disparities in access to education in terms of the gender parity index point to imbalances in sub-African countries (Chad, Niger, Mali, Guinea, Mali) where the value of the index is below 0.8 and indicates a disparity in favour of men. These facts show that there is still a need for action on education at the global population level, including building and modernizing schools with access to electricity, basic hand-washing facilities and drinking water, but also access to computerized information and the Internet, a major problem being access to infrastructure and materials adapted for students with disabilities (Heleta & Bagus, 2021).

Under Sustainable Development Goal 5 (SDG5)—gender equality—the elimination of discrimination against women and girls is promoted (Eurostat, 2022); there are countries in the world such as Poland, Belarus, Romania, Belgium, the United Arab Emirates, Latvia, Portugal, etc., where the non-discrimination clause does not mention gender in the Constitution and the legislation does not provide for non-discrimination on the basis of gender in employment (Our World in Data team, 2023k). Other aspects show that there is a vulnerability in countries such as India, Madagascar, Ethiopia and Nigeria in terms of gender equality in employment and economic benefits below 40% in 2022 as shown in Fig. 1.16.

Other issues promoted under this Sustainable Development Goal include reducing violence against women, marriage of young girls, reducing the average daily time spent in the family, such as unpaid domestic work, women's access to politics and business management, ensuring equal access to health and reproductive health care and access to property rights.

Sustainable Development Goal 10 (SDG10)—reducing inequality—aims to address disparities in income and opportunity within and between countries on the premise of eradicating global poverty (Eurostat, 2022). This goal recognizes that while economic growth and globalization have raised living standards and reduced poverty in many areas around the world, the benefits have not been evenly distributed (Bhandari, 2024). Increased inequalities can undermine social cohesion, generate instability and reduce the capacity of societies to sustain sustainable development.

The Gini coefficient is a statistical measure that quantifies the degree of income inequality in a given region or country (Charles et al., 2022). According to Fig. 1.17, by the year 2022, the Gini coefficient varied significantly by country, revealing differences in the economic structure,

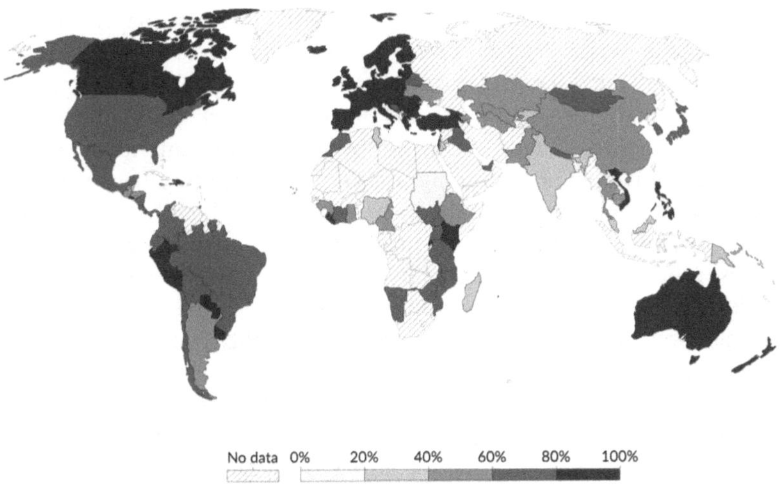


**Fig. 1.16** Gender equality in access to the global labour market in 2022. Source: Our World in Data (Our World in Data team, 2023k)

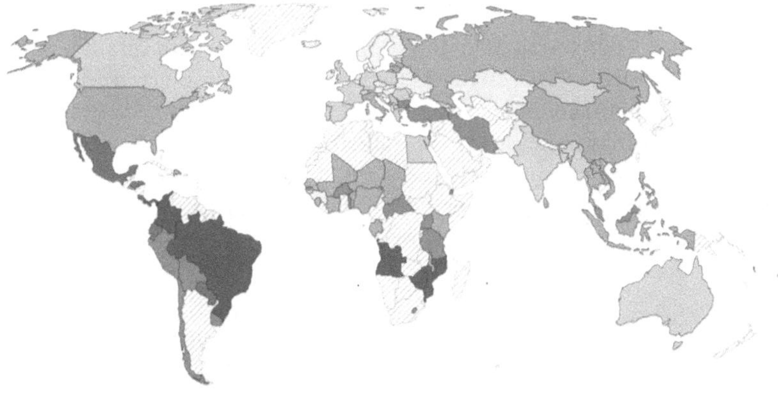


**Fig. 1.17** Income inequality—global Gini coefficient in 2022. Source: Our World in Data (Our World in Data team, 2023j)

social policies, level of development and history of inequality in each country. Scandinavian countries such as Denmark, Sweden and Norway are representative for their relatively low levels of income inequality, with Gini coefficients between 0.25 and 0.36, due to their social protection systems. On the other hand, many countries in Latin America and Sub-Saharan Africa had some of the highest Gini coefficients, at 0.41 indicating significant levels of income inequality.

The objective of reducing inequality within and between countries includes reducing income inequality, promoting social and economic inclusion, ensuring equal opportunities and eliminating discrimination, adopting fiscal and social policies to promote equality, improving the regulation of financial markets, strengthening the representation of developing countries in global economic and financial institutions and addressing the issue of migration of people (Gannon et al., 2022). The regulatory effects of taxation have been shown to reduce the spillover effects of uncertainty on economic growth in the EU. Badiu and co-authors (Badiu (Cazacu) et al., 2024) have shown in a study that financial independence and solvency promote excessive taxation in emerging markets and developing countries and are correlated with the macroeconomic performance of the country concerned. The results also indicate that the tax burden can be a barrier to the sustainable development of firms, with direct repercussions on consumers. Attractiveness for investors is also affected and remains a priority for companies.

The findings of the study will allow the identification of the main impediments and opportunities of tax policy on industry performance to promote a sustainable development of the industry and to establish a sustainable tax regime that protects investors.

## Sustainable Resource Consumption Targets

*Sustainable Development Goal 6 (SDG6)*—clean water and sanitation—is an important objective of the Sustainable Development Agenda, and is a particular concern in countries with limited water resources such as Africa and South-East Asia, where less than 10% to less than 40% of the population have access to and use safely managed drinking water (Hasan et al., 2019). This goal addresses important water-related issues such as ensuring access to clean drinking water, sustainable management of water resources, improving water quality, reducing pollution and hazardous waste, increasing water use efficiency and ensuring that everyone has access to sanitation and hygiene services (J. A. Silva, 2023).

As of 2020 there are no reports on this issue for some countries in Africa, Oceania, Australia and South America, as shown in Fig. 1.18.

In the context of the current geopolitical climate, Ukraine is facing significant problems with the safe use of canal water services. Other issues considered when defining Sustainable Development Goal 9 are the use of safely managed sanitation services and hand-washing facilities, where we note difficulties, particularly for countries in Africa, United Arab Emirates, Nigeria, Zambia and the Middle East (Tajikistan). An interesting statistic shows that the share of safely treated domestic wastewater is deficient in Russia and Mongolia and in some African countries, with shares of less than 13% (Our World in Data team, 2023f).

Productivity and water use efficiency show that over the period 1982–2020 the highest increase in productivity of more than $1000, respectively, from $327 to $1348 per cubic metre is achieved by Luxembourg, followed by Monaco ($1252). Other situations of significant increase in yield to $360.52 per cubic metre are realized by Great Britain, followed by Australia and Botswana with about $80–90 per cubic

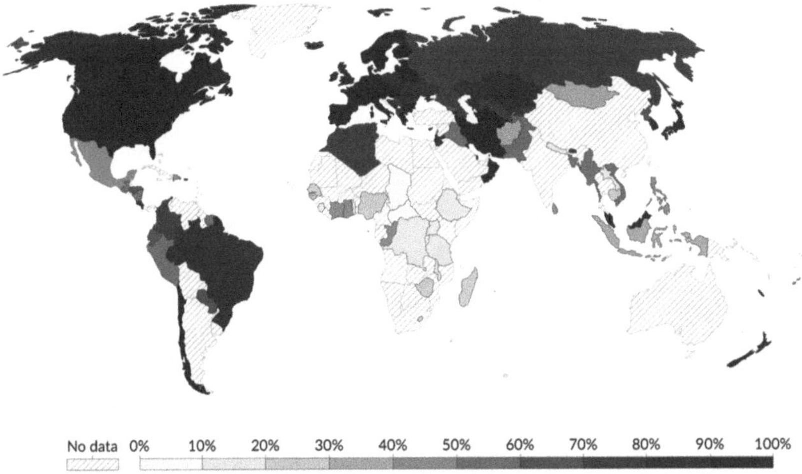


**Fig. 1.18** Share of global population use of drinking water from controlled sources in 2022. Source: Adapted by author according to Our World in Data (Our World in Data team, 2023f)

metre (Our World in Data team, 2023f). The level of water stress of freshwater farms as a share of domestic resources is maximized and assessed by the United Nations as being at an extremely high level of stress in North African countries such as Mauritania, Algeria, Libya, Egypt, Sudan, Saudi Arabia and Middle East countries (Pakistan, Kazakhstan), countries where freshwater withdrawals exceed 100% of total renewable resources, the maximum being reached by Egypt in 2017 with 6420% freshwater withdrawals from domestic resources.

*Sustainable Development Goal 7 (SDG7)*—affordable and clean energy—aims to ensure access to sustainable energy in the context of increasing energy consumption to support the global economy and household energy consumption, driven by technological progress (Swain & Karimu, 2020). According to Fig. 1.19, access to electricity in the year 2021 was for most continents within the parameters of 90% and 100%; however, for the African continent, in countries such as South Sudan only 7.24% of the population had access to electricity. In other countries in Central Saharan Africa, Burkina Faso, Niger, Mali, Chad, Mali, Chad, Burundi, Central African Republic and the Democratic Republic of Congo, no more than 20% of the population had access to a source of electricity.

Access to clean cooking fuels and access to renewable energy are other priorities under this objective (Marcillo-Delgado et al., 2019) (which is a

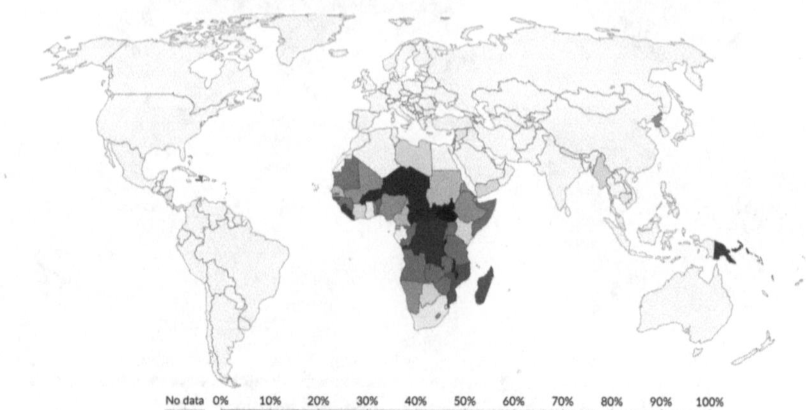


**Fig. 1.19** Global electricity access in 2021. Source: Adapted by author according to Our World in Data (Our World in Data team, 2023e)

problem for European countries, the United States, China and Australia, where the share of final energy consumption from renewable sources is less than 20%). Energy efficiency is a particular issue in the context of the energy crisis in Europe, which has increased energy costs and has raised the issue of promoting access to clean energy technologies and investments and expanding energy services (Yu et al., 2021).

*Sustainable Development Goal 12 (SDG12)*—responsible consumption and production—aims to promote resource consumption efficiency based on sustainable consumption patterns leading to enhanced economic completeness and poverty reduction (Di Vaio et al., 2020). Food waste is an important element of the Sustainable Development Agenda, with the 2030 Agenda's goal of halving per capita food waste and reducing food losses along the production and supply chains (Ardra & Barua, 2022). Another issue targeted under this goal is waste management and encouraging businesses to adopt sustainable practices and sustainability reporting (Salvador et al., 2021).

According to Fig. 1.20, across the globe, the most compliant countries that have developed integrated reporting systems on sustainability indicators are those in North America (United States, Canada), Europe (Sweden, Germany, France, United Kingdom), Asia (China and India) and Australia (Our World in Data team, 2023i).

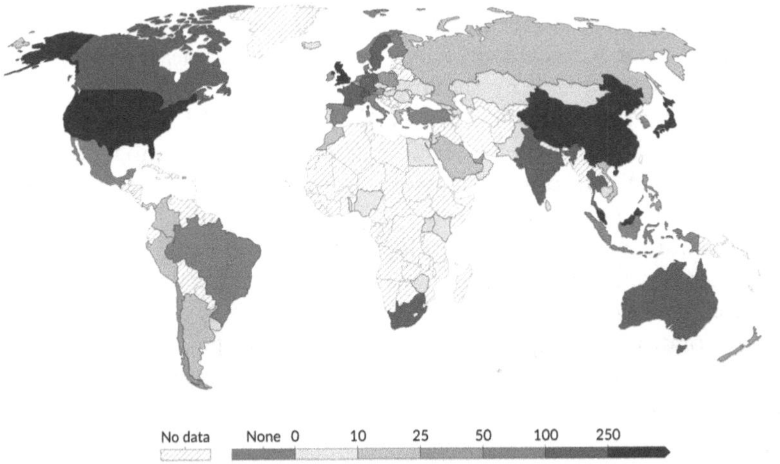


**Fig. 1.20** Corporate sustainability reporting in 2021. Source: Adapted by author according to Our World in Data (Our World in Data team, 2023i)

The objective aims inter alia at promoting sustainable practices and understanding of sustainable lifestyles, supporting scientific and technological capacity for sustainable consumption and production and tools to monitor the impact of sustainable development on industry and tourism (Eurostat, 2022).

## Environmental Protection Objectives

*Sustainable Development Goal 13 (SDG13)*—climate action—builds on the premise of developing affordable solutions for the transition to a cleaner and more resilient economy. Building resilience and capacity to climate change disasters is a major objective under SDG13 (Yin et al., 2022). Disaster risk management at the national level is thus addressed through the adoption of disaster risk reduction policies as agreed in the Sendai Framework Agreement (United Nations, 2025). By 2030, the Agenda's objectives on this theme aim to strengthen resilience and adaptive capacity to climate-related hazards and natural disasters across the globe (Gupta et al., 2024).

Figure 1.21 shows that the countries that have not adopted disaster risk reduction policies and strategies by 2022 include Romania, Bangladesh, Sweden, Montenegro and Cameroon (index 0).

Sustainable Development Goal 13 aims, inter alia, to integrate climate change measures into national policies, strategies and planning, to build capacity to cope with climate change and, last but not least, to implement the commitment made by signing the UN Framework Convention on Climate Change (Iacobuţă et al., 2022). To date, $51.93 billion in support has been provided to developing countries impacting on climate change mitigation actions (Our World in Data team, 2023q).

*Sustainable Development Goal 14 (SDG14)*—aquatic life—aims at the conservation and sustainable development of the oceans, seas and marine resources because these resources contribute to maintaining a favourable living climate on Earth (Martin & Carnero, 2019). Ecosystem protection and restoration is the approach to sustainably manage and protect marine and coastal ecosystems to avoid significant adverse impacts. Countries using ecosystem approaches for marine management in 2021 are shown in Fig. 1.22.

Other SDG14 targets are (Eurostat, 2022): reducing ocean acidification, developing sustainable fishing practices, conserving coastal and marine areas, increasing the economic benefits of sustainable use of marine

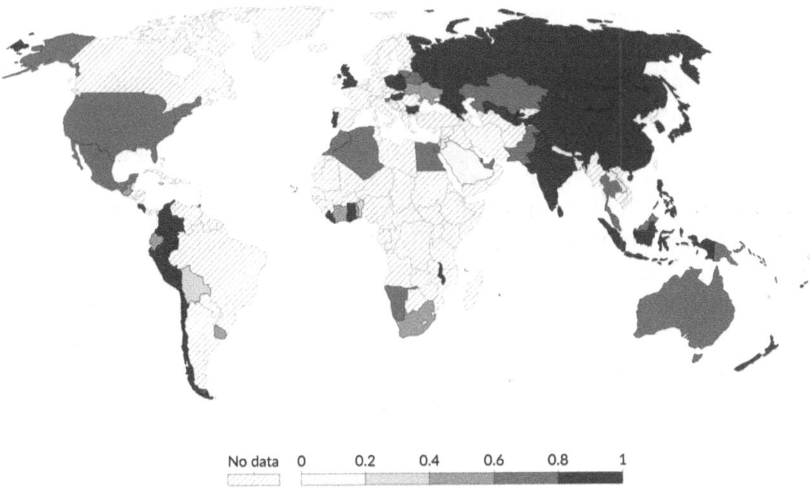


**Fig. 1.21** Global adoption of disaster risk policies in 2022. Source: Adapted by author according to Our World in Data (Our World in Data team, 2023q)

**Fig. 1.22** Countries using ecosystem approaches to marine management in 2021. Source: Reproduced by author according to Our World in Data (Our World in Data team, 2023b)

resources, supporting fishing communities, ensuring the international law of the sea.

*Sustainable Development Goal 15 (SDG15)*—sustainably managing forests, combating desertification, halting and reversing land degradation and protecting biodiversity (United Nations, 2015). This target is based on the premise of significant annual forest loss of 13 million hectares of forest per year and land desertification due to persistent degradation (3.6 billion hectares) (Scherer et al., 2018). The dynamics of the protected land area in 2021 is highlighted in Fig. 1.23.

Sustainable Development Goal 15 aims, inter alia, to conserve and restore terrestrial and freshwater ecosystems, restore degraded forests, halt desertification and restore degraded lands, secure mountain ecosystems, protect biodiversity and natural habitats, eliminate poaching and trafficking of protected species, develop sustainable policies for mainstreaming biodiversity (Eurostat, 2022).

The Sustainable Development Goals are an ambitious and comprehensive plan to tackle the most important global challenges such as poverty, inequality, climate change, environmental degradation, peace and justice by 2030.

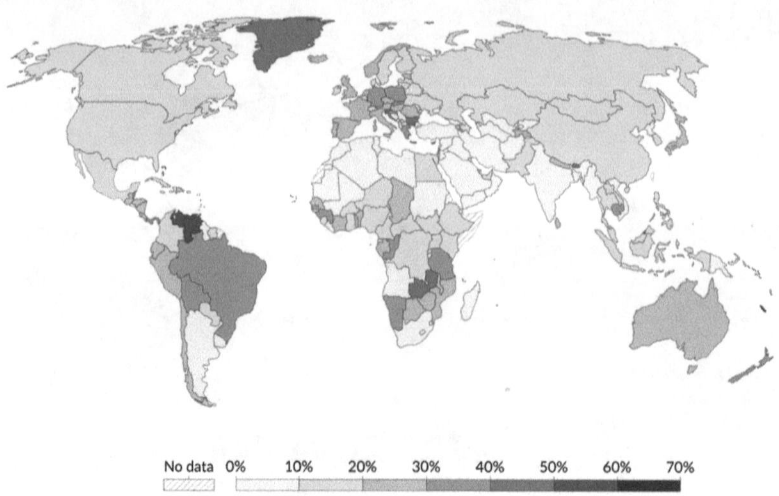


**Fig. 1.23** Dynamics of the area of land that is protected globally in the year 2021. Source: Taken by author according to Our World in Data (Our World in Data team, 2023p)

## Conclusions

Sustainable development is a fundamental necessity to ensure a balance between economic progress, social cohesion and environmental protection in the context of increasingly complex global challenges. Despite concerted efforts at international level, today's reality reflects the persistence of major problems such as extreme poverty, widening economic and social disparities and accelerated degradation of natural resources. These issues are aggravated by disruptive factors, including the intensification of natural disasters, the proliferation of international conflicts, the rise in violence and the spread of terrorism. Against this backdrop, achieving the 2030 Agenda goals remains a significant challenge, requiring effective monitoring mechanisms and adaptive policies capable of responding to global dynamics.

On environmental issues, climate change is one of the most pressing threats to the sustainability of the future. Increasing extreme weather events, such as prolonged droughts, devastating floods or violent storms, profoundly affect the ability of states to maintain ecological balance and protect their critical infrastructure. Desertification and degradation of agricultural land, including in European regions such as the Bărăgan Plain, lead to decreasing agricultural productivity, threatening global food security. At the same time, massive deforestation and forest fires are contributing to increased greenhouse gas emissions, thus exacerbating global warming.

Another major challenge is the depletion of natural resources, especially drinking water supplies and biodiversity. Industrial and urban pollution is affecting water and soil quality, causing major imbalances in ecosystems and endangering human health. On the other hand, biodiversity loss destabilizes food chains and reduces the capacity of the natural environment to provide essential ecosystem services such as pollination of agricultural crops, climate regulation and water purification. In this sense, protecting the environment can no longer be considered an option but an absolute priority in global development strategies.

From a socio-economic point of view, persistent inequalities between countries, as well as internal disparities within countries, accentuate the vulnerabilities of the population and create new barriers to sustainable development. Unequal access to essential services such as education, health and economic opportunities perpetuates cycles of poverty and hinders inclusive economic growth. Technological gaps between developed and developing countries also contribute to deepening the global economic divide, limiting the ability of some countries to adopt innovative solutions for sustainable development. In this context, international cooperation and technology transfer become essential to reduce inequalities and accelerate economic progress in disadvantaged regions.

A positive aspect of the current context is the unprecedented technological advances, which offer significant opportunities for implementing sustainable solutions. Digitization, artificial intelligence, automation and new renewable energy sources have the potential to fundamentally transform the way natural resources are used and to optimize industrial and economic processes. Global expansion of access to education and increased interconnectivity through communication networks are also enabling faster dissemination of knowledge and accelerating innovation in critical areas such as medicine, sustainable agriculture and energy efficiency. These factors can be basic pillars for sustainable development, provided that countries implement appropriate policies to integrate these technologies in an equitable and responsible way.

Another fundamental element for the success of sustainable development strategies is monitoring and reporting mechanisms, which ensure transparency of progress and allow policies to be adjusted to emerging realities. The High-Level Political Forum on Sustainable Development has become a central platform for assessing the implementation of the Sustainable Development Goals (SDGs), setting clear directions for action and promoting international cooperation. Its recent review has highlighted the need to step up efforts in areas such as quality education, gender equality, the protection of aquatic and terrestrial ecosystems and the development of global partnerships to implement the 2030 Agenda.

In 2022, the Forum focused its work on priority goals including education, gender equality, protection of marine and terrestrial life and strengthening international partnerships. In 2023, the focus shifted to key issues such as access to clean water, the transition to sustainable energy, industrial innovation and the development of smart cities. These initiatives reflect a continued commitment by the international community to achieve the Sustainable Development Goals but also underline the complexity of the challenges that need to be tackled in a coordinated and effective way.

Sustainable development must be seen as an urgent necessity, requiring concrete and adaptable action to current realities. The persistence of social, economic and environmental problems underlines that the strategies adopted must be flexible, integrated and based on principles of equity and global responsibility. International commitments and cooperation mechanisms must be strengthened to accelerate progress and ensure a balanced and sustainable future for all generations. Investments in education, technology and green infrastructure, together with inclusive and sustainable policies, will play a decisive role in achieving the goals set out in the 2030 Agenda and in transforming sustainable development from a challenge into a viable reality.

Under the 2030 Agenda for Sustainable Development, Goals 7, 8 and 9 play an important role in ensuring a sustainable, competitive and equitable economy based on access to clean energy, inclusive growth and modern infrastructure. These goals are interlinked and contribute to creating a resilient development model, where technological progress and innovation are used to optimize the use of resources and support economic development without compromising the environment.

Goal 7, Clean and affordable energy, is a fundamental pillar for sustainable development, as the transition to renewable energy sources is essential to reduce greenhouse gas emissions and reduce dependence on fossil fuels. Although significant progress has been made in the use of solar, wind and hydropower, major disparities remain between regions in terms of access to electricity. Particularly in developing countries, millions of people continue to lack adequate energy infrastructure, limiting economic growth and access to essential services such as education and health. In this regard, investments in the expansion of sustainable energy grids and the implementation of energy efficiency policies are important to achieve this objective.

Regarding Goal 8 decent work and growth is closely linked to sustainable development, as promoting an inclusive and sustainable economy contributes to reducing social inequalities and improving the living standards of the population. The creation of decent jobs, based on rights and social protection, is a priority to ensure a resilient economy. However, globalization and automation have led to rapid transformations in the labour market, requiring the skills of the workforce to adapt to new economic demands. The COVID-19 pandemic has had a devastating impact on jobs globally, exacerbating economic precariousness and highlighting the need for economic support and employee protection measures. Growth must be underpinned by policies that favour innovation, sustainability and social inclusion to avoid widening economic disparities.

Sustainable Development Goal 9, Industry, innovation and infrastructure, emphasizes the importance of modernizing infrastructure and stimulating technological innovation to support economic and social development. Efficient infrastructure is essential for the optimal functioning of national economies and for the provision of essential services such as transportation, telecommunications and access to drinking water. Investments in sustainable infrastructure based on clean technologies can help reduce the environmental impact of industrial activities and increase energy efficiency. Digitalization and automation also support productivity growth and facilitate the transition to a green economy.

Achieving Goals 7, 8 and 9 is essential to shaping a sustainable development model that reduces economic inequality, protects the environment and modernizes global infrastructure. While significant progress has been made, the challenges remain considerable and the implementation of integrated policies, based on international cooperation and sustainable investment, is necessary to accelerate the transition to a balanced and prosperous future.

## References

Abubakar, I. R., & Aina, Y. A. (2019). The prospects and challenges of developing more inclusive, safe, resilient and sustainable cities in Nigeria. *Land Use Policy, 87*, 104105. https://doi.org/10.1016/j.landusepol.2019.104105

Adom, P. K. (2024). The socioeconomic impact of climate change in developing countries over the next decades: A literature survey. *Heliyon, 10*(15), e35134. https://doi.org/10.1016/j.heliyon.2024.e35134

Akata, D. (2023). 1998 Russian financial crisis. In B. Açıkgöz (Ed.), *BT—Black swan: Economic crises* (Vol. II, pp. 145–156). Springer Nature Singapore. https://doi.org/10.1007/978-981-99-2318-2_9

Anukwonke, C. C., Tambe, E. B., Nwafor, D. C., & Malik, K. T. (2022). Climate change and interconnected risks to sustainable development. In S. A. Bandh (Ed.), *BT—Climate change: The social and scientific construct* (pp. 71–86). Springer International Publishing. https://doi.org/10.1007/978-3-030-86290-9_5

Ardra, S., & Barua, M. K. (2022). Halving food waste generation by 2030: The challenges and strategies of monitoring UN sustainable development goal target 12.3. *Journal of Cleaner Production, 380*, 135042. https://doi.org/10.1016/j.jclepro.2022.135042

Arora, N. K., & Mishra, I. (2022). Current scenario and future directions for sustainable development goal 2: A roadmap to zero hunger. *Environmental*

*Sustainability, 5*(2), 129–133. https://doi.org/10.1007/s42398-022-00235-8

Badiu (Cazacu), C. E., Bărbuță-Mișu, N., Chirita, M., Soare, I., Zlati, M. L., Fortea, C., & Antohi, V. M. (2024). Modelling the impact of VAT fiscality on branch-level performance in the construction industry—Evidence from Romania. *Economies, 12*(2), 30. https://doi.org/10.3390/economies12020030

Beccar-Varela, M. P., Mariani, M. C., Tweneboah, O. K., & Florescu, I. (2017). Analysis of the Lehman Brothers collapse and the flash crash event by applying wavelets methodologies. *Physica A: Statistical Mechanics and its Applications, 474*, 162–171. https://doi.org/10.1016/j.physa.2017.01.064

Bhandari, M. P. (2024). What is next for the sustainable development goals, what are the challenges concerning SDG 10—Reduced inequalities? *Sustainable Earth Reviews, 7*(1), 23. https://doi.org/10.1186/s42055-024-00093-8

Bhattacharya, R., & Bose, D. (2023). A review of the sustainable development goals to make headways through the COVID-19 pandemic era. *Environmental Progress & Sustainable Energy, 42*(4), e14093. https://doi.org/10.1002/ep.14093

Biermann, F., Hickmann, T., Sénit, C.-A., Beisheim, M., Bernstein, S., Chasek, P., Grob, L., Kim, R. E., Kotzé, L. J., Nilsson, M., Ordóñez Llanos, A., Okereke, C., Pradhan, P., Raven, R., Sun, Y., Vijge, M. J., van Vuuren, D., & Wicke, B. (2022). Scientific evidence on the political impact of the sustainable development goals. *Nature Sustainability, 5*(9), 795–800. https://doi.org/10.1038/s41893-022-00909-5

Calvo, T., Razafindrakoto, M., & Roubaud, F. (2019). Fear of the state in governance surveys? Empirical evidence from African countries. *World Development, 123*, 104609. https://doi.org/10.1016/j.worlddev.2019.104609

Chamut, S., Alhassan, M., Hameedaldeen, A., Kaplish, S., Yang, A. H., Wade, C. G., Alghamdi, S., Chamut, D., Novy, B. B., & Chandel, T. (2024). Every bite counts to achieve oral health: A scoping review on diet and oral health preventive practices. *International Journal for Equity in Health, 23*(1), 261. https://doi.org/10.1186/s12939-024-02279-0

Charles, V., Gherman, T., & Paliza, J. C. (2022). The Gini index: A modern measure of inequality. In V. Charles & A. Emrouznejad (Eds.), *BT—Modern indices for international economic diplomacy* (pp. 55–84). Springer International Publishing. https://doi.org/10.1007/978-3-030-84535-3_3

Coulibaly, A., & Yogo, U. T. (2020). The path to shared prosperity: Leveraging financial services outreach to create decent jobs in developing countries. *Economic Modelling, 87*, 131–147. https://doi.org/10.1016/j.econmod.2019.07.013

da Silva, F. R., De Paula, T. M., Gerhard, F., Victor, C., & de Freitas, A. A. F. (2024). Does tackling the sustainable development goals lead to life satisfaction?

*Environment, Development and Sustainability, 27*, 16797–16818. https://doi.org/10.1007/s10668-024-04640-3

Dahl, A. (2014). *Agenda 21. In global environmental change* (pp. 527–531). Springer Science + Business Media Dordrecht. https://doi.org/10.1007/978-94-007-5784-4_88

Dale, V. H., Joyce, L. A., McNulty, S., Neilson, R. P., Ayres, M. P., Flannigan, M. D., Hanson, P. J., Irland, L. C., Lugo, A. E., Peterson, C. J., Simberloff, D., Swanson, F. J., Stocks, B. J., & Wotton, B. M. (2001). Climate change and forest disturbances: Climate change can affect forests by altering the frequency, intensity, duration, and timing of fire, drought, introduced species, insect and pathogen outbreaks, hurricanes, windstorms, ice storms, or landslides. *BioScience, 51*(9), 723–734. https://doi.org/10.1641/0006-3568(2001)051[0723:CCAFD]2.0.CO;2

Di Vaio, A., Palladino, R., Hassan, R., & Escobar, O. (2020). Artificial intelligence and business models in the sustainable development goals perspective: A systematic literature review. *Journal of Business Research, 121*, 283–314. https://doi.org/10.1016/j.jbusres.2020.08.019

Dousa, M. (2019). European level of 2030 agenda for sustainable development. In R. Riha (Ed.), *10. Mezinarodni Konference Udrzitelny Rozvoj 2019: Vybrane Problemy Environmentalni a Regionalni Politiky. Selected issues on environmental and regional policy (Issue 10th international conference on sustainable development)* (pp. 24–33) WE-Conference Proceedings Citation Index.

El Bilali, H., Ottomano Palmisano, G., Bottalico, F., Cardone, G., & Capone, R. (2021). Chapter 3—Food security and nutrition in agro-food sustainability transitions. In C. M. Galanakis (Ed.), *Food security and nutrition* (pp. 57–86). Academic Press. https://doi.org/10.1016/B978-0-12-820521-1.00003-4

European Commission. (2019). *European green deal*. https://eur-lex.europa.eu/resource.html?uri=cellar:b828d165-1c22-11ea-8c1f-01aa75ed71a1.0020.02/DOC_1&format=PDF

European Parliament. (2011). Rio+20 earth summit. *Official Journal of the European Union*. https://www.europarl.europa.eu/doceo/document/TA-7-2011-0430_EN.html

Eurostat. (2022). *Sustainable development in the European Union*. https://doi.org/10.2785/313289

Farquharson, C., McNally, S., & Tahir, I. (2024). Education inequalities. *Oxford Open Economics, 3*(Suppl. 1), i760–i820. https://doi.org/10.1093/ooec/odad029

Gannon, K. E., Pettinotti, L., Conway, D., Surminski, S., Ndilanha, E., & Nyumba, T. (2022). Delivering the sustainable development goals through development corridors in East Africa: A Q-methodology approach to imagining development futures. *Environmental Science & Policy, 129*, 56–67. https://doi.org/10.1016/j.envsci.2021.12.013

Garicano, L., Rohner, D., & di Mauro, B. W. (2022). *Global economic consequences of the war in Ukraine: Sanctions, supply chains and sustainability.* CEPR Press. https://cepr.org/publications/books-and-reports/global-economic-consequences-war-ukraine-sanctions-supply-chains-and

Gitz, V., Meybeck, A., Lipper, L., Young, C., & Braatz, S. (2016). *Climate change and food security: Risks and responses.* Food and Agriculture Organization of the United Nations. https://www.fao.org/3/i5188e/I5188E.pdf

González-Pier, E., Barraza-Lloréns, M., Beyeler, N., Jamison, D., Knaul, F., Lozano, R., Yamey, G., & Sepúlveda, J. (2016). Mexico's path towards the sustainable development goal for health: An assessment of the feasibility of reducing premature mortality by 40% by 2030. *The Lancet Global Health, 4*(10), e714–e725. https://doi.org/10.1016/S2214-109X(16)30181-4

Gupta, A. K., Acharya, P., & Gupta, A. (2024). Climate change: Extremes, disasters and call for resilient development. In A. K. Gupta, A. Gupta, & P. Acharya (Eds.), *BT—Disaster risk and management under climate change* (pp. 3–25). Springer Nature Singapore. https://doi.org/10.1007/978-981-99-4105-6_1

Halkos, G., & Argyropoulou, G. (2022). Using environmental indicators in performance evaluation of sustainable development health goals. *Ecological Economics, 192*, 107263. https://doi.org/10.1016/j.ecolecon.2021.107263

Hansen, J., List, G., Downs, S., Carr, E. R., Diro, R., Baethgen, W., Kruczkiewicz, A., Braun, M., Furlow, J., Walsh, K., & Magima, N. (2022). Impact pathways from climate services to SDG2 ("zero hunger"): A synthesis of evidence. *Climate Risk Management, 35*, 100399. https://doi.org/10.1016/j.crm.2022.100399

Hansson, S., Arfvidsson, H., & Simon, D. (2019). Governance for sustainable urban development: The double function of SDG indicators. *Area Development and Policy, 4*(3), 217–235. https://doi.org/10.1080/23792949.2019.1585192

Hasan, M. M., Alauddin, M., Rashid Sarker, M. A., Jakaria, M., & Alamgir, M. (2019). Climate sensitivity of wheat yield in Bangladesh: Implications for the United Nations sustainable development goals 2 and 6. *Land Use Policy, 87*, 104023. https://doi.org/10.1016/j.landusepol.2019.104023

Heleta, S., & Bagus, T. (2021). Sustainable development goals and higher education: Leaving many behind. *Higher Education, 81*(1), 163–177. https://doi.org/10.1007/s10734-020-00573-8

Hendriks, S. L., & Babu, S. C. (2024). *Handbook on public policy and food security.* Edward Elgar Publishing. https://doi.org/10.4337/9781839105449

Hook, K., & Marcantonio, R. (2023). Environmental dimensions of conflict and paralyzed responses: The ongoing case of Ukraine and future implications for urban warfare. *Small Wars & Insurgencies, 34*(8), 1400–1428. https://doi.org/10.1080/09592318.2022.2035098

Hu, B., Peng, N., & Zhu, G. (2024). Sustainable finance in natural resource extraction: Navigating green recovery pathways. *Resources Policy, 96*, 105197. https://doi.org/10.1016/j.resourpol.2024.105197

Hughes, D., & Eduarda-Duarte, M. (2024). *Decent work, inclusion and sustainability*. Routledge. https://doi.org/10.4324/9781032662251

Iacobuţă, G. I., Brandi, C., Dzebo, A., & Elizalde Duron, S. D. (2022). Aligning climate and sustainable development finance through an SDG lens. The role of development assistance in implementing the Paris Agreement. *Global Environmental Change, 74*, 102509. https://doi.org/10.1016/j.gloenvcha.2022.102509

International Monetary Fund. (2022). *World economic outlook: Countering the cost-of-living crisis*. https://www.imf.org/en/publications/weo/issues/2022/10/11/world-economic-outlook-october-2022

Ki-Moon, B., & Secretary-General, U. N. (2015). *The millennium development goals report*. https://www.un.org/millenniumgoals/2015_MDG_Report/pdf/MDG%202015%20rev%20(July%201).pdf

Knez, M., Ranić, M., & Gurinović, M. (2024). Underutilized plants increase biodiversity, improve food and nutrition security, reduce malnutrition, and enhance human health and well-being. Let's put them back on the plate! *Nutrition Reviews, 82*(8), 1111–1124. https://doi.org/10.1093/nutrit/nuad103

Kufeoglu, S. (2022). *SDG-9: Industry, innovation and infrastructure* (pp. 349–369). Springer. https://doi.org/10.1007/978-3-031-07127-0_11

Lamichhane, S., Eğilmez, G., Gedik, R., Bhutta, M. K. S., & Erenay, B. (2021). Benchmarking OECD countries' sustainable development performance: A goal-specific principal component analysis approach. *Journal of Cleaner Production, 287*, 125040. https://doi.org/10.1016/j.jclepro.2020.125040

Liengpunsakul, S. (2021). Artificial intelligence and sustainable development in China. *The Chinese Economy, 54*(4), 235–248. https://doi.org/10.1080/10971475.2020.1857062. WE—Emerging Sources Citation Index (ESCI).

Ma, R., Abid, N., Yang, S., & Ahmad, F. (2023). From crisis to resilience: Strengthening climate action in OECD countries through environmental policy and energy transition. *Environmental Science and Pollution Research, 30*(54), 115480–115495. https://doi.org/10.1007/s11356-023-29970-z

Maheshwari, P., Kamble, S., Belhadi, A., & Kumar, S. (2024). UN sustainable development goals and management of non-instantaneous deteriorating items: A literature review and applications framework. *Annals of Operations Research*. https://doi.org/10.1007/s10479-024-06144-9

Mann, T., Atra, R. J., & Dowen, R. (2004). U.S. monetary policy indicators and international stock returns: 1970–2001. *International Review of Financial Analysis, 13*(4), 543–558. https://doi.org/10.1016/j.irfa.2004.02.025

Marcillo-Delgado, J. C., Ortego, M. I., & Pérez-Foguet, A. (2019). A compositional approach for modelling SDG7 indicators: Case study applied to electricity access. *Renewable and Sustainable Energy Reviews, 107*, 388–398. https://doi.org/10.1016/j.rser.2019.03.028

Martin, C. J., & Carnero, C. (2019). Evaluation of sustainable development in European Union countries. *Applied Sciences-Basel, 9*(22), 4880. https://doi.org/10.3390/app9224880. WE—Science Citation Index Expanded (SCI-EXPANDED) WE—Social Science Citation Index (SSCI).

Mason-D'Croz, D., Sulser, T. B., Wiebe, K., Rosegrant, M. W., Lowder, S. K., Nin-Pratt, A., Willenbockel, D., Robinson, S., Zhu, T., Cenacchi, N., Dunston, S., & Robertson, R. D. (2019). Agricultural investments and hunger in Africa modeling potential contributions to SDG2 – Zero Hunger. *World Development, 116*, 38–53. https://doi.org/10.1016/j.worlddev.2018.12.006

Micah, A. E., Su, Y., Bachmeier, S. D., Chapin, A., Cogswell, I. E., Crosby, S. W., Cunningham, B., Harle, A. C., Maddison, E. R., Moitra, M., Sahu, M., Schneider, M. T., Simpson, K. E., Stutzman, H. N., Tsakalos, G., Zende, R. R., Zlavog, B. S., Abbafati, C., Abebo, Z. H., et al. (2020). Health sector spending and spending on HIV/AIDS, tuberculosis, and malaria, and development assistance for health: Progress towards Sustainable Development Goal 3. *The Lancet, 396*(10252), 693–724. https://doi.org/10.1016/S0140-6736(20)30608-5

Moatsos, M., & Lazopoulos, A. (2021). Global poverty: A first estimation of its uncertainty. *World Development Perspectives, 22*, 100315. https://doi.org/10.1016/j.wdp.2021.100315

Mondejar, M. E., Avtar, R., Diaz, H. L. B., Dubey, R. K., Esteban, J., Gómez-Morales, A., Hallam, B., Mbungu, N. T., Okolo, C. C., Prasad, K. A., She, Q., & Garcia-Segura, S. (2021). Digitalization to achieve sustainable development goals: Steps towards a Smart Green Planet. *Science of the Total Environment, 794*, 148539. https://doi.org/10.1016/j.scitotenv.2021.148539

Najam, A. (2005). Developing countries and global environmental governance: From contestation to participation to engagement. *International Environmental Agreements: Politics, Law and Economics, 5*(3), 303–321. https://doi.org/10.1007/s10784-005-3807-6

OECD. (2001). *Sustainable development strategies What are they and how can development co-operation agencies support them?* The OECD Policy Briefs. https://www.oecd.org/dac/environment-development/1899857.pdf

Olaoye, O. O., Ibukun, C. O., Razzak, M., & Mose, N. (2021). Poverty prevalence and negative spillovers in Sub-Saharan Africa: A focus on extreme and multidimensional poverty in the region. *International Journal of Emerging Markets, 18*(9),2993–3021.https://doi.org/10.1108/IJOEM-01-2021-0028

Onishi, A. (1986). Alternative futures of the world economy, 1986-2000: Policy simulations by the FUGI global macroeconomic model. *IFAC Proceedings Volumes, 19*(10), 125–130. https://doi.org/10.1016/S1474-6670(17)59653-6

Our World in Data Team. (2023a). *Build resilient infrastructure, promote inclusive and sustainable industrialization and foster innovation.* https://ourworldindata.org. https://ourworldindata.org/sdgs/industry-innovation-infrastructure

Our World in Data Team. (2023b). *Conserve and sustainably use the oceans, seas and marine resources.* https://ourworldindata.org. https://ourworldindata.org/sdgs/life-below-water

Our World in Data Team. (2023c). *End hunger, achieve food security and improved nutrition and promote sustainable agriculture.* https://ourworldindata.org. https://ourworldindata.org/sdgs/zero-hunger#article-licence

Our World in Data Team. (2023d). *End poverty in all its forms everywhere.* https://ourworldindata.org. https://ourworldindata.org/sdgs/no-poverty#article-citation

Our World in Data Team. (2023e). *Ensure access to affordable, reliable, sustainable and modern energy for all.* https://ourworldindata.org. https://ourworldindata.org/sdgs/affordable-clean-energy

Our World in Data Team. (2023f). *Ensure access to water and sanitation for all.* https://ourworldindata.org. https://ourworldindata.org/sdgs/clean-water-sanitation

Our World in Data Team. (2023g). *Ensure healthy lives and promote well-being for all at all ages.* https://ourworldindata.org. https://ourworldindata.org/sdgs/good-health-wellbeing

Our World in Data Team. (2023h). *Ensure inclusive and quality education for all and promote lifelong learning.* https://ourworldindata.org. https://ourworldindata.org/sdgs/quality-education

Our World in Data Team. (2023i). *Ensure sustainable consumption and production patterns.* https://ourworldindata.org. https://ourworldindata.org/sdgs/responsible-consumption-production

Our World in Data Team. (2023j). Gini coefficient. https://ourworldindata.org. https://ourworldindata.org/grapher/economic-inequality-gini-index?time=latest

Our World in Data Team. (2023k). *Legal frameworks addressing gender equality in employment and economic benefits.* https://ourworldindata.org. https://ourworldindata.org/grapher/legal-frameworks-addressing-gender-equality-in-employment-and-economic-benefits?time=latest

Our World in Data Team. (2023l). *Make cities inclusive, safe, resilient and sustainable.* https://ourworldindata.org. https://ourworldindata.org/sdgs/sustainable-cities

Our World in Data Team. (2023m). *Promote just, peaceful and inclusive societies.* https://ourworldindata.org. https://ourworldindata.org/sdgs/peace-justice-institutions

Our World in Data Team. (2023n). *Promote sustained, inclusive and sustainable economic growth, full and productive employment and decent work for all.* https://ourworldindata.org. https://ourworldindata.org/sdgs/economic-growth

Our World in Data Team. (2023o). *Revitalize the global partnership for sustainable development.* https://ourworldindata.org. https://ourworldindata.org/sdgs/global-partnerships

Our World in Data Team. (2023p). *Sustainably manage forests, combat desertification, halt and reverse land degradation, halt biodiversity loss.* https://ourworldindata.org. https://ourworldindata.org/sdgs/life-on-land

Our World in Data Team. (2023q). *Take urgent action to combat climate change and its impacts.* https://ourworldindata.org. https://ourworldindata.org/sdgs/climate-action

Rai, S. M., Brown, B. D., & Ruwanpura, K. N. (2019). SDG 8: Decent work and economic growth – A gendered analysis. *World Development, 113*, 368–380. https://doi.org/10.1016/j.worlddev.2018.09.006

Rendtorff, J. D. (2019). Sustainable Development Goals and progressive business models for economic transformation. *Local Economy, 34*(6), 510–524. https://doi.org/10.1177/0269094219882270. WE—Emerging Sources Citation Index (ESCI).

Ritchie, R., & Mispy, O.-O. (2022). *Measuring progress towards the Sustainable Development Goals.* SDG-Tracker.org. https://sdg-tracker.org/energy

Rodionov, D. G., Pshenichnikov, V. V., & Zherebov, E. D. (2015). Currency crisis in Russia on the spun of 2014 and 2015: Causes and consequences. *Procedia—Social and Behavioral Sciences, 207*, 850–857. https://doi.org/10.1016/j.sbspro.2015.10.176

Roser, M., & Esteban, O.-O. (2022). Global extreme poverty. *Our World in Data, 1.* https://ourworldindata.org/extreme-poverty

Saleem, A., Anwar, S., Nawaz, T., Fahad, S., Saud, S., Ur Rahman, T., Khan, M. N. R., & Nawaz, T. (2024). Securing a sustainable future: The climate change threat to agriculture, food security, and sustainable development goals. *Journal of Umm Al-Qura University for Applied Sciences, 11*, 595–611. https://doi.org/10.1007/s43994-024-00177-3

Saleem, K. (2009). International linkage of the Russian market and the Russian financial crisis: A multivariate GARCH analysis. *Research in International Business and Finance, 23*(3), 243–256. https://doi.org/10.1016/j.ribaf.2008.09.003

Salvador, R., Puglieri, F. N., Halog, A., de Andrade, F. G., Piekarski, C. M., & De Francisco, A. C. (2021). Key aspects for designing business models for a circular bioeconomy. *Journal of Cleaner Production, 278*, 124341. https://doi.org/10.1016/j.jclepro.2020.124341

Scherer, L., Behrens, P., de Koning, A., Heijungs, R., Sprecher, B., & Tukker, A. (2018). Trade-offs between social and environmental Sustainable Development Goals. *Environmental Science & Policy, 90*, 65–72. https://doi.org/10.1016/j.envsci.2018.10.002. WE—Science Citation Index Expanded (SCI-EXPANDED) WE—Social Science Citation Index (SSCI).

Silva, J. A. (2023). Wastewater treatment and reuse for sustainable water resources management: A systematic literature review. *Sustainability, 15*(14), 10940. https://doi.org/10.3390/su151410940

Sosa, M., & Ortiz, E. (2015). Desequilibrios cambiarios y crisis: Canadá, México, Japón y Reino Unido vs dólar de EE.UU. (1994-2014). *Contaduría y Administración, 60*, 106–127. https://doi.org/10.1016/j.cya.2015.08.014

Swain, R. B., & Karimu, A. (2020). Renewable electricity and sustainable development goals in the EU. *World Development, 125*, 104693. https://doi.org/10.1016/j.worlddev.2019.104693. WE—Social Science Citation Index (SSCI).

Ulbrych, M. (2020). Progress in achieving sustainable industrial development—The case of the Czech Republic and Poland. *Comparative Economic Research-Central and Eastern Europe, 23*(4), 109–128. https://doi.org/10.18778/1508-2008.23.30. WE—Emerging Sources Citation Index (ESCI).

Underdal, A. (2010). Complexity and challenges of long-term environmental governance. *Global Environmental Change, 20*(3), 386–393. https://doi.org/10.1016/j.gloenvcha.2010.02.005

United Nations. (1987). Report of the world commission on environment and development. *Our Common Future*. https://www.are.admin.ch/are/en/home/media/publications/sustainable-development/brundtland-report.html

United Nations. (2015). *Transforming our world: The 2030 agenda for sustainable development*. Sustainabledevelopment.un.org. https://sustainabledevelopment.un.org/content/documents/21252030%20Agenda%20for%20Sustainable%20Development%20web.pdf

United Nations. (2024). *World social report 2024*. https://doi.org/10.18356/7f5d0efc-en

United Nations. (2025). *Sendai framework for disaster risk reduction 2015–2030*. https://www.preventionweb.net/files/43291_sendaiframeworkfordrren.pdf

Vrînceanu, A., Anghel, A., Bălăceanu, C., Lacatusu, A.-R., Musat, M., & Jinga, I. (2012). Land degradation on areas with desertification phenomenon risk in central Bărăgan plain. *Soil Forming Factors and Processes from the Temperate Zone, 9*.

World Health Organization. (2024). *Achieving well-being: A global framework for integrating well-being into public health utilizing a health promotion approach*. https://www.who.int/publications/i/item/9789240084858

Xu, Y., & Zhao, F. (2023). Impact of energy depletion, human development, and income distribution on natural resource sustainability. *Resources Policy, 83*, 103531. https://doi.org/10.1016/j.resourpol.2023.103531

Yang, S. Q., Zhao, W. W., Liu, Y. X., Cherubini, F., Fu, B. J., & Pereira, P. (2020). Prioritizing sustainable development goals and linking them to ecosystem services: A global expert's knowledge evaluation. *Geography and Sustainability, 1*(4), 321–330. https://doi.org/10.1016/j.geosus.2020.09.004. WE—Emerging Sources Citation Index (ESCI).

Yigit, S. (2021). An empirical perspective on the relationship between innovation performance and sustainable development. *Ege Academic Review, 21*(1), 47–57. https://doi.org/10.21121/eab.874020. WE—Emerging Sources Citation Index (ESCI).

Yin, C. C., Zhao, W. W., & Pereira, P. (2022). Soil conservation service underpins sustainable development goals. *Global Ecology and Conservation, 33*, e01974. https://doi.org/10.1016/j.gecco.2021.e01974. WE—Science Citation Index Expanded (SCI-EXPANDED).

Yu, M., Kubiczek, J., Ding, K., Jahanzeb, A., & Iqbal, N. (2021). Revisiting SDG-7 under energy efficiency vision 2050: The role of new economic models and mass digitalization in OECD. *Energy Efficiency, 15*(1), 2. https://doi.org/10.1007/s12053-021-10010-z

CHAPTER 2

# Synthesis of Economic Models of Sustainable Development on Clean Energy, Decent Work and Growth and Industry, Innovation and Infrastructure

## Introduction

In a global context characterized by economic, social and environmental challenges, economic models are fundamental tools for analysing sustainable development and informing public policy. These models are designed to assess the current dynamics of economies and to produce forecasts to support the development of effective economic strategies tailored to medium- and long-term sustainability objectives (Hariram et al., 2023; Stevanović et al., 2023). Through their ability to integrate multiple variables and provide alternative scenarios, economic models allow a better understanding of the impact of various policies on sustainable development, thus facilitating informed decision-making at governmental and international level (Pallaske, 2024; Son et al., 2023).

The complexity of these models derives from the multitude of parameters used, the different levels of data aggregation and the different ways of statistical validation. In the field of sustainable development, economic models are applied to analyse the interdependencies between economic growth, the use of natural resources and the social impacts of various public policies (Bieszk-Stolorz et al., 2024; Prado et al., 2019). Moreover, they are essential for monitoring progress towards the goals set by international organizations such as the United Nations 2030 Agenda (United Nations, 2015), which aims, among others, to transition to clean energy,



C. Fortea, *Sustainable Economic Development and the European Green Deal*, https://doi.org/10.1007/978-3-032-10326-0_2

promote decent work and strengthen economic infrastructure through innovation and technology (Jie & Lan, 2024).

A defining feature of economic models for sustainable development is their ability to integrate both quantitative and qualitative variables, providing a holistic perspective on how economic policy changes influence long-term sustainability (Debbarma & Choi, 2022; Y. Wang et al., 2024). These models are used to estimate the effects of renewable energy deployment on economic growth, to analyse the impact of job creation mechanisms on social cohesion and to assess the efficiency of investments in infrastructure and innovation.

For Sustainable Development Goal 7 (Clean and Affordable Energy), economic models are used to assess the cost-effectiveness of alternative energy sources, their impact on carbon reduction and the economic viability of energy transition policies (Bakhsh et al., 2024; Jayachandran et al., 2022). Also, for Objective 8 (Decent Work and Economic Growth), models are essential in analysing the relationship between employment policies, economic productivity and income distribution, providing solutions to reduce inequalities and increase social inclusion (Rai et al., 2019; Zehri et al., 2024). For Objective 9 (Industry, Innovation and Infrastructure), economic models are used to identify optimal investment strategies in infrastructure, digitization and emerging technologies to contribute to sustainable economic growth and reduce negative environmental impacts (Mondejar et al., 2021; Skare et al., 2024).

In this context, this chapter analyses the main economic models used in the field of sustainable development, with a focus on the interplay between energy, labour and infrastructure. It will examine the fundamental theoretical concepts underlying these models, the methodologies used to validate them, as well as the challenges and limitations encountered in their application at national and international level. This analysis aims to highlight the most effective economic approaches to support the transition towards a resilient, equitable and sustainable economic system capable of meeting current and future challenges.

## Economic Models in the Literature on Sustainable Development from the Perspective of Objective 7—Clean and Affordable Energy

Energy policy, through the Sustainable Development Goals, aims to ensure access to reliable and modern sustainable energy for all by ensuring universal access to energy services, substantially increasing the share of renewable energy in the global energy mix and doubling the global rate of energy efficiency improvement by 2030 (United Nations, 2015). These targets are based on strengthening international cooperation to facilitate access to clean energy research and technology and to promote investment in energy infrastructure, including the modernization of technology for the provision of energy services.

These issues have been the subject of concern of the High-Level Political Forum representatives on the basis of sessions dedicated to Goal 7. At the 2018 Forum on Transforming towards sustainable and resilient societies (United Nations, 2018), a ministerial declaration was adopted, where 46 countries presented their national voluntary values on efforts to realize SDG7 of the 2030 Agenda.

Over the period 2020–2022 there have been clear changes in the indicators for Objective 7, clean and affordable energy, with the most significant progress being made in improving energy efficiency and reducing greenhouse gas emissions. This has been made possible by making better use of alternative energy sources, developing clean and renewable energy exploitation facilities, mobilizing public attention on the importance of energy consumption, for example for heating homes, and this has been achieved by funding supranational house-warming projects (IRENA, 2021). The most challenging and vulnerable elements of Sustainable Development Goal 7 policy have been triggered by geopolitical conflicts that have generated energy crises, affecting many EU Member States. Thus, although European countries have developed the energy sector in a sustainable manner, the geopolitical crisis and the pandemic have reduced previous achievements, both in terms of energy availability and the existing alternatives for its transportation, given that alternative sources increase the pressure on transportation costs (IRENA, 2021). Generally speaking, by the year 2022 compared to the year 2010 electrification progress has increased from 83.2% to 90.5%, thus more than 77% of the global population without access to electricity currently lives in Sub-Saharan Africa alone; this percentage means more than 670 million people currently do not have access to energy sources (United Nations, 2022). Global investments are focused on improving energy efficiency, which according to the 2030 targets means that energy improvement should reach at least 2.6%, which is today only achieved in East and South-East Asian countries. Europe and North America are currently 0.7% behind the countries of East and South-East Asia, with the lowest rate of energy efficiency growth with the exception of Oceania and Latin America (compared to 2010, energy efficiency growth in Europe was only 0.2%) (United Nations, 2022). Promoting global sustainable development based on improving energy sustainability is a well-represented topic in the literature. Thus, in the field of fuels by studying more than 8000 published papers, we observe in the period 1975–2022 that they have aroused widespread interest in the academic world, being found in more than 52,800 citations, with a citation rate per article of 8.53 times and a Hirsch index of 79. Many of these articles were written in the period 2020–2022 benefiting from an increased research interest from year to year and likewise an interest expressed by the number of citations of the articles in the literature. After analysing the Web of Science database, the concept of energy within the field of study environmental sciences from the number of articles studied, 9627 articles were published in the period 1975–2022 with a wide addressability of interest in research results expressed by 59,481 citations in the literature, an average of 8.1 citations per article and a Hirsch index worth 78 points. The energy concept within the field of sustainable science and technology shows the same dynamism in the period 2020–2022 being studied a number of 6779 articles recognized in 53,333 refereed papers citing them with a citation rate of 10.02 times per article and a Hirsch index of 81 points. Within the domain multidisciplinary sciences and economics with application to the energy sector demonstrates an even higher interest of researchers; the citation rate of the 7405 articles analysed (on the Web of Science platform) is 14.35 times and the Hirsch index value exceeds 100 points.

The cluster analysis of research interest in the energy sector covers 8 clusters grouped according to the main areas of interest on consumption dynamics, renewable energy supply dynamics, climate issues, impact of the energy sector on sustainable economic growth, future of the energy sector, international regulatory areas on sustainable energy consumption, investment and governance related to the energy sector (Fig. 2.1). The figure is produced using the VOSviewer program, based on information collected from the Web of Science platform.

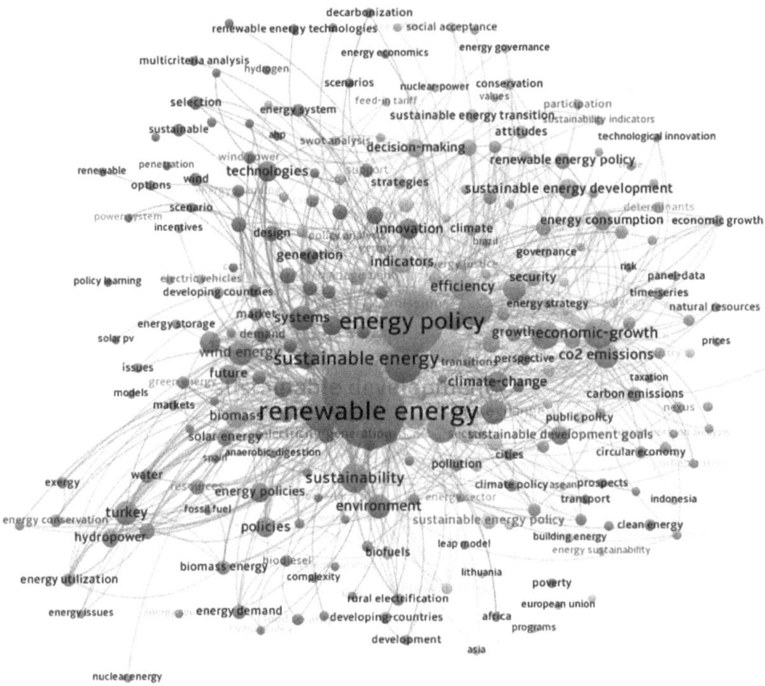


**Fig. 2.1** Bibliometric analysis on sustainable energy policies, 2019–2022. Source: Compiled by the author using VOSviewer software

In an integrated approach (Swain & Karimu, 2020), the impact of the energy industry on sustainable energy development is significant, as the production of goods and services and the distribution of these goods to the consuming population require energy resources continuously. In order to establish a framework between a number of renewable energy and environmental pollution parameters Cristea and co (Cristea et al., 2022) have used a number of machine learning techniques, panel data and time series prediction and forecasting techniques. Considering data for BRICS, G7 and EU countries they provided a tool for optimizing policy strategy in the sustainable energy production sector.

The results of the study indicated that the XGBoost model for renewable energy capacity prediction reveals that the highest importance of characteristics among the independent variables is associated with gas consumption for the G7, oil consumption for the EU bloc and GHG emissions for the BRICS. In addition, the predictions of the generalized additive model (GAM) for the EU bloc reveal a scenario of relatively constant renewable energy capacity if gas consumption increases, while increasing oil consumption leads to an increase in renewable energy capacity to a critical point, followed by a decrease. GAM models for the G7 revealed a scenario of an upward trend in renewable energy capacity as gas consumption increases and a downward trend in renewable energy capacity as oil consumption increases. In the case of the BRICS geopolitical bloc, the prediction scenario reveals that, over time, an increase in gas consumption leads to an increase in renewable energy production capacity.

Principal component analysis (PCA) revealed aspects of renewable energy production capacity and GHG emissions and $CO_2$ emissions, respectively, which are strongly correlated and integrated in the first component, which explains more than 60% of the variation. The resulting models represent a good predictive capacity and reveal specific particularities for each geopolitical block analysed. The prediction models conclude that the EU economic growth scenario is based on fossil energy sources in the first stage of development, followed by a transition to renewable energy sources once a tipping point is reached in the second stage of development. The decrease in renewable energy production capacity when oil consumption increases indicates that fossil fuels are trending in the G7 economy. In the case of BRICS, gas consumption is assumed to arise due to increasing industrial capacity, followed by increasing economic sustainability. In addition, the generalized additive models underline evolutionary scenarios with different particularities specific to each geopolitical bloc analysed.

The use of renewable energy is essential for sustainable consumption and environmental protection, especially in the context of the current energy crisis caused by political and military conflicts according to the authors (Gârdan et al., 2023). Research carried out by the collective of authors (Gârdan et al., 2023) aimed at using a sample of 1126 respondents to validate a theoretical model highlighting the complex relationship between specific variables such as environmental concern, renewable energy knowledge, perceived usefulness of renewable energy use, perceived ease of use of renewable energy, attitudes towards renewable energy use and behavioural intentions to use renewable energy. The results of the study showed that attitudes towards renewable energy use are strongly influenced by the other latent constructs, with perceived usefulness, social influence and environmental concern being among the most important determinants. In the authors' view behavioural intentions and actual renewable energy consumption behaviour are increasingly clearly expressed in decisions about the type of renewable energy technology preferred by consumers, and correlations with variables such as educational attainment and higher income are readily apparent.

In the opinion of Micu A. and collective (Micu et al., 2021) The Internet of Things (IoT) represents a transition to an enriched digital environment that connects smart objects and users, aiming to provide retailers with innovative ways to communicate with customers. Therefore, in research the authors set out to identify the openness of Romanian consumers to technological autonomy and the degree of acceptance of IoT services and technologies to address the Green Deal principle of low energy consumption. The study investigated the factors influencing the decision to purchase smart IoT devices and the customers' perception of the security of the data generated in this process. Based on the Technology Acceptance Model (TAM), this research proposed an alternative model consisting of 18 items measured on a Likert scale to identify the factors contributing to the consumer's perceived value and the behavioural precursors influencing the decision to purchase IoT products. The results of the study aimed to promote Smart Home IoT technologies and devices more effectively among Romanians, making it possible to control consumption and generate energy savings.

The current geopolitical context has brought an unprecedented energy crisis on the European energy market. The European Union has been forced to restrict its energy consumption and diversify its sources of supply due to its dependence on energy imports from Russia. Fortea and colleagues (Fortea et al., 2022) analysed the dynamics of the main energy indicators in Romania from a sustainable perspective and highlighted, through econometric modelling, the vulnerabilities induced by the current geopolitical context and the energy price crisis in Romania. The methods used included literature review, analysis of energy consumption and allocation dynamics in the period 2010–2020 according to Eurostat reports, as well as consumption trend modelling techniques to identify a valid econometric model adapted to the sustainable development objectives assumed by Romania. The results of the study are useful for national decision-makers in setting sustainable energy development policies for the period 2022–2030.

Besides the use of machine learning techniques such as XGBoost and generalized additive models in the analysis of the energy industry's impact on sustainable development, other advanced methods have been used to improve the accuracy of predictions and optimize renewable energy development strategies.

A notable example is artificial neural networks and deep learning models, which are increasingly being used to model the complex relationships between energy resource consumption, carbon emissions and renewable energy production. These models are able to learn non-linear models and integrate multiple factors, including government policies, energy market dynamics and climate change (Jin et al., 2024; Liang et al., 2024; R. Singh et al., 2024).

Another set of methods in recent use includes advanced econometric models, such as autoregressive lagged distribution models (ARDL) and error correction models (ECM). These models allow the investigation of short- and long-term causal relationships between fossil fuel consumption, renewable energy and environmental indicators, thus providing insights into the effectiveness of energy transition policies (Daly et al., 2024; Kripfganz & Schneider, 2023).

Also, approaches based on multi-objective optimization (Tudorică et al., 2024) are increasingly used to balance energy requirements and environmental impact. Genetic algorithms and methods based on swarm intelligence, such as particle swarm optimization (Delgarm et al., 2016; Ida Evangeline & Rathika, 2021), are used to identify the most efficient energy mixes and reduce dependence on fossil fuels.

Recent research has also explored the integration of renewable energy with smart grids and energy storage, using optimization techniques and machine learning algorithms to improve energy distribution and efficiency. For example, blockchain-based systems are being investigated to ensure transparency of transactions in the renewable energy sector, facilitating the integration of prosumers into the grid and improving the management of decentralized resources (Al Shareef et al., 2024; Khalid, 2024; Kiasari et al., 2024; Q. Wang et al., 2025). The diversification of renewable energy analysis and optimization methodologies contributes to a better understanding of the factors influencing the energy transition. The combined use of machine learning techniques, advanced econometrics and multi-objective optimization provides an integrated framework for the development of sustainable strategies in the energy sector.

A report by the International Energy Agency (IEA, 2022b) shows that the energy sector is currently facing an unprecedented crisis situation due to rising fuel prices, inflationary pressures and short supply chains, which creates an immediate need to accelerate the transformation of the sector towards increasing the share of renewable energy consumption and shifting towards the energy sustainability goals. Future directions are favourable for reallocating capital to the low-carbon energy industry and for increasing energy efficiency. These directions provide opportunities for sustainable growth of the sector and can tip the balance in adequately meeting growing energy demand. The global disparities and constraints in Sub-Saharan Africa are threats that need to be countered on the basis of a plan called by the International Energy Agency (IEA) the Net Zero Horizon 2050 Roadmap (IEA, 2022b). This report supports and promotes the financing of green energy and the transition to the green economy in emerging and developed economies. The geopolitical conflict triggered by Russia has revealed Europe's vulnerability to imported Russian energy resources, which was the subject of the Versailles meeting in March 2022, when European leaders decided to reduce energy dependence on Russian imports. The alternative sources targeted are fossil fuels supplied from other sources as well as accelerating investments to make the energy sector more efficient and increasing the share of renewables in total energy and other clean technology sources as an alternative to Russian products used for energy production in Europe. Cost pressures make energy security vulnerable and fuel inflation in crisis-hit economies. Investment in the energy economy has increased by more than 8% in 2022, but most of it is countermeasures to limit the effects of rising costs (Fig. 2.2).

Investments in energy are more necessary as the international economic climate is more vulnerable amid economic uncertainty, energy security and climate change concerns. Thus, total investments of $2.4 trillion have been estimated for the year 2022, mainly for energy efficiency, low-carbon fuel distribution and capital investment. Cost pressures are best represented in the oil fuel supply sector, but also affect clean energy technologies, which are represented by increases of 10–20% amid inflation and unavailability of some sub-assemblies (geopolitical conflict in Ukraine). The cost of energy bills paid by global consumers has reached a record figure of 2.2 in 2022 calculated at over $10 trillion, which has created social protection measures for the poor population through fiscal measures and price interventions (IEA, 2022b). In this context, some

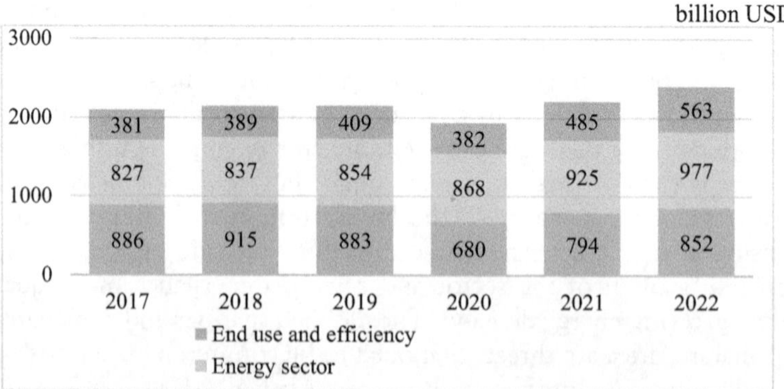


**Fig. 2.2** Global energy investment, 2017–2022. Source: Author based on IEA data (IEA, 2022a)

countries have opted to invest in the use of fossil fuels and have sought to diversify their sources of supply (case of the European Union).

Amid economic pressures and rising costs in the energy sector, investment alternatives have become a priority for many governments and private companies. These include expanding and improving renewable energy infrastructure, investing in energy storage and developing new energy efficiency technologies.

One area of growing interest is nuclear energy, which is seen as a viable solution for reducing carbon emissions and ensuring a steady flow of energy. Several countries, including the United States, France and China, have relaunched plans to build small modular reactors (SMRs), which offer significant advantages in terms of safety and operational flexibility (Holechek et al., 2022; International Atomic Energy Agency, 2022).

Another research direction is the development of green hydrogen technologies, which promise to play a key role in the global energy transition (Hassan, Algburi, et al., 2024; Hassan, Viktor, et al., 2024). Investment in high-efficiency electrolysers and the infrastructure needed to transport and store hydrogen is growing, with support from both governments and the private sector. The European Union has launched significant initiatives to create an internal market for hydrogen, and Japan and South Korea have established national strategies to integrate hydrogen into their energy mix (Alam et al., 2024; Cho et al., 2024; Genovese et al., 2023). In addition to these solutions, recent research (Aguilar et al., 2021; Biswas et al.,

2024; Safari et al., 2024) indicates a growing interest in the use of artificial intelligence and digital technologies to optimize energy consumption. AI-based energy management systems can help reduce losses and improve efficiency in distribution networks.

Faced with today's challenges, countries and investors are diversifying their strategies to ensure long-term energy security and sustainability. The transition to clean and efficient energy sources requires not only substantial funding but also collaboration between the public and private sectors and continuous technological advances to meet emerging global market demands. Clean energy investments are on track to exceed $1.4 trillion by 2022, which represents three-fourth of total energy investments. The growth rate for clean investment set by the 2015 Paris Agreement was 2% of GDP for signatory countries, yet as of 2020 this rate has increased to 12%, which shows the global interest in achieving climate goals and that important steps have been taken in this direction (IEA, 2022b). The largest investors at the 2021 level were China with $380 billion, followed by the European Union with $260 billion and the United States with $215 billion. It is estimated that at the level of 2022, the governments of the world's countries will invest more than $710 billion in clean energy. By area, the most important sectors attracting investment are: energy storage capacities—$20 billion in 2022; investments in hydrogen emission reduction technologies—$0.5 billion, with a 2030 target at the European Union level through the REPowerEU Energy Plan (European Commission, 2022); capital investment to reduce carbon emissions—$1.8 billion (Fig. 2.3).

Investment in clean energy is a central element of the global energy transition, with a significant impact on reducing greenhouse gas emissions and meeting the targets set by the Paris Agreement. According to recent literature, increased investment in renewable energy and sustainable infrastructure has been driven by more ambitious public policies as well as technological advances in areas such as energy storage, energy efficiency and the digitization of electricity grids (Dekeyrel & Fessler, 2024; K. A. Khan et al., 2023; Sun et al., 2024).

In addition, recent reports from the International Energy Agency show that investment in clean energy has outstripped investment in fossil fuels for the first time, marking a paradigm shift in the financing of the global energy sector (IRENA, 2024). Also, in the context of the energy crisis caused by geopolitical and economic factors, governments in developed countries have accelerated the implementation of strategies to diversify

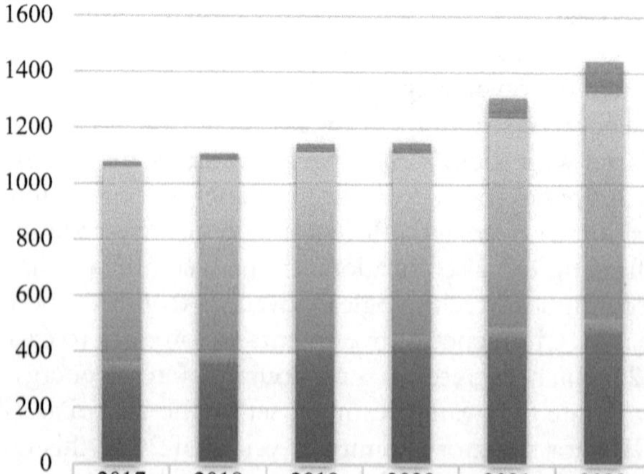


| | 2017 | 2018 | 2019 | 2020 | 2021 | 2022 |
|---|---|---|---|---|---|---|
| Electric vehicles | 5 | 13 | 19 | 27 | 55 | 93 |
| Low-carbon fuels | 11 | 10 | 10 | 10 | 16 | 19 |
| Grids and storage | 322 | 315 | 296 | 298 | 317 | 337 |
| Energy efficiency and other end-uses | 376 | 376 | 390 | 355 | 430 | 470 |
| Nuclear | 37 | 34 | 35 | 40 | 44 | 49 |
| Renewable energy | 326 | 359 | 393 | 418 | 446 | 472 |

**Fig. 2.3** Clean energy investment evolution, 2017–2022. Source: Author based on IEA data (IEA, 2022a)

energy sources and reduce dependence on traditional fuels, leading to significant increases in funding for solar, wind and green hydrogen (Bakhsh et al., 2024; Gajdzik et al., 2024; IRENA, 2022; Mesa Puyo et al., 2024).

Another key aspect of this process is the increasing interest of private and institutional investors in clean energy projects, amid growing awareness of climate risks and the increasing profitability of these investments. Venture capital funds and large energy corporations are reorienting their strategies towards sustainable technologies, and green financing mechanisms such as green bonds and impact funds are playing an increasingly important role in mobilizing the resources needed to transform the global energy system (Babic, 2024; Bhutta et al., 2022; Nasir & Ahmed, 2024).

Investments in fossil fuels are on an upward trend; this has been driven by the uncertain political climate which has led companies to behave cautiously about capital investment in the sector. The lowest investments are in coal supply, with almost $105 billion invested in coal supply chains, with an estimated 10% growth this year. The biggest investing countries in the sector have been China and India, mainly concerned with maintaining energy security and neglecting the Glasgow Agreement to reduce coal consumption. Thus in 2021, new coal mining capacities have been opened in China and other new capacities are in the planning stages. The upward trend in consumption is also evident in Europe amid energy security following the conflict in Ukraine. The oil and gas sector has seen similar variability in the wake of the war in Ukraine, with price increases of more than 30% at operators in the Middle East, Russia and South-East Asia (IEA, 2022b). Sustainable financing conditions for clean energy are affected by the much more volatile global financial markets during the pandemic and conflict in Ukraine. The efficiency and productivity of companies as measured by liquidity and equity profitability improved in 2022 compared to the periods prior to the outbreak of the COVID-19 pandemic. Oil and gas companies continued to increase their profits amid rising prices, while the cost of financing and raw materials were vulnerabilities for companies operating in the clean energy sector. The year 2021 signalled declining sustainability in the energy industry's debt insurance market with more than $1.7 trillion of insurance recorded, mostly green bonds to finance the green energy sector and green energy transmission.

Recent trends in the fossil fuel sector reflect complex dynamics influenced by geopolitical, economic and energy security factors. Rising investments in oil, gas and coal suggest a cautious approach by governments and companies in the context of uncertain energy supply and volatile international markets (Anh et al., 2024; S. Chen & Nouseen, 2025; Lin & Lan, 2025). These developments run counter to the decarbonization goals of the Paris Agreement and the Glasgow Climate Pact, highlighting the difficulty of energy transition in an unstable economic and political environment.

At the same time, the expansion of the extraction and transportation infrastructure for fossil fuels has led to an increase in global $CO_2$ emissions, with direct effects on accelerating climate change. According to the International Energy Agency (IEA, 2023), investment in oil and gas infrastructure has been driven in particular by demand growth in emerging economies, posing significant challenges for the implementation of sustainable energy transition policies.

On the other hand, financial conditions for clean energy have become more difficult amid macroeconomic instability and rising financing costs.

High interest rates and volatility in international financial markets have led to a slowdown in capital flows to green projects, which has affected the progress of renewable energy development plans globally (Murtaza & Luqman, 2025; Sultanuzzaman et al., 2024). While green bonds and other sustainable financing mechanisms continue to play an important role in supporting the transition, the accessibility of capital remains a challenge for clean energy companies compared to those in the fossil fuel industry, which benefit from higher profit margins and more consistent support from producer countries.

Research by energy experts (Madurai Elavarasan et al., 2021) aims to assess the impact of the global energy market on the economy in the context of economic, political and energy security uncertainties with the analysis of the challenges for technological development; thus most of the time a multilateral approach is proposed with the pursuit of changes on economic sustainability in the global context; the authors are oriented towards multilateral development strategies for boosting the transition to renewable energy consumption, digitalization of the energy sector and energy security.

Thus, some authors have focused in the study of energy efficiency on strategic development with a horizon of 2030, proposing new economic models for growth and digitalization of the sector (Yu et al., 2021). The proposed models aim at the distributive economy, increasing prosumers (personal carbon footprint), reducing social disparities and energy poverty and increasing the rate of investment in green energy. The energy models start from the standard efficiency function and through a matrix approach, where an energy efficiency indicator is proposed, which combines the above-mentioned models with energy digitalization and energy security:

$$EfE_{it} = \beta 0_{it} + \beta 1_{it} \sum_{i=1}^{n} \sum_{t=1}^{k} (MOD_{it}) + \beta 2_{it} \sum_{i=1}^{n} \sum_{t=1}^{k} (SECEn_{it}) + \varepsilon_{it} \qquad (2.1)$$

waves:

- $EfE_{it}$ is the energy efficiency index calculated by the authors (Yu et al., 2021) for 30 countries over the time horizon 2005–2018;
- $\beta$ are the model coefficients.
- ($MOD_{it}$) represents economic models for growth and digitalization of the sector: models on the distributive economy, increasing prosumerism (personal carbon footprint), reducing social

disparities and energy poverty and increasing the rate of investment in green energy.

- $SECEn_{it}$ is the energy security index.
- $\varepsilon_{it}$ is the residual of the econometric function.

According to the authors (Yu et al., 2021) the average energy efficiency index calculated at the level of the 30 countries is 56% for 2018, being better represented by the European countries (Austria, Belgium, Denmark, Italy, Poland, Hungary, Slovakia, Spain, Sweden, Poland, Hungary, Spain), where the average efficiency index at the level of 2018 is almost 60%, being exceeded by the values of New Zealand with 81%, Korea with 75% and the United States with 63%.

There are multiple models for the development of the energy sector in the literature. These models are summarized in Table 2.1.

The presented analysis reflects both the researchers' interest in the development of the energy sector and, more specifically, the alignment with the sustainable development targets projected for Horizon 2030 and Horizon 2050.

Thus, the global trend picture includes the development of renewable energy, namely biomass, hydropower, wind and solar. Another important aspect is the transition to the green sector in car manufacturing, the creation of electricity grids to power cars. According to researchers, the energy sector is conducive to sustainable environmental, economic and social development, as technologies will complement efforts to achieve Sustainable Development Goal 7, compatible with action to combat climate change. The complexity of the inter-relationship between SDG7 and the other Sustainable Development Goals motivates the development of scenarios for shifting energy consumption towards renewable energy sources and curbing carbon emissions associated with the energy industry.

## Economic Models in the Literature on Sustainable Development from the Perspective of Goal 8—Decent Work and Growth

Objective 8, decent work and growth, aims to promote socially inclusive sustainable economic growth and integrated, productive employment (Frey, 2017; Ralph & Arora, 2024). The resulting objectives aim at sustainable economic growth, diversification, innovation and improvement

**Table 2.1** Summary of the main economic models presented in the literature with reference to the implementation of Sustainable Development Goal 7

| *Author/year* | *Model conceptualization* | *Comments* |
|---|---|---|
| Kumar N.M., Chopra S.S., Chand A.A., Elavarasan R.M., Shafiullah G.M. (2020) | Proposes a framework for optimizing the hybrid energy system based on the key characteristics of the SDG7 Sustainable Development Goal of affordability, reliability, sustainability and timeliness (Kumar et al., 2020). | The authors select a few indicators for each characteristic (capital investment, energy security, renewable energy, carbon reduction, reliable power systems, etc.) The modelling considers these indicators to select the best feasible configuration of SDG7 through analysis and optimization techniques. The results recommend as a result of the sensitivity analysis solutions to increase investment in solar and wind energy utilization for the South India region with reduced consumption of petroleum products (diesel), with environmental and energy security impacts highlighted (Kumar et al., 2020). |
| Bansal S., Sharma G.D., Rahman M.M., Yadav A., Garg I. (2021) | The authors use indicators such as biological capacity, ecological footprint, energy consumption, Gini and financial development indexes, and the impact of commodity trade on economic growth to analyse the nexus of environmental, social and economic factors. The area of interest for which the research was conducted is South Asia (Bansal et al., 2021). | The research shows through the proposed statistical model with validation of working hypotheses that biological capacity, ecological footprint and energy consumption negatively influence economic growth; the following energy strategy elements are provided: policy-makers should focus on reducing regional inequalities (SDG5 and SDG10); this has beneficial long-term implications. Government bodies should encourage employment opportunities (SDG8) through feasible and sustainable financial plans. Governmental bodies should ensure and promote energy efficiency and reduction of energy consumption (SDG12) by shifting to clean and renewable energy (SDG7) using green technologies (SDG9) (Bansal et al., 2021). |

(*continued*)

**Table 2.1** (continued)

| *Author/year* | *Model conceptualization* | *Comments* |
|---|---|---|
| Sarkodie S. A., Ackom E., Bekun F.V., Owusu P.A. (2020) | Motivated by the Sustainable Development Goals (SDGs) and their impact by 2030, to examine the relationship between energy consumption (SDG7), climate (SDG13), economic growth and population growth in Kenya, Senegal and Eswatini. The authors used the Kernel of Least Squares (KRLS) automation technique and econometric methods such as Dynamic Ordinary Least Squares (DOLS) and Mean Group Estimation (PMG) models. The econometric techniques confirm the Environmental Kuznets Curve (EKC) hypothesis between income level and $CO_2$ emissions, while the machine learning method confirms the scale effect hypothesis (Sarkodie et al., 2020). | The authors find that while $CO_2$ emissions, population growth and income levels drive energy demand and use, economic development is driven by energy consumption and population dynamics. This demonstrates that income, population growth, energy and $CO_2$ emissions are inseparable, but require a collective participatory decision in realizing the SDGs (Sarkodie et al., 2020). |
| Aderemi T.A., Alejo A., Omoyele O. S., Olaoye O. P., Olanipekun W.D., Azuh D.E. (2022) | Based on the premise that the continued demand and use of energy in large quantities for industrial purposes has motivated the global advocacy for energy sustainability (SDG7), the authors used various econometric techniques to study the link between clean energy supply in Nigeria and industrial development between 1990 and 2019. The research aims to establish the nature of the long-run relationship, direction of causality and stochastic dynamic interaction between clean energy supply and industrial development in Nigeria. The authors find that the supply of clean energy and value-added output have evolved in inversely proportional relationship. Further evidence indicates that there is no feedback relationship between clean energy supply and industrial development. Also, the stochastic dynamic between clean energy supply and industrial development shows that the value-added output undergoes significant compression, while the variance decomposition of clean energy supply indicates similar effect on the behaviour of industrial development (Aderemi et al., 2022). | In the light of the findings from this study, the following recommendations are made for policy-makers in Nigeria; in achieving the Sustainable Development Goal (SDG7), clean energy supply could be explored for future industrial development in Nigeria with sustainable economic effects (Aderemi et al., 2022). |

Source: Author

of economic productivity, promotion of economic policies to support job creation, improved resource efficiency in consumption and production, full employment and decent work with equal pay (Chigbu & Nekhwevha, 2023; Stoian et al., 2019). Other outcome objectives are promoting youth employment; ending modern slavery, child trafficking and its exploitation; and promoting secure employment and other benefits for workers, such as universal access to banking, insurance and financial services (Rendtorff, 2019; Singla et al., 2023).

Sustainable Development Goal 8 is a centrepiece of the Sustainable Development Strategy, with indicators of progress being highly sensitive to conditions of uncertainty. For example, the pandemic that started in early 2020 has had the direct effect of lowering living standards, including in developed countries, which have been hit by unemployment and the economic crisis (Bundervoet et al., 2022; Karpunina et al., 2022). This period has seen a shift from working in the office to working at home, with the digital economic system being impacted to the detriment of the traditional economic system (Battisti et al., 2022; Yao et al., 2024). Women, young people and people with disabilities have suffered the most severe effects of the pandemic, representing the most affected population in terms of access to decent and secure employment (Debono & Garzia, 2022). The outbreak of geopolitical conflicts has exacerbated these vulnerabilities, with an observable impact on the annual growth rate of Gross Domestic Product (Fig. 2.4).

The results of the pandemic were manifested in reduced labour productivity, which worsened the overall situation of firms that were faced with supply and supply chain bottlenecks, rising raw material costs, inflation and problems in recruiting the necessary staff. At the same time, the pandemic and the geopolitical uncertainties have affected unemployment, which will reach 6.2% in 2022 compared to 5.4% in 2021, down from 6.6% in the year of the pandemic's onset (2020). In European countries, the level of unemployment has varied over the period by an average of 5–10 percentage points compared to the global average (5.5% in 2020 and 5.7% in 2022) as a result of the geopolitical conflict. Other features of the conditions of uncertainty have manifested themselves in the decreasing availability of jobs in the traditional economy and increasing jobs in the digital economy, the increasing number of children engaged in early child labour and the increasing risk of extreme poverty.

Figure 2.5 shows three important economic indicators at EU and Member State level: the employment rate; the percentage of young people

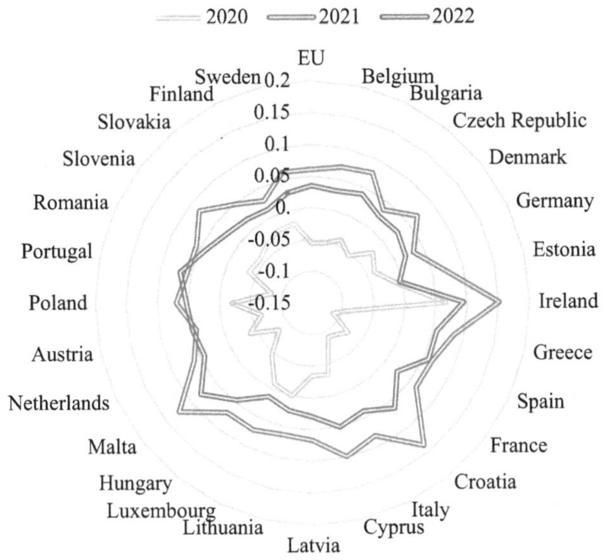


**Fig. 2.4** Annual GDP growth rate for EU member countries, 2020–2022. Source: Author based on Eurostat data (Eurostat, 2023a)

not in employment, education or training (NEETs); and the long-term unemployment rate. The employment rate reflects the percentage of employed persons in the population; a higher value indicates a larger active labour force. The highest values were recorded in the Czech Republic, Germany and Sweden, suggesting robust labour markets. On the other hand, Greece and Italy have significantly lower rates, which may indicate structural problems in their economies. NEET youth share is an indicator measuring economic inactivity and untapped potential among young people. Greece, Spain and Italy face major challenges here, with the highest NEET rates, suggesting difficulties in integrating young people into the labour market or education. The long-term unemployment rate shows the percentage of the unemployed who are out of work for a long period of time and is an indicator of rigidities and difficulties in the labour market. Greece and Spain have the highest rates, reflecting the impact of economic crises and deficiencies in employment and training policies. Comparing countries, there are significant variations between the Nordic and Southern economies. Nordic countries, such as Sweden and Denmark, tend to have higher employment rates and lower NEET and long-term unemployment

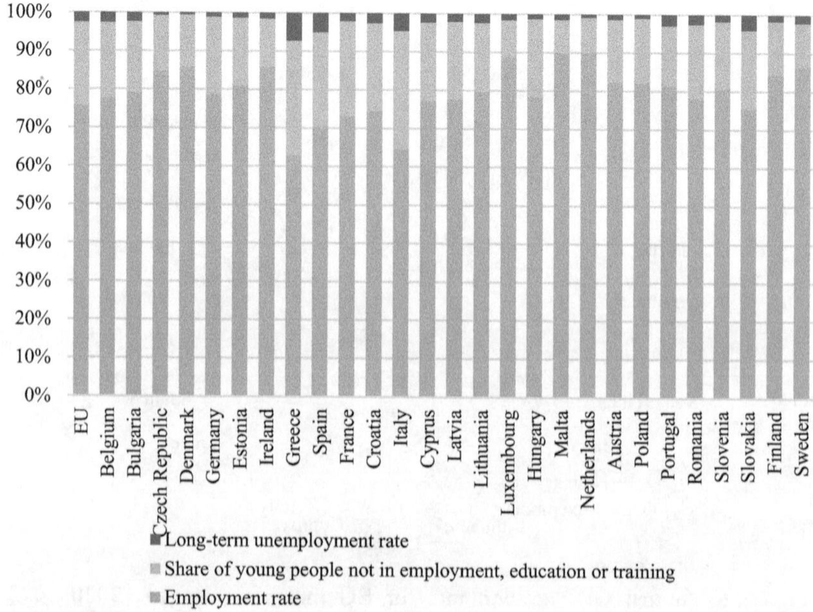


**Fig. 2.5** Evolution of outcome indicators for Sustainable Development Goal 8 by 2022 at European level. Source: Author based on Eurostat data (Eurostat, 2023b)

rates, indicating more flexible labour markets and more effective education and training systems. While Southern countries are struggling with higher unemployment and NEET youth rates, leading to structural reforms and policy interventions to improve the situation.

In the literature there are numerous concerns on sustainable development on impact levels on Sustainable Development Goal 8. Sustainable Development Goal 8 (SDG8) on "decent work and growth" is closely linked to the energy transition and economic sustainability, with major implications for the labour market, productivity and social inclusion. As stated in the literature (Ahmad et al., 2024; Pollin, 2023; Thake, 2025), the transition to a green economy creates both opportunities and challenges for achieving MDG 8, as it requires retraining of the workforce and restructuring of industrial sectors dependent on fossil fuels.

In this respect, studies show that investments in clean energy and the circular economy can create millions of jobs globally, contributing to sustainable economic growth (Kandpal et al., 2024; Mukherjee et al., 2023;

M. X. Wang et al., 2023). International Renewable Energy Agency (IRENA, 2023) estimates that the energy transition could generate more than 40 million jobs in the renewable energy sector by 2050, making up for losses in the fossil fuel industry. However, this transformation requires adequate training and social protection policies to ensure a just transition so that workers from traditional industries are integrated into the new economic sectors.

On the other hand, the literature emphasizes that economic sustainability depends not only on job growth but also on job quality (Berg et al., 2023; Bracarense & Bracarense Costa, 2024). There are now concerns about the precariousness of work in new green industries, where a significant proportion of the jobs created are temporary or low-paid, especially in developing regions (Baldry et al., 2024; OECD, 2024). Public policies must therefore aim not only to stimulate investment in the green economy but also to create fair and sustainable working conditions for all workers involved in the energy transition.

From the analysis of more than 8300 articles published between 1975 and 2022 (on the Web of Science platform), we found that the concept of sustainable economic development is well represented in the scientific community, being a growing area of interest, as demonstrated by the citation rate of articles: 7.92 citations per article, i.e. 27,378 articles in which 8300 articles are cited (Fig. 2.6). The figure is produced using the VOSviewer program with bibliometric information collected from the Web of Science platform.

In an interesting paper (Frey, 2017) it critically examines the Sustainable Development Goal from two perspectives: the business approach advocated by the International Organization of Employers (IOE) and the human right to full employment and decent work advocated by the International Trade Union Confederation (ITUC) and human rights NGOs. While full employment and decent work are indeed important in relation to Sustainable Development Goal 8, the 2030 Agenda pursues market-centred institutional arrangements that may present obstacles to achieving the goal. Specifically, the limitation of the human rights to full employment and decent work that sits on a business-oriented growth trend in SDG8 calls into question the 2030 Agenda's objectives. The article concludes that the SDG8 presents both opportunities for human rights monitoring and accountability and increased legitimacy for business.

Another approach to sustainable development from the SDG8 perspective by authors Bilek-Steindl S. and Url T. (Bilek-Steindl & Url, 2022)

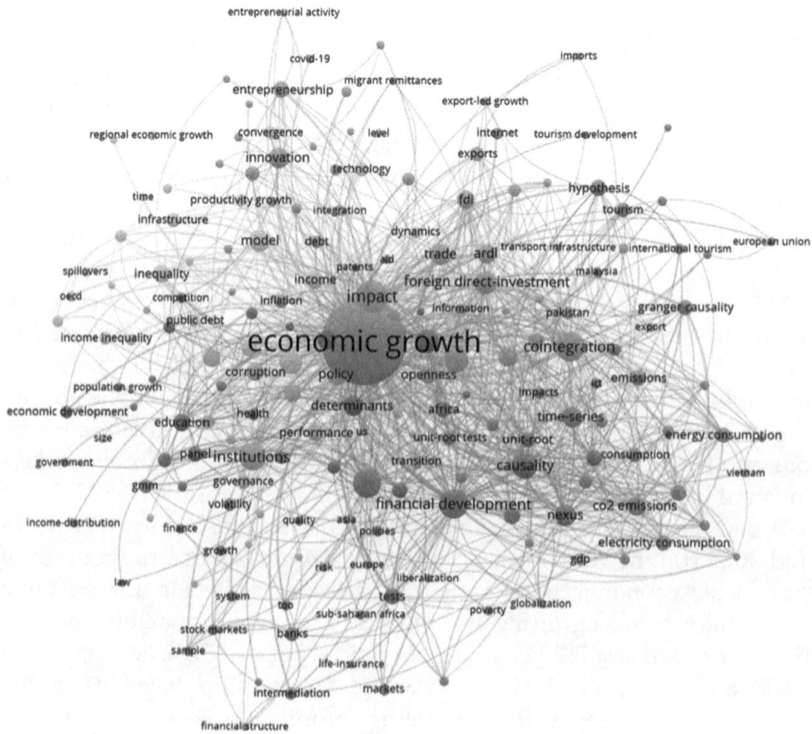


**Fig. 2.6** Bibliometric analysis on sustainable development from the perspective of Sustainable Development Goal 8, 2019–2022. Source: Author using VOSviewer software

starts with the implementation of dynamic factor models based on the quarterly data set monitored at the European Union level, namely: real GDP per capita, GDP investment rate, number of young people out of work and out of education, employment rate, long-term unemployment rate and work-related death rate. The period analysed by the conducted research was 1990–2020, the authors showing that the influences of economic or pandemic crises can significantly affect the level of achievement of sustainable development goals, including through seasonal influence (quarterly GDP), which picks up elements of uncertainty and affects the level of statistical significance of econometric models (which was observed for Austria in the period 2014–2019, a period when the level of significance coefficients of statistical tests were underrepresented in relation to the maximum allowable level of error representation).

A topical study (Rehman et al., 2024) investigates the increasingly important issue of sustainable tourism development through the lens of Big Data analysis, economic considerations and policy frameworks. Guided by the Theory of Planned Behaviour, seven hypotheses were formulated to explore how certain variables influence attitudes, subjective norms, perceived behavioural control, intentions and actual involvement in sustainable tourism, and using structural equation modelling (SEM) for data analysis, the authors found substantial evidence supporting the hypotheses.

Results showed that Big Data analysis significantly influences attitudes towards sustainable tourism. Economic factors shape societal norms and expectations of sustainable tourism, while policy frameworks affect individuals' perceived control over sustainable tourism activities. The study also confirmed that positive attitudes towards sustainable tourism led to higher intentions to engage in such practices, which in turn is predictive of actual engagement. In addition, societal norms and perceived behavioural control were found to be significant predictors of both intentions to engage and actual engagement in sustainable tourism practices.

Overall, the results indicate that Big Data analytics play a significant role in shaping attitudes and behaviours towards sustainable tourism. Economic and policy considerations were also found to be key determinants. This research not only fills an academic gap but also provides actionable insights for policy-makers and stakeholders in the tourism sector. Recent studies on sustainable development highlight the interdependencies between sustainable tourism, the circular economy, emerging technologies and public policies, reinforcing the importance of integrated approaches in achieving the Sustainable Development Goals (SDGs). Research by Rehman et al. (2024) on the use of Big Data in analysing sustainable tourism behaviour is complemented by Zhang and Deng's (Zhang & Deng, 2024), which explores the influence of artificial intelligence and machine learning algorithms on the optimization of tourism strategies, reducing negative environmental impacts through efficient management of tourism resources and flows.

A scenario-based research (Allen et al., 2016) highlights the significant implications of the implementation of the Sustainable Development Goals for the development of national economies. The research conducts a meta-analysis of over 80 econometric models of sustainable development, concluding that vertical (top-down) macroeconomic models of analysis are more appropriate for determining national and supranational long-term development scenarios, capitalizing on intra-sectoral synergies, while sectoral (bottom-up) models support the level of choice of interventions, quantification of technology needs or investments. Regarding econometric models applied to sustainable development, recent research by Pierre et al., 2024 (Pierre et al., 2024) and Giglio et al. (Giglio et al., 2023) emphasizes the importance of hybrid economic models, which combine top-down and bottom-up approaches to determine sustainable national development scenarios. This study supports the findings of Allen et al. (2016), demonstrating that the implementation of the SDGs requires effective coordination between macroeconomic strategies and policy interventions at the sectoral level.

Rendtorff J., in a research carried out in 2019 (Rendtorff, 2019), makes the connection between the Sustainable Development Goals and progressive business models for economic transformation. According to the author, the SDGs combine political goals with visions of economic development and social justice and are important for business ethics and corporate social responsibility. The aim of the research focused on the possibilities of Sustainable Development Goals to contribute to the development of business ethics and corporate sustainability.

The integration of ESG (Environmental, Social and Governance) principles into corporate strategies has become a central topic in the literature. The study by Martiny et al. (Martiny et al., 2024) confirms that the adoption of these practices not only improves corporate sustainability but also generates competitive advantages by making companies more attractive to responsible investors and consumers. These findings complement Rendtorff's (2019) analysis of the link between SDGs and progressive business models.

An interesting approach is that of the authors Stoian, Monterroso and Current (Stoian et al., 2019) who show that through combinations of different paradigms, the prioritizations of sustainable development goals are differentiated. Climate change is, in the authors' view, a vulnerability that all world governments should address as a matter of priority, and improving environmental conditions can help maximize synergies by reconciling government policies with sustainable development standards. Promoting decent work is necessary and the authors recommend integrated measures of economic growth and decent work that consider wider social and environmental impacts.

Climate change remains a key determinant of sustainable development strategies and the Gutner and Heltberg study (Gutner & Heltberg, 2025) emphasizes that adapting government policies to new climate challenges requires flexible financing mechanisms and transnational collaboration. This is in line with research by Stoian et al. (2019), which argues for the need for integrated measures to combat climate impacts and promote decent work.

Ionescu, Zlati and Antohi (Ionescu et al., 2021) approach the SDGs in an integrated manner, showing that sustainability can only be achieved by striving to improve all the goals and analysing on a number of five goals, namely SDG1, SDG4, SDG7, SDG8 and SDG9. The authors followed a cluster approach in identifying regional sustainable development at NUTS2 level in the European Union. The authors conclude that there are large disparities in sustainable development based on regional financial autonomy and administrative capacity; the cluster approach highlights the need for sustainable regional development based on corrective policies derived from the stability and volatility index defined using the proposed econometric model. The analysis of regional disparities in the achievement of the SDGs is extended by the study of D'Adamo and Rossi (D'Adamo & Rossi, 2024), which uses a Europe-wide clustering model to identify sustainability gaps and the impact of financial autonomy on administrative capacity to implement green policies. This approach confirms the results of Ionescu et al. (2021) and emphasizes the need for corrective policies based on balancing the distribution of resources and strengthening regional institutional capacities.

Thus, recent research reinforces the idea that sustainable development requires a multidimensional approach, where technological innovations, economic models and ethical principles are integrated into governance strategies and policy decisions. Advances in Big Data analytics, the circular economy and ESG policies offer viable solutions to overcome sustainability challenges and reduce regional inequalities.

In the literature, economic growth is an area of permanent interest as a reliable alternative to satisfying consumption needs in a growing population driven by demographic growth. These models are summarized in Table 2.2.

In the literature it has been shown through different economic models and methods that indicators of economic growth and human resource development develop objective synergies influenced by national and supranational economic interest (Rosato et al., 2021), being related to financial

**Table 2.2** Summary of the main economic models presented in the literature with reference to the implementation of Sustainable Development Goal 8

| *Authors/year* | *Research* | |
|---|---|---|
| Osińska M., Kufel T. Błażejowski M., Kufel P. (2020) | Objective | The authors propose to apply a non-linear time-series autoregressive mechanism to examine the possible relationship between the economic growth rate and its potential determinants, including the rate of public debt-to-GDP coverage ratio (Osińska et al., 2020). |
| | Indicators | GDP growth rate;<br>Industrial production growth rate;<br>Public debt;<br>Inflation rate;<br>Interest rate;<br>Unemployment rate |
| | Results | The models reveal different mechanisms of the dynamics of endogenous variables considering their dynamics over time. The authors have demonstrated based on working hypotheses that macroeconomic indicators in dynamics can adequately define clusters of development in European countries under the influence of the political factor. In a broader sense the authors show that the institutional organization in the Member States influences the level of their sustainable development (Osińska et al., 2020). |
| Agarkov G.A., Tarasyeva T.V. (2020) | Objective | The authors aim to estimate the proportional development of the economic system using the economic growth model. They start from the premise that one of the most important components of socio-economic systems of sustainable development is ensuring its economic security. The process of ensuring the economic security of the region consists in maintaining stable regional functioning with constant improvement of the socio-economic situation. The main parameters of the socio-economic system development affect the process of realization of economic security in the region (Agarkov & Tarasyeva, 2020). |
| | Indicators | The growth model (R. Solow);<br>GDP;<br>Capital per employee;<br>Optimal investment plan;<br>The model considers three factors: the size of capital K(t), labour L(t) at time t and also the volume of output Y(t), which is given by the Cobb-Douglas production function. To go to the relative values of the factors considered, we use labour productivity as a function of the capital-labour ratio. |
| | Results | According to the authors, the use of the modified Solow model makes it possible to predict the dynamics of the main macroeconomic indicators in the short and long term, as well as to assess the potential of regions to ensure sustainable proportional development (Agarkov & Tarasyeva, 2020). |

(*continued*)

**Table 2.2** (continued)

| *Authors/year* | *Research* | |
|---|---|---|
| Malik M. (2021) | Objective | The research uses the simultaneous equation modelling approach to investigate the three-way link between economic growth, energy consumption and environmental quality in Turkey for the period 1970–2014 (Malik, 2021). |
| | Indicators | The study uses the amount of physical capital, labour force, value added in production, trade openness, credit to the private sector and urbanization as control variables.<br>The econometric approach controls for problems of non-stationarity, endogeneity, correlation between errors and heteroscedasticity. The robustness of the results is checked using the three-stage least squares estimator (3SLS). |
| | Results | The statistical results of the paper support the existence of bidirectional causality between energy consumption and economic growth, $CO_2$ emissions and economic growth and $CO_2$ emissions and energy consumption. Moreover, the results indicate the existence of a monotonically increasing relationship between $CO_2$ emissions and economic growth, which implies the non-existence of the Environmental Kuznets Curve hypothesis in Turkey during the analysed period 1970–2014 (Malik, 2021). |
| Armeanu D.S., Joldes C.C., Gherghina S.C., Andrei J.V. (2021) | Objective | The authors aim to explore the link between energy consumption, $CO_2$ emissions, economic growth and urbanization worldwide. To achieve this goal, the authors used several advanced statistical techniques to analyse the complex relationships between these variables, study the cointegration between variables, the impulse response function to track the effect of a shock that arises and investigate the types of causality that are established by the Granger test. |
| | Indicators | Variables representing economic growth (GDP growth, growth per capita);<br>Variables representing energy consumption;<br>Variables representing $CO_2$ emissions;<br>Variables representing urbanization (urban population as percentage of total population);<br>Variables representing inexhaustible energy |
| | Results | The empirical results confirmed the presence of long-run associations. The impulse response functions (IRF) decompositions illustrated the extent to which renewable energy consumption, different types of energy, economic growth, $CO_2$ emissions, and urbanization are determined by innovations in the other variables of the systems. Following the Granger causality test, both unidirectional and bidirectional causal relationships were identified. |

(*continued*)

**Table 2.2** (continued)

| *Authors/year* | *Research* | |
|---|---|---|
| Traore A., Sene N. (2020) | Objective | The authors propose a model of economic growth in the context of factional drift.<br>The Caputo-Liouville derivative fractional growth model was considered.<br>The optimization problem solved by the Hamiltonian function was proposed for obtaining the optimal growth rate (Traore & Sene, 2020). |
| | Indicators | Fractional derivatives with singularity—Riemann-Liouville derivative, Caputo-Liouville derivative and their generalized forms.<br>Fractional derivatives, Caputo-Fabrizio derivative and Atangana-Baleanu derivative and their discrete forms. |
| | Results | The main conclusion was the strategy adopted to derive the growth rate equation with the classical derivative not the same as that adopted with the fractional model (Traore & Sene, 2020). |

Source: Author

indicators supporting economic growth. The financial indicators quantify the evolution of economic boom and crisis periods, which show cyclical trends with increased incidence rates due to an exogenous variable such as the economic growth memory or the impact of supranational sustainable development policies (M. K. Khan et al., 2021). Since the Second World War, economic growth models were initially developed multiplicatively and later design and forecasting elements, non-linear functions, auto-regression mechanisms, representational thresholds, factional analysis etc. were added.

Today, economic models are being used in the development of strategic plans for sustainable development as they are known as Agenda 2030 and Agenda 2050. However interrelated the development goals may be, it has been scientifically recognized that there are large development disparities in the global economy, mainly based on national institutional orientations (political regimes, patterns of administration and governance, integration into global economic clusters). In terms of SDG8 (Ribeiro-Duthie, 2020) the most important partnerships aim at sustaining economic growth so that these disparities are reduced with the effective development of supportive policies for productive activities, decent jobs, entrepreneurship, micro-enterprise development and ensuring access to financial services.

## Economic Models in the Literature on Sustainable Development from the Perspective of Objective 9—Industry, Innovation and Infrastructure

Sustainable Development Goal 9 meets the expectation of building a resilient infrastructure together with promoting inclusive and sustainable infrastructure and innovation (Mio et al., 2020). Industrial development has gone through several stages, from the extensive stage until the 1970s of the last century to the intensive stage based on technologization and efficiency, and later, with the development of the Internet, the issues of digitalization of industry became increasingly significant in building a resilient industry.

Sustainable Development Goal 9 (SDG9) plays a central role in promoting a sustainable economy by developing resilient infrastructure, supporting inclusive industrialization and stimulating innovation. Specialized studies (Chander et al., 2022; Rame et al., 2024; Rijwani et al., 2025) underlines that the industrial and technological transformations of the last decades have been catalysed by the rapid progress of digitalization and the implementation of Industry 4.0 concepts, which include artificial intelligence, the Internet of Things (IoT), blockchain and advanced automation. These technologies have helped to increase the efficiency of industrial processes, optimize supply chains and reduce environmental impacts, facilitating the transition towards a circular and sustainable economy (M. I. Khan et al., 2025; Rusch et al., 2023; Sánchez-García et al., 2024).

A key aspect of the implementation of SDG9 is the development of sustainable and smart infrastructure integrated into economic and social systems. According to research by D'Orazio (D'Orazio, 2025), public-private partnerships (PPPs) and innovative financing mechanisms, such as green bonds and impact funds, have become essential in attracting the investment needed to modernize infrastructure. In this context, Abu-Rayash and Dincer (Abu-Rayash & Dincer, 2025) highlights that smart infrastructure, based on digitization and energy efficiency, contributes to reducing socio-economic vulnerabilities, thus boosting the resilience of urban and rural communities. These results are also confirmed by the authors' analysis (Rani et al., 2024), which has demonstrated that the implementation of advanced technological solutions in transmission grids and electricity distribution systems leads to reductions in greenhouse gas emissions and increased efficiency in the use of natural resources.

Sustainable industrialization is also strongly correlated with the adoption of circular economy principles. Authors' study (Chabowski et al., 2023) has shown that the shift towards production models based on reuse and recycling of resources generates substantial economic benefits, both by reducing production costs and by increasing the competitiveness of firms in international markets. Other research (Ionaşcu & Noja, 2024; Surmeier et al., 2024; Wigger, 2023) has shown that investments in sustainable infrastructure contribute significantly to reducing regional disparities, facilitating the integration of less developed regions into global value chains and increasing economic and social cohesion at supranational level.

From a macroeconomic perspective, recently developed analytical models demonstrate that the implementation of resilient and sustainable infrastructures requires a multidimensional approach, combining efficient economic policies, advanced technologies and flexible financing mechanisms. According to Lv et al. (Lv et al., 2024) and Asfaw et al. (Asfaw et al., 2024), hybrid economic models, which combine macroeconomic (top-down) and sector-specific (bottom-up) approaches, are best suited to project long-term development scenarios and to identify the intra-sectoral synergies needed in the process of sustainable industrialization. These findings are in line with previous research (Field & Look, 2018; Linkov et al., 2022; Mahajan et al., 2022), which has emphasized that resilient infrastructure cannot be separated from coherent economic strategies and innovative supporting policies.

Specialized studies (Kulkov et al., 2024; Sharma & Gupta, 2024) emphasized that achieving the goals of SDG9 requires a profound structural transformation of the global economy, based on emerging technologies, sustainable innovation and economic policies adaptable to current challenges. The development of smart infrastructure and resilient industry is an essential prerequisite for sustainable economic growth, the reduction of regional inequalities and the effective integration of national economies into global production and distribution networks.

Industrial revolutions have unfolded successively, and we are now in the fifth industrial revolution (Fig. 2.7).

At EU level the development of Industry 5.0 is a key component of the economic and social transformation towards a sustainable economy. It represents the desideratum of efficient and productive development in a single goal and revitalization of the role and contribution of industry in society as a basis for prosperity and protection of ecosystems (M. Chen et al., 2021).

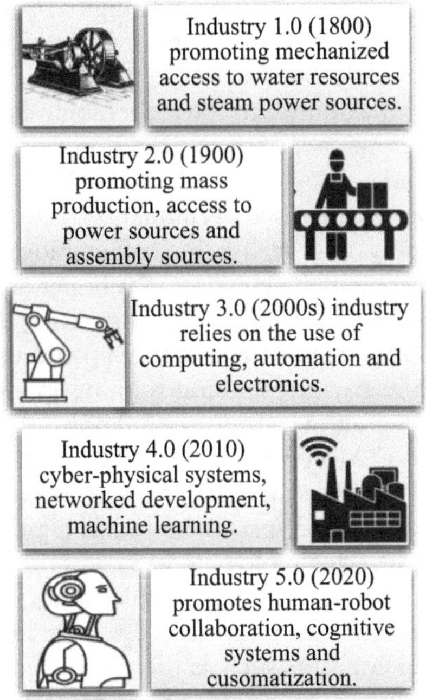


**Fig. 2.7** Industrial revolution. Source: Author

At European Union level, the transition to Industry 5.0 is recognized as an essential component of the process of economic and social transformation, with the main objective of reconciling technological progress with social needs and environmental protection (Industry 5.0, 2024; Schröder et al., 2024). In contrast to Industry 4.0, which focused on automation, digitalization and operational efficiency, Industry 5.0 emphasizes human-machine collaboration, sustainability and resilience, thus contributing to a more balanced and human-centric production model.

A fundamental aspect of Industry 5.0 is the integration of emerging technologies with industrial processes in a way that maximizes energy efficiency and the use of renewable resources. Specialized studies (Turner et al., 2022; Zong & Guan, 2024) have shown that the application of artificial intelligence (AI), the Internet of Things (IoT) and collaborative robotics can transform production chains into circular and adaptive systems, reducing waste and raw material consumption. To this end, research by Ashraf et al. (Ashraf et al., 2024) and Jianing et al. (Jianing et al., 2024) confirms that sustainable digitization of industry can help reduce the environmental footprint by striking a balance between productivity and ecosystem protection.

In addition to the technological component, Industry 5.0 brings to the fore the need for resilience and social inclusion. According to specialized studies (Suganya et al., 2024; Verma, 2024), this stage of industrial development aims to rehumanize economic processes, with a focus on the safety and well-being of employees, but also on reducing economic inequality by creating jobs better adapted to the needs of the digital society. Solvang et al. (Solvang et al., 2024) and Sheikh et al. (Sheikh et al., 2024) have shown that countries that invest in STEM education, digital infrastructure and innovation support schemes succeed in accelerating the integration of Industry 5.0 principles and boosting economic competitiveness. Moreover, some studies (Behera et al., 2024; Halim-Lim et al., 2025; Hossain et al., 2024) stressed that the adoption of production models based on sustainability and digitization enables emerging economies to reduce technological gaps with developed economies, facilitating global economic cohesion. In this context, the European Union is promoting an industrial strategy geared towards sustainability and innovation, integrating concepts such as the circular economy, carbon reduction and responsible use of natural resources (Baldassarre, 2025; Hojnik et al., 2024). According to Terzi et al.'s analysis (Terzi et al., 2023), recent European policies aim to redefine the role of industry as a pillar of the green and digital transition, transforming production into a factor of economic prosperity and ecosystem protection.

Recent literature confirms that Industry 5.0 is not just a continuation of digitization, but a new industrial model in which economic efficiency is coupled with social and environmental responsibility. This transformation process is a strategic opportunity for the EU to strengthen its global position in technology and sustainability, providing a balanced development framework between economic progress and environmental protection.

Figure 2.8 shows the main indicators for Sustainable Development Goal 9 at EU level for 2021.

The data presented in Fig. 2.8 show that countries such as Austria, Belgium, Denmark, Finland, Germany and Sweden have relatively higher R&D expenditure, suggesting that there is a correlation between the size of the economy and the resources allocated to R&D. Although the EU average for R&D expenditure is 1.49% of GDP, there are significant variations between member countries. Sweden, for example, invests more than

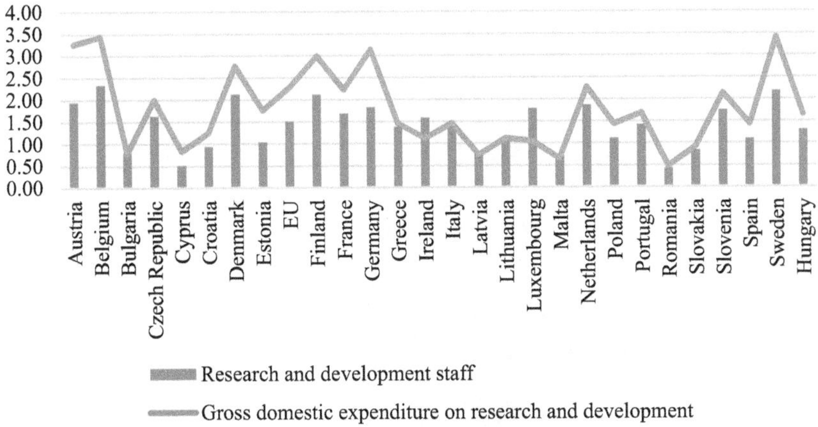


**Fig. 2.8** Evolution of key result indicators for Sustainable Development Goal 9 in 2021. Source: Author based on Eurostat data (Eurostat, 2023c)

3% of GDP in R&D, while other countries, such as Bulgaria and Malta, invest less than 1%. Increased spending on research and development contributes to innovation, economic growth and job creation in the research and technology industry.

From the analysis of 7850 articles selected for the period 2019–2022 (from the Web of Science platform), we can observe an increased interest represented by the Hirsh index of articles (39) and by the average citation rate of 2.63 citations per article, with over 20,600 articles cited in the papers, of which 18,797 articles without self-citations (Fig. 2.9).

The literature in the SDG9 research focuses on the inevitable digital transformation of economic organizations and society as a whole, and the term "digital economy" has become established (Palomares et al., 2021). From the perspective of sustainability, researchers are focused on the development of human resources to benefit from the opportunities offered by industrial revolutions, which requires the implementation of digital technologies in the education process and familiarization of human resources with cloud computing, data analytics and artificial intelligence technologies (Mio et al., 2020). These technologies implemented in developing countries can contribute to reducing extreme poverty rates and promoting gender equality. The benefits of investing in infrastructure and innovation, know-how development and the innovation process are

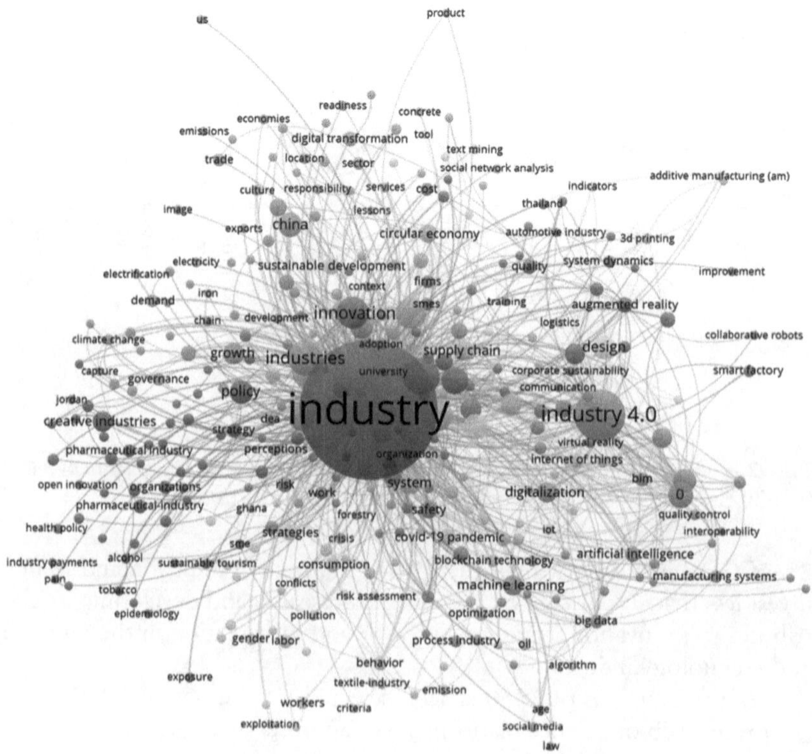


**Fig. 2.9** Bibliometric analysis on Sustainable Development Goal 9 between 2019 and 2022. Source: Author using VOSviewer software

all opportunities for implementing SDG9. The economic models presented in the literature are diverse, some of which are neural models for assessing synergies in sustainable development (Türkeli, 2020). The authors point out that the neural model can easily highlight the interdependencies between SDGs; the study was conducted on 162 countries and 17 SDGs (Türkeli, 2020). The synergy assessed based on the Fuzzy model shows common factors that are often related to local and national policies, performance targets, assumed reforms and development orientation through sustainable innovations. The importance of digital transformation in achieving Sustainable Development Goal (SDG) 9 is highlighted by various research studies (Almeida & Okon, 2024; Regona et al., 2024) which have aimed to promote resilient infrastructure, sustainable industrialization and encourage innovation. This transformation is essential for modernizing economies and adapting to contemporary challenges.

Central to this transformation is the development of human resources. The integration of digital technologies in the education process is essential to prepare the workforce to seize the opportunities offered by the new industrial revolutions (Manchanda & Arora, 2023). This involves familiarization with technologies such as cloud computing, data analytics and artificial intelligence. Implementing these technologies in developing countries can help reduce extreme poverty and promote gender equality.

Investments in infrastructure and innovation are also key to achieving SDG 9. Skills development and innovative processes offer significant opportunities in this regard. The economic models proposed in the literature are diverse; for example, neural models are used to assess synergies in sustainable development, highlighting the interdependencies between the different SDGs (Regona et al., 2024). In addition, fuzzy model-based assessments reveal common factors, often linked to local and national policies, performance targets, committed reforms and development guidelines through sustainable innovations (Abdullah et al., 2023). These assessments emphasize the importance of adaptable economic policies and effective governance to facilitate the transition to a digital and sustainable economy. Achieving SDG9 requires an integrated approach that combines digital transformation, human resource development, investment in infrastructure and innovation and the implementation of flexible and context-specific economic policies. Other sustainable development models under Sustainable Development Goal 9—Industry, Innovation and Infrastructure—have been reviewed in the literature and summarized in Table 2.3.

The adoption of the 2030 Agenda has meant taking on targets on inclusive and sustainable industrialization, innovation and supporting infrastructure systems. The difficulty in monitoring achievements in this area has arisen against the backdrop of rapid economic growth and the lack of historical data that can be tracked through indicators (Türkeli, 2020). Thus, efforts have been initiated at the level of supranational statistical structures affiliated to the United Nations, the European Commission or the OECD to construct global reporting to monitor technological progress, digitization or innovation (Kynčlová et al., 2020). Various development indices have subsequently been developed, such as the World Economic Forum's Inclusive Development Index. The scores estimated at

**Table 2.3** Summary of the main economic models presented in the literature with reference to the implementation of Sustainable Development Goal 9

| *Research* | | |
|---|---|---|
| Karobliene V., Pilinkiene V. (2021) | Objective | The purpose of this research study was to establish a framework for the relationship between the sharing economy and the Sustainable Development Goals (SDGs) set by the United Nations. There are 17 SDGs with 169 targets, which, in the scientific literature, are categorized into dimensions of sustainability: economic, social and environmental (Karobliene & Pilinkiene, 2021). |
| | Indicators | In this study, a theoretical model of the sharing economy was developed; a cluster analysis was conducted to determine the impact of the sharing economy on the EU countries in terms of the SDGs in the economic dimension.<br>– Gross domestic expenditure on R&D by sector (% of GDP)<br>– Human resources in science and technology (% of active population aged 25–64)<br>– R&D personnel (all sectors) (% of active population)<br>– Patent applications at the European Patent Office (number)<br>– Share of buses and trains in total passenger transport (% of total passenger/km by land)<br>– Medium and high-tech industry (including construction) (% of production value added) |
| | Results | Analysing the sharing economy from the perspective of sustainable economic development shows that this business model has a positive impact on the economic sustainability of countries in terms of the SDGs.<br>The sharing economy is a relevant theme with a significant impact to be recognized as a factor for the sustainable development of countries. In the research literature reviewed, the notion of "access over ownership" is a substantial factor in improving business performance for sustainability (Karobliene & Pilinkiene, 2021). |
| Kunkel S., Tyfield D. (2021) | Objective | In this article, applying the CPERI/CSPK approach (Cultural Political Economy of Research and Innovation/Complex Systems of Power-Knowledge approach), the authors argue that digital rebound should be a central parameter in research on digitization and sustainability.<br>Thinking strategically about different models of digitization, called the "human-machine associative model" and the "micro-efficiency model", may not only allow for changing the trajectory of digitization itself. It could also indirectly address the dominant policy regime of the system-level economy that will propel or contain the digital comeback (Kunkel & Tyfield, 2021). |
| | Indicators | $CO_2$ emissions per capita plotted against GDP per capita.<br>Global trends in material extraction. |
| | Get | The CPERI/CSPK method offers a heuristic approach, a conception that allows for strategic thinking by diverse agents about how specific socio-technical initiatives can also reshape the power/knowledge relations that constitute the emergent system-level relations of the emergent political economy itself (Kunkel & Tyfield, 2021). |

(*continued*)

**Table 2.3** (continued)

| *Research* | | |
|---|---|---|
| Kynčlová P., Upadhyaya S., Nice T. (2020) | Objective | Composite index as a measure for achieving Sustainable Development Goal 9 related to industry: the SDG9 Index. This article presents the SDG9 index as a measure of a country's progress towards achieving its industrial targets related to Sustainable Development Goal 9 (Kynčlová et al., 2020). |
| | Indicators | – Value added in manufacturing as a share of GDP and per capita;<br>– Employment in manufacturing as a share of total employment;<br>– Proportion of small industries in total industry value added;<br>– Proportion of small industries with a loan or line of credit;<br>– $CO_2$ emissions per unit of value added;<br>– Proportion of value added of medium and high-tech industry in total value added. |
| | Results | The article aims to provide a simple tool to help countries track performance in different dimensions of sustainable development and to enable policy-makers and researchers to develop strategies for achieving inclusive and sustainable industrial development. For this reason, the indicators for building the SDG-9 index are selected based on the global framework of indicators for monitoring the Sustainable Development Goals. By mainstreaming inclusive and sustainable industrial development into national policies, governments are expected to develop a solid understanding of the relationships, synergies and trade-offs between industry-specific strategies and policy instruments that lead to economic growth, social inclusion and environmental sustainability. The SDG-9 index shows that industrialized economies dominate the overall rankings as they perform best in all dimensions captured in the composite measure. Evidence indicates that developing countries at an early stage of industrialization have more opportunities to achieve inclusive industry, inclusive industrial development that is experiencing rapid economic growth and limited environmental damage. Labour-intensive industries, such as food and beverages, chemicals, non-metallic minerals, textiles and clothing, are most likely to generate the most significant employment, employment opportunities, as low wages can give developing countries a comparative advantage in these industries. As the least developed countries appear mostly at the bottom of the rankings, the SDG-9 rankings, there is a need for real political commitment and better institutional capacity to include inclusive and sustainable industrial development policies in countries' long-term strategies. Least developed countries (LDCs) are dominated by the agricultural sector and manufacturing relies on low-tech products and very low levels of pollution; yet these countries often face the most severe impacts of climate change. Achieving inclusive and sustainable industrial development in LDCs requires the introduction of policies that do not focus exclusively on economic growth, but more on structural transformation that will help create jobs while limiting environmental damage (Kynčlová et al., 2020). |

*(continued)*

**Table 2.3** (continued)

| *Research* | | |
|---|---|---|
| Costa J., Cancela D., Reis J. (2021) | Objective | The article aims to empirically test (in)compatibilities between these objectives even in developed economies such as the European Union. Countries in the European Union demonstrate that unless strong bridges are built to promote innovative networks at a transnational level, welfare and prosperity among these ecosystems will be compromised (Costa et al., 2021). |
| | Indicators | SOC_SUST Social Sustainability<br>ECO_SUST Economic sustainability<br>ENV_SUST Environmental sustainability<br>SUSTAINABILITY Sustainability<br>PA_EPO Number of patents filed at the European Patent Office<br>CORR_PIND Corruption Perceptions Index<br>HED_L High level of education<br>RD_GDP Gross domestic expenditure<br>ALE Average life expectancy<br>HDI Human Development Index<br>ENTREP Opportunity Entrepreneurship |
| | Results | The empirical results obtained by the models under analysis seem to point towards a pyramidal organization of goals rather than simultaneous achievement, and the top of the framework will be reached by the least advantaged if richer nations do not understand that there is only one environment, and the retardation of prosperity in some parts of the world will give those countries no alternative but to fully exploit all natural resources, regardless of responsible innovation. The aim of the article was to understand to what extent the UN plan is feasible, given its centrality for the near future of the whole world (Costa et al., 2021). |

Source: Author

global level have helped to build a picture of disparities that has subsequently contributed to improving regional development policies. The influence of the pandemic on the industrial sector was relevant in that it highlighted the importance of technological progress, innovation and resilient infrastructure for achieving sustainable goals. Developed economies have on average recovered faster than developing countries, including using digital technologies. One job in the production supply chain has been abolished due to bottlenecks put in place to combat the spread of disease. Globally, the job-frequency rate in the manufacturing sector has been declining since the onset of the pandemic, from 13.7% to 13.21% in the pandemic's inception year, with the impact particularly concentrated in developing countries.

## Conclusions

This chapter highlighted the progress made through the implementation of Sustainable Development Goal 7—clean and affordable energy; Sustainable Development Goal 8—decent work and growth; and Sustainable Development Goal 9—industry, innovation and infrastructure, as reflected in the economic models presented in the literature. The integration of the Sustainable Development Goals into econometric models is a fundamental line of research, aimed at analysing global challenges through a systemic and statistically grounded approach. In particular, goals aiming at the transition to renewable energy sources, sustainable economic growth and infrastructure development through innovation are frequently modelled in economic studies that aim to establish causal relationships between sustainability and economic development. A general trend highlighted in the literature is an increase in the intensity of research at times of emerging opportunity or vulnerability triggers that could influence the achievement of the targets set by the 2030 Agenda. The economic models identified are highly varied and generally reflect correlations between indicators of sustainable development, providing a quantitative perspective on progress and challenges. The findings of the studies reviewed usually include recommendations for implementable public policies to correct the shortcomings identified and contribute to achieving the SDGs in a coherent and sustainable manner. Regarding the economic models used for Objective 7, the literature shows a predilection for multiplicative and seasonal models, which allow the influence of climatic and economic factors on the transition to renewable energy sources to be analysed. For Objective 8, the econometric models used are mainly panel regression models or forecasting models based on multiplicative methodologies, with the aim of analysing labour market dynamics and the impact of economic policies on employment. In the case of Objective 9, the predominant models used are neural, dynamic and regression models, which facilitate a thorough understanding of the interactions between innovation, infrastructure and long-term economic performance.

The analysis of the results obtained using these economic models has revealed several structural vulnerabilities that affect the accuracy and applicability of the conclusions drawn. Among the main problems identified are the partial absence of key datasets, the lack of statistical homogeneity between different databases and the variability of uncertainty conditions that influence the accuracy of the predictions generated by the proposed models. These limitations underline the need for the development of improved methodologies for data collection and analysis, as well as for greater flexibility in adapting econometric models to changing economic and social conditions. The economic models analysed prove essential for understanding the complex interactions between economic development and sustainability, providing a sound analytical framework for testing the effectiveness of different economic policy strategies in achieving the Sustainable Development Goals. The literature uses simulations and models based on real data to assess the impact of various economic measures on sustainability, thereby facilitating the formulation of more effective public policies that are more adapted to the current context. The integration of new technologies, artificial intelligence and machine learning methods in econometric analysis is a promising direction for improving the predictive capacity of economic models, allowing a more nuanced and accurate approach to the relationship between growth, innovation and sustainability.

This chapter thus demonstrates that while economic models are essential tools for assessing progress towards sustainable development, they need continuous improvement to keep pace with global dynamics and new economic, social and environmental challenges. Integrating more robust and adaptable methodologies into econometric analysis can make a significant contribution to increasing the effectiveness of public policies and accelerating the transition towards a sustainable economic model that is capable of meeting today's needs without compromising the prospects of future generations.

## References

Abdullah, A., Saraswat, S., & Talib, F. (2023). Barriers and strategies for sustainable manufacturing implementation in SMEs: A hybrid fuzzy AHP-TOPSIS framework. *Sustainable Manufacturing and Service Economics, 2*, 100012. https://doi.org/10.1016/j.smse.2023.100012

Abu-Rayash, A., & Dincer, I. (2025). Development of an integrated model for environmentally and economically sustainable and smart cities. *Sustainable Energy Technologies and Assessments, 73*, 104096. https://doi.org/10.1016/j.seta.2024.104096

Aderemi, T. A., Alejo, A., Omoyele, O. S., Olaoye, O. P., Olanipekun, W. D., & Azuh, D. E. (2022). An econometric analysis of clean energy supply and industrial development in Nigeria: Implications for sustainable development.

*International Journal of Energy Economics and Policy, 12*(3), 209–215. https://doi.org/10.32479/ijeep.13109

Agarkov, G. A., & Tarasyeva, T. V. (2020). Estimation of economic system's proportional development using economic growth model. In T. Simos & C. Tsitouras (Eds.), *International conference on numerical analysis and applied mathematics (ICNAAM 2019) (Vol. 2293, Issue International Conference on Numerical Analysis and Applied Mathematics (ICNAAM))*. https://doi.org/10.1063/5.0030881. WE—Conference Proceedings Citation Index—Science (CPCI-S).

Aguilar, J., Garces-Jimenez, A., R-Moreno, M. D., & García, R. (2021). A systematic literature review on the use of artificial intelligence in energy self-management in smart buildings. *Renewable and Sustainable Energy Reviews, 151*, 111530. https://doi.org/10.1016/j.rser.2021.111530

Ahmad, P., Alnoor, A., & Mohamad Khan, T. N. (2024). The question of job losses in the fossil fuel economies during energy transition: Losses and gains. In S. Taneja, P. Kumar, B. Reepu, K. S. Balusamy, & S. Grima (Eds.), *Sustainability development through green economics* (Vol. 114, pp. 219–229). Emerald Publishing Limited. https://doi.org/10.1108/S1569-375920240000114013

Al Shareef, A. M., Seçkiner, S., Eid, B., & Abumeteir, H. (2024). Integration of blockchain with artificial intelligence technologies in the energy sector: A systematic review. *Frontiers in Energy Research, 12*, 1377950. https://doi.org/10.3389/fenrg.2024.1377950

Alam, S. N., Khalid, Z., Singh, B., & Guldhe, A. (2024). Integration of government policies on the global level for green hydrogen production. In *Green hydrogen economy for environmental sustainability. Volume 1: Fundamentals and feedstocks* (Vol. 1473, p. 1). American Chemical Society. https://doi.org/10.1021/bk-2024-1473.ch001

Allen, C., Metternicht, G., & Wiedmann, T. (2016). National pathways to the Sustainable Development Goals (SDGs): A comparative review of scenario modelling tools. *Environmental Science & Policy, 66*, 199–207. https://doi.org/10.1016/j.envsci.2016.09.008

Almeida, F., & Okon, E. (2024). Achieving sustainable development goals through digitalization in ports. *Business Strategy and the Environment, 33*(7), 6737–6747. https://doi.org/10.1002/bse.3842

Anh, D. L. T., Quang, N. T. T., & Anh, N. T. (2024). Investment decision and efficiency: Global insights on manufacturing firms amidst energy uncertainties. *Energy Economics, 137*, 107793. https://doi.org/10.1016/j.eneco.2024.107793

Asfaw, A. H., Teklu, G., Birhan, A., Eshetu, Y., Regasa, E., & Wondimu, T. (2024). Mathematical modeling of Ethiopia's energy demand by sectors and energy types, with forecasts for the next 30 years. *Heliyon, 10*(22), e40185. https://doi.org/10.1016/j.heliyon.2024.e40185

Ashraf, M. Z., Wei, W., Usman, M., & Mushtaq, S. (2024). How can natural resource dependence, environmental-related technologies and digital trade protect the environment: Redesigning SDGs policies for sustainable environment? *Resources Policy, 88*, 104456. https://doi.org/10.1016/j.resourpol.2023.104456

Babic, M. (2024). Green finance in the global energy transition: Actors, instruments, and politics. *Energy Research & Social Science, 111*, 103482. https://doi.org/10.1016/j.erss.2024.103482

Bakhsh, S., Zhang, W., Ali, K., & Oláh, J. (2024). Strategy towards sustainable energy transition: The effect of environmental governance, economic complexity and geopolitics. *Energy Strategy Reviews, 52*, 101330. https://doi.org/10.1016/j.esr.2024.101330

Baldassarre, B. (2025). Circular economy for resource security in the European Union (EU): Case study, research framework, and future directions. *Ecological Economics, 227*, 108345. https://doi.org/10.1016/j.ecolecon.2024.108345

Baldry, K., Koekemoer, E., & Olckers, C. (2024). Empirical research on decent work and precarious work for semi-skilled and unskilled blue-collar workers: A scoping review. *Australian Journal of Career Development, 33*(3), 268–285. https://doi.org/10.1177/10384162241286439

Bansal, S., Sharma, G. D., Rahman, M. M., Yadav, A., & Garg, I. (2021). Nexus between environmental, social and economic development in South Asia: Evidence from econometric models. *Heliyon, 7*(1), e05965. https://doi.org/10.1016/j.heliyon.2021.e05965

Battisti, E., Alfiero, S., & Leonidou, E. (2022). Remote working and digital transformation during the COVID-19 pandemic: Economic–financial impacts and psychological drivers for employees. *Journal of Business Research, 150*, 38–50. https://doi.org/10.1016/j.jbusres.2022.06.010

Behera, B., Haldar, A., & Sethi, N. (2024). Investigating the direct and indirect effects of Information and Communication Technology on economic growth in the emerging economies: Role of financial development, foreign direct investment, innovation, and institutional quality. *Information Technology for Development, 30*(1), 33–56. https://doi.org/10.1080/02681102.2023.2233463

Berg, J., Green, F., Nurski, L., & Spencer, D. A. (2023). Risks to job quality from digital technologies: Are industrial relations in Europe ready for the challenge? *European Journal of Industrial Relations, 29*(4), 347–365. https://doi.org/10.1177/09596801231178904

Bhutta, U. S., Tariq, A., Farrukh, M., Raza, A., & Iqbal, M. K. (2022). Green bonds for sustainable development: Review of literature on development and impact of green bonds. *Technological Forecasting and Social Change, 175*, 121378. https://doi.org/10.1016/j.techfore.2021.121378

Bieszk-Stolorz, B., Dmytrów, K., & Frąckiewicz, E. (2024). Multivariate analysis of the sustainable development of the silver economy in the European Union countries. *Sustainability, 16*(23), 10703. https://doi.org/10.3390/su162310703

Bilek-Steindl, S., & Url, T. (2022). Nowcasting and monitoring SDG 8. *Empirica, 49*(2), 313–345. https://doi.org/10.1007/s10663-022-09533-0

Biswas, P., Rashid, A., Biswas, A., Nasim, M. A., Al Chakraborty, S., Gupta, K. D., & George, R. (2024). AI-driven approaches for optimizing power consumption: A comprehensive survey. *Discover Artificial Intelligence, 4*(1), 116. https://doi.org/10.1007/s44163-024-00211-7

Bracarense, N., & Bracarense Costa, P. A. (2024). Green jobs: Sustainable path for environmental conservation and socio-economic stability and inclusion. *Review of Political Economy, 36*(1), 351–372. https://doi.org/10.1080/09538259.2022.2041311

Bundervoet, T., Dávalos, M. E., & Garcia, N. (2022). The short-term impacts of COVID-19 on households in developing countries: An overview based on a harmonized dataset of high-frequency surveys. *World Development, 153*, 105844. https://doi.org/10.1016/j.worlddev.2022.105844

Chabowski, B. R., Gabrielsson, P., Hult, G. T. M., & Morgeson, F. V. (2023). Sustainable international business model innovations for a globalizing circular economy: A review and synthesis, integrative framework, and opportunities for future research. *Journal of International Business Studies, 56*, 383–402. https://doi.org/10.1057/s41267-023-00652-9

Chander, B., Pal, S., De, D., & Buyya, R. (2022). Artificial intelligence-based Internet of Things for Industry 5.0. In S. Pal, D. De, & R. Buyya (Eds.), *BT—Artificial intelligence-based Internet of Things systems* (pp. 3–45). Springer International Publishing. https://doi.org/10.1007/978-3-030-87059-1_1

Chen, M., Sinha, A., Hu, K., & Shah, M. I. (2021). Impact of technological innovation on energy efficiency in industry 4.0 era: Moderation of shadow economy in sustainable development. *Technological Forecasting and Social Change, 164*, 120521. https://doi.org/10.1016/j.techfore.2020.120521

Chen, S., & Nouseen, S. (2025). Tackling economic policy uncertainty and improving energy security through clean energy change. *Energy, 315*, 134356. https://doi.org/10.1016/j.energy.2024.134356

Chigbu, B. I., & Nekhwevha, F. (2023). Exploring the concepts of decent work through the lens of SDG 8: Addressing challenges and inadequacies. *Frontiers in Sociology, 8*, 1266141. https://doi.org/10.3389/fsoc.2023.1266141

Cho, A., Kim, H., & Park, S. (2024). Resurgence of the hydrogen energy in South Korea's government strategies from 2005 to 2019. *International Journal of Hydrogen Energy, 65*, 844–854. https://doi.org/10.1016/j.ijhydene.2024.04.049

Costa, J., Cancela, D., & Reis, J. (2021). Neverland or Tomorrowland? Addressing (in)compatibility among the SDG pillars in Europe. *International Journal of Environmental Research and Public Health, 18*(22), 11858. https://doi.org/10.3390/ijerph182211858

Cristea, D. S., Zamfir, C. G., Simionov, I. A., Fortea, C., Ionescu, R. V., Zlati, M. L., Antohi, V. M., Munteanu, D., & Petrea, S. M. (2022). Renewable energy strategy analysis in relation to environmental pollution for BRICS, G7, and EU countries by using a machine learning framework and panel data analysis. *Frontiers in Environmental Science, 10*. https://doi.org/10.3389/fenvs.2022.1005806

D'Adamo, I., & Rossi, E. N. (2024). Impact of regional investment on the sustainable development goals: A group analysis of economic and territorial development. *Sustainable Development, 33*, 1816–1834. https://doi.org/10.1002/sd.3215

D'Orazio, P. (2025). Addressing climate risks through fiscal policy in emerging and developing economies: What do we know and what lies ahead? *Energy Research & Social Science, 119*, 103852. https://doi.org/10.1016/j.erss.2024.103852

Daly, H., Ahmed Abdulrahman, B. M., Khader Ahmed, S. A., Yahia Abdallah, A. E., Hasab Elkarim, S. H. E., Gomaa Sahal, M. S., Nureldeen, W., Mobarak, W., & Elshaabany, M. M. (2024). The dynamic relationships between oil products consumption and economic growth in Saudi Arabia: Using ARDL cointegration and Toda-Yamamoto Granger causality analysis. *Energy Strategy Reviews, 54*, 101470. https://doi.org/10.1016/j.esr.2024.101470

Debbarma, J., & Choi, Y. (2022). A taxonomy of green governance: A qualitative and quantitative analysis towards sustainable development. *Sustainable Cities and Society, 79*, 103693. https://doi.org/10.1016/j.scs.2022.103693

Debono, M., & Garzia, C. (2022). COVID-19 impact on the employment conditions of women, youth, people with disabilities, and atypical workers—Key findings. https://gwu.org.mt/wp-content/uploads/2022/09/Report-%E2%80%93-COVID-19-Impact-on-Employment-Conditions-1.pdf

Dekeyrel, S., & Fessler, M. (2024). Digitalisation: An enabler for the clean energy transition. *Journal of Energy & Natural Resources Law, 42*(2), 185–209. https://doi.org/10.1080/02646811.2023.2254103

Delgarm, N., Sajadi, B., Kowsary, F., & Delgarm, S. (2016). Multi-objective optimization of the building energy performance: A simulation-based approach by means of particle swarm optimization (PSO). *Applied Energy, 170*, 293–303. https://doi.org/10.1016/j.apenergy.2016.02.141

European Commission. (2022). *REPowerEU plan*. Europa.Eu. https://eur-lex.europa.eu/resource.html?uri=cellar:fc930f14-d7ae-11ec-a95f-01aa75ed71a1.0014.02/DOC_1&format=PDF

Eurostat. (2023a). *Real GDP growth rate—Volume*. Europa.Eu. https://ec.europa.eu/eurostat/databrowser/view/tec00115/default/table?lang=en
Eurostat. (2023b). *SDG 8—Decent work and economic growth*. Europa.Eu. https://ec.europa.eu/eurostat/statistics-explained/index.php?title=SDG_8_-_Decent_work_and_economic_growth
Eurostat. (2023c). *SDG 9—Industry, innovation and infrastructure*. Europa.Eu. https://ec.europa.eu/eurostat/statistics-explained/index.php?title=SDG_9_-_Industry,_innovation_and_infrastructure
Field, C., & Look, R. (2018). A value-based approach to infrastructure resilience. *Environment Systems and Decisions, 38*(3), 292–305. https://doi.org/10.1007/s10669-018-9701-x
Fortea, C., Zlati, M.-L., Antohi, V.-M., Ionescu, R.-V., & Cristea, D.-S. (2022). Analysis of the energy status in Romania from the sustainable development perspective in the current geopolitical context. *Economics and Applied Informatics, XXVII*(3), 52–59. https://doi.org/10.35219/eai15840409287
Frey, D. F. (2017). Economic growth, full employment and decent work: The means and ends in SDG 8. *The International Journal of Human Rights, 21*(8), 1164–1184. https://doi.org/10.1080/13642987.2017.1348709
Gajdzik, B., Wolniak, R., Nagaj, R., Žuromskaitė-Nagaj, B., & Grebski, W. W. (2024). The influence of the global energy crisis on energy efficiency: A comprehensive analysis. *Energies, 17*(4). https://doi.org/10.3390/en17040947
Gârdan, I. P., Micu, A., Paştiu, C. A., Micu, A. E., & Gârdan, D. A. (2023). Consumers' attitude towards renewable energy in the context of the energy crisis. *Energies, 16*(2), 676. https://doi.org/10.3390/en16020676
Genovese, M., Schlüter, A., Scionti, E., Piraino, F., Corigliano, O., & Fragiacomo, P. (2023). Power-to-hydrogen and hydrogen-to-X energy systems for the industry of the future in Europe. *International Journal of Hydrogen Energy, 48*(44), 16545–16568. https://doi.org/10.1016/j.ijhydene.2023.01.194
Giglio, E., Petracca, E., Paduano, B., Moscoloni, C., Giorgi, G., & Sirigu, S. A. (2023). Estimating the cost of wave energy converters at an early design stage: A bottom-up approach. *Sustainability, 15*(8), 6756. https://doi.org/10.3390/su15086756
Gutner, T., & Heltberg, R. (2025). Conceptualizing and evaluating how international organizations collaborate. *World Development, 186*, 106789. https://doi.org/10.1016/j.worlddev.2024.106789
Halim-Lim, S. A., Jamaludin, A. A., Islam, A. S. M. T., Weerabahu, S., & Priyono, A. (2025). Unlocking potential for a circular bioeconomy transition through digital innovation, lean manufacturing and green practices: A review. *Management of Environmental Quality: An International Journal, 36*(1), 130–154. https://doi.org/10.1108/MEQ-11-2023-0386

Hariram, N. P., Mekha, K. B., Suganthan, V., & Sudhakar, K. (2023). Sustainalism: An integrated socio-economic-environmental model to address sustainable development and sustainability. *Sustainability, 15*(13), 10682. https://doi.org/10.3390/su151310682. WE —Science Citation Index Expanded (SCI-EXPANDED) WE—Social Science Citation Index (SSCI).

Hassan, Q., Algburi, S., Sameen, A. Z., Salman, H. M., & Jaszczur, M. (2024). Green hydrogen: A pathway to a sustainable energy future. *International Journal of Hydrogen Energy, 50*, 310–333. https://doi.org/10.1016/j.ijhydene.2023.08.321

Hassan, Q., Viktor, P., Al-Musawi, T. J., Mahmood Ali, B., Algburi, S., Alzoubi, H. M., Khudhair Al-Jiboory, A., Zuhair Sameen, A., Salman, H. M., & Jaszczur, M. (2024). The renewable energy role in the global energy Transformations. *Renewable Energy Focus, 48*, 100545. https://doi.org/10.1016/j.ref.2024.100545

Hojnik, J., Ruzzier, M., Konečnik Ruzzier, M., Sučić, B., Soltwisch, B., & Rus, M. (2024). Review of EU projects with a focus on environmental quality: Innovation, eco-innovation, and circular-economy elements. *International Journal of Innovation Studies, 8*(1), 1–12. https://doi.org/10.1016/j.ijis.2023.10.001

Holechek, J. L., Geli, H. M. E., Sawalhah, M. N., & Valdez, R. (2022). A global assessment: Can renewable energy replace fossil fuels by 2050? *Sustainability, 14*(8), 4792. https://doi.org/10.3390/su14084792

Hossain, M. R., Rao, A., Sharma, G. D., Dev, D., & Kharbanda, A. (2024). Empowering energy transition: Green innovation, digital finance, and the path to sustainable prosperity through green finance initiatives. *Energy Economics, 136*, 107736. https://doi.org/10.1016/j.eneco.2024.107736

Ida Evangeline, S., & Rathika, P. (2021). A real-time multi-objective optimization framework for wind farm integrated power systems. *Journal of Power Sources, 498*, 229914. https://doi.org/10.1016/j.jpowsour.2021.229914

IEA. (2022a). *Energy investment in 2022.* www.Iea.org. https://www.iea.org/reports/world-energy-investment-2022/overview-and-key-findings

IEA. (2022b). *World energy investment 2022.* https://iea.blob.core.windows.net/assets/b0beda65-8a1d-46ae-87a2-f95947ec2714/WorldEnergyInvestment2022.pdf

IEA. (2023). *World energy outlook.* https://iea.blob.core.windows.net/assets/86ede39e-4436-42d7-ba2a-edf61467e070/WorldEnergyOutlook2023.pdf

Industry 5.0. (2024). *European commission.* https://research-and-innovation.ec.europa.eu/research-area/industrial-research-and-innovation/industry-50_en

International Atomic Energy Agency. (2022). *Climate change and nuclear power 2022.* https://www.iaea.org/sites/default/files/iaea-ccnp2022-body-web.pdf

Ionașcu, A., & Noja, G. G. (2024). Globalisation, economic integration, and labour market dynamics within the European Union. In S. Grima, I. Romānova, G. G. Noja, & T. Dorożyński (Eds.), *Economic development and resilience by EU member states* (Vol. 115, pp. 5–22). Emerald Publishing Limited. https://doi.org/10.1108/S1569-375920240000115002

Ionescu, R.-V., Zlati, M. L., & Antohi, V. M. (2021). European Union's regions between cohesion and sustainability. *Technological Forecasting and Social Change, 169*, 120862. https://doi.org/10.1016/j.techfore.2021.120862

IRENA. (2021). *Tracking SDG 7: The energy progress report 2021*. https://www.irena.org/-/media/Files/IRENA/Agency/Publication/2021/Jun/SDG7_Tracking_Progress_2021.pdf

IRENA. (2022). *Geopolitics of the energy transformation: The hydrogen factor*. https://www.irena.org/publications/2022/Jan/Geopolitics-of-the-Energy-Transformation-Hydrogen

IRENA. (2023). *World energy transitions outlook 2023: 1.5°C pathway*. https://mc-cd8320d4-36a1-40ac-83cc-3389-cdn-endpoint.azureedge.net/-/media/Files/IRENA/Agency/Publication/2023/Jun/IRENA_World_energy_transitions_outlook_v1_2023.pdf?rev=cc4522ff897a4e26a47906447c74bca6

IRENA. (2024). *World energy transitions outlook 2023*. https://www.irena.org/Digital-Report/World-Energy-Transitions-Outlook-2023

Jayachandran, M., Gatla, R. K., Rao, K. P., Rao, G. S., Mohammed, S., Milyani, A. H., Azhari, A. A., Kalaiarasy, C., & Geetha, S. (2022). Challenges in achieving sustainable development goal 7: Affordable and clean energy in light of nascent technologies. *Sustainable Energy Technologies and Assessments, 53*, 102692. https://doi.org/10.1016/j.seta.2022.102692

Jianing, P., Bai, K., Solangi, Y. A., Magazzino, C., & Ayaz, K. (2024). Examining the role of digitalization and technological innovation in promoting sustainable natural resource exploitation. *Resources Policy, 92*, 105036. https://doi.org/10.1016/j.resourpol.2024.105036

Jie, Y., & Lan, J. (2024). Dynamic linkages between human capital, natural resources, and economic growth—Impact on achieving sustainable development goals. *Heliyon, 10*(14), e33536. https://doi.org/10.1016/j.heliyon.2024.e33536

Jin, Y., Sharifi, A., Li, Z., Chen, S., Zeng, S., & Zhao, S. (2024). Carbon emission prediction models: A review. *Science of the Total Environment, 927*, 172319. https://doi.org/10.1016/j.scitotenv.2024.172319

Kandpal, V., Jaswal, A., Santibanez Gonzalez, E. D. R., & Agarwal, N. (2024). The economics of sustainable energy transition and the circular economy. In V. Kandpal, A. Jaswal, E. D. R. Santibanez Gonzalez, & N. Agarwal (Eds.), *BT—Sustainable energy transition: Circular economy and sustainable financing for environmental, social and governance (ESG) practices* (pp. 53–87). Springer Nature Switzerland. https://doi.org/10.1007/978-3-031-52943-6_2

Karobliene, V., & Pilinkiene, V. (2021). The sharing economy in the framework of sustainable development goals: Case of European Union countries. *Sustainability, 13*(15), 8312. https://doi.org/10.3390/su13158312

Karpunina, E. K., Moskovtceva, L. V., Zabelina, O. V., Zubareva, N. N., & Tsykora, A. V. (2022). Socio-economic impact of the COVID-19 pandemic on OECD countries. In E. G. Popkova & I. V. Andronova (Eds.), *Current problems of the world economy and international trade* (Vol. 42, pp. 103–114). Emerald Publishing Limited. https://doi.org/10.1108/S0190-128120220000042011

Khalid, M. (2024). Smart grids and renewable energy systems: Perspectives and grid integration challenges. *Energy Strategy Reviews, 51*, 101299. https://doi.org/10.1016/j.esr.2024.101299

Khan, K. A., Quamar, M. M., Al-Qahtani, F. H., Asif, M., Alqahtani, M., & Khalid, M. (2023). Smart grid infrastructure and renewable energy deployment: A conceptual review of Saudi Arabia. *Energy Strategy Reviews, 50*, 101247. https://doi.org/10.1016/j.esr.2023.101247

Khan, M. I., Yasmeen, T., Khan, M., Hadi, N. U., Asif, M., Farooq, M., & Al-Ghamdi, S. G. (2025). Integrating industry 4.0 for enhanced sustainability: Pathways and prospects. *Sustainable Production and Consumption, 54*, 149–189. https://doi.org/10.1016/j.spc.2024.12.012

Khan, M. K., Abbas, F., Godil, D. I., Sharif, A., Ahmed, Z., & Anser, M. K. (2021). Moving towards sustainability: How do natural resources, financial development, and economic growth interact with the ecological footprint in Malaysia? A dynamic ARDL approach. *Environmental Science and Pollution Research, 28*(39), 55579–55591. https://doi.org/10.1007/s11356-021-14686-9

Kiasari, M., Ghaffari, M., & Aly, H. H. (2024). A comprehensive review of the current status of smart grid technologies for renewable energies integration and future trends: The role of machine learning and energy storage systems. *Energies, 17*(16), 4128. https://doi.org/10.3390/en17164128

Kripfganz, S., & Schneider, D. C. (2023). ardl: Estimating autoregressive distributed lag and equilibrium correction models. *The Stata Journal, 23*(4), 983–1019. https://doi.org/10.1177/1536867X231212434

Kulkov, I., Kulkova, J., Rohrbeck, R., Menvielle, L., Kaartemo, V., & Makkonen, H. (2024). Artificial intelligence—Driven sustainable development: Examining organizational, technical, and processing approaches to achieving global goals. *Sustainable Development, 32*(3), 2253–2267. https://doi.org/10.1002/sd.2773

Kumar, N. M., Chopra, S. S., Chand, A. A., Elavarasan, R. M., & Shafiullah, G. M. (2020). Hybrid renewable energy microgrid for a residential community: A techno-economic and environmental perspective in the context of the SDG7. *Sustainability, 12*(10), 3944. https://doi.org/10.3390/su12103944

Kunkel, S., & Tyfield, D. (2021). Digitalisation, sustainable industrialisation and digital rebound—Asking the right questions for a strategic research agenda. *Energy Research & Social Science, 82*, 102295. https://doi.org/10.1016/j.erss.2021.102295

Kynčlová, P., Upadhyaya, S., & Nice, T. (2020). Composite index as a measure on achieving Sustainable Development Goal 9 (SDG-9) industry-related targets: The SDG-9 index. *Applied Energy, 265*, 114755. https://doi.org/10.1016/j.apenergy.2020.114755

Liang, W., Maesoumi, M., Basem, A., Jasim, D. J., Sultan, A. J., Al-Rubaye, A. H., & Zhang, J. (2024). Are hybrid approaches combining EKF-UKF and artificial neural networks key to unlocking the full potential of sustainable energy technologies and reducing environmental footprint? *Heliyon, 10*(18), e36746. https://doi.org/10.1016/j.heliyon.2024.e36746

Lin, B., & Lan, T. (2025). The influence of coal price uncertainty on investment and consumption dynamics: Evidence from China. *Energy Policy, 198*, 114517. https://doi.org/10.1016/j.enpol.2025.114517

Linkov, I., Trump, B. D., Trump, J., Pescaroli, G., Hynes, W., Mavrodieva, A., & Panda, A. (2022). Resilience stress testing for critical infrastructure. *International Journal of Disaster Risk Reduction, 82*, 103323. https://doi.org/10.1016/j.ijdrr.2022.103323

Lv, F., Wu, Q., Ren, H., Zhou, W., & Li, Q. (2024). On the design and analysis of long-term low-carbon roadmaps: A review and evaluation of available energy-economy-environment models. *Renewable and Sustainable Energy Reviews, 189*, 113899. https://doi.org/10.1016/j.rser.2023.113899

Madurai Elavarasan, R., Pugazhendhi, R., Jamal, T., Dyduch, J., Arif, M. T., Manoj Kumar, N., Shafiullah, G. M., Chopra, S. S., & Nadarajah, M. (2021). Envisioning the UN Sustainable Development Goals (SDGs) through the lens of energy sustainability (SDG 7) in the post-COVID-19 world. *Applied Energy, 292*, 116665. https://doi.org/10.1016/j.apenergy.2021.116665

Mahajan, S., Hausladen, C. I., Argota Sánchez-Vaquerizo, J., Korecki, M., & Helbing, D. (2022). Participatory resilience: Surviving, recovering and improving together. *Sustainable Cities and Society, 83*, 103942. https://doi.org/10.1016/j.scs.2022.103942

Malik, M. (2021). Economic growth, energy consumption, and environmental quality nexus in Turkey: Evidence from simultaneous equation models. *Environmental Science and Pollution Research, 28*, 41988–41999. https://doi.org/10.1007/s11356-021-13468-7

Manchanda, M., & Arora, J. (2023). Higher education's position in shaping the workforce of the future and the importance of adapting to the digital age. *International Journal of Educational Reform*. https://doi.org/10.1177/10567879231211285

Martiny, A., Taglialatela, J., Testa, F., & Iraldo, F. (2024). Determinants of environmental social and governance (ESG) performance: A systematic literature review. *Journal of Cleaner Production, 456*, 142213. https://doi.org/10.1016/j.jclepro.2024.142213

Mesa Puyo, D., Panton, A. J., Sridhar, T., Stuermer, M., Ungerer, C., & Zhang, A. T. (2024). *Key challenges faced by fossil fuel exporters during the energy transition* (Vol. 2024 (001)). International Monetary Fund. https://doi.org/10.5089/9798400270147.066

Micu, A., Micu, A.-E., Geru, M., Capatina, A., & Muntean, M.-C. (2021). The challenge for energy saving in smart homes: Exploring the interest for IoT devices acquisition in Romania. *Energies, 14*(22), 7589. https://doi.org/10.3390/en14227589

Mio, C., Panfilo, S., & Blundo, B. (2020). Sustainable development goals and the strategic role of business: A systematic literature review. *Business Strategy and the Environment, 29*(8), 3220–3245. https://doi.org/10.1002/bse.2568

Mondejar, M. E., Avtar, R., Diaz, H. L. B., Dubey, R. K., Esteban, J., Gómez-Morales, A., Hallam, B., Mbungu, N. T., Okolo, C. C., Prasad, K. A., She, Q., & Garcia-Segura, S. (2021). Digitalization to achieve sustainable development goals: Steps towards a Smart Green Planet. *Science of the Total Environment, 794*, 148539. https://doi.org/10.1016/j.scitotenv.2021.148539

Mukherjee, P. K., Das, B., Bhardwaj, P. K., Tampha, S., Singh, H. K., Chanu, L. D., Sharma, N., & Devi, S. I. (2023). Socio-economic sustainability with circular economy—An alternative approach. *Science of the Total Environment, 904*, 166630. https://doi.org/10.1016/j.scitotenv.2023.166630

Murtaza, G., & Luqman, M. (2025). Chapter 10—Environmental banking, renewable energy projects, and private investments crowd out. In H. Dinçer & S. Yüksel (Eds.), *Renewable energy projects and investments* (Interdisciplinary knowledge, analysis, opportunities, and outlook) (pp. 177–200). Elsevier. https://doi.org/10.1016/B978-0-443-29869-1.00010-6

Nasir, N., & Ahmed, W. (2024). Green finance initiatives and their potential to drive sustainable development. In N. Naifar (Ed.), *BT—Climate change and finance: Navigating the challenges and opportunities in capital markets* (pp. 3–29). Springer Nature Switzerland. https://doi.org/10.1007/978-3-031-56419-2_1

OECD. (2024). *OECD employment outlook 2024: The net-zero transition and the labour market*. https://www.oecd.org/en/publications/oecd-employment-outlook-2024_ac8b3538-en.html

Osińska, M., Kufel, T., Błażejowski, M., & Kufel, P. (2020). Modeling mechanism of economic growth using threshold autoregression models. *Empirical Economics, 58*(3), 1381–1430. https://doi.org/10.1007/s00181-018-1560-2

Pallaske, G. (2024). Analyzing sustainable development strategies through multi-method integration in the Green Economy Model. *Ecological Modelling, 496*, 110828. https://doi.org/10.1016/j.ecolmodel.2024.110828

Palomares, I., Martínez-Cámara, E., Montes, R., García-Moral, P., Chiachio, M., Chiachio, J., Alonso, S., Melero, F. J., Molina, D., Fernández, B., Moral, C., Marchena, R., de Vargas, J. P., & Herrera, F. (2021). A panoramic view and swot analysis of artificial intelligence for achieving the sustainable development goals by 2030: Progress and prospects. *Applied Intelligence, 51*(9), 6497–6527. https://doi.org/10.1007/s10489-021-02264-y

Pierre, C., Catherine, A.-P., Sylvain, B., & Catherine, M.-V. (2024). Beyond the "bottom-up" and "top-down" controversy: A methodological inquiry into hybrid modeling methods for hydrogen supply chains. *International Journal of Production Economics, 268*, 109091. https://doi.org/10.1016/j.ijpe.2023.109091

Pollin, R. (2023). Fossil fuel industry phase-out and just transition: Designing policies to protect workers' living standards. *Journal of Human Development and Capabilities, 24*(4), 539–568. https://doi.org/10.1080/19452829.2023.2241840

Prado, G., Piekarski, C., Luz, L., Souza, J., Salvador, R., & Francisco, A. (2019). Sustainable development and economic performance: Gaps and trends for future research. *Sustainable Development, 28*, 368–384. https://doi.org/10.1002/sd.1982

Rai, S. M., Brown, B. D., & Ruwanpura, K. N. (2019). SDG 8: Decent work and economic growth – A gendered analysis. *World Development, 113*, 368–380. https://doi.org/10.1016/j.worlddev.2018.09.006

Ralph, A., & Arora, A. (2024). Mapping the literature on decent work: A bibliometric analysis of sustainable development goal 8. *Sustainable Development, 32*(4), 3937–3952. https://doi.org/10.1002/sd.2879

Rame, R., Purwanto, P., & Sudarno, S. (2024). Industry 5.0 and sustainability: An overview of emerging trends and challenges for a green future. *Innovation and Green Development, 3*(4), 100173. https://doi.org/10.1016/j.igd.2024.100173

Rani, P., Parkash, V., & Sharma, N. K. (2024). Technological aspects, utilization and impact on power system for distributed generation: A comprehensive survey. *Renewable and Sustainable Energy Reviews, 192*, 114257. https://doi.org/10.1016/j.rser.2023.114257

Regona, M., Yigitcanlar, T., Hon, C., & Teo, M. (2024). Artificial intelligence and sustainable development goals: Systematic literature review of the construction industry. *Sustainable Cities and Society, 108*, 105499. https://doi.org/10.1016/j.scs.2024.105499

Rehman, S. u., Khan, S. N., Antohi, V. M., Bashir, S., Fareed, M., Fortea, C., & Cristian, N. P. (2024). Open innovation big data analytics and its influence on sustainable tourism development: A multi-dimensional assessment of economic, policy, and behavioral factors. *Journal of Open Innovation: Technology, Market, and Complexity, 10*(2), 100254. https://doi.org/10.1016/j.joitmc.2024.100254

Rendtorff, J. D. (2019). Sustainable Development Goals and progressive business models for economic transformation. *Local Economy, 34*(6), 510–524. https://doi.org/10.1177/0269094219882270. WE—Emerging Sources Citation Index (ESCI).

Ribeiro-Duthie, A. C. (2020). SDG 8 decent work and economic growth. In I. B. Franco, T. Chatterji, E. Derbyshire, & J. Tracey (Eds.), *BT—Actioning the global goals for local impact: Towards sustainability science, policy, education and practice* (pp. 117–133). Springer Singapore. https://doi.org/10.1007/978-981-32-9927-6_9

Rijwani, T., Kumari, S., Srinivas, R., Abhishek, K., Iyer, G., Vara, H., Dubey, S., Revathi, V., & Gupta, M. (2025). Industry 5.0: A review of emerging trends and transformative technologies in the next industrial revolution. *International Journal on Interactive Design and Manufacturing (IJIDeM), 19*(2), 667–679. https://doi.org/10.1007/s12008-024-01943-7

Rosato, P. F., Caputo, A., Valente, D., & Pizzi, S. (2021). 2030 Agenda and sustainable business models in tourism: A bibliometric analysis. *Ecological Indicators, 121*, 106978. https://doi.org/10.1016/j.ecolind.2020.106978

Rusch, M., Schöggl, J.-P., & Baumgartner, R. J. (2023). Application of digital technologies for sustainable product management in a circular economy: A review. *Business Strategy and the Environment, 32*(3), 1159–1174. https://doi.org/10.1002/bse.3099

Safari, A., Daneshvar, M., & Anvari-Moghaddam, A. (2024). Energy intelligence: A systematic review of artificial intelligence for energy management. *Applied Sciences, 14*(23), 11112. https://doi.org/10.3390/app142311112

Sánchez-García, E., Martínez-Falcó, J., Marco-Lajara, B., & Manresa-Marhuenda, E. (2024). Revolutionizing the circular economy through new technologies: A new era of sustainable progress. *Environmental Technology & Innovation, 33*, 103509. https://doi.org/10.1016/j.eti.2023.103509

Sarkodie, S. A., Ackom, E., Bekun, F. V., & Owusu, P. A. (2020). Energy–climate–economy–population nexus: An empirical analysis in Kenya, Senegal, and Eswatini. *Sustainability, 12*(15), 6202. https://doi.org/10.3390/su12156202

Schröder, A. J., Cuypers, M., & Götting, A. (2024). From Industry 4.0 to Industry 5.0: The triple transition digital, green and social. In D. Stroud, A. J. Schröder, L. Antonazzo, C. Behrend, V. Colla, A. Goti, & M. Weinel (Eds.), *BT—Industry 4.0 and the road to sustainable steelmaking in Europe: Recasting the future* (pp. 35–51). Springer International Publishing. https://doi.org/10.1007/978-3-031-35479-3_3

Sharma, R., & Gupta, H. (2024). Leveraging cognitive digital twins in Industry 5.0 for achieving sustainable development goal 9: An exploration of inclusive and sustainable industrialization strategies. *Journal of Cleaner Production, 448*, 141364. https://doi.org/10.1016/j.jclepro.2024.141364

Sheikh, R. A., Ahmed, I., Faqihi, A. Y. A., & Shehawy, Y. M. (2024). Global perspectives on navigating Industry 5.0 knowledge: Achieving resilience, sustainability, and human-centric innovation in manufacturing. *Journal of the Knowledge Economy*. https://doi.org/10.1007/s13132-024-02498-4

Singh, A. R., Kumar, R. S., Bajaj, M., Khadse, C. B., & Zaitsev, I. (2024). Machine learning-based energy management and power forecasting in grid-connected microgrids with multiple distributed energy sources. *Scientific Reports, 14*(1), 19207. https://doi.org/10.1038/s41598-024-70336-3

Singla, N., Sood, K., Grima, S., & Yadav, U. S. (2023). Target 8.8. In *The impact of climate change and sustainability standards on the insurance market* (pp. 373–392). Wiley. https://doi.org/10.1002/9781394167944.ch24

Skare, M., Gavurova, B., & Rigelsky, M. (2024). Quantification of the impact of innovations in industry and infrastructure for sustainable circular economy production and consumption. *Journal of Innovation & Knowledge, 9*(1), 100456. https://doi.org/10.1016/j.jik.2023.100456

Solvang, W. D., Solvang, B., Forgó, Z., Kaartinen, H., Yu, H., & Shu, B. (2024). Educational support for SMEs transitioning from Industry 4.0 to Industry 5.0—Insights and lessons learned from European cooperation projects. In *2024 IEEE/SICE International symposium on system integration (SII)* (pp. 1012–1017). https://doi.org/10.1109/SII58957.2024.10417242

Son, T. H., Weedon, Z., Yigitcanlar, T., Sanchez, T., Corchado, J. M., & Mehmood, R. (2023). Algorithmic urban planning for smart and sustainable development: Systematic review of the literature. *Sustainable Cities and Society, 94*, 104562. https://doi.org/10.1016/j.scs.2023.104562

Stevanović, M., Pavlićević, P., Vujinović, N., & Radovanović, M. (2023). International relations challenges and sustainable development in developing countries after 2022: Conceptualization of the risk assessment model. *Energy, Sustainability and Society, 13*(1), 48. https://doi.org/10.1186/s13705-023-00430-3

Stoian, D., Monterroso, I., & Current, D. (2019). *SDG 8: Decent work and economic growth – Potential impacts on forests and forest-dependent livelihoods* (pp. 237–278). Cambridge University Press. https://doi.org/10.1017/9781108765015.010

Suganya, G., Selvakumar, J., Varadharajan, P., & Pachiyappan, S. (2024). *Skill sets required to meet a human-centered Industry 5.0: A systematic literature review and bibliometric analysis* (pp. 231–252). IGI Global. https://doi.org/10.4018/979-8-3693-0782-3.ch014

Sultanuzzaman, M. R., Yahya, F., & Lee, C.-C. (2024). Exploring the complex interplay of green finance, business cycles, and energy development. *Energy, 306*, 132479. https://doi.org/10.1016/j.energy.2024.132479

Sun, C., Khan, A., Xue, J., & Huang, X. (2024). Are digital economy and financial structure driving renewable energy technology innovations: A major eight countries perspective. *Applied Energy, 362*, 122990. https://doi.org/10.1016/j.apenergy.2024.122990

Surmeier, A., Meyer, I., & Maleka, M. (2024). Living wages in global value chains: Pitfalls and pathways to successful implementation. *Organizational Dynamics, 54*, 101109. https://doi.org/10.1016/j.orgdyn.2024.101109

Swain, R. B., & Karimu, A. (2020). Renewable electricity and sustainable development goals in the EU. *World Development, 125*, 104693. https://doi.org/10.1016/j.worlddev.2019.104693. WE—Social Science Citation Index (SSCI).

Terzi, A., Sherwood, M., & Singh, A. (2023). European industrial policy for the green and digital revolution. *Science and Public Policy, 50*(5), 842–857. https://doi.org/10.1093/scipol/scad018

Thake, A. M. (2025). Chapter 13—Transitioning to a green economy—The impact on the labor market and workforce skills. In S. Grima, K. Sood, E. Özen, & R. D. Gonzi (Eds.), *Science of sustainable systems* (pp. 163–175). Elsevier. https://doi.org/10.1016/B978-0-443-23603-7.00013-3

Traore, A., & Sene, N. (2020). Model of economic growth in the context of fractional derivative. *Alexandria Engineering Journal, 59*(6), 4843–4850. https://doi.org/10.1016/j.aej.2020.08.047

Tudorică, B.-G., Bucur, C., Panait, M., Oprea, S.-V., & Bâra, A. (2024). Energetic equilibrium: Optimizing renewable and non-renewable energy sources via particle swarm optimization. *Utilities Policy, 87*, 101722. https://doi.org/10.1016/j.jup.2024.101722

Türkeli, S. (2020). Complexity and the sustainable development goals: A computational intelligence approach to support policy mix designs. *Journal of Sustainability Research, 2*(1), e200006. https://doi.org/10.20900/jsr20200006

Turner, C., Oyekan, J., Garn, W., Duggan, C., & Abdou, K. (2022). Industry 5.0 and the circular economy: Utilizing LCA with intelligent products. *Sustainability, 14*(22), 14847. https://doi.org/10.3390/su142214847

United Nations. (2015). *Transforming our world: The 2030 agenda for sustainable development*. Sustainabledevelopment.un.org. https://sustainabledevelopment.un.org/content/documents/21252030%20Agenda%20for%20Sustainable%20Development%20web.pdf

United Nations. (2018). *High-level political forum 2018*. Sustainable Development Goals Knowledge Platform. https://sustainabledevelopment.un.org/hlpf/2018

United Nations. (2022). *The sustainable development goals report 2022*. https://unstats.un.org/sdgs/report/2022/The-Sustainable-Development-Goals-Report-2022.pdf

Verma, D. (2024). Industry 5.0: A human-centric and sustainable approach to industrial development. *International Journal of Social Relevance & Concern, 12*, 17–21. https://doi.org/10.26821/IJSRC.12.5.2024.120507

Wang, M. X., Hossain, M. R., Mohammed, K. S., Cifuentes-Faura, J., & Cai, X. T. (2023). Heterogenous effects of circular economy, green energy and globalization on $CO_2$ emissions: Policy based analysis for sustainable development. *Renewable Energy, 211*, 789–801. https://doi.org/10.1016/j.renene.2023.05.033

Wang, Q., Li, Y., & Li, R. (2025). Integrating artificial intelligence in energy transition: A comprehensive review. *Energy Strategy Reviews, 57*, 101600. https://doi.org/10.1016/j.esr.2024.101600

Wang, Y., He, Z., Zou, J., Xie, H., & Bao, J. (2024). Energy transition for sustainable economy: What is the role of government governance and public concern? *Finance Research Letters, 69*, 106087. https://doi.org/10.1016/j.frl.2024.106087

Wigger, A. (2023). The new EU industrial policy and deepening structural asymmetries: Smart specialisation not so smart. *JCMS: Journal of Common Market Studies, 61*(1), 20–37. https://doi.org/10.1111/jcms.13366

Yao, X., Xu, Z., Škare, M., & Wang, X. (2024). Aftermath on COVID-19 technological and socioeconomic changes: A meta-analytic review. *Technological Forecasting and Social Change, 202*, 123322. https://doi.org/10.1016/j.techfore.2024.123322

Yu, M., Kubiczek, J., Ding, K., Jahanzeb, A., & Iqbal, N. (2021). Revisiting SDG-7 under energy efficiency vision 2050: The role of new economic models and mass digitalization in OECD. *Energy Efficiency, 15*(1), 2. https://doi.org/10.1007/s12053-021-10010-z

Zehri, C., Mohammed El Amin, B., Kadja, A., Inaam, Z., & Sekrafi, H. (2024). Exploring the nexus of decent work, financial inclusion, and economic growth: A study aligned with SDG 8. *Sustainable Futures, 7*, 100213. https://doi.org/10.1016/j.sftr.2024.100213

Zhang, Y., & Deng, B. (2024). Exploring the nexus of smart technologies and sustainable ecotourism: A systematic review. *Heliyon, 10*(11), e31996. https://doi.org/10.1016/j.heliyon.2024.e31996

Zong, Z., & Guan, Y. (2024). AI-driven intelligent data analytics and predictive analysis in Industry 4.0: Transforming knowledge, innovation, and efficiency. *Journal of the Knowledge Economy, 16*, 864–903. https://doi.org/10.1007/s13132-024-02001-z

CHAPTER 3

# Analysis of the Economy's Strategies for Achieving Sustainable Development Goal 7 and the Main Indicators for Sustainable Development Goal 7

## Introduction

In the context of the redefinition of energy governance paradigms at EU level, SDG7—"Clean and affordable energy"—takes on profound strategic implications, being integrated transversally into European climate, economic and social policies. In a period characterized by multiple crises—marked simultaneously by energy insecurity, the intensifying effects of climate change, volatile energy prices and growing social gaps—the transition to a sustainable energy system becomes not only an environmental objective, but a sine qua non for the economic resilience and political cohesion of the Union. Within this framework, the European Union has taken on the role of a global normative actor in defining and implementing ambitious standards for decarbonization, energy efficiency and digitization of energy infrastructure. Through flagship initiatives such as the European Green Deal, REPowerEU and the new Energy Governance Framework established by Regulation (EU) 2018/1999, clear directions are mapped out for achieving climate neutrality by 2050, with ambitious intermediate milestones for 2030. In this complex regulatory and institutional ecosystem, SDG7 becomes a critical interface between environmental objectives and socio-economic imperatives, calling for a rigorous synchronization between national and European policies. The research aims to investigate,



C. Fortea, *Sustainable Economic Development and the European Green Deal*, https://doi.org/10.1007/978-3-032-10326-0_3

in an integrated and comparative approach, the extent to which the national economic strategies developed by Romania converge with the European guidelines on sustainable energy. Emphasis is placed on a critical analysis of the main statistical indicators related to SDG7, in order to assess the progress achieved and the structural constraints that prevent full alignment with the European dynamics. In this sense, the analysis reflects not only the differences in trajectory between Romania and the EU average but also the untapped potential of a coherent energy policy based on technological innovation, effective governance and social equity.

## Analysis of Economic Strategies to Achieve Sustainable Development Goal 7

In the current geopolitical context, at least in the first part of 2022, Europe went through a period of energy crisis followed by an economic crisis amid its dependence on energy imports from Russia and the sanctions imposed on Russia to stop the war against Ukraine. A recovery plan called REPowerEU (European Commission, 2024) was based on finding solutions to increase energy independence. The main methods were accelerating to clean transition and creating a more resilient energy system for Europe.

The additional actions of the Energy Plan aim at increasing energy savings, diversifying sources of supply, combining reforms and investments in a smart way as well as accelerating Europe's clean energy transition. In this context the European Green Deal reinforced the selected strategic directions and steered Europe towards the proposed efficiency and climate neutrality thresholds based on the 2030 and 2050 projections of the European Agenda. European legislation, Regulation (EU) 2018/1999 of the European Parliament and of the Council of 11 December 2018 on the governance of the energy union and climate action (European Parliament, 2018b) currently emphasize incentivizing the use of renewable energy sources, creating responsible energy consumer behaviour and providing sustainable directions to combat climate change and reduce energy poverty.

According to the REPowerEU Plan (European Commission, 2024), by chapter the main achievements in the energy field were: creating responsible consumption behaviour, followed by increasing energy efficiency, the vital transition to a clean economy. National Energy and Climate Plans have been launched with a role in building investor confidence and in planning and encouraging the reduction of fossil fuel consumption. On a regional level, energy information and support measures have been developed to ensure citizens' co-involvement in reducing energy consumption. These objectives are part of the European Urban Initiative and the Smart and Climate Neutral Cities mission. According to REPowerEU the diversification of energy imports has been achieved by setting up the purchasing platform to perform the functions of a joint energy purchaser, a function that is doubled by aggregating European energy demand, optimal use of infrastructure for import, storage and transportation of energy products, supply control and stock replenishment.

Accelerating the clean energy transition of the European economy means increasing energy consumption from renewable sources, phasing out imports of fossil fuels and electrifying industrial sectors for hydrogen use. This objective aims to intensify the use of solar photovoltaic technology, the use of wind energy (Europe is the world leader in offshore wind energy), the exploitation of industrial heat and the acceleration of hydrogen development.

The European Union is a global leader in combating climate change, implementing a range of policies and measures to reduce greenhouse gas emissions and promote sustainable development.

These measures help reduce greenhouse gas emissions, increase the use of renewable energy, improve energy efficiency and protect the environment.

In the smart investment policy card, the REPowerEU Plan (European Commission, 2022) includes an important transformation through the dynamics of energy flows, respectively, cross-border connections impacting the integrated energy market. Another project, TEN-E aims to create European energy networks contributing to a more resilient infrastructure and a more diversified energy supply.

Smart investments also aim to ensure security in the acquisition of oil-based energy resources. In this regard, there are projects to expand infrastructure to provide viable solutions for countries affected by the scarcity of such resources. Another area where investment is needed is energy storage with the facilitation of the integration of renewable energy production. As an additional project, the European Union aims to enable the rapid development of offshore networks and cross-border hydrogen infrastructures.

In the area of smart investment financing, common provisions and regulations have been created (Regulation 2021/1060, Regulation 2021/2115) but also recovery and resilience mechanisms have been set up whose economic functionality is bifunctional as financing under the mechanism or loans for undistributed funds. The EIM-E, i.e. the Interconnecting Europe for Energy Facility, has been set up to finance urgent infrastructure projects to stimulate the implementation of REPowerEU.

Implementing REPowerEU (European Commission, 2022) started in 2022 with the signing of the plan at the European level after which a task force for the implementation of the energy platform was set up, and in July 2022 12 countries and the European Union launched the "Energy Pathway to Meet the Global Methane Commitment" to which Norway joined in the same month. In July the project of European interest in the hydrogen sector "PIIEC Hy2Tech" was approved, which aims to decarbonize industrial processes and includes 15 EU Member States.

December 2022 saw the launch of the new Industrial Alliance to boost the use of solar energy and increase energy security at European level; it is based on the EU Solar Energy Strategy and aims to reach the production targets of 30 GW by 2025 by bringing together industrial entities, research institutes, consumer associations etc. Other steps under the REPowerEU Plan were in December 2022 when the European Parliament and the Council of Europe signed a political agreement on REPowerEU funding which provides the possibility for Member States to access through their recovery and resilience plans funding for the targets in the plan.

The European Union (EU) plays a significant role in tackling climate change through five pillars: energy security, decarbonization, energy efficiency, the internal energy market, research, innovation and competitiveness (as shown in Fig. 3.1). The European Union aims to lead the global energy transition by achieving the objectives of the Paris Agreement, which aims to deliver clean energy. According to the National Integrated Energy and Climate Change Plan 2021–2030 (Ministry of Energy, 2020) the EU has set energy and climate targets for 2030, including reducing domestic greenhouse gas emissions by 40%, achieving 32% renewable energy consumption, improving energy efficiency by 32.5% and achieving interconnected electricity grids by 15% by 2030.

European Commission, through Regulation (EU) 2018/1999 on Energy Union Governance (European Parliament, 2018b), has analysed draft integrated national energy and climate plans, in particular in the field of renewable energy and energy efficiency.

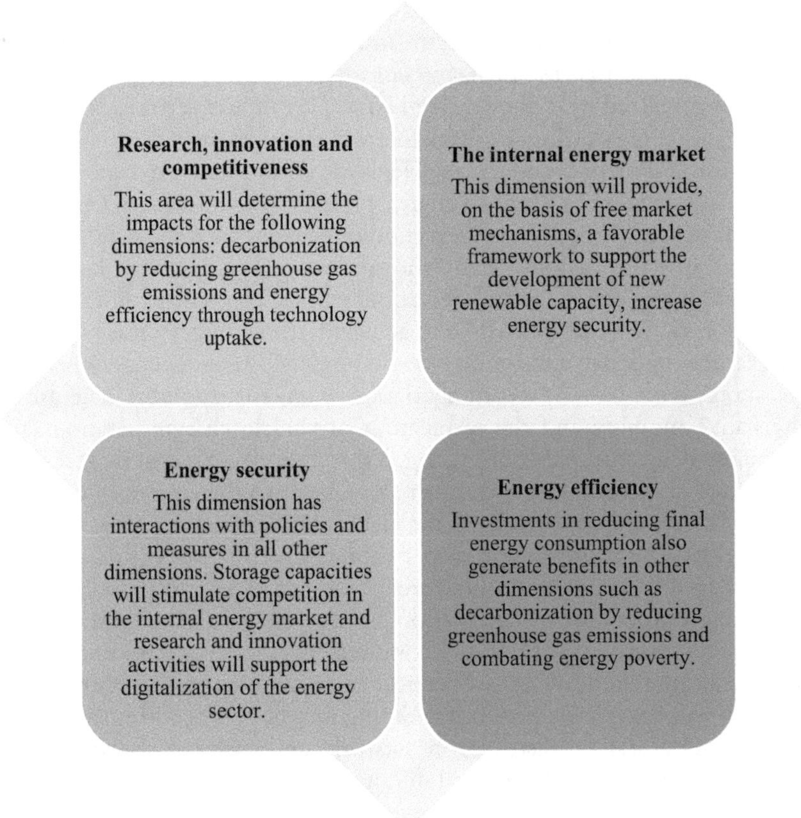


**Fig. 3.1** Main dimensions of the National Integrated Energy and Climate Change Plan, 2021–2030. Source: Prepared by the author according to the National Integrated Energy and Climate Change Plan 2021–2030 (Ministry of Energy, 2020)

In Romania, strategic energy development objectives according to the vision of the energy strategy (Ministry of Energy, 2022) aim at sustainable growth of the energy sector in line with EU targets for 2030 and 2050.

Romania has set out to achieve eight strategic objectives and implement a priority investment programme in line with the 2030 targets, and the National Energy and Climate Change Panel was launched. According to Romania's Energy Strategy 2022–2030, with a 2050 perspective (Ministry of Energy, 2022) the main objectives are to modernize the corporate governance system and to strengthen the institutional capacity on energy market regulation so that the management of state-owned energy companies is professionalized and modernized. To achieve Objective 2 on clean energy and energy efficiency, Romania will develop the energy system in line with EU directives and national legislation. The aim is to optimize the cost of financing and to reduce energy poverty, which will require significant investment throughout the technology chain. In Romania, with this objective in mind, a long-term renovation strategy has been launched, aimed at energy efficiency and decarbonization, i.e. controlling emissions and absorption. As an alternative to achieving these targets, it is proposed that large industrial consumers should improve their energy efficiency measures on the basis of recommendations from energy audits. The use of alternative mobility and the installation of vehicle charging stations are encouraged for the transport sector. Objective 3 is to ensure access to energy for all consumers, and under this objective the degree of connection of household consumers to the electricity distribution networks and the level of energy consumption per capita, which is currently 2.4 times lower than the European average, are monitored. The priority objective is to complete Romania's electrification and the capacity of the distribution systems in correlation with socio-economic development. Also in the field of natural gas, the level of connection of consumers to the distribution network will have to be improved. Emphasis will be placed on the development of natural gas distribution networks and ensuring access to thermal energy in single-industry coal mining areas.

Objective 4 aims to reduce energy poverty; the priorities of this objective being energy affordability and reducing challenges in the energy system by developing public policies for social assistance in the energy sector. Also under this chapter, the aim is to "regulate the status and legal regime of vulnerable consumers and how to finance them". Under Objective 5, competitive energy markets, it is proposed that the energy system should operate based on free markets and that the state should abolish its regulatory role. At the same time, Directive 2019/944 on common rules for the common energy market and Regulation 2019/941, Regulation 2019/942 and Regulation 2019/943 will be transposed into law.

The sixth objective envisages "increasing the capacity for education and innovation in the energy field and continuous training of human resources". It favours scientific and innovative research and the development of energy technology and know-how. The seventh objective is to transform Romania into a regional energy security provider by exploiting the hydrocarbon potential of the Black Sea and renewable sources in the region, while strengthening and modernizing networks, continuing the digitalization process and modernizing storage capacities and interconnection with neighbouring regions.

This objective will emphasize the efficient transition towards decarbonization and the consolidation of Romania's status as a regional energy security provider. The last objective is to "increase Romania's energy contribution to regional and European markets".

## Literature Review

There are numerous studies in the literature regarding energy efficiency on sustainable economic development. According to the Web of Science report, between 2000 and 2023, 309,246 articles were published under the criteria of energy efficiency and sustainable development. Researchers are interested in measures to improve energy efficiency, the role and importance of energy efficiency for sustainable development, energy efficiency assessment of the industrial sector, climate change and energy efficiency, reducing environmental impacts and greenhouse gas emissions, independence from non-renewable energy source to ensure sustainable development, economic financing focused on energy conservation, strategic energy efficiency targets, energy efficiency from the perspective of corporate social responsibility, energy efficiency measurement and management etc. (Fig. 3.2).

There are numerous studies in the literature on the impact of energy efficiency on sustainable economic development.

As regards the literature review on sustainable development of the economy through the transition to Sustainable Development Goal 7, clean and affordable energy, it has been structured according to the following reference areas:

### *Renewable Energy and Economic Growth*

In a study by Tutak M. and Brodny J. (Brodny & Tutak, 2022) the research shows a significant increase in the consumption of renewable energy in the period 2000–2019 and the existence of significant differences in the use of this type of energy in the analysed EU countries. The authors show that the increase in the consumption of renewable energy

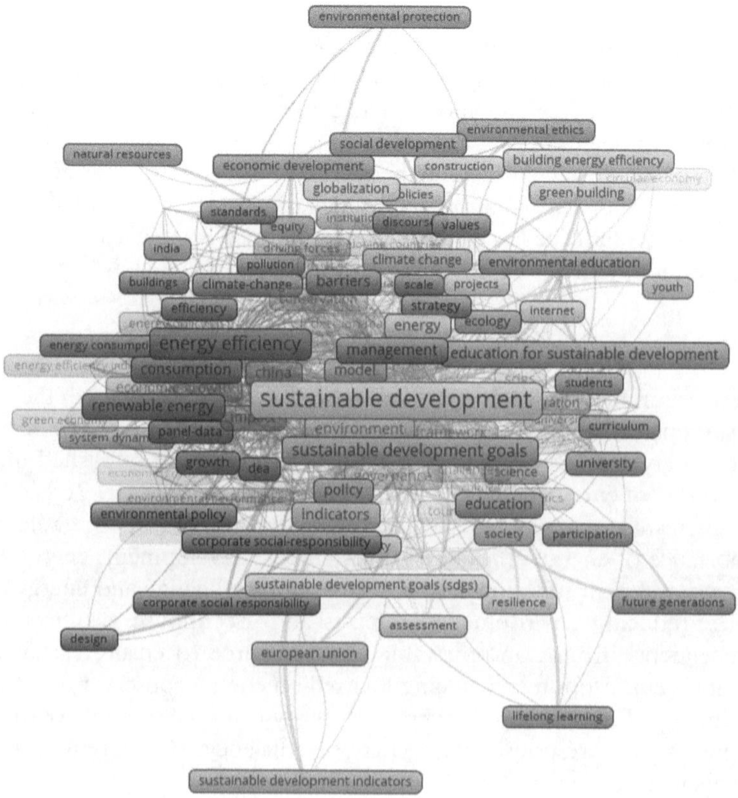


**Fig. 3.2** Bibliometric analysis of energy efficiency on sustainable economic development. Source: Author using VOSviewer software

has a positive effect on economic growth and reduction of greenhouse gas emissions. The study has a significant impact through the methodology presented, the Kohonen diagram is used and the cluster development of consumption from non-renewable sources is highlighted, with four dynamic clusters being identified in the period 2000–2019. Usman O., Alola A. and Akadiri S. (Usman et al., 2022) conduct a study based on an autoregressive vector panel and impulse response function to quantify the effects of renewable energy consumption in correlation with economic development, greenhouse gas emission reduction and environmental quality improvement. The period of the study is 2000–2017 and the results show that increased renewable energy consumption, economic growth and financial development in correlation with greenhouse gas reduction lead to sustainable development including environmental sustainability. The impact of the study is significant and is based on panel causality relationships, which indicate bidirectional causality with elements of sustainable development while renewable energy consumption demonstrates unidirectional causality with greenhouse gas emissions. The results have implications for the sustainable development of the production and consumption of goods. Another study conducted by Oncioiu I., Petrescu A.G., Grecu E. and Petrescu M. (Oncioiu et al., 2017) shows that the actual beneficiaries of a clean environment depend on the developers of renewable energy networks. The econometric analysis conducted by the authors establishes the factors that realize the awareness of consumers in Romania regarding the use of renewable energy. According to Dusmanescu D., Andrei J. and Subic J. (Dusmanescu et al., 2014), the specific characteristics of the use of renewable energy sources require an implementation process that must be adapted to regional particularities. This awareness according to the author Fanisi F. (Fanisi, 2011) has the effect of reducing greenhouse gas emissions by stimulating the building efficiency programme. According to Micu D.D., Braicu S.F., Czumbil L. and Stet D. (Micu et al., 2016), in order to achieve the targets of renewable energy utilization, modernization of distribution networks and re-capturing of lines for the integration of renewable energy into the grid are necessary. Czumbil L., Braicu S.F., Micu D.D., Stet D. and Ceclan, A. (Czumbil et al., 2017) present an analysis of load flows on a newly upgraded substation in the northern region of Romania; the results are useful for optimization and parameterization of power systems. According to Androniceanu A., Lazaroiu G. and Valter N. (Androniceanu et al., 2018) Romania has a great potential in the production of this type of energy and the revision of the Romanian energy policies especially in the field of renewable energy is a current priority.

### *Energy Efficiency and Economic Growth*

A group of researchers in Taiwan (Lin et al., 2023) studies by means of a regression model the energy efficiency of a number of 29 countries including EU Member States for the period 2015–2019. The results of the study show that in most Member States energy performance is good but by the date of finalization of the study the consumption of non-renewable energy is more efficient than renewable energy. Romania ranks among the top four countries that have improved energy efficiency after carbon redistribution. The impact of the study is high on the basis of public policy proposals on the European carbon market, inter-regional cooperation and promoting the implementation of carbon policies. In a study by Androniceanu A. (Androniceanu, 2012) it is shown that the orientation of strategies for increasing energy efficiency in Romania is made through the prism of the transition to clean transportation in Romania existing incentives of up to 5000 euro for the purchase of green cars and vehicles. The study carried out an analysis of energy consumption and showed that the usefulness of reducing environmental impact can be combined with real benefits of the transition to green transportation. According to Torok G. and Torok I. (Toeroek & Toeroek, 2014) the process of energy market liberalization will have multiple benefits in terms of increasing the efficiency of consumer-oriented service provision. Sanduleac M. (Sanduleac, 2018) shows that a vulnerability of the Romanian energy system is the storage system and the infrastructure for supplying electric vehicles. According to Carutasiu M.B., Ionescu C. and Necula H. (Carutasiu et al., 2017) the creation of a national guideline and strategies for the modernization of buildings are unavoidable elements in order to achieve energy efficiency.

### *Energy Productivity*

Kirikkaleli D., Addai K. and Castanho R.A. (Kirikkaleli et al., 2023) investigate the effect of financial stability and energy productivity on environmental degradation in Bulgaria. They show that both indicators on energy productivity and energy stability have positive effect on environmental degradation and economic growth has positive effect on greenhouse gas emissions. The study is one of the impacts through the public policy proposals on the development of smart energy technologies of financing to achieve energy productivity and to develop smart water infrastructure. The authors also propose controlling the use of fossil fuels and a policy of price stability for Bulgaria, which are also valid for Romania. The study "Dynamic Impact of Energy Productivity and Economic Growth on Environmental Sustainability in Southern European Countries" (Liu et al., 2023) analyses the effect of energy productivity on sustainable economic growth in the countries of Southern Europe, also taking into account the extent of carbon emissions in the region. The authors formulate public policy proposals for increasing energy efficiency and achieving sustainability goals in the region. The results of the study show that energy productivity has a positive, significant impact on reducing carbon emissions while economic growth has a negative impact on the same indicator.

### *Primary Energy Consumption*

The study by Azam A., Ateeq M., Shafique M. and Rafiq M. and Yuan J. (Azam et al., 2023) analyses the synergy between primary energy consumption, size of economic growth, availability of natural resources, quality of governance and financial development between 1990 and 2017. According to a group of authors (Azam et al., 2023) primary energy consumption positively influences economic growth. At the same time, the authors determine bidirectional causalities between primary energy consumption and economic growth and unidirectional causalities between primary energy consumption and natural resources and financial development. The impact of the study is high demonstrating the links between primary energy consumption, resource quality and governance on economic growth. The public policy proposals put forward are aimed at sustainable energy strategies, with the authors considering the energy sector as an important factor affecting economic growth. Bampatsou C., Halkos G. and Beneki C (Bampatsou et al., 2021) analyse the production process with its effect on gross domestic product through capital stocks, number of persons employed and primary energy consumption at the European Union level. They show that the consumption of renewable energy from biomass or recycled municipal waste has positive effect on productivity while carbon dioxide emissions have negative effects. The impact of the study for Romania is high, with the authors showing that Romania is on an upward slope in terms of primary energy sector productivity and technical efficiency improvement. At the same time there is a loss of productivity due to changes in production conditions. Productivity is mainly influenced using material resources, environmental degradation and increased use of municipal waste as an energy source.

### *Share of Renewable Energy in Gross Final Energy Consumption*

Halkos G. and Aslanidis P.S. (Halkos & Aslanidis, 2023) estimated the effect of energy efficiency and productivity on sustainable economic development. The study is carried out for the period 1995–2020 at the G20 group level. The results of the study show that including renewable energy consumption at the level of European countries, an improvement in productivity parameters was achieved in the analysed period, the results being differentiated after incorporating the negative carbon output. The impact is high by identifying the impact of technological change on energy productivity in the primary sector and of technical efficiency on the same parameter based on the scenario method.

### *Energy Import Dependency*

Carfora A., Pansini R.V. and Scandurra G. (Carfora et al., 2022) analyse the energy import needs of the European Union countries in the light of the current geopolitical context and the European renewable energy orientation. The analysis was carried out in the period 2007–2017 and it was shown that the development of the renewable energy sector significantly contributes to the reduction of energy import needs. The impact of the study is significant due to the statistical research carried out, which shows that at EU level achieving the targets for the use of renewable energy would effectively lead to a decrease in import dependency provided that new technology is used, and energy infrastructure is optimized.

## Analysis of the Main Sustainable Development Goal Indicators 7

It can be observed that the scientific interest in recent research in the international literature has focused on issues of economic growth through increased consumption of renewable energy, increased energy efficiency, monitoring of energy consumption and reduced energy import dependency. These issues are reflected in Eurostat statistics through specific indicators which will be analysed below (Eurostat, 2023).

Primary energy consumption indicator shows a country's total energy demand before any energy transition. It is used to track progress towards the EU's 2030 energy efficiency targets.

Final energy consumption is the total amount of energy consumed by a country's end-users, including transportation, households, services, agriculture and industry.

Final energy consumption in households per capita indicator shows the amount of energy consumed by each person in the household excluding transportation.

Energy productivity is the amount of economic output produced per unit of available gross energy.

The share of renewable energy in gross final consumption of energy according to the Renewable Energy Directive 2018/2001 (European Parliament, 2018a), the share of renewable energy consumption in final energy consumption.

Energy import dependency indicator shows the share of a country's energy needs that are met by imports from other countries.

The population unable to keep warm enough at home is the share of the population that cannot afford to keep warm enough at home.

The analysis of the primary energy consumption indicator at European Union level (CENPUE27) shows that in the period 2010–2021 it had a dynamic of 17.97%, i.e. from the minimum value of 1235.6 million tonnes of oil in 2020 to 1457.6 million tonnes of oil in 2010 (Fig. 3.3).

On trend the indicator showed an overall decreasing trend of 148.6 million tonnes of oil; the calculated overall average of the indicator being 1363.05 million tonnes of oil, with a standard error estimated by descriptive statistics of 16.034 million tonnes of oil (see Table 3.1). The dynamics of this indicator at European level have been changing continuously in

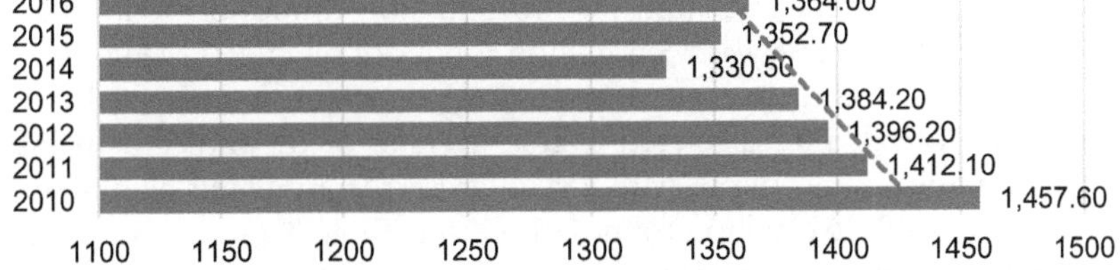


**Fig. 3.3** Dynamics of the indicator "primary energy consumption" at European level over the period 2010–2021. Source: Author based on Eurostat data

**Table 3.1** Comparative descriptive statistics of the indicator "primary energy consumption" at European and national level in the period 2010–2021

| *Primary energy consumption* | *European Union—27 countries* | *Romania* |
|---|---|---|
| Minim | 1235.60 | 30.10 |
| Maxim | 1457.60 | 33.50 |
| Average | 1363.0500 | 31.9170 |
| Standard error of the mean | 16.03400 | 0.36100 |
| Standard deviation | 55.54400 | 1.25000 |
| Variance | 3085.135 | 1.563 |
| Asymmetry | −0.792 | −0.204 |
| Asymmetry error | 0.637 | 0.637 |
| Flattening | 1.941 | −1.801 |
| Standard error of flattening | 1.232 | 1.232 |

Source: Author based on Eurostat data

recent years. In general, there has been a downward trend in primary energy consumption, reflecting the increased use of renewable energy sources and energy efficiency efforts. There are, however, significant differences between EU Member States, with some countries still recording high primary energy consumption while others have managed to significantly reduce their dependence on non-renewable energy resources. It is important that all countries invest in sustainable technologies and make clear commitments to reduce primary energy consumption in order to protect the environment and ensure sustainable development. It is also important for the European Union to provide financial and technical support for less developed Member States so that they can implement sustainable renewable energy solutions more quickly and effectively.

The analysis of the indicator "primary energy consumption" in Romania (CENPROM) reveals that in the period 2010–2021 it had a dynamic of 11.3%. The minimum threshold was 30.1 million tonnes of oil in 2014 and the maximum value was 33.5 million tonnes of oil in 2011 (Fig. 3.4).

On trend the indicator experienced an overall upward trend of 0.1 million tonnes of oil; the calculated overall average of the indicator being 31.917 million tonnes of oil, with a standard error estimated by descriptive statistics of 0.361 million tonnes of oil (see Table 3.1).

The analysis of the dynamic variations of the indicator in Romania compared to the European average shows that for our country, the overall

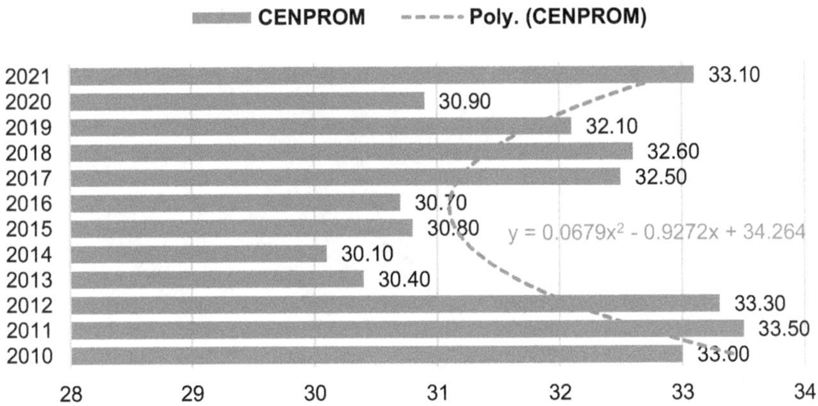


**Fig. 3.4** Dynamics of the indicator "primary energy consumption" at national level in the period 2010–2021. Source: Author based on Eurostat data

average of seasonal variations was higher than the European average, as shown in Fig. 3.5.

According to Eurostat (Eurostat, 2023), the EU is committed to reduce energy consumption by 20% by 2020 compared to baseline projections and the target for 2030 is to reduce energy consumption by at least 32.5%. Due to economic developments, the structure of industrial sectors, energy efficiency initiatives and weather conditions, primary energy consumption has changed over time. In 2020, the restrictions caused by the COVID-19 pandemic, such as travel blockages and travel restrictions, were a major factor affecting EU primary energy consumption, with the lowest levels of primary energy consumption in the period analysed. In 2021, energy consumption increased and exceeded the 2020 energy efficiency target by 5.8% (Eurostat, 2023). Given that this is still 9.5% below the 2030 target, continued efforts to increase efficiency in the coming years are needed.

Due to the limits imposed by the COVID-19 pandemic in 2020, primary and final energy consumption at EU level declined; this trend recovered in 2021 as countries relaxed their anti-COVID policies.

Diverging tensions between primary and final energy consumption often arise because of fundamental changes in the energy system, in particular the shift from electricity produced mainly from fossil fuels to wind and solar. Although final energy consumption will remain the same,

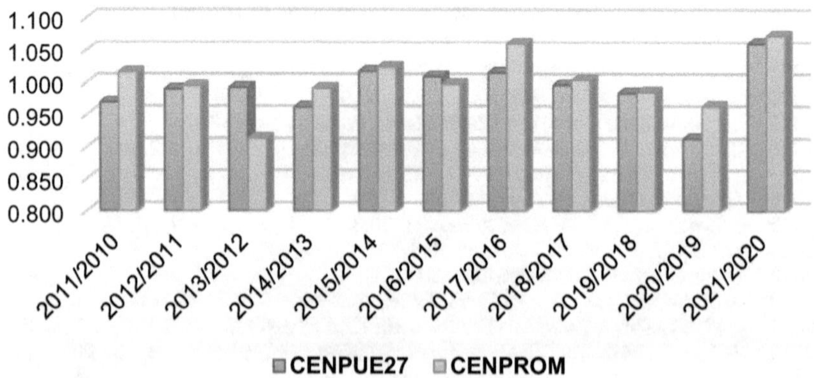


**Fig. 3.5** Analysis of the dynamic variations of the indicator "primary energy consumption" in Romania compared to the European average. Source: Author based on Eurostat data

primary energy consumption will decrease because of this change. In addition, transformation losses are a component of the industrial sector of the producing state and have a varied impact on the primary and final energy consumption of importers and exporters (Eurostat, 2023). Both primary energy consumption (resources needed to produce or import electricity) and final energy consumption (actual consumption by end-users) are affected by the amount of electricity used.

The analysis of the indicator "final energy consumption" at EU level (CENFUE27) shows that in the period 2010–2021 it had a dynamic of 13.09%. The minimum value of 905.9 million tonnes of oil was recorded in 2020 while the maximum value of 1024.5 million tonnes of oil in 2010 (Fig. 3.6).

On trend, the indicator experienced an overall downward trend of 56.6 million tonnes of oil; the calculated overall average of the indicator being 973.842 million tonnes of oil, with a standard error estimated by the descriptive statistics of 8.545 million tonnes of oil (see Table 3.2).

The analysis of the indicator "final energy consumption" (million tonnes of oil) in Romania (CENFROM) shows that in the analysed period 2010–2021 it had a dynamic of 17.05%, respectively, from the minimum value of 21.7 million tonnes of oil in 2014 to 25.4 million tonnes of oil in 2021 (see Fig. 3.7).

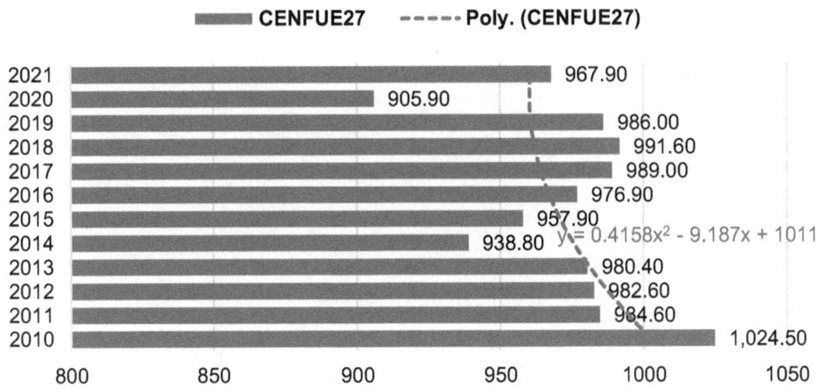


**Fig. 3.6** Dynamics of the indicator "final energy consumption" at European level over the period 2010–2021. Source: Author based on Eurostat data

**Table 3.2** Comparative descriptive statistics of the indicator "final energy consumption" at European and national level in the period 2010–2021

| *Final energy consumption* | *European Union—27 countries* | *Romania* |
|---|---|---|
| Minim | 905.90 | 21.70 |
| Maxim | 1024.50 | 25.40 |
| Average | 973.8420 | 22.9420 |
| Standard error of the mean | 8.54500 | 0.30900 |
| Standard deviation | 29.60000 | 1.07000 |
| Variance | 876.134 | 1.144 |
| Asymmetry | −0.916 | 0.998 |
| Asymmetry error | 0.637 | 0.637 |
| Flattening | 2.056 | 1.172 |
| Standard error of flattening | 1.232 | 1.232 |

Source: Author based on Eurostat data

On trend the indicator experienced an overall upward trend of 2.9 million tonnes of oil; the calculated overall average of the indicator being 22.942 million tonnes of oil, with a standard error estimated by descriptive statistics of 0.309 million tonnes of oil (see Table 3.2).

The analysis of the dynamic variations of the indicator in Romania compared to the European average shows that for our country, the overall

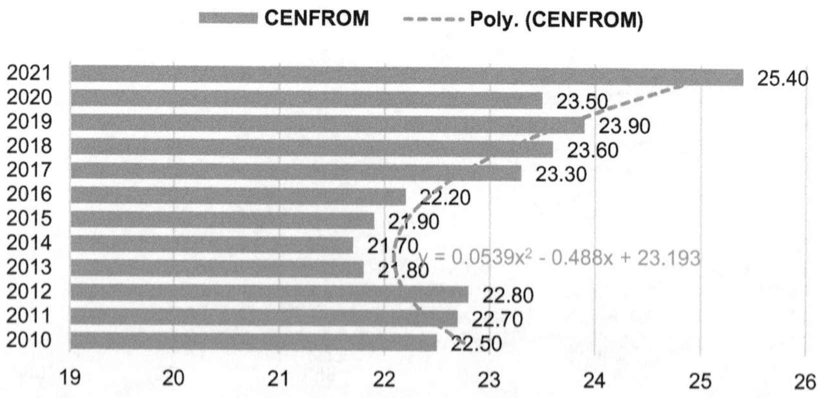


**Fig. 3.7** Dynamics of the indicator "final energy consumption" at national level in the period 2010–2021. Source: Author based on Eurostat data

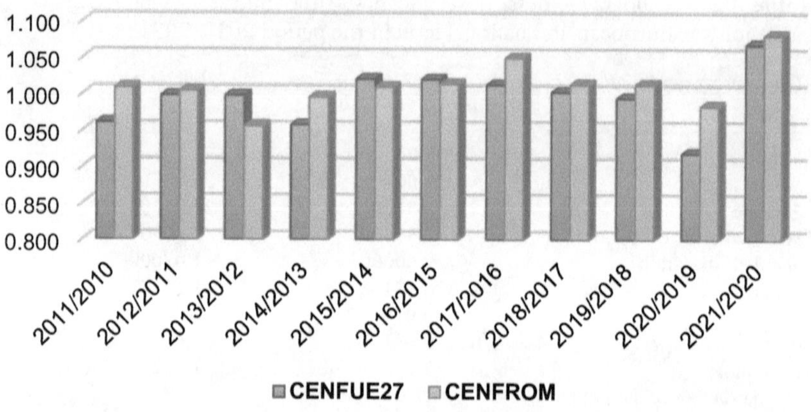


**Fig. 3.8** Analysis of the dynamic variations of the indicator "final energy consumption" in Romania compared to the European average. Source: Author based on Eurostat data

average of seasonal variations was higher than the European average, as shown in Fig. 3.8.

The analysis of the indicator "final energy consumption in households per capita" (kilogrammes of oil equivalent) at EU level (CENFGUE27) shows that in the period 2010–2021 it had a dynamic of 19.47%. The minimum value of 529 kilogrammes of oil was recorded in 2020 and the maximum value of 632 kilogrammes of oil in 2010 (Fig. 3.9).

On trend, the indicator showed an overall downward trend of 46 kilogrammes of oil; the calculated overall average of the indicator being 572.333 kilogrammes of oil, with a standard error estimated by descriptive statistics of 7.991 kilogrammes of oil (see Table 3.3).

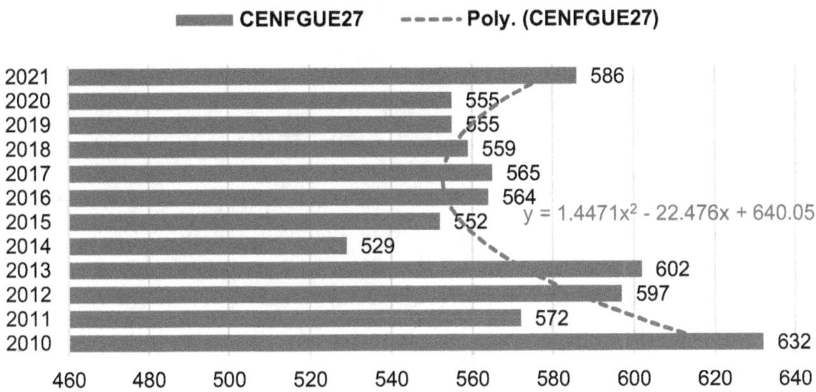


**Fig. 3.9** Dynamics of the indicator "household final energy consumption per capita" at European level over the period 2010–2021. Source: Author based on Eurostat data

**Table 3.3** Comparative descriptive statistics of the indicator "household final energy consumption per capita" at European and national level in the period 2010–2021

| *Household final energy consumption per capita* | *European Union—27 countries* | *Romania* |
|---|---|---|
| Minim | 529.00 | 372.00 |
| Maxim | 632.00 | 458.00 |
| Average | 572.3330 | 397.1670 |
| Standard error of the mean | 7.99100 | 6.73800 |
| Standard deviation | 27.68100 | 23.34300 |
| Variance | 766.242 | 544.879 |
| Asymmetry | 0.785 | 1.620 |
| Asymmetry error | 0.637 | 0.637 |
| Flattening | 0.736 | 3.845 |
| Standard error of flattening | 1.232 | 1.232 |

Source: Author based on Eurostat data

The analysis of the indicator "final energy consumption in households per capita" in Romania (CENFGROM) shows that in the analysed period 2010–2021 it had a dynamic of 23.12%, respectively, from the minimum value of 372 kilogrammes of oil in 2014 and 2015 to 458 kilogrammes of oil in 2021 (Fig. 3.10).

On trend the indicator showed an overall increasing trend of 58 kg oil; the calculated overall average of the indicator being 397.167 kg oil, with a standard error estimated by descriptive statistics of 6.738 kg oil (as shown in Table 3.3).

The analysis of the dynamic variations of the indicator in Romania compared to the European average shows that for our country, the overall average of seasonal variations has been higher than the European average in recent years, as shown in Fig. 3.11.

Final energy consumption in households accounts for a quarter of final energy consumption, with people using electricity mainly for lighting, heating, cooking and other uses. The share of energy consumed is influenced by the outside temperature, the energy efficiency of the building, the use of electrical appliances, the behaviour of the inhabitants and their economic situation (Eurostat, 2023). Over 60% of energy is consumed for heating in the winter months on average each year (Eurostat, 2023).

The analysis of the Energy Productivity indicator (Euro per kilogramme of oil) at the European Union level (WENUE27) reveals that in the period

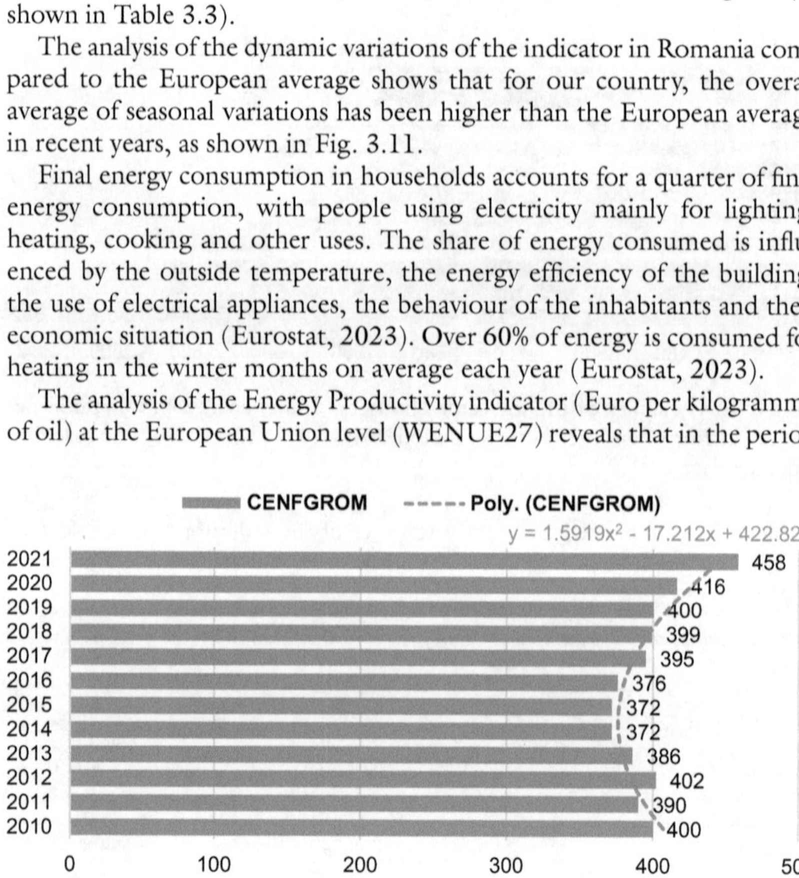


**Fig. 3.10** Dynamics of the indicator "household final energy consumption per capita" at national level in the period 2010–2021. Source: Author based on Eurostat data

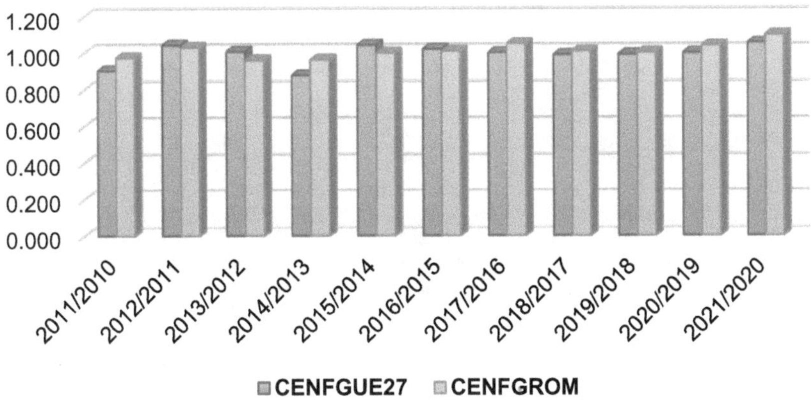


**Fig. 3.11** Analysis of the dynamic variations of the indicator "final energy consumption in households per capita" in Romania compared to the European average. Source: Author based on Eurostat data

2010–2021 it had a dynamic of 25.58%, i.e. from the minimum value of 6.84 euro per kilogramme of oil in 2010 to 8.59 euro per kilogramme of oil in 2020 (as shown in Fig. 3.12).

On trend the indicator showed an overall upward trend of 1.7 euro per kilogramme of oil; the overall calculated average of the indicator being 7.773 euro per kilogramme of oil, with a standard error estimated by descriptive statistics of 0.163 euro per kilogramme of oil (see Table 3.4).

The analysis of the energy productivity (Euro per kilogramme of oil) indicator (WENROM) at the Romanian level shows that in the period 2010–2021 it had a dynamic of 48.36%, respectively, from the minimum value of 3.66 euro per kilogramme of oil in 2010 to 5.43 euro per kilogramme of oil in 2019, as shown in Fig. 3.13.

On trend, the indicator showed an overall upward trend of 1.69 euro per kilogramme of oil; the calculated overall average of the indicator being 4.642 euro per kilogramme of oil, with a standard error estimated by descriptive statistics of 0.184 euro per kilogramme of oil (see Table 3.4).

The analysis of the dynamic variations of the indicator in Romania compared to the European average shows that for our country, the general average of seasonal variations was higher than the European average, as shown in Fig. 3.14.

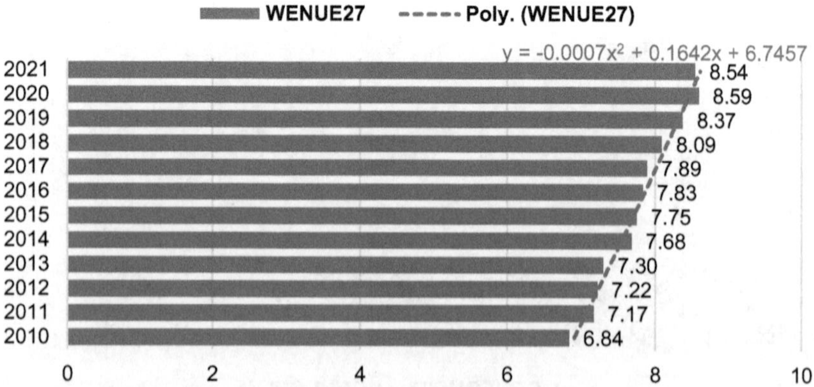


**Fig. 3.12** Dynamics of the energy productivity indicator at European level between 2010 and 2021. Source: Author based on Eurostat data

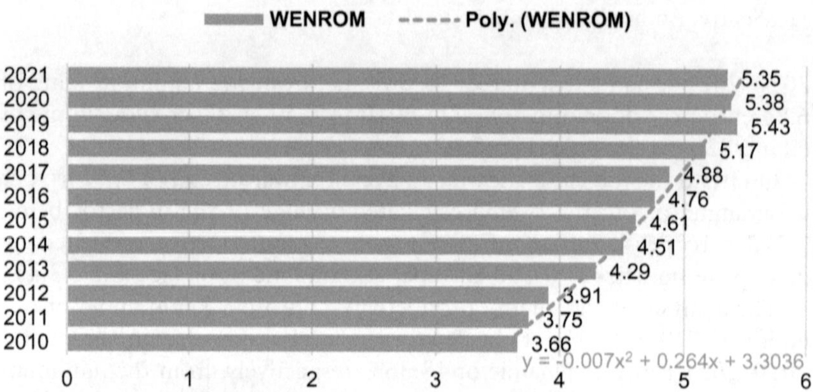


**Fig. 3.13** Energy productivity indicator dynamics at national level in the period 2010–2021. Source: Author based on Eurostat data

The analysis of the indicator "share of renewable energy in gross final consumption of energy" in the European Union (CENRUE27) shows that over the period 2010–2021 it has had a dynamic of 52.99%, i.e. from a minimum of 14.4% in 2010 to 22.03% in 2020 (Fig. 3.15).

On trend, the indicator showed an overall upward trend of 7.37%; the calculated overall average of the indicator being 18.003%, with a standard error estimated by descriptive statistics of 0.71% (as shown in Table 3.5).

**Table 3.4** Comparative descriptive statistics of the energy productivity indicator at European and national level in the period 2010–2021

| *Energy productivity* | *European Union—27 countries* | *Romania* |
|---|---|---|
| Minim | 6.84 | 3.66 |
| Maxim | 8.59 | 5.43 |
| Average | 7.7730 | 4.6420 |
| Standard error of the mean | 0.16300 | 0.18400 |
| Standard deviation | 0.56400 | 0.63600 |
| Variance | 0.318 | 0.405 |
| Asymmetry | −0.036 | −0.289 |
| Asymmetry error | 0.637 | 0.637 |
| Flattening | −0.983 | −1.266 |
| Standard error of flattening | 1.232 | 1.232 |

Source: Author based on Eurostat data

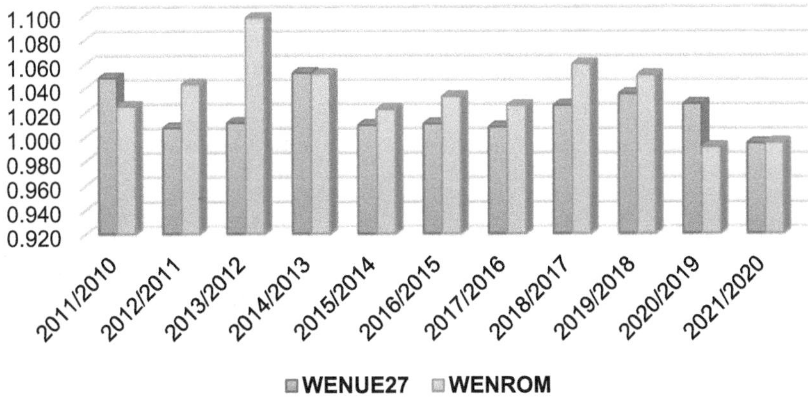


**Fig. 3.14** Analysis of the dynamic variations of the energy productivity indicator in Romania compared to the European average. Source: Author based on Eurostat data

The analysis of the indicator "share of renewable energy in gross final energy consumption" in Romania (CENRROM) shows that in the period 2010–2021 it had a dynamic of 15.13%, respectively, from the minimum value of 21.74% in 2011 to 25.03% in 2016, as shown in Fig. 3.16.

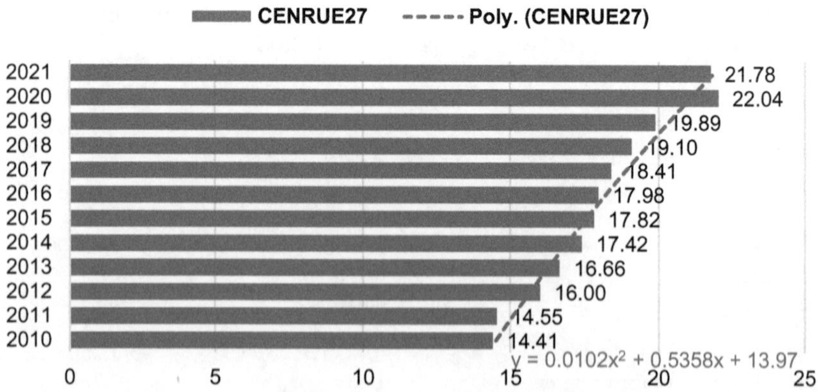


**Fig. 3.15** Dynamics of the indicator "share of renewable energy in gross final energy consumption" at European level in the period 2010–2021. Source: Author based on Eurostat data

**Table 3.5** Comparative descriptive statistics of the indicator "share of renewable energy in gross final energy consumption" at European and national level in the period 2010–2021

| *Share of renewable energy in gross final energy consumption* | *European Union—27 countries* | *Romania* |
|---|---|---|
| Minim | 14.41 | 21.74 |
| Maxim | 22.04 | 25.03 |
| Average | 18.0030 | 23.8870 |
| Standard error of the mean | 0.71000 | 0.28600 |
| Standard deviation | 2.45900 | 0.99000 |
| Variance | 6.045 | 0.981 |
| Asymmetry | 0.212 | −0.976 |
| Asymmetry error | 0.637 | 0.637 |
| Flattening | −0.535 | 0.407 |
| Standard error of flattening | 1.232 | 1.232 |

Source: Author based on Eurostat data

On trend, the indicator showed an overall upward trend of 0.762%; the calculated overall average of the indicator being 23.887%, with a standard error estimated by descriptive statistics of 0.286% (as shown in Table 3.5).

The analysis of the dynamic variations of the indicator in Romania compared to the European average shows that for our country, the general

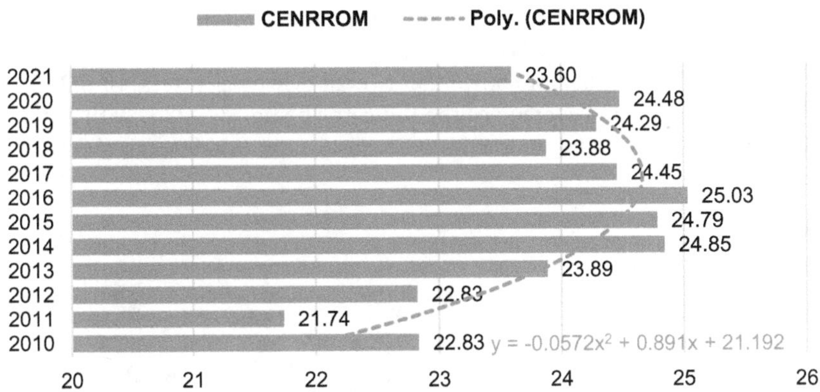


**Fig. 3.16** Renewable energy share in gross final energy consumption at national level in the period 2010–2021. Source: Author based on Eurostat data

average of seasonal variations was lower than the European average, as shown in Fig. 3.17.

To achieve a clean and secure energy system, by 2030, the European Union wants to expand its use of renewable energy from 32% to 42.5% of total gross energy consumption, with an additional 2.5%, allowing it to increase to 45% (Eurostat, 2023). Renewable energy sources are inexhaustible and renewable whereas fossil fuels regenerate over millions of years, are the main source of greenhouse gas emissions and have a major impact on climate change. In addition, imports of fossil fuels from outside the EU, such as crude oil and natural gas, expose consumers to high costs and supply risks, as has been seen in the aftermath of the Russian gas supply cut. The EU is therefore working to increase domestic energy production, especially from renewable sources, reduce energy consumption and build and modernize infrastructure to distribute clean energy between Member States (Eurostat, 2023).

In 2021, the share of renewable energy in gross final energy consumption at EU level varied from country to country due to differences in the availability of renewable sources as well as financial support and regulation. At European level, in 2021 the largest share of renewable energy was from solid biofuels 41.4%, wind energy 13.2% and hydropower 11.9% (Eurostat, 2023).

The analysis of the indicator "energy import dependency by products" at EU level (DEPIMPUE27) shows that in the period 2010–2021 it had a dynamic of 12.13%, i.e. from a minimum value of 53.93% in 2013 to 60.48% in 2019 (Fig. 3.18).

On trend, the indicator showed an overall downward trend of 0.243%; the calculated overall average of the indicator being 56.398%, with a standard error estimated by descriptive statistics of 0.519% (as shown in Table 3.6).

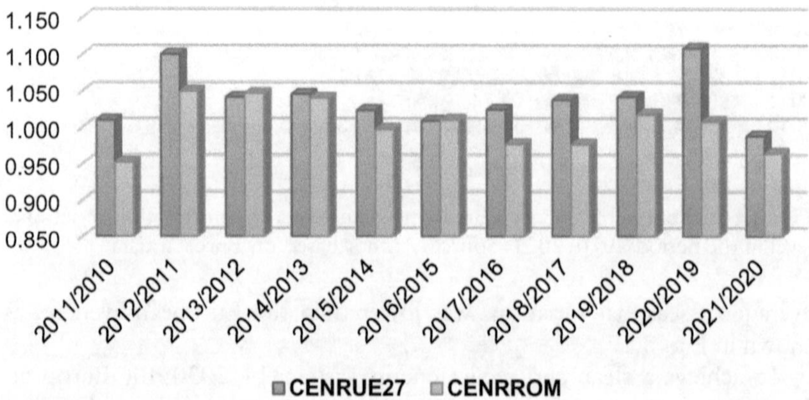


**Fig. 3.17** Analysis of dynamic variations of the indicator "share of renewable energy in gross final energy consumption" in Romania compared to the European average. Source: Author based on Eurostat data

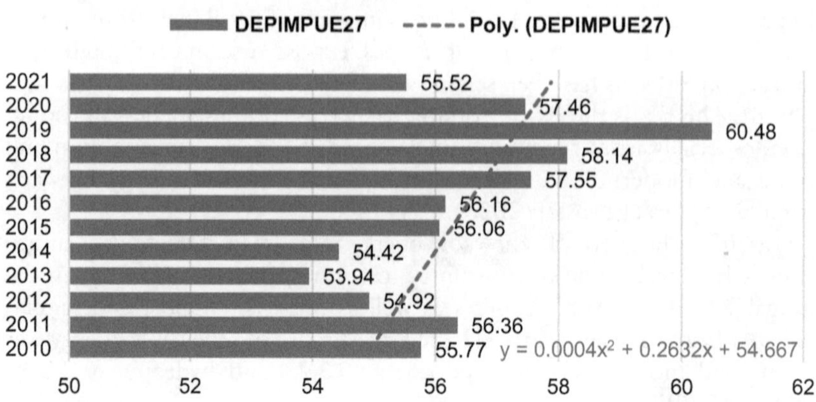


**Fig. 3.18** Dynamics of the indicator "energy import dependency by product" at European level over the period 2010–2021. Source: Author based on Eurostat data

The analysis of the indicator "energy import dependency by product" at the Romanian level (DEPIMPROM) reveals that in the analysed period 2010–2021 it had a dynamic of 89.91%, respectively, from the minimum value of 16.66% in 2014 to 31.64% in 2021 as shown in Fig. 3.19.

On trend, the indicator showed an overall upward trend of 10.25%; the calculated overall average of the indicator being 23.022%, with a standard error estimated by descriptive statistics of 1.419% (see Table 3.6).

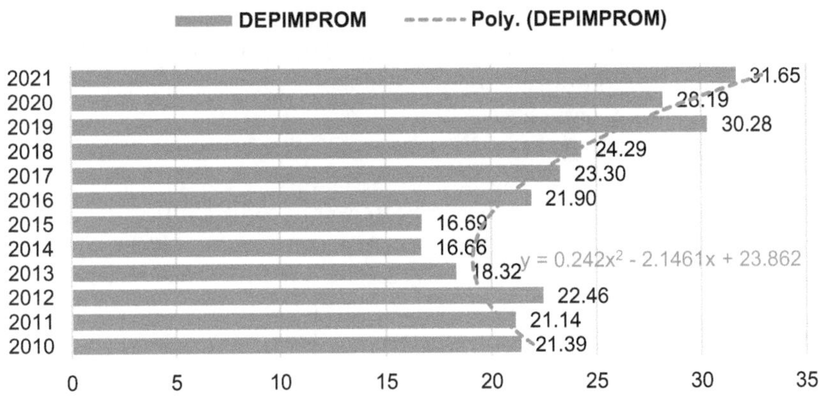


**Fig. 3.19** Dynamics of the indicator "energy import dependency by products" at national level in the period 2010–2021. Source: Author based on Eurostat data

**Table 3.6** Comparative descriptive statistics of the indicator "energy import dependency by products" at European and national level in the period 2010–2021

| *Energy import dependence by product* | *European Union—27 countries* | *Romania* |
|---|---|---|
| Minim | 53.94 | 16.66 |
| Maxim | 60.48 | 31.65 |
| Average | 56.3980 | 23.0220 |
| Standard error of the mean | 0.51900 | 1.41900 |
| Standard deviation | 1.79900 | 4.91700 |
| Variance | 3.238 | 24.178 |
| Asymmetry | 0.923 | 0.492 |
| Asymmetry error | 0.637 | 0.637 |
| Flattening | 1.193 | −0.588 |
| Standard error of flattening | 1.232 | 1.232 |

Source: Author based on Eurostat data

The analysis of the dynamic variations of the indicator in Romania compared to the European average shows that for our country, the general average of seasonal variations was higher than the European average, as shown in Fig. 3.20.

Fuel imports from outside the European Union remained an important source of energy in 2021 even though the last 10 years have seen a steady increase in renewable energy. Fuel imports contributed 55.6% of total gross energy measured by net imports (Eurostat, 2023).

The European Union has increased the use of renewable energy sources and decreased total energy consumption, while at the same time decreasing fossil fuel-based primary energy production due to depletable domestic sources, namely natural gas.

The largest net imports in 2021 were oil, 92% imported, with natural gas in second place 83.4% and solid fuels, mainly coal, in third place 37.3% imported. Only 1.8% of the net imports were produced from renewable energy sources, including biofuels, which accounted for 8.9% of the total net available energy. In 2021, Russia remained the EU's main energy supplier, supplying 44.1% of gas, 24.8% of petroleum products and 52.4% of non-EU imports of solid fuels (Eurostat, 2023). This demonstrates the EU's strong dependence on Russian energy imports, which saw a significant reduction in 2022 due to the geopolitical impact in Russia, with

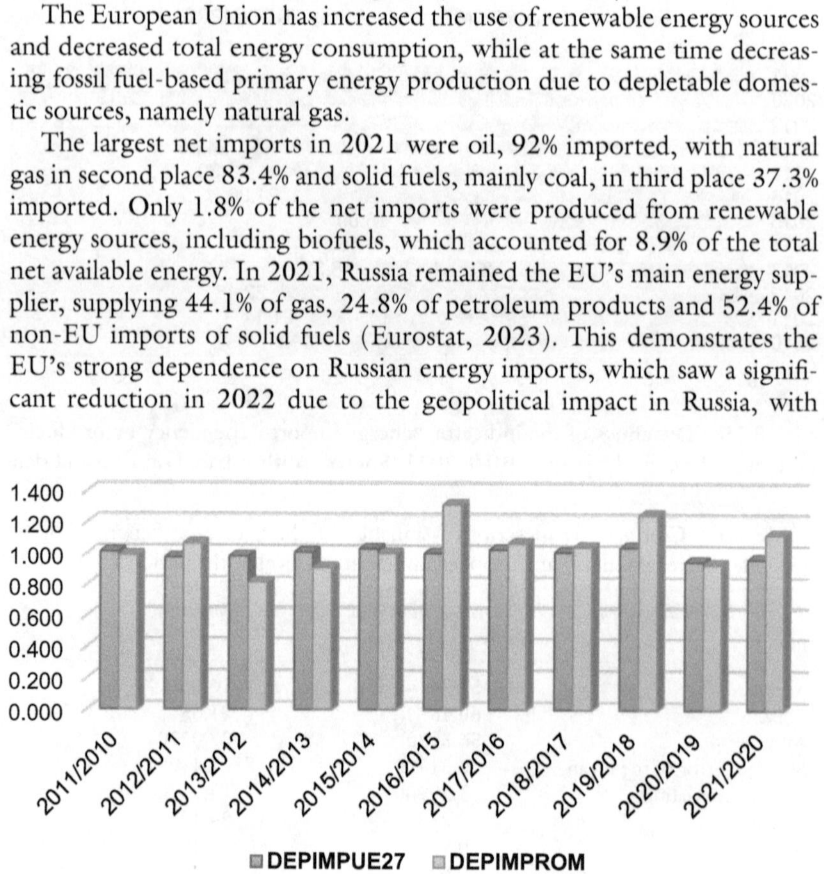


**Fig. 3.20** Analysis of the dynamic variations of energy import dependency by product in Romania compared to the European average. Source: Author based on Eurostat data

Russian natural gas exports to the EU being halted. The next sources on gas and oil supply, which supplied 18% of gas imports and 15.4% of oil imports, came from non-EU European countries, Norway and the United Kingdom (Eurostat, 2023). North America supplied 17.9% of solid fuels, the second largest source. These statistics do not take into account energy traded between Member States; they simply reflect total imports from outside the EU.

The analysis of the indicator "population unable to keep their homes sufficiently warm because of poverty" at European Union level (SARENUE27) shows that in the period 2010–2021 it had a dynamic of 62.32%. The minimum value of 6.9% was recorded in 2019 and 2021 and the maximum value of 11.2% in 2012 (Fig. 3.21).

On trend, the indicator experienced an overall downward trend of 3%; the calculated overall average of the indicator being 9.017%, with a standard error estimated by descriptive statistics of 0.45% (see Table 3.7).

The analysis of the indicator "population unable to keep their homes sufficiently warm due to poverty" in Romania (SARENROM) shows that in the period 2010–2021 this indicator had a dynamic of 116.13%. The minimum threshold was 9.3% in 2019, and the maximum threshold was 20.1% in 2010 according to Fig. 3.22.

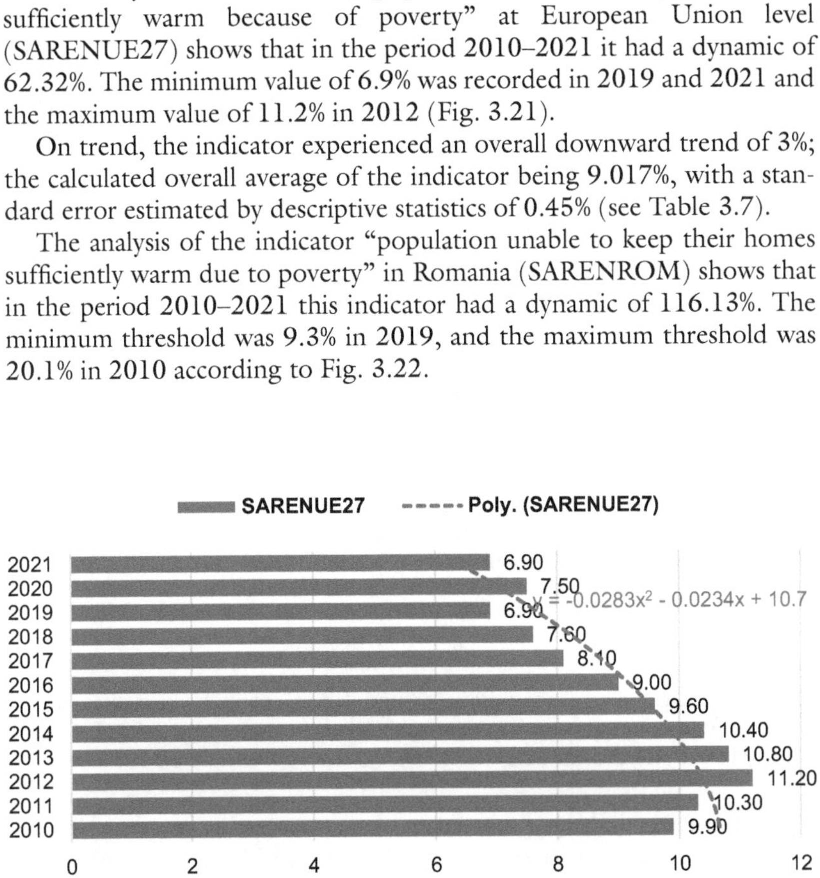


**Fig. 3.21** Dynamics of the indicator "population unable to keep their homes warm enough due to poverty" at EU level over the period 2010–2021. Source: Author based on Eurostat data

**Table 3.7** Comparative descriptive statistics of the indicator "population unable to keep their homes warm enough due to poverty" at EU and national level in the period 2010–2021

| *People unable to keep their homes warm enough because of poverty* | *European Union—27 countries* | *Romania* |
|---|---|---|
| Minim | 6.90 | 9.30 |
| Maxim | 11.20 | 20.10 |
| Average | 9.0170 | 12.9580 |
| Standard error of the mean | 0.45000 | 0.91400 |
| Standard deviation | 1.55900 | 3.16600 |
| Variance | 2.431 | 10.023 |
| Asymmetry | −0.125 | 0.882 |
| Asymmetry error | 0.637 | 0.637 |
| Flattening | −1.630 | 0.883 |
| Standard error of flattening | 1.232 | 1.232 |

Source: Author based on Eurostat data

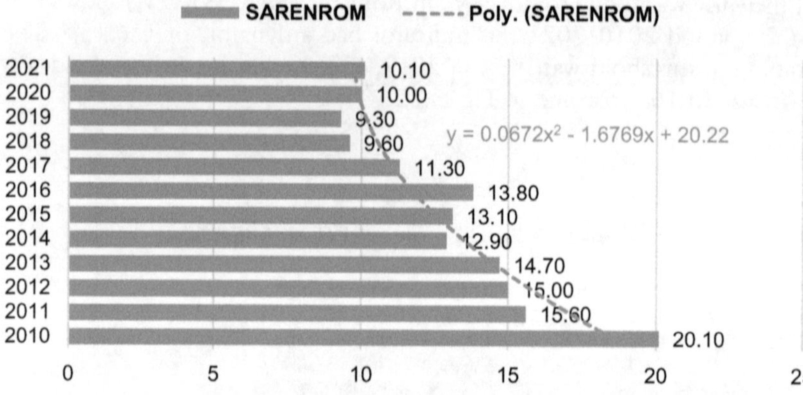


**Fig. 3.22** Dynamics of the indicator "population unable to keep their homes warm enough due to poverty" at national level in the period 2010–2021. Source: Author based on Eurostat data

On trend, the indicator showed an overall decreasing trend of 10%; the calculated overall average of the indicator being 12.958%, with a standard error estimated by descriptive statistics of 0.914% (as shown in Table 3.7).

The analysis of the dynamic variations of the indicator in Romania compared to the European average shows that for our country, the general average of seasonal variations was lower than the European average, as shown in Fig. 3.23.

The ability to maintain sufficient heating in the home is an indicator used to monitor access to affordable energy at EU level. Low energy access is closely linked to low-income, high-energy use and poor building efficiency standards.

The European Union has recently made progress in improving access to affordable energy. Thus, over the period under review, 2010–2021, there has been a steady decrease in the number of people who cannot afford to keep their homes sufficiently warm. People who are below the poverty line in terms of income are more likely to be unable to keep their homes sufficiently warm (Eurostat, 2023).

In 2021, less than 10% of the population in 20 EU Member States reported difficulties in keeping warm enough (Eurostat, 2023). The lowest number of people without access to heat was found in Northern and Western European countries due to cold winters. Especially in Southern and Eastern Europe, there seems to be a problem with lack of acceptable heat. Poor energy efficiency, insufficient heating systems and lower income levels impact on housing standards and fuel consumption (Eurostat, 2023).

The analysis shows that energy indicators in Europe have experienced a dynamic in line with European policies, thus energy consumption was

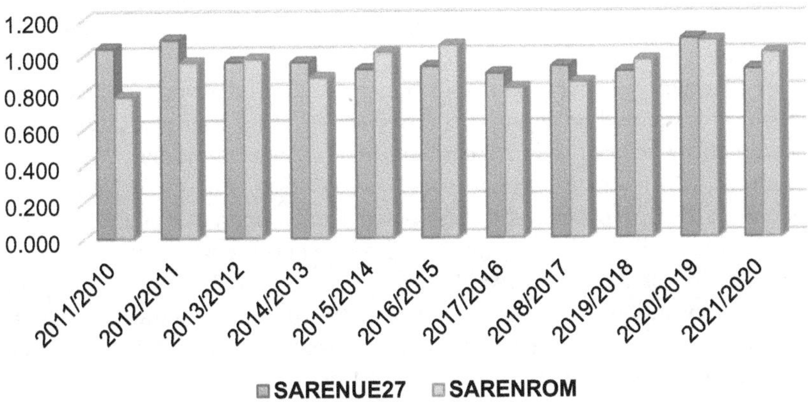


**Fig. 3.23** Analysis of the dynamic variations of the indicator "population unable to keep their homes sufficiently warm due to poverty" in Romania compared to the European average. Source: Author based on Eurostat data

reduced in the period analysed by 11%; the same dynamic was recorded at the level of final energy consumption indicator which was reduced by 5.5%; at household level there was a decrease of 7.3%; in contrast, in Romania primary energy consumption was maintained in the period analysed at 33 million tonnes of oil and primary energy consumption increased by 12.8%; at household level in Romania there was an increase of 14.5%. These results constitute the premises of a vulnerable energy policy and are supported by the results of the import dependency ratio, which increased in Romania by 48%. The only favourable evolution is the decrease of the population exposed to the risk of energy poverty, which will be reduced by 50% between 2010 and 2021.

## Conclusions

A multidimensional analysis of the economic strategies adopted to achieve Sustainable Development Goal 7 and its related headline indicators reveals significant momentum at EU level towards strengthening the energy transition and reducing structural vulnerabilities in energy security, efficiency and affordability. In an environment marked by unprecedented geopolitical and economic pressures, such as the 2022 energy crisis and the gradual decoupling from fossil fuel imports from Russia, the EU has reconfigured its energy architecture through strategic initiatives such as REPowerEU and the European Green Pact, with the aim of accelerating decarbonization, electrification of industrial sectors and the expansion of the use of renewable resources.

At the national level, Romania has implemented several policies and programmes aimed at aligning the objectives of its energy strategy with the directions set by the European Union, focusing on modernizing infrastructure, diversifying energy sources, reducing energy poverty and increasing energy productivity. However, the comparative analysis of relevant indicators—such as primary and final energy consumption, energy productivity, share of renewable energy in final consumption, import dependency and incidence of energy poverty—highlights a number of persistent gaps between Romania and the EU average, reflecting institutional, technological and socio-economic limitations.

While Romania is making progress in areas such as increasing the share of renewable energy and reducing energy poverty, other dimensions—such as energy dependency, end-use efficiency and network performance—require major structural interventions. The significant differences between

European and national trends in energy intensity and storage capacity point to the need for a sustained effort to modernize infrastructure, strengthen administrative capacity and stimulate investments in green technologies.

In conclusion, achieving SDG7 in Romania requires a strategic recalibration of energy policies, accompanied by a firm commitment to convergence with European sustainability standards. In this respect, the coherent integration of national objectives into the European energy architecture, the financial support provided through the recovery and resilience mechanisms and the increased involvement of local and regional players are imperative. Only through an integrated, systemic and fair approach can a just energy transition be guaranteed, which effectively serves both the environmental and the economic and social interests of Romanian society within a sustainable and interconnected Europe.

## References


Androniceanu, A. (2012). Strategic thinking and ethical behavior in the Romanian energy sector. In C. Bratianu, G. Bratucu, D. Lixandroiu, N. A. Pop, & S. Vaduva (Eds.), *Business excellence challenges during the economic crisis* (Vol. 1, pp. 15–19). Editura Univ Transilvania Brasov.

Androniceanu, A., Lazaroiu, G., & Valter, N. (2018). Management of the renewable energies—Current status and priorities for Romania. In K. S. Soliman (Ed.), *Innovation management and education excellence through vision 2020* (Vol. I-XI, pp. 1871–1879). Int Business Information Management Assoc (IBIMA).

Azam, A., Ateeq, M., Shafique, M., Rafiq, M., & Yuan, J. (2023). Primary energy consumption-growth nexus: The role of natural resources, quality of government, and fixed capital formation. *Energy, 263*, 125570. https://doi.org/10.1016/j.energy.2022.125570

Bampatsou, C., Halkos, G., & Beneki, C. (2021). Energy and material flow management to improve EU productivity. *Economic Analysis and Policy, 70*, 83–93. https://doi.org/10.1016/j.eap.2021.02.003

Brodny, J., & Tutak, M. (2022). Analysis of the efficiency and structure of energy consumption in the industrial sector in the European Union countries between 1995 and 2019. *Science of the Total Environment, 808*, 152052. https://doi.org/10.1016/j.scitotenv.2021.152052

Carfora, A., Pansini, R. V., & Scandurra, G. (2022). Energy dependence, renewable energy generation and import demand: Are EU countries resilient? *Renewable Energy, 195*, 1262–1274. https://doi.org/10.1016/j.renene.2022.06.098

Carutasiu, M.-B., Ionescu, C., & Necula, H. (2017). Optimal technical and economic strategy for retrofitting residential buildings in Romania. *Proceedings of the International Conference on Business Excellence, 11*(1), 146–156. https://doi.org/10.1515/picbe-2017-0016

Czumbil, L., Braicu, S. F., Micu, D. D., Stet, D., & Ceclan, A. (2017). Analysis of load flow and short-circuit issues in a retrofitted 110/20 kV Romanian substation. In *2017 14th International conference on engineering of modern electric systems (EMES)* (pp. 13–16).

Dusmanescu, D., Andrei, J., & Subic, J. (2014). Scenario for implementation of renewable energy sources in Romania. In C. Luminita, C. Constantin, & I. F. Valeriu (Eds.), *1st International conference 'economic scientific research—theoretical, empirical and practical approaches', ESPERA 2013* (Vol. 8, pp. 300–305). Elsevier Science BV. https://doi.org/10.1016/S2212-5671(14)00094-X

European Commission. (2022). *REPowerEU plan*. Europa.Eu. https://eur-lex.europa.eu/legal-content/EN/TXT/?uri=COM%3A2022%3A230%3AFIN&qid=1653033742483

European Commission. (2024). *REPowerEU affordable, secure and sustainable energy for Europe*. Europa.Eu. https://commission.europa.eu/topics/energy/repowereu_en

European Parliament. (2018a). Directive (EU) 2018/2001 of the European Parliament and of the Council of 11 December 2018 on the promotion of the use of energy from renewable sources. *Official Journal of the European Union*. https://eur-lex.europa.eu/legal-content/EN/TXT/PDF/?uri=CELEX:32018L2001

European Parliament. (2018b). Regulation (EU) 2018/1999 of the European Parliament and of the Council of 11 December 2018 on the governance of the Energy Union and Climate Action, amending Regulations (EC) No 663/2009 and (EC) No 715/2009 of the European Parliament and of the Council. *Official Journal of the European Union, 77*. https://eur-lex.europa.eu/legal-content/EN/TXT/PDF/?uri=CELEX:32018R1999

Eurostat. (2023). *SDG 7—Affordable and clean energy*. Europa.Eu. https://ec.europa.eu/eurostat/statistics-explained/index.php?title=SDG_7_-_Affordable_and_clean_energy#Affordable_and_clean_energy_in_the_EU:_overview_and_key_trends

Fanisi, F. (2011). Energy performance certificates for buildings, at their beginning in Romania. In C. I. Murzea & A. Repanovici (Eds.), *Legal practice and international laws* (pp. 98–103). World Scientific and Engineering Acad and Soc.

Halkos, G. E., & Aslanidis, P.-S. C. (2023). Sustainable energy development in an era of geopolitical multi-crisis. Applying productivity indices within institutional framework. *Resources Policy, 85*, 103854. https://doi.org/10.1016/j.resourpol.2023.103854

Kirikkaleli, D., Addai, K., & Castanho, R. A. (2023). Energy productivity, financial stability, and environmental degradation in an Eastern European country: Evidence from novel Fourier approaches. *Heliyon, 9*(7), e18073. https://doi.org/10.1016/j.heliyon.2023.e18073

Lin, T.-Y., Chiu, Y.-H., Lin, Y.-N., Chang, T.-H., & Lin, P.-Y. (2023). Greenhouse gas emission indicators, energy consumption efficiency, and optimal carbon emission allowance allocation of the EU countries in 2030. *Gas Science and Engineering, 110*, 204902. https://doi.org/10.1016/j.jgsce.2023.204902

Liu, M., Chen, Z., Sowah, J. K., Ahmed, Z., & Kirikkaleli, D. (2023). The dynamic impact of energy productivity and economic growth on environmental sustainability in South European countries. *Gondwana Research, 115*, 116–127. https://doi.org/10.1016/j.gr.2022.11.012

Micu, D. D., Braicu, S. F., Czumbil, L., & Stet, D. (2016). Load flow and short-circuit analysis in a Romanian 110/20 kV retrofitted substation. In *2016 51st International universities power engineering conference (UPEC)*.

Ministry of Energy. (2020). *National integrated energy and climate change plan 2021–2030.* https://energie.gov.ro/. https://energie.gov.ro/wp-content/uploads/2019/02/PNIESC_RO_COM-1.pdf

Ministry of Energy. (2022). *Romania's energy strategy 2022–2030, with a view to 2050.* https://energie.gov.ro.

Oncioiu, I., Petrescu, A. G., Grecu, E., & Petrescu, M. (2017). Optimizing the renewable energy potential: Myth or future trend in Romania. *Energies, 10*(6), 759. https://doi.org/10.3390/en10060759

Sanduleac, M. (2018). Energy storage needs for clean power systems and the potential support from electrical vehicles a simplified assessment on Romanian case. In M. Gavrilas, C. Fosalau, C. G. Haba, & B. C. Neagu (Eds.), *2018 International conference and exposition on electrical and power engineering (EPE)* (pp. 458–463). IEEE.

Toeroek, G., & Toeroek, I. (2014). The liberalization of the Romanian energy market: Opportunities and challenges. In *Geoconference on ecology, economics, education and legislation, SGEM 2014* (Vol. III, pp. 471–478).

Usman, O., Alola, A. A., & Akadiri, S. S. (2022). Effects of domestic material consumption, renewable energy, and financial development on environmental sustainability in the EU-28: Evidence from a GMM panel-VAR. *Renewable Energy, 184*, 239–251. https://doi.org/10.1016/j.renene.2021.11.086

CHAPTER 4

# Modelling European Energy Sustainability Based on Sustainable Development Goal 7 Indicators

## Introduction

In a Europe at the crossroads of accelerated decarbonization imperatives, recurring energy crises and increasingly pressing geopolitical constraints, energy sustainability is becoming not just a component of the environmental agenda, but a fundamental pillar of economic resilience and strategic security. In this context, Sustainable Development Goal 7 (SDG7), which aims to ensure access to affordable, reliable, sustainable and modern energy for all, provides a normative and operational framework for assessing progress and formulating convergent policies within the European Union.

Modelling European energy sustainability based on SDG7 indicators requires an integrated approach that captures the interdependencies between sectoral energy consumption (agriculture and industry), the share of renewable energy in the energy mix, energy productivity, greenhouse gas emissions, industrial emissions intensity and the degree of external energy dependence. These dimensions are essential benchmarks for diagnosing the structural vulnerabilities of the European energy system and identifying the critical factors influencing the transition to a sustainable, low-carbon energy model.

This study contributes to the literature by applying a rigorous multiple linear regression methodology, accompanied by variable selection using the Backward Feature Selection (BFS) method, to a consolidated set of



C. Fortea, *Sustainable Economic Development and the European Green Deal*, https://doi.org/10.1007/978-3-032-10326-0_4

data collected from official sources (Eurostat, OECD). Through this empirical approach, nine functional models of energy sustainability are developed and validated, each reflecting a specific angle of analysis of the interactions between energy policies, sectoral consumption behaviours and environmental constraints. The results obtained highlight the differences in performance between Member States and allow for the development of a framework for analysing the impact of fiscal policies, energy productivity and the penetration of renewable sources on the sustainability of the energy system. This chapter therefore aims to provide a solid analytical basis for public policy decisions that support the green transition, reduce dependence on external resources and promote technological innovation in critical sectors of the European economy.

## Literature Review

The literature on energy sustainability in the European Union has developed significantly in recent decades in response to intensifying climate pressures, geopolitical instability and the commitments made by Member States under the Paris Agreement (United Nations, 2023) and the 2030 Agenda for Sustainable Development (European Commission, 2022b). At the heart of these debates is Sustainable Development Goal 7 (SDG7), which aims to ensure universal access to safe, affordable, sustainable and modern energy. SDG7 thus becomes an essential normative framework for analysing energy performance and formulating convergent policies among Member States (Madurai Elavarasan et al., 2022; Zarghami, 2025).

Against the backdrop of these transformations, the literature highlights a dual trend: on the one hand, the emergence of post-carbon paradigms and green innovations (Wennick, 2024; Żywiołek et al., 2025), and on the other hand, the accentuation of disparities between EU countries in terms of their ability to adapt to these paradigms (Calafat-Marzal et al., 2025; Sabato & Mandelli, 2024). Recent studies indicate that coherent energy policies must be contextualized according to the economic structure, infrastructure maturity and institutional dynamics of each Member State (Brodny et al., 2024; Georgescu et al., 2025; Manta et al., 2025; Radtke, 2025). This differentiated approach is supported by comparative literature, which identifies divergent models of energy governance in Central and Eastern Europe compared to Western Europe and the Nordic countries.

One of the major trends in contemporary literature is related to the expansion of renewable energies. Quantitative studies have documented the positive impact of green energy on reducing greenhouse gas emissions, improving air quality and reducing dependence on external energy sources. For example, various studies (European Environment Agency, 2025c; Gajdzik et al., 2024; Paraschiv & Paraschiv, 2023) highlight that the accelerated implementation of solar, wind and hydroelectric energy has contributed significantly to the decarbonization of the production and consumption sectors. Furthermore, the literature indicates that the integration of renewable energies positively influences the energy independence of states, strengthening resilience to external shocks such as geopolitical fluctuations in the fossil fuel market (European Environment Agency, 2025b; Guarascio et al., 2025; Gueye et al., 2025; Proedrou, 2023).

However, the integration of renewable technologies into national energy systems is deeply uneven across countries, as highlighted by cross-country research identifying multiple barriers. These include limited administrative capacity to implement support schemes, deficiencies in network infrastructure, lack of interoperability of storage systems and low levels of energy literacy in certain regions (Dekeyrel & Fessler, 2024; Psara et al., 2022). In addition, comparative studies suggest that Eastern European countries face significant delays in achieving the Fit for 55 targets (European Council, 2023), mainly due to fiscal constraints and dependence on conventional energy sources (Borozan et al., 2021; Romaldi et al., 2024; Safarzadeh & Di Maria, 2025). At the same time, some advanced analyses propose the use of technology diffusion and adoption models to assess the dynamics of renewable integration, highlighting the role of proactive public policies and local community participation in accelerating the transition (Csedő et al., 2025; Radtke, 2025; Tsoutsos & Stamboulis, 2005).

Another important conceptual pillar is energy productivity, often used as a proxy indicator for resource efficiency in the economy. Improving energy efficiency is crucial for decoupling economic growth from environmental degradation, a key principle of the green economy. Recent studies highlight that energy efficiency policies can generate double benefits: reducing emissions intensity and increasing economic competitiveness, in particular by lowering energy costs and stimulating technological innovation (Dogan et al., 2023; European Environment Agency, 2025a; Özkan et al., 2023). Empirical research also shows that investments in energy efficiency have a significant multiplier effect on GDP, being positively correlated with employment growth and SME dynamism (Dirma et al., 2024; Firtescu et al., 2025; OECD/UNDP, 2025).

The differences in energy performance between EU countries can be explained by a combination of structural and institutional factors. These include the degree of digitization of energy infrastructure—through the use of smart sensors, advanced metering systems and consumption management platforms—as well as the level of integration of smart grids (Abdessadak et al., 2025; Campana et al., 2025; Rodriguez-Perez et al., 2024). At the same time, energy efficiency is influenced by the availability of public and private funds for building renovation, industrial equipment modernization and transport logistics optimization, areas in which European funds such as the Recovery and Resilience Facility (RRF) (European Union, 2024) play a central role.

Another key factor is the existence of functional green certificate markets and economic incentive schemes that value the positive externalities of reducing energy consumption. The literature indicates that the effectiveness of these mechanisms depends on regulatory stability, administrative transparency and the level of participation of economic actors (Borowiecki et al., 2023; Farid et al., 2024; Gonzalez-Torres et al., 2023). In addition, some research suggests that the impact of energy efficiency on sustainability is amplified when it is coupled with participatory, integrative and results-oriented energy governance (Basílio, 2025; Dai et al., 2025; Faure et al., 2022).

The literature also shows that energy sustainability must be analysed in relation to the resilience of energy systems. The COVID-19 pandemic has highlighted the importance of energy security, network flexibility and crisis response capacity. Post-2020 studies explore energy resilience as a critical dimension of sustainability, highlighting the need for infrastructure redundancy, advanced storage and distributed energy sources (Bauwens et al., 2024; Rejeb et al., 2024). In this sense, the literature defines resilience not only as resistance to shocks but also as the ability to adapt institutionally and technologically to volatile contexts. For example, the integration of distributed energy resources (DERs), the digitization of networks and the diversification of the energy mix are considered essential for increasing crisis absorption capacity (Almihat & Munda, 2025; López González & Garcia Rendon, 2022; Twaisan & Barışçı, 2022).

At the same time, the connections between energy resilience and just transition are highlighted, in which the social dimension of energy security—accessibility, equity and protection of vulnerable consumers—plays a central role. In this context, SDG7 increasingly intersects with SDG11 (sustainable cities), SDG12 (responsible consumption) and SDG13 (climate action), reflecting the need for multi-scalar and integrative governance (Immler & Sakkers, 2022; Ribeiro et al., 2025). Thus, cities are becoming key actors in strengthening energy resilience through sustainable urban infrastructure, smart energy management systems and decentralized community initiatives (Mishra & Singh, 2023; Mo & Liu, 2025; Umeike et al., 2025; Wei et al., 2024). This paradigm shift requires a transition from traditional energy security, focused on volume and stability, to energy resilience oriented towards flexibility, sustainability and adaptability.

On the fiscal side, the literature highlights that energy taxation policies, particularly those based on environmental principles, can act as a catalyst for behavioural change and investment in clean sources. The implementation of carbon taxes has contributed to significant reductions in emissions without negatively affecting macroeconomic performance (Dechezleprêtre et al., 2023; European Central Bank, 2025; Mengesha & Roy, 2025; Olasehinde-Williams, 2024; Pan et al., 2024). Econometric studies suggest that energy taxes can stimulate innovation in clean technologies and encourage energy efficiency in industry and transport (Aydin et al., 2025; García-Quevedo & Jové-Llopis, 2021; Rasoulinezhad, 2025).

However, other research draws attention to the possible regressive effects of green taxation on vulnerable groups or energy-intensive sectors such as agriculture. In this regard, analyses (Cevik et al., 2023; Köppl & Schratzenstaller, 2023; Smeets Křístková et al., 2025) indicate that the distributional impact of carbon taxes should be mitigated through targeted compensation mechanisms, green subsidies or investments in sustainable public infrastructure. At the same time, the literature shows that the uniform application of such taxes can lead to regional imbalances, especially in regions dependent on energy-intensive industries or with incomes below the national average (Brzezinski & Kaczan, 2025; Timilsina, 2022; Zhao & Lin, 2025).

To reduce social and economic risks, flexible approaches are recommended, such as the gradual introduction of taxes, their adaptation to sectoral specificities and the implementation of a complementary policy framework that includes investments in vocational training, technological innovation and social protection. Thus, energy taxation becomes not only a tool for internalizing external costs but also a lever for reconfiguring the economic structure in a sustainable and inclusive direction.

Sectoral energy consumption is a frequently analysed topic in recent empirical literature and is recognized as a critical dimension of energy sustainability, as it reflects the efficiency with which resources are used in major economic activities. In particular, the industrial sector is considered both an engine of economic growth and a significant source of emissions. Recent research shows that heavy industries, such as steel, cement, and chemical production, contribute disproportionately to energy intensity and total emissions, requiring specific decarbonization measures, such as process electrification and the use of green hydrogen (Küfeoğlu, 2024; van der Spek et al., 2022; Zhou et al., 2024).

At the same time, the agricultural sector is often identified as being slower to adopt clean technologies due to financial constraints, lack of infrastructure and fragmented policies. The intensive use of fossil fuel engines, inefficient irrigation and rudimentary heating systems in small farms generates disproportionate consumption relative to the sector's added value (Chalkias & Stathatos, 2024; Eurostat, 2024c; Rindermann et al., 2023). The energy transition in agriculture is often delayed by a lack of access to green finance, unstable agricultural policies and weak institutional capacity in rural areas (Geng et al., 2024; Touch et al., 2024).

This creates a complex equation between energy efficiency, sectoral productivity and long-term sustainability, which requires differentiated approaches depending on the profile of each sector. The literature highlights the importance of integrated analyses that combine energy intensity indicators, technological performance and socio-economic factors for a nuanced assessment of the energy transition (Karpavicius et al., 2025; Lamprousis & Golfinopoulos, 2025; Soto et al., 2025). In this regard, public policies must support the convergence of decarbonization and economic competitiveness objectives through targeted incentives, public-private partnerships and investments in infrastructure tailored to the needs of each sector.

Contemporary literature also explores the relationship between industrial emissions intensity and regulatory instruments in an increasingly sophisticated manner, integrating economic, technological and institutional perspectives. Emissions intensity per unit of GDP is a critical indicator for assessing progress towards decarbonising the economy, as it is influenced not only by the level of industrial production but also by the type of technologies used and the public policies adopted. Studies show the transition to low-carbon energy sources, such as renewable energy, electrification and green hydrogen (Luderer et al., 2022; Mingolla et al., 2024; Zhang et al., 2024).

This intensity is influenced by the energy mix, sectoral structure and implementation of cap-and-trade systems (ETS). The EU ETS has been extensively analysed in the literature for its ability to reduce industrial emissions through price signals and incentives for technological innovation (Eslahi et al., 2025; European Commission, 2023; Karmaker et al., 2025). Recent research suggests that the effectiveness of the ETS increases when combined with other environmental policies, such as technology standards or subsidies for industrial modernization (Amendola, 2025; Böning et al., 2023).

At the same time, the performance of regulatory systems is influenced by the volatility of certificate prices, carbon leakage risks and the ability of firms to adapt to new market conditions. Thus, the literature calls for gradual reforms of ETS systems, such as expanding their scope, integrating them with other regional markets and using the revenues generated to finance the green transition (Borowiecki et al., 2023; Haywood & Jakob, 2023; Marchewka-Bartkowiak, 2023). The analysis of emission intensity and associated regulatory instruments provides an integrative perspective on industrial sustainability, in which energy efficiency, decarbonization and economic competitiveness must be balanced through flexible, transparent and long-term policies.

Energy import dependency is another key area in energy sustainability analysis, with direct implications for energy sovereignty and the resilience of national systems to geopolitical shocks. The literature highlights that excessive exposure to the volatility of international fossil fuel markets can make national economies vulnerable, affecting price stability, industrial competitiveness and security of supply (Basdekis et al., 2024; Cardinale et al., 2024; Li et al., 2023; S. Yang & Fu, 2025).

Reducing this dependence through energy diversification, smart storage, the development of interconnection infrastructure and the exploitation of domestic renewable resources is an essential strategy for achieving SDG7 (affordable and clean energy) and SDG13 (climate action). Recent studies emphasize the importance of investing in battery storage, hydrogen or regional interconnections, which can mitigate seasonal imbalances and external shocks (Blanchard, 2024; Hoffart et al., 2024; Wang et al., 2025).

More recently, in the context of the energy crisis triggered by the war in Ukraine, literature highlights the increased focus on energy autonomy, diversification of natural gas suppliers, reduction of dependence on Russia and acceleration of the transition to green infrastructure. Initiatives such as REPowerEU have been analysed as systemic responses aimed at reducing fossil fuel imports by stimulating investment in renewable energy, energy efficiency and hydrogen (European Commission, 2022a; European Investment Bank, 2025; Igliński et al., 2024; Vezzoni, 2023). Research also highlights that energy autonomy must be understood within a common European framework based on solidarity, integrated planning and cross-border coordination, in which more vulnerable countries receive adequate technical and financial support (Costa & Campanini, 2024; Domac et al., 2025; European Environment Agency, 2025a; Paleari, 2024).

Thus, reducing energy dependence becomes not only a national security objective but also a fundamental pillar of ecological transition and socio-economic resilience in the European Union.

The development of econometric modelling methods applied to energy sustainability has evolved significantly in recent years, in parallel with the diversification of data sources and analytical paradigms. In addition to classic multiple linear regression and panel models (with fixed and random effects), researchers have begun to integrate advanced techniques from the field of machine learning and artificial intelligence. These include algorithms such as Random Forest, Support Vector Machines, Gradient Boosting Machines (GBM), XGBoost and artificial neural networks (ANN), applied to identify non-linear relationships and complex interactions between energy, economic and environmental variables.

At the same time, modern variable selection methods, such as Best Subset Selection (BFS), Least Absolute Shrinkage and Selection Operator (LASSO), Elastic Net or Principal Component Analysis (PCA), are used to build robust predictive models capable of avoiding multicollinearity and overfitting. In this context, the BFS method is valued for its ability to eliminate irrelevant variables and build compact, yet statistically and semantically meaningful models with high theoretical significance.

Recent literature increasingly supports the combination of classical approaches with machine learning-based approaches in a hybrid framework to improve prediction accuracy and the generalizability of results. Applied studies on energy consumption forecasting or the assessment of the impact of energy efficiency policies use ensemble models that integrate OLS regression with methods such as bagging or boosting to capture systemic variability (Dostmohammadi et al., 2024; Rondón-Cordero et al., 2025; V. Santos et al., 2025). Techniques for interpreting complex models, such as SHAP (SHapley Additive exPlanations), allow for a deeper understanding of the contribution of each variable, facilitating evidence-based decisions in energy policies (Machlev et al., 2022; M. R. Santos et al., 2024; C. Yang et al., 2024).

Overall, this methodological evolution reflects a broader trend in applied sciences—the shift from deterministic models to probabilistic, data-driven approaches that allow for a better understanding of uncertainty and the dynamics of energy sustainability in the context of SDG7.

Another emerging body of literature addresses the intersection between energy sustainability and digitalization, particularly through the concept of "smart energy systems". The integration of distributed energy sources, the digitalization of networks and the use of blockchain or AI technologies enable consumption optimization, loss reduction and increased system flexibility. At the same time, energy digital twins, green certificate traceability and demand prediction algorithms are innovations described in the literature as transformative for the future of sustainable energy.

In conclusion, the academic literature provides a dense and diverse framework for interpreting energy sustainability in the European Union, but methodological and application gaps remain. This chapter responds to these challenges by developing nine functional models based on SDG7 and applying a rigorous linear regression methodology with BFS selection, providing a valuable tool for the formulation of sustainable public policies adapted to the current European context.

An analysis of the literature on energy sustainability in the European Union reveals an increasingly complex and interconnected conceptual framework, in which SDG7 acts as a cross-cutting axis between the objectives of environmental protection, social inclusion and economic development. Against the backdrop of the accelerated energy transition, contemporary literature explores the multidimensionality of this objective, combining perspectives from economics, engineering, public policy and social sciences. At the same time, there is a shift from fragmented sectoral approaches to systemic analyses that integrate structural variables such as digitalization, governance, resilience and energy equity.

A growing number of studies emphasize the importance of contextualizing energy strategies according to national and regional specificities. This territorial diversity in performance and administrative capacities requires differentiated policies, alongside the strengthening of convergence towards common European objectives. The literature draws attention to the risk of widening gaps between Member States in the absence of adequate correction and support mechanisms for countries with high structural vulnerabilities.

From a methodological point of view, there is a shift from descriptive models to predictive and prescriptive techniques using artificial intelligence, variable selection algorithms and spatiotemporal models. These methods allow for a deeper understanding of the complex relationships between SDG7 indicators and other relevant dimensions of sustainability.

However, the literature remains limited in terms of integrated assessment of energy policy effectiveness, longitudinal analysis of the impact of structural reforms and investigation of indirect effects on social inequalities, energy migration or labour market transformations. In addition, the relationship between sustainability and energy security in the context of recent geopolitical conflicts requires more rigorous exploration.

In this context, the present research proposes an original methodological contribution by developing and testing nine functional models based on SDG7 and applying BFS selection to optimize the explanatory structure. These results can inform differentiated but coherent policies at the EU level to achieve a fair, sustainable and resilient energy transition.

## Methodology

In the current global context, characterized by a growing concern about climate change and the impact of activities on the environment, energy sustainability has become an important area for research and action. Recognized for its commitment to environmental protection and sustainable development, the European Union has stepped up its efforts to implement energy strategies that respond to these challenges. In this context, Sustainable Development Goal 7 (SDG7), which aims to ensure access to affordable, secure, sustainable and modern energy for all, provides a valuable framework for assessing and guiding progress in this area.

The specific SDG7 indicators relate to increasing the share of renewable energy in the energy mix, improving energy efficiency, ensuring universal energy access and promoting the clean use of fuels and technologies, representing variables in the modelling of energy sustainability. These indicators not only measure current performance but, by analysing future trends and projections, help to identify the opportunities and challenges facing the European Union in the transition towards a green economy. This study therefore aims to explore how modelling European energy sustainability, based on Sustainable Development Goal 7 indicators, contributes to the development of effective solutions to achieve the Sustainable Development Goals.

The BFS (Backward Feature Selection) method was applied to determine the European energy sustainability model.

To determine the model, we used the indicators presented in Table 4.1. Data were collected from Eurostat and OECD and then modelled using the statistical program Python.

Previously the set of indicators presented above was subjected to the log normalization procedure using Logit linear regression analysis. In this way the normalization of the data was obtained by transforming them to a Gaussian normal distribution, reducing the effects of heteroscedasticity and reducing the influences of extreme values (increasing the robustness of the model).

Linear regression using the dependent variable Y or its logarithm is modelled as a linear function of one or more independent variables. The equation can be formulated as follows:

**Table 4.1** Presentation of indicators

| *Symbol* | *Indicator name* | *Unit of measurement* | *Source* |
|---|---|---|---|
| SDG7FZEP | Total primary energy supply | Tonnes of oil equivalent, million | OECD (OECD, 2025) |
| SDG7APER | Renewable energy production | % total energy supply | OECD (OECD, 2025) |
| SDG7CENAG | Energy consumption in agriculture | % of total energy consumption | OECD (OECD, 2025) |
| SDG7CENI | Energy consumption in industry | % of total energy consumption | OECD (OECD, 2025) |
| SDG7VFEN | Energy-related tax revenues | % of total environmental tax revenues | OECD (OECD, 2025) |
| SDG7PREN | Energy productivity | Euro per kilogramme of oil | Eurostat (Eurostat, 2024b) |
| SDG7IMPEN | Dependence on energy imports | % | Eurostat (Eurostat, 2024) |
| SDG7ENGS | Net greenhouse gas emissions | Index, 1990 = 100 | Eurostat (Eurostat, 2025) |
| SDG7INEMT | Industrial air emissions intensity | Grammes per euro | OECD (OECD, 2025) |

Source: Author

$$\ln(Y) = \beta_1 \ln(X_1) + \beta_2 \ln(X_2) + \ldots + \beta_n \ln(X_n) + \varepsilon \qquad (4.1)$$

where,

$\ln(Y)$—natural logarithm of the dependent variable, representing an indicator of Sustainable Development Goal 7;
$\beta_1, \beta_2, \beta_n$—are the coefficients reflecting the sensitivity of the logarithm of variable $Y$ to a percentage change in each indicator $X_i$;
$\ln(X_1), \ln(X_2), \ln(X_n)$—are the natural logarithms of the selected indicators
$\varepsilon$—is the constant.

The application of the BFS method involves the gradual elimination of variables Xi that contribute least to the model, using criteria such as p-value, adjusted coefficient of determination (adjusted $R^2$) or variance inflation factor (VIF). This process continues until every variable remaining in the model is significant, and the elimination of any additional variable would lead to a significant deterioration in model performance. The BFS method was applied until a valid solution was obtained, i.e. until the variance inflation factors of the indicators fell within the 10-point significance threshold, excluding multicollinearity. This ensured the performance of the models by monitoring the correlation coefficient and the mean squared error. This improved the prediction and increased the stability of the nine proposed models.

## Results and Discussions

The SDG7.1 model of European energy sustainability from the perspective of the SDG7APER indicator has renewable energy production as the selected dependent variable. The independent variables are SDG7FZEP representing total primary energy supply, SDG7CENAG representing energy consumption in agriculture, SDG7CENI representing energy consumption in industry, SDG7VFEN representing energy-related tax revenues, SDG7PREN representing energy productivity, SDG7IMPEN representing energy import dependence, SDG7ENGS representing net greenhouse gas emissions. A linear regression model is constructed with the independent variables defined above for which regression coefficients have been calculated according to Eq. (4.2).

$$\begin{aligned}SDG7APER = &-0.16 * SDG7FZEP + 0.49 * SDG7CENAG \\ &+1.20 * SDG7CENI + 1.17 * SDG7VFEN \\ &+0.72 * SDG7PREN - 0.18 * SDG7IMPEN \\ &-0.46 * SDG7ENGS - 2.35\end{aligned} \tag{4.2}$$

According to the regression equation for the SDG7.1 model, the influence of the independent variables on the dependent variable is observed in the case of the variable SDG7FZEP representing the total primary energy supply. There is an inverse influence on the dependent variable, i.e. a 1% increase in total primary energy supply leads to a 0.16% decrease in renewable energy production, suggesting that high dependence on traditional primary energy sources may inhibit the development or integration of renewable energy sources. In the case of the variable SDG7CENAG representing energy consumption in agriculture, there is a positive influence on the dependent variable, i.e. a 1% increase in energy consumption in agriculture leads to a 0.49% increase in renewable energy production, indicating a trend towards the adoption of renewable technologies in this sector in response to the need for sustainability and energy efficiency. In the case of the variable SDG7CENI representing energy consumption in industry, there is a positive influence on the dependent variable, i.e. a 1% increase in energy consumption in industry leads to a 1.2% increase in renewable energy production, suggesting that the industrial sector could be an important driver for the adoption of renewable energy, due to initiatives to reduce emissions and improve energy efficiency. In the case of the variable SDG7VFEN representing energy-related tax revenues, there is a positive influence on the dependent variable, i.e. a 1% increase in energy-related tax revenues leads to a 1.17% increase in renewable energy production, indicating that tax policies and government revenues in the energy sector can support the development of renewable energy. In the case of the variable SDG7PREN representing energy productivity, there is a positive influence on the dependent variable, i.e. a 1% increase in energy productivity leads to a 0.72% increase in renewable energy production, emphasizing the importance of energy efficiency as a factor supporting the use of renewable energy sources. With respect to SDG7IMPEN representing energy import dependence, there is an inverse influence on the dependent variable, i.e. a 1% increase in energy import dependence leads to a 0.18% decrease in renewable energy production, suggesting that countries more dependent on energy imports may be less inclined to develop domestic renewable sources. In the case of the SDG7ENGS variable representing net greenhouse gas emissions, there is an inverse influence on the dependent variable, i.e. a 1% increase in net greenhouse gas emissions leads to a 0.46% decrease in renewable energy production, indicating that increasing greenhouse gas emissions may be associated with a higher dependence on fossil fuels and a lower use of renewable energy sources. These results provide insights for the formulation of energy and environmental policies, highlighting the need to promote energy efficiency, innovation in the energy sector and the uptake of renewable energy sources to reduce fossil fuel dependency and environmental impacts.

Figure 4.1 shows the ranking of the importance of the predictors related to the influence on the dependent variable SDG7APER.

Figure 4.1 shows that the SDG7.1 model is mainly characterized by the direct influence of the change in industrial energy consumption, followed by the direct influence of energy-related tax revenues. An inverse influence is net greenhouse gas emissions. The use of renewable energy in industry would significantly reduce the impact of carbon emissions. Energy-related tax revenues show the link between the energy sector and taxation, with higher tax revenues reflecting higher energy prices or an efficient tax policy influencing infrastructure development as well as investment in renewable energy.

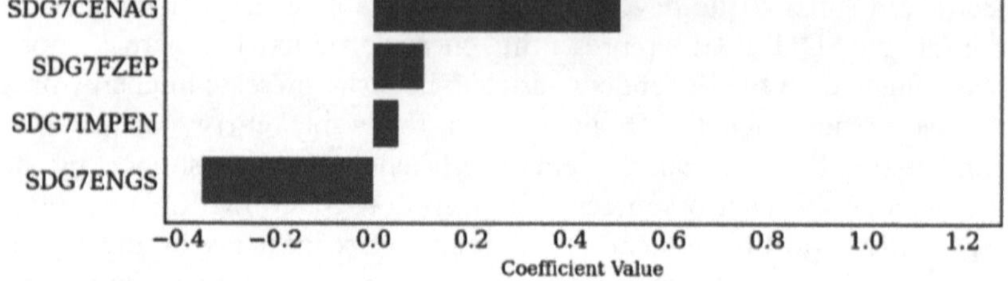


**Fig. 4.1** Importance of predictors related to the influence on the variable SDG7APER. Source: Developed by the author using Python

The SDG7.2 model of European energy sustainability from the perspective of the SDG7CENAG indicator has the selected dependent variable agricultural energy consumption. The independent variables are SDG7FZEP representing total primary energy supply, SDG7APER representing renewable energy supply, SDG7CENI representing energy consumption in industry, SDG7VFEN representing energy-related tax revenues, SDG7PREN representing energy productivity, SDG7IMPEN representing energy import dependence, SDG7ENGS representing net greenhouse gas emissions, SDG7INEMT representing air emissions intensity of industry. A linear regression model is constructed with the independent variables defined above for which the regression coefficients have been calculated according to Eq. (4.3).

$$\begin{aligned} \mathrm{SDG7CENAG} &= 0.16 * \mathrm{SDG7FZEP} + 0.25 * \mathrm{SDG7APER} \\ &-0.78 * \mathrm{SDG7CENI} - 1.77 * \mathrm{SDG7VFEN} \\ &-0.14 * \mathrm{SDG7PREN} - 0.24 * \mathrm{SDG7IMPEN} \\ &+0.17 * \mathrm{SDG7ENGS} + 0.25 * \mathrm{SDG7INEMT} + 5.41 \end{aligned} \tag{4.3}$$

For Model SDG7.2 it can be observed that the influence of the independent variables on the dependent variable is in the case of the variable SDG7FZEP representing total primary energy supply, a positive effect on the dependent variable is observed respectively a 1% increase in total primary energy supply leads to a 0.16% increase in energy consumption in agriculture, indicating that an increase in primary energy availability stimulates energy consumption in the agricultural sector, due to increased activity and technological expansion. As for the variable SDG7APER representing renewable energy production, a positive influence on the dependent variable is found, i.e. a 1% increase in renewable energy production leads to a 0.25% increase in energy consumption in agriculture. The positive relationship suggests that an increase in renewable energy use is associated with an increase in energy consumption in agriculture, indicating the adoption of renewable technologies in this sector. In the case of the variable SDG7CENI representing energy consumption in industry, there is an inverse influence on the dependent variable, i.e. a 1% increase in energy consumption in industry leads to a 0.78% decrease in energy consumption in agriculture. The presence of an inverse relationship between industrial and agricultural energy consumption indicates a competition for energy resources or a reallocation of energy resources from agriculture to industry in the context of limited supply. According to the variable SDG7VFEN representing energy-related tax revenues, there is an inverse influence on the dependent variable, i.e. a 1% increase in energy-related tax revenues leads to a 1.77% decrease in agricultural energy consumption. The inverse relationship reveals that an increase in energy-related tax revenue may decrease energy consumption in agriculture due to the increase in energy costs for farmers. As for the variable SDG7PREN representing energy productivity, an inverse influence on the dependent variable is found, i.e. a 1% increase in energy productivity leads to a 0.14% decrease in energy consumption in agriculture. This influence indicates that higher energy efficiency at the national level may be associated with lower energy consumption in agriculture, suggesting a possible optimization of energy use in this sector. In the case of the variable SDG7IMPEN representing energy import dependence, there is an inverse influence on the dependent variable, i.e. a 1% increase in energy import dependence leads to a 0.24% decrease in energy consumption in agriculture. This reflects the fact that countries that are more dependent on energy imports tend to implement energy efficiency measures in key sectors, including agriculture, to reduce vulnerability to international market fluctuations. According to the variable SDG7ENGS representing net greenhouse gas emissions, there is a positive influence on the dependent variable, i.e. a 1% increase in net greenhouse gas emissions leads to a 0.17% increase in energy consumption in agriculture, suggesting that an increase in greenhouse gas emissions is associated with higher energy consumption in agriculture due to the intensive use of chemical fertilizers and mechanization, which increase fossil fuel consumption. As for the variable SDG7INEMT representing the intensity of atmospheric emissions from industry, a positive influence on the dependent variable is found, i.e. a 1% increase in the intensity of atmospheric emissions from industry leads to a 0.25% increase in energy consumption in agriculture. This correlation indicates that an increase in emissions intensity in industry is associated with higher energy consumption in agriculture, suggesting that less efficient or more polluting industrial practices may also be reflected in agricultural practices. These results emphasize the interdependence between various energy and environmental factors and the agricultural sector, highlighting the need to address energy consumption in agriculture as part of an integrated energy and environmental policy strategy that promotes sustainability and energy efficiency.

Figure 4.2 shows the ranking of the importance of the predictors related to the influence on the dependent variable SDG7CENAG.

Figure 4.2 shows that the SDG7.2 model is mainly characterized by the inverse influence of the change in energy-related tax revenues, i.e. an increase in energy tax revenues is associated with a decrease in the dependent variable suggesting that an increase in energy taxes and tax revenues discourages certain activities in the energy sector. A negative impact of energy-related tax revenues shows that high taxes decrease energy consumption, which is beneficial for the environment but has a negative impact on economic growth. Similarly, a negative impact of energy consumption in industry points to energy use efficiency as the key to achieving the goals of reducing carbon emissions and improving sustainability.

The variable that represents a vulnerability of European sustainable energy development in terms of energy consumption in agriculture is energy productivity.

Figure 4.3 is based on the ranking of SDG7.2 vulnerability indicators determined for the reference year 2021. The states with the weakest distribution of the dependent variable are Slovakia, Slovenia and Lithuania; these states record low values of energy productivity being in the back half of the ranking, respectively, Slovenia (15th place), Slovakia (22nd place) and Lithuania (20th place).

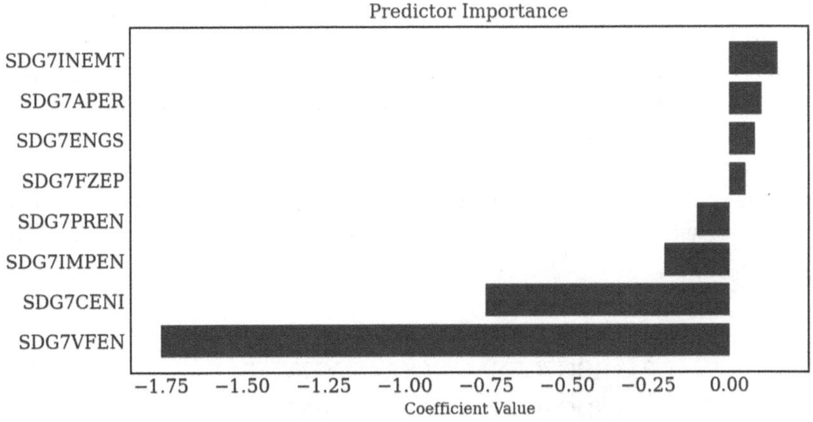


**Fig. 4.2** Importance of predictors related to influence on the variable SDG7CENAG. Source: Developed by the author using Python

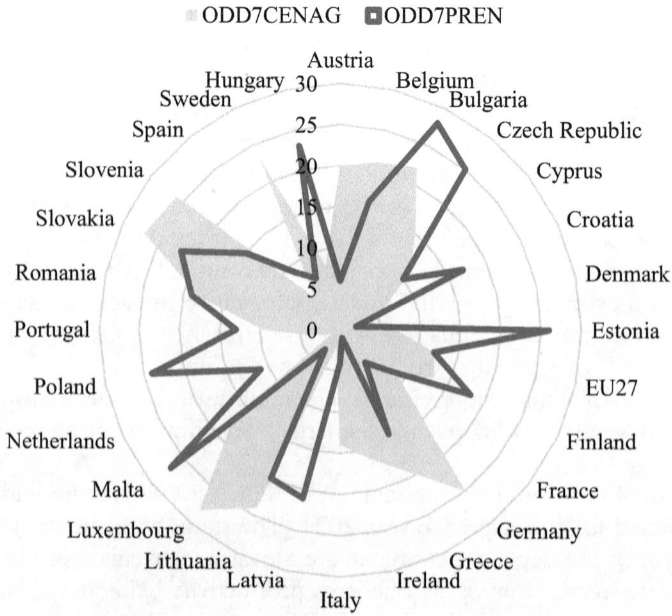


**Fig. 4.3** Vulnerability diagram of the variable SDG7CENAG. Source: Author

The SDG7.3 model of European energy sustainability from the perspective of the SDG7CENI indicator has the selected dependent variable industrial energy consumption. The independent variables are SDG7FZEP—total primary energy supply, SDG7APER—renewable energy supply, SDG7CENAG—energy consumption in agriculture, SDG7VFEN—energy-related tax revenues, SDG7PREN—energy productivity, SDG7INEMT—air emissions intensity of industry. A linear regression model is constructed with the independent variables defined above for which regression coefficients have been calculated according to Eq. (4.4):

$$\begin{aligned} SDG7CENI &= 0.11 * SDG7FZEP + 0.20 * SDG7APER \\ &-0.24 * SDG7CENAG - 0.66 * SDG7VFEN \\ &-0.14 * SDG7PREN + 0.09 * SDG7INEMT + 2.87 \end{aligned} \tag{4.4}$$

According to the regression equation for Model SDG7.3 it is observed that the influence of the independent variables on the dependent variable is in the case of the variable SDG7FZEP representing the total primary energy supply, which demonstrates a statistically positive effect on the dependent variable, i.e. a 1% increase in the total primary energy supply leads to a 0.11% increase in energy consumption in industry. This suggests that the higher availability of primary energy stimulates industrial activity and hence energy consumption in this sector. As for the variable SDG7APER representing renewable energy supply, there is a positive influence on the dependent variable, i.e. a 1% increase in renewable energy production leads to a 0.2% increase in industrial energy consumption, due to the increasing integration of renewable sources in the industrial energy mix. In the case of the variable SDG7CENAG representing energy consumption in agriculture, there is an inverse influence on the dependent variable, i.e. a 1% increase in energy consumption in agriculture leads to a 0.24% decrease in energy consumption in industry, suggesting a reallocation of energy resources between sectors or differences in energy policy priorities between agriculture and industry. According to the variable SDG7VFEN representing energy-related tax revenues, there is an inverse influence on the dependent variable, i.e. a 1% increase in energy-related tax revenues leads to a 0.66% decrease in energy consumption in industry reflecting the impact of higher energy taxation policies and energy costs on industrial energy consumption. In the case of the variable SDG7PREN representing energy productivity, there is an inverse influence on the dependent variable, i.e. a 1% increase in energy productivity leads to a 0.14% decrease in industrial energy consumption, suggesting that higher energy efficiency can reduce energy requirements in industrial processes. In the case of the SDG7INEMT variable representing the intensity of air emissions in industry, a positive influence on the dependent variable is found, i.e. a 1% increase in the intensity of air emissions in industry leads to a 0.09% increase in energy consumption in industry, indicating that industrial activities with higher emissions may be more energy intensive. These results emphasize the interlinkages between the availability and type of energy sources, energy efficiency, fiscal policies and energy consumption in the industrial sector. They highlight the importance of adopting balanced energy and environmental strategies that promote both growth and sustainability in industry.

Figure 4.4 shows the ranking of the importance of the predictors related to the influence on the dependent variable SDG7CENI.

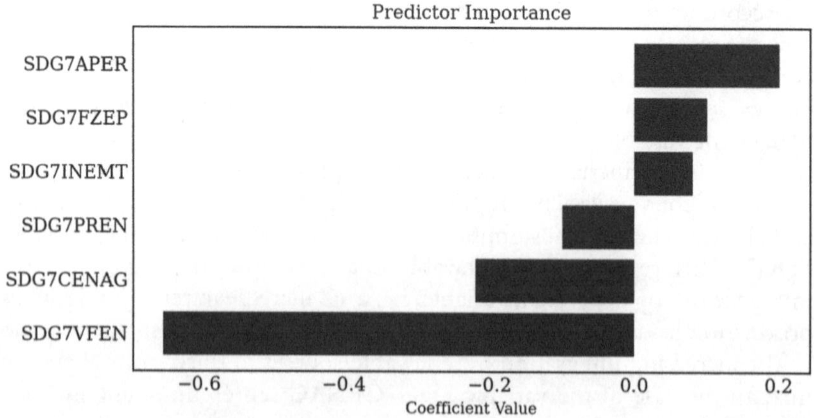


**Fig. 4.4** Importance of predictors related to influence on the variable SDG7CENI. Source: Developed by the author using Python

Figure 4.4 shows that the SDG7.3 model is mainly characterized by the inverse influence of the change in energy-related tax revenues, i.e. an increase in energy tax revenues is associated with a decrease in the dependent variable suggesting that an increase in energy taxes and tax revenues discourages certain activities in the energy sector. A significant positive impact of renewable energy production leads to increased use of renewable energy which is important for reducing environmental pollution. At the same time, a smaller negative impact of energy-related tax revenues suggests that these revenues are not as critical for achieving sustainability goals in this specific model.

The variable that represents a vulnerability of European energy sustainability in terms of energy consumption in industry is energy productivity.

Figure 4.5 was realized based on the ranking of SDG7.3 vulnerability indicators determined for the reference year 2021. The states with the weakest distribution of the dependent variable are Estonia, Lithuania and Croatia; these states record low values of energy productivity being in the back half of the ranking, respectively, Estonia (rank 26), Lithuania (rank 20) and Croatia (rank 17).

Energy sustainability models pivoted on energy consumption at industrial and agricultural branch level have demonstrated that the main vulnerability is energy productivity which affects Member States' energy security by directly influencing the national energy balance. In general, developed

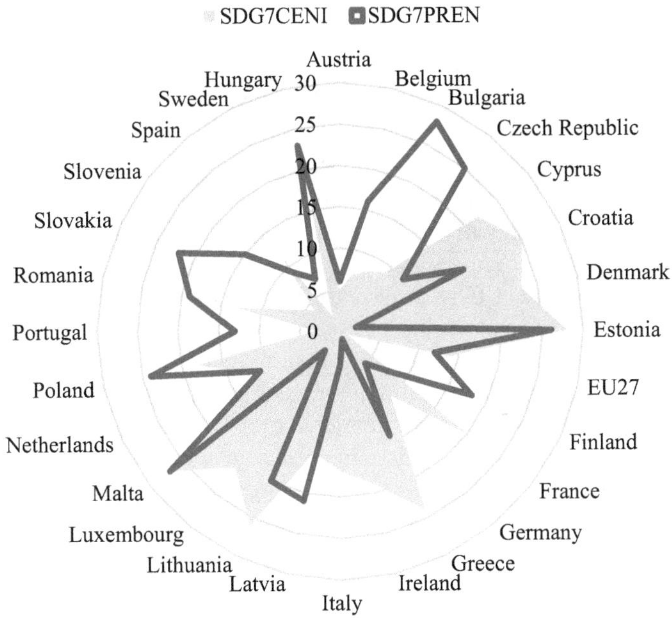


**Fig. 4.5** Diagram of vulnerabilities of the variable SDG7CENI. Source: Author

European countries have built energy policies based on the use of renewable and other unconventional sources of electricity. In contrast, emerging countries have remained dependent on energy productivity to maintain their national energy balance.

The SDG7.4 model of European energy sustainability from the perspective of the SDG7ENGS indicator has the selected dependent variable net greenhouse gas emissions. The independent variables are: SDG7APER—renewable energy supply, SDG7CENAG—energy consumption in agriculture, SDG7VFEN—energy-related tax revenues, SDG7PREN—energy productivity, SDG7IMPEN—energy import dependence, SDG7INEMT—air emission intensity of industry. A linear regression model is constructed with the independent variables defined above for which regression coefficients have been calculated according to Eq. (4.5).

$$SDG7ENGS = -0.18 * SDG7APER + 0.10 * SDG7CENAG$$
$$-0.73 * SDG7VFEN + 0.34 * SDG7PREN \quad (4.5)$$
$$+0.19 * SDG7IMPEN + 0.13 * SDG7INEMT + 3.39$$

For Model SDG7.4 it is observed that the influence of the independent variables on the dependent variable is in the case of the variable SDG7APER representing the supply of renewable energy, the results indicate a negative effect on the dependent variable, i.e. a 1% increase in renewable energy production leads to a 0.18% decrease in net greenhouse gas emissions. There is an inverse relationship between renewable energy supply and net greenhouse gas emissions, indicating that an increase in renewable energy use is associated with a reduction in emissions, reflecting the positive environmental impact of renewable energy. As for the variable SDG7CENAG representing energy consumption in agriculture, there is a positive influence on the dependent variable, i.e. a 1% increase in energy consumption in agriculture leads to a 0.1% increase in net greenhouse gas emissions, due to the use of fossil fuels and less efficient energy technologies in this sector. According to the variable SDG7VFEN representing energy-related tax revenues, there is an inverse influence on the dependent variable, i.e. a 1% increase in energy-related tax revenues leads to a 0.73% decrease in net greenhouse gas emissions. The inverse relationship indicates that an increase in energy-related tax revenues is associated with a decrease in GHG emissions, suggesting that tax policies can encourage energy efficiency and reduce dependence on fossil fuels. In the case of the variable SDG7PREN representing energy productivity, there is a positive influence on the dependent variable, i.e. a 1% increase in energy productivity leads to a 0.34% increase in net greenhouse gas emissions. This could reflect the fact that in some cases, increasing energy efficiency leads to an increase in economic activities, which in turn may increase net GHG emissions. In the case of the variable SDG7IMPEN representing energy import dependence, a positive influence on the dependent variable is found, i.e. a 1% increase in energy import dependence leads to a 0.19% increase in net greenhouse gas emissions. The direct relationship indicates that a higher energy import dependence is associated with an increase in GHG emissions, since the imported energy comes from less sustainable sources or due to emissions associated with energy transportation. These results underline the importance of adopting integrated energy and environment policy strategies that promote the use of renewable energy, energy efficiency and reduce energy import dependency in order to minimize the environmental impact of human activities and combat climate change.

Figure 4.6 shows the ranking of the importance of the predictors related to the influence on the dependent variable SDG7ENGS.

Figure 4.6 shows that the SDG7.4 model is characterized by the direct influence of energy productivity, which shows that more efficient energy use has a significant impact in reducing net greenhouse gas emissions. A significant inverse influence on the dependent variable is exerted by energy-related tax revenues. The variable that represents a vulnerability of European energy sustainability in terms of net GHG emissions is renewable energy supply.

The SDG7.5 model of European energy sustainability from the perspective of the SDG7FZEP indicator is the selected dependent variable that signifies the total primary energy supply. The independent variables are SDG7APER—renewable energy supply, SDG7CENAG—energy consumption in agriculture, SDG7CENI—energy consumption in industry, SDG7VFEN—energy-related tax revenues, SDG7PREN—energy productivity, SDG7INEMT—air emission intensity of industry. A linear regression model is constructed with the independent variables defined above for which regression coefficients were calculated according to Eq. (4.6):

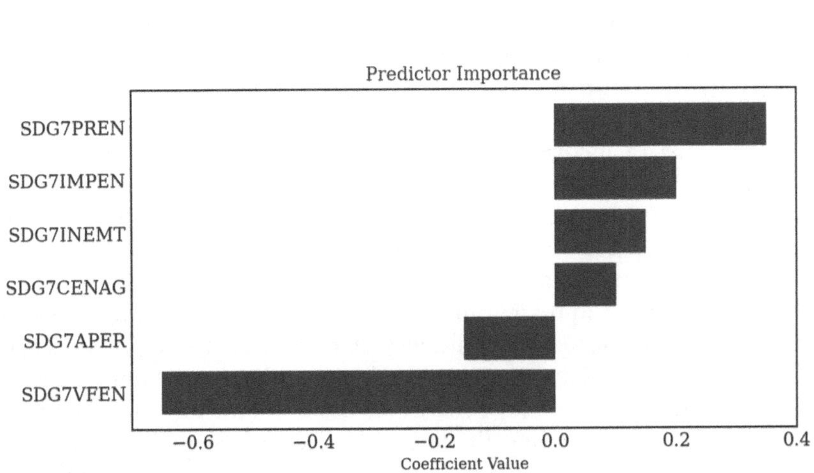


**Fig. 4.6** Importance of predictors related to influence on the variable SDG7ENGS. Source: Developed by the author using Python

$$\begin{aligned} SDG7FZEP &= -0.72 * SDG7APER + 1.51 * SDG7CENAG \\ &+3.33 * SDG7CENI + 5.42 * SDG7VFEN \\ &+1.07 * SDG7PREN - 0.67 * SDG7INEMT - 16.76 \end{aligned} \tag{4.6}$$

According to the regression equation for the SDG7.5 model, the influence of the independent variables on the dependent variable is observed. In the case of the variable SDG7APER representing the supply of renewable energy, there is an inverse influence on the dependent variable, i.e. a 1% increase in the production of renewable energy leads to a 0.72% decrease in the total supply of primary energy. This influence suggests that the integration of renewables reduces dependence on fossil fuels and other traditional primary energy sources. In the case of the variable SDG7CENAG representing energy consumption in agriculture, there is a positive influence on the dependent variable, i.e. a 1% increase in energy consumption in agriculture leads to a 1.51% increase in total primary energy supply, reflecting the increased energy needs of the agricultural sector for mechanization and production. In the case of the variable SDG7CENI representing energy consumption in industry, there is a positive influence on the dependent variable, i.e. a 1% increase in energy consumption in industry leads to a 3.33% increase in total primary energy supply. This suggests that the industrial sector is a major consumer of primary energy, and the increase in consumption in this sector leads to a significant increase in primary energy supply, emphasizing the role of industry in the global energy dynamics. In the case of the variable SDG7VFEN representing energy-related tax revenues, there is a positive influence on the dependent variable, i.e. a 1% increase in energy-related tax revenues leads to a 5.42% increase in total primary energy supply, reflecting investments and policies that promote the exploitation of energy sources. In the case of the variable SDG7PREN representing energy productivity, there is a positive influence on the dependent variable, i.e. a 1% increase in energy productivity leads to a 1.07% increase in total primary energy supply. The direct relationship indicates that higher energy efficiency at the national level is associated with increased primary energy supply, due to technological improvement and optimization of the use of energy resources. In the case of the variable SDG7INEMT representing the intensity of air emissions from industry, there is an inverse influence on the dependent variable, i.e. a 1% increase in the intensity of air emissions from industry leads to a 0.67% decrease in total primary energy supply. The inverse relationship suggests that an increase in industrial emissions intensity is associated with a decrease in total primary energy supply. This indicates a transition to cleaner energy sources or an effort to reduce energy consumption in industry in response to environmental pressures.

These results highlight the complex interdependence between the different aspects of the energy system and their impact on primary energy supply, underlining the need to adopt balanced energy policies that promote sustainability, efficiency and reduce environmental impacts while meeting the energy needs of the agricultural and industrial sectors.

Figure 4.7 shows the ranking of the importance of the predictors related to the influence on the dependent variable SDG7FZEP.

According to Fig. 4.7 energy-related tax revenue has the largest positive coefficient, suggesting that energy-related tax revenue is a strong factor affecting the dependent variable of the model. Renewable energy supply has a small and negative coefficient, indicating that an increase in renewable energy output is associated with a decrease in the dependent variable, highlighting that renewable energy has an inverse effect on the model variable of interest due to the associated costs.

The SDG7.6 model of European energy sustainability from the perspective of the SDG7IMPEN indicator is the selected dependent variable that signifies the dependence on energy imports. The independent variables are SDG7APER—renewable energy supply, SDG7CENAG—energy

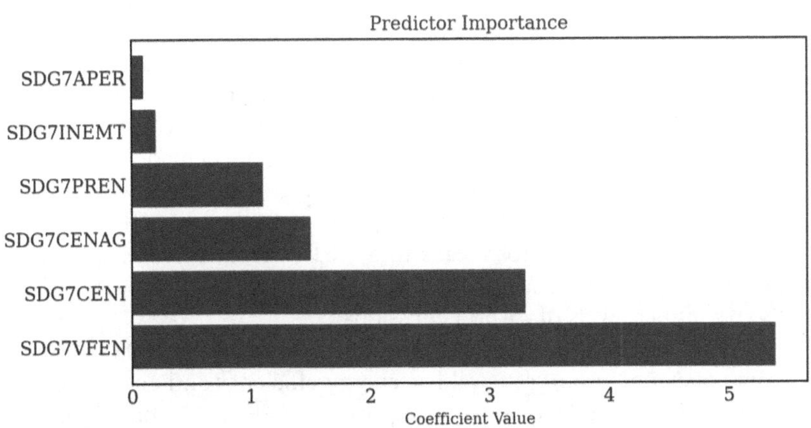


**Fig. 4.7** Importance of predictors related to influence on the variable SDG7FZEP. Source: Developed by the author using Python

consumption in agriculture, SDG7PREN—energy productivity, SDG7ENGS—net greenhouse gas emissions. A linear regression model is constructed with the independent variables defined above for which regression coefficients have been calculated according to Eq. (4.7):

$$\begin{aligned} SDG7IMPEN &= -0.15 * SDG7APER - 0.40 * SDG7CENAG \\ &+0.24 * SDG7PREN + 0.51 * SDG7ENGS + 2.01 \end{aligned} \tag{4.7}$$

For Model SDG7.6 it is observed that the influence of the independent variables on the dependent variable is in the case of the variable SDG7APER representing the supply of renewable energy, the results indicate a negative effect on the dependent variable, i.e. a 1% increase in the supply of renewable energy leads to a 0.15% decrease in the dependence on energy imports. There is an inverse relationship between renewable energy use and energy import dependence, indicating that an increase in the use of renewable energy can reduce the need to import energy. This emphasizes the potential of renewable energy to improve energy security by diversifying energy sources. With respect to the variable SDG7CENAG representing energy consumption in agriculture, there is an inverse influence on the dependent variable, i.e. a 1% increase in energy consumption in agriculture leads to a 0.4% decrease in energy import dependence. This could reflect increased energy efficiency and self-sufficiency in the agricultural sector, possibly through the use of biofuels or other renewable technologies. According to the variable SDG7PREN representing energy productivity, there is a positive influence on the dependent variable, i.e. a 1% increase in energy productivity leads to a 0.24% increase in energy import dependence. This reflects a more energy-intensive economy which, although efficient, depends on external sources to meet energy demand. In the case of the variable SDG7ENGS representing net greenhouse gas emissions, there is a positive influence on the dependent variable, i.e. a 1% increase in net greenhouse gas emissions leads to a 0.51% increase in energy import dependence, indicating a link between dependence on imported fossil fuels and higher levels of carbon emissions.

The results presented above underline the complex interplay between energy policy, the use of renewables, energy efficiency and environmental impacts in the context of energy import dependency. It highlights the need to promote renewable energy sources and energy efficiency to reduce import dependency and address climate change challenges.

Figure 4.8 shows the ranking of the importance of the predictors related to the influence on the dependent variable SDG7IMPEN.

According to Fig. 4.8 net greenhouse gas emissions have the largest positive coefficient, suggesting that it has the largest positive influence on the dependent variable followed by energy productivity. The weakest influence on the dependent variable is energy consumption in agriculture representing efforts to reduce energy consumption in agriculture that help to decrease greenhouse gas emissions. This is relevant in the context of the energy sustainability model, where higher energy use in agriculture is considered negative for sustainability or energy efficiency goals.

The SDG7.7 model of European energy sustainability from the perspective of the SDG7INEMT indicator has the selected dependent variable air emissions intensity from industry. The independent variables are SDG7FZEP—total primary energy supply, SDG7CENAG—energy consumption in agriculture, SDG7CENI—energy consumption in industry, SDG7VFEN—energy-related tax revenues, SDG7PREN—energy productivity, SDG7ENGS—net greenhouse gas emissions. A linear regression model is constructed with the independent variables defined above for which regression coefficients have been calculated according to Eq. (4.8):

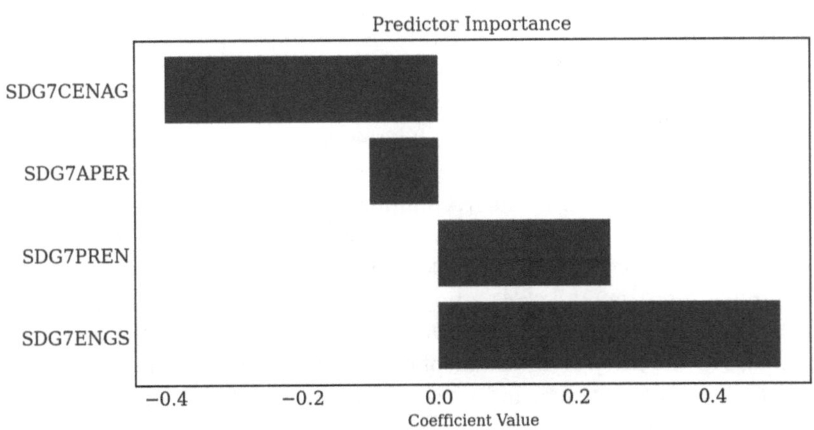


**Fig. 4.8** Importance of predictors related to the influence on the variable SDG7IMPEN. Source: Developed by the author using Python

$$\begin{aligned} SDG7INEMT &= -0.23 * SDG7FZEP + 0.81 * SDG7CENAG \\ &+0.94 * SDG7CENI + 3.86 * SDG7VFEN \\ &-0.53 * SDG7PREN + 0.57 * SDG7ENGS - 11.69 \end{aligned} \tag{4.8}$$

For Model SDG7.7 it is observed that the influence of the independent variables on the dependent variable is in the case of the variable SDG7FZEP representing total primary energy supply, a negative association with the dependent variable is observed, i.e. a 1% increase in total primary energy supply leads to a 0.23% decrease in the air emission intensity of industry possibly indicating improved energy efficiency or a shift to cleaner energy sources as energy availability increases. In the case of the SDG7CENAG variable representing energy consumption in agriculture, there is a positive influence on the dependent variable, i.e. a 1% increase in energy consumption in agriculture leads to a 0.81% increase in the air emission intensity of industry, due to the sharing of more polluting energy sources between these sectors. In the case of the variable SDG7CENI representing energy consumption in industry, there is a positive influence on the dependent variable, i.e. a 1% increase in energy consumption in industry leads to a 0.94% increase in the intensity of atmospheric emissions in industry, emphasizing the direct impact of industrial activity on greenhouse gas emissions. In the case of the variable SDG7VFEN representing energy-related tax revenues, there is a positive influence on the dependent variable, i.e. a 1% increase in energy-related tax revenues leads to a 3.86% increase in the intensity of air emissions from industry, due to insufficient carbon taxation or tax incentives for fossil fuels.

In the case of the variable SDG7PREN representing energy productivity, there is an inverse influence on the dependent variable, i.e. a 1% increase in energy productivity determines a 0.53% decrease in the intensity of atmospheric emissions from industry, highlighting the importance of energy efficiency in reducing the environmental impact of industrial activities. In the case of the variable SDG7ENGS representing net greenhouse gas emissions, there is a positive influence on the dependent variable, i.e. a 1% increase in net greenhouse gas emissions leads to a 0.57% increase in the intensity of atmospheric emissions from industry, indicating a close link between industrial emissions and the overall emissions profile of a country.

The results presented above highlight the complexity and interconnections between the different aspects of energy consumption, energy-related fiscal policy, energy efficiency and environmental impacts in the industrial context highlighting the need for integrated policies that promote clean energy sources, energy efficiency and mitigation measures to reduce the negative environmental impacts of the industrial sector.

Figure 4.9 shows the ranking of the importance of the predictors related to the influence on the dependent variable SDG7INEMT.

Figure 4.9 shows that the largest influence on the dependent variable is energy-related tax revenues, suggesting that higher tax revenues are associated with higher industrial emissions intensity. This argues that higher energy taxes may lead to higher production costs, which induce industries to use less efficient or more polluting technologies. Energy consumption in industry has a positive influence, indicating that higher energy consumption in the industrial sector is associated with higher emission intensities, suggesting that industry is a major source of emissions and that energy efficiency in this sector is important to reduce GHG emissions. The weakest influence on the dependent variable is energy productivity, indicating that more efficient energy use does not reduce emissions per unit of output to a significant extent in this model of energy sustainability.

The SDG7.8 model of European energy sustainability from the perspective of the SDG7PREN indicator has energy productivity as the selected dependent variable. The independent variables are

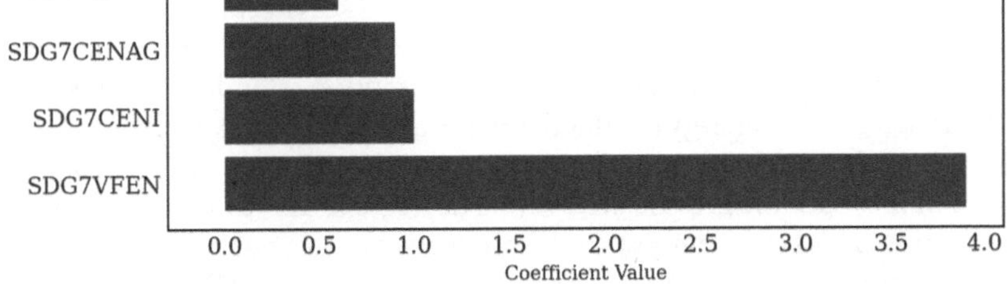


**Fig. 4.9** Importance of predictors related to influence on the variable SDG7INEMT. Source: Developed by the author using Python

SDG7FZEP—total primary energy supply, SDG7APER—renewable energy supply, SDG7CENAG—energy consumption in agriculture, SDG7CENI—energy consumption in industry, SDG7IMPEN—energy import dependence, SDG7ENGS—net greenhouse gas emissions, SDG7INEMT—air emissions intensity of industry. A linear regression model is constructed with the independent variables defined above for which regression coefficients have been calculated according to Eq. (4.9):

$$\begin{aligned} SDG7PREN &= 0.08 * SDG7FZEP + 0.32 * SDG7APER \\ &-0.06 * SDG7CENAG - 0.33 * SDG7CENI \\ &+0.14 * SDG7IMPEN + 0.42 * SDG7ENGS \\ &-0.18 * SDG7INEMT - 1.01 \end{aligned} \tag{4.9}$$

For the SDG7.8 model it is observed that the influence of the independent variables on the dependent variable is in the case of the variable SDG7FZEP representing the total primary energy supply, a positive relationship with the dependent variable emerges, i.e. a 1% increase in the total primary energy supply leads to a 0.08% increase in energy productivity. This suggests that higher energy availability may lead to more efficient uses or innovations that improve energy productivity. Regarding the variable SDG7APER renewable energy supply, there is a positive influence on the dependent variable, i.e. a 1% increase in renewable energy production leads to a 0.32% increase in energy productivity. This influence may reflect efficiency in the growth of renewable technologies or a transition to more sustainable and less carbon-intensive energy sources. According to the variable SDG7CENAG representing energy consumption in agriculture, there is an inverse influence on the dependent variable, i.e. a 1% increase in energy consumption in agriculture leads to a 0.06% decrease in energy productivity. In the case of the variable SDG7CENI representing energy consumption in industry, there is an inverse influence on the dependent variable, i.e. a 1% increase in energy consumption in industry leads to a 0.33% decrease in energy productivity. Both variables show an inverse relationship with energy productivity, indicating that higher energy consumption in these sectors is associated with a decrease in energy efficiency in the economy. This could suggest that these sectors have a potential to improve their energy efficiency. In the case of the variable SDG7IMPEN representing energy import dependence, there is a positive influence on the dependent variable, i.e. a 1% increase in energy import dependence leads to a

0.14% increase in energy productivity. This reflects the need for import-dependent economies to use energy more efficiently to offset the costs and vulnerabilities associated with dependence on external sources. For the SDG7ENGS indicator of net greenhouse gas emissions, there is a positive influence on the dependent variable, i.e. a 1% increase in net greenhouse gas emissions leads to a 0.42% increase in energy productivity. This result indicates the need to decouple the increase in energy efficiency from the increase in emissions, possibly through the adoption of low-emission technologies. In the case of the variable SDG7INEMT representing the intensity of atmospheric emissions from industry, an inverse influence on the dependent variable is found, i.e. a 1% increase in the intensity of atmospheric emissions from industry leads to a 0.18% decrease in energy productivity. This indicates that industrial activities with higher emissions are less energy efficient and that there is potential for improvements in this sector.

These findings reflect the complexity of relationships between energy sources, energy use in different sectors, environmental impacts and overall energy efficiency. They highlight the importance of integrating renewable energy sources, improving energy efficiency in all sectors and addressing greenhouse gas emissions to improve energy and economic sustainability.

Figure 4.10 shows the ranking of the importance of the predictors related to their influence on the dependent variable SDG7PREN.

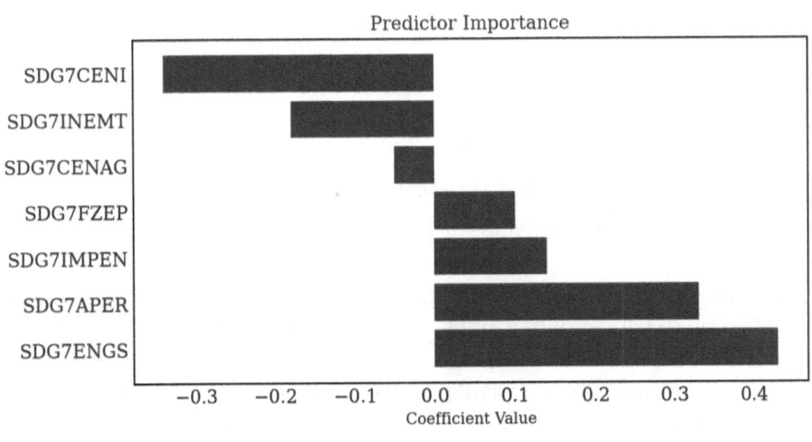


**Fig. 4.10** Importance of predictors related to the influence on the variable SDG7PREN. Source: Developed by the author using Python

Figure 4.10 shows that the largest influence on the dependent variable is net greenhouse gas emissions, indicating that an increase in net greenhouse gas emissions is associated with an improvement in energy productivity. This result indicates that industries that emit more GHGs are the most energy efficient, due to modern technologies or production scales that allow for higher energy efficiency.

Renewable energy production has a direct influence on the dependent variable, indicating that an increase in renewable energy utilization is associated with better energy productivity which indicates an increase in the efficiency of renewable technologies. An inverse influence on the dependent variable is represented by industrial energy consumption and industrial air emissions intensity, suggesting that an increase in industrial energy consumption or emissions intensity may be associated with a decrease in energy productivity indicating that some industries consume a lot of energy without producing a proportional output as well as that industries with higher emissions are less energy efficient.

The SDG7.9 model of European energy sustainability from the perspective of the SDG7VFEN indicator has the selected dependent variable energy-related tax revenues. The independent variables are: SDG7FZEP—total primary energy supply, SDG7APER—renewable energy supply, SDG7CENAG—agricultural energy consumption, SDG7CENI—industrial energy consumption, SDG7ENGS—net greenhouse gas emissions, SDG7INEMT—intensity of air emissions from industry. A linear regression model is constructed with the independent variables defined above for which regression coefficients have been calculated according to Eq. (4.10).

$$\begin{aligned} SDG7VFEN &= 0.04 * SDG7FZEP + 0.03 * SDG7APER \\ &-0.15 * SDG7CENAG - 0.16 * SDG7CENI \\ &-0.10 * SDG7ENGS + 0.11 * SDG7INEMT + 2.70 \end{aligned} \tag{4.10}$$

For Model SDG7.9 it is observed that the influence of the independent variables on the dependent variable is in the case of the variable SDG7FZEP representing the total primary energy supply, the results indicate a positive effect on the dependent variable, i.e. a 1% increase in the total primary energy supply leads to a 0.04% increase in energy-related tax revenues, indicating that an increase in the availability of primary energy can lead to an increase in tax revenues, possibly through increased economic activities and taxation of energy resources. As for the SDG7APER indicator of renewable energy production, there is a positive influence on the dependent variable, i.e. a 1% increase in renewable energy supply leads to a 0.03% increase in energy-related tax revenues, reflecting tax incentives for investment in renewable energy sources or efficient taxation of renewable energy sources.

In the case of the variable SDG7CENAG representing energy consumption in agriculture, there is an inverse influence on the dependent variable, i.e. a 1% increase in energy consumption in agriculture leads to a 0.15% decrease in energy-related tax revenues. According to the variable SDG7CENI, representing energy consumption in industry, there is an inverse influence on the dependent variable, i.e. a 1% increase in energy consumption in industry leads to a 0.16% decrease in energy-related tax revenues. Both variables have inverse relationships with energy-related tax revenues, suggesting that higher energy consumption in these sectors may reduce tax revenues, possibly due to subsidies or tax exemptions given to these sectors to support production and competitiveness. In the case of the SDG7ENGS variable representing net greenhouse gas emissions, there is an inverse influence on the dependent variable, i.e. a 1% increase in net greenhouse gas emissions leads to a 0.1% decrease in energy-related tax revenues. This indicates that an effective environmental policy that reduces emissions can increase tax revenues, either by taxing emissions or by promoting cleaner and more profitable energy sources. In the case of the variable SDG7INEMT representing the intensity of air emissions from industry, there is a positive influence on the dependent variable, i.e. a 1% increase in the intensity of air emissions from industry leads to a 0.11% increase in energy-related tax revenues, possibly indicating that industry is subject to higher taxation on its emissions or that more energy-intensive industrial activities are more profitable and therefore generate more tax revenues.

Figure 4.11 shows the ranking of the importance of predictors related to the influence on the dependent variable SDG7VFEN.

Figure 4.11 shows that the most significant inverse influences on the dependent variable are energy consumption in agriculture and energy consumption in industry. A significant influence on the dependent variable is exerted by the intensity of air emissions from industry, which indicates that an increase in emissions intensity from industry is associated with an increase in energy-related tax revenues suggesting that industries that

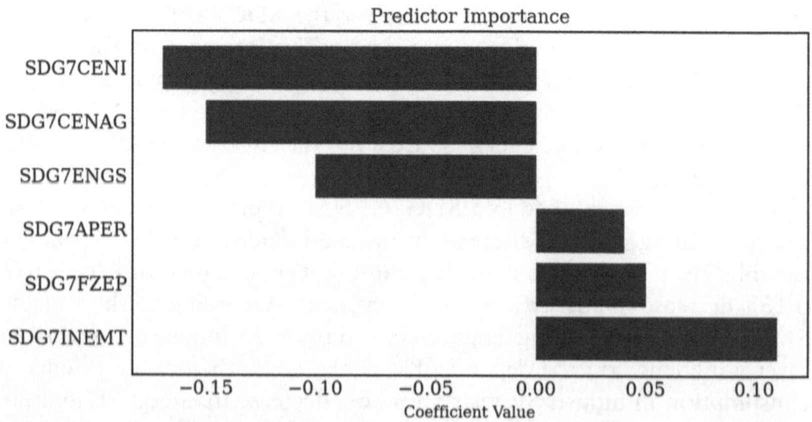


**Fig. 4.11** Importance of predictors related to the influence on the variable SDG7VFEN. Source: Developed by the author using Python

**Table 4.2** Validation of energy sustainability models

| *Model* | *Dependent variable* | *Coefficient of determination* | *Residue standard deviation (RMSE)* |
|---|---|---|---|
| SDG7.1 | SDG7APER | 0.4599 | 0.5126 |
| SDG7.2 | SDG7CENAG | 0.5350 | 0.3488 |
| SDG7.3 | SDG7CENI | 0.5093 | 0.1970 |
| SDG7.4 | SDG7ENGS | 0.4447 | 0.2884 |
| SDG7.5 | SDG7FZEP | 0.5617 | 1.0480 |
| SDG7.6 | SDG7IMPEN | 0.3956 | 0.4548 |
| SDG7.7 | SDG7INEMT | 0.6115 | 0.6136 |
| SDG7.8 | SDG7PREN | 0.5234 | 0.3065 |
| SDG7.9 | SDG7VFEN | 0.6042 | 0.1041 |

Source: Developed by the author using Python

pollute more may be subject to higher taxes on emissions, leading to higher tax revenues.

The regression functions were tested on the significance level and residual standard deviation of residuals (RMSE) data are presented in Table 4.2.

It is observed that the standard deviation falls in the range (0.1041–1.0480). Maximizing the statistical significance of the model indicates Model SDG7.7 as statistically relevant with a significance of 61.15% and a standard deviation of the residuals of 0.61 (which confirms that for the prediction right there are deviations of the normal distribution on average of 0.6 points).

The VIF variance inflation factor analysis was used to test for multicollinearities among the independent variables of the proposed regression models and is presented in Table 4.3.

From Table 4.3 the homogeneity of the proposed models is significant, with the largest deviations from the trend line being recorded for SDG7.6, SDG7.4 and SDG7.2. However, the models have a range of error representation that tends to be 0 in almost all cases being statistically well determined and relevant for the purpose. The multicollinearity of the models has been tested, the inflation factors being below the threshold of multicollinearity representation (VIF<10), which demonstrates that the evaluated models are opportune for determining the causal relationships of energy sustainability on composite factors.

The validated energy sustainability model assumed an integrated approach to the efficient use of energy resources and the development of renewable energy sources. The proposed model quantified the segregated weaknesses of the proposed indicators correlations (total primary energy supply, renewable energy supply, agricultural energy consumption, industrial energy consumption, energy-related tax revenues, energy productivity, energy import dependency, net greenhouse gas emissions, industrial air emissions intensity), vulnerabilities whose mitigation relies on reducing energy consumption by implementing modern and innovative technologies and maximizing the use of green renewable energy. Energy sustainability as determined by the nine regression equations implies reducing greenhouse gas emissions and promoting responsible use of conventional energy. A limitation of this model is the cost of implementing modern and innovative technologies. There is also some uncertainty about the long-term efficiency and sustainability of these technologies. The study shows that investing in energy sustainability is important for protecting the environment and ensuring sustainable economic development. In addition, long-term benefits such as reduced pollution and job creation in green industry can outweigh the initial costs. By adopting modern and innovative technologies, we can reduce dependence on finite resources and environmental pollution, thus contributing to the long-term sustainability of the economy. Investments in renewable energy can also bring significant economic benefits by creating new business opportunities and jobs in the green energy sector. Switching to renewable energy will reduce dependence on finite resources and help diversify energy sources. By adopting

**Table 4.3** The homogeneity table of sustainable energy development models

| *sModel* | *Dependent variable* | *Independent variables* | *P* | *VIF* |
|---|---|---|---|---|
| SDG7.1 | **SDG7APER** 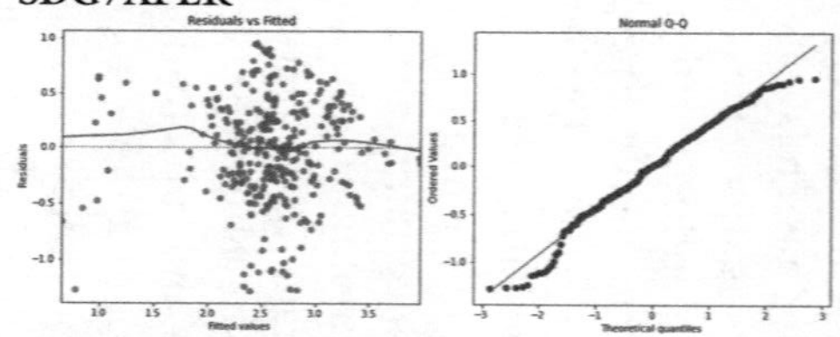 | SDG7FZEP | 8.865e−14 | 1.6825 |
| | | SDG7CENAG | 3.22e−15 | 1.4455 |
| | | SDG7CENI | 1.888e−25 | 1.3804 |
| | | SDG7VFEN | 1.83e−10 | 1.3673 |
| | | SDG7PREN | 1.417e−22 | 1.4566 |
| | | SDG7IMPEN | 0.00124 | 1.6292 |
| | | SDG7ENGS | 1.817e−08 | 1.5425 |
| | | SDG7FZEP | 8.865e−14 | 1.6825 |
| SDG7.2 | **SDG7CENAG** 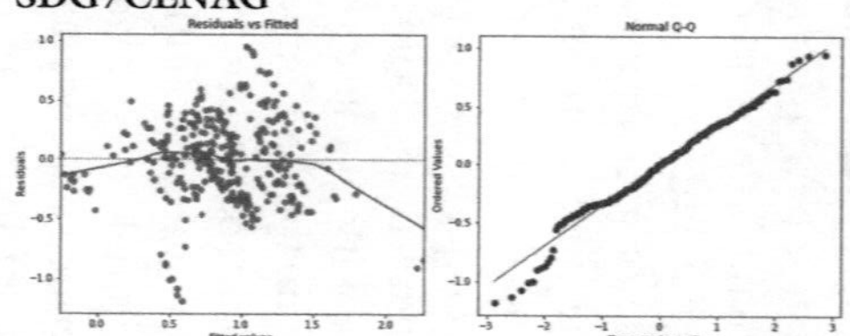 | SDG7FZEP | 6.209e−22 | 1.7500 |
| | | SDG7APER | 3.824e−10 | 1.8667 |
| | | SDG7CENI | 5.219e−17 | 1.6753 |
| | | SDG7VFEN | 7.87e−25 | 1.8715 |
| | | SDG7PREN | 0.02025 | 2.1265 |
| | | SDG7IMPEN | 6.574e−09 | 1.5213 |
| | | SDG7ENGS | 0.008104 | 1.7996 |
| | | SDG7INEMT | 6.11e−18 | 2.0978 |
| SDG7.3 | **SDG7CENI** 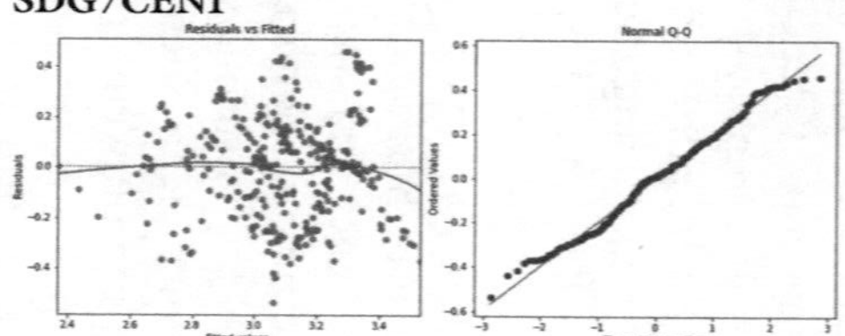 | SDG7FZEP | 3.77e−37 | 1.4119 |
| | | SDG7APER | 2.247e−24 | 1.2518 |
| | | SDG7CENAG | 6.793e−19 | 1.5541 |
| | | SDG7VFEN | 1.796e−11 | 2.1171 |
| | | SDG7PREN | 1.733e−06 | 1.4876 |
| | | SDG7INEMT | 2.341e−08 | 2.1652 |

| | | | | |
|---|---|---|---|---|
| SDG7.4 | **SDG7ENGS** 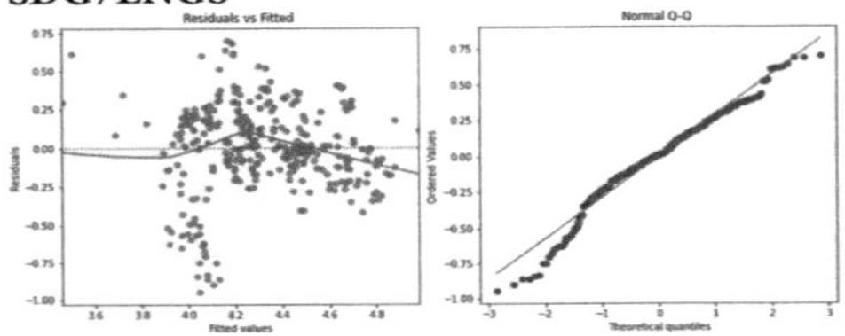  | SDG7APER | 8.524e−10 | 1.4191 |
| | | SDG7CENAG | 0.009715 | 1.5622 |
| | | SDG7VFEN | 1.121e−08 | 1.7032 |
| | | SDG7PREN | 4.214e−13 | 1.6243 |
| | | SDG7IMPEN | 1.111e−08 | 1.5258 |
| | | SDG7INEMT | 5.684e−09 | 2.0347 |
| SDG7.5 | **SDG7FZEP** 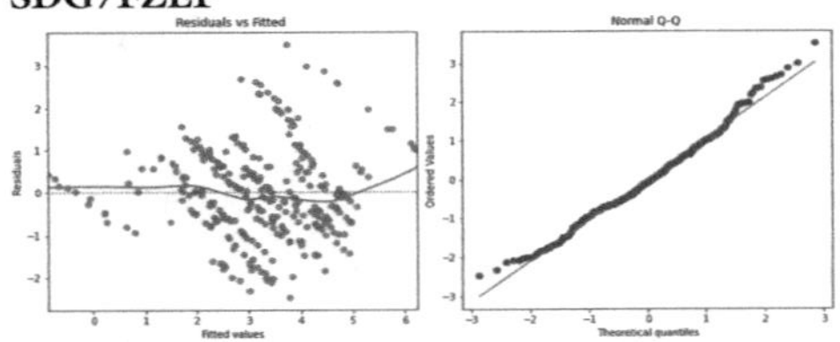  | SDG7APER | 7.127e−11 | 1.5112 |
| | | SDG7CENAG | 2.265e−25 | 1.4194 |
| | | SDG7CENI | 3.77e−37 | 1.2611 |
| | | SDG7VFEN | 7.483e−28 | 1.6841 |
| | | SDG7PREN | 1.101e−11 | 1.3850 |
| | | SDG7INEMT | 3.768e−15 | 1.9707 |
| SDG7.6 | **SDG7IMPEN** 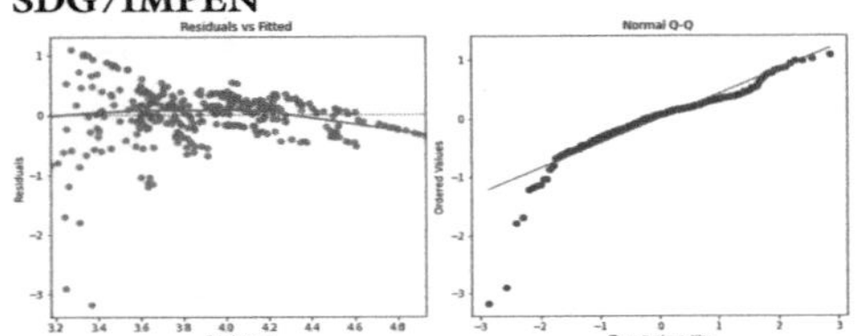  | SDG7APER | 0.0004865 | 1.3348 |
| | | SDG7CENAG | 4.127e−14 | 1.1295 |
| | | SDG7PREN | 0.0001341 | 1.2780 |
| | | SDG7ENGS | 8.303e−11 | 1.4106 |

(*continued*)

**Table 4.3** (continued)

| *sModel* | *Dependent variable* | *Independent variables* | *P* | *VIF* |
|---|---|---|---|---|
| SDG7.7 | **SDG7INEMT** 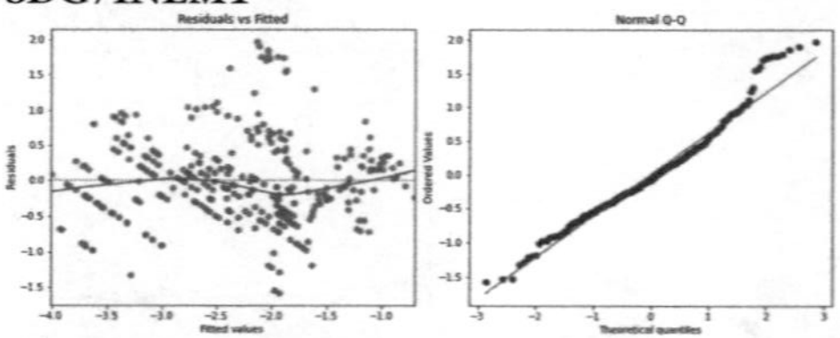  | SDG7FZEP | 4.485e−16 | 1.6815 |
| | | SDG7CENAG | 5.665e−26 | 1.1592 |
| | | SDG7CENI | 6.668e−11 | 1.3681 |
| | | SDG7VFEN | 8.769e−44 | 1.3673 |
| | | SDG7PREN | 7.044e−09 | 1.4297 |
| | | SDG7ENGS | 1.235e−08 | 1.2730 |
| SDG7.8 | **SDG7PREN** 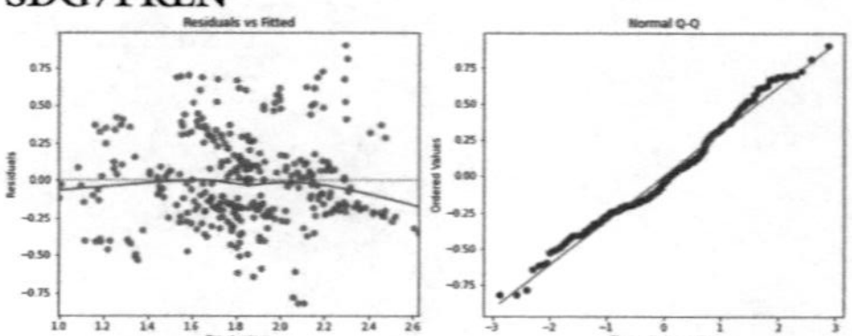  | SDG7FZEP | 2.068e−10 | 1.4923 |
| | | SDG7APER | 1.213e−21 | 1.5148 |
| | | SDG7CENAG | 0.09174 | 1.5748 |
| | | SDG7CENI | 2.371e−05 | 1.7498 |
| | | SDG7IMPEN | 0.0001042 | 1.6114 |
| | | SDG7ENGS | 5.767e−15 | 1.4349 |
| | | SDG7INEMT | 3.376e−20 | 1.2142 |
| SDG7.9 | **SDG7VFEN** 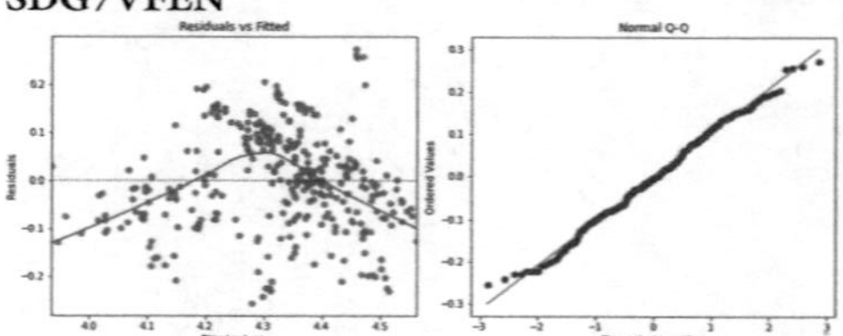  | SDG7FZEP | 1.007e−24 | 1.4875 |
| | | SDG7APER | 0.000267 | 1.5020 |
| | | SDG7CENAG | 6.936e−28 | 1.3133 |
| | | SDG7CENI | 2.237e−09 | 1.7443 |
| | | SDG7ENGS | 3.421e−10 | 1.1401 |
| | | SDG7INEMT | 7.487e−50 | 1.2136 |

Source: Developed by the author using Python

sustainable practices and promoting green innovations, we can create a cleaner and healthier environment for future generations.

## Conclusions

Modelling energy sustainability in the European Union based on indicators related to Sustainable Development Goal 7 reveals a complex configuration of causal relationships and interdependencies between energy production factors, energy fiscal policies, energy efficiency and productivity, sectoral consumption and environmental pressures. By applying multiple linear regression methodology and using the BFS variable selection technique, the study has outlined a robust framework for interpreting the key variables that define the sustainable trajectory of the European energy system.

The results obtained by estimating the nine valid econometric models indicate that energy sustainability is not determined by a single isolable factor, but by a systemic interaction between energy consumption in agriculture and industry, the share of energy from renewable sources, the level of greenhouse gas emissions, industrial emission intensity, energy productivity and import dependence. Among the most influential variables with a positive impact on sustainability are the increase in the share of renewable energy and the improvement of energy productivity, while high levels of emissions and external energy dependence are negatively correlated with sustainability objectives.

At the same time, SDG7.2 (energy consumption in agriculture), SDG7.3 (industrial energy consumption) and SDG7.7 (industrial emissions intensity) highlight the critical role of energy fiscal policies, with energy tax revenues having a significant influence but with mixed effects depending on the sector analysed. Similarly, the analysis of national vulnerabilities shows that Member States with low levels of energy productivity and a low share of renewable sources remain exposed to risks related to energy security and the inability to sustain European climate objectives in the long term.

The conclusions of this exercise therefore highlight the need for an integrated approach to energy and climate policies, in which energy efficiency, the decarbonization of industrial sectors and fiscal incentives for technological innovation in renewable energy become converging priorities. In addition, reducing dependence on energy imports, coupled with the development of domestic clean production capacities, is essential for strengthening the European Union's strategic autonomy. Overall, the proposed models provide a valuable analytical tool for assessing Member States' performance in the energy transition and can form the basis for evidence-based public policies that contribute to achieving the Sustainable Development Goals in a balanced, fair and sustainable manner across the European Union.

## References

Abdessadak, A., Ghennioui, H., Thirion-Moreau, N., Elbhiri, B., Abraim, M., & Merzouk, S. (2025). Digital twin technology and artificial intelligence in energy transition: A comprehensive systematic review of applications. *Energy Reports, 13*, 5196–5218. https://doi.org/10.1016/j.egyr.2025.04.060

Almihat, M. G. M., & Munda, J. L. (2025). The role of smart grid technologies in urban and sustainable energy planning. *Energies, 18*(7), 1618. https://doi.org/10.3390/en18071618

Amendola, M. (2025). Winners and losers of the EU carbon border adjustment mechanism. An intra-EU issue? *Energy Economics, 142*, 108139. https://doi.org/10.1016/j.eneco.2024.108139

Aydin, M., Degirmenci, T., Ahmed, Z., & Apergis, N. (2025). Do the energy taxes, green technological innovation, and energy productivity enable the green energy transition in EU countries? Evidence from novel panel data estimators. *Renewable Energy, 249*, 123236. https://doi.org/10.1016/j.renene.2025.123236

Basdekis, C., Christopoulos, A. G., Katsampoxakis, I., & Xanthopoulos, S. (2024). Trends and challenges after the impact of COVID-19 and the energy crisis on financial markets. *Energies, 17*(15), 3857. https://doi.org/10.3390/en17153857

Basílio, M. (2025). Renewable energy and energy efficiency: An exploratory study in EU countries. *Sustainable Futures, 9*, 100514. https://doi.org/10.1016/j.sftr.2025.100514

Bauwens, T., Wade, R., & Burke, M. (2024). The energy commons: A systematic review, paradoxes, and ways forward. *Energy Research & Social Science, 118*, 103776. https://doi.org/10.1016/j.erss.2024.103776

Blanchard, A. (2024). Strategic investments: Electrolysis vs. storage for Europe's energy security in the hydrogen era. *Energy Policy, 195*, 114371. https://doi.org/10.1016/j.enpol.2024.114371

Böning, J., Di Nino, V., & Folger, T. (2023). Benefits and costs of the ETS in the EU, a lesson learned for the CBAM design. *SSRN Electronic Journal, 2764*. https://doi.org/10.2139/ssrn.4335984

Borowiecki, M., Giménez, J. C., Giovannelli, F., & Vanni, F. (2023). *Accelerating the EU's green transition* (p. 1777). OECD. https://doi.org/10.1787/bed2b6df-en

Borozan, S., Mateska, A. K., & Krstevski, P. (2021). Progress of the electricity sectors in South East Europe: Challenges and opportunities in achieving compliance with EU energy policy. *Energy Reports, 7*, 8730–8741. https://doi.org/10.1016/j.egyr.2021.11.203

Brodny, J., Tutak, M., & Grebski, W. (2024). Empirical assessment of the efficiency of Poland's energy transition process in the context of implementing the European Union's energy policy. *Energies, 17*(11), 2689. https://doi.org/10.3390/en17112689

Brzezinski, M., & Kaczan, M. (2025). Carbon taxes in Europe do not hurt the poor: Evidence from existing taxation schemes. *Ecological Economics, 233*, 108585. https://doi.org/10.1016/j.ecolecon.2025.108585

Calafat-Marzal, C., Vega, V., Sanz-Torro, V., & Puertas, R. (2025). Assessment of the resilience factors associated with European green efficiency. *Science of the Total Environment, 966*, 178643. https://doi.org/10.1016/j.scitotenv.2025.178643

Campana, P., Censi, R., Ruggieri, R., & Amendola, C. (2025). Smart grids and sustainability: The impact of digital technologies on the energy transition. *Energies, 18*(9), 2149. https://doi.org/10.3390/en18092149

Cardinale, R., Cardinale, I., & Zupic, I. (2024). The EU's vulnerability to gas price and supply shocks: The role of mismatches between policy beliefs and changing international gas markets. *Energy Economics, 131*, 107383. https://doi.org/10.1016/j.eneco.2024.107383

Cevik, S., Ilahi, N., Krogulski, K., Li, G. B., Mohona, S., & Zhao, Y. (2023). *Climate change mitigation and policy spillovers in the EU's immediate neighborhood*. IMF Working Papers 23/246. https://doi.org/10.5089/9798400259401.001.A000

Chalkias, D. A., & Stathatos, E. (2024). Energy and agriculture. In D. A. Chalkias & E. Stathatos (Eds.), *The emergence of agrivoltaics: Current status, challenges and future opportunities* (pp. 9–37). Springer International Publishing. https://doi.org/10.1007/978-3-031-48861-0_2

Costa, V., & Campanini, F. (2024). Community-centred energy planning: Within and beyond administrative borders. *Sustainability, 16*(5), 2049. https://doi.org/10.3390/su16052049

Csedő, Z., Zavarkó, M., Sára, Z., & Pörzse, G. (2025). Exploring the role of transdisciplinary research in accelerating sustainability transition: An empirical analysis of environmental innovation drivers in Central European energy sector. *Energy Research & Social Science, 127*, 104222. https://doi.org/10.1016/j.erss.2025.104222

Dai, J., Mehmood, U., & Nassani, A. A. (2025). Empowering sustainability through energy efficiency, green innovations, and the sharing economy: Insights from G7 economies. *Energy, 318*, 134768. https://doi.org/10.1016/j.energy.2025.134768

Dechezleprêtre, A., Nachtigall, D., & Venmans, F. (2023). The joint impact of the European Union emissions trading system on carbon emissions and economic performance. *Journal of Environmental Economics and Management, 118*, 102758. https://doi.org/10.1016/j.jeem.2022.102758

Dekeyrel, S., & Fessler, M. (2024). Digitalisation: An enabler for the clean energy transition. *Journal of Energy & Natural Resources Law, 42*(2), 185–209. https://doi.org/10.1080/02646811.2023.2254103

Dirma, V., Neverauskienė, L., Tvaronaviciene, M., Danilevičienė, I., & Tamošiūnienė, R. (2024). The impact of renewable energy development on economic growth. *Energies, 17*, 6328. https://doi.org/10.3390/en17246328

Dogan, E., Hodžić, S., & Šikić, T. F. (2023). Do energy and environmental taxes stimulate or inhibit renewable energy deployment in the European Union? *Renewable Energy, 202*, 1138–1145. https://doi.org/10.1016/j.renene.2022.11.107

Domac, J., Šegon, V., & Dumitriu, F. (2025). *European energy independence through investing in renewables: Empowering freedom*. Routledge. https://doi.org/10.4324/9781003617075

Dostmohammadi, M., Pedram, M. Z., Hoseinzadeh, S., & Garcia, D. A. (2024). A GA-stacking ensemble approach for forecasting energy consumption in a smart household: A comparative study of ensemble methods. *Journal of Environmental Management, 364*, 121264. https://doi.org/10.1016/j.jenvman.2024.121264

Eslahi, E., Creti, A., & Sanin, M.-E. (2025). Signal received? Carbon price and financial–environmental performance prioritization in EU ETS firms. *International Review of Financial Analysis, 105*, 104348. https://doi.org/10.1016/j.irfa.2025.104348

European Central Bank. (2025). *Assessing the macroeconomic effects of climate change transition policies*. https://www.ecb.europa.eu/press/economic-bulletin/focus/2024/html/ecb.ebbox202401_04~92ad3c032a.en.html

European Commission. (2022a). *REPowerEU affordable, secure and sustainable energy for Europe*. https://commission.europa.eu/topics/energy/repowereu_en

European Commission. (2022b). *The 2030 agenda for sustainable development and the SDGs*. https://ec.europa.eu/environment/sustainable-development/SDGs/index_en.htm

European Commission. (2023). *About the EU ETS*. https://climate.ec.europa.eu/eu-action/eu-emissions-trading-system-eu-ets/about-eu-ets_en

European Council. (2023). *Fit for 55.* https://www.consilium.europa.eu/en/policies/green-deal/fit-for-55-the-eu-plan-for-a-green-transition/

European Environment Agency. (2025a). *Renewables, electrification and flexibility – For a competitive EU energy system transformation by 2030.* https://www.eea.europa.eu/en/analysis/publications/renewables-electrification-and-flexibility-for-a-competitive-eu-energy-system

European Environment Agency. (2025b). *Renewables and electrification: Key to cutting costs and powering EU's clean industry and competitiveness.* https://www.eea.europa.eu/en/newsroom/news/renewables-and-electrification-key-to-cutting-costs-and-powering-eus-clean-industry-and-competitiveness

European Environment Agency. (2025c). *Share of energy consumption from renewable sources in Europe.* https://www.eea.europa.eu/en/analysis/indicators/share-of-energy-consumption-from

European Investment Bank. (2025). *REPowerEU and the EIB.* https://www.eib.org/en/projects/topics/energy-natural-resources/energy/repowereu

European Union. (2024). *The recovery and resilience facility.* https://commission.europa.eu/business-economy-euro/economic-recovery/recovery-and-resilience-facility_en

Eurostat. (2024). *Energy import dependency by products.* Europa.Eu. https://ec.europa.eu/eurostat/databrowser/view/sdg_07_50/default/table?lang=en&category=sdg.sdg_07

Eurostat. (2024b). *Energy productivity.* https://ec.europa.eu/eurostat/databrowser/view/sdg_07_30/default/table?lang=en

Eurostat. (2024c). *Fossil fuel reliance in EU increased slightly in 2022.* https://ec.europa.eu/eurostat/web/products-eurostat-news/w/ddn-20240130-2

Eurostat. (2025). *Domestic net greenhouse gas emissions.* https://ec.europa.eu/eurostat/databrowser/view/sdg_13_10/default/table?lang=en

Farid, H. M. A., Iram, S., Shakeel, H. M., & Hill, R. (2024). Enhancing stakeholder engagement in building energy performance assessment: A state-of-the-art literature survey. *Energy Strategy Reviews, 56*, 101560. https://doi.org/10.1016/j.esr.2024.101560

Faure, C., Guetlein, M.-C., Schleich, J., Tu, G., Whitmarsh, L., & Whittle, C. (2022). Household acceptability of energy efficiency policies in the European Union: Policy characteristics trade-offs and the role of trust in government and environmental identity. *Ecological Economics, 192*, 107267. https://doi.org/10.1016/j.ecolecon.2021.107267

Firtescu, B. N., Bostan, I., Grosu, M., Droj, L., & Mihalciuc, C. C. (2025). Increasing the share of renewable energy sources (RESs) in the specific portfolio by using the taxation mechanism: Study at the level of EU states. *Economic Analysis and Policy, 85*, 1534–1549. https://doi.org/10.1016/j.eap.2025.02.007

Gajdzik, B., Nagaj, R., Wolniak, R., Bałaga, D., Žuromskaitė, B., & Grebski, W. W. (2024). Renewable energy share in European industry: Analysis and extrapolation of trends in EU countries. *Energies, 17*(11), 2476. https://doi.org/10.3390/en17112476

García-Quevedo, J., & Jové-Llopis, E. (2021). Environmental policies and energy efficiency investments. An industry-level analysis. *Energy Policy, 156*, 112461. https://doi.org/10.1016/j.enpol.2021.112461

Geng, G., Shen, Y., & Dong, C. (2024). The impact of green finance on agricultural non-point source pollution: Analysis of the role of environmental regulation and rural land transfer. *Land, 13*(9), 1516. https://doi.org/10.3390/land13091516

Georgescu, L. P., Fortea, C., Antohi, V. M., Balsalobre-Lorente, D., Zlati, M. L., & Barbuta-Misu, N. (2025). Economic, technological and environmental drivers of the circular economy in the European Union: A panel data analysis. *Environmental Sciences Europe, 37*(1), 76. https://doi.org/10.1186/s12302-025-01119-4

Gonzalez-Torres, M., Bertoldi, P., Castellazzi, L., & Perez-Lombard, L. (2023). Review of EU product energy efficiency policies: What have we achieved in 40 years? *Journal of Cleaner Production, 421*, 138442. https://doi.org/10.1016/j.jclepro.2023.138442

Guarascio, D., Reljic, J., & Zezza, F. (2025). Energy vulnerability and resilience in the EU: Concepts, empirics and policy. *Journal of Industrial and Business Economics, 52*, 683–726. https://doi.org/10.1007/s40812-025-00340-9

Gueye, S., Karanfil, F., & Omgba, L. D. (2025). Navigating the energy transition in the EU: Renewables, critical raw materials and emerging vulnerabilities. *Ecological Economics, 237*, 108696. https://doi.org/10.1016/j.ecolecon.2025.108696

Haywood, L., & Jakob, M. (2023). The role of the emissions trading scheme 2 in the policy mix to decarbonize road transport in the European Union. *Transport Policy, 139*, 99–108. https://doi.org/10.1016/j.tranpol.2023.06.003

Hoffart, F. M., D'Orazio, P., Holz, F., & Kemfert, C. (2024). Exploring the interdependence of climate, finance, energy, and geopolitics: A conceptual framework for systemic risks amidst multiple crises. *Applied Energy, 361*, 122885. https://doi.org/10.1016/j.apenergy.2024.122885

Igliński, B., Kiełkowska, U., Mazurek, K., Drużyński, S., Pietrzak, M. B., Kumar, G., Veeramuthu, A., Skrzatek, M., Zinecker, M., & Piechota, G. (2024). Renewable energy transition in Europe in the context of renewable energy transition processes in the world. A review. *Heliyon, 10*(24), e40997. https://doi.org/10.1016/j.heliyon.2024.e40997

Immler, N. L., & Sakkers, H. (2022). The UN-Sustainable Development Goals going local: Learning from localising human rights. *The International Journal of Human Rights, 26*(2), 262–284. https://doi.org/10.1080/13642987.2021.1913411

Karmaker, S. C., Sen, K. K., Chapman, A. J., Mohiuddin, G., & Saha, B. B. (2025). Innovation under Cap-and-Trade: How emission trading systems propel decarbonization. *Next Energy, 7*, 100220. https://doi.org/10.1016/j.nxener.2024.100220

Karpavicius, T., Balezentis, T., & Streimikiene, D. (2025). Energy security indicators for sustainable energy development: Application to electricity sector in the context of state economic decisions. *Sustainable Development, 33*(1), 1381–1400. https://doi.org/10.1002/sd.3190

Köppl, A., & Schratzenstaller, M. (2023). Carbon taxation: A review of the empirical literature. *Journal of Economic Surveys, 37*(4), 1353–1388. https://doi.org/10.1111/joes.12531

Küfeoğlu, S. (2024). Industrial process emissions. In S. Küfeoğlu (Ed.), *Net zero: Decarbonizing the global economies* (pp. 341–414). Springer Nature Switzerland. https://doi.org/10.1007/978-3-031-70322-5_7

Lamprousis, G., & Golfinopoulos, S. (2025). The Integrated Energy Community Performance Index (IECPI): A multidimensional tool for evaluating energy communities. *Urban Science, 9*, 264. https://doi.org/10.3390/urbansci9070264

Li, Z., Hasan, M. M., & Lu, Z. (2023). Assessing financial factors for oil supply disruptions and its impact on oil supply security and transportation risks. *Environmental Science and Pollution Research, 30*(12), 33695–33710. https://doi.org/10.1007/s11356-022-24541-0

López González, D. M., & Garcia Rendon, J. (2022). Opportunities and challenges of mainstreaming distributed energy resources towards the transition to more efficient and resilient energy markets. *Renewable and Sustainable Energy Reviews, 157*, 112018. https://doi.org/10.1016/j.rser.2021.112018

Luderer, G., Madeddu, S., Merfort, L., Ueckerdt, F., Pehl, M., Pietzcker, R., Rottoli, M., Schreyer, F., Bauer, N., Baumstark, L., Bertram, C., Dirnaichner, A., Humpenöder, F., Levesque, A., Popp, A., Rodrigues, R., Strefler, J., & Kriegler, E. (2022). Impact of declining renewable energy costs on electrification in low-emission scenarios. *Nature Energy, 7*(1), 32–42. https://doi.org/10.1038/s41560-021-00937-z

Machlev, R., Heistrene, L., Perl, M., Levy, K. Y., Belikov, J., Mannor, S., & Levron, Y. (2022). Explainable Artificial Intelligence (XAI) techniques for energy and power systems: Review, challenges and opportunities. *Energy and AI, 9*, 100169. https://doi.org/10.1016/j.egyai.2022.100169

Madurai Elavarasan, R., Pugazhendhi, R., Irfan, M., Mihet-Popa, L., Campana, P. E., & Khan, I. A. (2022). A novel Sustainable Development Goal 7 composite index as the paradigm for energy sustainability assessment: A case study from Europe. *Applied Energy, 307*, 118173. https://doi.org/10.1016/j.apenergy.2021.118173

Manta, A. G., Gherțescu, C., Bădîrcea, R. M., Manta, L. F., Popescu, J., & Lăpădat, C. V. (2025). How does the interplay between banking performance, digitalization, and renewable energy consumption shape sustainable development in European Union countries? *Energies, 18*(3), 571. https://doi.org/10.3390/en18030571

Marchewka-Bartkowiak, K. (2023). The European Union Emission Trading System and its role for green budgeting development—The case of EU member states. *Current Opinion in Environmental Sustainability, 65*, 101390. https://doi.org/10.1016/j.cosust.2023.101390

Mengesha, I., & Roy, D. (2025). Carbon pricing drives critical transition to green growth. *Nature Communications, 16*(1), 1321. https://doi.org/10.1038/s41467-025-56540-3

Mingolla, S., Gabrielli, P., Manzotti, A., Robson, M. J., Rouwenhorst, K., Ciucci, F., Sansavini, G., Klemun, M. M., & Lu, Z. (2024). Effects of emissions caps on the costs and feasibility of low-carbon hydrogen in the European ammonia industry. *Nature Communications, 15*(1), 3753. https://doi.org/10.1038/s41467-024-48145-z

Mishra, P., & Singh, G. (2023). Energy management systems in sustainable smart cities based on the Internet of energy: A technical review. *Energies, 16*, 6903. 1–36. https://doi.org/10.3390/en16196903

Mo, S., & Liu, X. (2025). Strengthening the resilience of urban energy systems amid renewable energy transition: A new method based on double machine learning. *Energy Policy, 206*, 114776. https://doi.org/10.1016/j.enpol.2025.114776

OECD. (2025). *Green growth.* https://data-explorer.oecd.org/vis?df[ds]=DisseminateFinalDMZ&df[id]=DSD_GG%40DF_GREEN_GROWTH&df[ag]=OECD.ENV.EPI&dq=AUS....&pd=2017%2C&to[TIME_PERIOD]=false

OECD/UNDP. (2025). *Investing in climate for growth and development: The case for enhanced NDCs.* OECD. https://doi.org/10.1787/16b7cbc7-en

Olasehinde-Williams, G. (2024). Carbon pricing and aggregate macroeconomic performance in the Eurozone: A contribution to the climate policy debate using the EU ETS and Macroeconomic Performance Index. *Environmental Science and Pollution Research, 31*(19), 28290–28305. https://doi.org/10.1007/s11356-024-32676-5

Özkan, O., Alola, A. A., & Adebayo, T. S. (2023). Environmental benefits of non-renewable energy efficiency and renewable energy intensity in the USA and EU: Examining the role of clean technologies. *Sustainable Energy Technologies and Assessments, 58*, 103315. https://doi.org/10.1016/j.seta.2023.103315

Paleari, S. (2024). The role of strategic autonomy in the EU green transition. *Sustainability, 16*(6), 2597. https://doi.org/10.3390/su16062597

Pan, J., Cross, J. L., Zou, X., & Zhang, B. (2024). To tax or to trade? A global review of carbon emissions reduction strategies. *Energy Strategy Reviews, 55*, 101508. https://doi.org/10.1016/j.esr.2024.101508

Paraschiv, L. S., & Paraschiv, S. (2023). Contribution of renewable energy (hydro, wind, solar and biomass) to decarbonization and transformation of the electricity generation sector for sustainable development. *Energy Reports, 9*, 535–544. https://doi.org/10.1016/j.egyr.2023.07.024

Proedrou, F. (2023). EU decarbonization under geopolitical pressure: Changing paradigms and implications for energy and climate policy. *Sustainability, 15*(6), 5083. https://doi.org/10.3390/su15065083

Psara, K., Papadimitriou, C., Efstratiadi, M., Tsakanikas, S., Papadopoulos, P., & Tobin, P. (2022). European energy regulatory, socioeconomic, and organizational aspects: An analysis of barriers related to data-driven services across electricity sectors. *Energies, 15*(6), 2197. https://doi.org/10.3390/en15062197

Radtke, J. (2025). Understanding the complexity of governing energy transitions: Introducing an integrated approach of policy and transition perspectives. *Environmental Policy and Governance, 35*, 595–614. https://doi.org/10.1002/eet.2158

Rasoulinezhad, E. (2025). Green taxes innovation and energy imports in advancing renewable transitions in developing countries. *Resources Policy, 102*, 105517. https://doi.org/10.1016/j.resourpol.2025.105517

Rejeb, A., Rejeb, K., Zrelli, I., Kayikci, Y., & Hassoun, A. (2024). The research landscape of industry 5.0: A scientific mapping based on bibliometric and topic modeling techniques. *Flexible Services and Manufacturing Journal*. https://doi.org/10.1007/s10696-024-09584-4

Ribeiro, J. D., Falanga, R., & Moniz, J. (2025). Assessing the role of democratic innovations in environmental sustainability: A systematic literature review. *Sustainable Development, 33*, 7775–7790. https://doi.org/10.1002/sd.3545

Rindermann, R., Sachs, W., & Santarius, T. (2023). Slow trade-sound farming a multilateral framework for sustainable markets in agriculture.

Rodriguez-Perez, N., Matanza, J., Lopez, G., Cossent, R., Chaves Avila, J. P., Mateo, C., Gomez San Roman, T., & Sanchez Fornie, M. A. (2024). Measuring the digitalisation of electricity distribution systems in Europe: Towards the smart grid. *International Journal of Electrical Power & Energy Systems, 159*, 110009. https://doi.org/10.1016/j.ijepes.2024.110009

Romaldi, G., Zoboli, R., Speck, S., Tagliapietra, S., Paleari, S., Pronti, A., & D'Amato, A. (2024). Investment needs and gaps for the sustainability transition in Europe: Rethinking the European Green Deal as an EU industrial strategy. https://www.eionet.europa.eu/etcs/etc-ce/products/etc-ce-report-2024-8-investment-needs-and-gaps-for-the-sustainability-transition-in-europe-rethinking-the-european-green-deal-as-an-eu-industrial-strategy

Rondón-Cordero, V. H., Montuori, L., Alcázar-Ortega, M., & Siano, P. (2025). Advancements in hybrid and ensemble ML models for energy consumption forecasting: Results and challenges of their applications. *Renewable and Sustainable Energy Reviews, 224*, 116095. https://doi.org/10.1016/j.rser.2025.116095

Sabato, S., & Mandelli, M. (2024). Towards an EU framework for a just transition: Welfare policies and politics for the socio-ecological transition. *European Political Science, 23*(1), 14–26. https://doi.org/10.1057/s41304-023-00458-1

Safarzadeh, H., & Di Maria, F. (2025). How to fit energy demand under the constraint of EU 2030 and FIT for 55 goals: An Italian case study. *Sustainability, 17*(8), 3743. https://doi.org/10.3390/su17083743

Santos, M. R., Guedes, A., & Sanchez-Gendriz, I. (2024). SHapley Additive exPlanations (SHAP) for efficient feature selection in rolling bearing fault diagnosis. *Machine Learning and Knowledge Extraction, 6*(1), 316–341. https://doi.org/10.3390/make6010016

Santos, V., da Silva, M., & de Freitas Santos, H. (2025). Modeling and forecasting of energy consumption in urban environments: Exploring the potential of machine learning in energy consumption prediction. https://www.researchgate.net/publication/393472362_Modeling_and_Forecasting_of_Energy_Consumption_in_Urban_Environments_Exploring_the_Potential_of_Machine_Learning_in_Energy_Consumption_Prediction/stats

Smeets Křístková, Z., Cui, H. D., Rokicki, B., M'Barek, R., van Meijl, H., & Boysen-Urban, K. (2025). European green bonds, carbon tax and crowding-out: The economic, social and environmental impacts of the EU's green investments under different financing scenarios. *Renewable and Sustainable Energy Reviews, 211*, 115330. https://doi.org/10.1016/j.rser.2025.115330

Soto, G. H., Nghiem, X.-H., & Martinez-Cobas, X. (2025). Analyzing the role of main energy transition policies upon renewable energy penetration in the EU: An assessment of energy productivity and low carbon economies. *Environmental and Sustainability Indicators, 25*, 100573. https://doi.org/10.1016/j.indic.2024.100573

Timilsina, G. R. (2022). Carbon taxes. *Journal of Economic Literature, 60*(4), 1456–1502. https://doi.org/10.1257/jel.20211560

Touch, V., Tan, D. K. Y., Cook, B. R., Liu, D. L., Cross, R., Tran, T. A., Utomo, A., Yous, S., Grunbuhel, C., & Cowie, A. (2024). Smallholder farmers' challenges and opportunities: Implications for agricultural production, environment and food security. *Journal of Environmental Management, 370*, 122536. https://doi.org/10.1016/j.jenvman.2024.122536

Tsoutsos, T. D., & Stamboulis, Y. A. (2005). The sustainable diffusion of renewable energy technologies as an example of an innovation-focused policy. *Technovation, 25*(7), 753–761. https://doi.org/10.1016/j.technovation.2003.12.003

Twaisan, K., & Barışçı, N. (2022). Integrated distributed energy resources (DER) and microgrids: Modeling and optimization of DERs. *Electronics, 11*(18), 2816. https://doi.org/10.3390/electronics11182816

Umeike, R., Dao, T., & Crawford, S. (2025). State-of-the-art review of resilient smart cities: Progress and challenges. *Urban Governance, 5*(2), 222–239. https://doi.org/10.1016/j.ugj.2025.05.007

United Nations. (2023). *The Paris Agreement.* https://unfccc.int/process-and-meetings/the-paris-agreement

van der Spek, M., Banet, C., Bauer, C., Gabrielli, P., Goldthorpe, W., Mazzotti, M., Munkejord, S. T., Røkke, N. A., Shah, N., Sunny, N., Sutter, D., Trusler, J. M., & Gazzani, M. (2022). Perspective on the hydrogen economy as a pathway to reach net-zero $CO_2$ emissions in Europe. *Energy & Environmental Science, 15*(3), 1034–1077. https://doi.org/10.1039/D1EE02118D

Vezzoni, R. (2023). Green growth for whom, how and why? The REPowerEU plan and the inconsistencies of European Union energy policy. *Energy Research & Social Science, 101*, 103134. https://doi.org/10.1016/j.erss.2023.103134

Wang, Z., Imran, M., Karacan, R., Xu, J., Mirzaliev, S., & Wang, L. (2025). Advancing the hydrogen economy: Optimizing renewable energy for decarbonization and resilience in net-zero networks. *International Journal of Hydrogen Energy, 119*, 406–415. https://doi.org/10.1016/j.ijhydene.2025.03.152

Wei, Y., Yuan, H., & Li, H. (2024). Exploring the contribution of advanced systems in smart city development for the regeneration of urban industrial heritage. *Buildings, 14*, 583. https://doi.org/10.3390/buildings14030583

Wennick, D. (2024). How ideas shape the EU's climate policy: Moving toward the sufficiency paradigm for the EU ETS. *European Policy Analysis, 10*(2), 206–224. https://doi.org/10.1002/epa2.1186

Yang, C., Guan, X., Xu, Q., Xing, W., Chen, X., Chen, J., & Jia, P. (2024). How can SHAP (SHapley Additive exPlanations) interpretations improve deep learning based urban cellular automata model? *Computers, Environment and Urban Systems, 111*, 102133. https://doi.org/10.1016/j.compenvurbsys.2024.102133

Yang, S., & Fu, Y. (2025). Interconnectedness among supply chain disruptions, energy crisis, and oil market volatility on economic resilience. *Energy Economics, 143*, 108290. https://doi.org/10.1016/j.eneco.2025.108290

Zarghami, S. A. (2025). The role of economic policies in achieving sustainable development goal 7: Insights from OECD and European countries. *Applied Energy, 377*, 124558. https://doi.org/10.1016/j.apenergy.2024.124558

Zhang, Q., Wang, L., Chen, W., & Zhang, C. (2024). Assessing the impact of hydrogen trade towards low-carbon energy transition. *Applied Energy, 376*, 124233. https://doi.org/10.1016/j.apenergy.2024.124233

Zhao, H., & Lin, B. (2025). Rising inequality in the European Union under stringent climate policy: Internal challenges of carbon border adjustment mechanism. *Energy Economics, 142*, 108180. https://doi.org/10.1016/j.eneco.2025.108180

Zhou, Z., Zeng, C., Li, K., Yang, Y., Zhao, K., & Wang, Z. (2024). Decomposition of the decoupling between electricity $CO_2$ emissions and economic growth: A production and consumption perspective. *Energy, 293*, 130644. https://doi.org/10.1016/j.energy.2024.130644

Żywiołek, J., Wolniak, R., & Grebski, W. W. (2025). From traditional to digital: The paradigm shift in the energy sector through green innovation. *Energy Reports, 14*, 1–16. https://doi.org/10.1016/j.egyr.2025.05.080

CHAPTER 5

# New Models of Impact on European Energy Sustainability Using Panel Data Analysis

## Introduction

In a European context characterized by multiple transitions on ecological, digital and social, Sustainable Development Goal 8 (SDG 8), which aims to promote sustained, inclusive and sustainable economic growth, as well as full and productive employment, becomes a fundamental strategic benchmark in building a resilient and equitable economy. This dimension has become increasingly relevant in the wake of the overlapping crises of the last decade: the sovereign debt crisis, the COVID-19 pandemic and the instability generated by the conflict in Ukraine—which have exposed deep structural vulnerabilities in the economic growth models and social protection systems of the European Union Member States.

Against this backdrop, progress towards SDG 8 can no longer be measured solely in terms of traditional macroeconomic performance but must integrate qualitative and structural variables such as resource efficiency, income distribution equity, employment in green sectors and the degree of technological innovation. In this regard, the statistical indicators of SDG 8, such as GDP per capita, employment rate, labour productivity, long-term unemployment and the share of young people who are not in education, employment or training (NEET), provide a comprehensive framework for assessing sustainable economic convergence among Member States.



C. Fortea, *Sustainable Economic Development and the European Green Deal*, https://doi.org/10.1007/978-3-032-10326-0_5

This chapter aims to provide a rigorous empirical modelling of the relationship between sustainable development and economic performance in the European Union, based on a set of key variables associated with SDG 8 targets. By applying multiple regression models, complemented by variable selection using the Backward Feature Selection (BFS) algorithm, the analysis identifies the most relevant determinants of sustainable economic growth in the EU and outlines distinct statistical profiles at Member State level.

The chapter thus makes a significant contribution to the literature, not only by empirically validating hypotheses about the interdependence between employment, productivity and economic inclusion but also by providing public policy directions aimed at balancing competitiveness objectives with the imperatives of social cohesion and just transition. In this sense, the proposed analysis provides a relevant framework for understanding how the European Union can simultaneously advance towards economic prosperity and societal sustainability, in line with the vision of the 2030 Agenda.

## Modelling the Impact of Energy Sustainability by Quantifying the Correlated Balance of Energy Efficiency on Greenhouse Gas Emissions

The achievement of climate neutrality is a major European objective, which is underpinned by far-reaching reforms of the European economy, including in the field of energy. Achieving energy efficiency is a means of minimizing greenhouse gas emissions, for which substantial resources have been allocated at European level. The literature review conducted in Chap. 3 highlighted the concern of researchers to identify econometric models to help monitor vulnerabilities in achieving climate neutrality. Utilizing a complex methodology (based on Dynamic Ordinary Least Squares [DOLS], Fully Modified Ordinary Least Squares [FMOLS], Mean-Group [MG] and Pooled Mean-Group [PMG] regression and estimation models) Sarkodie et al. (2020) demonstrate the inseparable link of emissions with energy use, energy consumption and population dynamics.

In the context of a growing global aspiration for wealth accumulation and economic progress, the intensive exploitation of natural resources for various industries has led to an increase in emissions of pollutants, especially carbon dioxide. Now, more than ever, it is important than ever to find solutions for energy security, economic stability, job security, reducing biodiversity loss, as well as for combating climate change and global warming. In a recent research Mitić and colleagues (Mitić et al., 2023) have explored the causal relationship between $CO_2$ emissions, economic growth, available energy and employment for a panel of eight SEE countries over the period 1995–2019, with results showing a bidirectional short-run causality between $CO_2$ emissions and employment and between available energy and employment, as well as a unidirectional causality between available energy and employment and GDP.

The role of economic policy in boosting energy efficiency from theoretical, empirical and existing policy perspective to assess the relationship between energy efficiency and economic policy a research was conducted by Mushafiq et al. (2023), who tried to identify existing problems from the perspective of energy efficiency policies. In another study Wang et al. (2016) analysed the relationship between economic growth, energy consumption and $CO_2$ emissions for governments to develop energy saving and emission reduction strategies to cope with climate change impacts; the authors investigated the co-interesting, time-dynamic and casual relationships that exist between economic growth, energy consumption and $CO_2$ emissions. The relationship between per capita carbon dioxide emissions, economic complexity index, renewable energy and inward foreign direct investment using panel data for the BRICS countries over the period 1995–2020 was analysed by Balsalobre-Lorente et al. (2023). Maintaining environmental sustainability has become a priority on the agenda of almost all nations today. The association between digital finance, financial inclusion, renewable energy and institutional quality with environmental sustainability is realized in a research (Ansari et al., 2024) which supports the United Nations Sustainable Development Goals, in particular SDG11 for sustainable societies and SDG13 to mitigate vulnerability to climate change. The authors used data from 2004 to 2021 to explore the relationship between the studied variables. Using the autoregressive with lagged distribution (ARDL) model, symmetric long-run and short-run relationships between the variables were examined. The study also investigates the moderate impact on environmental sustainability by analysing the interaction term between institutional quality and digital finance. The results showed that financial inclusion and digital finance can help developing countries to achieve environmental sustainability. The study also underlines the vital role of renewable energy sources in reducing long-term carbon emissions. Moreover, the interaction between digital finance and institutional quality holds positive prospects for advancing environmental sustainability.

These findings emphasize the need to redefine financial inclusion and give top priority to environmental sustainability projects. They provide valuable insights for policy-makers and digital financial service providers in less developed countries. In addition, the study highlights the importance of robust financial institutions that prioritize renewable energy and institutional integrity for financial health and long-term growth.

Numerous studies have analysed the relationship between the amount of primary energy consumed and greenhouse gas emissions. AlShafeey and Rashdan (2023) examined how energy policy and energy production technologies affect greenhouse gas emissions. Thus in the economic and energy literature, there is a wide range of studies analysing how energy policy and technologies influence greenhouse gas emissions (Grubb et al., 2021; Li et al., 2021; Osobajo et al., 2020; Wang & Azam, 2024). Other researches (Firtescu et al., 2023; Hassan, 2023; Holechek et al., 2022) have argued that the implementation of taxes or regulations that penalize greenhouse gas emissions can reduce dependence on fossil fuels and promote the use of less polluting energy sources such as renewables. Empirical studies have shown that such policies have led to significant decreases in greenhouse gas emissions in countries where they have been implemented. The role of technological innovation in reducing greenhouse gas emissions has been captured in the literature. Investments in research and development for more energy-efficient technologies and renewable energy sources can reduce dependence on fossil fuels and thus reduce associated greenhouse gas emissions [155–157]. The analysis of the costs and benefits of energy policy is supported in various specialized studies (Doan et al., 2023; Gudlaugsson et al., 2023), showing that switching to cleaner energy sources can have long-term economic benefits. Although initially there may be transition costs, the savings realized by reducing climate change damages and increasing energy efficiency can outweigh the initial costs and lead to a more sustainable and resilient economy.

The empirical studies and economic models used in this research provide a deep understanding of how energy policy and technologies can influence greenhouse gas emissions and provide guidance for effective public policy-making to combat climate change. The literature therefore provides substantial evidence by which we can formulate the following hypothesis:

H1—there is a significant direct dependence between the amount of primary energy supplied and the level of greenhouse gas emissions.

In the face of the increasingly evident challenges of climate change and the need to reduce greenhouse gas emissions, it is of interest to explore the interdependence between energy policies and environmental impacts. Thus, economic, political and environmental factors contribute to the phenomenon of increasing energy import dependency with effects on the level of greenhouse gas emissions.

Empirical studies and economic modelling in the literature show that increased dependence on fossil fuel imports is associated with increased greenhouse gas emissions. For example, a study by Azni et al. (2023) shows that the world's long-standing reliance on fossil fuel energy has produced numerous negative impacts, and long-term dependence on fossil fuels has increased carbon emissions and accelerated climate change. Empirical findings from another study have shown that the use of natural gas, oil and coal-based energy reduces environmental sustainability, with oil consumption having the most significant impact (Adebayo et al., 2021). The energy sector being one of the main contributors to environmental degradation. Pan and colleagues (2024) examined the impact of energy imports and natural resource revenues on environmental degradation in the Asia-Pacific Economic Cooperation (APEC) countries over the period 1990–2020, using revenues minus the production cost of natural gas and renewable electricity production as moderating variables, and found that importing energy from countries specializing in renewable energy can help reduce dependence on fossil fuels. This diversification of energy sources reduces the global carbon footprint and contributes to a cleaner environment.

Analysis of data from different countries shows that the processes of extraction and transportation of imported fossil fuels are often associated with significant greenhouse gas emissions. For example, a report by the International Energy Agency (International Energy Agency, 2021) shows that maritime and land transportation of oil and natural gas can lead to significant emissions of $CO_2$, methane and other greenhouse gases. Another report by the International Renewable Energy Agency (International Renewable Energy Agency, 2023) shows that the events of recent years have highlighted the cost that centralized energy systems, heavily dependent on fossil fuels, are having on the global economy. Oil and gas prices are reaching new highs, with the crisis in Ukraine adding new levels of concern and uncertainty. The COVID-19 pandemic continues to hamper recovery efforts, while citizens around the world are concerned about the affordability of their energy bills. At the same time, the impacts of man-made climate change are becoming increasingly evident globally. The Intergovernmental Panel on Climate Change (IPCC) warns that between 3.3 and 3.6 billion people already live in environments highly vulnerable to climate change.

Vulnerability to price fluctuations and political instability was an important aspect of study. The literature has shown that dependence on energy imports can expose a country to risks associated with price fluctuations and political instability in supplier countries (Kim et al., 2024). These risks may lead to a reassessment of energy policy and an increase in the consumption of domestic fossil fuels, which may contribute to increased greenhouse gas emissions. Other studies [166–168] have shown that oil price fluctuations can have a significant impact on energy policy and GHG emissions in importing countries. During periods of low prices, oil and gas consumption may increase, which may increase greenhouse gas emissions. A country's energy policy can influence the level of dependence on energy imports and hence greenhouse gas emissions. Policies that favour traditional energy sources, such as oil and natural gas, can lead to an increase in import dependence and greenhouse gas emissions (Carfora et al., 2022). Analysis of energy policies in various countries shows that some governments are taking measures to encourage the use of domestic energy resources, which can reduce import dependence and help reduce greenhouse gas emissions associated with the transportation and extraction of imported fossil fuels (IRENA, 2024). Several economic models and simulations have been used to assess the impact of increased energy import dependence on long-term greenhouse gas emissions. These models have taken into account factors such as energy policy, energy price developments and international economic interactions to forecast the evolution of greenhouse gas emissions under different scenarios (Carton et al., 2023; Osman et al., 2023). The analysis of economic simulations and general equilibrium models have shown that reducing energy import dependence and switching to cleaner energy sources can significantly contribute to reducing greenhouse gas emissions. These studies provide important guidance for the development of public policies and strategies to manage energy dependency in the context of the fight against climate change.

By analysing these issues, we can provide a better understanding of the environmental implications of energy import dependency and identify possible courses of action for a more sustainable and responsible energy policy in terms of greenhouse gas emissions.

The analysis of the relationship between energy policies and greenhouse gas emissions has recently become a topic of interest for researchers in the current context of climate change and efforts to combat it, the following working hypothesis can be formulated:

H2—increasing dependence on energy imports has a long-term effect on increasing greenhouse gas emissions.

Current climate change and sustainability concerns on analysing the relationship between energy fiscal policies and greenhouse gas emissions are significant, where the need for a transition to cleaner energy sources is confronted with the economic and political challenges of increasing sectoral activity in the energy sector.

Studies in economics and energy policy have identified a direct link between increased fossil fuel consumption and increased greenhouse gas emissions. Yamaka and colleagues (2021) analysed the economic and energy impacts on climate change as measured by greenhouse gas emissions in China and the United States. The results of the study showed that the impact of economic factors for China and the United States is slightly different; economic factors in China increase greenhouse gas emissions, while in the United States there is a decrease in greenhouse gas emissions, and renewable energy production leads to sustainable development in both the United States and China. Another study examined the links between renewable and non-renewable energy use, $CO_2$ emissions and economic growth in developed, developing, least developed and transition economies between 1990 and 2019 in 152 countries (Dissanayake et al., 2023). The findings of the study showed that GDP and $CO_2$ have a bidirectional relationship in transition economies, a unidirectional relationship in developing countries and no significant association in developed and least developed countries. It is therefore important to focus on actions to reduce $CO_2$ emissions and develop renewable energy while stimulating the economy. Other studies have shown that every percentage increase in oil and coal consumption is associated with a proportional increase in $CO_2$ (Jiang & Sun, 2023; McKinsey & Company, 2024).

Economic models that have analysed different growth scenarios have shown that higher sectoral activity can lead to higher energy demand, most of which comes from traditional sources such as oil and coal. This trend may directly contribute to increased greenhouse gas emissions (Farghali et al., 2023a; Lindholt & Wei, 2023; van Vuuren et al., 2017). Various empirical studies and economic simulations have shown that an increase in oil and gas consumption is associated with a direct increase in $CO_2$ (Mitić et al., 2023; Onofrei et al., 2022; Osobajo et al., 2020; Alaganthiran & Anaba, 2022).

The trend to promote the exploitation of more polluting resources is also reported in the literature which shows that some government policies may favour the exploitation of more polluting resources, such as oil and natural gas, to increase energy tax revenues. This trend may lead to increased activity in the sector and, by extension, to increased greenhouse gas emissions (Aquilas et al., 2024; Azam et al., 2023; Yanyan Zhang et al., 2022b).

Analysis of tax policies in different countries shows that subsidies and tax incentives to the fossil fuel industry can create an enabling environment for increased activity in this sector; subsidies to the fossil fuel industry have contributed significantly to increased exploitation of more polluting resources and increased greenhouse gas emissions (OECD, 2013, 2021; United Nations Environment Programme, 2019). The impact of fossil fuel subsidy policy is studied in the literature. Studies show that subsidies to the fossil fuel industry can encourage increased consumption and exploitation of fossil fuels, thus leading to higher $CO_2$ (Black et al., 2023; de Bruin & Yakut, 2023; van den Bergh et al., 2024) and the elimination of fossil fuel subsidies could significantly reduce global $CO_2$ emissions by 2030 (Arzaghi & Squalli, 2023; Bassi et al., 2023). Fiscal and economic policies can have a significant impact on the activity of the energy sector and thus on greenhouse gas emissions. Policies that promote the exploitation of more polluting resources or that do not consider the external costs of pollution can contribute to increased greenhouse gas emissions.

Analysis of the effectiveness of fiscal instruments and analysis of energy subsidy policies can significantly influence the energy mix and the level of greenhouse gas emissions. Studies in the literature that have been conducted to assess the effectiveness of fiscal instruments and subsidy policies in reducing greenhouse gas emissions have shown that the introduction of fiscal taxes and the removal or substantial reduction of fossil fuel subsidies can influence energy production and consumption decisions, thus having a direct impact on the environment and climate change can reduce $CO_2$

emissions and encourage the transition to cleaner energy sources (Antimiani et al., 2023; Hussain et al., 2023; Li et al., 2024).

By analysing the literature and the complex interactions between fiscal policy, energy sector activity and greenhouse gas emissions, the following working hypothesis can be formulated:

H3—the increase in energy tax revenues because of increased sectoral activity has a significant direct impact on the increase in greenhouse gas emissions.

This underlines the need for a balanced approach to sustainable energy and fiscal policy to promote an efficient transition to a cleaner and more environmentally sustainable energy system.

These studies support the desirability of developing a new econometric impact model capable of quantifying the effect of primary energy production, energy sector focalization and energy import dependence on net greenhouse gas emissions as a sensitivity indicator of energy sustainability.

The following indicators were used to develop the econometric model: net greenhouse gas emissions (SDG7ENGS), total primary energy supply (SDG7FZEP), energy import dependence (SDG7IMPEN) and energy-related tax revenues (SDG7VFEN).

These indicators have been assessed on the basis of descriptive statistics for the period 2010–2021 considering national developments for each indicator for all EU Member States, the database being organized in panel data as presented in Table 4.1. The results of the descriptive analysis are presented in Table 5.1.

The descriptive statistics table shows a trend of polarization of the mean average of the selected dependent variable at the level of 80% of the

**Table 5.1** Descriptive statistics

| *Variable* | *SDG7ENGS* | *SDG7IMPEN* | *SDG7FZEP* | *SDG7VFEN* |
|---|---|---|---|---|
| Comments | 324 | 324 | 324 | 324 |
| Average | 80.40 | 56.77 | 52.77 | 75.41 |
| Standard deviation | 28.01 | 24.39 | 74.19 | 11.35 |
| Minim | 22.1 | −16.23 | 0.6 | 45.55 |
| Maxim | 162.6 | 104.13 | 329.55 | 93.43 |

Source: Author

amount of greenhouse gas emissions in 1990. At the same time, we observe a standard deviation of the frequency of the dependent variable of 28%, a significant amount that captures the effects of policy changes to protect the environment and combat climate change. The other regression indicators contain smaller standard deviations (SDG7IMPEN and SDG7VFEN), while SDG7FZEP has a very large standard deviation which confirms significant changes at Member State level and in the dynamics of the indicator. Regarding the dependence on energy imports, it can be observed that the average frequency is 56.67%, which represents a significant dependence threshold. The total supply of primary energy shows a tendency for a marked dispersion of values in relation to the calculated average of 52.77 million tonnes of oil equivalent, with the Member States exceeding the average by up to six times during the period analysed, but also with values close to 0, which indicates a disparity in energy policies that is assimilated to a low efficiency in this area. The fight against climate change has involved identifying polluting industries at European level, including the energy industry. To support environmental reforms, the European Union has established an energy-related tax policy which, according to the energy-related tax revenue indicator, averages 75.41% of total environmental tax revenue.

Variable testing was carried out as a preliminary step in the conceptualization of the model, the first tests being the autocorrelation tests presented in Table 5.2.

According to the results in Table 5.2, there is a lack of autocorrelation, the values of the coefficients being lower than the autocorrelation threshold of 0.7, which allows modelling the data.

**Table 5.2** Correlation matrix of the variables of the energy sustainability impact model by quantifying the correlation balance of energy efficiency on greenhouse gas emissions

| *Variable* | *SDG7ENGS* | *SDG7IMPEN* | *SDG7FZEP* | *SDG7VFEN* |
|---|---|---|---|---|
| SDG7ENGS | 1.000 | | | |
| SDG7IMPEN | 0.5003 | 1.000 | | |
| SDG7FZEP | −0.0169 | −0.0146 | 1.000 | |
| SDG7VFEN | −0.3635 | −0.1282 | 0.0738 | 1.000 |

Source: Author

The Levin-Lin-Chin, Breitung, Im-Pesaran-Shin, ADF-Fisher Chi-square, PP-Fisher Chi-square and Hadri stationarity tests were applied. The results are presented centralized in Table 5.3.

Five different two-order (order 0 and order 1) stationarity tests were applied for four data series (SDG7IENGS, SDG7IMPEN, SDG7FZEP, SDG7VFFEN). The tests aim to determine the stationarity of the data by rejecting the null hypothesis. The value of the statistical test and the associated p-value confirm the stationarity of 0 or 1 order of the variables.

The Levin-Lin-Chin test tested the null hypothesis that the series is non-stationary. Significant negative values ($p < 0.05$) for SDG7IENGS, SDG7IMPEN and SDG7FZEP suggest rejection of the null hypothesis and indicate stationarity of the series at 0 order. The indicator SDG7VFEN has a lower statistical value (−2.165) with a p-value (0.015), still indicating stationarity at order 1. By the Breitung test, similar to Levin-Lin-Chin, non-stationarity of the data was tested. According to this test most of the results are negative and significant except for SDG7IMPEN at order 0, indicating stationarity at order 1 for most data series. Another hypothesis test for non-stationarity is Im-Pesaran-Shin. Mixed results were obtained, i.e. some series are stationary at order 1 (SDG7IMPEN, SDG7VFEN), while others show no clear stationarity.

The ADF-Fisher Chi-square test tests for non-stationarity using an augmented Dickey-Fuller test applied for each individual series. In this test, p-values are varied; for SDG7FZEP and SDG7VFEN at order 1, p-values are extremely small, indicating stationarity. The PP-Fisher Chi-square test uses the Phillips-Perron method to test for stationarity. The test results indicate that SDG7IENGS and SDG7FZEP are stationary at order 1, according to very small p-values. The Hadri test applied to test stationarity confirmed the alternative hypothesis and rejected the null hypothesis for all variables. In this case, all series are stationary, with small p-values at both orders.

In conclusion, the SDG7IENGS, SDG7IMPEN and SDG7VFEN series are first-order integrated, while the SDG7FZEP series is 0-order integrated. For this reason, we use an ARDL model.

The data were checked for cointegration using the Pedroni cointegration test presented in Table 5.4.

By analysing Table 5.4 we can say that we reject the null hypothesis and accept the alternative hypothesis, i.e. the series are cointegrated.

To determine the type of model (PMG—Pooled Mean Group or MG—Mean Group) the Hausman test was applied, where the null hypothesis

**Table 5.3** Stationarity tests

| *The stationarity test* | *SDG7IENGS* | | *SDG7IMPEN* | | *SDG7FZEP* | | *SDG7VFEN* | |
|---|---|---|---|---|---|---|---|---|
| | *Order 0* | *Order 1* | *Order 0* | *Order 1* | *Order 0* | *Order 1* | *Order 0* | *Order 1* |
| Levin-Lin-Chin | −3.958 | NA | −3.4772 | NA | −5.508 | NA | −2.165 | NA |
| | (0.000) | | (0.000) | | (0.000) | | (0.015) | |
| Breitung | −3.072 | NA | 1.591 | −3.647 | −3.275 | NA | −1.611 | −3.200 |
| | (0.001) | | (0.944) | (0.001) | (0.001) | | (0.054) | (0.001) |
| Im-Pesaran-Shin | −1.351 | −0.519 | −0.782 | −3.142 | −1.030 | −0.141 | 0.449 | −4.019 |
| | (0.088) | (0.302) | (0.217) | (0.000) | (0.151) | (0.444) | (0.673) | (0.000) |
| ADF-Fisher | 67.553 | 59.824 | 59.790 | 111.344 | 59.102 | 55.457 | 47.448 | 137.555 |
| Chi-square | (0.101) | (0.2726) | (0.274) | (0.000) | (0.294) | (0.420) | (0.723) | (0.000) |
| PP-Fisher | 55.371 | 118.486 | 134.248 | NA | 103.864 | NA | 85.067 | NA |
| Chi-square | (0.423) | (0.000) | (0.000) | | (0.000) | | (0.004) | |
| Hadri | 7.697 | 11.649 | 8.3418 | 14.113 | 8.558 | 9.214 | 9.699 | 14.441 |
| | (0.000) | (0.000) | (0.000) | (0.000) | (0.000) | (0.000) | (0.000) | (0.000) |

Source: Author

**Table 5.4** Pedroni residual cointegration test

*Pedroni residual cointegration test*

Series: SDG7ENGS, SDG7FZEP, SDG7IMPEN, SDG7VFEN
Sample: 2010–2021
Remarks included: 324
Cross-sections included: 27
Null hypothesis: No cointegration
The trend hypothesis: No deterministic trend
User-specified lag length: 1
Automatic Newey-West and Bartlett Kernel bandwidth selection
Alternative hypothesis: common AR coefficients (within dimension).

| | Statistic | Prob. | Statistics Considered | Prob. |
|---|---|---|---|---|
| Panel v-Statistic | −1.560354 | 0.9407 | −1.770854 | 0.9617 |
| Rho-Statistic Panel | 3.190112 | 0.9993 | 2.370297 | 0.9911 |
| Panel PP-Statistic | −0.013541 | 0.4946 | −2.323004 | 0.0101 |
| Panel ADF-Statistic | 1.306943 | 0.9044 | 0.385178 | 0.6499 |

Alternative hypothesis: individual AR coefficients (between dimensions)

| | Statistic | Prob. |
|---|---|---|
| Group rho-Statistic | 4.738881 | 1.0000 |
| Group PP-Statistic | −3.020294 | 0.0013 |
| Group ADF-Statistic | 1.138660 | 0.8726 |

Source: Author

means that the model is MG and the alternative hypothesis PMG model (see Table 5.5).

After applying the Hausman test, it was concluded that the null hypothesis is rejected and the alternative hypothesis is accepted, and the PMG model will be used. The Pooled Mean Group (PMG) model, developed by Pesaran, Shin and Smith (Pesaran et al., 1999), is an extension of the MG model. This model is used when it is assumed that there is a common long-run relationship between variables in different cross-sections, but short-run behaviour may vary. PMG is efficient for long-run estimates while retaining the flexibility to model group-specific dynamics in the short run. The PMG model is often preferred in situations where there is reason to believe that long-run relationships are stable across groups, but short-run adjustments may differ.

In the literature, the PMG model has been applied in various fields, including studies related to energy policy and its impact on the environment (Bosah et al., 2021; Isiksal & Assi, 2022; Li et al., 2023b). Using

**Table 5.5** Hausman test

| *Variable* | *Coefficients* | | *Difference* | *Standard error* |
|---|---|---|---|---|
| | *(b)* *mg* | *(B)* *pmg* | *(b-B)* | |
| SDG7IMPEN | 3.826,174 | 0.401509 | 3.424,665 | 21.0611 |
| SDG7FZEP | −9.709,461 | 0.6,008,449 | −10.31031 | 142.6438 |
| SDG7VFEN | 3.75,895 | −1.759,012 | 5.517,962 | 15.7165 |

b = consistent under null and alternative hypothesis; obtained from xtpmg
B = inconsistent under alternative hypothesis, efficient under null hypothesis; obtained from xtpmg
Test: Null hypothesis: The difference in coefficients is not systematic
$Chi^2$ (2) = 0.24, Prob>$chi^2$ = 0.9713

Source: Author

PMG in these contexts has allowed researchers to analyse the complex relationships between macroeconomic variables, energy policy and greenhouse gas emissions in a more comprehensive and rigorous way (Georgescu et al., 2024; Sreenu, 2022). The PMG model has been used to analyse the relationships between economic variables and regional development in different countries and regions (Ben-Salha et al., 2021; Jouini, 2015). By applying PMG, researchers can investigate how economic policy and structural factors influence economic growth and regional disparities (Aksoy, 2019; Chu et al., 2023; Udeagha & Muchapondwa, 2022). These analyses are important for the design of public policies that promote balanced and sustainable regional development. In the field of finance and capital markets, the PMG model has been used to study the interdependencies between global and local financial markets (Lone et al., 2023; Tabash et al., 2023), the association between digital finance, financial inclusion, renewable energy and institutional quality with sustainability (Ansari et al., 2024; Jebli & Hakimi, 2023). Research has examined how changes in international capital markets affect local financial markets and vice versa. Using GMP in this context allows a deeper understanding of the transmission of financial shocks and the stability of the financial system. Economic and social analyses related to urbanization and urban mobility have also benefited from the application of the PMG model (Ecer et al., 2023; Hongxing et al., 2021; Liu et al., 2023). Research in this area has investigated the impact of urban policy and transport infrastructure on the quality of life in cities and on population mobility. The use of PMG allows to assess the effectiveness of different urban policies and to identify best practices for managing urban population growth and mobility.

In all these areas, the literature points out that the application of the PMG model brings significant benefits in understanding and analysing the complex relationships between relevant variables. This method allows researchers to investigate more precisely and rigorously the impact of different policies and phenomena on economic and social outcomes, contributing to more effective policy-making and to the development of strategies that are better oriented towards sustainability and sustainable economic growth.

The ARDL model equation is as follows:

$$y_{i,t} = \sum_{i=1}^{p} \delta_i y_{i,t-j} + \sum_{j=0}^{q} \beta_{ij} x_{i,t-j} + \varphi_i + e_{i,t} \quad (5.1)$$

waves:

- $y_{i,\,t}$—is the dependent variable, net greenhouse gas emissions (SDG7ENGS);
- $x_{i,\,t}$—are the integrated or cointegrated independent variables I(0) or I(1), total primary energy supply (SDG7FZEP), energy import dependence (SDG7IMPEN) and energy-related tax revenue (SDG7VFEN)
- $\delta_i$—are the coefficients of the lagged dependent variables
- $\beta_{ij}$—are the coefficients of the independent variables
- $\varphi_i$—is the unit specific to fixed bills
- p,q—are the optional delay values
- $e_{i,\,t}$—is the error.

Econometric model evaluation tests were applied, and the results are presented in Table 5.6.

The Pooled Mean Group (PMG) model with specification (2,1,2,0) provides a detailed understanding of the long-run and short-run relationships between environmental and energy economic variables. The model estimation results for the selected variables show a strong dependence of the evolution of greenhouse gas emissions on the evolution of the regressors (SDG7FZEP, SDG7IMPEN and DD7VFEN).

**Table 5.6** PMG model summary (2,1,2,0)

| *Variable* | *Coefficient* | *Standard error* | *t-Statistic* | *Prob.* |
|---|---|---|---|---|
| | Long-term coefficients (grouped) | | | |
| SDG7FZEP | 1.785569 | 0.085941 | 20.77667 | 0.0000 |
| SDG7IMPEN | 0.461086 | 0.045242 | 10.19165 | 0.0000 |
| SDG7VFEN | 0.441718 | 0.045220 | 9.768252 | 0.0000 |
| | Short-term coefficients (group average) | | | |
| COINTEQ | −0.108218 | 0.043335 | −2.497272 | 0.0131 |
| D(SDG7ENGS(−1)) | −0.007596 | 0.081536 | −0.093158 | 0.9258 |
| D(SDG7FZEP) | 10.82284 | 4.788432 | 2.260206 | 0.0246 |
| D(SDG7IMPEN) | −0.214472 | 0.207543 | −1.033386 | 0.3024 |
| D(SDG7IMPEN(−1)) | −0.222044 | 0.156585 | −1.418040 | 0.1574 |
| Log-Likelihood: | −606.2111 | | | |

Source: Author

In the long run all three variables have a positive impact on the dependent variable. In addition, all these variables are statistically significant.

The coefficient of SDG7FZEP is 1.78 with a standard error of 0.085, showing a t-statistic of 20.77, implying extremely high statistical significance ($p = 0.0000$) and suggesting that each unit added to the total primary energy supply has a positive and significant long-run impact on the dependent variable. This positive and significant coefficient for the indicator SDG7FZEP indicates a direct impact of increased energy supply on the dependent variable. These aspects demonstrate Hypothesis I1—there is a significant direct dependence between the amount of primary energy supplied and the level of greenhouse gas emissions. In the context of sustainable development, this suggests that an increase in the availability of energy, including renewables, is important to sustain economic growth and to facilitate the transition to cleaner and more energy-efficient technologies. In Europe, investments in green energy and energy infrastructure have an important role to play in achieving sustainability goals.

The results obtained for the validation of Hypothesis H1 are consistent with the findings in the literature on the relationship between primary energy supply and the level of greenhouse gas emissions (Chien et al., 2022; He et al., 2022; Mohsin et al., 2021). Previous studies have also found a positive association between the amount of primary energy used and greenhouse gas emissions, supporting the hypothesis that there is a significant direct dependence between these two variables (Ali et al., 2021; Deng et al., 2020; Wang et al., 2022). Various studies have analysed empirical data to assess the link between primary energy consumption and GHG emissions in different countries or regions (Chien et al., 2022; Nawaz et al., 2021). These studies provide direct evidence of a positive association between energy supply and greenhouse gas emissions.

As for the SDG7FZEP coefficient, the positive and significant value, as well as the long-term impact on the dependent variable, is in line with the findings in the literature. These findings confirm that increasing primary energy supply, including renewables, can have a positive and significant effect on the level of GHG emissions (Azam et al., 2021; Chien et al., 2022; Mostafaeipour et al., 2022).

In the context of sustainable development, the results suggest that an increase in energy availability is useful for sustaining economic growth and facilitating the transition to cleaner and more energy-efficient technologies (Alam et al., 2022). Investments in green energy and energy infrastructure have been recognized as having an important role to play in achieving sustainability goals, and the results underline their importance in the context of climate change for achieving climate neutrality.

In conclusion, the results obtained are consistent with the literature and support the hypothesis that there is a significant direct dependence between the amount of primary energy supplied and the level of greenhouse gas emissions. These findings underline the importance of continuing efforts to promote sustainable energy sources and to implement policies and investments that support the transition towards a cleaner and more sustainable energy system.

The SDG7IMPEN indicator has a coefficient of 0.46, a standard error of 0.045 and a t-statistic of 10.19, with high statistical significance ($p = 0.0000$) indicating that an increase in energy import dependence is associated with a significant long-term increase in greenhouse gas emissions. These findings support working Hypothesis 2—increasing energy import dependence has a long-run effect on increasing GHG emissions. Increasing energy import dependence is a challenge for sustainability as dependence on external resources can be volatile and undermine energy security. Europe needs to balance the need for imports with the development of domestic renewable energy production capacities to reduce dependence and improve resilience to global market fluctuations.

The results obtained in the validation of Hypothesis 2, indicating a significant association between energy import dependence and increased greenhouse gas emissions, are consistent with previous research in the literature. These findings reflect recurring concerns in the energy and environmental fields about the negative impacts of energy import dependence on energy sustainability and security and on the environment. The positive association between dependence on energy imports and increased greenhouse gas emissions is also found in other studies (Rehman et al., 2021; Wenlong et al., 2023). This is because energy imports, especially from conventional sources such as fossil fuels, are associated with higher emissions compared to domestic energy production or renewable sources. In this context, the results highlight once again the importance of managing energy import dependency and promoting cleaner and more sustainable energy mixes. At the same time, the finding that increasing import dependence may undermine energy security and create vulnerabilities to global market fluctuations is in line with the literature that has highlighted the risks associated with excessive reliance on external energy sources (Cevik, 2024; Zhu et al., 2023). These risks include exposure to sudden price changes or geopolitical instability in supplying regions. The results obtained indicate that a significant long-term increase in greenhouse gas emissions in association with an increase in energy import dependence is in line with the findings of previous studies which have shown that this dependence has negative long-term environmental effects.

The analysis of the impact of increasing import dependence on energy sustainability and security is an important disputed topic in the literature. The results of the analysis highlight these challenges and emphasize the need to develop domestic renewable energy production capacities to reduce dependence and improve resilience to global market fluctuations (Hasselqvist et al., 2022; Juhola et al., 2024; Osman et al., 2023).

The results obtained make a useful contribution to the literature on the relationship between energy import dependence and greenhouse gas emissions, emphasizing the need to adopt energy policies and strategies that promote energy independence and sustainability in line with sustainable development, environmental and climate objectives. This extensive link between the results of the analysis and the literature reinforces the conclusions and their relevance in the context of the current energy and environment debates.

The coefficient of the SDG7VFEN indicator is 0.44, standard error of 0.045 and t-statistic of 9.76 ($p = 0.0000$) signifying a positive long-run relationship between energy-related tax revenues and the dependent variable (SDG7ENGS). This demonstrates working hypothesis I3—increasing energy-related tax revenues as an effect of increased sectoral activity has a significant direct impact on the growth of greenhouse gas emissions.

The positive impact of energy-related tax revenues suggests that energy taxes (e.g. carbon or fossil fuel taxes) have a significant role in shaping consumer and industry behaviour. These revenues can be reinvested in sustainable development projects, including renewable energy subsidies, energy efficiency and green infrastructure projects. In Europe, the strategic use of tax revenues can accelerate the transition to a cleaner and less fossil fuel dependent economy. There is ample research to support the conclusions from the validation of Hypothesis 3, which shows a significant positive relationship between energy-related tax revenues and greenhouse gas emissions growth. Previous studies have shown a positive relationship between energy-related tax revenues and the level of greenhouse gas emissions (Nong et al., 2021; Zhang et al., 2021, 2022b). This is due to the fact that taxes and charges on energy consumed, particularly on fossil fuels, can influence consumer and industrial behaviour, leading to more intensive use of more carbon-intensive energy sources. Some authors (Aziz et al., 2024; Li et al., 2023b) stress the importance of fiscal policies in promoting responsible energy behaviour and reducing greenhouse gas emissions. Carbon or fossil fuel taxes are seen as effective tools for internalizing the social and environmental costs associated with the use of these non-renewable resources (Nchofoung et al., 2023; Sarpong et al., 2023; Wolde-Rufael & Mulat-weldemeskel, 2023). An important aspect highlighted by recent studies is the need to reinvest tax revenues from the energy sector in sustainable development projects (Filipović et al., 2022; Hassan, 2023; He et al., 2023). These may include subsidizing renewable energy, promoting energy efficiency and investing in green infrastructure such as smart grids and sustainable transport.

Therefore, the results of the analysis are in line with previous research and support Hypothesis 3, highlighting the importance of tax policy in shaping energy behaviour and promoting a cleaner and more sustainable economy. The strategic use of tax revenues from the energy sector can play a significant role in accelerating the transition towards a less fossil-fuel dependent economy and in achieving sustainability and greenhouse gas emission reduction goals in line with global commitments, including the Paris Agreement.

In the short run there is cointegration between the variables, so there is a link between them in the long run at the 5% level. Any deviation from long-run equilibrium is speed-corrected at a level of 22.56%. The variables that have a positive impact on the variable SDG7INEMT are D(SDG7FZEP), D(SDG7FZEP(-1)), D(SDG7CENI), i.e. the first-order differences of the current variables SDG7FZEP and SDG7CENI, and the first-order difference of the variable SDG7FZEP at a previous point in time. All other variables in the model have a negative impact.

The effects of the model have been underpinned by the significant investments in green energy and energy infrastructure that have marked the last decade, underlining Europe's commitment to achieving sustainability goals. At the same time, regulations on carbon emissions, the introduction and adjustment of carbon taxes and initiatives to improve energy efficiency in industries and households have been focal points during this period. Energy import dependency continued to be a challenge, with fluctuations in global energy resource prices directly influencing greenhouse gas emissions. Energy crises, such as the one in 2021 when gas and oil prices reached historic highs, demonstrated Europe's vulnerability to external shocks. In conclusion, the PMG model highlights the complex interconnections between energy policies, economic behaviour and environmental impacts. The model suggests the need for sustainable energy development by continuing to invest in green technologies and by optimizing fiscal and import policies to encourage greener behaviour for a friendlier and more sustainable environment.

## Modelling the Impact of Energy Sustainability by Quantifying the Sectoral Sensitivity of Energy Efficiency on Industrial Air Emission Intensity

Industrial activity is known to have a significant impact on the environment, with the European Union campaigning for the transition to green industry and to protect the environment by reducing the intensity of air emissions from industry.

In recent times, concerns about climate change and the negative impacts of greenhouse gas emissions have increased significantly, leading to a growing interest in the development of renewable energy sources and the reduction of air pollution (Jaiswal et al., 2022; Shivanna, 2022; Wang & Azam, 2024). A number of studies have shown that domestic production of green energy, such as solar, wind and hydro energy, contributes significantly to reducing industrial air pollution (Ahmed Ali et al., 2020; Chen et al., 2023, 2024; Osman et al., 2023; Paraschiv & Paraschiv, 2023). These energy sources generate no greenhouse gas emissions and produce no air pollutants, in contrast to fossil fuels traditionally used in industry. To ensure the efficiency and sustainability of renewable energy sources, some studies (Ganda, 2018; Hassan et al., 2022; IRENA, 2024; Xie et al., 2023) have shown that green energy investments are associated with a decrease in greenhouse gas intensity and an improvement in air quality in industries such as power generation and industrial production. Appropriate policies and measures to promote green energy according to some researchers (Chen et al., 2024; Falcone, 2023; Lu et al., 2020; Seetharaman et al., 2019) help the deployment and development of renewable energy sources and the development of policies that include green energy subsidies, regulated tariffs and investments in sustainable energy infrastructure.

Some studies have shown that increasing domestic green energy production not only reduces air pollution but also helps promote more sustainable economic and industrial development (Ahmed et al., 2022; Chen et al., 2023; Chou et al., 2023). Investing in green energy generates sustainable jobs, stimulates technological innovation and supports sustainability and corporate social responsibility goals. Other studies (Seddighi et al., 2023; Wang et al., 2023; Zhang et al., 2022a) have shown that the transition to green energy sources has significant environmental and health benefits. Reducing greenhouse gas emissions and air pollutants improves air quality, reduces risks to human health and protects fragile ecosystems. Promoting green energy is a permanent strategy in the fight against climate change and in achieving a healthier and more sustainable environment for future generations. To emphasize the importance of the transition to green energy sources for reducing air pollution and promoting sustainable and environmentally responsible development, I propose the following hypothesis:

H1—Increased domestic (green) energy production has a lasting effect on decreasing air pollution due to the intensity of air emissions from industry.

Hypothesis H1 proposes that increasing domestic energy production, in particular green energy, can have a lasting effect on decreasing pollution due to the intensity of air emissions from industry. This hypothesis suggests that the transition to cleaner and more sustainable energy sources can help reduce negative environmental impacts and improve industrial air quality.

Research on the relationship between primary energy supply and the intensity of air emissions from industry has become increasingly relevant because of climate change and environmental degradation. In a world of increasing energy consumption, it is of interest to understand whether there is a direct and strong link between these two variables or whether other factors, such as clean technologies and environmental policies, may influence this relationship. Some studies in the literature (Altıntaş & Kassouri, 2020; Anser et al., 2024; Gawusu et al., 2022; Jahanger et al., 2023) have shown that an increase in primary energy supply can be accompanied by significant improvements in energy efficiency and the adoption of clean technologies in industrial processes. For example, the introduction of more energy-efficient technologies and the use of renewable energy sources can reduce the intensity of air emissions, even with an increase in primary energy consumption. Other studies (Lin & Zhang, 2023; Muhammad et al., 2022; Xu & Xu, 2022) have analysed the role of policy and regulation in influencing the relationship between primary energy supply and industrial air emissions intensity. Policies aimed at promoting green energy, limiting emissions and improving energy efficiency can mitigate the direct link between primary energy consumption and greenhouse gas emissions. Research on decarbonization and switching to renewable energy sources [154,260–262] has shown that a structural change in the energy mix, with an increase in the share of renewable energy sources and a reduction in the use of fossil fuels, can weaken the direct link between primary energy supply and air emissions from industry. This is particularly relevant in the context of decarbonization strategies and commitments under international climate change agreements.

One aspect of interest studied in the literature has been the importance of R&D investment for the realization of cleaner technologies and energy innovation (Bilgili et al., 2023; McLaughlin et al., 2023; Yasemi et al., 2023). Emerging technologies such as carbon capture and storage or more efficient production processes could reduce the intensity of atmospheric emissions, even in the context of increased primary energy consumption.

In the context of the research presented in the literature, the following hypothesis can be formulated:

H2—primary energy supply has a weak direct influence on the increase in air emissions intensity from industry.

Primary energy supply is not the only factor influencing the intensity of air emissions from industry; environmental policies, technological innovations and companies' strategic decisions can play a crucial role in shaping this relationship. It is therefore essential to consider a holistic approach and analyse the complex interactions between these factors in order to develop effective strategies to reduce emissions and protect the environment.

In recent times, air quality issues and the impact of pollution on human health and the environment have increased significantly. Industry is recognized as one of the main sources of particulate emissions into the atmosphere, which can have adverse effects on air quality and public health.

Industrial processes and combustion are two important topics presented by specialized studies (Larki et al., 2023; Osman et al., 2022) which highlight that most industrial processes involve the combustion of fossil fuels or other operations that generate particulate matter in the air. Energy consumption in these processes can be a major factor in the generation of particulate emissions, either directly through the combustion process or indirectly using energy to power the equipment and machinery involved in production.

Energy and environment research (Fayyazbakhsh et al., 2022; Lelieveld et al., 2023) have shown that the choice of fuels in industrial processes has a substantial impact on air quality and particulate emissions. Fossil fuels such as coal and oil are recognized to generate significant amounts of particulate matter in the atmosphere during the combustion process and are considered among the main sources of air pollution. On the other hand, cleaner fuels such as natural gas or renewable energy sources have significant advantages in terms of particulate emissions. Studies have shown that the use of these cleaner energy sources can significantly reduce particulate emissions into the atmosphere, helping to improve air quality and protect human health and the environment (Pan et al., 2024; Sanyal & Wuebbles, 2022; Sofia et al., 2020; Zeng et al., 2022). Thus, the type of fuel used in industrial processes plays a crucial role in managing and reducing air pollution and particulate emissions, and the adoption of more sustainable energy sources can contribute to a cleaner and healthier environment for all citizens.

A major importance in environmental and engineering research should be given to the implementation of advanced pollution control technologies in the industrial sector, with the main goal of significantly reducing particulate emissions (Haque & Sharif, 2021; Sahu et al., 2021). These technologies are an essential pillar in the efforts to protect air quality and combat air pollution, as they allow the elimination or substantial reduction of particulate emissions to ambient air. Pollution control technologies adopted in industrial processes include a diverse range of innovative devices and systems. These include particulate filters, which operate by trapping solid or liquid particles in the exhaust gas stream. Emission abatement systems are also used to convert or neutralize toxic substances in exhaust gases, thereby reducing the negative impact on the environment. In addition, there are other advanced pollutant capture and neutralization devices, such as electrostatic precipitators and adsorption systems, which are designed to remove pollutants from exhaust gases through various filtration and chemical reaction mechanisms. Effective implementation of these pollution control technologies in industries is essential to reduce the negative impact on human health and the environment. Through the use of these advanced technologies, a significant reduction in particulate emissions can be achieved and thus an improvement in air quality can be achieved, helping to protect the health of the population and preserving the environment for future generations.

Public health and ecology studies (Enyoh et al., 2020; Kaur & Pandey, 2021; Petropoulou et al., 2023; Xu et al., 2022) have highlighted the serious consequences of exposure to airborne particulate matter on human health and the ecological balance. The negative impact of these particles is not only limited to respiratory diseases, but also extends to damage to the cardiovascular system, creating an increased risk for diseases such as asthma, bronchitis and heart disease. In parallel, particles in the air have a profound impact on the environment, influencing soil and water quality. Particulate deposition can affect soil fertility and disturb the chemical balance of soil, with consequences for plant growth and crop yields (Ullah et al., 2023; Zhai et al., 2024). At the same time, particles can reach water sources, compromising water quality and affecting aquatic life (Giri, 2021; Woodward et al., 2021). In addition to these issues, impacts on biodiversity and ecosystems are also significant. Particulate deposition can affect species habitats and disrupt food chains, with consequences for biodiversity and fragile ecosystems (Kumar et al., 2021; Lincoln et al., 2022). It is thus clear that particulate emissions from industry pose a threat not only to human health but also to the integrity and functioning of terrestrial and aquatic ecosystems. In this context, it is of real interest to implement effective measures to reduce particulate emissions from industry and to protect both human health and the environment. The adoption of sustainable pollution control policies and technologies can contribute to improving air quality and preserving biodiversity, ensuring a healthy and balanced environment for all forms of life.

Studies in the literature have shown that reducing energy consumption in industry and adopting cleaner and more emission-efficient technologies contribute to reducing air pollution and protecting public health. It is therefore important to develop and implement effective policies and measures to reduce energy consumption in industry and to promote more sustainable and environmentally responsible production. Following the literature review, we hypothesized the following:

H3—energy consumption in industry is a risk factor on the increase of particle-emitting pollution from industry.

Energy consumption in industry, through combustion processes and other associated operations, can contribute significantly to emissions of particulate matter into the atmosphere. These particles can have various negative effects on human health and the environment, including increasing the risk of respiratory diseases, affecting the quality of soil and ecosystems and reducing atmospheric visibility.

The following indicators were used to develop the econometric model: industrial air emissions intensity (SDG7INEMT), total primary energy supply (SDG7FZEP), energy import dependence (SDG7IMPEN) and industrial energy consumption (SDG7CENI).

These indicators have been assessed based on descriptive statistics for the period 2010–2021 considering the national developments of each indicator for all EU Member States, and the database being organized in panel data as presented in Table 4.1. The results of the descriptive analysis are presented in Table 5.7.

**Table 5.7** Descriptive statistics

| *Variable* | *SDG7INEMT* | *SDG7IMPEN* | *SDG7FZEP* | *SDG7CENI* |
|---|---|---|---|---|
| Comments | 324 | 324 | 324 | 324 |
| Average | 0.15 | 56.67 | 52.77 | 22.88 |
| Standard deviation | 0.17 | 24.39 | 74.19 | 6.65 |
| Minim | 0.01 | −16.23 | 0.6 | 9.97 |
| Maxim | 0.86 | 104.13 | 329.55 | 43.21 |

Source: Author

As for the dependent variable it can be observed that the mean value is at the level of 0.15 grammes per euro closer to the minimum value of 0.01 grammes than to the maximum value, which confirms an asymptotic distribution to the left of the Gaussian distribution graph. The standard deviation is slightly above the mean value which indicates that there is a disparity of emission limitation policies in industry at European level. The other regression indicators contain smaller standard deviations (SDG7IMPEN and SDG7CENI), while SDG7FZEP has a very large standard deviation which confirms significant changes at Member State level and in the dynamics of the indicator. Regarding the dependence on energy imports, it can be observed that the average frequency is 56.67%, which represents a significant dependence threshold. The total supply of primary energy shows a tendency for a marked dispersion of values in relation to the calculated average of 52.77 million tonnes of oil equivalent, with the Member States exceeding the average by up to six times during the period analysed, but also with values close to 0, which indicates a disparity in energy policies that is assimilated to a low efficiency in this area. Energy consumption in industry is on average 22.88% of total energy consumption, which confirms the importance of the industrial sector in terms of energy policy.

Variable testing was carried out as a preliminary step in the conceptualization of the model, the first tests being the autocorrelation tests presented in Table 5.8.

According to the results in Table 3.17, there is a lack of autocorrelation, the values of the coefficients being lower than the autocorrelation threshold of 0.7, which allows modelling the data.

**Table 5.8** Variable correlation matrix of the energy sustainability impact model by quantifying the sectoral sensitivity of energy efficiency on industrial air emissions intensity

| *Variable* | *SDG7INEMT* | *SDG7IMPEN* | *SDG7FZEP* | *SDG7CENI* |
|---|---|---|---|---|
| SDG7INEMT | 1.000 | | | |
| SDG7IMPEN | −0.1196 | 1.000 | | |
| SDG7FZEP | −0.2569 | −0.0146 | 1.000 | |
| SDG7CENI | −0.0661 | −0.2618 | 0.0874 | 1.000 |

Source: Author

The Levin-Lin-Chin, Breitung, Im-Pesaran-Shin, ADF-Fisher Chi-square, PP-Fisher Chi-square and Hadri stationarity tests were applied. The results are presented centralized in Table 5.9.

The Levin-Lin-Chu test was able to demonstrate stationarity of the data by significant results ($p < 0.05$) after removing individual effects. Another test for detecting unit roots in panel data is the Breitung Test. According to the results in Table 3.18 higher p-values indicate no stationarity, while small values (usually below 0.05) indicate stationarity. The test results confirm first-order stationarity for all variables except SDG7FZEP which has 0-order stationarity. Application of the Im-Pesaran-Shin test confirms stationarity for all data series. The combination of ADF tests applied separately to each series, with results aggregated by Chi-square test, confirms stationarity of order 1 for all variables except SDG7CENI which has stationarity of order 0. PP-Fisher Chi-square indicates stationarity for all data series.

The Hadri test resulted in very low p-values suggesting stationarity of the series.

The SDG7INEMT and SDG7IMPEN series are first-order integrates, while the SDG7FZEP and SDG7CENI series are 0-order integrates. For this reason, we use an ARDL model.

The ARDL model equation is shown below:

$$y_{i,t} = \sum_{i=1}^{p} \delta_i y_{i,t-j} + \sum_{j=0}^{q} \beta_{ij} x_{i,t-j} + \varphi_i + e_{i,t} \tag{5.2}$$

where:

$y_{i,\ t}$—is the dependent variable, industrial air emission intensity (SDG7INEMT)

$x_{i,\ t}$—are the integrated or cointegrated independent variables I(0) or I(1), (total primary energy supply (SDG7FZEP), energy import dependence (SDG7IMPEN) and industrial energy consumption (SDG7CENI))

$\delta_i$—are the coefficients of the lagged dependent variables

$\beta_{ij}$—are the coefficients of the independent variables

$\varphi_i$—is the unit specific to fixed bills

p,q—are the optional delay values

$e_{i,\ t}$—is the error.

**Table 5.9** Stationarity tests

| *The stationarity test* | *SDG7INEMT* | | *SDG7IMPEN* | | *SDG7FZEP* | | *SDG7CENI* | |
|---|---|---|---|---|---|---|---|---|
| | *Order 0* | *Order 1* | *Order 0* | *Order 1* | *Order 0* | *Order 1* | *Order 0* | *Order 1* |
| Levin-Lin-Chin | −6.679 | NA | −3.4772 | NA | −5.508 | NA | −10.496 | NA |
| | (0.000) | | (0.000) | | (0.000) | | (0.000) | |
| Breitung | −0.598 | −3.647 | 1.591 | −3.647 | −3.275 | NA | 3.821 | −2.188 |
| | (0.275) | (0.001) | (0.944) | (0.001) | (0.001) | | (0.999) | (0.014) |
| Im-Pesaran-Shin | −0.245 | −3.142 | −0.782 | −3.142 | −1.030 | −0.141 | −1.377 | −3.351 |
| | (0.403) | (0.000) | (0.217) | (0.000) | (0.151) | (0.444) | (0.084) | (0.000) |
| ADF-Fisher | 53.760 | 111.344 | 59.790 | 111.344 | 59.102 | 55.457 | 82.135 | NA |
| Chi-square | (0.484) | (0.000) | (0.274) | (0.000) | (0.294) | (0.420) | (0.008) | |
| PP-Fisher | 105.405 | NA | 134.248 | NA | 103.864 | NA | 101.778 | NA |
| Chi-square | (0.000) | | (0.000) | | (0.000) | | (0.000) | |
| Hadri | 14.905 | 38.257 | 8.3418 | 14.113 | 8.558 | 9.214 | 11.109 | 14.544 |
| | (0.000) | (0.000) | (0.000) | (0.000) | (0.000) | (0.000) | (0.000) | (0.000) |

Source: Author

We checked the cointegration of the data series using the Pedroni cointegration test presented in Table 5.10.

Analysing Table 5.10 and taking into account the null hypothesis, we can say that the series are not cointegrated.

To establish the type of model (PMG—Pooled Mean Group or MG—Mean Group) the Hausman test was applied, where the null hypothesis means that the model is MG and the alternative hypothesis PMG model as shown in Table 5.11.

The application of the test led to the conclusion that the null hypothesis is rejected, and the alternative hypothesis is accepted.

The ARDL model was evaluated, and the results are presented in Table 5.12.

The data in Table 5.12 show that in the long run the variable SDG7IMPEN has a negative impact on the variable SDG7INEMT at a 5% significance level while the variables SDG7FZEP and SDG7CENI have a positive impact on the variable SDG7INEMT at a 5% significance level.

**Table 5.10** Pedroni cointegration test

*Series SDG7INEMT SDG7IMPEN SDG7FZEP SDG7CENI*

Sample: 2010–2021
Remarks included: 324
Cross-sections included: 27
Null hypothesis: No cointegration
The trend hypothesis: No deterministic trend
User-specified lag length: 1
Automatic Newey-West and Bartlett Kernel bandwidth selection
Alternative hypothesis: common AR coefficients (within dimension)

| | Statistic | Prob. | Statistics Considered | Prob. |
|---|---|---|---|---|
| Panel v-Statistic | −1.875204 | 0.9696 | −2.219433 | 0.9868 |
| Rho-Statistic Panel | 2.668876 | 0.9962 | 3.099979 | 0.9990 |
| Panel PP-Statistic | −5.472945 | 0.0000 | −0.167275 | 0.4336 |
| Panel ADF-Statistic | −3.395608 | 0.0003 | −0.419103 | 0.3376 |

Alternative hypothesis: individual AR coefficients (between dimensions)

| | Statistic | Prob. |
|---|---|---|
| Group rho-Statistic | 4.988527 | 1.0000 |
| Group PP-Statistic | −2.324329 | 0.0101 |
| Group ADF-Statistic | −1.571414 | 0.0580 |

Source: Author

**Table 5.11** Hausman test

| *Variable* | *Coefficients* | | *Difference* | *Standard error* |
|---|---|---|---|---|
| | *(b)* *mg* | *(B)* *pmg* | *(b-B)* | |
| SDG7IMPEN | −0.0114722 | 0.000629 | −0.0121012 | 0.048285 |
| SDG7FZEP | −0.0370775 | −0.0005076 | −0.0365699 | 0.2,358,838 |
| SDG7CENI | 0.0236917 | 0.0292509 | −0.0055593 | 0.040814 |

b = consistent under null and alternative hypothesis; obtained from xtpmg
B = inconsistent under alternative hypothesis, efficient under null hypothesis; obtained from xtpmg
Test: null hypothesis: the difference in coefficients is not systematic
$Chi^2$ (2) = 0.09; Prob>$chi^2$ = 0.9925

Source: Author

**Table 5.12** PMG model summary

| *Variable* | *Coefficient* | *Standard error* | *t-statistic* | *Prob.* |
|---|---|---|---|---|
| | Long-term coefficients (grouped) | | | |
| SDG7IMPEN | −0.000174 | 3.75E-08 | −4643.263 | 0.0000 |
| SDG7FZEP | 8.75E-06 | 3.05E-06 | 2.868378 | 0.0045 |
| SDG7CENI | 0.001277 | 3.17E-06 | 402.3016 | 0.0000 |
| | Short-term coefficients (group average) | | | |
| COINTEQ | −0.225642 | 0.082894 | −2.722047 | 0.0069 |
| D(SDG7INEMT(−1)) | −0.293340 | 0.115859 | −2.531866 | 0.0119 |
| D(SDG7IMPEN) | −0.006546 | 0.005961 | −1.098003 | 0.2732 |
| D(SDG7IMPEN(−1)) | −0.002936 | 0.003211 | −0.914235 | 0.3614 |
| D(SDG7FZEP) | 0.015130 | 0.013892 | 1.089113 | 0.2771 |
| D(SDG7FZEP(−1)) | 0.001306 | 0.015382 | 0.084930 | 0.9324 |
| D(SDG7CENI) | 0.003521 | 0.003185 | 1.105256 | 0.2701 |
| D(SDG7CENI(−1)) | −0.012227 | 0.014557 | −0.839974 | 0.4017 |
| Log-likelihood: | 1224.131 | | | |

Source: Author

The coefficient of the SDG7IMPEN indicator is −0.0001, with a very small standard error (3.75E-08) and a significant t-statistic (−4643.263). The probability value (0.0000) suggests that the variable has a significant negative and consistent long-term negative impact on reducing the intensity of industrial air emissions. This demonstrates working Hypothesis 1—increasing domestic (green) energy production has a lasting effect on decreasing pollution due to air emission intensity from industry. In the context of sustainable development, this indicates that high import dependence may be economically or environmentally unsustainable, negatively influencing the trade balance and contributing to resource scarcity. The results obtained for the validation of Hypothesis 1 are in line with research in the literature, which argues that increasing domestic green energy production can have a significant and sustainable effect on reducing air pollution from industry. Some energy and environmental studies (Chien et al., 2022; Mohsin et al., 2021; Olabi & Abdelkareem, 2022) have shown that switching to renewable energy sources can have a significant impact in reducing greenhouse gas emissions. The uptake of green energy, such as solar, wind and hydropower, according to some researchers (Chen et al., 2022, 2023; Nwokolo et al., 2023) can reduce dependence on fossil fuels, the main emitters of greenhouse gases, and help reduce pollutant emissions from the industrial sector. This transition to cleaner energy sources is recognized as one of the most effective strategies to combat climate change and promote a more sustainable and environmentally friendly economy.

Energy and environmental studies emphasize the importance of energy efficiency investments and technological innovations to reduce air pollution from industry (García-Quevedo & Jové-Llopis, 2021; Paramati et al., 2022; Wang & Wang, 2020; Wen et al., 2022). More efficient and advanced technologies can have a significant impact in reducing fossil fuel consumption and thus associated emissions. By optimizing industrial processes and implementing innovative technological solutions, the amount of fuel required for production can be reduced, leading to lower pollutant emissions and improved air quality. Thus, investment in energy efficiency and technological innovation is a key pillar in efforts to combat air pollution and promote a cleaner and healthier environment. Other specialized studies (Pata et al., 2023; Ullah et al., 2024; Yilanci et al., 2023; Yanyan Zhang et al., 2022b) emphasize that increased dependence on energy imports can have unsustainable consequences both economically and environmentally. Energy imports often involve long-distance transportation, generating additional greenhouse gas emissions and having a negative impact on air quality. In addition, this dependence can create vulnerabilities to price fluctuations and market instability, affecting the balance of trade and creating risks to energy security. Thus, reducing import dependency and promoting the use of domestic resources and renewable energy sources are key strategies for building a more sustainable economy and a healthier environment. Extensive literature studies (Bashir et al., 2022; Neves et al., 2020; Zhao et al., 2022) highlight that the adoption of policies and regulations oriented towards the promotion of renewable energies can have a significant impact in reducing air pollution from industry. These policies include a diverse range of instruments, such as subsidies, fiscal incentives and financial support mechanisms, which are designed to encourage investment in clean and sustainable technologies. By stimulating the development and deployment of renewable energy, these policies can help accelerate the transition to a more efficient and greener energy system. Moreover, promoting renewable energy can also have beneficial effects on sustainable economic growth, generating jobs and stimulating energy innovation. Coherent and effective policies and regulations in support of renewable energy are therefore an essential step towards building a cleaner economy and a healthier environment.

Therefore, the results obtained for the validation of Hypothesis 1 are consistent with the findings in the literature and support the importance of promoting domestic green energy production in the efforts to reduce air pollution from industry.

The coefficient of the SDG7FZEP indicator is 8.75E-06, with a standard error of 3.05E-06, a t-statistic of 2.86 and a p-value of 0.0045, which indicates sufficient statistical significance to consider the positive effect of this variable. This demonstrates working Hypothesis 2—primary energy supply has weak direct influence on the increase in air emissions intensity from industry. The positive long-run coefficient shows that this variable supports the performance of the dependent variable. This correlation demonstrates the need for energy efficiency to ensure sustainability, a process that must be based on an increase in innovation, thus contributing to sustainable economic growth by optimizing resource use and reducing waste. The results obtained in the validation of Hypothesis 2 are consistent with several studies in the literature that have examined the relationship between primary energy supply and the intensity of air emissions from industry. Specifically, these findings support the idea that primary energy supply has relatively little influence on the increase in air emissions intensity, in the sense that there is no direct or strong correlation between these two variables (Chen et al., 2023; Hao, 2022; Li et al., 2023a; Pan et al., 2024). Studies in the literature that have investigated the link between energy consumption and the level of pollution generated in industrial processes have brought to the fore the complexity of this relationship and the variability of results in different contexts. Many of these studies have examined different aspects of energy consumption and greenhouse gas emissions, considering a wide range of factors that may influence this relationship. Some studies have shown that the type of fuel used in industrial processes can significantly influence the level of pollution (Awewomom et al., 2024; Kalak, 2023; Yue et al., 2021). For example, fossil fuels such as coal and oil have been associated with higher greenhouse gas emissions compared to renewable or lower emitting energy sources such as natural gas (Gyamfi et al., 2021; Mohammad et al., 2021). Another important component is the energy efficiency of industrial processes. Studies have shown that adopting more energy-efficient technologies and implementing measures to reduce energy consumption can contribute to lower greenhouse gas emissions, even with increasing energy consumption (Akdag & Yıldırım, 2020; EEA, 2023; IRENA, 2024; Oloruntobi et al., 2023). The policy and legislative context also have a significant impact on the relationship between energy consumption and pollution. According to researchers (Lu et al., 2020; Wang & Liang, 2022) policies that promote the use of renewable energy, impose strict energy efficiency standards or implement measures to reduce emissions can influence the direction and magnitude of this impact. Furthermore, studies in the literature (Farhana et al., 2022; International Renewable Energy Agency, 2023; Kumar et al., 2023; Osman et al., 2023) have shown that increased energy efficiency and the adoption of cleaner technologies can significantly reduce the environmental impacts of industrial processes, even with a moderate increase in energy consumption. Therefore, the results obtained from the analysis indicate a relatively weak influence of primary energy supply on the intensity of atmospheric emissions, which are consistent with the findings of these studies. It is important to continue research in this area and to develop policies and strategies that promote energy efficiency and encourage the uptake of cleaner technologies in industry, thus contributing to achieving sustainable economic growth and protecting the environment.

The SDG7CENI indicator has a coefficient of 0.001 and a standard error of 3.17E-06, with a t-statistic of 402.3016 and a probability of 0.0000, indicating a very significant and strong long-term influence on the intensity of air emissions from industry. This demonstrates the working Hypothesis 3—energy consumption in industry is a risk factor on the increase of pollution assimilated to particulate emissions from industry. To eliminate these vulnerabilities, we believe that investments are needed to promote sustainable development by financing green infrastructure, renewable energy projects, or by stimulating innovations in clean technologies. The results obtained in the analysis of the SDG7CENI indicator confirm Hypothesis 3, showing that energy consumption in industry is indeed associated with a significant increase in the intensity of atmospheric emissions, including particulate emissions. These findings are consistent with extensive research in the literature that has investigated the impact of energy consumption on air pollution in the industrial sector (Bildirici & Çoban Kayıkçı, 2024; Gao et al., 2023; Meng et al., 2019). One of the main factors contributing to this association is the high level of industrial activity associated with high energy consumption. More specifically, industrial processes that require a large amount of energy to operate can generate significant emissions of pollutants into the atmosphere, including particulate matter of various sizes.

Research has emphasized that this link between energy consumption and particulate matter emissions may also be influenced by other variables such as the type of fuel used, the energy efficiency of industrial processes and environmental and energy policies (Butt et al., 2023; Farghali et al., 2023b; Nevskaya et al., 2023). For example, the use of fossil fuels in industrial processes may be associated with higher emissions of particulate matter compared to renewable or cleaner energy sources such as solar or wind energy (Algarni et al., 2023; Dincer & Aydin, 2023; Sikiru et al., 2024).

To address these problems and reduce the impact of pollution on the environment and human health, various measures and policies have been proposed. Investments in green infrastructure, such as pollutant filtration systems and emission reduction measures, can help improve air quality and reduce the negative impacts of air pollution on human health and the environment. Promoting the use of renewable energy and clean technologies in industrial processes can also be key to reducing emissions of particulate matter and other air pollutants. These strategies can help to strike a balance between economic development needs and environmental protection by promoting a sustainable approach to industry and energy consumption. It is also important to consider the economic and social impacts of these measures. Some policies and regulations may have high upfront costs for industry or affect their competitiveness in the global market. It is therefore essential to balance environmental and economic objectives. The relationship between energy consumption in industry and particulate emission intensity is complex and influenced by several factors. Addressing this issue requires an integrated analysis and a comprehensive strategy combining energy efficiency measures, environmental policies and incentives for the use of renewable energies to promote sustainable industry and protect the environment.

In the short run there is cointegration between the variables, so there is a link between them in the long run at the 5% level. Any deviation from long-run equilibrium is speed-corrected at a level of 22.56%. The variables that have a positive impact on the variable SDG7INEMT are D(SDG7FZEP), D(SDG7FZEP(-1)), D(SDG7CENI), i.e. the first-order differences of the current variables SDG7FZEP and SDG7CENI, and the first-order difference of the variable SDG7FZEP at a previous point in time. All other variables in the model have a negative impact.

In conclusion, the long-run models are more robust and consistent in showing the effects of variables on the model compared to the short-run effects, which are less significant and more variable. The impact model of energy sustainability by quantifying the sectoral sensitivity of energy efficiency on the intensity of air emissions from industry has highlighted the sensitivity of the energy sector on the industrial branch demonstrating that there are vulnerabilities induced by the development of this sector on the environmental quality aspect that transforms the sustainability objectives into challenges for the fastest possible implementation of new green technological innovations and ensuring environmental protection against pollution.

## Conclusions

The empirical results of modelling the relationship between SDG8 indicators and economic performance highlight the multifactorial and deeply structural nature of sustainable development in the European Union. Multiple regression analysis, supported by variable selection using the Backward Feature Selection (BFS) method, identified the most relevant determinants of sustainable economic growth, in particular labour productivity, employment rate, share of NEETs and greenhouse gas emissions intensity.

On the one hand, a robust positive correlation between labour productivity and GDP growth per capita was confirmed, suggesting that investment in innovation, digitization and vocational training remain essential for strengthening economic competitiveness in the EU. At the same time, employment rates and a decline in the share of young people not in employment, education or training (NEET) are proving to be key factors in reducing social exclusion and increasing labour market inclusion, which directly contribute to the social sustainability of the European economic model.

On the other hand, the analysis also reveals some tensions between economic performance and environmental sustainability, particularly in countries where GHG emissions remain high in relation to economic growth. This finding highlights the importance of a just transition, in which economic growth is decoupled from environmental pressures through the adoption of green industrial policies and the reorientation of investment towards clean technologies.

The chapter's conclusions support the need for an integrated approach, in which the economic, social and environmental dimensions of sustainable development are addressed in a coherent public policy framework, calibrated differently at the level of Member States. Romania and other emerging economies in Central and Eastern Europe need to step up their efforts to ensure sustainable convergence, reducing both productivity gaps and persistent social vulnerabilities.

Overall, this research provides a solid empirical basis for formulating policies aimed at balancing economic growth and employment objectives with the imperatives of environmental sustainability and social inclusion, in line with the transformed vision of the 2030 Agenda for Sustainable Development.

## References

Adebayo, T. S., Awosusi, A. A., Oladipupo, S. D., Agyekum, E. B., Jayakumar, A., & Kumar, N. M. (2021). Dominance of fossil fuels in Japan's National Energy mix and implications for environmental sustainability. *International Journal of Environmental Research and Public Health, 18*(14). https://doi.org/10.3390/ijerph18147347

Ahmed Ali, K., Ahmad, M. I., & Yusup, Y. (2020). Issues, impacts, and mitigations of carbon dioxide emissions in the building sector. *Sustainability, 12*(18). https://doi.org/10.3390/su12187427

Ahmed, F., Kousar, S., Pervaiz, A., Trinidad-Segovia, J. E., Del Pilar Casado-Belmonte, M., & Ahmed, W. (2022). Role of green innovation, trade and energy to promote green economic growth: A case of South Asian Nations. *Environmental Science and Pollution Research International, 29*(5), 6871–6885. https://doi.org/10.1007/s11356-021-15881-4

Akdag, S., & Yıldırım, H. (2020). Toward a sustainable mitigation approach of energy efficiency to greenhouse gas emissions in the European countries. *Heliyon, 6*(3). https://doi.org/10.1016/j.heliyon.2020.e03396

Aksoy, T. (2019). Structural reforms and growth in developing countries. *Journal of Economic Policy Reform, 22*(4), 325–350. https://doi.org/10.1080/17487870.2018.1424629

Alaganthiran, R., & Anaba, M. I. (2022). The effects of economic growth on carbon dioxide emissions in selected sub-Saharan African (SSA) countries. *Heliyon, 8*(11), e11193. https://doi.org/10.1016/j.heliyon.2022.e11193

Alam, M. S., Alam, M. N., Murshed, M., Mahmood, H., & Alam, R. (2022). Pathways to securing environmentally sustainable economic growth through efficient use of energy: A bootstrapped ARDL analysis. *Environmental Science and Pollution Research, 29*(33), 50025–50039. https://doi.org/10.1007/s11356-022-19410-9

Algarni, S., Tirth, V., Alqahtani, T., Alshehery, S., & Kshirsagar, P. (2023). Contribution of renewable energy sources to the environmental impacts and economic benefits for sustainable development. *Sustainable Energy Technologies and Assessments, 56*, 103098. https://doi.org/10.1016/j.seta.2023.103098

Ali, M. U., Gong, Z., Ali, M. U., Wu, X., & Yao, C. (2021). Fossil energy consumption, economic development, inward FDI impact on CO2 emissions in Pakistan: Testing EKC hypothesis through ARDL model. *International Journal of Finance & Economics, 26*(3), 3210–3221. https://doi.org/10.1002/ijfe.1958

AlShafeey, M., & Rashdan, O. (2023). Quantifying the impact of energy consumption sources on GHG emissions in major economies: A machine learning approach. *Energy Strategy Reviews, 49*, 101159. https://doi.org/10.1016/j.esr.2023.101159

Altıntaş, H., & Kassouri, Y. (2020). The impact of energy technology innovations on cleaner energy supply and carbon footprints in Europe: A linear versus nonlinear approach. *Journal of Cleaner Production, 276*, 124140. https://doi.org/10.1016/j.jclepro.2020.124140

Ansari, M. A. A., Sajid, M., Khan, S. N., Antohi, V. M., Fortea, C., & Zlati, M. L. (2024). Unveiling the effect of renewable energy and financial inclusion towards sustainable environment: Does interaction of digital finance and institutional quality matter? *Sustainable Futures*, 100196. https://doi.org/10.1016/j.sftr.2024.100196

Anser, M. K., Khan, K. A., Umar, M., Awosusi, A. A., & Shamansurova, Z. (2024). Formulating sustainable development policy for a developed nation: Exploring the role of renewable energy, natural gas efficiency and oil efficiency towards decarbonization. *International Journal of Sustainable Development & World Ecology, 31*(3), 247–263. https://doi.org/10.1080/13504509.2023.2268586

Antimiani, A., Costantini, V., & Paglialunga, E. (2023). Fossil fuels subsidy removal and the EU carbon neutrality policy. *Energy Economics, 119*, 106524. https://doi.org/10.1016/j.eneco.2023.106524

Aquilas, N. A., Ngangnchi, F. H., & Mbella, M. E. (2024). Industrialization and environmental sustainability in Africa: The moderating effects of renewable and non-renewable energy consumption. *Heliyon, 10*(4), e25681. https://doi.org/10.1016/j.heliyon.2024.e25681

Arzaghi, M., & Squalli, J. (2023). The environmental impact of fossil fuel subsidy policies. *Energy Economics, 126*, 106980. https://doi.org/10.1016/j.eneco.2023.106980

Awewomom, J., Dzeble, F., Takyi, Y. D., Ashie, W. B., Ettey, E. N. Y. O., Afua, P. E., Sackey, L. N. A., Opoku, F., & Akoto, O. (2024). Addressing global environmental pollution using environmental control techniques: a focus on environmental policy and preventive environmental management. *Discover Environment, 2*(1), 8. https://doi.org/10.1007/s44274-024-00033-5

Azam, A., Rafiq, M., Shafique, M., Zhang, H., & Yuan, J. (2021). Analyzing the effect of natural gas, nuclear energy and renewable energy on GDP and carbon emissions: A multi-variate panel data analysis. *Energy, 219*, 119592. https://doi.org/10.1016/j.energy.2020.119592

Azam, W., Khan, I., & Ali, S. A. (2023). Alternative energy and natural resources in determining environmental sustainability: A look at the role of government final consumption expenditures in France. *Environmental Science and Pollution Research, 30*(1), 1949–1965. https://doi.org/10.1007/s11356-022-22334-z

Aziz, N., Hossain, B., & Lamb, L. (2024). The effectiveness of environmental protection policies on greenhouse gas emissions. *Journal of Cleaner Production, 450*, 141868. https://doi.org/10.1016/j.jclepro.2024.141868

Azni, M. A., Md Khalid, R., Hasran, U. A., & Kamarudin, S. K. (2023). Review of the effects of fossil fuels and the need for a hydrogen fuel cell policy in Malaysia. *Sustainability, 15*(5). https://doi.org/10.3390/su15054033

Balsalobre-Lorente, D., dos Santos, C., Parente, C., Leitão, N. C., & Cantos-Cantos, J. M. (2023). The influence of economic complexity processes and renewable energy on CO2 emissions of BRICS. What about industry 4.0? *Resources Policy, 82*, 103547. https://doi.org/10.1016/j.resourpol.2023.103547

Bashir, M. F., Ma, B., Bashir, M. A., Radulescu, M., & Shahzad, U. (2022). Investigating the role of environmental taxes and regulations for renewable energy consumption: Evidence from developed economies. *Economic Research-Ekonomska Istraživanja, 35*(1), 1262–1284. https://doi.org/10.1080/1331677X.2021.1962383

Bassi, A. M., Pallaske, G., Bridle, R., & Bajaj, K. (2023). Emission reduction via fossil fuel subsidy removal and carbon pricing, creating synergies with revenue recycling. In *World* (Vol. 4, issue 2, pp. 225–240). https://doi.org/10.3390/world4020016

Ben-Salha, O., Dachraoui, H., & Sebri, M. (2021). Natural resource rents and economic growth in the top resource-abundant countries: A PMG estimation.

*Resources Policy, 74*, 101229. https://doi.org/10.1016/j.resourpol.2018.07.005

Bildirici, M., & Çoban Kayıkçı, F. (2024). Energy consumption, energy intensity, economic growth, FDI, urbanization, PM2.5 concentrations nexus. *Environment, Development and Sustainability, 26*(2), 5047–5065. https://doi.org/10.1007/s10668-023-02923-9

Bilgili, F., Balsalobre-Lorente, D., Kuskaya, S., Alnour, M., Onderol, S., & Hoque, M. E. (2023). Are research and development on energy efficiency and energy sources effective in the level of CO2 emissions? Fresh evidence from EU data. *Environment, Development and Sustainability*. https://doi.org/10.1007/s10668-023-03641-y

Black, S., Liu, A. A., Parry, I., & Vernon, N. (2023). *IMF Fossil Fuel Subsidies Data: 2023 Update.*

Bosah, C. P., Li, S., Ampofo, G. K. M., & Liu, K. (2021). Dynamic nexus between energy consumption, economic growth, and urbanization with carbon emission: Evidence from panel PMG-ARDL estimation. *Environmental Science and Pollution Research, 28*(43), 61201–61212. https://doi.org/10.1007/s11356-021-14943-x

Butt, H. M. M., Khan, I., & Xia, E. J. (2023). How do energy supply and energy use link to environmental degradation in China? *Environmental Science and Pollution Research*. https://doi.org/10.1007/s11356-023-28960-5

Carfora, A., Pansini, R. V., & Scandurra, G. (2022). Energy dependence, renewable energy generation and import demand: Are EU countries resilient? *Renewable Energy, 195*, 1262–1274. https://doi.org/10.1016/j.renene.2022.06.098

Carton, B., Evans, C., Muir, D. V., & Voigts, S. (2023). Getting to know GMMET: The global macroeconomic model for the energy transition. *IMF Working Papers, 2023*(269), A001. https://doi.org/10.5089/9798400262326.001.A001

Cevik, S. (2024). Climate change and energy security: The dilemma or opportunity of the century? *Environmental Economics and Policy Studies*. https://doi.org/10.1007/s10018-023-00391-z

Chen, L., Msigwa, G., Yang, M., Osman, A. I., Fawzy, S., Rooney, D. W., & Yap, P.-S. (2022). Strategies to achieve a carbon neutral society: A review. *Environmental Chemistry Letters, 20*(4), 2277–2310. https://doi.org/10.1007/s10311-022-01435-8

Chen, X. H., Tee, K., Elnahass, M., & Ahmed, R. (2023). Assessing the environmental impacts of renewable energy sources: A case study on air pollution and carbon emissions in China. *Journal of Environmental Management, 345*, 118525. https://doi.org/10.1016/j.jenvman.2023.118525

Chen, L., Hu, Y., Wang, R., Li, X., Chen, Z., Hua, J., Osman, A. I., Farghali, M., Huang, L., Li, J., Dong, L., Rooney, D. W., & Yap, P.-S. (2024). Green building practices to integrate renewable energy in the construction sector: A review. *Environmental Chemistry Letters, 22*(2), 751–784. https://doi.org/10.1007/s10311-023-01675-2

Chien, F., Hsu, C.-C., Ozturk, I., Sharif, A., & Sadiq, M. (2022). The role of renewable energy and urbanization towards greenhouse gas emission in top Asian countries: Evidence from advance panel estimations. *Renewable Energy, 186*, 207–216. https://doi.org/10.1016/j.renene.2021.12.118

Chou, C.-H., Ngo, S. L., & Tran, P. P. (2023). Renewable energy integration for sustainable economic growth: Insights and challenges via bibliometric analysis. *Sustainability, 15*(20). https://doi.org/10.3390/su152015030

Chu, L. K., Doğan, B., Abakah, E. J. A., Ghosh, S., & Albeni, M. (2023). Impact of economic policy uncertainty, geopolitical risk, and economic complexity on carbon emissions and ecological footprint: An investigation of the E7 countries. *Environmental Science and Pollution Research, 30*(12), 34406–34427. https://doi.org/10.1007/s11356-022-24682-2

de Bruin, K., & Yakut, A. M. (2023). The impacts of removing fossil fuel subsidies and increasing carbon taxation in Ireland. *Environmental and Resource Economics, 85*(3), 741–782. https://doi.org/10.1007/s10640-023-00782-6

Deng, Q., Alvarado, R., Toledo, E., & Caraguay, L. (2020). Greenhouse gas emissions, non-renewable energy consumption, and output in South America: The role of the productive structure. *Environmental Science and Pollution Research, 27*(13), 14477–14491. https://doi.org/10.1007/s11356-020-07693-9

Dincer, I., & Aydin, M. I. (2023). New paradigms in sustainable energy systems with hydrogen. *Energy Conversion and Management, 283*, 116950. https://doi.org/10.1016/j.enconman.2023.116950

Dissanayake, H., Perera, N., Abeykoon, S., Samson, D., Jayathilaka, R., Jayasinghe, M., & Yapa, S. (2023). Nexus between carbon emissions, energy consumption, and economic growth: Evidence from global economies. *PLoS One, 18*(6), e0287579. https://doi.org/10.1371/journal.pone.0287579

Doan, B., Vo, D. H., & Pham, H. (2023). The net economic benefits of power plants: International evidence{*}. *Energy Policy, 175.* https://doi.org/10.1016/j.enpol.2023.113478

Ecer, F., Küçükönder, H., Kayapınar Kaya, S., & Faruk Görçün, Ö. (2023). Sustainability performance analysis of micro-mobility solutions in urban transportation with a novel IVFNN-Delphi-LOPCOW-CoCoSo framework. *Transportation Research Part A: Policy and Practice, 172*, 103667. https://doi.org/10.1016/j.tra.2023.103667

EEA. (2023). *Accelerating the energy efficiency renovation of residential buildings — A behavioural approach.* European Environment Agency. https://www.eea.europa.eu/publications/accelerating-the-energy-efficiency

Enyoh, C. E., Verla, A. W., Qingyue, W., Ohiagu, F. O., Chowdhury, A. H., Enyoh, E. C., Chowdhury, T., Verla, E. N., & Chinwendu, U. P. (2020). An overview of emerging pollutants in air: Method of analysis and potential public health concern from human environmental exposure. *Trends in Environmental Analytical Chemistry, 28*, e00107. https://doi.org/10.1016/j.teac.2020.e00107

Falcone, P. M. (2023). Sustainable energy policies in developing countries: A review of challenges and opportunities. *Energies, 16*(18). https://doi.org/10.3390/en16186682

Farghali, M., Osman, A. I., Chen, Z., Abdelhaleem, A., Ihara, I., Mohamed, I. M. A., Yap, P.-S., & Rooney, D. W. (2023a). Social, environmental, and economic consequences of integrating renewable energies in the electricity sector: A review. *Environmental Chemistry Letters, 21*(3), 1381–1418. https://doi.org/10.1007/s10311-023-01587-1

Farghali, M., Osman, A. I., Mohamed, I. M. A., Chen, Z., Chen, L., Ihara, I., Yap, P.-S., & Rooney, D. W. (2023b). Strategies to save energy in the context of the energy crisis: A review. *Environmental Chemistry Letters, 21*(4), 2003–2039. https://doi.org/10.1007/s10311-023-01591-5

Farhana, K., Kadirgama, K., Mahamude, A. S. F., & Mica, M. T. (2022). Energy consumption, environmental impact, and implementation of renewable energy resources in global textile industries: An overview towards circularity and sustainability. *Materials Circular Economy, 4*(1), 15. https://doi.org/10.1007/s42824-022-00059-1

Fayyazbakhsh, A., Bell, M. L., Zhu, X., Mei, X., Koutný, M., Hajinajaf, N., & Zhang, Y. (2022). Engine emissions with air pollutants and greenhouse gases and their control technologies. *Journal of Cleaner Production, 376*, 134260. https://doi.org/10.1016/j.jclepro.2022.134260

Filipović, S., Lior, N., & Radovanović, M. (2022). The green deal—just transition and sustainable development goals Nexus. *Renewable and Sustainable Energy Reviews, 168*, 112759. https://doi.org/10.1016/j.rser.2022.112759

Firtescu, B. N., Brinza, F., Grosu, M., Doaca, E. M., & Siriteanu, A. A. (2023). The effects of energy taxes level on greenhouse gas emissions in the environmental policy measures framework. *Frontiers in Environmental Science, 10*. https://doi.org/10.3389/fenvs.2022.965841

Ganda, F. (2018). The influence of green energy investments on environmental quality in OECD countries. *Environmental Quality Management, 28*(2), 17–29. https://doi.org/10.1002/tqem.21595

Gao, J., Duan, C., Song, J., Ma, L., & Cai, W. (2023). PM2.5 can help adjust building's energy consumption. *Journal of Environmental Management, 331*, 117235. https://doi.org/10.1016/j.jenvman.2023.117235

García-Quevedo, J., & Jové-Llopis, E. (2021). Environmental policies and energy efficiency investments. An industry-level analysis. *Energy Policy, 156*, 112461. https://doi.org/10.1016/j.enpol.2021.112461

Gawusu, S., Zhang, X., Jamatutu, S. A., Ahmed, A., Amadu, A. A., & Djam Miensah, E. (2022). The dynamics of green supply chain management within the framework of renewable energy. *International Journal of Energy Research, 46*(2), 684–711. https://doi.org/10.1002/er.7278

Georgescu, I. A., Oprea, S.-V., & Bâra, A. (2024). Investigating the relationship between macroeconomic indicators, renewables and pollution across diverse regions in the globalization era. *Applied Energy, 363*, 123077. https://doi.org/10.1016/j.apenergy.2024.123077

Giri, S. (2021). Water quality prospective in twenty first century: Status of water quality in major river basins, contemporary strategies and impediments: A review. *Environmental Pollution, 271*, 116332. https://doi.org/10.1016/j.envpol.2020.116332

Grubb, M., Drummond, P., Poncia, A., McDowall, W., Popp, D., Samadi, S., Penasco, C., Gillingham, K. T., Smulders, S., Glachant, M., Hassall, G., Mizuno, E., Rubin, E. S., Dechezleprêtre, A., & Pavan, G. (2021). Induced innovation in energy technologies and systems: A review of evidence and potential implications for CO2 mitigation. *Environmental Research Letters, 16*(4), 43007. https://doi.org/10.1088/1748-9326/abde07

Gudlaugsson, B., Ahmed, T. G., Dawood, H., Ogwumike, C., Short, M., & Dawood, N. (2023). Cost and environmental benefit analysis: An assessment of renewable energy integration and smart solution technologies in the InteGRIDy project. *Cleaner Energy Systems, 5*, 100071. https://doi.org/10.1016/j.cles.2023.100071

Gyamfi, B. A., Adedoyin, F. F., Bein, M. A., Bekun, F. V., & Agozie, D. Q. (2021). The anthropogenic consequences of energy consumption in E7 economies: Juxtaposing roles of renewable, coal, nuclear, oil and gas energy: Evidence from panel quantile method. *Journal of Cleaner Production, 295*, 126373. https://doi.org/10.1016/j.jclepro.2021.126373

Hao, Y. (2022). Effect of economic indicators, renewable energy consumption and human development on climate change: An empirical analysis based on panel data of selected countries. *Frontiers in Energy Research, 10*. https://doi.org/10.3389/fenrg.2022.841497

Haque, M. S., & Sharif, S. (2021). The need for an effective environmental engineering education to meet the growing environmental pollution in Bangladesh. *Cleaner Engineering and Technology, 4*, 100114. https://doi.org/10.1016/j.clet.2021.100114

Hassan, T. (2023). Taxing energy to tackle greenhouse gases: Evaluating the role of financial risk in high-income economies. *Environmental Science and Pollution Research International, 30*(57), 120103–120119. https://doi.org/10.1007/s11356-023-30310-4

Hassan, S. T., Batool, B., Sadiq, M., & Zhu, B. (2022). How do green energy investment, economic policy uncertainty, and natural resources affect greenhouse gas emissions? A Markov-switching equilibrium approach. *Environmental Impact Assessment Review, 97*, 106887. https://doi.org/10.1016/j.eiar.2022.106887

Hasselqvist, H., Renström, S., Strömberg, H., & Håkansson, M. (2022). Household energy resilience: Shifting perspectives to reveal opportunities for renewable energy futures in affluent contexts. *Energy Research & Social Science, 88*, 102498. https://doi.org/10.1016/j.erss.2022.102498

He, Y., Li, X., Huang, P., & Wang, J. (2022). Exploring the road toward environmental sustainability: Natural resources, renewable energy consumption, economic growth, and greenhouse gas emissions. *Sustainability, 14*(3). https://doi.org/10.3390/su14031579

He, J. M., Iqbal, W., & Su, F. L. (2023). Nexus between renewable energy investment, green finance, and sustainable development: Role of industrial structure and technical innovations. *Renewable Energy, 210*, 715–724. https://doi.org/10.1016/j.renene.2023.04.010

Holechek, J. L., Geli, H. M. E., Sawalhah, M. N., & Valdez, R. (2022). A global assessment: Can renewable energy replace fossil fuels by 2050? *Sustainability, 14*(8). https://doi.org/10.3390/su14084792

Hongxing, Y., Abban, O. J., Boadi, A. D., & Ankomah-Asare, E. T. (2021). Exploring the relationship between economic growth, energy consumption, urbanization, trade, and CO2 emissions: A PMG-ARDL panel data analysis on regional classification along 81 BRI economies. *Environmental Science and Pollution Research, 28*(46), 66366–66388. https://doi.org/10.1007/s11356-021-15660-1

Hussain, S. A., Razi, F., Hewage, K., & Sadiq, R. (2023). The perspective of energy poverty and 1st energy crisis of green transition. *Energy, 275*, 127487. https://doi.org/10.1016/j.energy.2023.127487

International Energy Agency. (2021). *Global Energy Review: CO2 Emissions in 2021.*

International Renewable Energy Agency. (2023). *World Energy Transitions Outlook 2022.* https://www.irena.org/Digital-Report/World-Energy-Transitions-Outlook-2022

IRENA. (2024). *World Energy Transitions Outlook 2023.* https://www.irena.org/Digital-Report/World-Energy-Transitions-Outlook-2023

Isiksal, A. Z., & Assi, A. F. (2022). Determinants of sustainable energy demand in the European economic area: Evidence from the PMG-ARDL model. *Technological Forecasting and Social Change, 183*, 121901. https://doi.org/10.1016/j.techfore.2022.121901

Jahanger, A., Ozturk, I., Chukwuma Onwe, J., Joseph, T. E., & Razib Hossain, M. (2023). Do technology and renewable energy contribute to energy efficiency and carbon neutrality? Evidence from top ten manufacturing countries. *Sustainable Energy Technologies and Assessments, 56*, 103084. https://doi.org/10.1016/j.seta.2023.103084

Jaiswal, K. K., Chowdhury, C. R., Yadav, D., Verma, R., Dutta, S., Jaiswal, K. S., SangmeshB, & Karuppasamy, K. S. K. (2022). Renewable and sustainable clean energy development and impact on social, economic, and environmental health. *Energy Nexus, 7*, 100118. https://doi.org/10.1016/j.nexus.2022.100118

Jebli, M. B., & Hakimi, A. (2023). How do financial inclusion and renewable energy collaborate with environmental quality? Evidence for top ten countries in technological advancement. *Environmental Science and Pollution Research, 30*(11), 31755–31767. https://doi.org/10.1007/s11356-022-24430-6

Jiang, W., & Sun, Y. (2023). Which is the more important factor of carbon emission, coal consumption or industrial structure? *Energy Policy, 176*, 113508. https://doi.org/10.1016/j.enpol.2023.113508

Jouini, J. (2015). Linkage between international trade and economic growth in GCC countries: Empirical evidence from PMG estimation approach. *The Journal of International Trade & Economic Development, 24*(3), 341–372. https://doi.org/10.1080/09638199.2014.904394

Juhola, S., Laurila, A.-G., Groundstroem, F., & Klein, J. (2024). Climate risks to the renewable energy sector: Assessment and adaptation within energy companies. *Business Strategy and the Environment, 33*(3), 1906–1919. https://doi.org/10.1002/bse.3580

Kalak, T. (2023). Potential use of industrial biomass waste as a sustainable energy source in the future. *Energies, 16*(4). https://doi.org/10.3390/en16041783

Kaur, R., & Pandey, P. (2021). Air pollution, climate change, and human health in Indian cities: A brief review. *Frontiers in Sustainable Cities, 3*. https://doi.org/10.3389/frsc.2021.705131

Kim, J., Panton, A. J., & Schwerhoff, G. (2024). Energy security and The green transition. *IMF Working Papers, 2024*(006), A001. https://doi.org/10.5089/9798400263743.001.A001

Kumar, R., Verma, A., Shome, A., Sinha, R., Sinha, S., Jha, P. K., Kumar, R., Kumar, P., Shubham, Das, S., Sharma, P., & Vara Prasad, P. V. (2021). Impacts of plastic pollution on ecosystem services, sustainable development goals, and need to focus on circular economy and policy interventions. *Sustainability, 13*(17). https://doi.org/10.3390/su13179963

Kumar, R., Gupta, S. K., Wang, H.-C., Kumari, C. S., & Korlam, S. S. (2023). From Efficiency to Sustainability: Exploring the Potential of 6G for a Greener Future. *Sustainability, 15*(23). https://doi.org/10.3390/su152316387

Larki, I., Zahedi, A., Asadi, M., Forootan, M. M., Farajollahi, M., Ahmadi, R., & Ahmadi, A. (2023). Mitigation approaches and techniques for combustion power plants flue gas emissions: A comprehensive review. *Science of the Total Environment, 903*, 166108. https://doi.org/10.1016/j.scitotenv.2023.166108

Lelieveld, J., Haines, A., Burnett, R., Tonne, C., Klingmüller, K., Münzel, T., & Pozzer, A. (2023). Air pollution deaths attributable to fossil fuels: Observational and modelling study. *BMJ (Clinical research ed.), 383*, e077784. https://doi.org/10.1136/bmj-2023-077784

Li, Y., Yang, X., Ran, Q., Wu, H., Irfan, M., & Ahmad, M. (2021). Energy structure, digital economy, and carbon emissions: Evidence from China. *Environmental Science and Pollution Research International, 28*(45), 64606–64629. https://doi.org/10.1007/s11356-021-15304-4

Li, J., Irfan, M., Samad, S., Ali, B., Zhang, Y., Badulescu, D., & Badulescu, A. (2023a). The relationship between energy consumption, CO2 emissions, economic growth, and health indicators. *International Journal of Environmental Research and Public Health, 20*(3). https://doi.org/10.3390/ijerph20032325

Li, S., Samour, A., Irfan, M., & Ali, M. (2023b). Role of renewable energy and fiscal policy on trade adjusted carbon emissions: Evaluating the role of environmental policy stringency. *Renewable Energy, 205*, 156–165. https://doi.org/10.1016/j.renene.2023.01.047

Li, Z., Zhao, Q., Guo, H., & Huang, R. (2024). Impact of fossil fuel subsidies on energy-saving technological change in China. *Energy, 286*, 129265. https://doi.org/10.1016/j.energy.2023.129265

Lin, B., & Zhang, A. (2023). Can government environmental regulation promote low-carbon development in heavy polluting industries? Evidence from China's new environmental protection law. *Environmental Impact Assessment Review, 99*, 106991. https://doi.org/10.1016/j.eiar.2022.106991

Lincoln, S., Andrews, B., Birchenough, S. N. R., Chowdhury, P., Engelhard, G. H., Harrod, O., Pinnegar, J. K., & Townhill, B. L. (2022). Marine litter and climate change: Inextricably connected threats to the world's oceans. *Science of the Total Environment, 837*, 155709. https://doi.org/10.1016/j.scitotenv.2022.155709

Lindholt, L., & Wei, T. (2023). The effects on energy markets of Achieving a 1.5 °C scenario. *International Journal of Environmental Research and Public Health, 20*(5). https://doi.org/10.3390/ijerph20054341

Liu, H., Wong, W.-K., The Cong, P., Nassani, A. A., Haffar, M., & Abu-Rumman, A. (2023). Linkage among urbanization, energy consumption, economic growth and carbon emissions. Panel data analysis for China using ARDL model. *Fuel, 332*, 126122. https://doi.org/10.1016/j.fuel.2022.126122

Lone, U. M., Darzi, M. A., & Islam, K. U. (2023). Macroeconomic variables and stock market performance: A PMG/ARDL approach for BRICS economies. *Macroeconomics and Finance in Emerging Market Economies, 16*(2), 300–325. https://doi.org/10.1080/17520843.2021.1983704

Lu, Y., Khan, Z. A., Alvarez-Alvarado, M. S., Zhang, Y., Huang, Z., & Imran, M. (2020). A critical review of sustainable energy policies for the promotion of renewable energy sources. *Sustainability, 12*(12). https://doi.org/10.3390/su12125078

McKinsey & Company. (2024). *Global energy perspective 2023: CO2 emissions outlook.* https://www.mckinsey.com/industries/oil-and-gas/our-insights/global-energy-perspective-2023-co2-emissions-outlook#/

McLaughlin, H., Littlefield, A. A., Menefee, M., Kinzer, A., Hull, T., Sovacool, B. K., Bazilian, M. D., Kim, J., & Griffiths, S. (2023). Carbon capture utilization and storage in review: Sociotechnical implications for a carbon reliant world. *Renewable and Sustainable Energy Reviews, 177*, 113215. https://doi.org/10.1016/j.rser.2023.113215

Meng, J., Yang, H., Yi, K., Liu, J., Guan, D., Liu, Z., Mi, Z., Coffman, D. M., Wang, X., Zhong, Q., Huang, T., Meng, W., & Tao, S. (2019). The slowdown in global air-pollutant emission growth and driving factors. *One Earth, 1*(1), 138–148. https://doi.org/10.1016/j.oneear.2019.08.013

Mitić, P., Fedajev, A., Radulescu, M., & Rehman, A. (2023). The relationship between CO2 emissions, economic growth, available energy, and employment in SEE countries. *Environmental Science and Pollution Research, 30*(6), 16140–16155. https://doi.org/10.1007/s11356-022-23356-3

Mohammad, N., Mohamad Ishak, W. W., Mustapa, S. I., & Ayodele, B. V. (2021). Natural gas as a key alternative energy source in sustainable renewable energy transition: A mini review. *Frontiers in Energy Research, 9.* https://doi.org/10.3389/fenrg.2021.625023

Mohsin, M., Kamran, H. W., Atif Nawaz, M., Sajjad Hussain, M., & Dahri, A. S. (2021). Assessing the impact of transition from nonrenewable to renewable energy consumption on economic growth-environmental nexus from developing Asian economies. *Journal of Environmental Management, 284*(February), 1–8. https://doi.org/10.1016/j.jenvman.2021.111999

Mostafaeipour, A., Bidokhti, A., Fakhrzad, M.-B., Sadegheih, A., & Zare Mehrjerdi, Y. (2022). A new model for the use of renewable electricity to reduce carbon dioxide emissions. *Energy, 238*, 121602. https://doi.org/10.1016/j.energy.2021.121602

Muhammad, S., Pan, Y., Agha, M. H., Umar, M., & Chen, S. (2022). Industrial structure, energy intensity and environmental efficiency across developed and developing economies: The intermediary role of primary, secondary and tertiary industry. *Energy, 247*, 123576. https://doi.org/10.1016/j.energy.2022.123576

Mushafiq, M., Arisar, M. M., Tariq, H., & Czapp, S. (2023). Energy efficiency and economic policy: Comprehensive theoretical, empirical, and policy review. *Energies, 16*(5). https://doi.org/10.3390/en16052381

Nawaz, M. A., Hussain, M. S., Kamran, H. W., Ehsanullah, S., Maheen, R., & Shair, F. (2021). Trilemma association of energy consumption, carbon emission, and economic growth of BRICS and OECD regions: Quantile regression estimation. *Environmental Science and Pollution Research, 28*(13), 16014–16028. https://doi.org/10.1007/s11356-020-11823-8

Nchofoung, T. N., Fotio, H. K., & Miamo, C. W. (2023). Green taxation and renewable energy technologies adoption: A global evidence. *Renewable Energy Focus, 44*, 334–343. https://doi.org/10.1016/j.ref.2023.01.010

Neves, S. A., Marques, A. C., & Patrício, M. (2020). Determinants of CO2 emissions in European Union countries: Does environmental regulation reduce environmental pollution? *Economic Analysis and Policy, 68*, 114–125. https://doi.org/10.1016/j.eap.2020.09.005

Nevskaya, M. A., Raikhlin, S. M., Vinogradova, V. V., Belyaev, V. V., & Khaikin, M. M. (2023). A study of factors affecting national energy efficiency. *Energies, 16*(13). https://doi.org/10.3390/en16135170

Nong, D., Simshauser, P., & Nguyen, D. B. (2021). Greenhouse gas emissions vs CO2 emissions: Comparative analysis of a global carbon tax. *Applied Energy, 298*, 117223. https://doi.org/10.1016/j.apenergy.2021.117223

Nwokolo, S. C., Meyer, E. L., & Ahia, C. C. (2023). Credible pathways to catching up with climate goals in Nigeria. *Climate, 11*(9). https://doi.org/10.3390/cli11090196

OECD. (2013). *Analysing energy subsidies in the countries of eastern Europe, Caucasus and central Asia.* https://www.oecd.org/env/outreach/energy_subsidies.pdf

OECD. (2021). *Update on recent progress in reform of inefficient fossil-fuel subsidies that encourage wasteful consumption.* https://www.oecd.org/fossil-fuels/publicationsandfurtherreading/OECD-IEA-G20-Fossil-Fuel-Subsidies-Reform-Update-2021.pdf

Olabi, A. G., & Abdelkareem, M. A. (2022). Renewable energy and climate change. *Renewable and Sustainable Energy Reviews, 158*, 112111. https://doi.org/10.1016/j.rser.2022.112111

Oloruntobi, O., Mokhtar, K., Mohd Rozar, N., Gohari, A., Asif, S., & Chuah, L. F. (2023). Effective technologies and practices for reducing pollution in warehouses—A review. *Cleaner Engineering and Technology, 13*, 100622. https://doi.org/10.1016/j.clet.2023.100622

Onofrei, M., Vatamanu, A. F., & Cigu, E. (2022). The relationship between economic growth and CO2 emissions in EU countries: A cointegration analysis. *Frontiers in Environmental Science, 10.* https://doi.org/10.3389/fenvs.2022.934885

Osman, A. I., Mehta, N., Elgarahy, A. M., Hefny, M., Al-Hinai, A., Al-Muhtaseb, A. H., & Rooney, D. W. (2022). Hydrogen production, storage, utilisation and environmental impacts: A review. *Environmental Chemistry Letters, 20*(1), 153–188. https://doi.org/10.1007/s10311-021-01322-8

Osman, A. I., Chen, L., Yang, M., Msigwa, G., Farghali, M., Fawzy, S., Rooney, D. W., & Yap, P.-S. (2023). Cost, environmental impact, and resilience of renewable energy under a changing climate: A review. *Environmental Chemistry Letters, 21*(2), 741–764. https://doi.org/10.1007/s10311-022-01532-8

Osobajo, O. A., Otitoju, A., Otitoju, M. A., & Oke, A. (2020). The impact of energy consumption and economic growth on carbon dioxide emissions. *Sustainability, 12*(19). https://doi.org/10.3390/su12197965

Pan, A., Xu, S., & Zaidi, S. A. H. (2024). Environmental impact of energy imports: Natural resources income and natural gas production profitability in the Asia-Pacific economic cooperation countries. *Geoscience Frontiers, 15*(2), 101756. https://doi.org/10.1016/j.gsf.2023.101756

Paramati, S. R., Shahzad, U., & Doğan, B. (2022). The role of environmental technology for energy demand and energy efficiency: Evidence from OECD countries. *Renewable and Sustainable Energy Reviews, 153*, 111735. https://doi.org/10.1016/j.rser.2021.111735

Paraschiv, L. S., & Paraschiv, S. (2023). Contribution of renewable energy (hydro, wind, solar and biomass) to decarbonization and transformation of the electricity generation sector for sustainable development. *Energy Reports, 9*, 535–544. https://doi.org/10.1016/j.egyr.2023.07.024

Pata, U. K., Alola, A. A., Erdogan, S., & Kartal, M. T. (2023). The influence of income, economic policy uncertainty, geopolitical risk, and urbanization on renewable energy investments in G7 countries. *Energy Economics, 128*, 107172. https://doi.org/10.1016/j.eneco.2023.107172

Pesaran, M. H., Shin, Y., & Smith, R. P. (1999). Pooled mean group estimation of dynamic heterogeneous panels. *Journal of the American Statistical Association, 94*(446), 621–634. https://doi.org/10.1080/01621459.1999.10474156

Petropoulou, P., Artopoulou, I., Kalemikerakis, I., & Govina, O. (2023). Environment and public health: Air pollution and chronic diseases. In *Environmental sciences proceedings* (Vol. 26, issue 1). https://doi.org/10.3390/environsciproc2023026118.

Rehman, A., Ma, H., Radulescu, M., Sinisi, C. I., Paunescu, L. M., Alam, M. D. S., & Alvarado, R. (2021). The energy mix dilemma and environmental sustainability: Interaction among greenhouse gas emissions, nuclear energy, urban agglomeration, and economic growth. *Energies, 14*(22). https://doi.org/10.3390/en14227703

Sahu, M., Malyan, V., & Mayya, Y. S. (2021). In S. P. Singh, K. Rathinam, T. Gupta, & A. K. Agarwal (Eds.), *Technologies for controlling particulate matter emissions from industries BT —Pollution control technologies: Current status and future prospects* (pp. 253–290). Springer Singapore. https://doi.org/10.1007/978-981-16-0858-2_12

Sanyal, S., & Wuebbles, D. J. (2022). The potential impact of a clean energy society on air quality. *Earth's Future, 10*(6), e2021EF002558. https://doi.org/10.1029/2021EF002558

Sarkodie, S. A., Ackom, E., Bekun, F. V., & Owusu, P. A. (2020). Energy–climate–economy–population nexus: An empirical analysis in Kenya, Senegal, and Eswatini. *Sustainability, 12*(15). https://doi.org/10.3390/su12156202

Sarpong, K. A., Xu, W., Gyamfi, B. A., & Ofori, E. K. (2023). Can environmental taxes and green-energy offer carbon-free E7 economies? An empirical analysis in the framework of COP-26. *Environmental Science and Pollution Research, 30*(18), 51726–51739. https://doi.org/10.1007/s11356-023-25904-x

Seddighi, S., Anthony, E. J., Seddighi, H., & Johnsson, F. (2023). The interplay between energy technologies and human health: Implications for energy transition. *Energy Reports, 9*, 5592–5611. https://doi.org/10.1016/j.egyr.2023.04.351

Seetharaman, M. K., Patwa, N., Saravanan, & Gupta, Y. (2019). Breaking barriers in deployment of renewable energy. *Heliyon, 5*(1), e01166. https://doi.org/10.1016/j.heliyon.2019.e01166

Shivanna, K. R. (2022). Climate change and its impact on biodiversity and human welfare. *Proceedings of the Indian National Science Academy. Part A, Physical Sciences, 88*(2), 160–171. https://doi.org/10.1007/s43538-022-00073-6

Sikiru, S., Oladosu, T. L., Amosa, T. I., Olutoki, J. O., Ansari, M. N. M., Abioye, K. J., Rehman, Z. U., & Soleimani, H. (2024). Hydrogen-powered horizons: Transformative technologies in clean energy generation, distribution, and storage for sustainable innovation. *International Journal of Hydrogen Energy, 56*, 1152–1182. https://doi.org/10.1016/j.ijhydene.2023.12.186

Sofia, D., Gioiella, F., Lotrecchiano, N., & Giuliano, A. (2020). Mitigation strategies for reducing air pollution. *Environmental Science and Pollution Research, 27*(16), 19226–19235. https://doi.org/10.1007/s11356-020-08647-x

Sreenu, N. (2022). Impact of FDI, crude oil price and economic growth on CO2 emission in India:—symmetric and asymmetric analysis through ARDL and non -linear ARDL approach. *Environmental Science and Pollution Research, 29*(28), 42452–42465. https://doi.org/10.1007/s11356-022-19597-x

Tabash, M. I., Sheikh, U. A., Matar, A., Ahmed, A., & Tran, D. K. (2023). Do financial crises matter for nonlinear exchange rate and stock market cointegration? A heterogeneous nonlinear panel data model with PMG approach. *International Journal of Financial Studies, 11*(1). https://doi.org/10.3390/ijfs11010007

Udeagha, M. C., & Muchapondwa, E. (2022). Investigating the moderating role of economic policy uncertainty in environmental Kuznets curve for South Africa: Evidence from the novel dynamic ARDL simulations approach. *Environmental Science and Pollution Research, 29*(51), 77199–77237. https://doi.org/10.1007/s11356-022-21107-y

Ullah, S., Liu, Q., Wang, S., Jan, A. U., Sharif, H. M. A., Ditta, A., Wang, G., & Cheng, H. (2023). Sources, impacts, factors affecting Cr uptake in plants, and mechanisms behind phytoremediation of Cr-contaminated soils. *Science of the*

*Total Environment, 899*, 165726. https://doi.org/10.1016/j.scitotenv.2023.165726

Ullah, S., Luo, R., Adebayo, T. S., & Kartal, M. T. (2024). Paving the ways toward sustainable development: The asymmetric effect of economic complexity, renewable electricity, and foreign direct investment on the environmental sustainability in BRICS-T. *Environment, Development and Sustainability, 26*(4), 9115–9139. https://doi.org/10.1007/s10668-023-03085-4

United Nations Environment Programme. (2019). *Measuring fossil fuel subsidies in the context of the sustainable development goals.*

van den Bergh, J., van Beers, C., & King, L. C. (2024). Prioritize carbon pricing over fossil-fuel subsidy reform. *IScience, 27*(1), 108584. https://doi.org/10.1016/j.isci.2023.108584

van Vuuren, D. P., Stehfest, E., Gernaat, D. E. H. J., Doelman, J. C., van den Berg, M., Harmsen, M., de Boer, H. S., Bouwman, L. F., Daioglou, V., Edelenbosch, O. Y., Girod, B., Kram, T., Lassaletta, L., Lucas, P. L., van Meijl, H., Müller, C., van Ruijven, B. J., van der Sluis, S., & Tabeau, A. (2017). Energy, land-use and greenhouse gas emissions trajectories under a green growth paradigm. *Global Environmental Change, 42*, 237–250. https://doi.org/10.1016/j.gloenvcha.2016.05.008

Wang, J., & Azam, W. (2024). Natural resource scarcity, fossil fuel energy consumption, and total greenhouse gas emissions in top emitting countries. *Geoscience Frontiers, 15*(2), 101757. https://doi.org/10.1016/j.gsf.2023.101757

Wang, P., & Liang, S. (2022). Environmental regulations and energy efficiency: The mediating role of climate change and technological innovation. In *Frontiers in Environmental Science* (Vol. 10). https://doi.org/10.3389/fenvs.2022.909082

Wang, H., & Wang, M. (2020). Effects of technological innovation on energy efficiency in China: Evidence from dynamic panel of 284 cities. *Science of the Total Environment, 709*, 136172. https://doi.org/10.1016/j.scitotenv.2019.136172

Wang, S., Li, Q., Fang, C., & Zhou, C. (2016). The relationship between economic growth, energy consumption, and CO2 emissions: Empirical evidence from China. *Science of the Total Environment, 542*, 360–371. https://doi.org/10.1016/j.scitotenv.2015.10.027

Wang, Q.-J., Feng, G.-F., Wang, H.-J., & Chang, C.-P. (2022). The influence of political ideology on greenhouse gas emissions. *Global Environmental Change, 74*, 102496. https://doi.org/10.1016/j.gloenvcha.2022.102496

Wang, H., Gu, K., Sun, H., & Xiao, H. (2023). Reconfirmation of the symbiosis on carbon emissions and air pollution: A spatial spillover perspective. *Science of the Total Environment, 858*, 159906. https://doi.org/10.1016/j.scitotenv.2022.159906

Wen, J., Okolo, C. V., Ugwuoke, I. C., & Kolani, K. (2022). Research on influencing factors of renewable energy, energy efficiency, on technological innovation. Does trade, investment and human capital development matter? *Energy Policy, 160*, 112718. https://doi.org/10.1016/j.enpol.2021.112718

Wenlong, Z., Tien, N. H., Sibghatullah, A., Asih, D., Soelton, M., & Ramli, Y. (2023). Impact of energy efficiency, technology innovation, institutional quality, and trade openness on greenhouse gas emissions in ten Asian economies. *Environmental Science and Pollution Research, 30*(15), 43024–43039. https://doi.org/10.1007/s11356-022-20079-3

Wolde-Rufael, Y., & Mulat-weldemeskel, E. (2023). Effectiveness of environmental taxes and environmental stringent policies on CO2 emissions: The European experience. *Environment, Development and Sustainability, 25*(6), 5211–5239. https://doi.org/10.1007/s10668-022-02262-1

Woodward, J., Li, J., Rothwell, J., & Hurley, R. (2021). Acute riverine microplastic contamination due to avoidable releases of untreated wastewater. *Nature Sustainability, 4*(9), 793–802. https://doi.org/10.1038/s41893-021-00718-2

Xie, Y., Xu, M., Pu, J., Pan, Y., Liu, X., Zhang, Y., & Xu, S. (2023). Large-scale renewable energy brings regionally disproportional air quality and health cobenefits in China. *IScience, 26*(8). https://doi.org/10.1016/j.isci.2023.107459

Xu, B., & Xu, R. (2022). Assessing the role of environmental regulations in improving energy efficiency and reducing CO2 emissions: Evidence from the logistics industry. *Environmental Impact Assessment Review, 96*, 106831. https://doi.org/10.1016/j.eiar.2022.106831

Xu, H., Jia, Y., Sun, Z., Su, J., Liu, Q. S., Zhou, Q., & Jiang, G. (2022). Environmental pollution, a hidden culprit for health issues. *Eco-Environment & Health, 1*(1), 31–45. https://doi.org/10.1016/j.eehl.2022.04.003

Yamaka, W., Phadkantha, R., & Rakpho, P. (2021). Economic and energy impacts on greenhouse gas emissions: A case study of China and the USA. *Energy Reports, 7*, 240–247. https://doi.org/10.1016/j.egyr.2021.06.040

Yasemi, S., Khalili, Y., Sanati, A., & Bagheri, M. (2023). Carbon capture and storage: Application in the oil and gas industry. *Sustainability, 15*(19). https://doi.org/10.3390/su151914486

Yilanci, V., Candan, G., & Shah, M. I. (2023). Identifying the roles of energy and economic factors on environmental degradation in MINT economies: A hesitant fuzzy analytic hierarchy process. *Environmental Science and Pollution Research, 30*(19), 55768–55781. https://doi.org/10.1007/s11356-023-26142-x

Yue, H., Worrell, E., Crijns-Graus, W., & Zhang, S. (2021). The potential of industrial electricity savings to reduce air pollution from coal-fired power generation in China. *Journal of Cleaner Production, 301*, 126978. https://doi.org/10.1016/j.jclepro.2021.126978

Zeng, J., Bao, R., & McFarland, M. (2022). Clean energy substitution: The effect of transitioning from coal to gas on air pollution. *Energy Economics, 107*, 105816. https://doi.org/10.1016/j.eneco.2022.105816

Zhai, Y., Bai, J., Chang, P., Liu, Z., Wang, Y., Liu, G., Cui, B., Peijnenburg, W., & Vijver, M. G. (2024). Microplastics in terrestrial ecosystem: Exploring the menace to the soil-plant-microbe interactions. *TrAC Trends in Analytical Chemistry, 174*, 117667. https://doi.org/10.1016/j.trac.2024.117667

Zhang, Y., Abbas, M., Koura, Y. H., Su, Y., & Iqbal, W. (2021). The impact trilemma of energy prices, taxation, and population on industrial and residential greenhouse gas emissions in Europe. *Environmental Science and Pollution Research, 28*(6), 6913–6928. https://doi.org/10.1007/s11356-020-10618-1

Zhang, L., Xu, M., Chen, H., Li, Y., & Chen, S. (2022a). Globalization, Green Economy and Environmental Challenges: State of the Art Review for Practical Implications. In *Frontiers in Environmental Science* (Vol. 10). https://doi.org/10.3389/fenvs.2022.870271

Zhang, Y., Khan, I., & Zafar, M. W. (2022b). Assessing environmental quality through natural resources, energy resources, and tax revenues. *Environmental Science and Pollution Research, 29*(59), 89029–89044. https://doi.org/10.1007/s11356-022-22005-z

Zhao, X., Mahendru, M., Ma, X., Rao, A., & Shang, Y. (2022). Impacts of environmental regulations on green economic growth in China: New guidelines regarding renewable energy and energy efficiency. *Renewable Energy, 187*, 728–742. https://doi.org/10.1016/j.renene.2022.01.076

Zhu, B., Deng, Y., & Hu, X. (2023). Global energy security: Do internal and external risk spillovers matter? A multilayer network method. *Energy Economics, 126*, 106961. https://doi.org/10.1016/j.eneco.2023.106961

CHAPTER 6

# Energy Efficiency Analysis of Romania Compared to EU Member States Using the DEA Method

## Introduction

In a European landscape marked by accelerated energy transition and ambitious decarbonization targets, Sustainable Development Goal 7 (SDG7), which aims to ensure access to affordable, reliable, sustainable and clean energy for all, plays a strategic role in the integrated architecture of the European Green Deal and the sustainability policy framework. However, simply quantifying progress through aggregate indicators is not sufficient to reflect the complexity and heterogeneity of energy performance across Member States. Thus, assessing ecological efficiency becomes crucial to understanding how energy resources are transformed into productive outputs while minimizing negative environmental impacts, in particular greenhouse gas emissions.

In this context, the Data Envelopment Analysis (DEA) method proves to be an appropriate analytical tool, as it allows for a relative assessment of performance between decision-making units (countries) in relation to an empirically constructed efficiency frontier, without imposing a pre-established production function. The model considers a number of relevant inputs (energy consumption, environmental protection expenditure, economic inputs) as well as desired outputs (share of renewable energy, GDP per capita) to estimate the ecological efficiency scores of EU Member States.



C. Fortea, *Sustainable Economic Development and the European Green Deal*, https://doi.org/10.1007/978-3-032-10326-0_6

The main objective of this research is to identify both countries that are at the efficiency frontier and can serve as benchmarks for good practice in the field of sustainable energy transition, and those countries that are operating below their estimated potential and require strategic interventions to optimize their energy and environmental policies. In this way, the DEA analysis provides a valuable benchmarking framework for the formulation of differentiated and evidence-based policies, thereby supporting a fair and efficient energy transition across the European Union.

## Literature Review

With the European energy transition and the commitments made by the European Union through the European Green (European Commission, 2023a), energy efficiency has become a key pillar of sustainable development policies. The United Nations Sustainable Development Goal (SDG) 7, which aims to ensure access to affordable, reliable, sustainable and modern energy for all, highlights the strategic role of energy efficiency in promoting sustainability, reducing greenhouse gas emissions and increasing economic competitiveness. Beyond traditional quantitative approaches, such as per capita energy consumption analysis or renewable source shares, the literature emphasizes the importance of an integrative assessment that captures the complexity of transforming energy resources into positive economic and environmental outcomes (Algarni et al., 2023; Bakhsh et al., 2024; Yang et al., 2024). In this regard, non-parametric methods, in particular Data Envelopment Analysis (DEA), provide a robust methodological framework for measuring relative performance between states without imposing a pre-established production function (Camanho et al., 2024; Mergoni et al., 2025; Murillo Zamorano & Vega-Cervera, 2001). This literature review section analyses, in a structured manner, four main directions: the conceptual foundations of energy efficiency, the assessment methods used in the literature, relevant empirical studies applied in the EU context and the main determinants of energy efficiency at the national and European levels.

### *Conceptual Foundations of Energy Efficiency and SDG7*

Energy efficiency is widely recognized as one of the most important factors in achieving energy sustainability and reducing greenhouse gas emissions. Essentially, it reflects the ability of an economic or technological system to achieve maximum output from a minimum amount of energy input (Ibrahim et al., 2023; Işık et al., 2024; Wang et al., 2021, 2022). This concept transcends simple consumption reduction and also includes technological optimization processes, industrial innovation, and behavioural changes geared towards energy saving and smart energy use (Chu & Wang, 2024; Gorina et al., 2024; Wu et al., 2023).

Within the 2030 Agenda for Sustainable Development (European Commission, 2022; United Nations, 2015), SDG7 aims to ensure access to affordable, reliable, sustainable and modern energy for all, emphasizing the importance of increasing the share of energy from renewable sources and the global rate of improvement in energy efficiency. The European Union has taken up these objectives through a series of strategic instruments, in particular the "Fit for 55" package (European Council, 2023) and the Energy Efficiency Directive (EU Directive 2023/1791) (European Union, 2023), which set binding targets for reducing final and primary energy consumption.

Recent academic literature conceptualizes energy efficiency as a systemic element at the intersection of energy policies, ecological transition and socio-economic sustainability (Barragán-Ocaña et al., 2025; Del Duca et al., 2024; European Environment Agency, 2024; Mushafiq et al., 2023; Wang et al., 2025b). This approach integrates three fundamental dimensions: technical (equipment and infrastructure efficiency), economic (energy productivity) and institutional (regulations and administrative capacity).

In theory, energy efficiency is analysed within two dominant paradigms. The first is the neoclassical perspective, which associates efficiency with optimized production functions and economies of scale, while the second is the evolutionary-institutionalist perspective, which emphasizes the role of institutional context, innovation and public policies in generating efficient trajectories (Brancaccio et al., 2022; Gaeta et al., 2021; Giraudet & Missemer, 2023).

In particular, in European literature, energy efficiency is frequently correlated with indicators such as energy intensity (energy consumed per unit of GDP), energy productivity (GDP per unit of energy) and the share of energy from renewable sources (Caglar & Yavuz, 2023; Özkan et al., 2023; Quito et al., 2023; Török, 2025; Zhang et al., 2021). At the same time, energy efficiency is seen as a catalyst for "decoupling" economic growth from environmental impact, a phenomenon known as "decoupling" (Cautisanu & Hatmanu, 2023; Nyangchak, 2022; Palmer & Floyd, 2025; Zhang & Wei, 2024).

In this context, energy efficiency is analysed not only as a result but also as a process governed by a complex set of factors: fiscal and environmental regulations, the level of investment in R&D, the degree of digitization of energy infrastructure, consumer behaviour and the national economic structure (Alola et al., 2023; Axenbeck et al., 2024; Mahmood et al., 2022; Shabalov et al., 2021). Therefore, energy efficiency assessment must reflect this multidimensionality, avoid simplistic generalizations and use robust models capable of capturing the heterogeneity of national systems.

The conceptual foundations of energy efficiency require a systemic, integrative and contextualized understanding. As the European Union strengthens its path towards climate neutrality, energy efficiency will continue to play a central role in the convergence of economic, social and environmental objectives. In this regard, integrating SDG7 objectives into national and regional policies requires not only political commitments but also refined analytical tools capable of differentiating between the actual performance and latent potential of each Member State.

### *Methodological Approaches in Energy Efficiency Analysis: Focus on DEA*

Energy efficiency assessment has undergone significant methodological diversification over the past two decades, amid growing pressures related to climate change and the energy transition. Among the most commonly used methods in the literature are stochastic frontier analysis (SFA), multiple regression analysis, methods based on artificial intelligence (neural networks, genetic algorithms), but especially Data Envelopment Analysis (DEA), which has established itself as a benchmark method in inter-country and inter-regional comparative studies (Chen et al., 2022; Narayanan et al., 2022; Paulet & Mavoori, 2021).

DEA is a non-parametric efficiency analysis technique that uses linear optimization to construct an efficient production frontier based on a set of empirical inputs and outputs. Unlike traditional econometric methods, DEA does not impose a pre-established production function and allows the relative performance of comparable decision-making units (DMUs), such as states or regions, to be evaluated (Banker et al., 1984; Charnes et al., 1978). This flexibility is essential in the analysis of complex energy systems, which are characterized by structural heterogeneity and multiple objectives.

In the field of energy efficiency, DEA is frequently used to measure countries' ability to transform energy resources (inputs such as primary energy consumption, environmental protection expenditure, GHG emissions) into economic and environmental outcomes (outputs such as GDP per capita, share of renewable energy, energy productivity) (Addis, 2025; Lin et al., 2023; Tang et al., 2023; Xue et al., 2022).

The classic DEA model assumes two basic configurations: the constant returns to scale (CCR) model and the variable returns to scale (BCC) model. The CCR model, introduced by Charnes, Cooper and Rhodes (Charnes et al., 1978), is appropriate when the units analysed operate at an optimal scale, while the BCC model, proposed by Banker et al. (Banker et al., 1984), allows for the capture of efficiency variations generated by scalability. In energy efficiency studies, the choice of model depends on the nature of the data and the purpose of the analysis: static benchmarking, dynamic evaluation or identification of technological frontiers (Iqbal et al., 2025; Panwar et al., 2022; Rostamzadeh et al., 2021).

An important contribution to the development of DEA is the introduction of distance measures and input- or output-oriented models. In the case of energy transition, input-oriented models are often preferred, as they aim to reduce consumption and emissions while maintaining the desired level of economic and environmental outputs (Bakhsh et al., 2024; Benfica & Marques, 2024; Henriques et al., 2022). At the same time, DEA models can integrate undesirable outputs, such as $CO_2$ emissions or industrial pollutants, through adaptations such as the slack-based measure (SBM) model (Emrouznejad et al., 2025; Huang, 2023).

A major advantage of DEA is its ability to identify efficient units (with a score of 1) that define the efficiency frontier, as well as inefficient ones, for which adjustments to inputs or increases in outputs can be recommended (Omrani et al., 2023; Vaseei et al., 2024). In addition, DEA results can be interpreted in terms of improvement potential, benchmarking and differentiated policy formulation, depending on the profile of each unit analysed.

Applied literature confirms the broad applicability of DEA in energy efficiency analyses at the national, regional and sectoral levels. For example, Fidanoski et al. (2021) apply a DEA model to analyse the energy performance of OECD countries, and Shu et al. (2024) evaluate the energy systems of 168 countries. In the European Union, DEA has been used to compare the performance of Member States against SDG7 targets, identifying both efficiency leaders and regions with potential for optimization (Saha et al., 2024; Simeonovski et al., 2021).

Recent extensions of the method include dynamic DEA models, which allow for the analysis of time variations in efficiency (Malmquist index) (Lou et al., 2024), DEA with moving windows (window analysis), which captures performance in variable contexts (Sueyoshi & Goto, 2025), and the integration of DEA with other quantitative methods, such as PCA (Principal Component Analysis) (Omrani et al., 2019) or fuzzy analysis (Fuzzy DEA), to manage uncertainty and multidimensionality (Davoudabadi et al., 2021).

In Romania's case, applying the DEA method to energy efficiency analysis allows us to identify its relative position compared to other Member States, as well as the main areas where policy interventions and investments can bring the greatest benefits. Studies show that Romania performs well in terms of the share of renewable energy and energy tax revenues, but still faces challenges related to industrial emission intensity and consumption efficiency in agriculture and industry (Ceausescu et al., 2025; European Union, 2024a; Niță et al., 2025; OECD, 2024).

The DEA is a robust and flexible methodological tool for assessing energy efficiency in diverse economic and institutional contexts. Its ability to integrate multiple variables, enable contextualized benchmarking and generate relevant operational information recommends it as one of the most effective methods for analysing energy sustainability. The choice of this method in the present research is justified both by its extensive validation in the literature and by its suitability for the comparative and evaluative objectives of the study.

### *Empirical Studies on Energy Efficiency in the European Union*

The empirical literature on energy efficiency in the European Union (EU) has expanded significantly, particularly in the last decade, against the backdrop of intensified climate commitments and the need to base public policies on evidence. Studies using the DEA method have stood out for their ability to highlight not only the relative performance of Member States but also the trajectories of convergence or divergence in relation to decarbonization and energy sustainability objectives (Fazio et al., 2024; Lacko et al., 2024).

One of the research directions on energy efficiency at the European Union level has focused on the use of output-oriented DEA models, in which the performance of Member States was assessed by reporting the resources used—such as energy consumption and capital—to economic and environmental outcomes, such as GDP and $CO_2$ emissions (Makridou et al., 2015; Matsumoto et al., 2020; Simeonovski et al., 2021). The conclusions of these initial studies highlighted the superior performance of the Nordic countries, characterized by mature energy systems and effective public policies, while countries in Central and Eastern Europe generally showed lower levels of efficiency, which can be explained by structural, institutional and technological gaps.

Other European studies (Basilio, 2025; Demiral & Sağlam, 2021; Gökgöz & Yalçın, 2023) used output-oriented non-parametric DEA models to assess the energy performance of Member States, taking into account inputs such as energy consumption and capital, and economic and environmental outputs. The results revealed relatively higher efficiency in the Nordic countries and persistent deficits in Central and Eastern Europe, suggesting a correlation between the level of economic development, institutional maturity and energy performance.

In Romania's case, recent studies based on the DEA method suggest an upward trend in energy efficiency in certain periods, especially when public policies have supported the increase in the share of renewable sources and the reduction of industrial emissions. Between 2010 and 2017, Romania's energy performance approached the efficiency frontier in years marked by sustained investment from European funds and the implementation of fiscal measures favourable to the green transition. However, the literature indicates a trend of stagnation since 2018, which can be explained by structural constraints in the energy system, including high import dependence, outdated infrastructure and limited administrative capacity to absorb funds earmarked for efficiency (European Commission, 2023b; European Environment Agency, 2022). These developments reflect the complexity of the Romanian energy context, where potential performance is often mitigated by institutional and economic factors that hinder sustainable progress.

Similar results are confirmed by other analyses carried out for Eastern Europe. Thus, the application of the DEA BCC model in comparative studies between countries such as Romania, Lithuania and the Czech Republic indicates a general trend of improving energy productivity, supported by the integration of renewable sources and the support of

European policies (Krejnus et al., 2023; Sotiroski et al., 2023). However, industrial emissions relative to economic output remain high in these countries, reflecting persistent challenges in modernizing the industrial sector and implementing low-emission technologies.

At the European aggregate level, numerous studies have investigated how differences in energy efficiency between Member States can be explained by structural and institutional factors, using combined DEA models and panel regressions (Chodakowska et al., 2025; Iqbal et al., 2025). These studies have shown that high energy efficiency performance is often associated with a favourable sectoral structure (low share of energy-intensive industries), a high degree of market liberalization, sustained investment in efficient technologies and the existence of coherent, stable and well-implemented policies. Such findings support the idea that energy efficiency is not only a consequence of technological progress, but also of a solid and predictable institutional framework (Anwar et al., 2021; Yavuz et al., 2023; Zhang & Dilanchiev, 2022).

An important aspect highlighted by empirical literature is the impact of crises on energy efficiency. For example, the 2008 financial crisis generated a slight artificial increase in efficiency through a decline in industrial production, while the COVID-19 pandemic led to a temporary reduction in emissions, but also to a destabilization of efficiency policies (Gajewski, 2022; Qin et al., 2024; Schaupp, 2023). The conflict in Ukraine has also led to a reconfiguration of energy strategies, affecting the performance of countries such as Germany and the Netherlands, which were dependent on Russian gas imports.

Empirical studies based on DEA provide a detailed and comparative picture of how EU Member States manage energy resources in relation to efficiency and sustainability objectives. They highlight the importance of dynamic assessments tailored to the national context and the usefulness of benchmarking for the formulation of differentiated policies. The case of Romania reveals both notable progress and a continuing need for technological modernization and institutional strengthening in order to achieve the performance of the leading EU countries.

### *Determinants of Energy Efficiency in EU Member States*

Identifying and analysing the factors that determine energy efficiency in European Union Member States is essential for understanding differences in energy performance and for developing appropriate public policies. The literature has presented a wide range of structural, institutional, technological and behavioural factors that influence energy efficiency, and the interaction between them varies significantly across countries (Gajdzik et al., 2024; Kim & Medal, 2024; Papadakis & Katsaprakakis, 2023).

A first major determinant is economic structure. Countries with a high share of energy-intensive industries (such as Poland, Bulgaria or the Czech Republic) face additional challenges in reducing consumption and emissions compared to countries where services and creative sectors are dominant (European Union, 2024b; Manowska et al., 2024; Saboori et al., 2024; Sompolska-Rzechuła et al., 2024). In this regard, changing the economic structure in favour of high value-added and low energy consumption sectors is considered an effective indirect strategy for increasing efficiency.

Another important factor is the level of investment in research and development (R&D) and technological innovation. Countries that allocate substantial resources to the development of clean technologies, the thermal rehabilitation of buildings and the digitization of energy networks (smart grids) consistently perform better (Dimian et al., 2025; Fernandez et al., 2024; Mahmood et al., 2024; Prieto González et al., 2021). Countries such as Germany, Sweden and Denmark are recognized for their innovation ecosystems and policies to support efficiency through fiscal instruments and coherent regulations (Cefis & Scrofani, 2025; Chen et al., 2023; Teixeira & Tavares-Lehmann, 2022; Wang et al., 2025a).

At the institutional level, the quality of governance and the coherence of energy policies are another key determinant. According to specialist studies (Gajdzik et al., 2023; Kwilinski et al., 2023; Ni et al., 2022), energy efficiency is positively correlated with the stability of the legislative framework, the administrative capacity to implement European directives and the transparency of resource allocation. Countries with a clear national strategy and dedicated institutions (energy efficiency agencies, specialized funds) achieve significantly better performance.

The fiscal and economic dimensions also play an essential role. Pricing policies (energy taxes, differentiated tariffs, subsidies for efficient equipment) influence both consumer behaviour and firms' investment decisions (Coady et al., 2023; Fotiou et al., 2022; Kruse-Andersen & Sørensen, 2022). Carbon taxes and green certificate systems have proven to be effective tools in reducing energy intensity, especially in the Nordic countries and Germany (Al-Abdulqader et al., 2025; Bolat et al., 2023; European Environmental Bureau, 2021).

Energy dependence and the national energy mix also influence energy efficiency. Countries that are heavily dependent on imports (Italy, Lithuania, Hungary) are more exposed to price fluctuations and are systemically vulnerable, while countries with a diversified mix and investments in renewable sources (Austria, Spain) have more room for manoeuvre in the transition to efficiency (Dolphin et al., 2024; European Commission, 2025; International Monetary Fund, 2025).

Demographic and social factors, such as urbanization, education and average income, also influence energy efficiency. Recent studies have shown that urban populations are, on average, more energy efficient than rural populations due to compact infrastructure, public transportation and access to modern technologies (Almatar, 2024; Dai et al., 2025). At the same time, citizens' awareness of efficiency issues and access to information lead to more rational consumption behaviours.

A revealing example is the differences between Romania and Western European countries. Although Romania has made significant progress in the use of renewable sources and in reducing industrial emissions, challenges remain related to structural inefficiencies in the building and transport sectors, the lack of a long-term integrated strategy and the limited capacity to implement European funds for energy efficiency (Lamb et al., 2022; OECD, 2024; Panton, 2023).

Recent literature increasingly highlights the importance of digitizing energy infrastructure and adopting smart energy solutions. The use of smart meters, artificial intelligence in consumption management and integrated monitoring platforms can generate significant energy savings and contribute to systemic efficiency (Rajaperumal & Columbus, 2025; Safari et al., 2024; Sargiotis, 2025; Ukoba et al., 2024).

Energy efficiency is the result of a complex set of interconnected factors. There is no universal solution, and the performance of each Member State depends on how these determinants are managed strategically, integrated and contextualized. With a view to achieving SDG7 and climate neutrality, the analysis of these factors provides informed decision-making support for the development of effective, equitable and sustainable public policies in the European Union.

The literature convincingly demonstrates that energy efficiency is not only a technical indicator of energy performance but also an expression of the capacity of economic systems to adapt to a sustainable, equitable and competitive model. Within the European Union, differences in energy efficiency between Member States reflect the variety of economic structures, levels of development, public policies and availability of resources. Applying the DEA method in comparative efficiency analysis allows not only the identification of performance frontiers but also the highlighting of opportunities for improvement without penalizing national diversity. Thus, studies investigating energy efficiency in the EU, including those focusing on Romania, contribute to the formulation of differentiated, evidence-based policies to achieve SDG7 and the transition to a clean energy system. The integration of these perspectives into the theoretical and empirical framework of the present research underpins the choice of the DEA model and justifies the relevance of the comparative assessment between Romania and the other EU Member States.

## Methodology

DEA (Data Envelopment Analysis) is an effective way of assessing the energy performance and efficiency of different countries. This method uses a set of indicators and variables to measure and compare energy consumption and production between different countries. By identifying the most efficient countries and identifying strategies, the DEA method provides valuable information for improving long-term energy efficiency. This approach helps to identify and promote best practices in energy use and can serve as a basis for decision-making to implement energy efficiency policies and measures. DEA can also help increase competitiveness, reduce costs and protect the environment by promoting the efficient use of energy resources. DEA provides an objective perspective on the energy performance of different sectors or regions, thus enabling the identification and improvement of energy use weaknesses. Through the application of the DEA method, innovative technological solutions and efficient energy management strategies can be identified and evaluated, thus contributing to the sustainable development of society. The application of DEA in the field of energy efficiency can bring multiple benefits at both macro and micro economic levels, contributing to sustainable development objectives and reducing environmental impacts.

We propose to perform the energy efficiency analysis of Romania in the European context, and we will use the DEA method for which the following inputs and outputs have been established according to Table 6.1.

The following working hypotheses were established to demonstrate energy efficiency:

**Table 6.1** Presentation of indicators

| *Symbol* | *Indicator name* | *Unit of measurement* | *Source* | *Tip* |
|---|---|---|---|---|
| SDG7FZEP | Total primary energy supply | Tonnes of oil equivalent, million | OECD (2025) | Input |
| SDG7APER | Renewable energy production | % total energy supply | OECD (2025) | Output |
| SDG7CENAG | Energy consumption in agriculture | % of total energy consumption | OECD (2025) | Input |
| SDG7CENI | Energy consumption in industry | % of total energy consumption | OECD (2025) | Input |
| SDG7VFEN | Energy-related tax revenues | % of total environmental tax revenues | OECD (2025) | Output |
| SDG7PREN | Energy productivity | Euro per kilogramme of oil | Eurostat (2024b) | Output |
| SDG7IMPEN | Dependence on energy imports | % | Eurostat (2024a) | Input |
| SDG7ENGS | Net greenhouse gas emissions | Index, 1990=100 | Eurostat (2025) | Input |
| SDG7INEMT | Industrial air emissions intensity | Grammes per euro | OECD (2025) | Input |

Source: Author

H1: Most European countries are energy efficient.

H2: The European Union picks up the efficiency trend of Member States showing a fluctuation in energy efficiency in relation to elements of economic and geopolitical uncertainty.

H3: Romania was among the countries with full energy efficiency during the period analysed.

H4: The most energy inefficient countries are Finland, Belgium and the Netherlands

Data Envelopment analysis (DEA) can be used as a technique based on linear programming and optimization to evaluate the efficiency of each unit, and in order to improve the efficiency of each unit, a benchmark set for an inefficient unit is determined and the efficiency of different units can be compared with the efficiency limit.

## Results and Discussions

In this study, 28 decision-making units (DMUs) represented by the 28 states and the European average were used and investigated with respect to 6 inputs and 3 outputs for the period 2010–2021. The type of DEA analysis used in this study is the radial model based on the CRS model (constant returns to scale model) using the IN (input) approach. The efficiency value obtained by the defined model is shown in Table 6.2.

Table 6.2 shows that the countries that are fully energy efficient over the whole period 2010–2021 are Austria, Czech Republic, Cyprus, Denmark, Estonia, Germany, Ireland, Latvia, Lithuania, Luxembourg, Malta, Romania, Slovenia, Cyprus, and Sweden. This demonstrates working Hypothesis 1. Some countries such as Bulgaria, Croatia, France, Hungary and Slovakia achieved energy efficiency only during certain

**Table 6.2** The SDG7 effectiveness scoreboard at EU Member State level and European average

| DMU | 2010 | 2011 | 2012 | 2013 | 2014 | 2015 | 2016 | 2017 | 2018 | 2019 | 2020 | 2021 |
|---|---|---|---|---|---|---|---|---|---|---|---|---|
| Austria | 1.000 | 1.000 | 1.000 | 1.000 | 1.000 | 1.000 | 1.000 | 1.000 | 1.000 | 1.000 | 1.000 | 1.000 |
| Belgium | 0.598 | 0.612 | 0.612 | 0.589 | 0.588 | 0.578 | 0.617 | 0.639 | 0.621 | 0.628 | 0.580 | 0.567 |
| Bulgaria | 0.962 | 0.944 | 1.000 | 1.000 | 1.000 | 1.000 | 1.000 | 1.000 | 1.000 | 1.000 | 1.000 | 1.000 |
| Czech Republic | 1.000 | 1.000 | 1.000 | 1.000 | 1.000 | 1.000 | 1.000 | 1.000 | 1.000 | 1.000 | 1.000 | 1.000 |
| Cyprus | 1.000 | 1.000 | 1.000 | 1.000 | 1.000 | 1.000 | 1.000 | 1.000 | 1.000 | 1.000 | 1.000 | 1.000 |
| Croatia | 0.964 | 0.978 | 1.000 | 1.000 | 1.000 | 1.000 | 1.000 | 1.000 | 1.000 | 1.000 | 0.897 | 0.834 |
| Denmark | 1.000 | 1.000 | 1.000 | 1.000 | 1.000 | 1.000 | 1.000 | 1.000 | 1.000 | 1.000 | 1.000 | 1.000 |
| Estonia | 1.000 | 1.000 | 1.000 | 1.000 | 1.000 | 1.000 | 1.000 | 1.000 | 1.000 | 1.000 | 1.000 | 1.000 |
| EU 27 | 0.930 | 0.937 | 0.963 | 1.000 | 1.000 | 1.000 | 1.000 | 1.000 | 0.997 | 0.771 | 1.000 | 0.753 |
| Finland | 0.799 | 0.820 | 0.840 | 0.887 | 0.865 | 0.826 | 0.876 | 0.892 | 0.960 | 0.953 | 0.858 | 0.876 |
| France | 0.862 | 0.838 | 0.858 | 0.854 | 0.864 | 0.912 | 0.905 | 0.918 | 0.996 | 1.000 | 1.000 | 0.909 |
| Germany | 1.000 | 1.000 | 1.000 | 1.000 | 1.000 | 1.000 | 1.000 | 1.000 | 1.000 | 1.000 | 1.000 | 1.000 |
| Greece | 0.871 | 0.914 | 0.934 | 0.939 | 0.897 | 0.899 | 0.887 | 0.896 | 0.885 | 0.898 | 0.868 | 0.845 |
| Ireland | 1.000 | 1.000 | 1.000 | 1.000 | 1.000 | 1.000 | 1.000 | 1.000 | 1.000 | 1.000 | 1.000 | 1.000 |
| Italy | 0.928 | 0.894 | 0.901 | 0.957 | 0.955 | 0.872 | 0.871 | 0.828 | 0.869 | 0.861 | 0.838 | 0.785 |
| Latvia | 1.000 | 1.000 | 1.000 | 1.000 | 1.000 | 1.000 | 1.000 | 1.000 | 1.000 | 1.000 | 1.000 | 1.000 |
| Lithuania | 1.000 | 1.000 | 1.000 | 1.000 | 1.000 | 1.000 | 1.000 | 1.000 | 1.000 | 1.000 | 1.000 | 1.000 |
| Luxembourg | 1.000 | 1.000 | 1.000 | 1.000 | 1.000 | 1.000 | 1.000 | 1.000 | 1.000 | 1.000 | 1.000 | 1.000 |
| Malta | 1.000 | 1.000 | 1.000 | 1.000 | 1.000 | 1.000 | 1.000 | 1.000 | 1.000 | 1.000 | 1.000 | 1.000 |
| Netherlands | 0.543 | 0.555 | 0.575 | 0.678 | 0.623 | 0.573 | 0.568 | 0.575 | 0.600 | 0.633 | 0.633 | 0.637 |
| Poland | 0.954 | 0.976 | 0.952 | 0.969 | 0.991 | 0.955 | 0.968 | 0.936 | 0.968 | 0.860 | 0.927 | 0.774 |
| Portugal | 0.891 | 0.862 | 0.752 | 0.833 | 0.847 | 0.714 | 0.825 | 0.660 | 0.752 | 0.750 | 0.709 | 0.693 |
| Romania | 1.000 | 1.000 | 1.000 | 1.000 | 1.000 | 1.000 | 1.000 | 1.000 | 1.000 | 1.000 | 1.000 | 1.000 |
| Slovakia | 0.941 | 0.890 | 0.921 | 0.966 | 0.951 | 0.985 | 0.994 | 0.989 | 1.000 | 1.000 | 1.000 | 1.000 |
| Slovenia | 1.000 | 1.000 | 1.000 | 1.000 | 1.000 | 1.000 | 1.000 | 1.000 | 1.000 | 1.000 | 1.000 | 1.000 |
| Spain | 0.837 | 0.798 | 0.770 | 0.790 | 0.796 | 0.814 | 0.785 | 0.760 | 0.789 | 0.734 | 0.742 | 0.654 |
| Sweden | 1.000 | 1.000 | 1.000 | 1.000 | 1.000 | 1.000 | 1.000 | 1.000 | 1.000 | 1.000 | 1.000 | 1.000 |
| Hungary | 1.000 | 1.000 | 0.977 | 0.912 | 0.835 | 0.912 | 0.864 | 0.813 | 0.827 | 0.739 | 0.813 | 0.740 |

Source: Author

periods. Among them Slovakia had an improvement in energy efficiency during the last period of the analysis (after 2018); the rest of the partially energy-efficient countries experienced reductions in energy efficiency due to the outbreak of geopolitical conflict while Hungary experienced an increased energy inefficiency intensity after 2011, a trend that continued until the end of the period. At the EU level it is found to reach energy efficiency in the period 2013–2017 and in the year 2020. We assess that the economic crisis in 2010 and 2012, the Brexit crisis in the period 2018–2019 and the geopolitical conflict triggered by Russia's aggression against Ukraine are the main elements that influenced European energy security. Working Hypothesis 2 is demonstrated. The most energy-efficient countries are Austria, the Czech Republic, Cyprus, Denmark, Estonia, Germany, Ireland, Latvia, Lithuania, Luxembourg, Malta, Romania, Slovenia and Sweden. This demonstrates working Hypothesis 3. At the other extreme are Finland, Belgium and the Netherlands. Working Hypothesis 4 is demonstrated.

Using the DEA method, the efficiency of the analysed unit is projected to the maximum level, and the process is completed by equating the efficiency thresholds to 1 for as many compared units as possible. Thus, efficiency benchmarks are obtained for each analysed DMU.

Table 6.3 presents Romania's efficiency benchmarks per year for the European average and Slovakia.

Table 6.3 shows that Romania is an efficiency benchmark for the EU (in 2011 and 2018) as well as for Slovakia for the period 2010–2017, with Slovakia becoming energy efficient from 2018. Together with Romania, Denmark is also an efficiency benchmark for the EU (2010–2012, 2018–2019 and 2021). Other partial efficiency benchmarks are Germany, Lithuania, Luxembourg, the Czech Republic, Estonia, Hungary, Estonia and Ireland. For Slovakia together with Romania, Luxembourg, Sweden, Lithuania, Germany, Slovenia, Czech Republic and Denmark are efficiency benchmarks.

Table 6.4 shows the efficiency benchmark ranking of the Romanian model in relation to other energy-efficient countries by determining the frequency ranking by year and by energy-efficient Member State.

Table 6.4 shows that Romania ranks 4th to 12th among the energy-efficient European Member States as a reference model, with efficiency peaks in 2014, 2017 and 2018. In 2021 Romania has the ninth most efficient energy model out of the 16 efficiency benchmarks analysed.

**Table 6.3** Romania's efficiency benchmarks by year

| DMU | Year | Peer1 | Peer2 | Peer3 | Peer4 | Peer5 | Peer6 |
|---|---|---|---|---|---|---|---|
| EU27 | 2010 | Czech Republic | Denmark | Estonia | Germany | Lithuania | Hungary |
| | 2011 | Denmark | Germany | Lithuania | Luxembourg | Romania | Hungary |
| | 2012 | Czech Republic | Denmark | Germany | Lithuania | Luxembourg | - |
| | 2013 | EU27 | - | - | - | - | - |
| | 2014 | EU27 | - | - | - | - | - |
| | 2015 | EU27 | - | - | - | - | - |
| | 2016 | EU27 | - | - | - | - | - |
| | 2017 | EU27 | - | - | - | - | - |
| | 2018 | Czech Republic | Denmark | Lithuania | Luxembourg | Romania | - |
| | 2019 | Czech Republic | Denmark | Estonia | Germany | Ireland | Luxembourg |
| | 2020 | EU27 | - | - | - | - | - |
| | 2021 | Denmark | Estonia | Germany | Ireland | Lithuania | - |
| Slovakia | 2010 | Germany | Lithuania | Luxembourg | Romania | Slovenia | - |
| | 2011 | Lithuania | Luxembourg | Romania | Slovenia | Sweden | - |
| | 2012 | Lithuania | Luxembourg | Romania | Slovenia | Sweden | |
| | 2013 | Germany | Lithuania | Luxembourg | Romania | Sweden | - |
| | 2014 | Czech Republic | Lithuania | Luxembourg | Romania | Sweden | - |
| | 2015 | Denmark | Lithuania | Luxembourg | Romania | Sweden | - |
| | 2016 | Czech Republic | Lithuania | Luxembourg | Romania | Sweden | - |
| | 2017 | Germany | Lithuania | Luxembourg | Romania | Sweden | - |
| | 2018 | Slovakia | - | - | - | - | - |
| | 2019 | Slovakia | - | - | - | - | - |
| | 2020 | Slovakia | - | - | - | - | - |
| | 2021 | Slovakia | - | - | - | - | - |

Source: Author

The values of λ (lambdas = weights for equal units) were determined, which represent the combination of equal units used to construct each virtual unit. The values of λ are shown in Table 6.5.

It can be seen from Table 6.5 that the highest values of lambdas coefficients with maximum annual frequency are those of Slovakia, which recommends this country for determining the efficiency correspondences of the Romanian model for SDG7.

Tables 6.6 and 6.7 present the values of the variables for the energy efficiency model, showing the weights attributable by the DEA method to the input values (Table 6.6) and output values (Table 6.7), respectively.

Table 6.6 shows that the significantly different from 0 weights of the improvable input variables for Romania are air emissions intensity from industry (SDG7INEMT) followed by energy consumption in agriculture (SDG7CENAG) and energy consumption in industry (SDG7CENI). At

**Table 6.4** Frequency ranking of benchmarks by year for energy-efficient Member States

| Year | 2010 | 2011 | 2012 | 2013 | 2014 | 2015 | 2016 | 2017 | 2018 | 2019 | 2020 | 2021 |
|---|---|---|---|---|---|---|---|---|---|---|---|---|
| Ranking | EN 10/14 | EN 10/14 | EN 12/16 | EN 7/17 | EN 4/17 | EN 8/17 | EN 6/17 | EN 4/17 | EN 4/17 | EN 7/17 | EN 10/17 | EN 9/16 |
| Peer frequencies | Austria (5) | Austria (4) | Austria (4) | Austria (4) | Austria (4) | Austria (1) | Austria (2) | Austria (1) | Austria (2) | Austria (1) | Austria (1) | Austria (1) |
| | Czech Republic (3) | Czech Republic (2) | Bulgaria (1) | Bulgaria (1) | Bulgaria (1) | Bulgaria (1) | Bulgaria (1) | Bulgaria (1) | Bulgaria (1) | Bulgaria (1) | Bulgaria (1) | Bulgaria (1) |
| | Cyprus (2) | Cyprus (2) | Czech Republic (6) | Czech Republic (6) | Czech Republic (7) | Czech Republic (6) | Czech Republic (8) | Czech Republic (5) | Czech Republic (6) | Czech Republic (7) | Czech Republic (8) | Czech Republic (5) |
| | Denmark (12) | Denmark (11) | Cyprus (2) | Cyprus (1) | Cyprus (1) | Cyprus (1) | Cyprus (1) | Cyprus (2) | Cyprus (1) | Cyprus (2) | Cyprus (1) | Cyprus (1) |
| | Estonia (5) | Estonia (6) | Croatia (1) | Croatia (3) | Croatia (2) | Croatia (2) | Croatia (1) | Croatia (1) | Croatia (1) | Croatia (1) | Denmark (8) | Denmark (6) |
| | Germany (5) | Germany (4) | Denmark (12) | Denmark (11) | Denmark (9) | Denmark (11) | Denmark (10) | Denmark (10) | Denmark (12) | Denmark (9) | Estonia (11) | Estonia (13) |
| | Ireland (1) | Ireland (1) | Estonia (5) | Estonia (4) | Estonia (3) | Estonia (6) | Estonia (5) | Estonia (4) | Estonia (4) | Estonia (11) | EU27 (3) | Germany (6) |
| | Latvia (5) | Latvia (5) | Germany (4) | EU27 (7) | EU27 (6) | EU27 (8) | EU27 (8) | EU27 (7) | Germany (3) | France (2) | France (4) | Ireland (6) |
| | Lithuania (9) | Lithuania (10) | Ireland (1) | Germany (5) | Germany (3) | Germany (2) | Germany (2) | Germany (3) | Ireland (2) | Germany (4) | Germany (3) | Latvia (1) |
| | Luxembourg (9) | Luxembourg (8) | Latvia (5) | Ireland (1) | Ireland (1) | Ireland (1) | Ireland (1) | Ireland (1) | Latvia (3) | Ireland (2) | Ireland (1) | Lithuania (13) |
| | Malta (2) | Malta (1) | Lithuania (12) | Latvia (4) | Latvia (3) | Latvia (2) | Latvia (3) | Latvia (3) | Lithuania (12) | Latvia (2) | Latvia (1) | Luxembourg (7) |
| | Romania (3) | Romania (4) | Luxembourg (9) | Lithuania (8) | Lithuania (11) | Lithuania (9) | Lithuania (12) | Lithuania (12) | Luxembourg (9) | Lithuania (10) | Lithuania (10) | Malta (1) |
| | Slovenia (4) | Slovenia (6) | Malta (2) | Luxembourg (10) | Luxembourg (9) | Luxembourg (11) | Luxembourg (8) | Luxembourg (9) | Malta (1) | Luxembourg (8) | Luxembourg (7) | Romania (1) |
| | Sweden (4) | Sweden (6) | Romania (2) | Malta (1) | Malta (1) | Malta (1) | Malta (1) | Malta (1) | Romania (6) | Malta (1) | Malta (1) | Slovakia (1) |
| | Hungary (6) | Hungary (5) | Slovenia (3) | Romania (5) | Romania (8) | Romania (4) | Romania (7) | Romania (7) | Slovakia (1) | Romania (2) | Romania (1) | Slovenia (1) |
| | | | Sweden (6) | Slovenia (3) | Slovenia (2) | Slovenia (1) | Slovenia (2) | Slovenia (1) | Slovenia (1) | Slovakia (1) | Slovakia (1) | Sweden (5) |
| | | | | Sweden (6) | Sweden (8) | Sweden (6) | Sweden (6) | Sweden (6) | Sweden (4) | Slovenia (1) | Slovenia (2) | |

Source: Author

EU level the significantly different from 0 weights of the improvable input variables are air emissions intensity from industry (SDG7INEMT) followed by energy consumption in industry (SDG7CENI) and energy consumption in agriculture (SDG7CENAG). At the Slovakian level all input indicators, i.e. primary energy supply, energy consumption in industry, energy consumption in agriculture, energy import dependency, net greenhouse gas emissions and air emissions intensity of industry need to be improved compared to the Romanian efficiency model to achieve energy efficiency in the perspective of the SDG7.

Table 6.7 shows that in the case of Romania the significantly different weights of the improved output variables from 0 are related to

**Table 6.5** Lambdas coefficients of the reference unit Romania

| DMU/year | Romania | | | | | | | | | | | |
|---|---|---|---|---|---|---|---|---|---|---|---|---|
| | 2010 | 2011 | 2012 | 2013 | 2014 | 2015 | 2016 | 2017 | 2018 | 2019 | 2020 | 2021 |
| Austria | 0.000 | 0.000 | 0.000 | 0.000 | 0.000 | 0.000 | 0.000 | 0.000 | 0.000 | 0.000 | 0.000 | 0.000 |
| Belgium | 0.000 | 0.000 | 0.000 | 0.000 | 0.000 | 0.043 | 0.085 | 0.005 | 0.000 | 0.000 | 0.000 | 0.000 |
| Bulgaria | 0.355 | 0.376 | 0.000 | 0.000 | 0.000 | 0.000 | 0.000 | 0.000 | 0.000 | 0.000 | 0.000 | 0.000 |
| Czech Republic | 0.000 | 0.000 | 0.000 | 0.000 | 0.000 | 0.000 | 0.000 | 0.000 | 0.000 | 0.000 | 0.000 | 0.000 |
| Cyprus | 0.000 | 0.000 | 0.000 | 0.000 | 0.000 | 0.000 | 0.000 | 0.000 | 0.000 | 0.000 | 0.000 | 0.000 |
| Croatia | 0.000 | 0.000 | 0.000 | 0.000 | 0.000 | 0.000 | 0.000 | 0.000 | 0.000 | 0.000 | 0.000 | 0.000 |
| Denmark | 0.000 | 0.000 | 0.000 | 0.000 | 0.000 | 0.000 | 0.000 | 0.000 | 0.000 | 0.000 | 0.000 | 0.000 |
| Estonia | 0.000 | 0.000 | 0.000 | 0.000 | 0.000 | 0.000 | 0.000 | 0.000 | 0.000 | 0.000 | 0.000 | 0.000 |
| EU27 | 0.000 | 0.098 | 0.000 | 0.000 | 0.000 | 0.000 | 0.000 | 0.000 | 0.083 | 0.000 | 0.000 | 0.000 |
| Finland | 0.000 | 0.000 | 0.000 | 0.000 | 0.000 | 0.000 | 0.000 | 0.000 | 0.000 | 0.000 | 0.000 | 0.000 |
| France | 0.000 | 0.000 | 0.000 | 0.000 | 0.035 | 0.000 | 0.065 | 0.050 | 0.044 | 0.000 | 0.000 | 0.000 |
| Germany | 0.000 | 0.000 | 0.000 | 0.000 | 0.000 | 0.000 | 0.000 | 0.000 | 0.000 | 0.000 | 0.000 | 0.000 |
| Greece | 0.000 | 0.000 | 0.000 | 0.078 | 0.157 | 0.127 | 0.079 | 0.000 | 0.010 | 0.000 | 0.000 | 0.000 |
| Ireland | 0.000 | 0.000 | 0.000 | 0.000 | 0.000 | 0.000 | 0.000 | 0.000 | 0.000 | 0.000 | 0.000 | 0.000 |
| Italy | 0.000 | 0.000 | 0.000 | 0.000 | 0.000 | 0.000 | 0.000 | 0.007 | 0.018 | 0.110 | 0.000 | 0.000 |
| Latvia | 0.000 | 0.000 | 0.000 | 0.000 | 0.000 | 0.000 | 0.000 | 0.000 | 0.000 | 0.000 | 0.000 | 0.000 |
| Lithuania | 0.000 | 0.000 | 0.000 | 0.000 | 0.000 | 0.000 | 0.000 | 0.000 | 0.000 | 0.000 | 0.000 | 0.000 |
| Luxembourg | 0.000 | 0.000 | 0.000 | 0.000 | 0.000 | 0.000 | 0.000 | 0.000 | 0.000 | 0.000 | 0.000 | 0.000 |
| Malta | 0.000 | 0.000 | 0.000 | 0.000 | 0.000 | 0.000 | 0.000 | 0.000 | 0.000 | 0.000 | 0.000 | 0.000 |
| Netherlands | 0.000 | 0.000 | 0.000 | 0.056 | 0.022 | 0.000 | 0.005 | 0.000 | 0.000 | 0.000 | 0.000 | 0.000 |
| Poland | 0.000 | 0.000 | 0.000 | 0.000 | 0.077 | 0.000 | 0.000 | 0.000 | 0.000 | 0.000 | 0.000 | 0.000 |
| Portugal | 0.000 | 0.000 | 0.000 | 0.000 | 0.000 | 0.000 | 0.000 | 0.000 | 0.000 | 0.000 | 0.000 | 0.000 |
| Romania | 1.000 | 1.000 | 1.000 | 1.000 | 1.000 | 1.000 | 1.000 | 1.000 | 1.000 | 1.000 | 1.000 | 1.000 |
| Slovakia | 0.195 | 0.103 | 0.111 | 0.170 | 0.078 | 0.107 | 0.102 | 0.025 | 0.000 | 0.000 | 0.000 | 0.000 |
| Slovenia | 0.000 | 0.000 | 0.000 | 0.000 | 0.000 | 0.000 | 0.000 | 0.000 | 0.000 | 0.000 | 0.000 | 0.000 |
| Spain | 0.000 | 0.000 | 0.000 | 0.016 | 0.067 | 0.000 | 0.118 | 0.101 | 0.153 | 0.000 | 0.000 | 0.000 |
| Sweden | 0.000 | 0.000 | 0.000 | 0.000 | 0.000 | 0.000 | 0.000 | 0.000 | 0.000 | 0.000 | 0.000 | 0.000 |
| Hungary | 0.000 | 0.000 | 0.000 | 0.000 | 0.000 | 0.000 | 0.000 | 0.047 | 0.000 | 0.000 | 0.000 | 0.000 |

Source: Author

energy-related tax revenues as a percentage of environmental tax revenues. In the case of the EU to these is added energy productivity, while for Slovakia the improvable output variables concern energy-related tax revenues as a percentage of environmental tax revenues.

The input and output vulnerabilities related to each unit are shown in Tables 6.8 and 6.9, respectively.

Table 6.8 shows that Romania has no input vulnerabilities. From the perspective of the Romanian EU-wide energy efficiency model,

**Table 6.6** Weights for the input variable values of the energy efficiency model

| *DMU* | *Romania* | | | | | | *EU27* | | | | | |
|---|---|---|---|---|---|---|---|---|---|---|---|---|
| *Indicator/ year* | *SDG7 IMPEN* | *SDG7 ENGS* | *SDG7 INEMT* | *SDG7 FZEP* | *SDG7 CENAG* | *SDG7 CENI* | *SDG7 IMPEN* | *SDG7 ENGS* | *SDG7 INEMT* | *SDG7 FZEP* | *SDG7 CENAG* | *SDG7 CENI* |
| 2010 | 0.006 | 0 | 0.406 | 0 | 0.09 | 0.022 | 0.006 | 0 | 0.322 | 0 | 0.066 | 0.021 |
| 2011 | 0.005 | 0 | 0 | 0 | 0.113 | 0.024 | 0.006 | 0 | 0.455 | 0 | 0.063 | 0.02 |
| 2012 | 0.005 | 0.001 | 0 | 0 | 0.111 | 0.023 | 0.005 | 0 | 0.842 | 0 | 0.055 | 0.021 |
| 2013 | 0.004 | 0 | 0 | 0 | 0.16 | 0.023 | 0.003 | 0 | 0.307 | 0 | 0 | 0.033 |
| 2014 | 0.003 | 0 | 0 | 0 | 0.185 | 0.022 | 0.003 | 0 | 0.459 | 0 | 0 | 0.029 |
| 2015 | 0.005 | 0 | 0 | 0 | 0.102 | 0.026 | 0.001 | 0 | 0.392 | 0 | 0 | 0.039 |
| 2016 | 0.005 | 0 | 0 | 0 | 0.127 | 0.024 | 0.001 | 0 | 0.133 | 0 | 0.015 | 0.037 |
| 2017 | 0.005 | 0 | 0.413 | 0 | 0.073 | 0.025 | 0.004 | 0 | 0.344 | 0 | 0.061 | 0.02 |
| 2018 | 0.004 | 0.005 | 0 | 0 | 0 | 0.028 | 0.006 | 0 | 1.113 | 0 | 0.027 | 0.021 |
| 2019 | 0.005 | 0.001 | 0 | 0 | 0.117 | 0.021 | 0.007 | 0.001 | 1.773 | 0 | 0.049 | 0.013 |
| 2020 | 0.006 | 0 | 0.776 | 0 | 0.089 | 0.019 | 0.005 | 0 | 1.721 | 0 | 0 | 0.025 |
| 2021 | 0.003 | 0.012 | 0 | 0 | 0 | 0.023 | 0.005 | 0 | 3.532 | 0 | 0.026 | 0.017 |
| | Slovakia | | | | | | | | | | | |
| | SDG7 IMPEN | SDG7 ENGS | SDG7 INEMT | SDG7 FZEP | SDG7 CENAG | SDG7 CENI | | | | | | |
| 2010 | 0.006 | 0.003 | 1.108 | 0.001 | 0.259 | 0 | | | | | | |
| 2011 | 0.005 | 0.003 | 1.271 | 0.001 | 0.213 | 0 | | | | | | |
| 2012 | 0.006 | 0.003 | 0.552 | 0.003 | 0.239 | 0 | | | | | | |
| 2013 | 0.005 | 0.004 | 0.941 | 0.001 | 0.269 | 0 | | | | | | |
| 2014 | 0.008 | 0.002 | 2.182 | 0.006 | 0.094 | 0 | | | | | | |
| 2015 | 0.008 | 0.002 | 2.132 | 0.009 | 0.049 | 0 | | | | | | |
| 2016 | 0.008 | 0.002 | 1.978 | 0.006 | 0.124 | 0 | | | | | | |
| 2017 | 0.006 | 0.003 | 1.847 | 0.001 | 0.236 | 0 | | | | | | |
| 2018 | 0.009 | 0.001 | 1.58 | 0.009 | 0.127 | 0 | | | | | | |
| 2019 | 0.002 | 0.003 | 10.095 | 0.001 | 0.139 | 0 | | | | | | |
| 2020 | 0.008 | 0.001 | 1.833 | 0 | 0.162 | 0.007 | | | | | | |
| 2021 | 0.008 | 0.001 | 1.215 | 0.005 | 0.172 | 0.004 | | | | | | |

Source: Author

**Table 6.7** Weights for the output variable values of the energy efficiency model

| *DMU* | *Romania* | | | *EU27* | | | *Slovakia* | | |
|---|---|---|---|---|---|---|---|---|---|
| *Indicator/year* | *SDG7VFEN* | *SDG7PREN* | *SDG7APER* | *SDG7VFEN* | *SDG7PREN* | *SDG7APER* | *SDG7VFEN* | *SDG7PREN* | *SDG7APER* |
| 2010 | 0.009 | 0 | 0.013 | 0.01 | 0.006 | 0 | 0.012 | 0 | 0 |
| 2011 | 0.011 | 0 | 0.004 | 0.01 | 0.007 | 0 | 0.011 | 0 | 0 |
| 2012 | 0.012 | 0 | 0 | 0.011 | 0.002 | 0 | 0.012 | 0 | 0 |
| 2013 | 0.008 | 0 | 0.018 | 0.009 | 0 | 0 | 0.013 | 0 | 0 |
| 2014 | 0.007 | 0 | 0.02 | 0.009 | 0 | 0 | 0.012 | 0 | 0 |
| 2015 | 0.008 | 0 | 0.014 | 0.009 | 0 | 0 | 0.013 | 0 | 0 |
| 2016 | 0.007 | 0.026 | 0.012 | 0.008 | 0.008 | 0 | 0.013 | 0 | 0 |
| 2017 | 0.011 | 0 | 0 | 0.009 | 0 | 0 | 0.012 | 0 | 0 |
| 2018 | 0.011 | 0 | 0 | 0.01 | 0.005 | 0 | 0.012 | 0 | 0 |
| 2019 | 0.011 | 0 | 0 | 0.009 | 0.021 | 0 | 0.01 | 0.017 | 0.006 |
| 2020 | 0.011 | 0 | 0 | 0.009 | 0.01 | 0 | 0.013 | 0 | 0 |
| 2021 | 0.011 | 0 | 0 | 0.009 | 0.012 | 0 | 0.013 | 0 | 0 |

Source: Author

**Table 6.8** Input vulnerabilities affecting the achievement of energy efficiency in the analysed regions

| *DMU* | *Romania* | | | | | | *EU27* | | | | | |
|---|---|---|---|---|---|---|---|---|---|---|---|---|
| *Indicator/ year* | *SDG7 IMPEN* | *SDG7 ENGS* | *SDG7 INEMT* | *SDG7 FZEP* | *SDG7 CENAG* | *SDG7 CENI* | *SDG7 IMPEN* | *SDG7 ENGS* | *SDG7 INEMT* | *SDG7 FZEP* | *SDG7 CENAG* | *SDG7 CENI* |
| 2010 | 0 | 0 | 0 | 0 | 0 | 0 | 0 | 0 | 0 | 1248.693 | 0 | 0 |
| 2011 | 0 | 0 | 0 | 0 | 0 | 0 | 0 | 0 | 0 | 1265.041 | 0 | 0 |
| 2012 | 0 | 0 | 0 | 0 | 0 | 0 | 0 | 8.408 | 0 | 1356.13 | 0 | 0 |
| 2013 | 0 | 0 | 0 | 0 | 0 | 0 | 0 | 0 | 0 | 0 | 0 | 0 |
| 2014 | 0 | 0 | 0 | 0 | 0 | 0 | 0 | 0 | 0 | 0 | 0 | 0 |
| 2015 | 0 | 0 | 0 | 0 | 0 | 0 | 0 | 0 | 0 | 0 | 0 | 0 |
| 2016 | 0 | 0 | 0 | 0 | 0 | 0 | 0 | 0 | 0 | 0 | 0 | 0 |
| 2017 | 0 | 0 | 0 | 0 | 0 | 0 | 0 | 0 | 0 | 0 | 0 | 0 |
| 2018 | 0 | 0 | 0 | 0 | 0 | 0 | 0 | 9.231 | 0 | 1399.475 | 0 | 0 |
| 2019 | 0 | 0 | 0 | 0 | 0 | 0 | 0 | 0 | 0 | 965.267 | 0 | 0 |
| 2020 | 0 | 0 | 0 | 0 | 0 | 0 | 0 | 0 | 0 | 0 | 0 | 0 |
| 2021 | 0 | 0 | 0 | 0 | 0 | 0 | 0 | 1.48 | 0 | 781.351 | 0 | 0 |
| | Slovakia | | | | | | | | | | | |
| | SDG7 IMPEN | SDG7 ENGS | SDG7 INEMT | SDG7 FZEP | SDG7 CENAG | SDG7 CENI | | | | | | |
| 2010 | 0 | 0 | 0 | 0 | 0 | 8.149 | | | | | | |
| 2011 | 0 | 0 | 0 | 0 | 0 | 5.926 | | | | | | |
| 2012 | 0 | 0 | 0 | 0 | 0 | 9.342 | | | | | | |
| 2013 | 0 | 0 | 0 | 0 | 0 | 9.873 | | | | | | |
| 2014 | 0 | 0 | 0 | 0 | 0 | 13.513 | | | | | | |
| 2015 | 0 | 0 | 0 | 0 | 0 | 12.333 | | | | | | |
| 2016 | 0 | 0 | 0 | 0 | 0 | 13.284 | | | | | | |
| 2017 | 0 | 0 | 0 | 0 | 0 | 11.822 | | | | | | |
| 2018 | 0 | 0 | 0 | 0 | 0 | 0 | | | | | | |
| 2019 | 0 | 0 | 0 | 0 | 0 | 0 | | | | | | |
| 2020 | 0 | 0 | 0 | 0 | 0 | 0 | | | | | | |
| 2021 | 0 | 0 | 0 | 0 | 0 | 0 | | | | | | |

Source: Author

**Table 6.9** Output vulnerabilities affecting the achievement of energy efficiency in the analysed regions

| *Year* | *Romania* | | | *EU27* | | | *Slovakia* | | |
|---|---|---|---|---|---|---|---|---|---|
| | *SDG7VFEN* | *SDG7PREN* | *SDG7APER* | *SDG7VFEN* | *SDG7PREN* | *SDG7APER* | *SDG7VFEN* | *SDG7PREN* | *SDG7APER* |
| 2010 | 0 | 0 | 0 | 0 | 0 | 1.276 | 0 | 1.577 | 1.237 |
| 2011 | 0 | 0 | 0 | 0 | 0 | 1.703 | 0 | 1.564 | 5.096 |
| 2012 | 0 | 0 | 0 | 0 | 0 | 0.347 | 0 | 1.403 | 5.585 |
| 2013 | 0 | 0 | 0 | 0 | 0 | 0 | 0 | 2.521 | 3.606 |
| 2014 | 0 | 0 | 0 | 0 | 0 | 0 | 0 | 1.587 | 2.026 |
| 2015 | 0 | 0 | 0 | 0 | 0 | 0 | 0 | 3.609 | 8.064 |
| 2016 | 0 | 0 | 0 | 0 | 0 | 0 | 0 | 1.818 | 1.777 |
| 2017 | 0 | 0 | 0 | 0 | 0 | 0 | 0 | 2.822 | 8.915 |
| 2018 | 0 | 0 | 0 | 0 | 0 | 5.22 | 0 | 0 | 0 |
| 2019 | 0 | 0 | 0 | 0 | 0 | 0.749 | 0 | 0 | 0 |
| 2020 | 0 | 0 | 0 | 0 | 0 | 0 | 0 | 0 | 0 |
| 2021 | 0 | 0 | 0 | 0 | 0 | 1.522 | 0 | 0 | 0 |

Source: Author

vulnerabilities are registered in terms of net greenhouse gas emissions and in terms of total primary energy supply. Also, from the perspective of the energy efficiency model for Slovakia, vulnerabilities have been identified in energy consumption in industry.

It can be seen from Table 6.9 that Romania does not register output vulnerabilities affecting energy efficiency. At the EU level, with reference to the Romanian efficiency model, there are vulnerabilities in the supply of renewable energy and in Slovakia, in addition to renewable energy production, the deficiencies also concern energy productivity.

Based on these vulnerabilities, the input and output efficiency targets for the analysed regions were designed. Table 6.10 shows the actual values and efficiency thresholds of each input.

Table 6.11 shows that Romania does not record differences between the input values and the proposed efficiency threshold values for all the variables analysed. At the European level in relation to the Romanian model, the largest reductions in inputs concern the whole primary energy supply, followed by the reduction of import dependency, the reduction of greenhouse gas emissions and the decrease of energy consumption in industry. The fewest deviations from the efficiency thresholds concern the intensity of air emissions in industry. Also, from Table 6.10 in the case of Slovakia the largest deviations from the efficiency threshold are for energy consumption in industry followed by energy import dependence and net greenhouse gas emissions.

Table 6.11 shows the actual values and output efficiency thresholds for the analysed regions.

Table 6.11 shows that Romania does not register vulnerabilities in reaching the output efficiency thresholds during the analysed period. At the European level, the Romanian model shows the need to increase the production of renewable energy, while Slovakia adds the need to improve energy productivity.

The analysis of Romania's energy efficiency compared to EU Member States using the DEA method has shown that Romania is energy efficient compared to other EU Member States. However, there are still significant opportunities to improve energy efficiency in the country. The implementation of appropriate policies and measures could contribute to reducing energy consumption and optimizing the use of energy resources, which would have a positive impact on the environment and the national economy. For example, investing in energy infrastructure, retrofitting buildings and promoting the use of renewable energy could help reduce

**Table 6.10** Actual values and input efficiency thresholds of the analysed regions

| *Tip* | | *Entry* | *Efficiency threshold* | *Entry* | *Efficiency threshold* | *Entry* | *Efficiency threshold* | *Entry* | *Efficiency threshold* | *Entry* | *Efficiency threshold* | *Entry* | *Efficiency threshold* |
|---|---|---|---|---|---|---|---|---|---|---|---|---|---|
| DMU | An | SDG7IMPEN | | SDG7ENGS | | SDG7INEMT | | SDG7FZEP | | SDG7CENAG | | SDG7CENI | |
| Romania | 2010 | 21.39 | 21.39 | 39.20 | 39.20 | 0.31 | 0.31 | 34.92 | 34.92 | 1.67 | 1.67 | 27.80 | 27.80 |
| | 2011 | 21.14 | 21.14 | 41.80 | 41.80 | 0.27 | 0.27 | 35.69 | 35.69 | 1.81 | 1.81 | 28.58 | 28.58 |
| | 2012 | 22.46 | 22.46 | 39.80 | 39.80 | 0.29 | 0.29 | 34.83 | 34.83 | 2.06 | 2.06 | 26.90 | 26.90 |
| | 2013 | 18.32 | 18.32 | 34.60 | 34.60 | 0.28 | 0.28 | 31.78 | 31.78 | 2.05 | 2.05 | 26.45 | 26.45 |
| | 2014 | 16.66 | 16.66 | 29.50 | 29.50 | 0.25 | 0.25 | 31.44 | 31.44 | 1.85 | 1.85 | 27.29 | 27.29 |
| | 2015 | 16.69 | 16.69 | 29.40 | 29.40 | 0.25 | 0.25 | 31.68 | 31.68 | 2.04 | 2.04 | 27.46 | 27.46 |
| | 2016 | 21.90 | 21.90 | 27.70 | 27.70 | 0.24 | 0.24 | 31.61 | 31.61 | 1.99 | 1.99 | 26.31 | 26.31 |
| | 2017 | 23.30 | 23.30 | 30.00 | 30.00 | 0.22 | 0.22 | 33.17 | 33.17 | 2.08 | 2.08 | 26.03 | 26.03 |
| | 2018 | 24.29 | 24.29 | 31.20 | 31.20 | 0.20 | 0.20 | 33.44 | 33.44 | 2.33 | 2.33 | 26.36 | 26.36 |
| | 2019 | 30.28 | 30.28 | 29.70 | 29.70 | 0.21 | 0.21 | 33.03 | 33.03 | 2.26 | 2.26 | 26.12 | 26.12 |
| | 2020 | 28.19 | 28.19 | 26.90 | 26.90 | 0.20 | 0.20 | 32.15 | 32.15 | 2.16 | 2.16 | 25.34 | 25.34 |
| | 2021 | 31.65 | 31.65 | 29.00 | 29.00 | 0.21 | 0.21 | 31.27 | 31.27 | 2.06 | 2.06 | 24.56 | 24.56 |

(*continued*)

**Table 6.10** (continued)

| *Tip* | | *Entry* | *Efficiency threshold* | *Entry* | *Efficiency threshold* | *Entry* | *Efficiency threshold* | *Entry* | *Efficiency threshold* | *Entry* | *Efficiency threshold* | *Entry* | *Efficiency threshold* |
|---|---|---|---|---|---|---|---|---|---|---|---|---|---|
| EU27 | 2010 | 55.77 | 51.87 | 83.40 | 77.57 | 0.10 | 0.09 | 1527.19 | 171.72 | 2.49 | 2.32 | 23.08 | 21.47 |
| | 2011 | 56.36 | 52.78 | 81.20 | 76.05 | 0.09 | 0.08 | 1479.03 | 120.14 | 2.53 | 2.37 | 24.08 | 22.55 |
| | 2012 | 54.92 | 52.89 | 79.70 | 68.35 | 0.08 | 0.08 | 1460.37 | 50.32 | 2.51 | 2.42 | 23.69 | 22.82 |
| | 2013 | 53.94 | 53.94 | 77.90 | 77.90 | 0.08 | 0.08 | 1444.80 | 1444.80 | 2.57 | 2.57 | 23.56 | 23.56 |
| | 2014 | 54.42 | 54.42 | 75.20 | 75.20 | 0.08 | 0.08 | 1391.90 | 1391.90 | 2.62 | 2.62 | 24.13 | 24.13 |
| | 2015 | 56.06 | 56.06 | 76.40 | 76.40 | 0.07 | 0.07 | 1408.50 | 1408.50 | 2.59 | 2.59 | 23.67 | 23.67 |
| | 2016 | 56.16 | 56.16 | 76.60 | 76.60 | 0.07 | 0.07 | 1419.17 | 1419.17 | 2.59 | 2.59 | 23.71 | 23.71 |
| | 2017 | 57.55 | 57.55 | 78.70 | 78.70 | 0.07 | 0.07 | 1443.28 | 1443.28 | 2.57 | 2.57 | 23.55 | 23.55 |
| | 2018 | 58.14 | 57.96 | 76.90 | 67.43 | 0.07 | 0.07 | 1431.59 | 27.72 | 2.84 | 2.83 | 23.81 | 23.74 |
| | 2019 | 60.48 | 46.61 | 73.80 | 56.87 | 0.06 | 0.05 | 1406.91 | 118.92 | 2.86 | 2.20 | 23.61 | 18.19 |
| | 2020 | 57.46 | 57.46 | 66.20 | 66.20 | 0.07 | 0.07 | 1310.73 | 1310.73 | 3.04 | 3.04 | 24.06 | 24.06 |
| | 2021 | 55.52 | 41.80 | 70.30 | 51.44 | 0.06 | 0.05 | 1214.55 | 133.01 | 3.22 | 2.42 | 24.51 | 18.45 |
| Slovakia | 2010 | 64.45 | 60.67 | 63.10 | 59.40 | 0.14 | 0.13 | 17.83 | 16.78 | 1.17 | 1.10 | 28.20 | 18.40 |
| | 2011 | 65.93 | 58.66 | 61.10 | 54.36 | 0.12 | 0.11 | 17.35 | 15.44 | 1.43 | 1.27 | 29.70 | 20.50 |
| | 2012 | 61.63 | 56.75 | 55.70 | 51.29 | 0.12 | 0.11 | 16.66 | 15.34 | 1.41 | 1.30 | 32.11 | 20.23 |
| | 2013 | 60.83 | 58.77 | 54.00 | 52.17 | 0.11 | 0.11 | 16.95 | 16.38 | 1.25 | 1.21 | 30.25 | 19.35 |
| | 2014 | 62.14 | 59.09 | 54.30 | 51.64 | 0.09 | 0.09 | 15.95 | 15.17 | 1.42 | 1.35 | 33.85 | 18.68 |
| | 2015 | 60.10 | 59.21 | 54.70 | 53.89 | 0.08 | 0.08 | 16.39 | 16.15 | 1.51 | 1.49 | 33.65 | 20.82 |
| | 2016 | 60.55 | 60.18 | 55.30 | 54.96 | 0.07 | 0.07 | 16.50 | 16.40 | 1.50 | 1.49 | 32.61 | 19.12 |
| | 2017 | 64.85 | 64.15 | 57.20 | 56.59 | 0.07 | 0.07 | 17.40 | 17.21 | 1.30 | 1.29 | 31.56 | 19.40 |
| | 2018 | 63.68 | 63.68 | 58.50 | 58.50 | 0.06 | 0.06 | 17.32 | 17.32 | 1.19 | 1.19 | 33.11 | 33.11 |
| | 2019 | 69.76 | 69.76 | 53.70 | 53.70 | 0.05 | 0.05 | 17.06 | 17.06 | 1.15 | 1.15 | 31.23 | 31.23 |
| | 2020 | 56.33 | 56.33 | 45.80 | 45.80 | 0.05 | 0.05 | 16.55 | 16.55 | 1.22 | 1.22 | 29.55 | 29.55 |
| | 2021 | 52.58 | 52.58 | 52.20 | 52.20 | 0.05 | 0.05 | 17.77 | 17.77 | 1.29 | 1.29 | 27.87 | 27.87 |

Source: Author

**Table 6.11** Actual values and output efficiency thresholds for the analysed regions

| *Tip* | | *Exit* | *Efficiency threshold* | *Exit* | *Efficiency threshold* | *Exit* | *Efficiency threshold* |
|---|---|---|---|---|---|---|---|
| *DMU* | *Year* | *SDG7VFEN* | | *SDG7PREN* | | *SDG7APER* | |
| Romania | 2010 | 84.48 | 84.48 | 3.66 | 3.66 | 16.78 | 16.78 |
| | 2011 | 87.43 | 87.43 | 3.75 | 3.75 | 14.20 | 14.20 |
| | 2012 | 86.29 | 86.29 | 3.91 | 3.91 | 14.92 | 14.92 |
| | 2013 | 85.89 | 85.89 | 4.29 | 4.29 | 17.47 | 17.47 |
| | 2014 | 88.47 | 88.47 | 4.51 | 4.51 | 19.48 | 19.48 |
| | 2015 | 89.43 | 89.43 | 4.61 | 4.61 | 18.86 | 18.86 |
| | 2016 | 89.62 | 89.62 | 4.76 | 4.76 | 19.59 | 19.59 |
| | 2017 | 92.71 | 92.71 | 4.88 | 4.88 | 18.21 | 18.21 |
| | 2018 | 93.15 | 93.15 | 5.17 | 5.17 | 18.06 | 18.06 |
| | 2019 | 91.98 | 91.98 | 5.43 | 5.43 | 18.20 | 18.20 |
| | 2020 | 90.89 | 90.89 | 5.38 | 5.38 | 18.63 | 18.63 |
| | 2021 | 89.80 | 89.80 | 5.35 | 5.35 | 19.06 | 19.06 |
| EU27 | 2010 | 87.29 | 87.29 | 6.84 | 6.84 | 11.20 | 12.48 |
| | 2011 | 86.63 | 86.63 | 7.17 | 7.17 | 11.28 | 12.98 |
| | 2012 | 87.75 | 87.75 | 7.22 | 7.22 | 12.62 | 12.97 |
| | 2013 | 106.93 | 106.93 | 7.30 | 7.30 | 13.38 | 13.38 |
| | 2014 | 112.92 | 112.92 | 7.68 | 7.68 | 13.84 | 13.84 |
| | 2015 | 112.11 | 112.11 | 7.75 | 7.75 | 14.04 | 14.04 |
| | 2016 | 113.40 | 113.40 | 7.83 | 7.83 | 14.12 | 14.12 |
| | 2017 | 111.34 | 111.34 | 7.89 | 7.89 | 14.15 | 14.15 |
| | 2018 | 92.57 | 92.57 | 8.09 | 8.09 | 14.89 | 20.11 |
| | 2019 | 68.35 | 68.35 | 8.37 | 8.37 | 15.61 | 16.36 |
| | 2020 | 97.52 | 97.52 | 8.59 | 8.59 | 17.28 | 17.28 |
| | 2021 | 70.81 | 70.81 | 8.54 | 8.54 | 18.95 | 20.47 |
| Slovakia | 2010 | 77.01 | 77.01 | 3.88 | 5.46 | 7.43 | 8.67 |
| | 2011 | 77.83 | 77.83 | 4.11 | 5.67 | 7.45 | 12.55 |
| | 2012 | 77.35 | 77.35 | 4.32 | 5.72 | 8.16 | 13.75 |
| | 2013 | 76.53 | 76.53 | 4.30 | 6.82 | 8.31 | 11.92 |
| | 2014 | 76.63 | 76.63 | 4.69 | 6.28 | 8.90 | 10.93 |
| | 2015 | 78.50 | 78.50 | 4.78 | 8.39 | 9.61 | 17.67 |
| | 2016 | 79.03 | 79.03 | 4.85 | 6.67 | 9.56 | 11.34 |
| | 2017 | 79.56 | 79.56 | 4.73 | 7.55 | 9.15 | 18.07 |
| | 2018 | 81.50 | 81.50 | 4.98 | 4.98 | 9.13 | 9.13 |
| | 2019 | 81.24 | 81.24 | 5.11 | 5.11 | 12.68 | 12.68 |
| | 2020 | 78.79 | 78.79 | 5.11 | 5.11 | 12.66 | 12.66 |
| | 2021 | 76.34 | 76.34 | 4.87 | 4.87 | 11.69 | 11.69 |

Source: Author

dependence on fossil fuels and increase energy efficiency. At the same time, education and public awareness of the importance of saving and using energy responsibly could play an important role in improving energy efficiency in Romania. By implementing these measures, Romania could become an example of energy efficiency in Europe and contribute to achieving the European Union's sustainability objectives. At the same time, the Romanian government should provide financial and fiscal support for investments in renewable energy and the modernization of buildings, so that these measures become accessible to all citizens. There is also a need for close cooperation between the public and private sectors to develop and implement advanced energy technologies. By promoting a favourable environment for innovation and investment in the energy sector, Romania can create a competitive and sustainable market which will bring long-term benefits for both the environment and the economy.

## Conclusions

The results obtained by applying the Data Envelopment Analysis (DEA) method to the Member States of the European Union, in the context of assessing progress towards Sustainable Development Goal 7, highlight significant variations in their environmental performance. The analysis showed that only a small subset of countries manages to efficiently transform energy and economic resources into desired outputs (clean energy, added value), while keeping greenhouse gas emissions at levels compatible with the green transition.

This finding highlights that environmental efficiency is not an automatic result of economic development, but reflects a combination of structural, institutional and technological factors, such as the quality of energy governance, the maturity of markets for renewable sources, the degree of industrial innovation and the efficiency of public resource allocation for the energy transition. Countries that combine a diversified energy mix, a high share of renewable energy and active fiscal policies in the field of environmental protection tend to be at the efficiency frontier.

In contrast, countries below this frontier show potential for improvement in reducing emissions intensity and optimizing energy inputs without compromising economic development. This suboptimal positioning should not be interpreted solely as a performance deficit, but as a signal for the need for structural reforms and closer alignment of national strategies with the European Union's climate and energy objectives. Beyond its descriptive dimension, the application of the DEA model adds significant operational value to the analysis, providing a benchmarking tool that enables policy-makers to identify best practices, areas of inefficiency and priority areas for intervention. Thus, this research not only contributes to advancing the methodological framework for assessing energy sustainability but also provides an empirical basis for formulating differentiated public policies tailored to the specificities of each economy, with a view to strengthening environmental performance and achieving SDG7 in a fair and efficient manner.

In conclusion, the transition to a sustainable, fair and competitive European energy system requires not only investment in green infrastructure but also a firm commitment to optimizing resource use and increasing environmental efficiency within a collaborative and evidence-based governance framework. Only through such an integrated approach can coherence between energy performance and climate responsibility within the European project be guaranteed.

## References

Addis, A. K. (2025). Sustainability and efficiency analysis of 42 countries: Super SBM-DEA model and the GML productivity index with undesirable outputs. *Ecological Indicators, 177*, 113767. https://doi.org/10.1016/j.ecolind.2025.113767

Al-Abdulqader, K. S., Ibrahim, A.-J., Ong, J., & Khalifa, A. A. (2025). Does carbon pricing matter? Evidence from a global sample. *Energies, 18*(5). https://doi.org/10.3390/en18051030

Algarni, S., Tirth, V., Alqahtani, T., Alshehery, S., & Kshirsagar, P. (2023). Contribution of renewable energy sources to the environmental impacts and economic benefits for sustainable development. *Sustainable Energy Technologies and Assessments, 56*, 103098. https://doi.org/10.1016/j.seta.2023.103098

Almatar, K. M. (2024). Increasing electric vehicles infrastructure in urban areas for efficiently employing renewable energy. *Environment, Development and Sustainability, 26*(10), 26183–26204. https://doi.org/10.1007/s10668-023-03723-x

Alola, A. A., Özkan, O., & Usman, O. (2023). Role of non-renewable energy efficiency and renewable energy in driving environmental sustainability in India: Evidence from the load capacity factor hypothesis. *Energies, 16*(6). https://doi.org/10.3390/en16062847

Anwar, A., Chaudhary, A. R., Malik, S., & Bassim, M. (2021). Modelling the macroeconomic determinants of carbon dioxide emissions in the G-7 countries: The roles of technological innovation and institutional quality improvement. *Global Business Review, 26*(3), 823–845. https://doi.org/10.1177/09721509211039392

Axenbeck, J., Berner, A., & Kneib, T. (2024). What drives the relationship between digitalization and energy demand? Exploring heterogeneity in German manufacturing firms. *Journal of Environmental Management, 369*, 122317. https://doi.org/10.1016/j.jenvman.2024.122317

Bakhsh, S., Zhang, W., Ali, K., & Oláh, J. (2024). Strategy towards sustainable energy transition: The effect of environmental governance, economic complexity and geopolitics. *Energy Strategy Reviews, 52*, 101330. https://doi.org/10.1016/j.esr.2024.101330

Banker, R. D., Charnes, A., & Cooper, W. W. (1984). Some models for estimating technical and scale inefficiencies in data envelopment analysis. *Management Science, 30*(9), 1078–1092. http://www.jstor.org/stable/2631725

Barragán-Ocaña, A., Cecilio-Ayala, E., Silva-Borjas, P., Cortés-Ruiz, J. A., & Hernandez-Cardona, E.-Y. (2025). Policies and sustainable energy transition in the global environment: Challenges for Latin America. *Heliyon, 11*(6), e42295. https://doi.org/10.1016/j.heliyon.2025.e42295

Basilio, M. (2025). Renewable energy and energy efficiency: An exploratory study in EU countries. *Sustainable Futures, 9*, 100514. https://doi.org/10.1016/j.sftr.2025.100514

Benfica, V., & Marques, A. C. (2024). Technological and financial development as drivers of Latin America's energy transition. *Renewable Energy, 237*, 121664. https://doi.org/10.1016/j.renene.2024.121664

Bolat, C. K., Soytas, U., Akinoglu, B., & Nazlioglu, S. (2023). Is there a macroeconomic carbon rebound effect in EU ETS? *Energy Economics, 125*, 106879. https://doi.org/10.1016/j.eneco.2023.106879

Brancaccio, E., Gallegati, M., & Giammetti, R. (2022). Neoclassical influences in agent-based literature: A systematic review. *Journal of Economic Surveys, 36*(2), 350–385. https://doi.org/10.1111/joes.12470

Caglar, A. E., & Yavuz, E. (2023). The role of environmental protection expenditures and renewable energy consumption in the context of ecological challenges: Insights from the European Union with the novel panel econometric approach. *Journal of Environmental Management, 331*, 117317. https://doi.org/10.1016/j.jenvman.2023.117317

Camanho, A. S., Silva, M. C., Piran, F. S., & Lacerda, D. P. (2024). A literature review of economic efficiency assessments using data envelopment analysis. *European Journal of Operational Research, 315*(1), 1–18. https://doi.org/10.1016/j.ejor.2023.07.027

Cautisanu, C., & Hatmanu, M. (2023). A study of the decoupling of economic growth from CO2 and HFCs emissions in the EU27 countries. *Energies, 16*(14). https://doi.org/10.3390/en16145546

Ceausescu, A. I., Alecsoiu, O.-R., Panagoret, A. A., Chirculescu, M.-F., Panagoret, D. M., & Nitu, R. V. (2025). Electricity generation from fossil fuels and environmental sustainability in Romania: Investigating the influence of renewable energy, financial development and urbanization. *Applied Economics*, 1–16. https://doi.org/10.1080/00036846.2025.2494766

Cefis, E., & Scrofani, S. (2025). European national innovation policies: A review of policy designs and scopes. In L. Aldieri (Ed.), *Technological evolution: How innovations are changing our future* (pp. 41–65). Springer Nature. https://doi.org/10.1007/978-3-031-85814-7_3

Charnes, A., Cooper, W. W., & Rhodes, E. (1978). Measuring the efficiency of decision making units. *European Journal of Operational Research, 2*(6), 429–444. https://doi.org/10.1016/0377-2217(78)90138-8

Chen, C., Loft, L., & Matzdorf, B. (2023). Lost in action: Climate friendly use of European peatlands needs coherence and incentive-based policies. *Environmental Science & Policy, 145*, 104–115. https://doi.org/10.1016/j.envsci.2023.04.010

Chen, J., Du, M., & Huang, C. (2022). Efficiency and its influencing factors of urban water sector in China and major OECD countries. *Journal of Cleaner Production, 373*, 133885. https://doi.org/10.1016/j.jclepro.2022.133885

Chodakowska, E., Nazarko, J., & Nazarko, Ł. (2025). Efficiency of renewable energy potential utilization in European Union: Towards responsible net-zero policy. *Energies, 18*(5). https://doi.org/10.3390/en18051175

Chu, Z., & Wang, Y. (2024). Efficiency improvement in energy consumption: A novel deep learning based model for leading a greener Economic recovery. *Sustainable Cities and Society, 108*, 105427. https://doi.org/10.1016/j.scs.2024.105427

Coady, D., Jahan, S., Machado, F., & Gu, M. (2023). The distributional and fiscal implications of public utility pricing. *IMF Working Papers, 2023*(118), A001. https://doi.org/10.5089/9798400243141.001.A001

Dai, J., Mehmood, U., & Nassani, A. A. (2025). Empowering sustainability through energy efficiency, green innovations, and the sharing economy: Insights from G7 economies. *Energy, 318*, 134768. https://doi.org/10.1016/j.energy.2025.134768

Davoudabadi, R., Mousavi, S. M., & Mohagheghi, V. (2021). A new decision model based on DEA and simulation to evaluate renewable energy projects under interval-valued intuitionistic fuzzy uncertainty. *Renewable Energy, 164*, 1588–1601. https://doi.org/10.1016/j.renene.2020.09.089

Del Duca, V., Ponsiglione, C., Primario, S., & Strazzullo, S. (2024). Towards economic, environmental, and societal sustainable world: Reviewing the interplay of methodologies, variables, and impacts in energy transition models. *Journal of Cleaner Production, 479*, 144074. https://doi.org/10.1016/j.jclepro.2024.144074

Demiral, E. E., & Sağlam, Ü. (2021). Eco-efficiency and Eco-productivity assessments of the states in the United States: A two-stage non-parametric analysis. *Applied Energy, 303*, 117649. https://doi.org/10.1016/j.apenergy.2021.117649

Dimian, G. C., Maftei, M., Jablonský, J., Marin, E., & Olaru, S. M. (2025). The influence of digitalization on greenhouse gas emissions in European Union. The analysis of mediating effect of renewable energy consumption. *Journal Of The Knowledge Economy*. https://doi.org/10.1007/s13132-025-02657-1

Dolphin, G., Duval, R. A., Rojas-Romagosa, H., & Sher, G. (2024). The energy security gains from strengthening Europe's climate action. *Departmental Papers, 2024*(005), A001. https://doi.org/10.5089/9798400265655.087.A001

Emrouznejad, A., Brzezicki, Ł., & Lu, C. (2025). Development and evolution of slacks-based measure models in data envelopment analysis: A comprehensive review of the literature. *Journal of Economic Surveys, n/a*(n/a). https://doi.org/10.1111/joes.12682

European Commission. (2022). *The 2030 agenda for sustainable development and the SDGs.* https://ec.europa.eu/environment/sustainable-development/SDGs/index_en.htm

European Commission. (2023a). *A European Green Deal.* https://commission.europa.eu/strategy-and-policy/priorities-2019-2024/european-green-deal_en.

European Commission. (2023b). *Assessment of progress towards the objectives of the Energy Union and Climate Action highlights the need for EU countries to focus on implementation.* https://energy.ec.europa.eu/news/assessment-progress-towards-objectives-energy-union-and-climate-action-highlights-need-eu-countries-2023-10-26_en

European Commission. (2025). *Economic forecast for Lithuania.* https://economy-finance.ec.europa.eu/economic-surveillance-eu-economies/lithuania/economic-forecast-lithuania_en

European Council. (2023). *Fit for 55.* https://www.consilium.europa.eu/en/policies/green-deal/fit-for-55-the-eu-plan-for-a-green-transition/

European Environment Agency. (2022). *Trends and projections in Europe reports.* https://www.eea.europa.eu/themes/climate/trends-and-projections-in-europe

European Environment Agency. (2024). *Delivering justice in sustainability transitions.*https://www.eea.europa.eu/publications/delivering-justice-in-sustainability-transitions

European Environmental Bureau. (2021). *A carbon pricing blueprint for the EU.*

European Union. (2023). Directive (EU) 2023/1791 of the European Parliament and of the Council of 13 September 2023 on energy efficiency and amending Regulation (EU) 2023/955. https://eur-lex.europa.eu/eli/dir/2023/1791/oj/eng

European Union. (2024a). 2024 Country Report - Romania Accompanying the document Recommendation for a COUNCIL RECOMMENDATION on the economic, social, employment, structural and budgetary policies of Romania. https://op.europa.eu/en/publication-detail/-/publication/5045e494-2e4a-11ef-a61b-01aa75ed71a1/language-en

European Union. (2024b). *The future of European competitiveness*. https://commission.europa.eu/document/download/ec1409c1-d4b4-4882-8bdd-3519f86bbb92_en?filename=ThefutureofEuropeancompetitiveness_In-depthanalysisandrecommendations_0.pdf

Eurostat. (2024a). *Energy import dependency by products*. Europa.Eu. https://ec.europa.eu/eurostat/databrowser/view/sdg_07_50/default/table?lang=en&category=sdg.sdg_07

Eurostat. (2024b). *Energy productivity*. https://ec.europa.eu/eurostat/databrowser/view/sdg_07_30/default/table?lang=en

Eurostat. (2025). *Domestic net greenhouse gas emissions*. https://ec.europa.eu/eurostat/databrowser/view/sdg_13_10/default/table?lang=en

Fazio, G., Maioli, S., & Rujimora, N. (2024). Building back greener, levelling-up or both? An assessment of the economic and environmental efficiency transition of UK regions. *Papers in Regional Science, 103*(6), 100053. https://doi.org/10.1016/j.pirs.2024.100053

Fernandez, M. I., Go, Y. I., Wong, D. M. L., & Früh, W.-G. (2024). Review of challenges and key enablers in energy systems towards net zero target: Renewables, storage, buildings, & grid technologies. *Heliyon, 10*(23), e40691. https://doi.org/10.1016/j.heliyon.2024.e40691

Fidanoski, F., Simeonovski, K., & Cvetkoska, V. (2021). Energy efficiency in OECD countries: A DEA approach. *Energies, 14*(4). https://doi.org/10.3390/en14041185

Fotiou, T., Capros, P., & Fragkos, P. (2022). Policy modelling for ambitious energy efficiency investment in the eu residential buildings. *Energies, 15*(6). https://doi.org/10.3390/en15062233

Gaeta, G. L., Ghinoi, S., Silvestri, F., & Tassinari, M. (2021). Innovation in the solid waste management industry: Integrating neoclassical and complexity theory perspectives. *Waste Management, 120*, 50–58. https://doi.org/10.1016/j.wasman.2020.11.009

Gajdzik, B., Wolniak, R., Nagaj, R., Grebski, W. W., & Romanyshyn, T. (2023). Barriers to renewable energy source (RES) installations as determinants of energy consumption in EU countries. *Energies, 16*(21). https://doi.org/10.3390/en16217364

Gajdzik, B., Wolniak, R., Nagaj, R., Žuromskaitė-Nagaj, B., & Grebski, W. W. (2024). The influence of the global energy crisis on energy efficiency: A comprehensive analysis. *Energies, 17*(4). https://doi.org/10.3390/en17040947

Gajewski, P. (2022). Regional resilience to the Covid-19 shock in Polish regions: How is it different from resilience to the 2008 global financial crisis? *Regional Studies, Regional Science, 9*(1), 672–684. https://doi.org/10.1080/21681376.2022.2137426

Giraudet, L.-G., & Missemer, A. (2023). The history of energy efficiency in economics: Breakpoints and regularities. *Energy Research & Social Science, 97*, 102973. https://doi.org/10.1016/j.erss.2023.102973

Gökgöz, F., & Yalçın, E. (2023). An environmental, energy, and economic efficiency analysis for the energy market in European Union. *Environmental Progress & Sustainable Energy, 42*(4), e14068. https://doi.org/10.1002/ep.14068

Gorina, L., Korneeva, E., Kovaleva, O., & Strielkowski, W. (2024). Energy-saving technologies and energy efficiency in the post-COVID era. *Sustainable Development, 32*(5), 5294–5310. https://doi.org/10.1002/sd.2978

Henriques, C. O., Gouveia, C. M., Tenente, M., & da Silva, P. P. (2022). Employing value-based DEA in the eco-efficiency assessment of the electricity sector. *Economic Analysis and Policy, 73*, 826–844. https://doi.org/10.1016/j.eap.2022.01.010

Huang, S. (2023). The comprehensive environmental efficiency analysis based on a new data envelopment analysis: The super slack based measure network three-stage data envelopment analysis approach. *Journal of Cleaner Production, 400*, 136689. https://doi.org/10.1016/j.jclepro.2023.136689

Ibrahim, M. D., Alola, A. A., & Ferreira, D. C. (2023). Assessing sustainable development goals attainment through energy-environmental efficiency: The case of Latin American and Caribbean countries. *Sustainable Energy Technologies and Assessments, 57*, 103219. https://doi.org/10.1016/j.seta.2023.103219

International Monetary Fund. (2025). *World Economic Outlook. A Critical Juncture amid Policies Shift*. International Monetary Fund. https://elibrary.imf.org/display/book/9798400289583/9798400289583.xml?cid=555872-com-dsp-crossref

Iqbal, M., Ma, J., Mushtaq, Z., Ahmad, N., Yousaf, M. Z., Tarawneh, B., Khan, W., Pushkarna, M., & Zaitsev, I. (2025). Energy efficiency evaluation of construction projects using data envelopment analysis and Tobit regression. *Scientific Reports, 15*(1), 11444. https://doi.org/10.1038/s41598-025-90671-3

Işık, C., Ongan, S., Islam, H., Balsalobre-Lorente, D., & Sharif, A. (2024). ECON-ESG factors on energy efficiency: Fostering sustainable development in ECON-growth-paradox countries. *Gondwana Research, 135*, 103–115. https://doi.org/10.1016/j.gr.2024.07.020

Kim, A., & Medal, L. (2024). Factors influencing energy-efficiency retrofits in commercial and institutional buildings: A systematic literature review. *Journal of Facility Management Education and Research, 7*, 42–63. https://doi.org/10.22361/jfmer/181200

Krejnus, M., Štofková, J., Stofkova, K., & Binasova, V. (2023). The use of the DEA method for measuring the efficiency of electronic public administration as part of the digitization of the economy and society. *Applied Sciences, 13*, 3672. https://doi.org/10.3390/app13063672

Kruse-Andersen, P. K., & Sørensen, P. B. (2022). Optimal energy taxes and subsidies under a cost-effective unilateral climate policy: Addressing carbon leakage. *Energy Economics, 109*, 105928. https://doi.org/10.1016/j.eneco.2022.105928

Kwilinski, A., Lyulyov, O., & Pimonenko, T. (2023). The impact of digital business on energy efficiency in EU countries. *Information (Basel), 14*(9). https://doi.org/10.3390/info14090480

Lacko, R., Hajduová, Z., & Dula, R. (2024). Development of environmental performance and circular economy in the European Union countries: The case of "post-2004" members. *Frontiers in Environmental Science, 12*, 2024. https://doi.org/10.3389/fenvs.2024.1467370

Lamb, W. F., Grubb, M., Diluiso, F., & Minx, J. C. (2022). Countries with sustained greenhouse gas emissions reductions: An analysis of trends and progress by sector. *Climate Policy, 22*(1), 1–17. https://doi.org/10.1080/14693062.2021.1990831

Lin, S.-W., Lo, H.-W., & Gul, M. (2023). An assessment model for national sustainable development based on the hybrid DEA and modified TOPSIS techniques. *Complex & Intelligent Systems, 9*(5), 5449–5466. https://doi.org/10.1007/s40747-023-01034-2

Lou, Y., Yang, G., Guan, Z., Chen, X., Pan, H., Wang, T., & Zheng, H. (2024). A parallel data envelopment analysis and Malmquist productivity index model of virtual frontier for evaluating scientific and technological innovation efficiency at universities. *Decision Analytics Journal, 10*, 100384. https://doi.org/10.1016/j.dajour.2023.100384

Mahmood, M., Chowdhury, P., Yeassin, R., Hasan, M., Ahmad, T., & Chowdhury, N.-U.-R. (2024). Impacts of digitalization on smart grids, renewable energy, and demand response: An updated review of current applications. *Energy Conversion and Management: X, 24*, 100790. https://doi.org/10.1016/j.ecmx.2024.100790

Mahmood, N., Zhao, Y., Lou, Q., & Geng, J. (2022). Role of environmental regulations and eco-innovation in energy structure transition for green growth: Evidence from OECD. *Technological Forecasting and Social Change, 183*, 121890. https://doi.org/10.1016/j.techfore.2022.121890

Makridou, G., Andriosopoulos, K., Doumpos, M., & Zopounidis, C. (2015). A two-stage approach for energy efficiency analysis in European Union countries. *The Energy Journal, 36*(2), 47–69. http://www.jstor.org/stable/24695747

Manowska, A., Bluszcz, A., Chomiak-Orsa, I., & Wowra, R. (2024). Towards energy transformation: A case study of EU countries. *Energies, 17*(7). https://doi.org/10.3390/en17071778

Matsumoto, K., Makridou, G., & Doumpos, M. (2020). Evaluating environmental performance using data envelopment analysis: The case of European countries. *Journal of Cleaner Production, 272*, 122637. https://doi.org/10.1016/j.jclepro.2020.122637

Mergoni, A., Emrouznejad, A., & De Witte, K. (2025). Fifty years of data envelopment analysis. *European Journal of Operational Research, 326*(3), 389–412. https://doi.org/10.1016/j.ejor.2024.12.049

Murillo Zamorano, L. R., & Vega-Cervera, J. (2001). The use of parametric and non-parametric frontier methods to measure the productive efficiency in the industrial sector. *International Journal of Production Economics, 69*, 265–275. https://doi.org/10.1016/S0925-5273(00)00027-X

Mushafiq, M., Arisar, M. M., Tariq, H., & Czapp, S. (2023). Energy efficiency and economic policy: Comprehensive theoretical, empirical, and policy review. *Energies, 16*(5). https://doi.org/10.3390/en16052381

Narayanan, E., binti Ismail, W. R., & bin Mustafa, Z. (2022). A data-envelopment analysis-based systematic review of the literature on innovation performance. *Heliyon, 8*(12), e11925. https://doi.org/10.1016/j.heliyon.2022.e11925

Ni, Z., Yang, J., & Razzaq, A. (2022). How do natural resources, digitalization, and institutional governance contribute to ecological sustainability through load capacity factors in highly resource-consuming economies? *Resources Policy, 79*, 103068. https://doi.org/10.1016/j.resourpol.2022.103068

Niță, D., Stoicuța, N., Nițescu, A., Isac, C., & Dobre-Baron, O. (2025). The impact of the transition to a green economy on Romania's economic growth. *Energy, Sustainability and Society, 15*(1), 19. https://doi.org/10.1186/s13705-025-00520-4

Nyangchak, N. (2022). Emerging green industry toward net-zero economy: A systematic review. *Journal of Cleaner Production, 378*, 134622. https://doi.org/10.1016/j.jclepro.2022.134622

OECD. (2024). *Decarbonising Romania's economy*. https://doi.org/10.1787/256205df-en.

OECD. (2025). *Green growth*. https://data-explorer.oecd.org/vis?df[ds]=DisseminateFinalDMZ&df[id]=DSD_GG%40DF_GREEN_GROWTH&df[ag]=OECD.ENV.EPI&dq=AUS....&pd=2017%2C&to[TIME_PERIOD]=false

Omrani, H., Oveysi, Z., Emrouznejad, A., & Teplova, T. (2023). A mixed-integer network DEA with shared inputs and undesirable outputs for performance evaluation: Efficiency measurement of bank branches. *Journal of the Operational Research Society, 74*(4), 1150–1165. https://doi.org/10.1080/01605682.2022.2064783

Omrani, H., Valipour, M., & Jafari Mamakani, S. (2019). Construct a composite indicator based on integrating common weight data envelopment analysis and principal component analysis models: An application for finding development degree of provinces in Iran. *Socio-Economic Planning Sciences, 68*, 100618. https://doi.org/10.1016/j.seps.2018.02.005

Özkan, O., Alola, A. A., & Adebayo, T. S. (2023). Environmental benefits of non-renewable energy efficiency and renewable energy intensity in the USA and EU: Examining the role of clean technologies. *Sustainable Energy Technologies and Assessments, 58*, 103315. https://doi.org/10.1016/j.seta.2023.103315

Palmer, G., & Floyd, J. (2025). Unravelling connections: Energy, economic growth, and decoupling through a historical lens. *New Political Economy, 30*(4), 508–525. https://doi.org/10.1080/13563467.2025.2453574

Panton, A. J. (2023). Making Romania fit and resilient for the net-zero transition. *Selected Issues Papers, 2023*(063), A001. https://doi.org/10.5089/9798400263736.018.A001

Panwar, A., Olfati, M., Pant, M., & Snasel, V. (2022). A review on the 40 years of existence of data envelopment analysis models: Historic development and current trends. *Archives of Computational Methods in Engineering, 29*(7), 5397–5426. https://doi.org/10.1007/s11831-022-09770-3

Papadakis, N., & Katsaprakakis, D. (2023). A review of energy efficiency interventions in public buildings. *Energies, 16*, 6329. https://doi.org/10.3390/en16176329

Paulet, E., & Mavoori, H. (2021). Cross-regional analysis of banking efficiency drivers. *Applied Economics, 53*(18), 2042–2065. https://doi.org/10.1080/00036846.2020.1855312

Prieto González, L., Fensel, A., Gómez Berbís, J. M., Popa, A., & de Amescua Seco, A. (2021). A survey on energy efficiency in smart homes and smart grids. *Energies, 14*(21). https://doi.org/10.3390/en14217273

Qin, M., Zhu, Y., Xie, X., Shao, X., & Lobonţ, O.-R. (2024). The impact of climate risk on technological progress under the fourth industrial era. *Technological Forecasting and Social Change, 202*, 123325. https://doi.org/10.1016/j.techfore.2024.123325

Quito, B., del Río-Rama, M. d. l. C., Álvarez- García, J., & Bekun, F. V. (2023). Spatiotemporal influencing factors of energy efficiency in 43 European countries: A spatial econometric analysis. *Renewable and Sustainable Energy Reviews, 182*, 113340. https://doi.org/10.1016/j.rser.2023.113340

Rajaperumal, T. A., & Columbus, C. C. (2025). Transforming the electrical grid: the role of AI in advancing smart, sustainable, and secure energy systems. *Energy Informatics, 8*(1), 51. https://doi.org/10.1186/s42162-024-00461-w

Rostamzadeh, R., Akbarian, O., Banaitis, A., & Soltani, Z. (2021). Application of DEA in benchmarking: A systematic literature review from 2003–2020.

*Technological and Economic Development of Economy, 27*(1 SE-Articles), 175–222. https://doi.org/10.3846/tede.2021.13406

Saboori, B., Goltabar, S., & Ranjbar, O. (2024). Rethinking diversification: Assessing the impact of energy concentration on climate change in rentier and non-rentier countries. *Energy Strategy Reviews, 56*, 101563. https://doi.org/10.1016/j.esr.2024.101563

Safari, A., Daneshvar, M., & Anvari-Moghaddam, A. (2024). Energy intelligence: A systematic review of artificial intelligence for energy management. *Applied Sciences, 14*(23). https://doi.org/10.3390/app142311112

Saha, A., Mishra, A., Rani, P., Deveci, M., Debnath, B., Jamil, N., & Mahmoud, M. (2024). An optimization model-based DEA-MARCOS approach for assessing EU countries towards achieving sustainable development goals. *Environmental Science & Policy, 162*. https://doi.org/10.1016/j.envsci.2024.103913

Sargiotis, D. (2025). Smart infrastructure for sustainable energy consumption: Leveraging AI and big data. *International Journal of Research Publication and Reviews, 6*, 3838–3849. https://doi.org/10.55248/gengpi.6.0125.0526

Schaupp, S. (2023). COVID-19, economic crises and digitalisation: How algorithmic management became an alternative to automation. *New Technology, Work and Employment, 38*(2), 311–329. https://doi.org/10.1111/ntwe.12246

Shabalov, M. Y., Zhukovskiy, Y. L., Buldysko, A. D., Gil, B., & Starshaia, V. V. (2021). The influence of technological changes in energy efficiency on the infrastructure deterioration in the energy sector. *Energy Reports, 7*, 2664–2680. https://doi.org/10.1016/j.egyr.2021.05.001

Shu, T., Liao, X., Yang, S., & Yu, T. (2024). Towards sustainability: Evaluating energy efficiency with a super-efficiency SBM-DEA model across 168 economies. *Applied Energy, 376*, 124254. https://doi.org/10.1016/j.apenergy.2024.124254

Simeonovski, K., Kaftandzieva, T., & Brock, G. (2021). Energy efficiency management across EU countries: A DEA approach. *Energies, 14*, 2619. https://doi.org/10.3390/en14092619

Sompolska-Rzechuła, A., Bąk, I., Becker, A., Marjak, H., & Perzyńska, J. (2024). The use of renewable energy sources and environmental degradation in EU countries. *Sustainability, 16*(23). https://doi.org/10.3390/su162310416

Sotiroski, K., Péter, K., Marcikić, H., Sedlak, O., Lakić, V., & Radovanov, B. (2023). Assessing sustainable economic development efficiency: A DEA approach. *Strategic Management, 29*, 43. https://doi.org/10.5937/StraMan2300039S

Sueyoshi, T., & Goto, M. (2025). Intermediate Model for SDGs: Three time structures. In T. Sueyoshi & M. Goto (Eds.), *Environment and sustainability for ESG and SDGs: Measured by data envelopment analysis in time horizon* (pp.99–130).SpringerNatureSingapore.https://doi.org/10.1007/978-981-96-2464-5_5

Tang, Y., Ding, H., Shan, X., & Wang, X. (2023). Application of the novel three-stage DEA model to evaluate total-factor energy efficiency: A case study based on 30 provinces and 8 comprehensive economic zones of China. *Results in Engineering, 20*, 101417. https://doi.org/10.1016/j.rineng.2023.101417

Teixeira, J. E., & Tavares-Lehmann, A. T. C. P. (2022). Industry 4.0 in the European Union: Policies and national strategies. *Technological Forecasting And Social Change, 180*, 121664. https://doi.org/10.1016/j.techfore.2022.121664

Török, L. (2025). Economic drivers of renewable energy growth in the European Union: Evidence from a panel data analysis (2015–2023). *Energies, 18*(13). https://doi.org/10.3390/en18133363

Ukoba, K., Olatunji, K. O., Adeoye, E., Jen, T.-C., & Madyira, D. M. (2024). Optimizing renewable energy systems through artificial intelligence: Review and future prospects. *Energy & Environment, 35*(7), 3833–3879. https://doi.org/10.1177/0958305X241256293

United Nations. (2015). *Transforming our world: the 2030 Agenda for Sustainable Development*. https://sdgs.un.org/2030agenda

Vaseei, M., Daneshmand-Mehr, M., Bazrafshan, M., & Kanafi, A. G. (2024). A network data envelopment analysis to evaluate the performance of a sustainable supply chain using bootstrap simulation. *Journal of Engineering Research, 12*(4), 904–915. https://doi.org/10.1016/j.jer.2023.10.003

Wang, C., Nazar, R., Ali, S., & Meo, M. S. (2025a). Eco-friendly algorithms: Artificial intelligence and green finance in European intelligent nations. *Technology in Society, 83*, 102960. https://doi.org/10.1016/j.techsoc.2025.102960

Wang, Q., Wang, X., & Li, R. (2025b). Energy transition and environmental sustainability: The interplay with natural resource rents and trade openness. *Humanities and Social Sciences Communications, 12*(1), 1152. https://doi.org/10.1057/s41599-025-05521-4

Wang, R., Wang, Q., & Yao, S. (2021). Evaluation and difference analysis of regional energy efficiency in China under the carbon neutrality targets: Insights from DEA and Theil models. *Journal of Environmental Management, 293*, 112958. https://doi.org/10.1016/j.jenvman.2021.112958

Wang, S., Sun, L., & Iqbal, S. (2022). Green financing role on renewable energy dependence and energy transition in E7 economies. *Renewable Energy, 200*, 1561–1572. https://doi.org/10.1016/j.renene.2022.10.067

Wu, H., Han, M., & Shen, Y. (2023). Technology-driven energy revolution: The impact of digital technology on energy efficiency and its mechanism. *Frontiers in Energy Research, 11*, 2023. https://doi.org/10.3389/fenrg.2023.1242580

Xue, Y., Mohsin, M., Taghizadeh-Hesary, F., & Iqbal, N. (2022). Environmental performance assessment of energy-consuming sectors through novel data envelopment analysis. *Frontiers in Energy Research, 9*, 2021. https://doi.org/10.3389/fenrg.2021.713546

Yang, Y., Xia, S., Huang, P., & Qian, J. (2024). Energy transition: Connotations, mechanisms and effects. *Energy Strategy Reviews, 52*, 101320. https://doi.org/10.1016/j.esr.2024.101320

Yavuz, O., Uner, M. M., Okumus, F., & Karatepe, O. M. (2023). Industry 4.0 technologies, sustainable operations practices and their impacts on sustainable performance. *Journal of Cleaner Production, 387*, 135951. https://doi.org/10.1016/j.jclepro.2023.135951

Zhang, J., Patwary, A. K., Sun, H., Raza, M., Taghizadeh-Hesary, F., & Iram, R. (2021). Measuring energy and environmental efficiency interactions towards CO2 emissions reduction without slowing economic growth in central and western Europe. *Journal of Environmental Management, 279*, 111704. https://doi.org/10.1016/j.jenvman.2020.111704

Zhang, M., & Wei, X. (2024). Resource efficiency, cultural industry, and green economic growth: A synergistic approach. *Resources Policy, 90*, 104769. https://doi.org/10.1016/j.resourpol.2024.104769

Zhang, Y., & Dilanchiev, A. (2022). Economic recovery, industrial structure and natural resource utilization efficiency in China: Effect on green economic recovery. *Resources Policy, 79*, 102958. https://doi.org/10.1016/j.resourpol.2022.102958

CHAPTER 7

# Proposed Sustainable Development Solutions from the Perspective of Sustainable Development Goal 7

The analysis of the Romanian economy's strategies for achieving the SDG7 has highlighted that research, innovation and competitiveness, the internal energy market, energy security and energy efficiency are the main dimensions of the National Integrated Energy and Climate Change Plan for Horizon 2050, which aims to achieve eight strategic objectives and implement a priority investment program in this field. From a strategic point of view, the objectives are aimed at strengthening institutional capacity for energy market regulation, achieving clean energy and energy efficiency, ensuring access to energy for all consumers, reducing energy poverty, competitive energy markets, increasing the capacity for education and innovation in the energy sector, transforming Romania into a regional energy security provider and increasing Romania's energy contribution to regional markets. From the analysis of the main indicators related to the SDG7 we observed that the primary energy consumption is on an oscillating slope being on the increase since 2017; the same trend is also registered by the final energy consumption at national level while the final energy consumption in households has assumed a slightly increasing variation compared to the decreasing trend at European level. These aspects show that Romania has vulnerabilities in achieving the objectives proposed by the National Integrated Energy and Climate Change Plan, being far from the more favourable developments recorded in the European Union. However, there are also favourable points such as the increase in energy



C. Fortea, *Sustainable Economic Development and the European Green Deal*, https://doi.org/10.1007/978-3-032-10326-0_7

productivity at national level or the decrease in the energy poverty rate. The picture of vulnerabilities is completed by an unfavourable dynamic since 2018 of the shares of renewable energy in gross energy consumption and the increase of energy import dependence by almost 50% in the period 2010–2021 (from 21.39% to 31.65%), so that the analysis carried out has demonstrated the need to improve energy solutions to achieve energy sustainability at the national level.

The study of the econometric models aimed at determining energy sustainability revealed several vulnerabilities as shown in Chap. 4, which motivated the proposal of policies to address these vulnerabilities as follows:

The **SDG7.1 model** of European energy sustainability from the perspective of the SDG7APER indicator (renewable energy production) explains the direct influence of the change in energy consumption and energy-related tax revenues in relation to the change in renewable energy production. The main findings indicate that renewable energy supply is a feature with a strong environmental impact, which needs to be correlated with the size of industrial energy consumption affecting energy security for countries with lower energy production (Bashir et al., 2025; Sompolska-Rzechuła et al., 2024). At European level, the best performing countries are Sweden, Latvia, Finland and Austria, with Malta, Luxembourg and Cyprus at the bottom of the list, with renewable energy production up to 10 times lower than the top-ranked countries.

To improve renewable energy supply at European level, effective public policies can include strategies such as financial incentives, supportive regulation and transnational collaboration (Grafström et al., 2023; Hoicka et al., 2021). They can be geared towards promoting investment in innovative technologies, facilitating the integration of renewables into existing grids and encouraging sustainable consumption. A relevant example would be the European Recovery Plan (European Commission, 2024f), which aims to accelerate the green transition with substantial funding. It includes initiatives such as the "Renewal Wave", aimed at doubling the rate of renovation of buildings to increase energy efficiency, and dedicated funds to develop clean energy infrastructure. The European Green Deal (European Commission, 2023a) is also an ambitious strategy to transform the EU into a modern, resource-efficient and competitive economy by ensuring that the transition to clean energy is fair and inclusive for all. In the case of Romania (ranked 10th in Europe according to the overall average of renewable energy production over the period 2010–2021), public policies to improve renewable energy production must be anchored in the national context and in line with the National Energy Strategy (Romanian Ministry of Energy, 2025). The main public policy guidelines should be oriented towards incentives for investments in renewable energy; modernization of the energy infrastructure; education and awareness programmes on the need to use renewable energy sources; and regulation of renewable energy consumption. The Romanian government can support the renewable energy sector through subsidies, tax credits or other forms of financial support to encourage users to invest in renewable energy sources such as solar, wind or biomass. Encouraging public-private collaboration to develop and implement large-scale renewable energy projects, including wind farms and solar farms, is also a useful tool. Investments in upgrading the electricity grid are significant milestones for improving the integration of renewable energy sources, reducing energy losses and improving energy efficiency. A public policy initiative to increase public awareness and acceptance of renewable energy, including educational campaigns and training programmes on green technologies, is a public policy with a long-term effect. The success of these efforts relies on the implementation of legislative frameworks that facilitate the development of renewable energy projects, including streamlining permitting processes and setting ambitious national clean energy targets.

The **SDG7.2 model** of European energy sustainability from the perspective of the SDG7CENAG indicator (energy consumption in agriculture) shows an inverse relationship with changes in tax revenues and industrial energy consumption. The Netherlands, Denmark, Poland and Latvia rank first in Europe. These countries benefit from suitable climate and humidity conditions for agricultural activities, with the challenge of energy sustainability crystallizing in energy productivity. Luxembourg, Slovakia, Slovenia and Malta rank last in terms of energy consumption in agriculture.

European agriculture, like other sectors, is a significant consumer of electricity, used in irrigation, ventilation, heating and lighting in greenhouses, as well as in processing and packaging operations (Maraveas et al., 2023; Paris et al., 2022). Energy efficiency in agriculture is important for reducing operational costs and mitigating environmental impacts (Jensen et al., 2025; Ragazou et al., 2022). The main public policies to achieve energy sustainability from this perspective are promotion of energy efficiency technologies; support for renewable energy in agriculture; energy auditing and advisory programs; funds and subsidies for energy improvements. Stimulating the uptake of energy-saving technologies such as efficient irrigation systems, low-energy equipment and automation solutions in greenhouses is an active policy with an impact on reducing energy risks in Member States (Castro et al., 2024). Pro-actively, governments can encourage farms to become energy producers by installing solar panels, wind turbines or using biomass for energy production, thus contributing to energy self-sufficiency (Bełdycka-Bórawska et al., 2025; Majeed et al., 2023; Pestisha et al., 2025). Recommended measures also include offering energy audit services for farms to identify opportunities to reduce energy consumption and improve energy efficiency. The allocation of European and national funds for investments in energy efficiency and renewable energy sources in the agricultural sector is another priority area for achieving energy sustainability in European agriculture (Castillo-Díaz et al., 2025; Doran et al., 2025; Prigoreanu et al., 2024).

The **SDG7.3 model** of European energy sustainability from the perspective of the SDG7CENI indicator (energy consumption in industry) shows similarity with the SDG7.2 model and in this case the model is characterized by the inverse influence of the variation of tax revenue and energy consumption in agriculture. The main public policies are to improve renewable energy production and increase energy productivity.

The **SDG7.4 model** of European energy sustainability from the perspective of the SDG7ENGS indicator (net greenhouse gas emissions) is characterized by the direct influence of energy productivity and the significant inverse influence of tax revenues. At European level the countries with the highest greenhouse gas emissions are Cyprus, Spain, Ireland and Austria. Lithuania, Romania, Sweden, Estonia and Slovakia are at the opposite pole as exponents of green policies or against the background of significant deindustrialization. At European level, public policies to reduce greenhouse gas emissions should focus on the transition to a low-carbon economy and stimulate investment in sustainable technologies and solutions. Key policy directions include: the development of the EU Emissions Trading System; the implementation of emission performance standards regulations; financing the green transition; and the promotion of renewable energy and energy efficiency. The EU Emissions Trading System is the central pillar of the EU's climate change policy, capping total greenhouse gas emissions and allowing economic operators to buy or sell emission permits, thus incentivizing emission reductions at least cost (Borowiecki et al., 2023; European Commission, 2023d). The EU has set strict emission standards for cars and light commercial vehicles, as well as for other industrial sectors, to encourage the development and uptake of low-emission technologies. The European Green Deal is an ambitious set of policy initiatives aimed at transforming the EU into a modern, resource-efficient and competitive economy, with the goal of eliminating net greenhouse gas emissions by 2050. The EU and Member States must promote an appropriate financial policy to support the transition to the green economy (European Commission, 2025a; Vela Almeida et al., 2023). The Just Transition Fund financial programme (European Union, 2024) and the Recovery and Resilience Mechanism have already been developed in this regard, but we believe that these efforts are not sufficient to fully address the elimination of greenhouse gas emissions. EU renewable energy and energy efficiency policies and directives aim to increase the use of renewable energy and improve energy efficiency in all sectors of the economy (Brugger et al., 2021; Dogan et al., 2023; European Commission, 2025c).

The **SDG7.5 model** of European energy sustainability from the perspective of the SDG7FZEP indicator (total primary energy supply) is directly influenced by the level of energy-related tax revenues and energy consumption in industry. In Europe the highest levels of primary energy supply are recorded in Germany, France, Italy and Spain. Malta, Cyprus, Luxembourg, Latvia, Estonia and Slovenia are at the opposite pole. Public policies at European level on primary energy supply focus on diversifying sources, ensuring energy security and the transition to cleaner and renewable energy sources. Within this framework, the main policy directions should be geared towards achieving the objectives of the EU Energy Strategy to 2030 (European Commission, 2024b), effective implementation of the Energy Union, the Sustainable Energy and Climate Action Plan (European Commission, 2025b) and the Connecting Europe Facility (European Commission, 2024a). The EU Energy Strategy sets ambitious targets for reducing greenhouse gas emissions, increasing the share of renewable energy and improving energy efficiency. The strategy encourages investment in new technologies and energy infrastructure to ensure a sustainable and secure supply of primary energy. As part of the efforts to create an integrated energy market in the EU, the Energy Union has been developed which aims to secure affordable energy supplies, increase reliance on the EU's own energy sources, such as renewable energy, and reduce dependence on imports. At the moment, the effects of the implementation of the Energy Union are favourable, but the European community does not yet enjoy energy independence, and further efforts are needed to expand the Energy Union and ensure energy security in the

European area. The European Union has also implemented the European Interconnection Mechanism (European Commission, 2024a), which supports the development of energy infrastructure for interconnecting national energy networks, with a supporting role in ensuring security of supply and integration of the EU energy market (European Commission, 2025d).

The **SDG7.6 model** of European energy sustainability from the perspective of the SDG7IMPEN indicator (energy import dependence) shows strong significant correlations with the level of net greenhouse gas emissions (positive correlation) and with energy consumption in agriculture (inverse correlation). At European level, the most import-dependent countries are Malta, Luxembourg and Ireland. At the other end of the scale, Estonia, Denmark, Romania, Sweden and the Czech Republic have the lowest levels of energy import dependence. The main public policies at European level should focus on reducing energy import dependency and may include diversified strategies to ensure energy security and to promote the energy autonomy of the European Union. These include diversifying energy sources; increasing energy efficiency; energy network interconnectivity; creating strategic energy reserves; and promoting energy research and innovation. At European level, policy-makers have implemented measures to encourage investment in alternative energy sources such as solar, wind, hydro and biomass to reduce dependence on imported fossil fuels, but energy infrastructure is still poor, and targeted plans are needed to create sustainable renewable energy flows (European Environment Agency, 2025a, 2025b; Majeed et al., 2023; Nwagu et al., 2025). Through directives and regulations, the EU is promoting improved energy efficiency in all sectors, from buildings and transport to industry, thus contributing to lower overall energy demand, but the EU's Green Deal and Climate Neutrality Agreement (United Nations, 2023) targets are still low. Sustained efforts are needed for regional implementation of regulations and traceability of energy sustainability measures such as strengthening and extending electricity and gas networks between Member States to allow better distribution of domestic energy resources, thus reducing the need for imports. Regarding strategic energy reserves, steps have been taken to establish minimum strategic reserve ceilings for oil and gas for each EU Member State, a vulnerability being the increase in seasonal industrial and agricultural consumption which may affect strategic reserves. These factors need to be monitored, and policies formulated in the framework of the SDG7.2 and SDG7.3 models. Investments in R&D for new and improved energy technologies are essential to reduce import dependency and advance the energy transition.

The **SDG7.7 model** of European energy sustainability from the perspective of the SDG7INEMT indicator (industrial air emissions intensity) is significantly influenced by changes in energy-related tax revenues that are associated with higher industrial emissions intensity. At European level the countries with the highest industrial air emissions are Portugal, Latvia, Bulgaria and Estonia. Malta, Denmark, Germany, Austria and Ireland are at the opposite pole. Public policies at European level focused on reducing the intensity of air emissions from industry include several initiatives and regulations aimed at minimizing the environmental impact of industrial activities. They focus on encouraging the uptake of clean technologies, streamlining industrial processes and promoting the circular economy. Main lines of action include implementation of the EU Emissions Trading Scheme (European Commission, 2024c); implementation of the provisions of the Industrial Emissions Directive (European Commission, 2024e); circular economy initiatives; funding and subsidies for clean technologies; and regulations on emission performance standards. The EU has set specific emission standards for various industrial sectors, obliging companies to improve efficiency and reduce pollution. These standards are being implemented and monitored at national level to ensure that the measure is effective and meets policy objectives.

The **SDG7.8 model** of European energy sustainability from the perspective of the SDG7PREN indicator (energy productivity) is significantly determined by the variation in greenhouse gas emissions and renewable energy supply. The most energy-productive countries in Europe are Ireland, Luxembourg and Denmark, which benefit from advanced technologies and good energy infrastructure. At the opposite pole are Bulgaria, Estonia, Malta, the Czech Republic and Poland. Romania ranks 20th in the ranking of Member States on the performance of the indicator analysed. Public policies at European level on energy productivity focus on improving the efficiency with which energy is used in all sectors of the economy in order to support sustainable economic growth, reduce greenhouse gas emissions and improve energy security. The most important lines of action are implementation of the Energy Efficiency Directive (European Commission, 2023b); implementation of the EU strategy for the renovation of buildings; acceleration of measures on energy labelling and eco-design standards; implementation of the Energy Efficiency Action Plan (European Commission, 2023c); and funding for energy efficiency investments. We appreciate that better implementation of the measures set out in the Energy Efficiency Directive is needed to promote energy efficiency and achieve the strategic objectives of a 32.5% reduction in EU energy consumption by 2030 (Parlamentul European, 2024). We welcome the need to monitor national implementation of the Energy Efficiency Action Plan, i.e. actions to improve energy efficiency throughout the economy, including in the industrial, transport and buildings sectors. In this respect the EU provides access to finance and fiscal incentives to support investments in energy efficiency measures, such as the modernization of energy infrastructure and the uptake of innovative technologies.

The **SDG7.9 model** of European energy sustainability from the perspective of the SDG7VFEN (energy-related tax revenues) indicator is significantly influenced by the positive variation in emissions intensity from industry and the inverse variation in industrial and agricultural energy consumption intensity. In order to support energy sustainability, it is essential that European policies balance the need for tax revenues, which finance clean energy and energy efficiency investments, with the objectives of reducing emissions and improving energy efficiency.

The main own contribution in terms of energy sustainability is the regression-based development of the energy sustainability function determined on the basis of the unit weighting of the significance of the developed energy sustainability models, characterized by equation (SEN):

$$\begin{aligned} SEN = {} & 0.099 * \overline{APER_{ODD7.1}} + 0.115 * \overline{CENAG_{ODD7.2}} + 0.11 * \overline{CENI_{ODD7.3}} \\ & + 0.096 * \overline{ENGS_{ODD7.4}} + 0.121 * \overline{FZEP_{ODD7.5}} + 0.085 * \overline{IMPEN_{ODD7.6}} \\ & + 0.132 * \overline{INEMT_{ODD7.7}} + 0.113 * \overline{PREN_{ODD7.8}} + 0.13 * \overline{VFEN_{ODD7.9}} \end{aligned} \tag{7.1}$$

First, the energy sustainability function demonstrates that at Member State level there are co-occurrences of sustainability in the renewable energy sector development segment in correlation with primary energy supply and industrial energy consumption, which means that the achievement of clean energy targets is closely dependent on energy security and sustainable economic development policies (C1). Secondly, the sustainability of energy sources is correlated with import dependence, the level of taxation of revenues and total primary energy supply. This correlation means that energy security objectives can be achieved if relevant policies are implemented both in terms of securing energy sources and in terms of energy sector taxation (C2—economic and financial policies to secure energy sources). Thirdly, the energy sustainability function implies the transition to a green economy and the monitoring of emissions at European level with effects on environmental protection and combating climate warming (C3—policies on environmental protection and combating climate warming).

We have developed two new European energy sustainability impact models using panel data analysis, namely the sustainability impact model by quantifying the correlated balance of energy efficiency on greenhouse gas emissions and the energy sustainability impact model by quantifying the sectoral sensitivity of energy efficiency on the intensity of air emissions from industry. The first model highlights the complex interconnections between energy policies, economic behaviour and environmental impacts. The model suggests the need for sustainable energy development through continued investments in green technologies and by optimizing fiscal and import policies to encourage greener behaviour for a friendlier and more sustainable environment including for Romania. The second model has highlighted the sensitivity of the energy sector on the industrial branch, demonstrating that there are vulnerabilities induced by the development of this sector on the quality of the environment, which transforms the sustainability objectives into challenges for the rapid implementation of new green technological innovations and ensuring environmental protection against pollution. Both models are applicable to Romania and support the need for reform in the energy sector to achieve energy sustainability.

Chapter 6 applied the DEA energy efficiency analysis and demonstrated that most European countries are energy efficient, and the European Union is taking over the efficiency trend of the Member States showing a fluctuation of energy efficiency in relation to economic and geopolitical uncertainties. The method revealed large disparities in efficiency scores under the influence of multiple crises (economic, pandemic, social, geopolitical). We assess that the following public policies to increase energy efficiency at the European level are relevant considering maximizing the productivity of each unit of energy consumed in order to reduce both costs and environmental impact:

Impose minimum efficiency standards for household and industrial electrical equipment, vehicles and buildings to ensure energy efficiency is maximized.

Provide subsidies, tax rebates, tax credits or other financial incentives for investments in clean energy and energy-efficient technologies, energy renovations of buildings and the purchase of energy-efficient equipment.
Implement programs to facilitate access to energy audits for the industrial and agricultural sectors, along with energy certifications to reduce the tax burden on energy-efficient consumers.
Promote R&D investment in the energy and environment sectors.

The analysis in this chapter has allowed the formulation of two strategies for sustainable energy development in Romania (as shown in Fig. 7.1) based on the hierarchical cluster analysis of indicators by the Average linkage method using the proximity matrix of energy sustainability for Romania for the period 2010–2021 and the multi-annual cluster links based on the real Euclidean distances calculated in the proximity matrix (Table 7.1), thus determining 11 clusters for the analysed period.

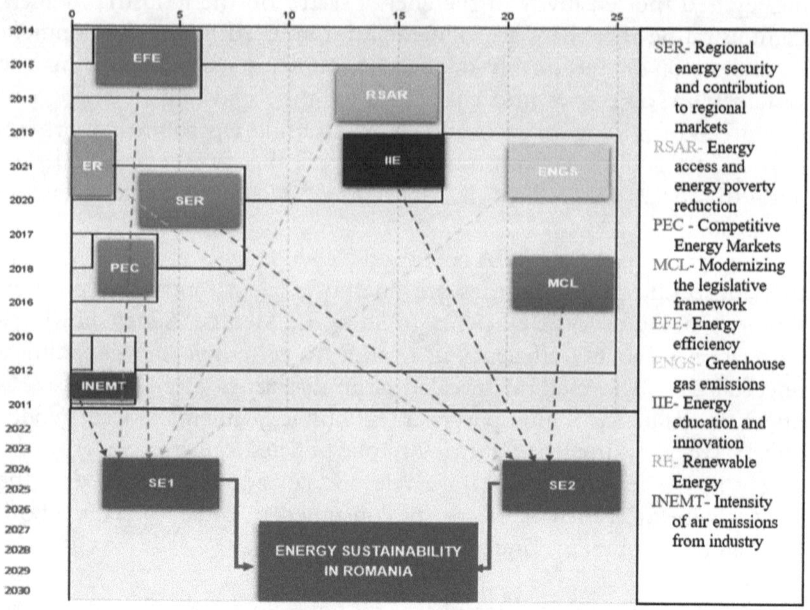


**Fig. 7.1** Cluster dendogram of Romanian energy sustainability from the perspective of the proposed new strategies. Source: Author

**Table 7.1** Energy proximity matrix in Romania (based on Euclidean real distances)

| *Years* | *2010* | *2011* | *2012* | *2013* | *2014* | *2015* | *2016* | *2017* | *2018* | *2019* | *2020* | *2021* |
|---|---|---|---|---|---|---|---|---|---|---|---|---|
| 2010 | 0.000 | 23.412 | 9.274 | 45.273 | 152.802 | 158.615 | 181.319 | 165.926 | 156.209 | 237.434 | 258.976 | 269.647 |
| 2011 | 23.412 | 0.000 | 11.211 | 93.031 | 220.627 | 217.406 | 256.089 | 202.069 | 182.183 | 282.808 | 329.123 | 341.860 |
| 2012 | 9.274 | 11.211 | 0.000 | 60.492 | 177.326 | 177.564 | 191.068 | 153.245 | 138.120 | 212.502 | 245.962 | 250.785 |
| 2013 | 45.273 | 93.031 | 60.492 | 0.000 | 40.373 | 45.294 | 79.108 | 95.481 | 103.880 | 207.693 | 185.628 | 231.826 |
| 2014 | 152.802 | 220.627 | 177.326 | 40.373 | 0.000 | 1.450 | 33.104 | 68.701 | 90.559 | 204.416 | 151.442 | 235.129 |
| 2015 | 158.615 | 217.406 | 177.564 | 45.294 | 1.450 | 0.000 | 31.956 | 59.573 | 80.186 | 196.057 | 146.010 | 233.266 |
| 2016 | 181.319 | 256.089 | 191.068 | 79.108 | 33.104 | 31.956 | 0.000 | 21.237 | 36.401 | 84.301 | 44.386 | 100.598 |
| 2017 | 165.926 | 202.069 | 153.245 | 95.481 | 68.701 | 59.573 | 21.237 | 0.000 | 2.965 | 49.706 | 38.784 | 85.905 |
| 2018 | 156.209 | 182.183 | 138.120 | 103.880 | 90.559 | 80.186 | 36.401 | 2.965 | 0.000 | 39.817 | 41.910 | 79.286 |
| 2019 | 237.434 | 282.808 | 212.502 | 207.693 | 204.416 | 196.057 | 84.301 | 49.706 | 39.817 | 0.000 | 14.977 | 13.437 |
| 2020 | 258.976 | 329.123 | 245.962 | 185.628 | 151.442 | 146.010 | 44.386 | 38.784 | 41.910 | 14.977 | 0.000 | 19.148 |
| 2021 | 269.647 | 341.860 | 250.785 | 231.826 | 235.129 | 233.266 | 100.598 | 85.905 | 79.286 | 13.437 | 19.148 | 0.000 |

Source: Prepared by the author using the statistical program SPSS vs 26

The proximity matrix reflects the distances between the annual values for the energy sustainability indicators in Romania (SDG7FZEP, SDG7APER, SDG7CENAG, SDG7CENI, SDG7VFEN, SDG7PREN, SDG7IMPEN, SDG7ENGS and SDG7INEMT) for the period 2010–2021. In this context, the differences in the values of the indicators by year suggest differences in the policies adopted/implemented in Romania. Large increases are observed between the consecutive years 2010–2011 and 2019–2020; these increases indicate significant changes in energy policy, increasing renewable energy production (2019–2020) or changes in industrial and agricultural energy consumption (2010–2011). Small changes in the years 2017–2018 indicate possible stability in policy and consumption, suggesting increased efficiency or implementation of constant sustainability measures. The impact of indicators by year categorizes the periods into three development stages:

- The initial stabilization period from 2010 to 2014 shows significant changes due to adaptation to EU rules on sustainability and renewable energy. The introduction of renewable energy subsidies and improved energy efficiency in industry and agriculture explain these variations.
- Energy efficiency improvements from 2015 to 2017 show a downward trend in variances, suggesting better management of energy consumption and adaptation to new technologies that improve energy productivity. Policies to reduce greenhouse gas emissions and increase energy-related tax revenues contribute to this trend.
- The period of continuous progress and stabilization from 2018 to 2021 corresponds to a stage of energy maturity. Continued efforts to reduce import dependency and increase the use of renewable energy show a continuous adaptation to sustainability goals.

We propose the Strategy (SE1) for sustainable energy development from a climate neutral perspective—monitoring and reducing the polluting effects of the energy industry should be achieved by limiting energy imports and increasing the share of renewable energy in the energy mix. At the same time, the favourable results will be supported by the reduction of environmental taxes according to the polluter pays principle.

We propose the Strategy (SE2) for sustainable energy development—the normalization of energy consumption in agriculture and industry must be achieved with the support of the development of renewable energy production as a share of total energy production by introducing appropriate taxes for conventional energy users in the two branches to support the efforts of transition to climate neutrality and to encourage the implementation of green energy solutions in industry and agriculture.

Forecasting the implementation of the proposed policy mix for 2030 will result in:

- Continued development of renewable technologies and energy storage solutions to reduce costs and improve efficiency, accelerating the transition to a green economy.
- Romania's commitments to international climate agreements and EU sustainability policies will help shape the energy future. Renewable energy and carbon taxes will significantly influence the dynamics of the sector.
- Increase renewable energy production by expanding and diversifying sources.
- For the horizon 2030 in terms of the proposed strategies, energy efficiency through the implementation of emerging technologies and the reduction of final energy consumption are envisaged.
- By increasing domestic production, Romania could reduce its dependence on energy imports.
- EU and national policies aimed at reducing emissions could lead to a continuation of the downward trend in greenhouse gas emissions to reach the 2030 targets.
- Sustainability can also be stimulated by EU initiatives promoting energy efficiency and the uptake of green technologies at national level.

The analysis of the proximity matrix and of the trends regarding the evolution of energy sustainability indicators (from the perspective of the implementation of the proposed strategies) suggests that Romania is on a favourable slope in terms of energy sustainability for Horizon 2030 (European Commission, 2024d). The proposed strategy can be used by national decision-makers to adjust the initiated energy policies and recalculate the efficiency targets in the perspective of the National Energy Efficiency Strategy for Horizon 2030.

## References


Bashir, M. F., Pata, U. K., & Shahzad, L. (2025). Linking climate change, energy transition and renewable energy investments to combat energy security risks: Evidence from top energy consuming economies. *Energy, 314*, 134175. https://doi.org/10.1016/j.energy.2024.134175

Bełdycka-Bórawska, A., Wyszomierski, R., Bórawski, P., & Trębska, P. (2025). Economic performance of the producers of biomass for energy generation in the context of national and European policies—A case study of Poland. *Energies, 18*(15). https://doi.org/10.3390/en18154042

Borowiecki, M., Giménez, J. C., Giovannelli, F., & Vanni, F. (2023). Accelerating the EU's green transition. 1777. https://doi.org/10.1787/bed2b6df-en

Brugger, H., Eichhammer, W., Mikova, N., & Dönitz, E. (2021). Energy efficiency vision 2050: How will new societal trends influence future energy demand in the European countries? *Energy Policy, 152*, 112216. https://doi.org/10.1016/j.enpol.2021.112216

Castillo-Díaz, F. J., Belmonte-Ureña, L. J., Gálvez-Sánchez, F. J., & Camacho-Ferre, F. (2025). Sustainable technological innovations in agriculture: Financial challenges and investment priorities under the European green deal. *Journal of Environmental Management, 389*, 126150. https://doi.org/10.1016/j.jenvman.2025.126150

Castro, R. P., Dinho da Silva, P., & Pires, L. C. (2024). Advances in solutions to improve the energy performance of agricultural greenhouses: A comprehensive review. *Applied Sciences, 14*(14). https://doi.org/10.3390/app14146158

Dogan, E., Hodžić, S., & Šikić, T. F. (2023). Do energy and environmental taxes stimulate or inhibit renewable energy deployment in the European Union? *Renewable Energy, 202*, 1138–1145. https://doi.org/10.1016/j.renene.2022.11.107

Doran, N. M., Badareu, G., Doran, M. D., Firu, M. A., & Staicu, A. L. (2025). Evaluating the impact of EU expenditures under agricultural priorities on energy sustainability in CEE countries. *Agriculture, 15*(4). https://doi.org/10.3390/agriculture15040417

European Commission. (2023a). *A European green deal*. https://commission.europa.eu/strategy-and-policy/priorities-2019-2024/european-green-deal_en

European Commission. (2023b). *Energy efficiency directive*. https://energy.ec.europa.eu/topics/energy-efficiency/energy-efficiency-targets-directive-and-rules/energy-efficiency-directive_en

European Commission. (2023c). *National Energy Efficiency Action Plans*. https://joint-research-centre.ec.europa.eu/scientific-activities-z/energy-efficiency/support-energy-efficiency-directive-eed/national-energy-efficiency-action-plans-neeaps_en?utm_source=chatgpt.com

European Commission. (2023d). *Pricing agricultural emissions and rewarding climate action in the agri-food value chain*. Publications Office of the European Union. https://doi.org/10.2834/200

European Commission. (2024a). *Connecting Europe facility - CEF digital*. https://digital-strategy.ec.europa.eu/en/activities/cef-digital

European Commission. (2024b). *Energy research and innovation strategy*. https://research-and-innovation.ec.europa.eu/research-area/energy/strategy_en

European Commission. (2024c). *EU emissions trading system*. https://climate.ec.europa.eu/eu-action/eu-emissions-trading-system-eu-ets_en

European Commission. (2024d). *Horizon Europe*. https://research-and-innovation.ec.europa.eu/funding/funding-opportunities/funding-programmes-and-open-calls/horizon-europe_en

European Commission. (2024e). *Industrial and livestock rearing emissions directive (IED 2.0)*. https://environment.ec.europa.eu/topics/industrial-emissions-and-safety/industrial-and-livestock-rearing-emissions-directive-ied-20_en

European Commission. (2024f). *Recovery and resilience plans*. https://reform-support.ec.europa.eu/what-we-do/recovery-and-resilience-plans_en

European Commission. (2025a). *Green transition*. https://reform-support.ec.europa.eu/what-we-do/green-transition_en

European Commission. (2025b). *How to develop a sustainable energy and climate action plan (SECAP)*. https://managenergy.ec.europa.eu/publications/how-develop-sustainable-energy-and-climate-action-plan-secap_en?utm_source=chatgpt.com

European Commission. (2025c). *Renewable energy targets*. https://energy.ec.europa.eu/topics/renewable-energy/renewable-energy-directive-targets-and-rules/renewable-energy-targets_en

European Commission. (2025d). *Trans-European networks for energy*. https://energy.ec.europa.eu/topics/infrastructure/trans-european-networks-energy_en

European Environment Agency. (2025a). *Renewable energy*. https://www.eea.europa.eu/en/topics/in-depth/renewable-energy

European Environment Agency. (2025b). *Renewables, electrification and flexibility - For a competitive EU energy system transformation by 2030*. https://www.eea.europa.eu/en/analysis/publications/renewables-electrification-and-flexibility-for-a-competitive-eu-energy-system

European Union. (2024). *Just transition fund*. https://www.europarl.europa.eu/factsheets/en/sheet/214/just-transition-fund

Grafström, J., Söderholm, P., Gawel, E., Lehmann, P., & Strunz, S. (2023). Government support to renewable energy R&D: Drivers and strategic interactions among EU Member States. *Economics of Innovation and New Technology, 32*(1), 1–24. https://doi.org/10.1080/10438599.2020.1857499

Hoicka, C. E., Lowitzsch, J., Brisbois, M. C., Kumar, A., & Ramirez Camargo, L. (2021). Implementing a just renewable energy transition: Policy advice for transposing the new European rules for renewable energy communities. *Energy Policy, 156*, 112435. https://doi.org/10.1016/j.enpol.2021.112435

Jensen, T. A., Antille, D. L., & Tullberg, J. N. (2025). Improving on-farm energy use efficiency by optimizing machinery operations and management: A review. *Agricultural Research, 14*(1), 15–33. https://doi.org/10.1007/s40003-024-00824-5

Majeed, Y., Khan, M. U., Waseem, M., Zahid, U., Mahmood, F., Majeed, F., Sultan, M., & Raza, A. (2023). Renewable energy as an alternative source for energy management in agriculture. *Energy Reports, 10*, 344–359. https://doi.org/10.1016/j.egyr.2023.06.032

Maraveas, C., Karavas, C.-S., Loukatos, D., Bartzanas, T., Arvanitis, K. G., & Symeonaki, E. (2023). Agricultural greenhouses: Resource management technologies and perspectives for zero greenhouse gas emissions. *Agriculture, 13*(7). https://doi.org/10.3390/agriculture13071464

Nwagu, C. N., Ujah, C. O., Kallon, D. V. V., & Aigbodion, V. S. (2025). Integrating solar and wind energy into the electricity grid for improved power accessibility. *Unconventional Resources, 5*, 100129. https://doi.org/10.1016/j.uncres.2024.100129

Paris, B., Vandorou, F., Balafoutis, A. T., Vaiopoulos, K., Kyriakarakos, G., Manolakos, D., & Papadakis, G. (2022). Energy use in open-field agriculture in the EU: A critical review recommending energy efficiency measures and renewable energy sources adoption. *Renewable and Sustainable Energy Reviews, 158*, 112098. https://doi.org/10.1016/j.rser.2022.112098

Parlamentul European. (2024). *EFICIENȚA ENERGETICĂ*. https://www.europarl.europa.eu/

Pestisha, A., Bai, A., Sertolli, A., Bytyqi, N., & Balogh, P. (2025). Farmers' willingness to achieve energy self-sufficiency in Kosovo. *Energies, 18*, 1332. https://doi.org/10.3390/en18061332

Prigoreanu, I., Ungureanu, B. A., Ungureanu, G., & Ignat, G. (2024). Analysis of sustainable energy and environmental policies in agriculture in the EU regarding the European green deal. *Energies, 17*(24). https://doi.org/10.3390/en17246428

Ragazou, K., Garefalakis, A., Zafeiriou, E., & Passas, I. (2022). Agriculture 5.0: A new strategic management mode for a cut cost and an energy efficient agriculture sector. *Energies, 15*(9). https://doi.org/10.3390/en15093113

Romanian Ministry of Energy. (2025). *Romania's Energy Strategy 2025–2035, with a view to 2050*. https://energie.gov.ro/strategiei-energetice-a-romaniei-2025-2035-cu-perspectiva-anului-2050/

Sompolska-Rzechuła, A., Bąk, I., Becker, A., Marjak, H., & Perzyńska, J. (2024). The use of renewable energy sources and environmental degradation in EU countries. *Sustainability, 16*(23). https://doi.org/10.3390/su162310416

United Nations. (2023). *The Paris agreement*. https://unfccc.int/process-and-meetings/the-paris-agreement

Vela Almeida, D., Kolinjivadi, V., Ferrando, T., Roy, B., Herrera, H., Vecchione Gonçalves, M., & Van Hecken, G. (2023). The "greening" of empire: The European green deal as the EU first agenda. *Political Geography, 105*, 102925. https://doi.org/10.1016/j.polgeo.2023.102925

CHAPTER 8

# Analysis of the Economy's Strategies to Achieve the Sustainable Development Goals and the Main SDG 8 Indicators

## Introduction

In a period marked by major economic transitions, successive crises and structural challenges related to inequality, unemployment and sustainability, sustainable development has become a central strategic objective in European Union governance. The adoption of the 2030 Agenda and the integration of the Sustainable Development Goals (SDGs) into European public policies signal a reconfiguration of socio-economic priorities, with an emphasis on inclusion, equity and resilience. In this context, SDG8, which aims to promote sustainable economic growth, full and productive employment and decent work for all, is particularly relevant to the analysis of Member States' economic performance.

This chapter aims to investigate, from an integrated perspective, the evolution of key indicators associated with SDG8 in Romania and the European Union during the period 2010–2021, in the context of the post-2008 financial crisis, the COVID-19 pandemic and recent geopolitical tensions. Using an analytical approach based on data provided by Eurostat, the dimensions of the risk of poverty in work, the long-term unemployment rate, the employment rate, investment as a share of GDP and the evolution of real GDP per capita are examined, providing a nuanced picture of the progress and gaps between Romania and the European average.



C. Fortea, *Sustainable Economic Development and the European Green Deal*, https://doi.org/10.1007/978-3-032-10326-0_8

The novelty of the approach lies in the application of a longitudinal comparative analysis of economic and social performance through the lens of SDG8 indicators, highlighting the internal dynamics of each indicator, regional trends and implications for economic and social cohesion. In particular, the paper aims to: assess the consistency of public policies in Romania with sustainable development goals, identify persistent vulnerabilities and formulate policy directions for convergence with the European average.

This analysis makes a relevant contribution to the literature by strategically linking SDG8 indicators to the fundamentals of sustainable development in an emerging economy, while providing empirical support for optimizing public interventions at the national and European levels.

## Analysis of the Romanian Economy's Strategies for Achieving Sustainable Development Goal 8

Sustainable development is part of the European Union's 2030 Agenda (United Nations, 2020), based on the need to realize the limits of global growth based on the finite nature of some natural resources, the pressure of demographic growth and the need for social security. Thus, the three pillars through which the 2030 Agenda supports sustainable development are social equity, economic growth enabling all countries to ensure the necessary parameters for a decent quality of life and the preservation of the environment, available resources and the implementation of new non-polluting technologies. In this context, several stages of setting the Sustainable Development Strategy based on concretely defined, monitorable indicators and targets aimed at a specialized but unitary approach to sustainable development have been carried out. Thus, sustainable development currently includes 17 objectives and a significant number of indicators as they are found in the Wider Europe Strategy implemented since 2006. The continuation of this strategy was launched in 2010 with the Europe 2020 Strategy (European Commission, 2020) which promoted smart growth based on innovation, research and education; also through this strategy was familiarized for sustainable development based on decarbonization and energy efficiency and inclusive development based towards poverty reduction. The 2030 Agenda thus integrates the Sustainable Development Goals into European policies as set out in the Commission Communication "Next steps for a sustainable European future—European action for sustainability". The 17 Sustainable Development Goals are thus brought together in the European Union's policy, becoming priority sustainable development objectives for Romania as a Member State. At the United Nations General Assembly in 2015, when the UN Agenda 2030 was signed, concrete actions were set out to achieve the 17 goals. The main goals aim to secure world peace and prosperity, eradicate poverty and protect the planet (United Nations, 2020). The Paris Agreement on Climate Change signed the European Green Pact (European Commission, 2019b) which is the global framework for cooperation on sustainable development. The signatory states of the European Green Pact have committed themselves to achieve all economic, environmental and governance actions to effectively combat climate change. At European level, the main effects of the implementation of sustainable development lie in the creation of a free and democratic European area in which European citizens can achieve unprecedented levels of prosperity. In terms of life expectancy, Europe is today the continent with the highest life expectancy. Social protection systems are being strengthened by European social policy and European economies are progressing economically and technologically thanks to structural reforms and strict monitoring of the public debt ratio in the European area. According to the "Reflection Paper Towards a Sustainable Europe", adult employment rates in the EU have been gradually increasing and thus labour productivity. In terms of cohesion policy, the EU advocates the reduction of regional disparities based on the principle of upward convergence established through specific programmes and measures for which the EU has provided and is providing funding.

In terms of European strategies, the Juncker Commission has launched sustainable public policies, such as the European Pillar of Social Rights, the Trade for All Strategy, the promotion of the circular economy through the Europe on the Move Strategy, the Blue Growth Strategy, the Urban Agenda. Several action plans have also been launched, followed up and implemented such as the Sustainable Finance Action Plan, the Nature Action Plan, the Energy Efficiency Action Plan. The EU's most ambitious project is the one that aims to be climate neutral in Europe by 2050. The means that have been and are being used to implement strategic policies include social dialogue, the establishment of public-private partnerships, private voluntary action, public governance and civil action. The multi-annual financial frameworks have created multiple opportunities for the practical implementation of sustainable development policies, with the latest multi-annual financial plan launched for the period 2021–2027. It takes sectoral policies for sustainable development and translates them into financing guidelines in line with the objectives set; in addition the Commission aims to reduce the effects of multiple crises such as the economic and financial crisis in Europe. From a strategic point of view, this implies strengthening national growth rates, reducing Member States' public debt levels and maintaining fiscal discipline to increase economic resilience and cohesion, thus making the European economy less exposed to structural vulnerabilities.

A collective of authors (Ionescu et al., 2023) set out to determine a structured dynamic model of monetary policy using information from the literature and the study of the evolution of the financial components of macroeconomic aggregates in a non-euro member state (Romania). The methods consisted of an empirical study of causality in monetary aggregates from the literature and an analytical approach to the consolidation of dynamic databases over a 16-year period (2007–2022) and their statistical modelling. This research examined the impact of uncertainty on Romania's monetary policy during the period under analysis and how this uncertainty changes the dependence relationships between monetary policy indicators and GDP deflator derivatives. The results of the two-stage modelling, respectively, for the periods 2007–2019 and 2007–2022, highlighted, through a comparison, the vulnerabilities induced by periods of uncertainty and pandemics on the evolution of monetary policy indicators, useful aspects for financial policy-makers in correcting monetary policy elements based on the picture of vulnerabilities instrumented because of the analysis and modelling.

The directions in which funding efforts are directed are investment in research and innovation, the creation of efficient public services and ensuring an adequate level of environmental protection (OECD, 2020). At the same time, from a strategic point of view, the aim is to ensure the sustainability of pension systems and budgetary systems within the functional framework of the single market. Reducing the pressure on the environment means, according to the 2030 Strategy (European Commission, 2019a), reducing the economic dependence on the consumption of non-renewable materials and increasing the use of renewable sources; in this direction the challenges are due to the excessive growth of excessive consumption of resources and environmental damage through climate change. Another strategic direction, such as equal opportunities, is being implemented with consequences in terms of fostering social inclusion and guaranteeing free access to the labour market for the European population.

Another strategic direction is that of the transition to the green economy so that progress has been made on the level of employment in the environmental sector and technologies have been developed to reduce carbon dioxide emissions. In economic terms, technology exports have outpaced imports since 2015, making the European economy an efficient sustainable growth economy. In terms of green growth, important steps towards sustainable development have been made in agriculture, in the raw materials sector, in the energy sector and in city administrations, where modern infrastructure has been developed in line with the new guidelines. To stimulate sustainable development and private sector development, the EU has financed smart and sustainable development projects, while advocating for the phasing out of funding for projects that do not converge towards economic, social and environmental sustainability. With the launch in 2015 of the European Fund for Strategic Investments, the foundations have been laid for the implementation of investment plans aimed at developing the renewable energy sector, developing the research and development sector and developing the infrastructure sector. Social entrepreneurship and sustainable infrastructure are being advocated. Several smart changes to the financial system have been adopted by the EU to support sustainable development. The following measures have been taken: the use of taxonomy in defining sustainable economic activities and impact investing in the field, the creation of standards for green financial products, the integration of sustainability into investment advice, the development of benchmarks on sustainable growth, the strengthening of transparency on corporate reporting and the integration of sustainability into prudential requirements to manage risks and protect financial stability. Other measures that are actively advocated in the European area are the fight against tax evasion, the creation of sustainable and fair competition, the taxation of sources of pollution by introducing the "polluter pays" etc.

According to the National Strategy for Sustainable Development of Romania 2030 (Government of Romania, 2018) the EU and Romania are promoting investments in education, skills training, research and development, business efficiency reforms, improvement of the labour market, introduction of sustainable social protection systems.

The outbreak of conflict in Ukraine has presented the EU with a social and financial challenge. On the one hand Ukrainian refugees needed asylum and access to the labour market and the education system and, on the other hand, the limitation of energy imports from Russia triggered the energy crisis followed by inflation and increasing economic hardship for the population at risk of poverty in Europe. In this context to stimulate social recovery, the EU proposed several measures such as the implementation of the NextGeneration program and the equitable transition to a greener and more digitalized economy. The social impact of the crisis has largely been deepening inequality, inflation and the emergence of energy poverty.

The current geopolitical context has exacerbated the energy crisis, motivating once again the need to transition to the green economy. In this context, the objectives of the European Agenda call for an increased focus on sustainable development in the transition to a green economy. Eastern European countries face major economic disadvantages that slow down the implementation of this objective in the region. Fortea and colleagues (Fortea et al., 2023) have developed an econometric representation of sustainable development from a green economy perspective in Eastern European countries. The methods used are empirical (literature review) and analytical, i.e. designing a model of sustainable development from the perspective of transition to green economy in Eastern European countries. The results of the study highlighted the differences in the development of Eastern European countries compared to the European average and identified the possibilities of catching up with the observed difficulties. The EU economy has been affected because of the geopolitical conflict by trade and financial disruptions, with the agricultural and energy sectors being the hardest hit, with rising energy prices having profound implications for European agriculture.

In the National Action Plan for 2022–2030 (Government of Romania, 2022), Romania aims to achieve the sustainable development goals, to this end the Department for Sustainable Development has been set up, the Action Plan contains 4 priority directions and 12 specific objectives in an integrated and multidimensional approach to sustainable development. The strategic directions and objectives for sustainable development in Romania are presented in Fig. 8.1.

For the implementation of these strategic directions and objectives, four monitoring and evaluation principles are applied: accountability, transparency, cooperation and efficiency. These principles make it possible to quantify the accountability, transparency, cooperation and collaboration of Romanian public bodies in order to implement the Sustainable Development Action Plan (Government of Romania, 2022).

**Consolidating and extending the governance framework for Sustainable Development**

- Objective 1: Develop and strengthen the regulatory and inter-institutional cooperation framework for the implementation of the NRDS 2030
- Objective 2: National budget planning framework for the implementation of SDG-based budgeting
- Objective 3: Support local authorities to incorporate the principles and values of sustainable development into local policies and strategies
- Objective 4: Support and stimulate business and civil society to adopt the concept of sustainable development
- Objective 5: Strengthening the RDI system to build anticipatory capacity for evidence-based public policy making for sustainable development

**Support the Implementation of the NRDSDS 2030 through Education and Training Programs for Sustainable Development**

- Objective 6: Training human resources in the field of sustainable development
- Objective 7: Develop specific tools for education for sustainable development at all stages of education

**Promoting the Principles and Values of the Sustainable Development Concept**

- Objective 8: Promote the concepts of sustainable development with the aim of achieving the NRDS 2030 targets
- Objective 9: Communication in support of the implementation of the NRDS 2030

**Monitoring and Evaluating the Implementation of the NRDSDS 2030**

- Objective 10: Monitoring and evaluation mechanism for the implementation of the NRDSDS 2030
- Objective 11: Reporting on the status of implementation of the NRDDS 2030
- Objective 12: Linking the implementation of sectoral policies to achieve the 2030 NRDSDS targets

**Fig. 8.1** Strategic directions and objectives for sustainable development in Romania. Source: Prepared by the author according to the National Action Plan for 2022–2030 (Government of Romania, 2022)

Economic growth is a real direction of action guiding national economies and has been discussed by many authors, as evidenced by many publications dedicated to this field. To analyse them, a synthetic review was carried out according to the general principles of literature review as shown in Fig. 8.2. The Web of Science database was used to search for the phrase "economic growth" used in the titles, abstracts and keywords of the publications included in this database. In the year 2023, the total number of papers identified on the Web of Science platform was 9982 articles recognized in 4633 scholarly papers that cited them (without self-citations) with a citation rate of 0.46 times per article and a Hirsch index of 17 points.

These publications address various research issues including economic growth and labour investment efficiency (Singh, 2023), the impact of environmental regulation on economic growth, economic growth and the impact of R&D investment, employment structure, industrial structure and the impact on economic growth (Zhou et al., 2023), unidirectional

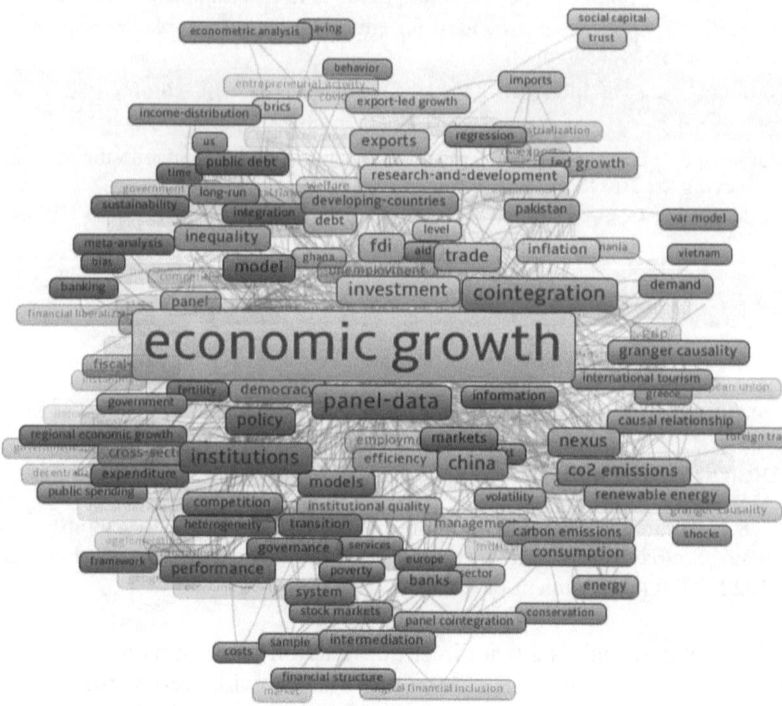


Fig. 8.2 Bibliometric analysis on economic growth. Source: Author using VOSviewer software

causality of renewable energy to long-term economic growth, impact of income inequality on economic growth (Acheampong et al., 2023).

The review of the literature on the correlation of SD indicators is presented below.

### *Risk of In-work Poverty*

In a study by Gioachin F., Marx I and Scherer S. (2023) the risk of poverty is analysed in a socio-economic context, finding through econometric modelling that it is stratified according to social class, with a marked dynamics in recent years. The impact of the research is substantial, as it demonstrates that poverty risk is stratified according to differences between social classes; moreover, the upper classes have continued to maintain high levels of economic security. Low-skilled and unskilled employees, according to the research, have the highest exposure to poverty, and in Southern Europe they are joined by the lower middle class based on the prevalence of single-earner households. Benedetti I. and Crescenzi F. (2023) show that the social, economic, financial and health crises have contributed to increasing inequalities among socially vulnerable groups. The contribution of their study is substantial, as the authors explicitly link the dimension of social exclusion to the heightened uncertainty generated by international pandemic and geopolitical events. Another study by Polizzi A., Struffolino A. and Van Winkle Z. (2022) shows that the formation of a marital or non-marital residential union protects individuals from in-work poverty and that single-earner families exhibit a significant poverty risk. The impact is high because the study connects demographic, family and poverty processes and highlights the importance of methodological considerations in analysing disparities across EU Member States.

### *Sustainable Economic Growth and Investment in Technology*

Diane F. Frey (2017) shows that the Global Agenda for Sustainable Development includes goals of economic growth, enterprise creation, ensuring productivity and technological innovation. She concludes the importance of monitoring human rights, increasing social accountability and the legitimacy provided by SDG8 actions for a sound approach to economic growth. Parka J, Ryu D and Lee K. (2019) examine the determinants of the national economic dimension compared to conventional determinants of per capita income growth. It thus connects macroeconomic size (GDP) with citizens' quality of life. The paper demonstrates that there are global differences in the balance between the two factors, which are relatively interdependent in the era of globalization.

An interesting approach by Destefanis S. and Rehman N. (2023) examines the effect of different forms of investment on employment at the European regional level. The authors find that only in NUT2 regions with medium to high levels of innovation the impact of R&D on new job creation is significant; in the other regions the employment-generating indicator is gross fixed capital formation. The impact is significant showing that reaching the technological frontier favours positive employment externalities.

### *Employment Rate*

Manuchehr Irandoust (2023) conducts an analysis of the impact of active labour market policies on the welfare level of citizens based on the Granger causality test in bootstrap panel; it was shown that active labour market policies lead to reduced unemployment and have an effect on increasing employment rates. The impact is significant, with the segregated data analysis showing that the phenomenon has a higher success rate for women than for men.

Another study by Ferraro S., Männasoo K. and Tasane H. (2023) analysed how support activities targeting research, development and innovation through the European Union Cohesion Policy Program 2014–2020 affect employment, productivity and export intensity of small and medium-sized enterprises in the EU member state Estonia. The final policy of this state aims at R&D-driven productivity and employment growth, together with stronger export competitiveness. Study results show a positive short-term effect on labour productivity and employment.

### *Long-Term Unemployment Rate*

The study by Caporale G.M., Gil-Alana L. and Trejo P.C. (2022) investigates the persistence of unemployment in the 27 Member States using fractional data integration methods. In developed countries such as Belgium, France, Luxembourg the level of persistence is subunitary while in countries such as Bulgaria and Romania significant negative trends are observed. The impact is high as the authors show that the seasonal persistence of unemployment was seasonally influenced by uncertainty and the results support the hysteresis hypothesis (inertia of development based on historical data). The authors of "Unemployment Shocks and Material Deprivation in Europe European Union: A Synthetic Control Approach" (Ayala et al., 2023) analyse the level of material deprivation of citizens (poverty) based on the significant change in the level of unemployment. It applied the synthetic control methodology of distributional analysis and found that unemployment shocks have a significant and rapid impact on material deprivation. The impact is high through the link between poverty level and unemployment shocks.

### *Young People Neither in Employment Nor in Education and Training (NEET)*

Papadakis N., Amanakib E., Drakakia M. and Saridakia S. (2020) show that employment status is affected by educational capital and family background. Research results document the intergenerational transmission of poverty because of the recession that limits the chances of a decent life for young people. In addition, the phenomenon of migration of highly qualified young people, which has an impact on the economic environment in the state of origin (Greece), is brought to attention. Another study by Rahmani H. and Groot W. (2023) presents the significant aspects of youth employment by correlating educational attainment with family influence quantifying critical impact indicators such as educational attainment, work experience and skills as well as physical and mental health. The authors also present other influencing factors such as social inequality, household income, education and occupational status. The study's contribution is of moderate impact, as it advances theoretical models concerning the effectiveness of early programmes and interventions aimed at facilitating youth labour market integration.

Sustainable development as shown in the literature is a complex, integrating phenomenon, which requires adequate resources and policies to reduce the risk of poverty, increase employment, reduce unemployment, ensure technological progress, being of interest policies dedicated to young people to ensure their early integration into the labour market and to make the most of their skills and experience.

## Analysis of Key Indicators on Sustainable Development Goal 8

It can be noted that the scientific interest shown in the international literature through recent research is focused on issues of economic growth through the reduction of the risk of poverty, increasing employment, reducing unemployment rates and ensuring the technological process.

Economic growth and fair working conditions are essential for the development and prosperity of European countries and for the well-being of their citizens. Monitoring SDG8 in the context of the European Union involves examining trends in employment, decent work and economic growth. The EU has made significant progress on SDG8, which has led to an improved workforce in Europe. At the same time, the EU is insisting on reaching the 2030 targets for the overall employment rate and the share of young people without access to employment, either in education or in training. As a result, working conditions have improved, leading to fewer fatal accidents at work and fewer people out of work.

Economic growth is important for prosperity and well-being, but it can also harm the environment. The European Union has adopted the Green Deal strategy (European Commission, 2019b) to transform the EU into a modern, efficient, fair and competitive economy.

These aspects are reflected by Eurostat statistics through specific indicators which will be analysed below (Eurostat, 2023):

- RSAR—The risk of in-work poverty is an indicator of inequality in income distribution and structural problems in the economy and labour market. It refers to the situation of people who are employed, but their earned income is not sufficient to lift them above the poverty line.
- PIB—Real gross domestic product per capita is an indicator calculated as the ratio of real GDP to the average population of the same year.
- INVPIB—Investment as a share of GDP is an indicator that shows gross fixed capital formation for the economy, government and business and household sectors as a percentage of GDP.
- ROFM—The long-term unemployment rate is the share of the labour force aged 15–74 who have been unemployed for at least 12 months. Unemployment has a negative impact on society because

it increases the risk that a person will stop looking for a job and fall into poverty.

- RSOM—Employment rate indicates the percentage of persons employed in relation to the total population.

The analysis of the at-risk-of-work poverty indicator at European Union level (EU27 at-risk-of-work poverty rate) shows that over the period 2010–2021 it has increased by 15.29%, from a minimum of 8.5% in 2010 to 9.8% in 2016 (Fig. 8.3).

Figure 8.3 shows that the risk of in-work poverty has fluctuated slightly over the years, with an overall decreasing trend, as indicated by the polynomial trend equation $y = -0.0323x^2 + 0.4341x + 8.1023$. On trend the indicator has experienced an overall upward trend of 0.4%; the calculated overall average of the indicator is 9.17%, with a standard error estimated by calculating descriptive statistics of 0.11% (see Table 8.1).

The analysis of the indicator on the risk of in-work poverty in Romania (RSARROM) shows that in the period 2010–2021 it had a dynamic of 32.89%. The minimum value of 14.9% was recorded in 2014 and the maximum value of 19.8% in 2020 (Fig. 8.4).

On trend, the indicator experienced an overall downward trend of 2.4%; the calculated overall average of the indicator being 17.55%, with a standard error estimated by descriptive statistics of 0.50% (as shown in

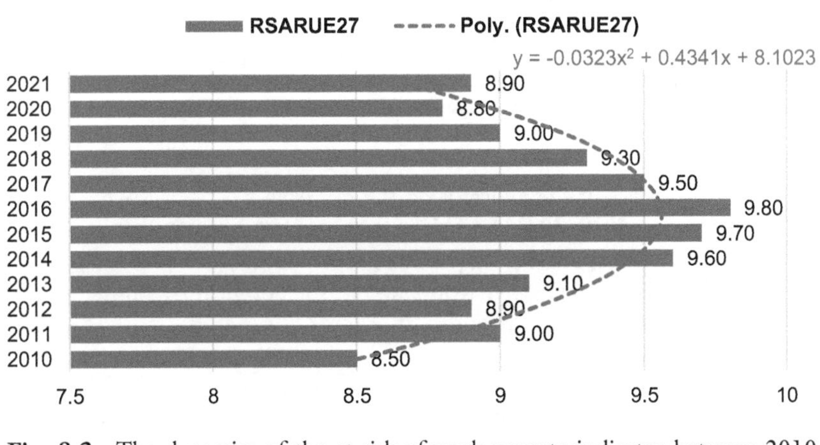


**Fig. 8.3** The dynamics of the at-risk-of-work poverty indicator between 2010 and 2021. Source: Author based on Eurostat data

**Table 8.1** Comparative descriptive statistics of the at-risk-of-work poverty indicator at European and national level over the period 2010–2021

| *The risk of in-work poverty* | *European Union—27 countries* | *Romania* |
|---|---|---|
| Minim | 8.50 | 14.90 |
| Maxim | 9.80 | 19.80 |
| Average | 9.17 | 17.55 |
| Standard error of the mean | 0.11 | 0.50 |
| Standard deviation | 0.40 | 1.74 |
| Variance | 0.16 | 3.04 |
| Asymmetry | 0.14 | −0.46 |
| Asymmetry error | 0.63 | 0.63 |
| Flattening | −0.95 | −1.53 |
| Standard error of flattening | 1.23 | 1.23 |

Source: Author based on Eurostat data

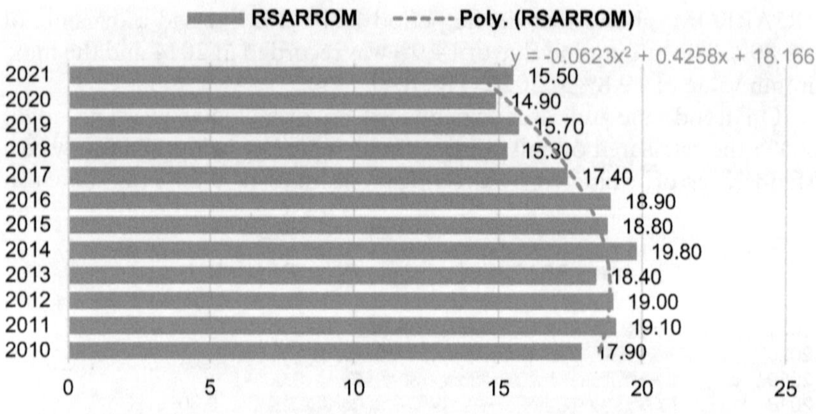


**Fig. 8.4** Dynamics of the indicator on the risk of in-work poverty at national level in the period 2010–2021. Source: Author based on Eurostat data

Table 4.1). This suggests that Romania faces a significantly higher risk of in-work poverty than the European average.

The analysis of the dynamic variation of the indicator in Romania compared to the European average shows that for Romania, the overall average seasonal variation was lower than the European average, as shown in Fig. 8.5. The risk of in-work poverty is higher and more variable in

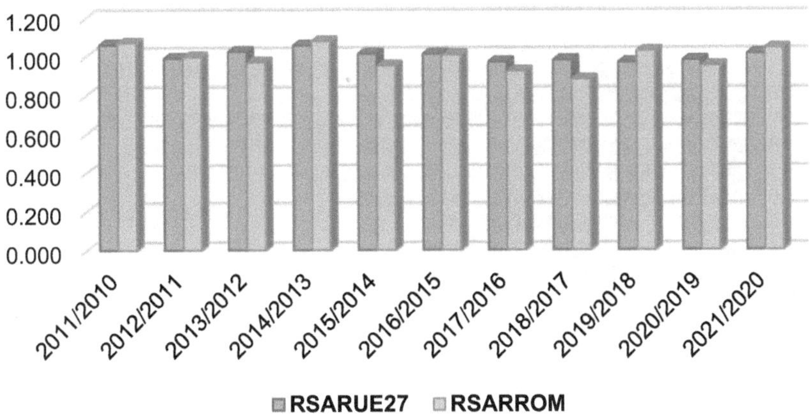


**Fig. 8.5** Analysis of the dynamic variations of the indicator on the risk of in-work poverty in Romania compared to the European average. Source: Author based on Eurostat data

Romania, which could reflect differences in economic structure, income inequality and the effectiveness of social protection systems that have significant implications for social cohesion and sustainable economic development.

Another important indicator is Gross Domestic Product being a macroeconomic indicator that helps measure a country's economic performance and is used to compare the size and economic health of different economies. The analysis of the real GDP per capita indicator at the European Union level (EU27 PIB27) shows that in the period 2010–2021 it has had a dynamic of 12.65%, i.e. from the minimum value of 24,900 euro per capita in 2010 to 28,050 euro per capita in 2019 as shown in Fig. 8.6.

Figure 4.6 shows a long-term upward trend reflected by the positive coefficient of the polynomial trend equation $y = 0.0974x^2 + 285.69x + 24415$. On trend the indicator has experienced an overall increasing trend of € 3010 per capita; the calculated overall average of the indicator being € 26,277.5 per capita, with a standard error estimated by descriptive statistics of € 335.022 per capita (see Table 8.2).

The analysis of the real GDP per capita indicator at the Romanian level (GDP per capita) shows that in the period 2010–2021 it had a dynamic of

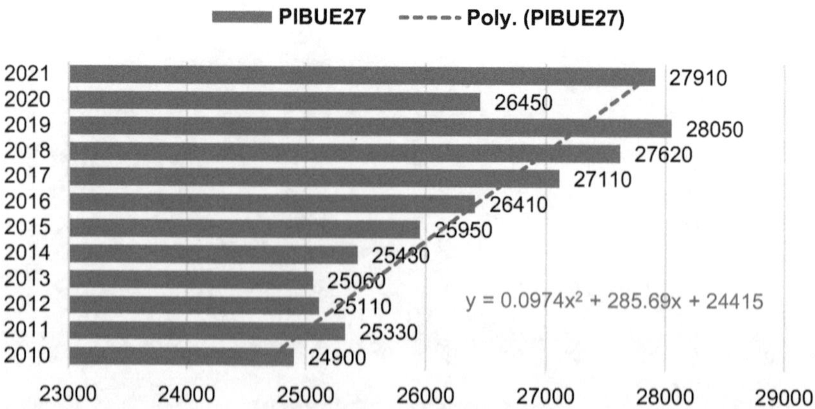


**Fig. 8.6** The dynamics of the real GDP per capita indicator at European level over the period 2010–2021. Source: Author based on Eurostat data

**Table 8.2** Comparative descriptive statistics of the real GDP per capita indicator at European and national level over the period 2010–2021

| *Real GDP per capita* | *European Union—27 countries* | *Romania* |
|---|---|---|
| Minim | 24,900.00 | 6340.00 |
| Maxim | 28,050.00 | 9610.00 |
| Average | 26,277.5000 | 7843.3330 |
| Standard error of the mean | 335.02200 | 330.56,300 |
| Standard deviation | 1160.54,900 | 1145.10,300 |
| Variance | 1,346,875.000 | 1,311,260.606 |
| Asymmetry | 0.378 | 0.293 |
| Asymmetry error | 0.637 | 0.637 |
| Flattening | −1.454 | −1.560 |
| Standard error of flattening | 1.232 | 1.232 |

Source: Author based on Eurostat data

51.58%, respectively, from the minimum value of 6340 euro per capita in 2010 to 9610 euro per capita in 2021 (Fig. 8.7).

On trend, the indicator showed a general upward trend of 3270 euro per inhabitant; the overall calculated average of the indicator being 7843.333 euro per inhabitant, with a standard error estimated by descriptive statistics of 330.563 euro per inhabitant (as shown in Table 8.2).

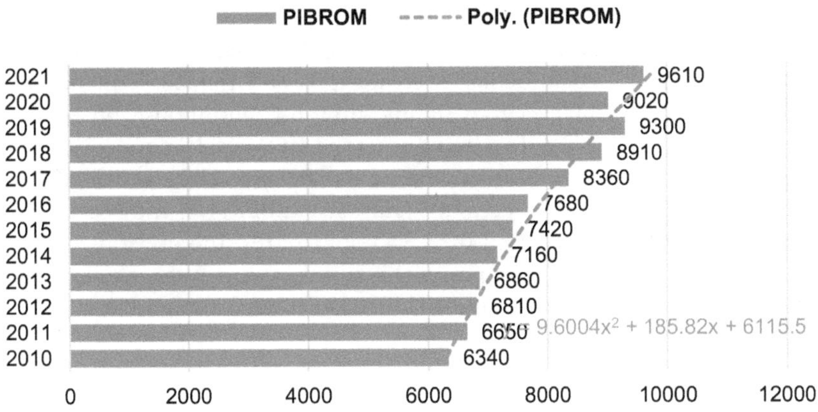


**Fig. 8.7** Dynamics of the real GDP per capita indicator at national level in the period 2010–2021. Source: Author based on Eurostat data

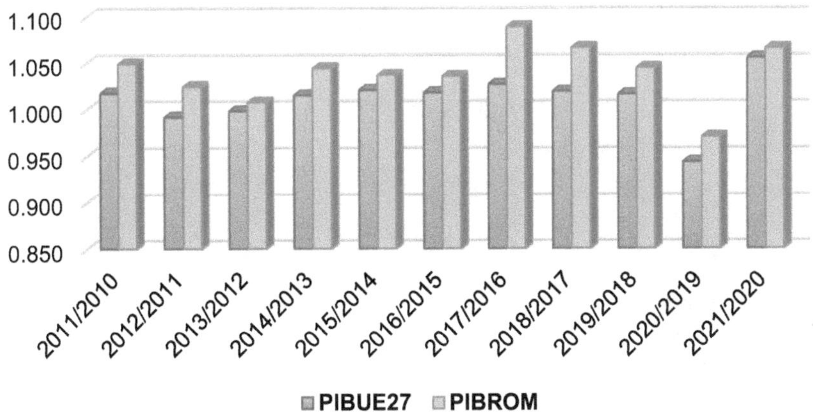


**Fig. 8.8** Analysis of the dynamic variations of the real GDP per capita indicator in Romania compared to the European average. Source: Author based on Eurostat data

The analysis of the dynamic variations of the indicator in Romania compared to the European average shows that for our country, the overall average of seasonal variations was higher than the European average, as shown in Fig. 8.8.

People's standard of living is based on the performance of the EU economy as measured by indicators, and GDP is a measure of the economy's potential to satisfy demand, create jobs and pursue growth. Real GDP per capita at EU level grew significantly and continuously on average between 2014 and 2019. In 2020 due to the COVID-19 pandemic leading to a significant reduction compared to 2019, in 2021 and 2022 the economy recovered from recession (Eurostat, 2023). In the year 2022, real GDP per capita increased by 3.3% compared to the previous year to €28,820, despite the economic repercussions of the Russian Ukrainian war and the mitigation measures of COVID-19, as shown in Fig. 8.9.

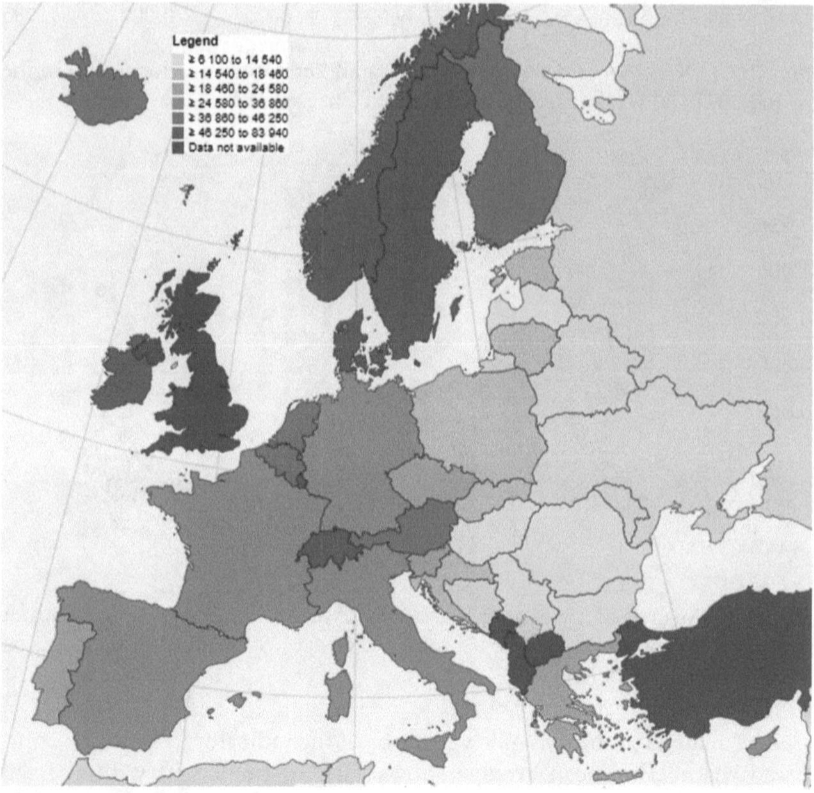


**Fig. 8.9** Real GDP per capita in the European Union. Source: Author based on Eurostat data (Eurostat, 2021)

The analysis of the indicator "investment share in GDP by institutional sectors" at EU level (INVPIBUE27) shows that in the period 2010–2021 it has had a dynamic of 12.45%, respectively, from a minimum of 20.08% in 2013 to 22.58% in 2019 (Fig. 8.10).

On trend, the indicator experienced an overall upward trend of 1.46%; the calculated overall average of the indicator being 21.208%, with a standard error estimated by descriptive statistics of 0.253% (as shown in Table 8.3).

The analysis of the indicator "investment share in GDP by institutional sectors" in Romania (INVPIBROM) shows that in the period 2010–2021 it had a dynamic of 30.78%. The minimum threshold was recorded in 2013 at 21.05% and the maximum value of 27.53% was recorded in 2019 (Fig. 8.11).

On trend, the indicator showed an overall downward trend of 4.76%; the calculated overall average of the indicator being 24.072%, with a standard error estimated by descriptive statistics of 0.615% (as shown in Table 8.3).

The analysis of the dynamic variations of the indicator in Romania compared to the European average shows that for our country, the general average of seasonal variations was lower than the European average, as

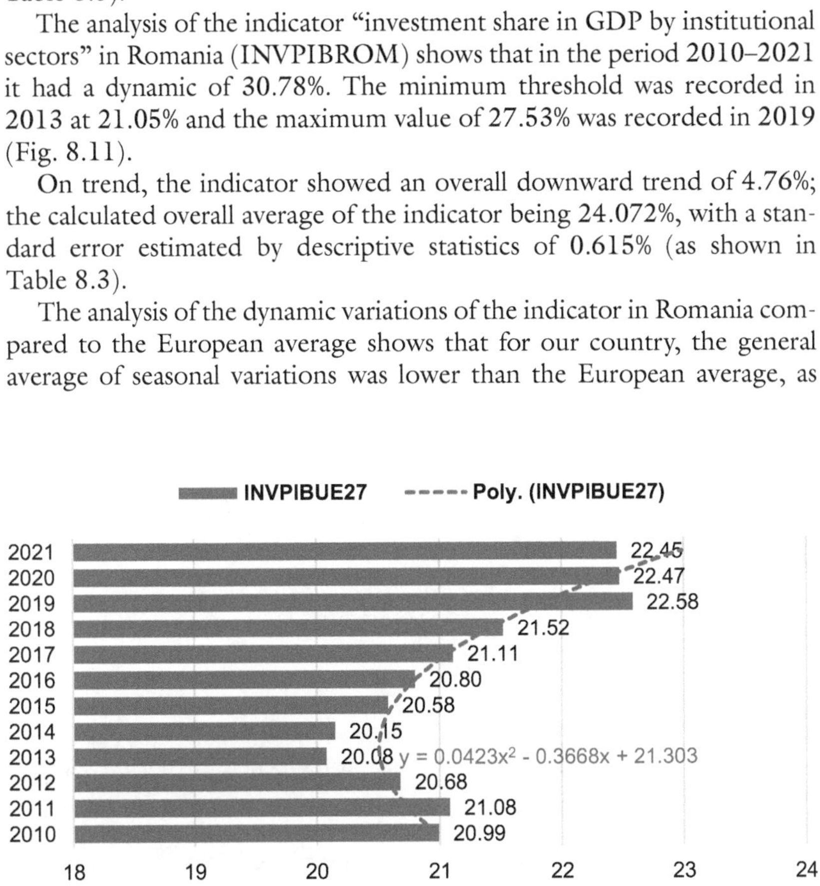


**Fig. 8.10** Dynamics of the indicator "investment share in GDP by total institutional sectors" at European level over the period 2010–2021. Source: Author based on Eurostat data

**Table 8.3** Comparative descriptive statistics of the indicator "share of investment in GDP by institutional sectors" at European and national level over the period 2010–2021

| *Share of investment in GDP by institutional sectors* | *European Union—27 countries* | *Romania* |
|---|---|---|
| Minim | 20.08 | 21.05 |
| Maxim | 22.58 | 27.53 |
| Average | 21.2080 | 24.0720 |
| Standard error of the mean | 0.25,300 | 0.61500 |
| Standard deviation | 0.87,500 | 2.13,100 |
| Variance | 0.765 | 4.541 |
| Asymmetry | 0.563 | 0.271 |
| Asymmetry error | 0.637 | 0.637 |
| Flattening | −0.910 | −0.858 |
| Standard error of flattening | 1.232 | 1.232 |

Source: Author based on Eurostat data

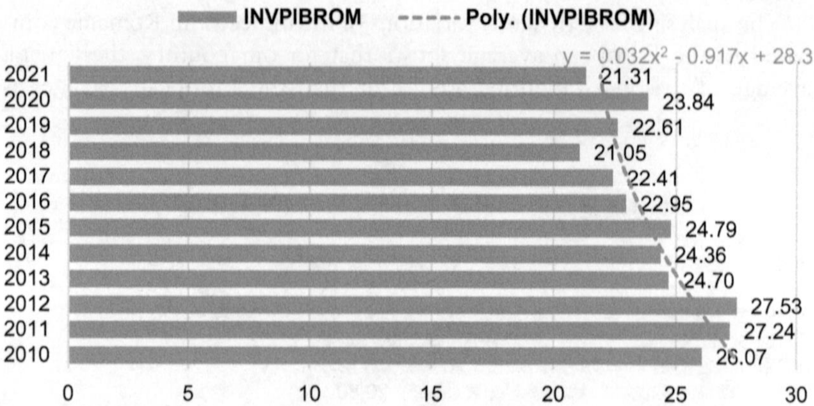


**Fig. 8.11** Dynamics of the indicator "share of investment in GDP by institutional sectors" at national level in Romania in the period 2010–2021. Source: Author based on Eurostat data

shown in Fig. 8.12. The share of investment in GDP is an indicator of economic growth, which increases the productive capacity of an economy.

The analysis of the employment rate in the European Union indicator (EU27 employment rate) reveals that in the period 2010–2021 it had a dynamic of 9.43%, respectively, from a minimum of 66.8% in 2013 to 73.1% in 2021 (Fig. 8.13).

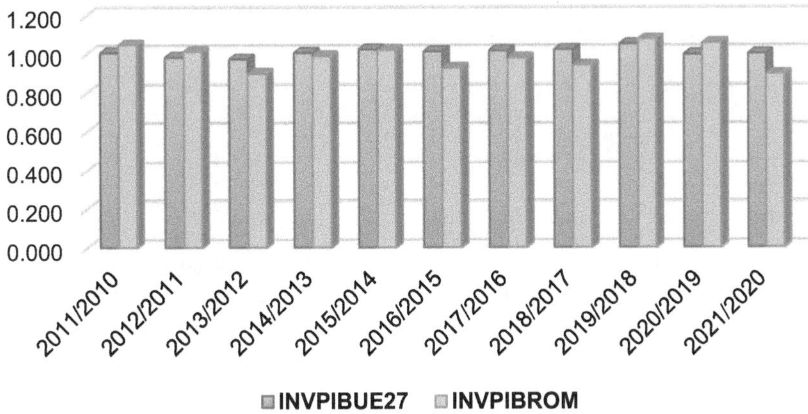


**Fig. 8.12** Analysis of the dynamic variations of the indicator "investment share in GDP by institutional sectors" in Romania compared to the European average. Source: Author based on Eurostat data

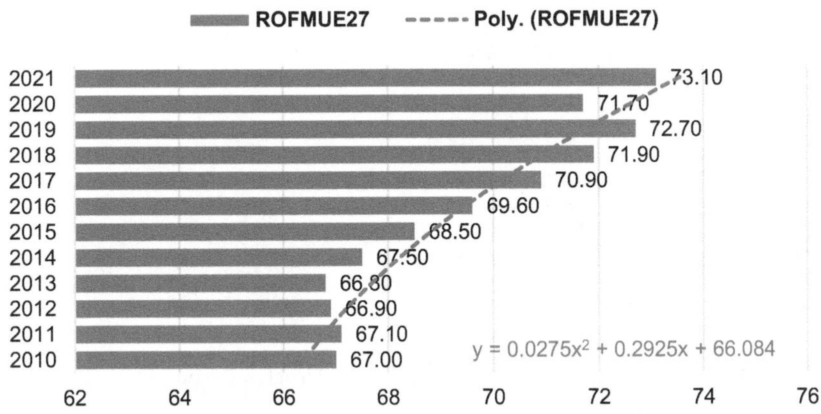


**Fig. 8.13** Employment rate dynamics at European level, 2010–2021. Source: Author based on Eurostat data

On trend the indicator showed an overall upward trend of 6.09%; the calculated overall average of the indicator being 69.47%, with a standard error estimated by descriptive statistics of 0.71% (as shown in Table 8.4).

The analysis of the employment rate in Romania (ROFMROM) indicator shows that in the period 2010–2021 it had a dynamic of 19.82%,

**Table 8.4** Comparative descriptive statistics of the employment rate indicator at European and national level over the period 2010–2021

| *Employment rate* | *European Union—27 countries* | *Romania* |
|---|---|---|
| Minim | 66.80 | 56.00 |
| Maxim | 73.10 | 67.10 |
| Average | 69.4750 | 60.6250 |
| Standard error of the mean | 0.71,100 | 1.15,300 |
| Standard deviation | 2.46500 | 3.99500 |
| Variance | 6.075 | 15.958 |
| Asymmetry | 0.262 | 0.329 |
| Asymmetry error | 0.637 | 0.637 |
| Flattening | −1.793 | −1.561 |
| Standard error of flattening | 1.232 | 1.232 |

Source: Author based on Eurostat data

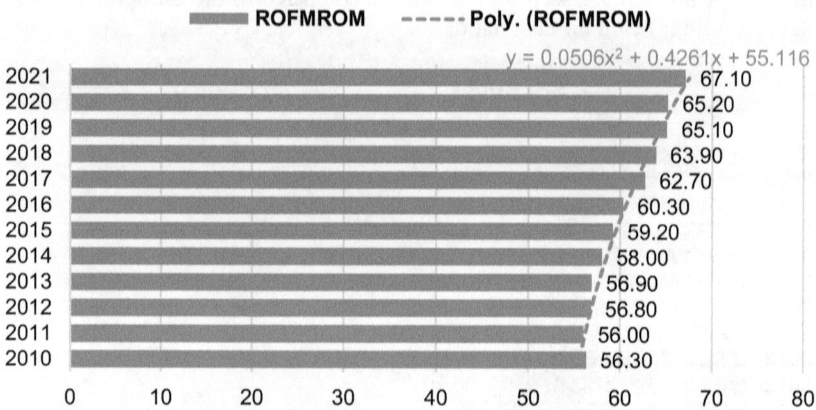


**Fig. 8.14** Employment rate dynamics at national level in the period 2010–2021. Source: Author based on Eurostat data

respectively, from the minimum value of 56% in 2011 to 67.1% in 2021, as shown in Fig. 8.14.

On trend, the indicator showed an overall upward trend of 10.8%; the calculated overall average of the indicator being 60.625%, with a standard error estimated by descriptive statistics of 1.153% (as shown in Table 8.4).

The analysis of the dynamic variations of the indicator in Romania compared to the European average shows that for our country, the overall

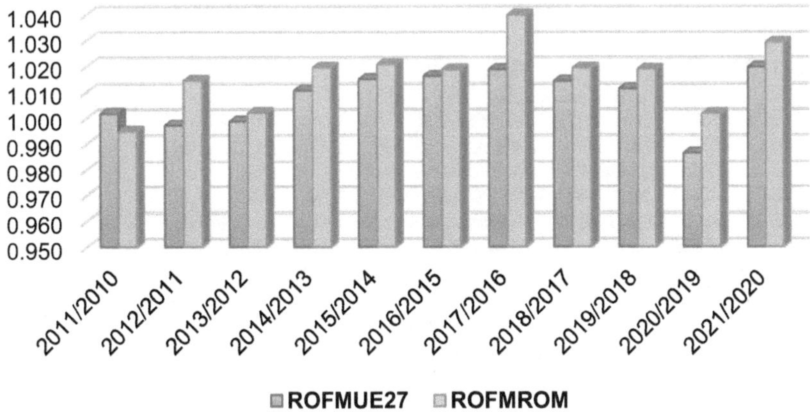


**Fig. 8.15** Analysis of the dynamic variations of the employment rate indicator in Romania compared to the European average. Source: Author based on Eurostat data

average of seasonal variations was higher than the European average, as shown in Fig. 8.15.

The employment rate in the EU reached 72.7% in 2019, but decreased slightly in 2020 due to the socio-economic impact of the pandemic and started to increase slightly in 2021 (Eurostat, 2023). Despite uncertain and challenging circumstances due to the war in Ukraine, employment reached a high level of 74.6% in 2022. The economic slowdown is expected to affect employment growth in 2023 and 2024 (Eurostat, 2023). However, if growth in 2017 continues, the EU is well positioned to reach an employment rate of 78% by 2030.

The analysis of the indicator "long-term unemployment rate" at European Union level (EU15 long-term unemployment rate27) shows that in the period 2010–2021 it had a dynamic of 116%. The minimum threshold was 2.5% in 2020 and the maximum threshold was 5.4% in 2013 and 2014 (Fig. 8.16).

On trend, the indicator showed an overall downward trend of 1.2%; the calculated overall average of the indicator being 4%, with a standard error estimated by descriptive statistics of 0.302% (as shown in Table 8.5).

The analysis of the indicator "long-term unemployment rate" in Romania (RSOMROM) shows that in the analysed period 2010–2021 it had a dynamic of 116.67%. The minimum value was recorded in 2020, i.e.

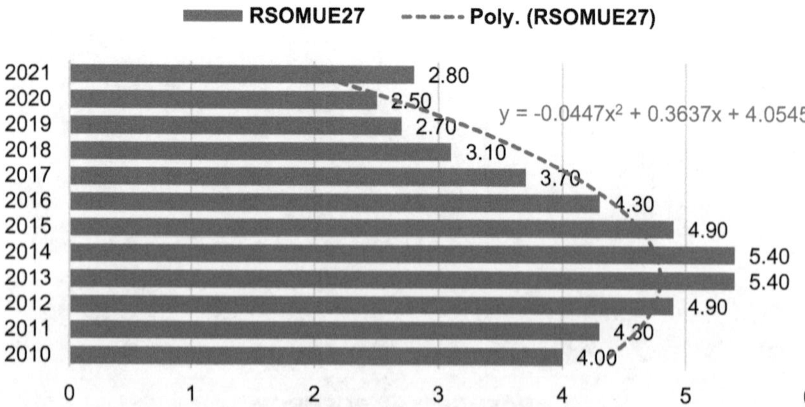


**Fig. 8.16** Long-term unemployment rate dynamics at European level, 2010–2021. Source: Author based on Eurostat data

**Table 8.5** Comparative descriptive statistics of the indicator "long-term unemployment rate" at European and national level over the period 2010–2021

| *Long-term unemployment rate* | *European Union—27 countries* | *Romania* |
|---|---|---|
| Minim | 2.50 | 1.80 |
| Maxim | 5.40 | 3.90 |
| Average | 4.0000 | 2.9170 |
| Standard error of the mean | 0.30,200 | 0.22,500 |
| Standard deviation | 1.04400 | 0.78000 |
| Variance | 1.091 | 0.609 |
| Asymmetry | −0.101 | −0.262 |
| Asymmetry error | 0.637 | 0.637 |
| Flattening | −1.429 | −1.840 |
| Standard error of flattening | 1.232 | 1.232 |

Source: Author based on Eurostat data

from a minimum value of 1.8% and the maximum value in 2014 at 3.9%, as shown in Fig. 8.17.

On trend, the indicator experienced an overall downward trend of 1%; the calculated overall average of the indicator being 2.917%, with a standard error estimated by descriptive statistics of 0.225% (see Table 4.7).

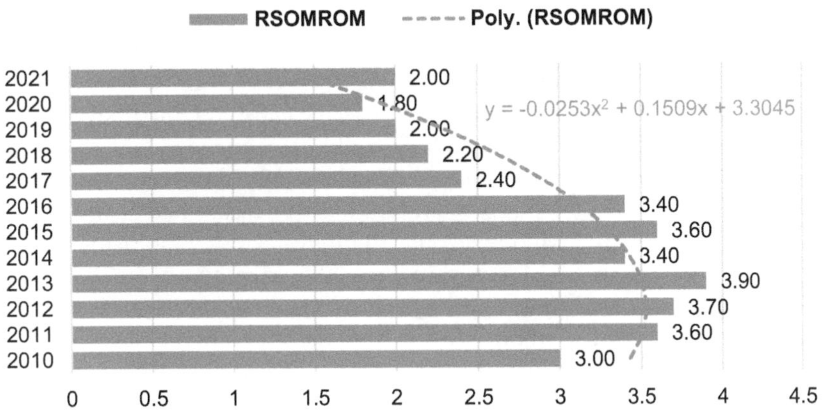


**Fig. 8.17** Long-term unemployment rate dynamics at national level in the period 2010–2021. Source: Author based on Eurostat data

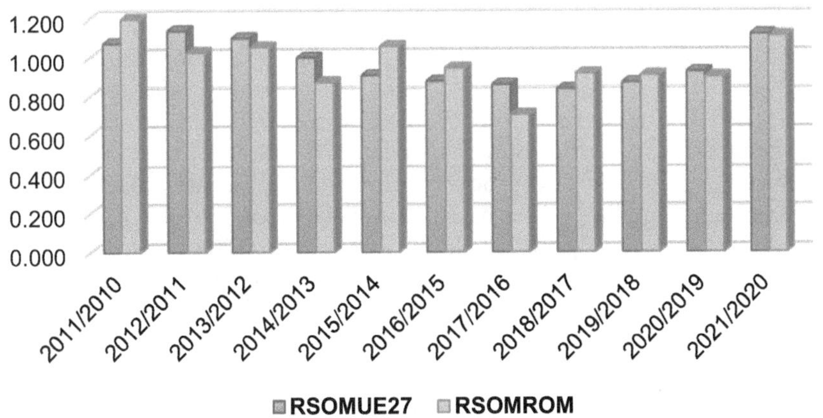


**Fig. 8.18** Analysis of dynamic changes in the long-term unemployment rate in Romania compared to the European average. Source: Author based on Eurostat data

The analysis of the dynamic variations of the indicator in Romania compared to the European average shows that for our country, the general average of seasonal variations was lower than the European average, as shown in Fig. 8.18.

Long-term unemployment is expected to increase because of the COVID-19 pandemic; this can be seen in the years 2020 and 2021. This could lead to reduced income prospects, depreciation of human capital, social cohesion, increased poverty and social exclusion (Eurostat, 2023). In addition, declining living standards could damage individual skills and health, hampering future gains (Eurostat, 2023). Between 2015 and 2020, the long-term unemployment rate was decreasing before this trend was halted due to the pandemic. The EU long-term unemployment rate increased by 3% in 2020 compared to 2021 due to the COVID-19 pandemic.

Economic growth is important for sustainable economic development and a better society by generating decent jobs, providing a decent income, security, social protection, better personal development, social inclusion and equal opportunities.

## Conclusions

The conclusions highlighted by the dynamic analysis of the main indicators of Sustainable Development Goal 8 for the period 2010–2021 reveal a dual picture of Romania's economic performance compared to the European Union average. On the one hand, there is a general trend towards alignment with European objectives on sustainable economic growth, employment and productive investment, against a backdrop of strengthened public policies and the availability of European structural funds. On the other hand, significant gaps remain in terms of the risk of poverty in work, the long-term unemployment rate and the employment rate, indicating unresolved structural vulnerabilities in the labour market and social protection systems.

More specifically, the analysis shows that Romania has made consistent progress in terms of real GDP growth per capita and the share of investment in GDP, signalling a sustained economic recovery process despite external shocks. However, higher risks of in-work poverty and volatile employment indicators underscore that the benefits of economic growth have not been distributed evenly across the working population. Similarly, although the long-term unemployment rate has followed a downward trend, persistent regional and social differences raise questions about the effectiveness of active employment measures.

Compared to the European average, Romania continues to face major challenges in fully achieving SDG8, particularly in terms of ensuring decent work and reducing social inequalities. This situation highlights the need for integrated policies that combine investment in sectors that generate sustainable jobs with reforms in education, vocational training and social cohesion.

In conclusion, achieving Sustainable Development Goal 8 in Romania requires not only maintaining the pace of economic growth, but also a strategic approach that ensures social inclusion, quality jobs and long-term sustainability. In this regard, continuing to allocate European resources, closely monitoring key indicators and pro-actively adapting public policies to social and economic realities remain essential conditions for convergence with European standards and for strengthening a fair and resilient economy.

## References

Acheampong, A. O., Adebayo, T. S., Dzator, J., & Koomson, I. (2023). Income inequality and economic growth in BRICS: Insights from non-parametric techniques. *The Journal of Economic Inequality.* https://doi.org/10.1007/s10888-023-09567-9

Ayala, L., Martín-Román, J., & Navarro, C. (2023). Unemployment shocks and material deprivation in the European Union: A synthetic control approach. *Economic Systems, 47*(1), 101053. https://doi.org/10.1016/j.ecosys.2022.101053

Benedetti, I., & Crescenzi, F. (2023). The role of income poverty and inequality indicators at regional level: An evaluation for Italy and Germany. *Socio-Economic Planning Sciences, 87*, 101540. https://doi.org/10.1016/j.seps.2023.101540

Caporale, G. M., Gil-Alana, L. A., & Trejo, P. V. (2022). Unemployment persistence in Europe: Evidence from the 27 EU countries. *Heliyon, 8*(2), e08898. https://doi.org/10.1016/j.heliyon.2022.e08898

Destefanis, S., & Rehman, N. U. (2023). Investment, innovation activities and employment across European regions. *Structural Change and Economic Dynamics, 65*, 474–490. https://doi.org/10.1016/j.strueco.2023.03.013

European Commission. (2019a). *A sustainable Europe by 2030.* Europa.Eu. https://commission.europa.eu/publications/sustainable-europe-2030_en

European Commission. (2019b). *The European green deal.* Europa.Eu. https://commission.europa.eu/strategy-and-policy/priorities-2019-2024/european-green-deal_en?prefLang=ro

European Commission. (2020). *EUROPE 2020 a European strategy for smart, sustainable and inclusive growth.* Europa.Eu. https://ec.europa.eu/eu2020/pdf/COMPLETENBARROSO007-Europe 2020-ENversion.pdf

Eurostat. (2021). *Sustainable development goals SDG8*. Europa.Eu. https://ec.europa.eu/eurostat/web/sdi/database/decent-work-and-economic-growth

Eurostat. (2023). *SDG 8 - decent work and economic growth*. Europa.Eu. https://ec.europa.eu/eurostat/statistics-explained/index.php?title=SDG_8_-_Decent_work_and_economic_growth#Decent_work_and_economic_growth_in_the_EU:_overview_and_key_trends

Ferraro, S., Männasoo, K., & Tasane, H. (2023). How the EU cohesion policy targeted at R&D and innovation impacts the productivity, employment and exports of SMEs in Estonia. *Evaluation and Program Planning, 97*, 102221. https://doi.org/10.1016/j.evalprogplan.2022.102221

Fortea, C., Zlati, M. L., & Lazarescu, I. (2023). Analysis of the sustainable development of the eastern European countries from the perspective of the transition to the green economy. *Ovidius University Annals, Economic Sciences Series, XXIII*(1), 914–922. https://stec.univ-ovidius.ro/html/anale/RO/2023-i1/Section 5/8.pdf

Frey, D. F. (2017). Economic growth, full employment and decent work: The means and ends in SDG 8. *The International Journal of Human Rights, 21*(8), 1164–1184. https://doi.org/10.1080/13642987.2017.1348709

Gioachin, F., Marx, I., & Scherer, S. (2023). Stratification of poverty risk: The importance of social class in four European countries. *Social Science Research, 110*, 102814. https://doi.org/10.1016/j.ssresearch.2022.102814

Government of Romania. (2018). *National Strategy for sustainable development of Romania 2030*. Paideia. https://www.edu.ro/sites/default/files/Strategia-nationala-pentru-dezvoltarea-durabila-a-României-2030.pdf

Government of Romania. (2022). *National Action Plan for the implementation of the National Strategy for sustainable development 2030*. Department for Sustainable Development. https://dezvoltaredurabila.gov.ro/planul-national-de-actiune-final

Ionescu, R. V., Fortea, C., Zlati, M. L., & Antohi, V. M. (2023). Studying differing impacts of various monetary aggregates on the real economy. *International Journal of Financial Studies, 11*(issue 4). https://doi.org/10.3390/ijfs11040140

Irandoust, M. (2023). Active labor market as an instrument to reduce unemployment. *Journal of Government and Economics, 9*, 100065. https://doi.org/10.1016/j.jge.2023.100065

OECD. (2020). *Romania: OECD scan of institutional mechanisms to deliver on the SDGs*. Oecd.Org. https://dezvoltaredurabila.gov.ro/web/wp-content/uploads/2020/09/Romania-Institutional-Scan_final.pdf

Papadakis, N., Amanaki, E., Drakaki, M., & Saridaki, S. (2020). Employment/unemployment, education and poverty in the Greek Youth, within the EU context. *International Journal of Educational Research, 99*, 101503. https://doi.org/10.1016/j.ijer.2019.101503

Park, J., Ryu, D., & Lee, K. (2019). What determines the economic size of a nation in the world: Determinants of a nation's share in world GDP vs. per capita GDP. *Structural Change and Economic Dynamics, 51*, 203–214. https://doi.org/10.1016/j.strueco.2019.09.001

Polizzi, A., Struffolino, E., & Van Winkle, Z. (2022). Family demographic processes and in-work poverty: A systematic review. *Advances in Life Course Research, 52*, 100462. https://doi.org/10.1016/j.alcr.2022.100462

Rahmani, H., & Groot, W. (2023). Risk factors of being a youth not in education, employment or training (NEET): A scoping review. *International Journal of Educational Research, 120*, 102198. https://doi.org/10.1016/j.ijer.2023.102198

Singh, A. (2023). Economic growth and labor investment efficiency. *International Review of Finance, n/a*(n/a). https://doi.org/10.1111/irfi.12415

United Nations. (2020). *Transforming our world: The 2030 agenda for sustainable development.* Sustainabledevelopment.Un.Org. https://sdgs.un.org/2030agenda

Zhou, C., Zheng, H., & Wan, S. (2023). Industrial structure, employment structure and economic growth—Evidence from China. *Sustainability, 15*(4). https://doi.org/10.3390/su15042890

CHAPTER 9

# Modelling European Economic Sustainability Based on Economic Indicators Related to Sustainable Development Goal 8

## Introduction

In the current context, characterized by the acceleration of the transition to a digital and green economy, the cumulative impact of economic, health and geopolitical crises and the need to strengthen social cohesion, analysing European economic sustainability through the lens of Sustainable Development Goal 8 (SDG8) is a methodological and strategic priority. This goal integrates essential dimensions of development—sustainable economic growth, quality employment, and the promotion of innovation—providing an analytical framework through which to assess the performance of EU Member States in achieving a balance between competitiveness, social equity and environmental protection.

The indicators associated with SDG8, such as real GDP per capita, employment rate, tax revenue from labour, NEET rate, Internet penetration rate or value added in the main economic sectors, are quantifiable benchmarks that allow for the investigation of causal relationships and interdependencies between the components of the real economy and the structural transformations generated by digitalization and globalization. Within this framework, this chapter develops an empirical approach based on advanced econometric methods—including the BFS regression selection procedure and multivariate linear modelling—to construct robust and statistically validated explanatory models capable of capturing not


C. Fortea, *Sustainable Economic Development and the European Green Deal*, https://doi.org/10.1007/978-3-032-10326-0_9

only the direct effects of economic factors but also the complex interactions between the social and technological dimensions of sustainability.

The analysis covers the period 2010–2021, marked by the implementation of the Europe 2020 Strategy, the intensification of green and digital transition policies and the major disruptions caused by the COVID-19 pandemic. This timeline allows us to identify structural patterns, highlight differences between Member States in terms of sustainable economic performance and identify persistent vulnerabilities, such as dependence on low-productivity sectors, persistent regional disparities, youth exclusion from the labour market and digital divides.

By linking the modelling results to the European Union's strategic directions—from the Digital Agenda and the European Green Deal to initiatives on the labour market and social inclusion—the chapter aims to provide a solid scientific basis for the formulation of integrated public policies geared towards increasing the economic resilience and structural adaptability of European economies. The research thus makes a significant contribution to understanding the mechanisms through which investments in human capital, digitalization and innovation, combined with coherent fiscal and social policies, can transform economic sustainability into a central vector of long-term development in the European Union.

## Literature Review

In economic and political literature, the concept of sustainability has become a central benchmark for understanding the dynamics of the European Union's development and for formulating public policies that ensure a balance between growth, social inclusion and environmental protection. In a global context marked by accelerated digitalization, recurring economic and health crises and pressures generated by the green transition, the analysis of economic sustainability takes on new theoretical and empirical dimensions. The objective of this section is to examine the most relevant contributions in the literature on modelling European economic sustainability through indicators associated with Sustainable Development Goal 8 (SDG8—Sustainable economic growth and decent work).

The literature review follows three main directions: on the one hand, clarifying the theoretical and conceptual foundations that explain the link between economic development and sustainability; on the other hand, the applied analysis of economic, social and technological indicators integrated into economic performance assessment models; and, finally, highlighting recent empirical contributions that show how digitization, ecological transition and public policies influence long-term outcomes. This approach provides a solid foundation for interpreting the econometric models presented in the chapter and for outlining directions for future research.

### *Theoretical Fundamentals of Economic Sustainability*

Political economy and development studies have highlighted, since the last decades of the twentieth century, that economic sustainability goes beyond the strict framework of maximizing gross domestic product and requires the integration of social and environmental dimensions into the analysis of national performance. Classical theories of economic growth, from the Harrod-Domar model to Solow's (Le-Van & Tran-Nam, 2023), have emphasized capital accumulation and total factor productivity, but have not taken sufficient account of negative externalities or intergenerational equity. In contrast, recent approaches inspired by the Brundtland Report (United Nations, 1987) and the United Nations' Agenda 2030 (European Commission, 2022b) highlight the idea of development that meets the needs of the present without compromising the ability of future generations to meet their own needs.

Along these lines, the current literature (Cattaneo et al., 2025; Crisp et al., 2023; Jansen et al., 2024) proposes models of "doughnut economics" and "beyond GDP", which include indicators of quality of life, social cohesion, resource use and institutional resilience. In the European context, the concept of a "social market economy", enshrined in the Treaty of Lisbon (European Union, 2008), provides a conceptual framework in which competitiveness is linked to social solidarity and environmental sustainability. This paradigm is also reflected in European economic policy, which seeks to integrate macroeconomic stability with social and climate objectives.

An essential element in the theoretical foundations is the distinction between "hard" and "soft" sustainability. The former considers natural capital to be irreplaceable and imposes strict limits on resource use, while the latter assumes that technological progress and investment in human capital can compensate for the degradation of natural resources. In the European debate, most studies (Diodato et al., 2023; Nieddu et al., 2022; Palmié et al., 2025) converge towards a hybrid model, in which digitalization and innovation can support the green transition, but only to the extent that they are accompanied by redistributive policies and strong regulation of externalities.

Thus, theoretical foundations reveal that economic sustainability is not simply a matter of reconciling growth and environmental protection objectives, but rather requires a complex architecture of institutions, market mechanisms and public policies (Annesi et al., 2024; Khan et al., 2025; Kirchherr et al., 2023). Recent literature has reinforced the idea that sustainable performance assessment must be multidimensional and include economic, social and technological indicators capable of reflecting the structural interdependencies of the European economy.

### *SDG 8 and Its Relevance for the European Union*

Sustainable Development Goal 8 (SDG8) is particularly significant within the European Union, where the aim is to combine economic growth with decent work, innovation and social inclusion. Unlike other goals that focus exclusively on environmental or social dimensions, SDG8 is integrative in nature, sitting at the intersection of competitiveness and equity. In the literature, this goal is often analysed in relation to European economic governance models and labour market policies.

Recent research (Eurostat, 2025a; Lafortune & Fuller, 2025; Lewandowska et al., 2024) highlights that Member States' performance in relation to SDG8 is extremely heterogeneous: Northern and Western European economies stand out with high employment and productivity rates, while Central and Eastern European countries face challenges related to migration, regional disparities and structural vulnerabilities. This divergence highlights the importance of adapting policies to national specificities while maintaining the common objectives set at the European level.

A central aspect of the literature concerns the relationship between GDP growth and the quality of employment. Specialized studies (Atay et al., 2025; Kolade & Owoseni, 2022; Soliman & Beram, 2025) show that in many emerging European economies there is a disconnect between GDP growth and the creation of decent jobs, a phenomenon known as "jobless growth". At the same time, the Eurofound report (Eurofound, 2022) draws attention to the precariousness of jobs and the increasing incidence of temporary contracts, which affect social cohesion and long-term sustainability.

The literature also explores the links between SDG8 and other goals of the 2030 Agenda. For example, the integration of SDG8 with SDG9 (innovation and infrastructure) and SDG13 (climate action) is considered crucial for the green and digital transition (Azmat et al., 2023; Raman et al., 2025; Sharifi et al., 2024). In this regard, European policies such as the European Green Deal and the Digital Decade are seen as instruments for achieving synergies between economic growth, sustainability and inclusion.

In conclusion, the literature establishes SDG8 as an essential objective for shaping economic sustainability in the European Union, providing a framework through which performance indicators can be interpreted not only from the perspective of economic efficiency but also from that of social equity and structural resilience.

### *Economic, Social and Technological Indicators Used in Modelling*

The literature emphasizes that the choice of indicators is an essential aspect in the construction of economic sustainability models. In the context of SDG8, classic economic indicators, such as GDP per capita or employment rate, are considered insufficient to capture the complexity of structural transformations in the European economy. Thus, recent research proposes the integration of additional social and technological variables that reflect the interdependencies between digitalization, social inclusion and economic performance (Azimi et al., 2025; Casau et al., 2024; Fan & Jackson, 2025).

Economic indicators remain fundamental, however, particularly through their ability to quantify the level of competitiveness and productivity. Per capita GDP is frequently used as a dependent variable in econometric models, while value added by sector (agriculture, industry, services) provides a detailed picture of the economic structure. At the same time, labour tax revenues and the in-work poverty rate are introduced to capture the link between taxation, employment quality and sustainability.

On the social front, indicators such as the NEET rate (young people who are not in employment, education or training), the risk of in-work poverty and the degree of labour market inclusion reflect structural vulnerabilities that can slow progress towards sustainability (Başol et al., 2023; International Labour Organization, 2024; Schmid et al., 2023). Recent literature highlights that these social dimensions have a direct influence on an economy's ability to maintain inclusive growth, with an impact on social cohesion and political stability (Ciucu et al., 2025; Eurofound, 2025; OECD, 2025).

With regards to the technological dimension, indicators on Internet access, high-speed network coverage, the share of ICT specialists and the level of Internet use by the population are increasingly being integrated into econometric models. Recent studies (Baffour Gyau et al., 2025; Capello et al., n.d.; Ho et al., 2025) show that digitization is a catalyst for productivity and innovation, but also a factor in reducing regional inequalities by increasing access to education and services.

In summary, the literature confirms the need to adopt a multidimensional framework of indicators, in which economic, social and technological dimensions are analysed simultaneously, in order to capture the complex mechanisms that define European economic sustainability.

### *The Impact of Digitalization and the Green Transition on Economic Performance*

An emerging consensus in recent literature is that digitalization and the green transition are the two main pillars of the structural transformation of the European economy. Digitalization is seen not only as a driver of productivity but also as an essential tool for achieving environmental goals and strengthening institutional resilience. At the same time, the green transition, reflected in the objectives of the European Green Deal (European Commission, 2023a), is redefining the criteria for competitiveness, with an emphasis on decarbonization, the circular economy and energy efficiency.

Empirical studies (de Clercq et al., 2023; Suhrab et al., 2024; Wang et al., 2025) show that investments in digital infrastructure and the expansion of broadband networks contribute significantly to GDP growth and the reduction of regional disparities. Furthermore, the share of ICT specialists and the degree of Internet usage are positively correlated with innovation and labour market performance (Hernández de Rojas et al., 2024; Minniti et al., 2025). However, the literature draws attention to the risk that digitization may accentuate social polarization through digital skill gaps and the exclusion of vulnerable groups (Grigorescu et al., 2025; Löfving et al., 2022).

The green transition is also analysed as a source of opportunities and challenges. On the one hand, the development of renewable energies, energy efficiency and eco-technological innovations generates new sectors of activity and jobs, strengthening economic resilience (Bajja et al., 2025; Han et al., 2025; Qamruzzaman & Karim, 2024). On the other hand, the literature points to high initial costs and the risk of deindustrialization for countries with high dependence on polluting industries (Akif Destek et al., 2024; European Environment Agency, 2024).

An interesting direction in recent research concerns the interaction between digitization and the green transition. Digital technologies such as artificial intelligence, blockchain and the Internet of Things are identified as key tools for monitoring emissions, optimizing resource consumption and developing circular economy models (Barteková & Börkey, 2022; Neligan et al., 2023; Schöggl et al., 2023). Thus, the literature paints a picture of a "double transition" that redefines European economic sustainability.

In conclusion, digitalization and the green transition are seen as factors of profound structural transformation, with effects on both competitiveness and social cohesion, which gives them a central role in economic sustainability models.

### *Vulnerability Factors: Unemployment, Poverty and NEET*

The literature emphasizes that economic sustainability cannot be analysed solely in terms of GDP growth or technological performance, but must also integrate the dimension of social vulnerabilities. In the European Union, the main challenges identified are structural unemployment, the risk of poverty in work and the high proportion of young people who are NEET.

With regard to unemployment, numerous studies (European Commission, 2024; International Labour Organization, 2025; Moridian et al., 2024) show that, although the overall employment rate has increased in many Member States, major disparities remain between regions and sectors. The phenomenon of "job polarization", whereby well-paid and low-paid jobs are growing simultaneously, while middle-level occupations are declining, is putting pressure on social cohesion and reducing labour market stability.

The risk of in-work poverty is another key vulnerability. Various reports and studies (European Commission, 2023b; Eurostat, 2024i, 2024f; Papadakis et al., 2022) show that a significant part of the employed population in the EU is below the poverty threshold due to temporary contracts, informal work and structural imbalances between productivity and wages. Specialized studies (Anjarwi, 2025; Hemerijck et al., 2023; Noubissi Domguia, 2023) highlight that in-work poverty not only diminishes quality of life but also affects fiscal sustainability by reducing tax revenues and increasing social spending.

The NEET category is considered by many authors (Heglum & Nilsen, 2025; Kang & Youn, 2024; Rahmani & Groot, 2023) to be a critical indicator of social exclusion and the risk of perpetuating intergenerational inequalities. Particularly in southern and eastern European countries, the high share of NEETs reflects a lack of education and training opportunities, external migration and the poor adaptability of education systems to labour market requirements (Caroleo et al., 2021; Eurostat, 2025b; Rocca et al., 2021). This phenomenon has direct implications for economic sustainability, as it affects the human capital base and reduces long-term competitiveness.

The literature emphasizes that social vulnerabilities are strongly correlated with the technological dimension and public policies (Khromova et al., 2025; Serrano-Bosquet et al., 2023; Stanojević, 2025). For example, access to high-speed Internet and digital training programs can contribute to the integration of NEETs and reduce structural unemployment (Tleppayev & Zeinolla, 2025; Xiong & Yu, 2024). At the same time, fiscal and redistributive policies play a decisive role in mitigating the risk of in-work poverty and stimulating inclusion (Ernst et al., 2025; Muñoz-Higueras et al., 2024).

Thus, recent literature emphasizes that economic sustainability is weakened by the existence of vulnerable social segments, and solutions involve a combination of active labour market policies, investment in education and digital support measures.

### *Econometric Models and Recent Empirical Contributions*

A distinctive feature of contemporary literature is the emphasis on developing complex econometric models that capture the interdependencies between economic, social and technological indicators. Panel data analyses, VAR models, SDM (spatial Durbin model) and variable selection techniques such as BFS (Backward Feature Selection) are frequently used to explain and predict economic sustainability in the European Union.

Empirical studies (Kalai et al., 2024; Magoutas et al., 2024; OECD, 2024a) have shown that the integration of digital variables, such as Internet usage and the proportion of ICT specialists, significantly increases the explanatory power of economic growth models. Furthermore, research applied to the post-COVID-19 crisis period (Bilal et al., 2024; Bürgel et al., 2023; Holl et al., 2024) shows that digitalization played a crucial role in economic resilience, facilitating the continuity of economic activities and adaptation to new working conditions.

Spatial models (SDM, SAR, SEM) have been used to highlight the existence of regional diffusion effects. For example, recent research (Liu & Lian, 2025; Tao et al., 2025; Zhang et al., 2025) shows that investments in digital infrastructure in one region generate positive externalities in neighbouring regions, strengthening economic convergence. These models allow for a more nuanced understanding of intra- and inter-state disparities, making them extremely useful for European cohesion policies.

A recent research direction aims to apply panel quantile regression to capture the differentiated impact of indicators on the distribution of economic performance (Ganda & Ruza, 2025; Georgescu et al., 2024; Labidi, 2025). This demonstrates that digitalization and the green transition have stronger effects on economies with average and weak performance, contributing to the reduction of gaps.

Recent empirical contributions demonstrate that multidimensional econometric models provide an in-depth understanding of the mechanisms of European economic sustainability and provide solid support for evidence-based public policy formulation.

Literature review reveals that economic sustainability in the European Union is the result of a complex combination of economic, social and technological factors, integrated into a multidimensional framework defined by SDG8. Theoretical foundations highlight the need to move beyond traditional growth paradigms and adopt models that include dimensions of equity and resilience. In this regard, the literature confirms the central role of SDG8 as an integrating objective, capable of linking competitiveness with social inclusion and the green transition.

The indicators used in the modelling show that economic performance should be assessed not only by GDP or employment rates but also by factors such as poverty risk, NEET rates or the degree of digitalization, which capture the complexity of structural transformations. Digitalization and the green transition are recognized as drivers of sustainability, but the literature warns of the risk that they may generate new forms of social and regional polarization. At the same time, vulnerabilities related to unemployment, poverty and youth exclusion highlight the need for proactive policies to strengthen human capital and reduce inequalities.

Recent empirical contributions demonstrate that advanced econometric models are indispensable tools for understanding the mechanisms of sustainability and informing public policy decisions. The results confirm that the interdependencies between the economy, society and technology must be analysed simultaneously within an integrated framework.

Overall, the literature provides a consensus that Europe's sustainable future depends on the interaction between digitalization, the green transition and inclusive social policies. This conclusion underpins the empirical analysis in the chapter and justifies the choice of indicators and methodology, highlighting the importance of an interdisciplinary approach and a long-term perspective in assessing economic sustainability.

## Methodology

Sustainable economic growth and decent work underpin the implementation of the Sustainable Development Goals and social progress in the European Union as well as worldwide. Sustainable Development Goal 8 (SDG8) provides an ambitious and comprehensive framework to address these challenges, emphasizing the need for an integrated approach that balances growth and social protection. In the European context, this goal takes on particular relevance given the region's commitment to the principles of the social market economy, which aims to combine economic efficiency with social justice and environmental protection.

Indicators specific to SDG8, such as Gross Domestic Product (GDP) per capita growth rate, employment rate, share of informal economy in GDP, innovation rate and other productivity indicators, provide valuable tools for measuring and assessing progress. Within the European Union, the use of these indicators for modelling economic sustainability allows the identification of region-specific trends, challenges and opportunities, facilitating the development of effective policies and strategies to achieve sustainable development goals. This study investigates the application of SDG8 indicators in modelling European economic sustainability, with a particular focus on analysing economic performance in the light of sustainability objectives. This analysis will include an assessment of the impact of European policy and initiatives at Member State level on the achievement of the SDG8 objectives, exploring the synergies and tensions between the different dimensions of sustainable development.

The BFS (Backward Feature Selection) method was applied to determine the European model of sustainable economic growth. The indicators presented in Table 9.1 were used to determine the economic sustainability models for the period 2010–2021.

**Table 9.1** Presentation of indicators

| *Symbol* | *Indicator name* | *Unit of measurement* | *Source* |
|---|---|---|---|
| SDG8VIMPM | Labour tax revenues | % GDP | OECD (2024b) |
| SDG8TNEET | Young people not in employment, education or training (NEET) | % | Eurostat (2024j) |
| SDG8ROCFM | Employment rate | % | Eurostat (2024a) |
| SDG8INTA | Level of internet access—Households | % | Eurostat (2024e) |
| SDG8UTINT | Internet usage by individuals | % | Eurostat (2024d) |
| SDG8ATIC | ICT specialists employed—Total | % | Eurostat (2024g) |
| SDG8AINT | High-speed internet coverage | % | Eurostat (2024b) |
| SDG8VAAG | Value added in agriculture | % | OECD (2024b) |
| SDG8VAIN | Value added in industry | % | OECD (2024b) |
| SDG8VASE | Value added in services | % | OECD (2024b) |
| SDG8PIBloc | GDP per capita | Euro per inhabitant | Eurostat (2024h) |
| SDG8RRSAR | Risk of in-work poverty | % | Eurostat (2024c) |

Source: Author

Data were collected from Eurostat and OECD and then modelled using the statistical program Python.

Previously the set of indicators presented above was subjected to the log normalization procedure using Logit linear regression analysis. In this way the normalization of the data was obtained by transforming them to a Gaussian normal distribution, reducing the effects of heteroscedasticity and reducing the influences of extreme values (increasing the robustness of the model).

Linear regression using the dependent variable Y or its logarithm which is modelled as a linear function of one or more independent variables. The equation can be formulated as follows:

$$\ln(Y) = \beta_1 \ln(X_1) + \beta_2 \ln(X_2) + \ldots + \beta_n \ln(X_n) + \varepsilon \quad (9.1)$$

where,

ln(Y)—the natural logarithm of the dependent variable, representing an indicator of Sustainable Development Goal 9;
$\beta_1$, $\beta_2$, $\beta_n$—are the coefficients reflecting the sensitivity of the logarithm of variable Y to a percentage change in each indicator X;i
$\ln(X_1)$, $\ln(X_2)$, $\ln(X_n)$—are the natural logarithms of the selected indicators;
ε—is the constant.

The application of the BFS method involves the gradual elimination of variables Xi that contribute least to the model, based on criteria such as p-value, adjusted coefficient of determination (adjusted R2) or variance inflation factor (VIF). This process continues until every remaining variable in the model is significant, and the elimination of any additional variable would lead to a significant deterioration in model performance. The BFS method was applied until a valid solution was obtained, i.e. until the variance inflation factors of the indicators fell within the 10-point significance threshold, excluding multicollinearity. This ensured the performance of the models by monitoring the correlation coefficient and the mean squared error. This improved the prediction and increased the stability of the 12 proposed models.

## Results and Discussions

The overall SDG8.1 model of European economic sustainability from the perspective of the SDG8GDPloc indicator with the selected dependent variable denoting gross domestic product per capita as the selected dependent variable. The independent variables are SDG8VAAG as value added in agriculture, SDG8VIMPM as income from taxes on labour, SDG8TNEET as the share of young people not in employment and not in education or training (NEET) in the total population, SDG8ROCFM as the employment rate, SDG8UTINT as the share of Internet usage by individuals, SDG8ATIC as the number of employed ICT specialists, SDG8AINT as high-speed Internet coverage. A linear regression model is constructed with the independent variables defined above for which regression coefficients have been calculated according to Equation (9.2).

$$\begin{aligned} \text{SDG8PIBloc} &= -0.45 * \text{SDG8VAAG} + 0.53 * \text{SDG8VIMPM} \\ &+ -0.27 * \text{SDG8TNEET} - 1.93 * \text{SDG8ROCFM} \\ &+ 0.86 * \text{SDG8UTINT} + 0.39 * \text{SDG8ATIC} \\ &+ -0.02 * \text{SDG8AINT} + 6.72 \end{aligned} \tag{9.2}$$

The level of statistical significance calculated using the coefficient of determination is 83.03%. According to the equation presented for the general model SDG8.1 it can be observed that the influence of independent variables on the dependent variable in the case of the variable SDG8VAAG representing the value added in agriculture, there is an inverse influence on the dependent variable, i.e. a 1% increase in the value added in agriculture causes a 0.45% decrease in GDP per capita. In the context of the analysed model, productivity growth in the agricultural sector has a negative effect on GDP per capita. This may indicate that a significant part of the population in the analysed economy is employed in agriculture, and productivity growth may reduce the number of jobs needed, thus having a negative impact on per capita income.

In the case of the variable SDG8VIMPM representing labour tax revenues, there is a positive influence on the dependent variable, i.e. a 1% increase in labour tax revenues leads to a 0.53% increase in GDP per capita; this reveals the importance of an efficient tax system to stimulate economic growth. This influence suggests that a strong tax base, supported by a well-paid labour force, contributes positively to the economy.

In the case of the variable SDG8TNEET representing the share of the total population of young people who are neither in employment nor in education or training (NEET), there is an inverse influence on the dependent variable, i.e. a 1% increase in the share of the total population of young people who are neither in employment nor in education or training (NEET) leads to a 0.27% decrease in GDP per capita. The negative impact of the increase in the share of young people neither in employment nor in education on GDP per capita shows the importance of integrating young people into the labour market or into education and training systems. This suggests that policies aimed at reducing NEET rates could have beneficial effects on overall economic performance.

Regarding the variable SDG8ROCFM representing the employment rate, there is an inverse influence on the dependent variable, i.e. a 1% increase in the employment rate leads to a 1.93% decrease in GDP per capita. In the context analysed, the increase in the employment rate is associated with less productive economic sectors, which contribute less to

GDP. In the case of the variable SDG8UTINT, the share of Internet usage by individuals, a positive influence on the dependent variable is found, i.e. a 1% increase in the share of Internet usage by individuals leads to a 0.86% increase in GDP per capita.

In the case of the variable SDG8ATIC representing the number of employed ICT specialists, a positive influence on the dependent variable is found, i.e. a 1% increase in the number of employed ICT specialists leads to a 0.39% increase in GDP per capita. These results underline the importance of ICT in stimulating economic growth. The increase in Internet usage and in the number of ICT professionals indicates a more digitized and innovative economy, which contributes positively to GDP per capita. In the case of the variable SDG8AINT representing high-speed Internet coverage, there is an inverse influence on the dependent variable, i.e. a 1% increase in high-speed Internet coverage leads to a 0.02% decrease in GDP per capita. The inverse relationship between high-speed Internet coverage and GDP per capita may suggest that, in the initial stages of high-speed Internet infrastructure deployment, the associated costs may outweigh the immediate benefits. In the long term, however, this investment is expected to generate economic growth.

Figure 9.1 shows the ranking of the importance of the predictors related to the influence on the dependent variable SDG8PIBloc.

Figure 9.1 shows that the overall pattern is mainly characterized by the inverse influence of the change in the employment rate, followed by the

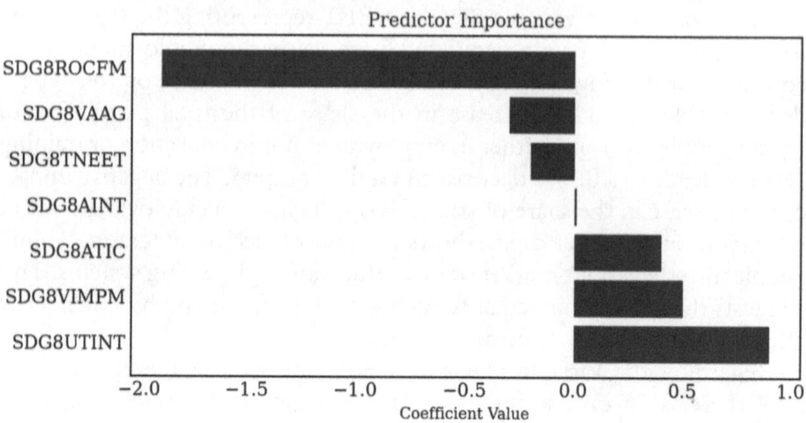


**Fig. 9.1** Importance of predictors related to the influence on the variable SDG8PIBloc. Source: Developed by the author using Python

direct influence of the share of individuals' Internet use and labour tax revenues. The weakest influence is the change in the high-speed Internet coverage indicator.

These aspects mean that the European economy is dependent on the quality and availability of labour, with social factors significantly influencing Europe's sustainable economic development. According to the authors (Bezrukova et al., 2022) digitization is the modern prerogative of a sustainable economy and the insignificant influence of high-speed Internet coverage is characterized by the high level of telecommunication and Internet service provision in Europe today. The European Union's Digital Single Market Strategy has paved the way for digital harmonization among EU Member States, with the aim of contributing to growth, boosting jobs, investment and innovation through three pillars: access, environment, economy and society (Gaftea et al., 2018).

Figure 9.2 is based on the vulnerability indicator rankings of the overall model SDG8.1 vulnerability indicators in 2021. According to the figure it is demonstrated that the countries with the weakest distribution of the dependent variable namely Bulgaria, Romania, Latvia, Hungary are in the top half of the ranking for the SDG8AINT indicator. Thus Bulgaria ranks 10th in Europe in terms of high-speed Internet coverage, Romania ranks 9th, Latvia ranks 5th and Hungary ranks 12th (European Commission, 2022a).

SDG8.2 model of European economic sustainability from the perspective of the SDG8AINT indicator, with high-speed Internet coverage as the selected dependent variable. The independent variables are: SDG8VAAG—the value added in agriculture, SDG8VIMPM—income from labour taxation, SDG8GDPloc—gross domestic product per capita, SDG8TNEET—share of the total population of young people neither in employment nor in education or training (NEET), SDG8ROCFM—employment rate, SDG8RRSAR—at-risk-of-work poverty rate, SDG8ATIC—number of employed ICT specialists. A linear regression model is constructed with the independent variables defined above for which regression coefficients were calculated according to Equation (9.3).

$$\begin{aligned}\text{SDG8AINT} = {} & 0.54 * \text{SDG8VAAG} - 0.78 * \text{SDG8VIMPM} \\ & -0.40 * \text{SDG8PIBloc} - 0.79 * \text{SDG8TNEET} \\ & +5.45 * \text{SDG8ROCFM} + 1.26 * \text{SDG8RRSAR} \\ & +1.29 * \text{SDG8ATIC} - 16.32\end{aligned} \tag{9.3}$$

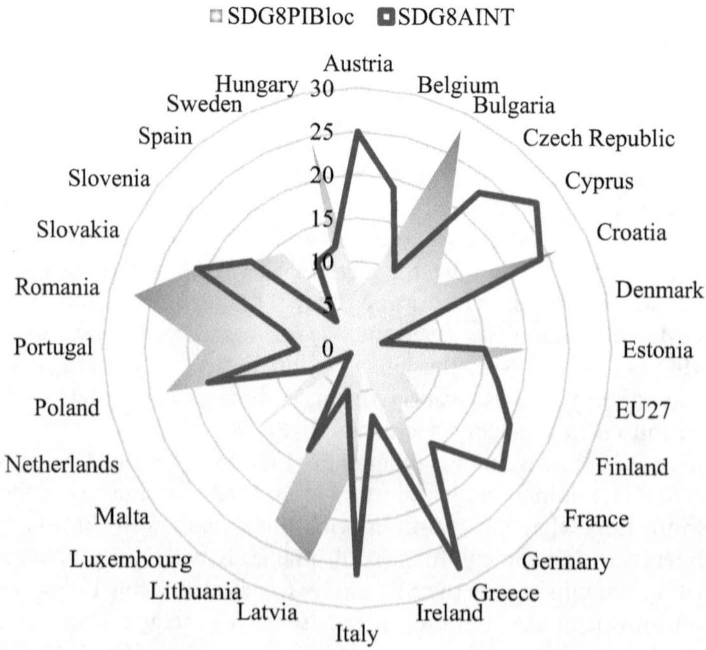


**Fig. 9.2** Vulnerabilities diagram of the variable SDG8PIBloc. Source: Author

The level of statistical significance calculated using the coefficient of determination is 36.38%. For Model SDG8.2 it is observed that the influence of the independent variables on the dependent variable is as follows: in the case of variable SDG8VAAG representing value added in agriculture, a positive influence on the dependent variable is observed, i.e. a 1% increase in value added in agriculture leads to a 0.54% increase in high-speed Internet coverage. The positive correlation relationship indicates that productivity improvements in the agricultural sector can stimulate investment in Internet infrastructure by increasing rural incomes and demand for digital services. In the case of the variable SDG8VIMPM representing labour tax revenues, there is an inverse influence on the dependent variable, i.e. a 1% increase in labour tax revenues leads to a 0.78% decrease in high-speed Internet coverage. In the case of the variable SDG8GDP per capita there is an inverse influence on the dependent variable, i.e. a 1% increase in GDP per capita leads to a 0.4% decrease in high-speed Internet coverage. The inverse influences of these variables on high-speed Internet coverage suggest that areas with higher tax incomes have already reached saturation in terms of Internet infrastructure. In the case of the variable SDG8TNEET, representing the share of the total population of young people neither in employment nor in education or training (NEET), there is an inverse influence on the dependent variable, i.e. a 1% increase in the share of the total population of young people neither in employment nor in education or training (NEET) leads to a 0.79% decrease in high-speed Internet coverage. The inverse relationship reveals the negative impact of social and economic exclusion on the development of digital infrastructure, indicating the need to address these issues to facilitate Internet access. In the case of the variable SDG8ROCFM representing the employment rate, there is a positive influence on the dependent variable, i.e. a 1% increase in the employment rate leads to a 5.45% increase in high-speed Internet coverage, indicating that a dynamic labour market and a higher employment rate are associated with a significant increase in high-speed Internet coverage, due to a higher demand for digital services and a higher investment capacity. In the case of the variable SDG8RRSAR representing the at-risk-of-work poverty rate, a positive influence on the dependent variable is found, i.e. a 1% increase in the at-risk-of-work poverty rate leads to a 1.26% increase in high-speed Internet coverage. The positive relationship indicates that, even in a low-income context, there is a consistent demand and need for Internet access, which may motivate investment in infrastructure improvements. In the case of the variable SDG8ATIC representing the number of ICT professionals employed, there is a positive influence on the dependent variable, i.e. a 1% increase in the number of ICT professionals employed leads to a 1.29% increase in high-speed Internet coverage. The positive relationship reveals the significant role of the ICT-skilled labour force in the development and maintenance of high-speed Internet infrastructure, indicating that a solid base of specialists can accelerate the expansion of Internet access.

Figure 9.3 shows the ranking of the importance of predictors related to the influence on the dependent variable SDG8AINT.

Figure 9.3 shows that the employment rate has the largest influence on the change in the dependent variable SDG8AINT—high-speed Internet coverage (European Commission, 2022a); tied for second place with significant influences are SDG8AINTand SDG8RSAR, showing that high-speed Internet coverage is sensitive to the demand for digital services (digital economy) and the existence of a sufficient number of ICT specialists employed in the digital economy. The weakest influences are the value

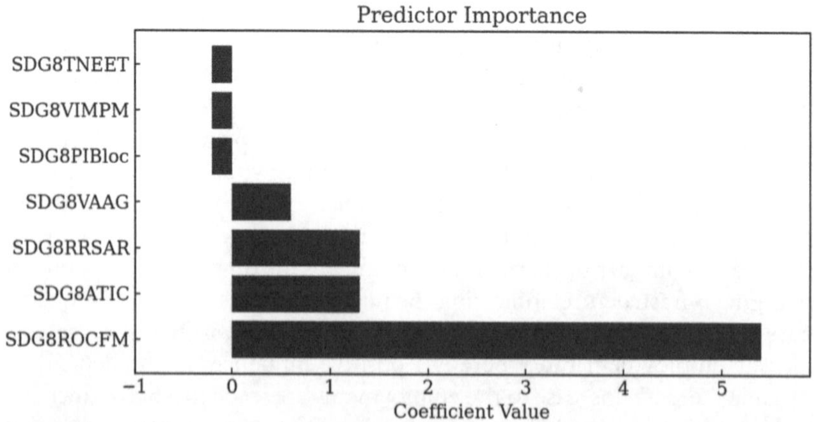


**Fig. 9.3** Importance of predictors related to influence on the variable SDG8AINT. Source: Developed by the author using Python

added in agriculture and the value of GDP per capita which shows that digitization is being implemented in a way that is not specific to economic development based on the overall impact of digitization (European Central Bank, 2023). It has been observed that labour tax revenues and the share of the total population of young people who are neither employed nor in education or training (NEET) show a low impact on the dependent variable and are often vulnerabilities for the progress of the digital economy, especially in countries where youth unemployment is a national phenomenon (Italy and Spain) (Başol et al., 2023) but also in countries where the tax regime is excessive (Abuselidze, 2021). The intensive use of digital technologies in recent years has led to the creation of new jobs and areas of employment, especially for young people, and has played an important role in tackling youth unemployment [360-363].

The SDG8.3 model of European economic sustainability from the perspective of the SDG8INTA indicator, with the selected dependent variable denoting the level of household Internet access. The independent variables are SDG8VIMPM representing labour tax revenues, SDG8RRSAR representing the at-risk-of-work poverty rate, SDG8UTINT representing the share of Internet usage by individuals, SDG8ATIC representing the number of employed ICT specialists. A linear regression model is constructed with the independent variables defined above for which regression coefficients have been calculated according to Equation (9.4).

$$\begin{aligned} SDG8INTA &= -0.02 * SDG8VIMPM + 0.04 * SDG8RRSAR \\ &+0.86 * SDG8UTINT + 0.05 * SDG8ATIC + 0.52 \end{aligned} \tag{9.4}$$

The level of statistical significance calculated using the coefficient of determination is 89.86%.

The SDG8.3 model analyses the impact of different economic and social variables on the level of household internet access, showing a number of relationships:

In the case of the variable SDG8VIMPM representing labour tax revenues, there is an inverse influence on the dependent variable, i.e. a 1% increase in labour tax revenues leads to a 0.02% decrease in the level of household Internet access, which indicates that in the context of a higher tax burden on labour, the ability of households to afford Internet services could be slightly reduced. This points to the need for careful weighting of tax policies so as not to reduce access to digital services. In the case of the SDG8RRSAR variable representing the at-risk-of-work poverty rate, there is a positive influence on the dependent variable, i.e. a 1% increase in the at-risk-of-work poverty rate leads to a 0.04% increase in the level of household Internet access. The positive relationship indicates that even with an increased risk of in-work poverty, household Internet access tends to increase. This reflects the growing importance of the Internet as an essential resource for seeking job opportunities, education and other services, even in lower-income households.

In the case of the variable SDG8UTINT representing the share of Internet use by individuals, there is a positive influence on the dependent variable, i.e. a 1% increase in the share of Internet use by individuals leads to a 0.86% increase in the level of Internet access by households. The positive relationship between Internet use by individuals and the level of household Internet access emphasizes a strong demand and need for connectivity among the population. This indicates that investments in Internet infrastructure and initiatives to increase accessibility are important in the context of achieving economic sustainability.

In the case of the variable SDG8ATIC representing the number of employed ICT specialists, there is a positive influence on the dependent variable, i.e. a 1% increase in the number of employed ICT specialists leads to a 0.05% increase in the level of household Internet access. The positive relationship between the number of ICT specialists and the level of household Internet access suggests that a larger ICT workforce can contribute to improving the digital infrastructure and therefore to expanding household Internet access. This reveals the importance of investing in ICT education and training not only for economic growth but also for improving access to digital services.

Figure 9.4 shows the ranking of the importance of the predictors related to the influence on the dependent variable SDG8INTA.

Figure 9.4 shows that the greatest influence on the dependent variable SDG8INTA is manifested by the indicator SDG8UTINT share of Internet use by individuals which shows that household Internet access depends significantly on the willingness of individuals to use the Internet which limits in some countries the sustainable development of the digital economy due to insufficient skills of individuals in using the Internet (Rosário & Dias, 2023). The digital economy helps sustainability through energy optimization, waste reduction, waste minimization and more efficient use of resources. It is also able to support interpersonal platforms, sustainable business models and the circular economy (Rosário & Dias, 2023).

The SDG8.4 model of European economic sustainability from the perspective of the SDG8ROCFM indicator has as selected dependent variable the employment rate. The independent variables in this model are: SDG8VASE representing value added in services, SDG8VIMPM representing income from labour taxation, SDG8PIBP representing GDP per capita, SDG8TNEET representing the share of the total population of young people neither in employment nor in education or training (NEET),

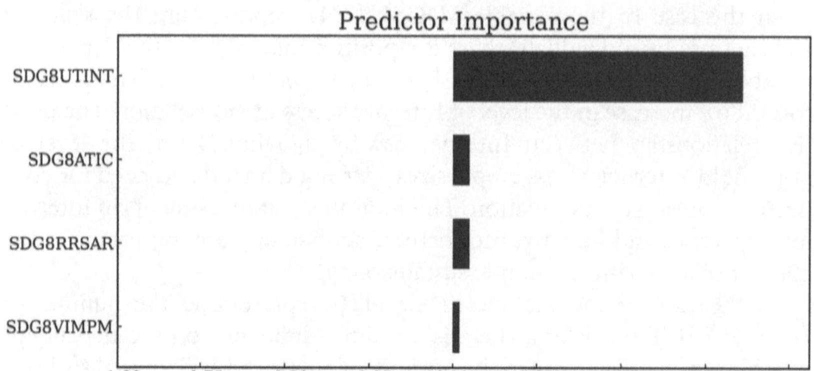


**Fig. 9.4** Importance of predictors related to influence on the variable SDG8INTA. Source: Developed by the author using Python

SDG8RRSAR as the at-risk-of-work poverty rate, SDG8UTINT as the share of Internet use by individuals, SDG8ATIC as the number of employed ICT specialists, SDG8AINT as the coverage of high-speed Internet. A linear regression model is constructed with the independent variables defined above for which regression coefficients have been calculated according to Equation (9.5).

$$\begin{aligned}\mathrm{SDG8ROCFM} = &-0.14 * \mathrm{SDG8VASE} - 0.009 * \mathrm{SDG8VIMPM}\\ &-0.04 * \mathrm{SDG8PIBloc} - 0.14 * \mathrm{SDG8TNEET}\\ &+0.002 * \mathrm{SDG8RRSAR} + 0.24 * \mathrm{SDG8UTINT}\\ &+0.04 * \mathrm{SDG8ATIC} + 0.004 * \mathrm{SDG8AINT} + 2.27\end{aligned} \tag{9.5}$$

The level of statistical significance calculated using the coefficient of determination is 81.2%. As shown by the regression equation for Model SDG8.4, the variable SDG8VASE (value added in services) exerts a statistically significant negative influence on the dependent variable: a 1% increase in value added in services corresponds to a 0.14% decline in the employment rate. This influence indicates that although services are becoming more efficient, this does not necessarily manifest itself in increased employment in the sector, possibly due to automation or increased efficiency reducing the need for human labour. In the case of the variable SDG8VIMPM representing labour tax revenues, there is an inverse influence on the dependent variable, i.e. a 1% increase in labour tax revenues leads to a 0.009% decrease in the employment rate. This indicates that higher taxes from labour taxation may discourage hiring or may encourage hiring practices that minimize tax liabilities, such as short-term contracts or self-employment, which may be less stable and therefore less beneficial for the overall employment rate. In the case of the variable SDG8GDPloc representing GDP per capita, there is an inverse influence on the dependent variable, i.e. a 1% increase in GDP per capita leads to a 0.04% decrease in the employment rate. This may reflect the fact that while the economy is growing, it does not necessarily create new jobs.

In the case of the variable SDG8TNEET, representing the share of the total population of young people neither in employment nor in education or training (NEET), there is an inverse influence on the dependent variable, i.e. a 1% increase in the share of the total population of young people neither in employment nor in education or training (NEET) leads to a 0.14% decrease in the employment rate. This indicates the importance of integrating young people into the labour force or into education and training systems in order to improve the labour market and prevent the long-term effects of unemployment or lack of skills on the economy.

Regarding the indicator SDG8RRSAR representing the at-risk-of-work poverty rate, a positive influence on the dependent variable is found, i.e. a 1% increase in the at-risk-of-work poverty rate leads to a 0.002% increase in the employment rate. In the case of the variable SDG8UTINT representing the share of Internet use by individuals, there is a positive influence on the dependent variable, i.e. a 1% increase in the share of Internet use by individuals leads to a 0.24% increase in the employment rate. This influence reveals the importance of access to technology and information, which can facilitate finding jobs, developing skills and participating in the digital economy, thus leading to better employment. In the case of the variable SDG8ATIC representing the number of employed ICT professionals, a positive influence on the dependent variable is found, i.e. a 1% increase in the number of employed ICT professionals leads to a 0.04% increase in the employment rate. This emphasizes the importance of the technology sector and the skilled ICT workforce for the economy as a whole, indicating that investments in ICT education and training have positive effects on employment.

According to the variable SDG8AINT representing high-speed Internet coverage, there is a positive influence on the dependent variable, i.e. a 1% increase in high-speed Internet coverage leads to a 0.004% increase in the employment rate. This indicates the role of technological infrastructure in facilitating economic activities and access to work, especially in areas that depend on fast and reliable Internet connectivity.

Figure 9.5 shows the ranking of the importance of predictors related to the influence on the dependent variable SDG8ROCFM.

Figure 9.5 shows that the significant direct influence of the independent variable the share of Internet usage by individuals determines the change in the employment rate, a significant aspect of the digital economy where the focus is on the skills of the workforce to use digital technologies (Başol et al., 2023). Figure 9.5 shows less significant influences on the dependent variable in terms of the share of the total population of young people neither in employment nor in education or training (NEETs) and value added in services. The variables that represent vulnerabilities of sustainable development in terms of employment rates are high-speed Internet coverage and the at-risk-of-work poverty rate.

The SDG8.5 model of European economic sustainability from the perspective of the SDG8RRSAR indicator is the selected dependent variable

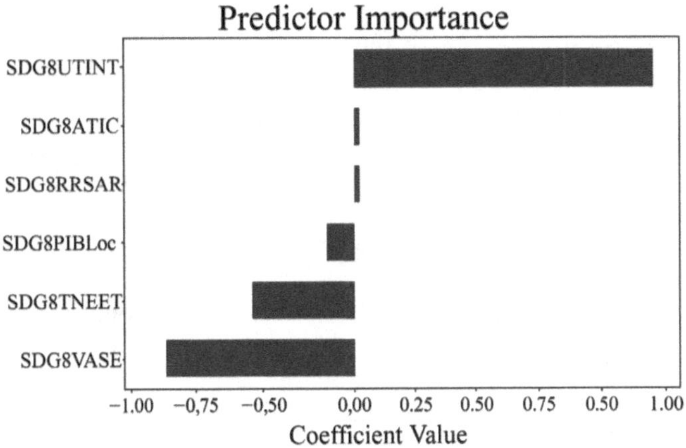


**Fig. 9.5** Importance of predictors related to influence on the variable SDG8ROCFM. Source: Developed by the author using Python

that signifies the at-risk-of-work poverty rate. The independent variables are SDG8VASE—value added in services, SDG8VIMPM—income from labour taxation, SDG8TNEET—share of the total population of young people neither in employment nor in education or training (NEET), SDG8ROCFM—employment rate, SDG8INTA—household Internet access level, SDG8ATIC—number of employed ICT specialists, SDG8AINT—high speed Internet coverage. A linear regression model is constructed with the independent variables defined above for which regression coefficients were calculated according to Equation (9.6).

$$\begin{aligned} SDG8RRSAR &= 1.03 * SDG8VASE + 0.12 * SDG8VIMPM \\ &+0.17 * SDG8TNEET - 0.73 * SDG8ROCFM \\ &+0.39 * SDG8INTA - 0.65 * SDG8ATIC \\ &+0.09 * SDG8AINT - 0.63 \end{aligned} \tag{9.6}$$

The level of statistical significance calculated using the coefficient of determination is 41.05%. As evidenced by the regression equation for Model SDG8.5, the variable SDG8VASE (value added in services) exerts a positive and statistically significant influence on the dependent variable: a 1% increase in value added in services corresponds to a 1.03% rise in the at-risk-of-work poverty rate. This suggests that while services are becoming more productive it is not necessarily improving working conditions or the incomes of workers in this sector, which may lead to an increase in the risk of poverty. In the case of the variable SDG8VIMPM representing labour tax revenues, we find a positive influence on the dependent variable, i.e. a 1% increase in labour tax revenues leads to a 0.12% increase in the at-risk-of-work poverty rate, indicating that, under higher labour taxation, workers' net incomes are affected, thus increasing the risk of poverty. In the case of the variable SDG8TNEET representing the share of the total population of young people who are neither in employment nor in education or training (NEET), there is a positive influence on the dependent variable, i.e. a 1% increase in the share of the total population of young people who are neither in employment nor in education or training (NEET) leads to a 0.17% increase in the at-risk-of-work poverty rate, emphasizing the link between the lack of employment or education among young people and poverty-related vulnerability. As for the SDG8ROCFM variable, the employment rate, there is an inverse influence on the dependent variable, i.e. a 1% increase in the employment rate leads to a 0.73% decrease in the at-risk-of-work poverty rate. This indicates that higher employment is associated with a reduction in in-work poverty, emphasizing the importance of job creation and access to jobs. According to the SDG8INTA variable representing the level of household Internet access, there is a positive influence on the dependent variable, i.e. a 1% increase in the level of household Internet access leads to a 0.39% increase in the at-risk-of-work poverty rate. This reveals that while Internet access can bring many benefits, there are aspects of the digital economy that can contribute to job insecurity or poor working conditions. In the case of the variable SDG8ATIC representing the number of employed ICT professionals, there is an inverse influence on the dependent variable, i.e. a 1% increase in the number of employed ICT professionals leads to a 0.65% decrease in the at-risk-of-work poverty rate. This highlights the positive role of ICT employment in reducing the risk of in-work poverty, due to better wages and more stable working conditions in this sector.

Figure 9.6 shows the hierarchy of importance of the predictors related to the influence on the dependent variable SDG8RRSAR.

Figure 9.6 shows that the most significant influence on the dependent variable is that of value added in services, which demonstrates the orientation towards the consumer economy, a major vulnerability for developing countries in achieving economic sustainability. Less significant influences are the number of ICT specialists employed and the employment rate. These aspects support the European economy's need for a skilled workforce and its present orientation towards the digital economy. The pattern of sustainability through poverty reduction is less influenced by variation in high-speed Internet coverage and labour tax revenues.

The SDG8.6 model of European economic sustainability from the perspective of the SDG8VIMPM indicator is the selected dependent variable denoting labour tax revenues. The independent variables are SDG8VAAG representing the value added in agriculture, SDG8GDPloc representing the gross domestic product per capita, SDG8TNEET representing the share of the total population of young people neither in employment nor in education or training (NEET), SDG8ROCFM as the employment rate, SDG8RRSAR as the at-risk-of-work poverty rate, SDG8INTA as the level of household Internet access, SDG8UTINT as the share of Internet use by individuals, SDG8AINT as the share of high-speed Internet coverage. A linear regression model is constructed with the independent variables defined above for which regression coefficients have been calculated according to Equation (9.7).

$$\begin{aligned} SDG8VIMPM &= 0.18 * SDG8VAAG + 0.33 * SDG8PIBloc \\ &-0.12 * SDG8TNEET + 0.003 * SDG8ROCFM \\ &+0.04 * SDG8RRSAR - 0.33 * SDG8INTA \\ &+0.57 * SDG8UTINT - 0.02 * SDG8AINT - 0.62 \end{aligned} \tag{9.7}$$

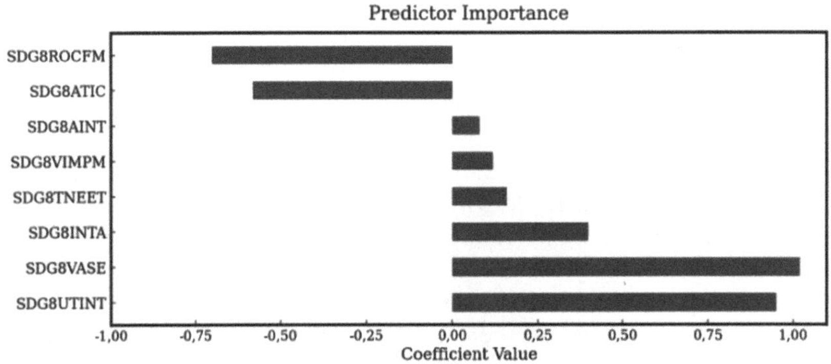


**Fig. 9.6** Importance of predictors related to the influence on the variable SDG8RRSAR. Source: Developed by the author using Python

The level of statistical significance calculated using the coefficient of determination is 45.57%. As evidenced by the regression equation for Model SDG8.6, the variable SDG8VAAG (value added in agriculture) exerts a positive and statistically significant influence on the dependent variable: a 1% increase in value added in agriculture corresponds to a 0.18% rise in labour tax revenue. This shows that productivity improvement in the agricultural sector can have a positive impact on the tax base due to the increase in labour income of workers in this sector.

In the case of the variable SDG8GDP per capita, a positive influence on the dependent variable is found, i.e. a 1% increase in GDP per capita leads to a 0.33% increase in labour tax revenues. This reflects the link between overall economic growth and the government's ability to generate tax revenues.

As for the variable SDG8TNEET, representing the share of the total population of young people who are neither employed nor in education or training (NEET), there is an inverse influence on the dependent variable, i.e. a 1% increase in the share of the total population of young people who are neither employed nor in education or training (NEET) leads to a 0.12% decrease in labour tax revenues. This underlines the negative impact of youth unemployment and lack of vocational education on the tax base.

In the case of the SDG8ROCFM indicator representing the employment rate, there is a positive influence on the dependent variable, i.e. a 1% increase in the employment rate leads to a 0.003% increase in labour tax revenues, emphasizing the importance of job creation for increasing government revenues. In the case of the variable SDG8RRSAR representing the at-risk-of-work poverty rate, there is a positive influence on the dependent variable, i.e. a 1% increase in the at-risk-of-work poverty rate leads to a 0.04% increase in labour tax revenues, which may indicate that even low-paid jobs contribute to the tax base. In the case of the variable SDG8INTA representing the level of household Internet access, there is an inverse influence on the dependent variable, i.e. a 1% increase in the level of household Internet access leads to a 0.33% decrease in labour tax revenues, indicating that higher connectivity does not always mean higher taxable income.

According to the variable SDG8UTINT representing the share of Internet use by individuals, there is a positive influence on the dependent variable, i.e. a 1% increase in the share of Internet use by individuals leads to a 0.57% increase in labour tax revenues, suggesting that digitalization has a positive impact on economic growth and taxable income.

In the case of the variable SDG8AINT representing high-speed Internet coverage, there is an inverse influence on the dependent variable, i.e. a 1% increase in high-speed Internet coverage leads to a 0.02% decrease in labour tax revenues, which may indicate that the benefits of faster connectivity do not necessarily mean an increase in taxable income.

Figure 9.7 shows the ranking of the importance of the predictors related to the influence on the dependent variable SDG8VIMPM.

Figure 9.7 shows that the dependent variable is significantly influenced by the share of Internet use by individuals which is characteristic of the digital economy, followed by economic growth as reflected by GDP per capita and less influenced by the level of Internet access by households. The vulnerabilities of European labour taxation are represented by the weak correlation of the dependent variable with the employment rate, high-speed Internet coverage and the at-risk-of-work poverty rate.

The SDG8.7 model of European economic sustainability from the perspective of the SDG8VASE indicator is the selected dependent variable that signifies value added in services. The independent variables are SDG8VAIN representing value added in industry, SDG8VIMPM representing labour tax revenue, SDG8TNEET representing the share of the total population of young people neither in employment nor in education or training (NEET), SDG8ROCFM representing the employment rate, SDG8RRSAR representing the at-risk-of-work poverty rate. A linear regression model is constructed with the previously defined independent

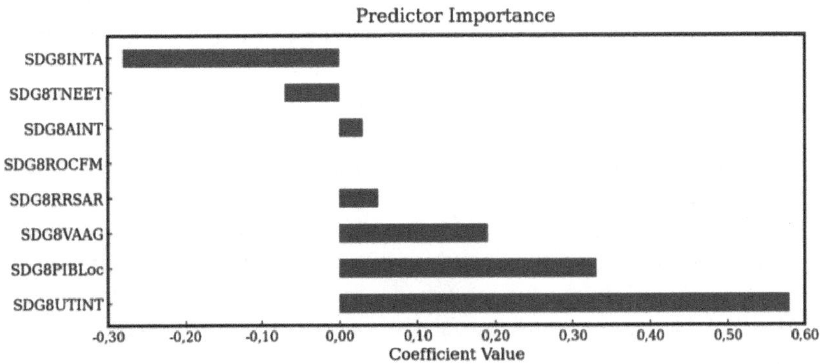


**Fig. 9.7** Importance of predictors related to the influence on the variable SDG8VIMPM. Source: Developed by the author using Python

variables for which regression coefficients have been calculated according to Equation (9.8).

$$\begin{aligned} \text{SDG8VASE} &= -0.35 * \text{SDG8VAIN} + 0.06 * \text{SDG8VIMPM} \\ &+0.03 * \text{SDG8TNEET} + 0.11 * \text{SDG8ROCFM} \\ &-0.01 * \text{SDG8RRSAR} + 2.33 \end{aligned} \tag{9.8}$$

The level of statistical significance calculated using the coefficient of determination is 95.74%. The regression results for Model SDG8.7 show that SDG8VAIN (value added in industry) has a negative effect on the dependent variable, such that a 1% increase in industrial value added results in a 0.35% reduction in value added in services. This may indicate that in some economies, the growth of the industrial sector may occur at the expense of the services sector, due to reallocation of resources or competition for labour and capital. In the case of the variable SDG8VIMPM representing labour tax revenues, there is a positive influence on the dependent variable, i.e. a 1% increase in labour tax revenues leads to a 0.06% increase in value added in services. This may reflect that a higher tax base, associated with higher labour tax revenues, corresponds to a healthier economy in which the service sector is improving. In the case of the variable SDG8TNEET representing the share of the total population of young people neither in employment nor in education or training (NEET), there is a positive influence on the dependent variable, i.e. a 1% increase in the share of the total population of young people neither in employment nor in education or training (NEET) leads to a 0.03% increase in value added in services. This might suggest that even in the context of a higher proportion of young people not in employment and not in education, there are factors in the services sector that can compensate for this, possibly through job creation or integration programs that involve these young people in the economy. In the case of the variable SDG8ROCFM representing the employment rate, there is a positive influence on the dependent variable, i.e. a 1% increase in the employment rate leads to a 0.11% increase in value added in services, emphasizing the importance of employment for the growth and development of the services sector. In the case of the variable SDG8RRSAR representing the at-risk-of-work poverty rate, an inverse influence on the dependent variable is found, i.e. a 1% increase in the at-risk-of-work poverty rate leads to a 0.01% decrease in the value added in services. This could indicate that an increase in in-work poverty may negatively affect the economic performance of the service sector by reducing purchasing power and demand for services.

Figure 9.8 shows the ranking of the importance of the predictors related to the influence on the dependent variable SDG8VASE.

Figure 9.8 shows that the dependent variable is little influenced by changes in value added in industry, which is normal in a developed economy. A significant influence is the employment rate. The vulnerabilities identified in the development of the service sector are related to the weak correlation of the change in the dependent variable with the indicators at-risk-of-work poverty rate and the share of the total population of young people neither in employment nor in education or training (NEET).

The SDG8.8 model of European economic sustainability from the perspective of the SDG8VAIN indicator is the selected dependent variable denoting value added in industry. The independent variables are SDG8VASE representing value added in services, SDG8VIMPM representing labour tax revenues, SDG8TNEET representing the share of the total population of young people neither in employment nor in education or training (NEET), SDG8ROCFM representing the employment rate, SDG8RRSAR representing the at-risk-of-work poverty rate, SDG8UTINT representing the share of Internet use by individuals. A linear regression model is constructed with the independent variables defined above for which regression coefficients have been calculated according to Equation (9.9).

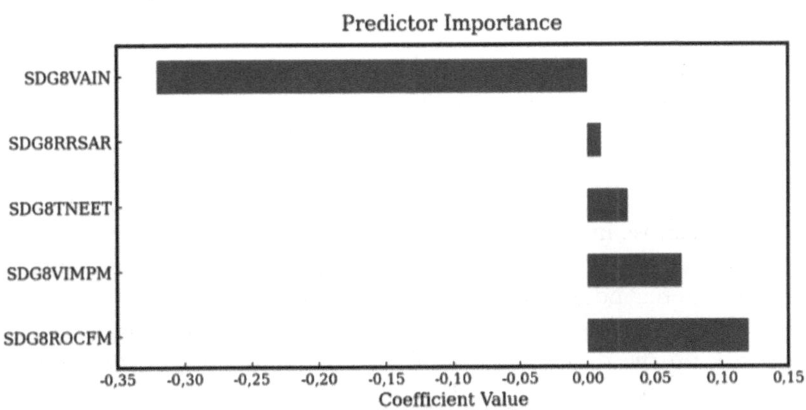


**Fig. 9.8** Importance of predictors related to influence on the variable SDG8VASE. Source: Developed by the author using Python

$$\begin{aligned} SDG8VAIN = & -2.65 * SDG8VASE + 0.17 * SDG8VIMPM \\ & +0.10 * SDG8TNEET + 0.47 * SDG8ROCFM \\ & -0.05 * SDG8RRSAR - 0.05 * SDG8UTINT + 6.05 \end{aligned} \tag{9.9}$$

The level of statistical significance calculated using the coefficient of determination is 95.90%. The estimation results for Model SDG8.8 show that SDG8VASE (value added in services) negatively influences the dependent variable, with a 1% rise in value added in services associated with a 2.65% reduction in value added in industry. This may suggest a reallocation of resources or investment from industry to services, which may have a negative impact on industrial output. In the case of the variable SDG8VIMPM representing labour tax revenues, there is a positive influence on the dependent variable, i.e. a 1% increase in labour tax revenues leads to a 0.17% increase in value added in industry. This reveals that a higher tax base associated with a healthy economy supports industrial output growth. In the case of the variable SDG8TNEET, representing the share of the total population of young people neither in employment nor in education or training (NEET), there is a positive influence on the dependent variable, i.e. a 1% increase in the share of the total population of young people neither in employment nor in education or training (NEET) leads to a 0.1% increase in value added in industry. This suggests that there are initiatives or programs that integrate these young people into the industrial sector, thus contributing to increased output. In the case of the variable SDG8ROCFM representing the employment rate, there is a positive influence on the dependent variable, i.e. a 1% increase in the employment rate leads to a 0.47% increase in the value added in industry, which shows the importance of employment to sustain industrial production. In the case of the variable SDG8RRSAR representing the at-risk-of-work poverty rate, there is an inverse influence on the dependent variable, i.e. a 1% increase in the at-risk-of-work poverty rate leads to a 0.05% decrease in the value added in industry. This indicates that poor labour conditions or low wages may negatively affect the productivity and efficiency of the industrial sector. In the case of the variable SDG8UTINT representing the share of Internet use by individuals, there is an inverse influence on the dependent variable, i.e. a 1% increase in the share of Internet use by individuals leads to a 0.05% decrease in value added in industry. This suggests that, despite the benefits of digitization, there are aspects of technology adoption that may have a negative impact on industrial output, possibly due to the distraction of the workforce or the reallocation of investment to the technology sector.

Figure 9.9 shows the ranking of the importance of the predictors related to the influence on the dependent variable SDG8VAIN.

Figure 9.9 shows a low influence of gross value added in services in explaining the change in the dependent variable (SDG8VAIN). The remaining influences reflect the existence of correlations between the change in the dependent variable and the employment rate. Vulnerabilities can be identified in the weak correlation of the dependent variable with the share of Internet use by individuals and the at-risk-of-work poverty rate.

Figure 9.10 is based on the SDG8.8 vulnerability indicator rankings in 2021. The figure shows that the last ranked countries in terms of gross value added in industry, i.e. Luxembourg, Greece, the Netherlands and Denmark, have top positions in Internet usage by individuals which has oriented the economy of these countries towards the service sector (the Netherlands, Luxembourg and Denmark). In addition, Greece and Luxembourg are in the top five countries with the highest poverty rates.

The SDG8.9 model of European economic sustainability from the perspective of the SDG8VAAG indicator is the selected dependent variable that signifies the value added in agriculture. The independent variables are SDG8VIMPM representing income from labour taxation, SDG8GDPlocal

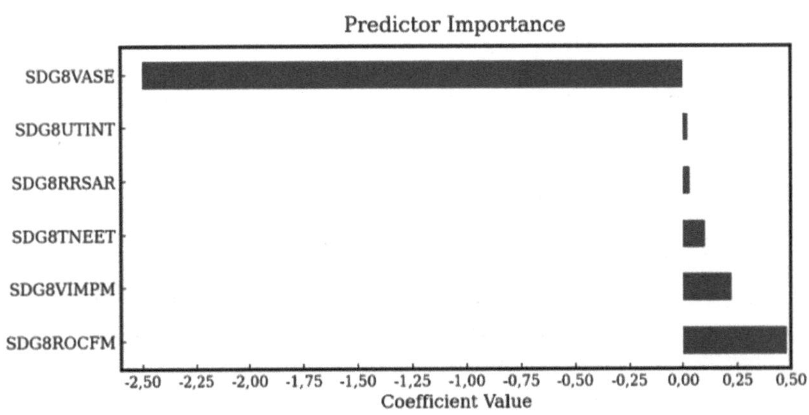


**Fig. 9.9** Importance of predictors related to the influence on the variable SDG8VAIN. Source: Developed by the author using Python

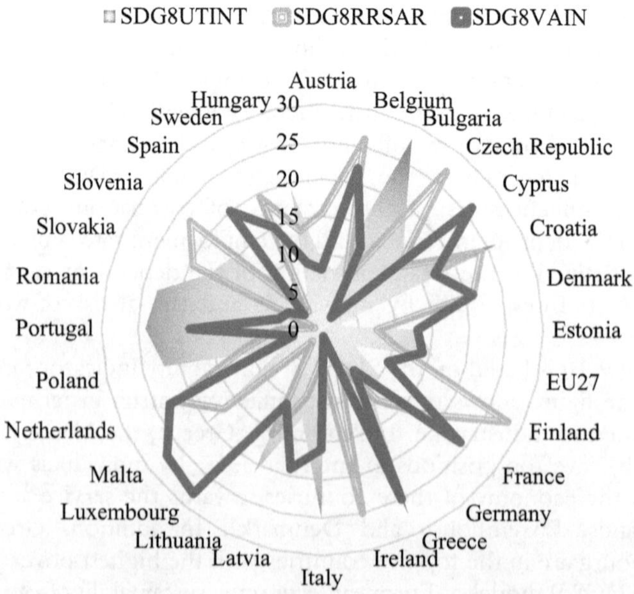


**Fig. 9.10** Vulnerabilities diagram of the variable SDG8VAIN. Source: Author

representing GDP per capita, SDG8TNEET representing the share of the total population of young people neither in employment nor in education or training (NEET), SDG8AINT representing high-speed Internet coverage. A linear regression model is constructed with the independent variables defined above for which regression coefficients have been calculated according to Equation (9.10).

$$\begin{aligned} SDG8VAAG &= 0.63 * SDG8VIMPM - 0.89 * SDG8PIBloc \\ &+ 0.32 * SDG8TNEET + 0.05 * SDG8AINT + 3.40 \end{aligned} \tag{9.10}$$

The level of statistical significance calculated using the coefficient of determination is 69.99%. As evidenced by the results of Model SDG8.9, SDG8VIMPM (labour tax revenue) exerts a statistically significant positive effect on the dependent variable: a 1% increase in labour tax revenue corresponds to a 0.63% increase in value added in agriculture. This indicates that a higher tax base, reflecting higher labour income and a healthier economy, is associated with an increase in productivity or investment in the agricultural sector. With respect to the variable SDG8GDP per capita GDP per capita, there is an inverse influence on the dependent variable, i.e. a 1% increase in GDP per capita leads to a 0.89% decrease in value added in agriculture. This may indicate that as economies grow and incomes rise, investment and resources may be reallocated from agriculture to other sectors, such as services or industry, which become more dominant in the economic structure. According to the variable SDG8TNEET, representing the share of the total population of young people neither in employment nor in education or training (NEET), there is a positive influence on the dependent variable, i.e. a 1% increase in the share of the total population of young people neither in employment nor in education or training (NEET) leads to a 0.32% increase in value added in agriculture. This could indicate that, in the absence of jobs or education opportunities, the agricultural sector may be an employment opportunity for these young people, thus contributing to increased agricultural output. In the case of the variable SDG8AINT representing high-speed Internet coverage, there is a positive influence on the dependent variable, i.e. a 1% increase in high-speed Internet coverage leads to a 0.05% increase in agricultural value added. This indicates that technology and connectivity can play a significant role in the modernization of agriculture by improving access to information, markets and new technologies, which can lead to increased efficiency and productivity.

Figure 9.11 shows the ranking of the importance of the predictors related to the influence on the dependent variable SDG8VAAG.

Figure 9.11 shows that the significant influences on the variation of the dependent variable are labour taxation (direct correlation) and the level of economic development represented by gross domestic product per capita (indirect correlation). Vulnerabilities are represented by the weak correlation of the dependent variable with the indicator of high-speed Internet coverage, which shows that digitalization in agriculture is still an element that hinders the achievement of sustainability of the European economy. In the opinion of Zlati and co (Zlati et al., 2023), investments made in agricultural cooperative companies support the creation and increase of added value and reduce specific risks, strengthening the role and status of agricultural producers in the food chain. In order to ensure sustainable development, it is necessary to enhance the role of agricultural producers in the food chain and increase the efficiency of agricultural activity, with a direct impact on European food security.

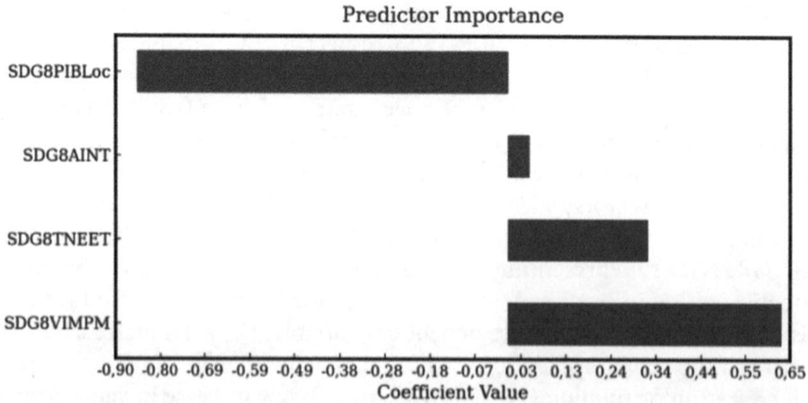


**Fig. 9.11** Importance of predictors related to influence on the variable SDG8VAAG. Source: Developed by the author using Python

The SDG8.10 model of European economic sustainability from the perspective of the SDG8ATIC indicator is the selected dependent variable that signifies the number of employed ICT specialists. The independent variables are SDG8GDPloc representing gross domestic product per capita, SDG8ROCFM representing the employment rate, SDG8RRSAR representing the at-risk-of-work poverty rate, SDG8INTA representing the level of household Internet access, SDG8AINT representing high-speed Internet coverage. A linear regression model is constructed with the independent variables defined above for which regression coefficients have been calculated according to Equation (9.11).

$$\begin{aligned} SDG8ATIC &= 0.21 * SDG8PIBloc + 0.54 * SDG8ROCFM \\ &-0.24 * SDG8RRSAR + 0.63 * SDG8INTA \\ &+0.02 * SDG8AINT - 2.78 \end{aligned} \tag{9.11}$$

The level of statistical significance calculated using the coefficient of determination is 74.67%. Model SDG8.10 demonstrates that SDG8GDP (GDP per capita) exerts a statistically significant positive influence on the dependent variable: a 1% increase in GDP per capita corresponds to a 0.21% rise in the number of ICT specialists employed. This suggests that developed economies with a higher GDP per capita tend to have a higher demand for ICT specialists, due to greater digitization and automation in various sectors. In the case of the variable SDG8ROCFM representing the employment rate, there is a positive influence on the dependent variable, i.e. a 1% increase in the employment rate leads to a 0.54% increase in the number of ICT specialists employed. This indicates that with a more dynamic labour market and higher employment rates, there are increased opportunities and greater needs for ICT professionals. In the case of the SDG8RRSAR variable representing the at-risk-of-work poverty rate, there is an inverse influence on the dependent variable, i.e. a 1% increase in the at-risk-of-work poverty rate leads to a 0.24% decrease in the number of employed ICT professionals. This may reflect the fact that in environments with a higher risk of in-work poverty, investments in technology and the hiring of ICT professionals may be lower, thus affecting the growth of the ICT sector. In the case of the SDG8INTA variable representing the level of household Internet access, a positive influence on the dependent variable is found, i.e. a 1% increase in the level of household Internet access leads to a 0.63% increase in the number of ICT professionals employed. This indicates a correlation between generalized Internet access and an increased demand for ICT professionals, possibly due to a greater integration of digital technologies in everyday life and business. In the case of the variable SDG8AINT representing high-speed Internet coverage, there is a positive influence on the dependent variable, i.e. a 1% increase in high-speed Internet coverage leads to a 0.02% increase in the number of ICT professionals employed. This suggests that improving the Internet infrastructure may have a positive, albeit small, impact on the employment of ICT specialists, supporting the need for advanced technological skills to fully reap the benefits of fast connectivity.

Figure 9.12 shows the ranking of the importance of the predictors related to the influence on the dependent variable SDG8ATIC.

Figure 9.12 shows that the strongest influences on the dependent variable are household Internet access and employment rate. The at-risk-of-work poverty rate does not significantly influence the prediction of the training of ICT specialists, which is a normal aspect of sustainable economic development.

The SDG8.11 model of European economic sustainability from the perspective of the SDG8TNEET indicator is the selected dependent variable that signifies the share of the total population of young people who are neither in employment nor in education or training (NEET). The independent variables are SDG8VAAG as value added in agriculture,

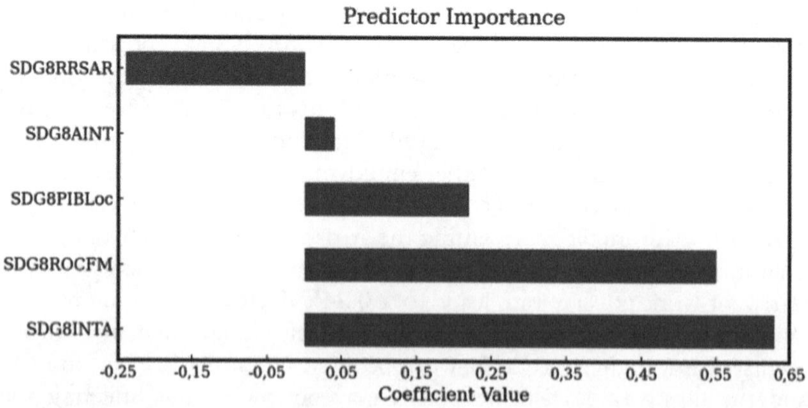


**Fig. 9.12** Importance of predictors related to the influence on the variable SDG8ATIC. Source: Developed by the author using Python

SDG8VASE as value added in services, SDG8VIMPM as income from labour taxation, SDG8PIBP as GDP per capita, SDG8ROCFM as employment rate, SDG8RRSAR as at-risk-of-work poverty rate, SDG8UTINT as share of Internet usage by individuals, SDG8AINT as high-speed Internet coverage. We construct a linear regression model with the independent variables defined above for which regression coefficients have been calculated according to Equation (9.12).

$$\begin{aligned} SDG8TNEET = 0.07 * SDG8VAAG - 0.43 * SDG8VASE \\ -0.10 * SDG8VIMPM - 0.12 * SDG8PIBloc \\ -2.77 * SDG8ROCFM + 0.08 * SDG8RRSAR \\ +0.32 * SDG8UTINT - 0.02 * SDG8AINT + 16.16 \end{aligned} \tag{9.12}$$

The level of statistical significance calculated using the coefficient of determination is 77.01%. Model SDG8.11 reveals a positive elasticity for SDG8VAAG (value added in agriculture), indicating that a 1% rise in agricultural value added generates a 0.xx increase in the dependent variable. This may suggest that, in some economies, growth in the agricultural sector does not necessarily translate into a reduction in the share of young NEETs, possibly due to the seasonal nature or low skill requirements in many agricultural jobs.

For the variable SDG8VASE representing value added in services, there is an inverse influence on the dependent variable, i.e. a 1% increase in value added in services leads to a 0.43% decrease in the share of young people out of the total population who are neither employed nor in education or training (NEET). This suggests that the expansion of the service sector may provide more employment and education opportunities for young people, thus contributing to a reduction in the share of NEET. In the case of the variable SDG8VIMPM representing labour tax revenues, there is an inverse influence on the dependent variable, i.e. a 1% increase in labour tax revenues leads to a 0.1% decrease in the share of the total population of young people neither in employment nor in education or training (NEET). This may reflect the fact that a healthier economy with higher labour tax revenues may better support the integration of young people into the labour market or the education system. In the case of the SDG8GDP per capita variable, there is an inverse influence on the dependent variable, i.e. a 1% increase in GDP per capita leads to a 0.12% decrease in the share of young people who are neither in employment nor in education or training (NEET) in the total population. This underlines the link between overall economic development and the ability to employ young people or include them in educational programmes. In the case of the variable SDG8ROCFM, the employment rate, there is an inverse influence on the dependent variable, i.e. a 1% increase in the employment rate leads to a 2.77% decrease in the share of young people who are neither employed nor in education or training (NEET) in the total population. This highlights the importance of job creation and a dynamic labour market for reducing the number of young NEETs. According to the SDG8RRSAR variable representing the at-risk-of-work poverty rate, there is a positive influence on the dependent variable, i.e. a 1% increase in the at-risk-of-work poverty rate leads to a 0.08% increase in the share of the total population of young people who are neither in employment nor in education or training (NEET). This may suggest that, with higher job insecurity and lower income, more young people may end up being classified as NEET. About the variable SDG8UTINT representing the share of Internet use by individuals, there is a positive influence on the dependent variable, i.e. a 1% increase in the share of Internet use by individuals leads to a 0.32% increase in the share of the total population of young people who are neither in employment nor in education or training (NEET). This may suggest that while Internet access provides educational and employment opportunities, there are other factors that may lead young people to move away from the labour market or education. In the case of the variable SDG8AINT representing high-speed Internet coverage, there is an inverse influence on the dependent variable, i.e. a 1% increase in high-speed Internet coverage leads to a 0.02% decrease in the share of the total population of young people who are neither in employment nor in education or training (NEET). This indicates that improving the technological infrastructure may help to reduce the share of NEET, possibly by facilitating access to information, educational resources and employment opportunities.

Figure 9.13 shows the ranking of the importance of the predictors related to the influence on the dependent variable SDG8TNEET.

Figure 9.13 shows a minor importance of the employment rate in the model for predicting SDG8TNEET, with SDG8UTINT being the most important predictor.

The SDG8.12 model of European economic sustainability from the perspective of the SDG8UTINT indicator is the selected dependent variable that signifies the share of Internet usage by individuals. The independent variables are SDG8VAIN as value added in industry, SDG8VIMPM as income from taxes on labour, SDG8GDPloc as gross domestic product per capita, SDG8TNEET as the share of young people out of the total population who are neither in employment nor in education or training (NEET), SDG8ROCFM as the employment rate, SDG8RRSAR as the at-risk-of-work poverty rate, SDG8INTA as the level of household

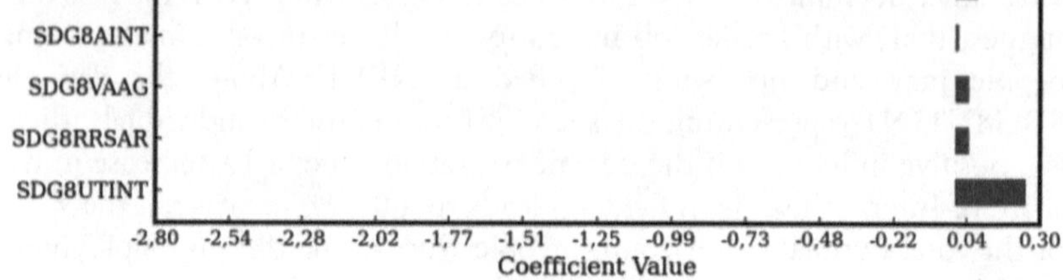


**Fig. 9.13** Importance of predictors related to influence on the variable SDG8TNEET. Source: Developed by the author using Python

Internet access. A linear regression model is constructed with the independent variables defined above for which regression coefficients have been calculated according to Equation (9.13).

$$\begin{aligned} SDG8UTINT = & -0.06 * SDG8VAIN + 0.05 * SDG8VIMPM \\ & +0.01 * SDG8PIBloc + 0.03 * SDG8TNEET \\ & +0.43 * SDG8ROCFM - 0.04 * SDG8RRSAR \\ & +0.74 * SDG8INTA - 0.85 \end{aligned} \quad (9.13)$$

The level of statistical significance calculated using the coefficient of determination is 92.87%. As evidenced by the results of Model SDG8.12, SDG8VAIN (value added in industry) exerts a statistically significant inverse effect on the dependent variable: a 1% increase in industrial value added corresponds to a 0.06% decline in individual Internet use. This may suggest that in economies more focused on industrial production, there may be less concentration on digital services and Internet access. With respect to the variable SDG8VIMPM representing labour tax revenues, there is a positive influence on the dependent variable, i.e. a 1% increase in labour tax revenues leads to a 0.05% increase in the share of Internet usage by individuals. This reflects the fact that a higher tax base, indicating higher household incomes, is associated with greater Internet accessibility and use. In the case of the SDG8GDP per capita variable, a positive influence on the dependent variable is found, i.e. a 1% increase in GDP per capita leads to a 0.01% increase in the share of individuals using the Internet. This highlights that general economic growth and income growth can have a positive impact on Internet access. According to the variable SDG8TNEET representing the share of the total population of young people neither in employment nor in education or training (NEET), there is a positive influence on the dependent variable, i.e. a 1% increase in the share of the total population of young people neither in employment nor in education or training (NEET) leads to a 0.03% increase in the share of individuals using the Internet. This could indicate that young NEETs may use the Internet as a means of information, alternative education or entertainment. In the case of the employment rate variable SDG8ROCFM, there is a positive influence on the dependent variable, i.e. a 1% increase in the employment rate leads to a 0.43% increase in the share of Internet usage by individuals. This suggests that a more dynamic labour market and more jobs are associated with higher Internet use, possibly due to job requirements or access to higher income. Regarding the SDG8RRSAR variable representing the at-risk-of-work poverty rate, there is an inverse influence on the dependent variable, i.e. a 1% increase in the at-risk-of-work poverty rate leads to a 0.04% decrease in the share of Internet use by individuals. This may indicate that poverty or low-income limits access to Internet and digital technologies. In the case of the SDG8INTA variable representing the level of household Internet access, there is a positive influence on the dependent variable, i.e. a 1% increase in the level of household Internet access leads to a 0.74% increase in the share of Internet use by individuals. This highlights the significant role of Internet infrastructure and accessibility in promoting digital use among the population.

Figure 9.14 shows the ranking of the importance of the predictors related to the influence on the dependent variable SDG8UTINT.

Figure 9.14 shows that the most significant influences on the dependent variable are the level of household Internet access and the employment rate. An inverse influence on the dependent variable is exerted by the at-risk-of-work poverty rate.

The regression functions were tested on the significance level and residual standard deviation of residuals (RMSE) data are presented in Table 9.2.

It is observed that the standard deviation falls in the range (0.0197–1.0471). Maximization of statistical significance indicates the general model SDG8.1 and models SDG8.3, SDG8.4, SDG8.7, SDG8.8,

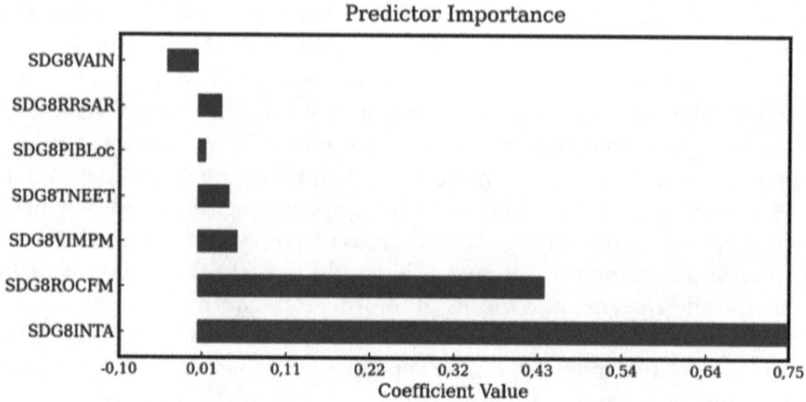


**Fig. 9.14** Importance of predictors related to influence on the variable SDG8UTINT. Source: Developed by the author using Python

**Table 9.2** Validation of economic sustainability models

| *Model* | *Dependent variable* | *Coefficient of determination* | *Residue standard deviation (RMSE)* |
|---|---|---|---|
| SDG8.1 | SDG8PIBloc | 0.8303 | 0.2553 |
| SDG8.2 | SDG8AINT | 0.3638 | 1.0471 |
| SDG8.3 | SDG8INTA | 0.8986 | 0.0510 |
| SDG8.4 | SDG8ROCFM | 0.8120 | 0.0404 |
| SDG8.5 | SDG8RRSAR | 0.4105 | 0.2977 |
| SDG8.6 | SDG8VIMPM | 0.4557 | 0.1977 |
| SDG8.7 | SDG8VASE | 0.9574 | 0.0197 |
| SDG8.8 | SDG8VAIN | 0.9590 | 0.0540 |
| SDG8.9 | SDG8VAAG | 0.6999 | 0.3645 |
| SDG8.10 | SDG8ATIC | 0.7467 | 0.1754 |
| SDG8.11 | SDG8TNEET | 0.7701 | 0.1795 |
| SDG8.12 | SDG8UTINT | 0.9287 | 0.0454 |

Source: Developed by the author using Python

SDG8.10, SDG8.11, SDG8.12 as statistically relevant with a significance greater than 70% and a standard deviation of residuals up to 0.3645 (which confirms that for the prediction right-hand side there are deviations from the normal distribution on the mean). The VIF variance inflation factor analysis was used to test for multicollinearity among the independent variables of the proposed regression models and is presented in Table 9.3.

From Table 9.3 it can be seen that the homogeneity of the proposed models is significant, with the largest deviations from the trend line being recorded for SDG8.2, SDG8.5 and SDG8.6. However, the models have a range of error representation that tends to 0 in almost all cases, being well statistically determined and relevant for the purpose. The multicollinearity of the models has been tested, the inflation factors being below the threshold of multicollinearity representation (VIF < 10) which demonstrates that the evaluated models are appropriate for determining the causal relationships of economic sustainability on composite factors.

To ensure European economic sustainability according to the modelling results, it is recommended to intensify investments in education and training to ensure a skilled and competitive workforce on the European market. We also believe that promoting digital inclusion and the development of high-speed Internet infrastructure will be of the utmost importance to support a sustainable European economy in the era of digitalization. Social factors directly influence economic development which, together

**Table 9.3** Table of homogeneity of sustainable economic development models

| *Model* | *Dependent variable* | *Independent variables* | *P* | *VIF* |
|---|---|---|---|---|
| SDG8.1 | **SDG8PIBloc** 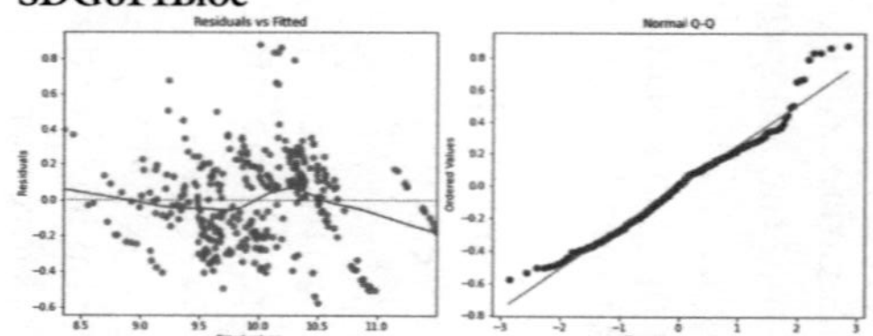 | SDG8VAAG | 6.317e-39 | 1.9724 |
| | | SDG8VIMPM | 1.374e-14 | 1.5459 |
| | | SDG8TNEET | 0.0003722 | 4.0992 |
| | | SDG8ROCFM | 5.707e-09 | 4.5025 |
| | | SDG8UTINT | $3.03 * 10^{-7}$ | 3.9536 |
| | | SDG8ATIC | 7.472e-08 | 3.0403 |
| | | SDG8AINT | 0.1163 | 1.3871 |
| SDG8.2 | **SDG8AINT** 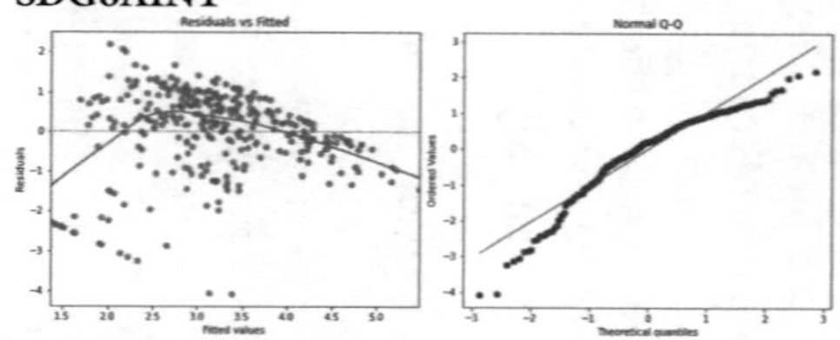 | SDG8VAAG | 0.0007581 | 3.3075 |
| | | SDG8VIMPM | 0.007952 | 1.8158 |
| | | SDG8PIBloc | 0.07079 | 5.5409 |
| | | SDG8TNEET | 0.01397 | 4.2455 |
| | | SDG8ROCFM | 1.109e-05 | 3.8243 |
| | | SDG8RRSAR | 1.332e-11 | 1.4339 |
| | | SDG8ATIC | 4.356e-05 | 3.4805 |
| SDG8.3 | **SDG8INTA** 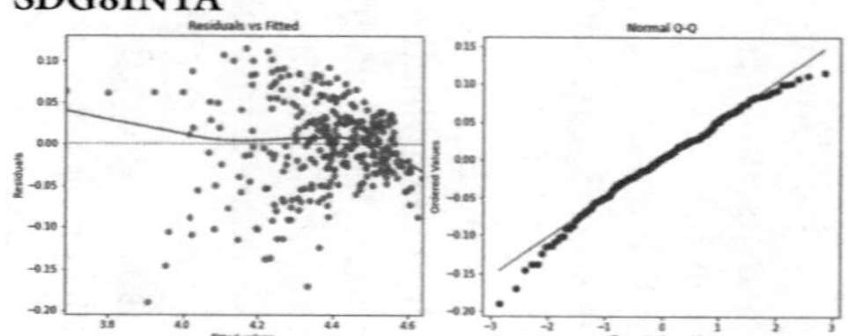 | SDG8VIMPM | 0.05262 | 1.4081 |
| | | SDG8RRSAR | 7.484e-08 | 1.3827 |
| | | SDG8UTINT | 2.755e-99 | 2.7632 |
| | | SDG8ATIC | 0.0002815 | 3.0817 |

| | | | | |
|---|---|---|---|---|
| SDG8.4 | **SDG8ROCFM** 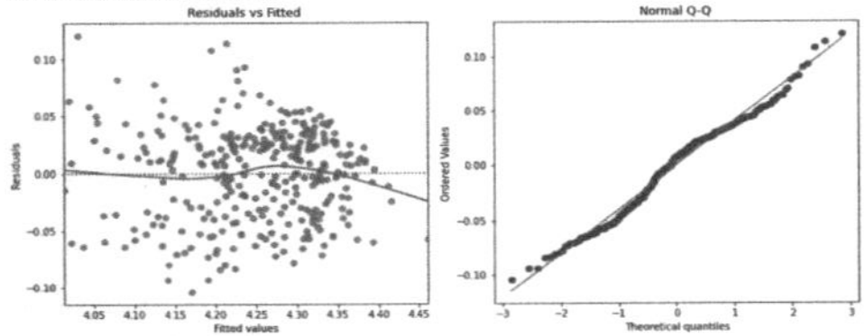  | SDG8VASE<br>SDG8VIMPM<br>SDG8PIBloc<br>SDG8TNEET<br>SDG8RRSAR<br>SDG8UTINT<br>SDG8ATIC<br>SDG8AINT | 5.02e-07<br>0.4093<br>4.816e-09<br>2.082e-40<br>0.7372<br>1.123e-19<br>0.001095<br>0.02442 | 22.8888<br>2.2955<br>3.4961<br>2.5722<br>1.8567<br>3.5718<br>3.8921<br>1.5826 |
| SDG8.5 | **SDG8RRSAR** 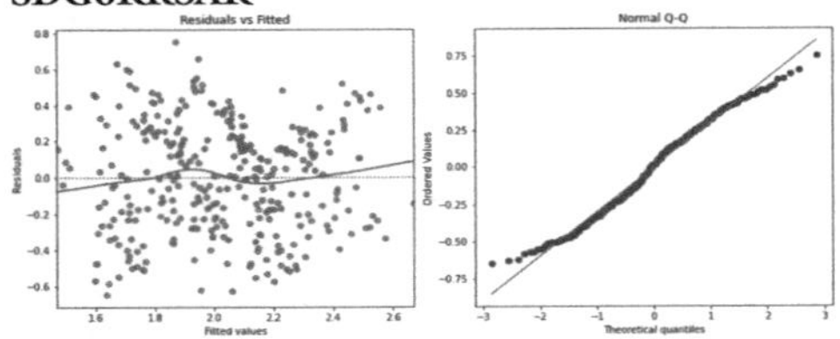  | SDG8VASE<br>SDG8VIMPM<br>SDG8TNEET<br>SDG8ROCFM<br>SDG8INTA<br>SDG8ATIC<br>SDG8AINT | 4.387e-07<br>0.1068<br>0.04161<br>0.04821<br>0.0306<br>5.52e-15<br>3.035e-10 | 23.8528<br>2.1561<br>4.2024<br>5.6271<br>9.3219<br>3.0064<br>1.3395 |
| SDG8.6 | **SDG8VIMPM** 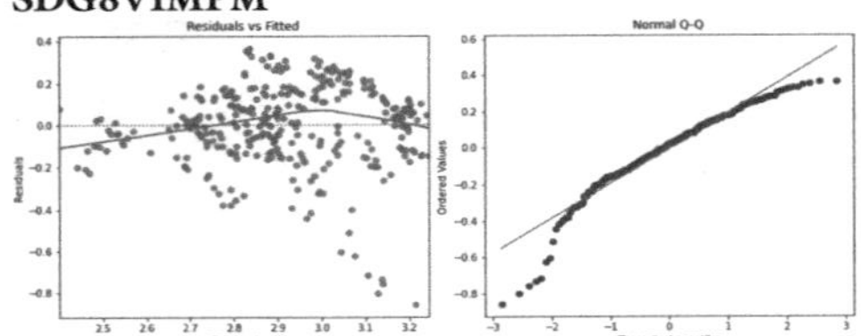  | SDG8VAAG<br>SDG8PIBloc<br>SDG8TNEET<br>SDG8ROCFM<br>SDG8RRSAR<br>SDG8INTA<br>SDG8UTINT<br>SDG8AINT | 4.871e-10<br>6.537e-17<br>0.04563<br>0.9888<br>0.2005<br>0.1158<br>0.01337<br>0.01116 | 3.2685<br>4.7237<br>4.6771<br>5.8054<br>1.6733<br>9.8441<br>13.9846<br>1.5644 |

*(continued)*

**Table 9.3** (continued)

| *Model* | *Dependent variable* | *Independent variables* | *P* | *VIF* |
|---|---|---|---|---|
| SDG8.7 | **SDG8VASE** 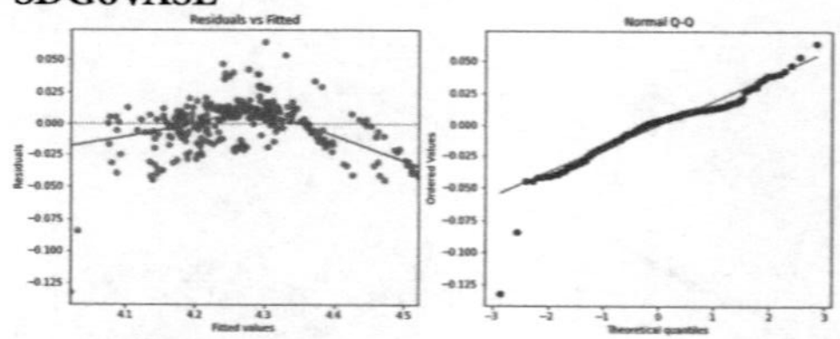 | SDG8VAIN | 6.73e-207 | 1.2676 |
| | | SDG8VIMPM | 1.195e-32 | 1.2582 |
| | | SDG8TNEET | 3.225e-07 | 3.9646 |
| | | SDG8ROCFM | 6.345e-08 | 3.4111 |
| | | SDG8RRSAR | 2.831e-06 | 1.3004 |
| SDG8.8 | **SDG8VAIN** 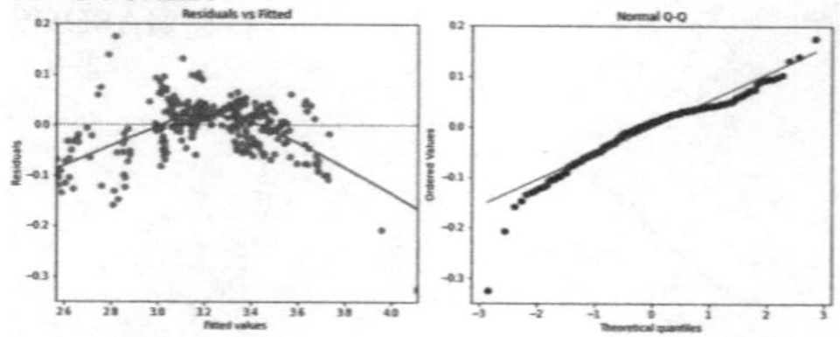 | SDG8VASE | 1.315e-193 | 1.4750 |
| | | SDG8VIMPM | 5.568e-31 | 1.4444 |
| | | SDG8TNEET | 1.31e-11 | 3.7294 |
| | | SDG8ROCFM | 4.251e-11 | 4.5921 |
| | | SDG8RRSAR | 8.521e-09, | 1.3301 |
| | | SDG8UTINT | 0.07509 | 3.5505 |
| SDG8.9 | **SDG8VAAG** 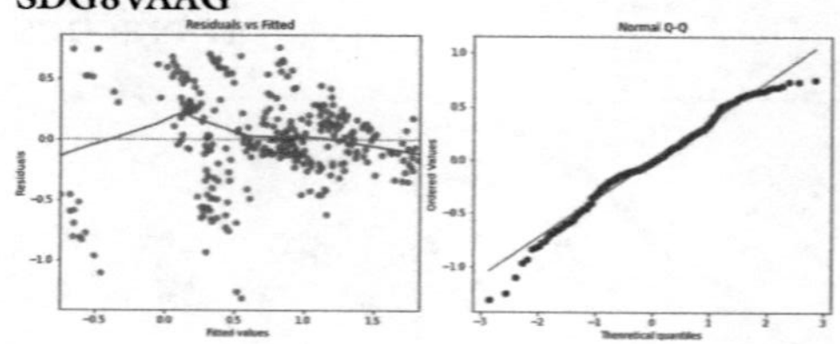 | SDG8VIMPM | 1.43e-10 | 1.6109 |
| | | SDG8PIBloc | 8.344e-53 | 2.1929 |
| | | SDG8TNEET | 1.576e-05 | 1.9503 |
| | | SDG8AINT | 0.001616 | 1.2236 |

| | | | | |
|---|---|---|---|---|
| SDG8.10 | **SDG8ATIC** 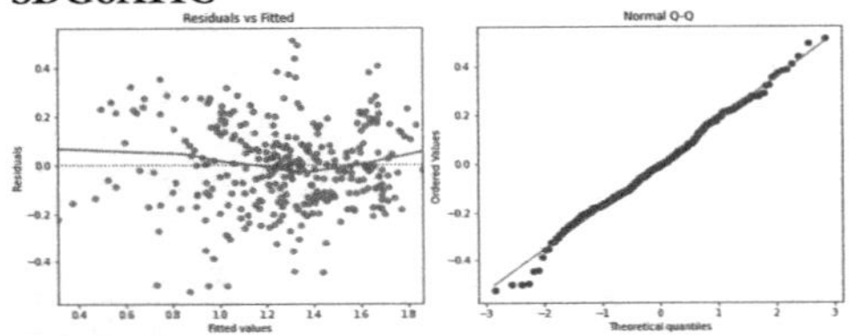  | SDG8PIBloc | 1.498e-20 | 1.9410 |
| | | SDG8ROCFM | 0.001323 | 2.5908 |
| | | SDG8RRSAR | 3.026e-15 | 1.3466 |
| | | SDG8INTA | 4.471e-09 | 2.9434 |
| | | SDG8AINT | 0.001716 | 1.4846 |
| SDG8.11 | **SDG8TNEET** 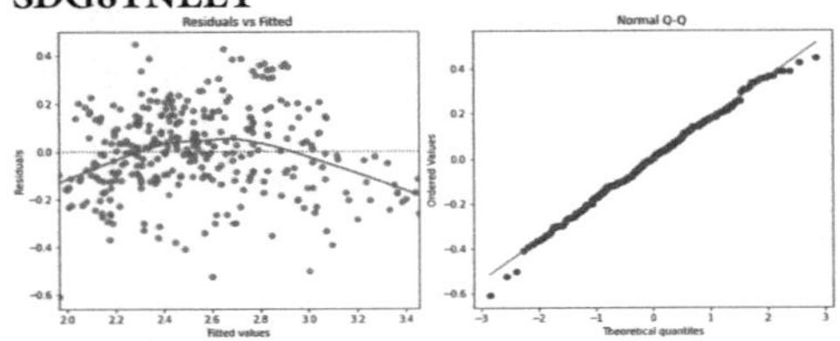  | SDG8VAAG | 0.005988 | 3.4704 |
| | | SDG8VASE | 0.001167 | 22.2356 |
| | | SDG8VIMPM | 0.03157 | 2.4223 |
| | | SDG8PIBloc | 0.001171 | 5.3465 |
| | | SDG8ROCFM | 6.213e-37 | 3.2542 |
| | | SDG8RRSAR | 0.006097 | 1.5582 |
| | | SDG8UTINT | 0.008121 | 4.3076 |
| | | SDG8AINT | 0.008351 | 1.5557 |
| SDG8.12 | **SDG8UTINT** 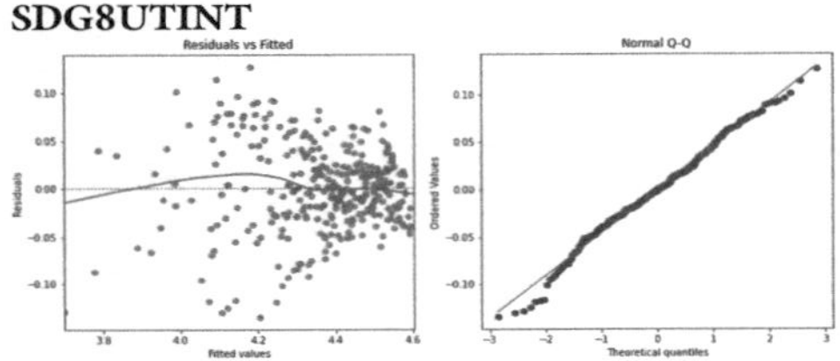  | SDG8VAIN | 4.189e-08 | 1.5343 |
| | | SDG8VIMPM | 6.078e-05 | 1.7133 |
| | | SDG8PIBloc | 0.03258 | 3.0038 |
| | | SDG8TNEET | 0.01166 | 4.4001 |
| | | SDG8ROCFM | 5.151e-13 | 4.6278 |
| | | SDG8RRSAR | 4.925e-10 | 1.3378 |
| | | SDG8INTA | 2.366e-85 | 2.9604 |

Source: Developed by the author using Python

with digitization, have an impact on the resilience of the European economy. European policies must be based on common strategies that promote access to quality digital education and facilitate the transition to a digital economy. In addition, it is important that the private sector is actively involved in these efforts, contributing to the development of innovative solutions and the creation of technology jobs. Digitization can improve the efficiency of business processes, facilitating access to information and services, reducing operational costs and opening new markets. It can also stimulate innovation through the use of emerging technologies such as artificial intelligence, blockchain and the Internet of Things (IoT). Promoting access to quality digital education is important for developing an adaptable workforce ready for the economy of the future. Digital education not only improves individual skills but also contributes to bridging the digital divide between different segments of the population. European policies should aim to coordinate Member States' efforts to ensure a smooth transition to digitization. This includes developing digital infrastructure, supporting start-ups and innovative businesses and establishing a regulatory framework to protect citizens' digital rights. Collaboration between the public and private sectors is essential to accelerate the digital transformation. The private sector can provide expertise, resources and innovative solutions that support European policy objectives while contributing to economic growth and job creation. The resilience of the European economy to external shocks, such as pandemics or financial crises, can be strengthened through digitization. Flexible and adaptable economic systems, underpinned by advanced technologies, are better able to manage disruptions and recover quickly.

The pandemic has disrupted all activities, highlighting the need to understand and rethink the complexities of economic resilience to better cope with future shocks. Authors (Apostu et al., 2022) consider that a key component that can signal the resilience potential of a socio-economic system is the smart response of cities, which use technology to make services more efficient. In this research the authors analysed the relationship between smart cities and urban resilience to determine whether urban resilience is significantly influenced by urban intelligence. The results of the study revealed that, at the European level, smart cities are significantly correlated with urban resilience. The analysis conducted by the authors demonstrated that urban resilience can be explained by variation in urban intelligence and that urban intelligence is correlated with all smart city dimensions, especially in the (post-)pandemic context; thus smart city development strategies play a significant role in increasing urban resilience, emphasizing the importance of integrating advanced technologies and innovation into urban policies to build stronger and more adaptable communities to future challenges.

By adopting an integrated and forward-looking approach, Europe can strengthen its position on the global stage and become a leader in innovation and technology. The European Union must promote public policies to combat the risk of poverty and to further motivate young people for inclusion in employment, as these are the essential keys to a sustainable future economy.

## Conclusions

The conclusions of the chapter highlight that the economic sustainability of the European Union, analysed through the indicators associated with Sustainable Development Goal 8 (SDG8), is the result of a complex balance between economic, social and technological factors, whose interaction determines both the level of performance and the structural vulnerabilities of Member States. Statistically validated econometric models have shown that factors such as digitization, measured by Internet access and usage, high-speed network coverage and the share of ICT specialists, contribute significantly to per capita GDP growth, improve employment and reduce regional disparities, provided that coherent public policies and an enabling fiscal framework are in place.

The results also highlighted that factors such as the NEET rate, the risk of in-work poverty or excessive dependence on low-productivity sectors (in particular traditional agriculture) can slow progress towards SDG8, requiring integrated interventions in education, vocational training and social inclusion. The analysis also showed that investment in human capital and digital infrastructure generates multiplier effects on the economy, but that the benefits are long-term and depend on the capacity of countries to absorb and capitalize on innovation.

Another major finding of the research is that European policies aimed at the green and digital transition must be linked to measures to stimulate the labour market and reduce inequalities in order to avoid creating imbalances between economic growth and social cohesion. The models presented have shown that, despite significant progress in digitization and economic integration, there are marked differences between Member States in terms of sustainable performance, which calls for closer policy coordination and differentiated support tailored to national and regional needs.

In conclusion, European economic sustainability depends on the strategic interconnection of three fundamental pillars: economic competitiveness based on innovation and digitalization, social inclusion through active labour market policies and environmental protection as an integrating element of development. Only through a coherent, multidimensional and empirically sound approach can the European Union strengthen its resilience, reduce identified vulnerabilities and turn SDG8 into a sustainable driver of long-term prosperity.

## References

Abuselidze, G. (2021). Optimality of tax policy on the basis of comparative analysis of income taxation. *European Journal of Sustainable Development, 9*(1), 272–293.

Akif Destek, M., Hossain, M. R., & Khan, Z. (2024). Premature deindustrialization and environmental degradation. *Gondwana Research, 127*, 199–210. https://doi.org/10.1016/j.gr.2023.06.006

Anjarwi, A. W. (2025). Tax burden and poverty in lower-middle-income countries: The moderating role of fiscal freedom. *Development Studies Research, 12*(1), 2466511. https://doi.org/10.1080/21665095.2025.2466511

Annesi, N., Battaglia, M., Ceglia, I., & Mercuri, F. (2024). Navigating paradoxes: Building a sustainable strategy for an integrated ESG corporate governance. *Management Decision, 63*(2), 531–559. https://doi.org/10.1108/MD-10-2023-2006

Apostu, S. A., Vasile, V., Vasile, R., & Rosak-Szyrocka, J. (2022). Do smart cities represent the key to urban resilience? Rethinking urban resilience. *International Journal of Environmental Research and Public Health, 19*(22). https://doi.org/10.3390/ijerph192215410

Atay, S., Müftüoğlu, C. T., Gülmez, N., & Şahin, M. (2025). Society 5.0 and human-centered technology: Redefining talent management in the digital age. *Sustainable Futures, 9*, 100733. https://doi.org/10.1016/j.sftr.2025.100733

Azimi, M. N., Rahman, M. M., & Maraseni, T. (2025). Advancing sustainable development goal 8 targets: The role of institutional quality, economic complexity, and state fragility in G20 nations (2000–2023). *Research in Globalization, 10*, 100278. https://doi.org/10.1016/j.resglo.2025.100278

Azmat, F., Lim, W. M., Moyeen, A., Voola, R., & Gupta, G. (2023). Convergence of business, innovation, and sustainability at the tipping point of the sustainable development goals. *Journal of Business Research, 167*, 114170. https://doi.org/10.1016/j.jbusres.2023.114170

Baffour Gyau, E., Li, Y., & Appiah, M. (2025). Global digital transformation: Discovering the impact of digitalization on income inequality in OECD countries, the moderating role of globalization. *Economic Change and Restructuring, 58*(1), 6. https://doi.org/10.1007/s10644-024-09843-2

Bajja, S., Sackitey, G. M., & Fumey, M. P. (2025). Technological innovation and cleaner energy consumption impact on economic growth and employment in the MENA region. *Environmental and Sustainability Indicators, 27*, 100806. https://doi.org/10.1016/j.indic.2025.100806

Barteková, E., & Börkey, P. (2022). Digitalisation for the transition to a resource efficient and circular economy. 192. https://doi.org/10.1787/6f6d18e7-en

Başol, O., Sevgi, H., & Yalçın, E. C. (2023). The effect of digitalization on youth unemployment for EU countries: Treat or threat? *Sustainability, 15*(14). https://doi.org/10.3390/su151411080

Bezrukova, N., L., H., H., C., L., V., O., K., & Y, K. (2022). Digitalization as a trend of modern development of the world economy. *WSEAS Transactions on Environment and Development, 18*, 120–129. https://doi.org/10.37394/232015.2022.18.13

Bilal, M., Aqib, S., & Raza, A. (2024). Strengthening economic resilience through ICT during the COVID-19 pandemic: Evidence from 100 countries. *Discover Sustainability, 5*(1), 534. https://doi.org/10.1007/s43621-024-00729-x

Bürgel, T. R., Hiebl, M. R. W., & Pielsticker, D. I. (2023). Digitalization and entrepreneurial firms' resilience to pandemic crises: Evidence from COVID-19 and the German Mittelstand. *Technological Forecasting and Social Change, 186*, 122135. https://doi.org/10.1016/j.techfore.2022.122135

Capello, R., Lenzi, C., & Panzera, E. (n.d.). Cities as catalysts of wage inequalities from digitalisation. *Spatial Economic Analysis*, 1–23. https://doi.org/10.1080/17421772.2025.2533478

Caroleo, F. E., Rocca, A., Neagu, G., & Keranova, D. (2021). NEETs and the process of transition from school to the labor market: A comparative analysis of Italy, Romania, and Bulgaria. *Youth & Society, 54*(2_suppl), 109S–129S. https://doi.org/10.1177/0044118X211056360

Casau, M., Ferreira Dias, M., & Leite Mota, G. (2024). Economics, happiness and climate change: Exploring new measures of progress. *Environment, Development and Sustainability*. https://doi.org/10.1007/s10668-024-05702-2

Cattaneo, C., Lemos, M. M. H., Humpert, V., Montlleo, M., Tello, E., & Demaria, F. (2025). Ecological economics into action: Lessons from the Barcelona City doughnut. *Ecological Economics, 236*, 108667. https://doi.org/10.1016/j.ecolecon.2025.108667

Ciucu, A., Vargas, V., Păuna, C., & Jigani, A.-I. (2025). Poverty, education, and decent work rates in central and eastern EU countries. *Standards, 5*(2). https://doi.org/10.3390/standards5020016

Crisp, R., Waite, D., Green, A., Hughes, C., Lupton, R., MacKinnon, D., & Pike, A. (2023). Beyond GDP in cities: Assessing alternative approaches to urban economic development. *Urban Studies, 61*(7), 1209–1229. https://doi.org/10.1177/00420980231187884

de Clercq, M., D'Haese, M., & Buysse, J. (2023). Economic growth and broadband access: The European urban-rural digital divide. *Telecommunications Policy, 47*(6), 102579. https://doi.org/10.1016/j.telpol.2023.102579

Diodato, D., Huergo, E., Moncada-Paternò-Castello, P., Rentocchini, F., & Timmermans, B. (2023). Introduction to the special issue on "the twin (digital and green) transition: handling the economic and social challenges". *Industry and Innovation, 30*(7), 755–765. https://doi.org/10.1080/13662716.2023.2254272

Ernst, E., Merola, R., & Reljic, J. (2025). Fiscal policy instruments for inclusive labor markets: A review. *Journal of Economic Surveys, n/a*(n/a). https://doi.org/10.1111/joes.12685

Eurofound. (2022). *Living and working in Europe 2022.* www.eurofound.europa.eu

Eurofound. (2025). *NEETs.* https://www.eurofound.europa.eu/en/topic/neets

European Central Bank. (2023). *Digitalisation and the economy.* Europa.Eu.

European Commission. (2022a). *Digital economy and society index (DESI) Romania.*

European Commission. (2022b). *The 2030 agenda for sustainable development and the SDGs.* https://ec.europa.eu/environment/sustainable-development/SDGs/index_en.htm

European Commission. (2023a). *A European green deal.* https://commission.europa.eu/strategy-and-policy/priorities-2019-2024/european-green-deal_en

European Commission. (2023b). *Working poverty not only diminishes quality of life, but also affects fiscal sustainability by reducing tax revenues and increasing social spending.*

European Commission. (2024). *Ninth report on economic, social and territorial cohesion.* https://ec.europa.eu/regional_policy/sources/reports/cohesion9/9CR_Report_FINAL.pdf

European Environment Agency. (2024). *Costs of industrial pollution from largest facilities decline in Europe but remain at 2% of EU GDP.*

European Union. (2008). Treaty of Lisbon. *Official Journal of the European Union.* https://eur-lex.europa.eu/legal-content/EN/TXT/?uri=celex%3A12007L%2FTXT

Eurostat. (2024a). *Employment rate.* Europa.Eu.

Eurostat. (2024b). *High-speed internet coverage, by type of area.* https://ec.europa.eu/eurostat/databrowser/view/sdg_17_60/default/table?lang=en&category=sdg.sdg_09

Eurostat. (2024c). *In work at-risk-of-poverty rate*. https://ec.europa.eu/eurostat/databrowser/view/sdg_01_41/default/table?lang=en

Eurostat. (2024d). *Internet use by individuals*. https://ec.europa.eu/eurostat/databrowser/view/tin00028/default/table?lang=en&category=t_isoc.t_isoc_i.t_isoc_iiu

Eurostat. (2024e). *Level of internet access - households*. https://ec.europa.eu/eurostat/databrowser/view/tin00134/default/table?lang=en&category=t_isoc.t_isoc_i.t_isoc_ici

Eurostat. (2024f). *People at risk of poverty or social exclusion in 2023*. https://ec.europa.eu/eurostat/web/products-eurostat-news/w/ddn-20240612-1

Eurostat. (2024g). *Percentage of the ICT personnel on total employment*. Europa.Eu.

Eurostat. (2024h). *Real GDP per capita*. https://ec.europa.eu/eurostat/databrowser/view/sdg_08_10/default/table?lang=en&category=sdg.sdg_08

Eurostat. (2024i). *Temporary and permanent employment - statistics*. https://ec.europa.eu/eurostat/statistics-explained/index.php?title=Temporary_and_permanent_employment_-_statistics

Eurostat. (2024j). *Young people neither in employment nor in education and training by sex*. https://ec.europa.eu/eurostat/databrowser/view/tesem150/default/table?lang=en

Eurostat. (2025a). *EU sustainable development indicators at regional level Print this page*. https://ec.europa.eu/eurostat/statistics-explained/index.php?title=EU_sustainable_development_indicators_at_regional_level

Eurostat. (2025b). *Statistics on young people neither in employment nor in education or training*. https://ec.europa.eu/eurostat/statistics-explained/index.php?title=Statistics_on_young_people_neither_in_employment_nor_in_education_or_training

Fan, Y., & Jackson, A. (2025). The relationship between technological innovation, human capital and civil liberties in advancing economic complexity and sustainable growth. *Frontiers in Environmental Science, 13*, 2025. https://doi.org/10.3389/fenvs.2025.1567322

Gaftea, V.-N., Ioniţă, A., Niţu, I., & Popa, I.-F. (2018). *România şi Piaţa Unică Digitală a Uniunii Europene*. Oportunităţi şi provocări. Institutul European Din România.

Ganda, F., & Ruza, C. (2025). Unveiling the non-linear dynamics: Quantile regression of financial development's impact on environmental degradation in BRICS and G7 nations. *Discover Sustainability, 6*(1), 60. https://doi.org/10.1007/s43621-025-00792-y

Georgescu, I., Nica, I., Delcea, C., Chiriță, N., & Ionescu, Ş. (2024). Assessing regional economic performance in Romania through panel ARDL and panel quantile regression models. *Sustainability, 16*(21). https://doi.org/10.3390/su16219287

Grigorescu, A., Alistar, T. V., & Lincaru, C. (2025). Digital skills, ethics, and integrity—The impact of risky internet use, a multivariate and spatial approach to understanding NEET vulnerability. *Systems, 13*(8). https://doi.org/10.3390/systems13080649

Han, S., Peng, D., Guo, Y., Aslam, M. U., & Xu, R. (2025). Harnessing technological innovation and renewable energy and their impact on environmental pollution in G-20 countries. *Scientific Reports, 15*(1), 2236. https://doi.org/10.1038/s41598-025-85182-0

Heglum, M. A., & Nilsen, W. (2025). A life course perspective on the NEET phenomenon: Long-term exclusion across cohorts, gender, and social origin among young adults in Norway. *Journal of Youth Studies, 28*(5), 807–827. https://doi.org/10.1080/13676261.2024.2305907

Hemerijck, A., Ronchi, S., & Plavgo, I. (2023). Social investment as a conceptual framework for analysing well-being returns and reforms in 21st century welfare states. *Socio-Economic Review, 21*(1), 479–500. https://doi.org/10.1093/ser/mwac035

Hernández de Rojas, F., Pita, P. R., & Pérez Martínez, J. E. (2024). Assessing the European association between digitalization and innovation. *Telecommunications Policy, 48*(7), 102810. https://doi.org/10.1016/j.telpol.2024.102810

Ho, T. L., Ngoc, L. H., & Ho, T. H. (2025). Digital inclusion or exclusion? Exploring the moderating role of governance in digitalization's impact on income inequality in developing countries. *Research in Globalization, 10*, 100283. https://doi.org/10.1016/j.resglo.2025.100283

Holl, A., Rama, R., & Hammond, H. (2024). COVID-19 and business digitalization: Unveiling the effects of concurrent strategies. *Journal of the Knowledge Economy*. https://doi.org/10.1007/s13132-024-02374-1

International Labour Organization. (2024). *Global Employment Trends for Youth 2024*. https://www.ilo.org/topics-and-sectors/youth-employment

International Labour Organization. (2025). *World Employment and Social Outlook: Trends 2025*. https://www.ilo.org/publications/flagship-reports/world-employment-and-social-outlook-trends-2025

Jansen, A., Wang, R., Behrens, P., & Hoekstra, R. (2024). Beyond GDP: A review and conceptual framework for measuring sustainable and inclusive wellbeing. *The Lancet Planetary Health, 8*(9), e695–e705. https://doi.org/10.1016/S2542-5196(24)00147-5

Kalai, M., Becha, H., & Helali, K. (2024). Effect of artificial intelligence on economic growth in European countries: A symmetric and asymmetric cointegration based on linear and non-linear ARDL approach. *Journal of Economic Structures, 13*(1), 22. https://doi.org/10.1186/s40008-024-00345-y

Kang, C., & Youn, M. (2024). Bridging the gender gap in NEET risk: Institutional influences on NEET status in different age groups. *SAGE Open, 14*(4), 21582440241294130. https://doi.org/10.1177/21582440241294126.

Khan, R. Z., Razak, L. A., & Premaratne, G. (2025). Green growth and sustainability: A systematic literature review on theories, measures and future directions. *Cleaner and Responsible Consumption, 17*, 100274. https://doi.org/10.1016/j.clrc.2025.100274

Khromova, S., Villalba Méndez, G., Eckelman, M. J., Herreros-Cantis, P., & Langemeyer, J. (2025). A social-ecological-technological vulnerability approach for assessing urban hydrological risks. *Ecological Indicators, 173*, 113334. https://doi.org/10.1016/j.ecolind.2025.113334

Kirchherr, J., Yang, N.-H. N., Schulze-Spüntrup, F., Heerink, M. J., & Hartley, K. (2023). Conceptualizing the circular economy (revisited): An analysis of 221 definitions. *Resources, Conservation and Recycling, 194*, 107001. https://doi.org/10.1016/j.resconrec.2023.107001

Kolade, O., & Owoseni, A. (2022). Employment 5.0: The work of the future and the future of work. *Technology in Society, 71*, 102086. https://doi.org/10.1016/j.techsoc.2022.102086

Labidi, M. A. (2025). An analysis of the relationship between economic complexity-energy and economic growth: Evidence from method of moment quantile regression. *Energy, 327*, 136412. https://doi.org/10.1016/j.energy.2025.136412

Lafortune, G., & Fuller, G. (2025). *SDG priorities for the new EU leadership*. Dublin University Press. https://s3.amazonaws.com/sustainabledevelopment.report/2025/europe-sustainable-development-report-2025.pdf

Le-Van, C., & Tran-Nam, B. (2023). Comparing the Harrod-Domar, Solow and Ramsey growth models and their implications for economic policies. *Fulbright Review of Economics and Policy, 3*(2), 167–183. https://doi.org/10.1108/FREP-06-2023-0022

Lewandowska, M. S., Kowalski, A. M., Majcherek, D., & Hegerty, S. W. (2024). Regional economic, social, and healthcare disparities among the European Union member states*. In S. Grima, I. Romānova, G. G. Noja, & T. Dorożyński (Eds.), *Economic development and resilience by EU member states* (Vol. 115, p. 0). Emerald Publishing Limited. https://doi.org/10.1108/S1569-375920240000115004

Liu, Y., & Lian, X. (2025). The spatial spillover effect of digital economy on regional tax revenue: An empirical study based on the decay boundary and spillover path. *International Review of Economics & Finance, 102*, 104352. https://doi.org/10.1016/j.iref.2025.104352

Löfving, L., Kamuf, V., Heleniak, T., Weck, S., & Norlén, G. (2022). Can digitalization be a tool to overcome spatial injustice in sparsely populated regions? The cases of digital Västerbotten (Sweden) and smart country side (Germany). *European Planning Studies, 30*(5), 917–934. https://doi.org/10.1080/09654313.2021.1928053

Magoutas, A. I., Chaideftou, M., Skandali, D., & Chountalas, P. T. (2024). Digital progression and economic growth: Analyzing the impact of ICT advancements on the GDP of European Union countries. *Economies, 12*(3). https://doi.org/10.3390/economies12030063

Minniti, A., Prettner, K., & Venturini, F. (2025). AI innovation and the labor share in European regions. *European Economic Review, 177*, 105043. https://doi.org/10.1016/j.euroecorev.2025.105043

Moridian, A., Radulescu, M., Kumar, P., Radu, M. T., & Mohammad, J. (2024). New insights on immigration, fiscal policy and unemployment rate in EU countries—A quantile regression approach. *Heliyon, 10*(13), e33519. https://doi.org/10.1016/j.heliyon.2024.e33519

Muñoz-Higueras, D., Köppe, S., Granell, R., & Fuenmayor, A. (2024). Non-take-up of in-work benefits: Determinants, benefit erosion and indexing. *Journal for Labour Market Research, 58*(1), 22. https://doi.org/10.1186/s12651-024-00385-8

Neligan, A., Baumgartner, R. J., Geissdoerfer, M., & Schöggl, J.-P. (2023). Circular disruption: Digitalisation as a driver of circular economy business models. *Business Strategy and the Environment, 32*(3), 1175–1188. https://doi.org/10.1002/bse.3100

Nieddu, M., Bertani, F., & Ponta, L. (2022). The sustainability transition and the digital transformation: Two challenges for agent-based macroeconomic models. *Review of Evolutionary Political Economy, 3*(1), 193–226. https://doi.org/10.1007/s43253-021-00060-5

Noubissi Domguia, E. (2023). Taxing for a better life? The impact of environmental taxes on income distribution and inclusive education. *Heliyon, 9*(11). https://doi.org/10.1016/j.heliyon.2023.e21443

OECD. (2024a). *Digital economy outlook 2024* (Vol. 1). Embracing the Technology Frontier. https://doi.org/10.1787/a1689dc5-en

OECD. (2024b). *Green growth indicators.* OECD.Stat.

OECD. (2025). *Opportunities for all: A framework for policy action on inclusive growth.* https://doi.org/10.1787/9789264301665-en.

Palmié, M., Aebersold, A., Oghazi, P., Pashkevich, N., & Gassmann, O. (2025). Digital-sustainable business models: Definition, systematic literature review, integrative framework and research agenda from a strategic management perspective. *International Journal of Management Reviews, 27*(3), 346–374. https://doi.org/10.1111/ijmr.12380

Papadakis, N., Drakaki, M., Saridaki, S., Amanaki, E., & Dimari, G. (2022). Educational capital/ level and its association with precarious work and social vulnerability among youth, in EU and Greece. *International Journal of Educational Research, 112*, 101921. https://doi.org/10.1016/j.ijer.2021.101921

Qamruzzaman, M., & Karim, S. (2024). Green energy, green innovation, and political stability led to green growth in OECD nations. *Energy Strategy Reviews, 55*, 101519. https://doi.org/10.1016/j.esr.2024.101519

Rahmani, H., & Groot, W. (2023). Risk factors of being a youth not in education, employment or training (NEET): A scoping review. *International Journal of Educational Research, 120*, 102198. https://doi.org/10.1016/j.ijer.2023.102198

Raman, R., Ray, S., Das, D., & Nedungadi, P. (2025). Innovations and barriers in sustainable and green finance for advancing sustainable development goals. *Frontiers in Environmental Science, 12*, 2024. https://doi.org/10.3389/fenvs.2024.1513204

Rocca, A., Neagu, G., & Tosun, J. (2021). School-work-transition of NEETS: A comparative analysis of European countries. *Youth & Society, 54*(2_suppl), 130S–152S. https://doi.org/10.1177/0044118X211051761

Rosário, A. T., & Dias, J. C. (2023). The new digital economy and sustainability: Challenges and opportunities. *Sustainability, 15*(14). https://doi.org/10.3390/su151410902

Schmid, G., Bellmann, L., Gazier, B., & Leschke, J. (2023). *Governing sustainable school to work transitions: Lessons for the EU* (Issue 197). Institute of Labor Economics (IZA). https://hdl.handle.net/10419/278330

Schöggl, J.-P., Rusch, M., Stumpf, L., & Baumgartner, R. J. (2023). Implementation of digital technologies for a circular economy and sustainability management in the manufacturing sector. *Sustainable Production and Consumption, 35*, 401–420. https://doi.org/10.1016/j.spc.2022.11.012

Serrano-Bosquet, F. J., Carreño Correa, L. M., & Giorgi, E. (2023). Review: Technological resources for vulnerable communities. *Technology in Society, 75*, 102354. https://doi.org/10.1016/j.techsoc.2023.102354

Sharifi, A., Allam, Z., Bibri, S. E., & Khavarian-Garmsir, A. R. (2024). Smart cities and sustainable development goals (SDGs): A systematic literature review of co-benefits and trade-offs. *Cities, 146*, 104659. https://doi.org/10.1016/j.cities.2023.104659

Soliman, P. E. N., & Beram, R. S. (2025). Sustainable development goals and unemployment: Worldwide evidence. *Journal of the Knowledge Economy*. https://doi.org/10.1007/s13132-025-02782-x

Stanojević, A. (2025). Algorithmic governance and social vulnerability: A value analysis of equality and trust. In J. Goossens, E. Keymolen, & A. Stanojević (Eds.), *Public governance and emerging technologies: Values, trust, and regulatory compliance* (pp. 335–354). Springer Nature. https://doi.org/10.1007/978-3-031-84748-6_15

Suhrab, M., Chen, P., & Ullah, A. (2024). Digital financial inclusion and income inequality nexus: Can technology innovation and infrastructure development help in achieving sustainable development goals? *Technology in Society, 76*, 102411. https://doi.org/10.1016/j.techsoc.2023.102411

Tao, M., San Pedro, M. J. P., Roubaud, D., & Tiwari, A. K. (2025). From digital clusters to urban environmental sustainability: New mechanisms and spillover effects. *Sustainable Development, n/a*(n/a). https://doi.org/10.1002/sd.3523

Tleppayev, A., & Zeinolla, S. (2025). Forecasting youth unemployment through educational and demographic indicators: A panel time-series approach. *Forecasting, 7*(3). https://doi.org/10.3390/forecast7030037

United Nations. (1987). *Report of the world commission on environment and development - our common future*. https://gat04-live-1517c8a4486c41609369c68f30c8-aa81074.divio-media.org/filer_public/6f/85/6f854236-56ab-4b42-810f-606d215c0499/cd_9127_extract_from_our_common_future_brundtland_report_1987_foreword_chpt_2.pdf

Wang, Z., Peng, D., Kong, Q., & Tan, F. (2025). Digital infrastructure and economic growth: Evidence from corporate investment efficiency. *International Review of Economics & Finance, 98*, 103854. https://doi.org/10.1016/j.iref.2025.103854

Xiong, B., & Yu, B. (2024). The impact of internet development on youth's job quality in the digital economy era: Transmission mechanism and empirical test. *Social Indicators Research, 175*(1), 269–294. https://doi.org/10.1007/s11205-024-03439-z

Zhang, H., Zhang, K., Yan, T., & Cao, X. (2025). The impact of digital infrastructure on regional green innovation efficiency through industrial agglomeration and diversification. *Humanities and Social Sciences Communications, 12*(1), 220. https://doi.org/10.1057/s41599-025-04512-9

Zlati, M. L., Florea, A. M., Antohi, V. M., Dinca, M. S., Bercu, F., Fortea, C., & Silvius, S. (2023). Financing Romanian agricultural cooperatives' investments for the 2023–2027 horizon. *Sustainability (Switzerland), 15*(3), 1–28. https://doi.org/10.3390/su15032306

CHAPTER 10

# Modelling the Impact of Economic Sustainability by Quantifying the Evolution of Economic Growth and Decent Work Factors

## Introduction

In the context of the multiple challenges generated by the transition to a green and digital economy, the intensification of globalization, and the cumulative impact of recent economic and health crises, analysing the interactions between economic development, innovation and sustainability has become a priority for both academia and policymakers. Within this framework, this chapter aims to investigate, through a rigorous econometric approach, the determinants of sustainable economic performance in the EU, with a focus on identifying the mechanisms through which investments in human capital, digital infrastructure, and innovation can contribute to increasing competitiveness and reducing regional disparities.

The analysis is based on a set of relevant indicators selected on the basis of the conceptual framework of the Sustainable Development Goals (SDGs) and European strategies for smart, sustainable and inclusive growth. To this end, the proposed methodology integrates advanced econometric techniques capable of capturing causal relationships and indirect effects between variables, providing a comprehensive overview of European economic dynamics. The analysis covers a period marked by the implementation of major public policies—from the Europe 2020 Strategy to the European Green Deal—but also by disruptive events such as the post-2008 financial crisis and the COVID-19 pandemic, which allows for



C. Fortea, *Sustainable Economic Development and the European Green Deal*, https://doi.org/10.1007/978-3-032-10326-0_10

an assessment of the resilience and adaptability of European economies in the face of structural changes.

By correlating the results obtained with the strategic priorities of the EU, the chapter aims not only to validate the hypotheses formulated, but also to formulate empirically based public policy recommendations to support the transition to a sustainable, competitive and inclusive economic growth model. This contribution is part of a broader effort to integrate empirical analysis and theoretical foundations into a coherent scientific approach that is relevant both for the specialized literature and for the decision-making process.

## Study of Literature and Hypotheses

In recent years the EU has experienced significant changes in the economy driven by globalization, digitalization, technological advances and domestic socio-political pressures. In this context, supporting sustainable economic growth has become a central priority for European policy. The Autoregressive Distributed Lag (ARDL) model applied in a panel data framework, such as the Pooled Mean Group (PMG) methodology, provides a robust tool for analysing the long- and short-term impact of different economic variables on the economic sustainability indicator. This methodology allows not only to identify dynamic relationships between variables, but also to adjust for the individual particularities of each Member State, while respecting the heterogeneity and interdependencies exhibited within the EU. The use of this model in assessing the impact of growth and decent work factors (Internet access, employment rate and risk of in-work poverty) on the GDP per capita deflator provides strategic guidance for policymakers to improve sustainable economic growth. By integrating these variables into the panel data analysis, we gain a deeper understanding of the factors that contribute to Europe's economic sustainability while identifying priority areas for intervention and development. At the same time, the model provides a solid basis for designing policies to promote equitable and sustainable growth across the EU. Thus, adopting a panel data-driven approach will play a significant role in shaping Europe's economic future, guiding the EU towards the goals of sustainable development and economic cohesion.

In today's digital age, access to the Internet has become a fundamental pillar of modern society, significantly influencing a wide range of socio-economic issues. From the way we interact and work to the way we consume information and run our businesses, the Internet is ubiquitous in our daily lives. This pervasiveness of the Internet has brought radical changes in the way the economy and society as a whole work. Widespread household Internet access has become a catalyst for economic and social progress. It facilitates not only connectivity and communication, but also democratization of access to information, education and business opportunities. Through the Internet, all people can access the same resources and knowledge, opening up new horizons of development and growth for everyone. Research has shown that Internet access can stimulate economic growth by facilitating communication (Cheng et al., 2021; Herman & Oliver, 2023) and access to information (Behera et al., 2024; Hussain et al., 2023) and creating business opportunities (Tan & Li, 2022; Brodny & Tutak, 2022). For example, the development of online platforms and e-commerce has opened up new avenues of interaction between consumers and producers, completely reshaping the way business is conducted (Ballerini et al., 2024; Ballerini et al., 2023). This has driven innovation and accelerated growth in the private sector (Battisti et al., 2022).

Digital inclusion and access to opportunities are two issues of concern that are closely linked to the availability and use of the Internet. Digital inclusion refers to equitable access to and participation in the digital world, including both access to the Internet and the digital skills needed to use technology effectively and productively. These issues are often associated with the economic and personal development opportunities offered by the Internet. Internet availability is a key factor for digital inclusion. Studies in the literature highlight that lack of Internet access can limit people's access to information, education, services and business opportunities (Anrijs et al., 2023). Especially in marginalized communities or rural areas, the lack of Internet infrastructure can create significant digital and social divides (Laskar, 2023).

In addition to Internet access, other research emphasizes the importance of digital competences for digital inclusion (Pérez-Escolar & Canet, 2023). These include skills such as navigating the Internet, using online tools and platforms, managing information and protecting personal data. Lack of these skills can create barriers to effective and productive use of the Internet, thus limiting the benefits associated with it.

Internet access and digital skills can open up new economic and personal development opportunities for individuals and communities. Through the Internet, people can access educational resources, search for jobs, participate in online training, and develop the skills needed to improve their economic situation and quality of life. The literature shows that digital inclusion can help reduce socio-economic gaps and increase social inclusion overall (Pérez-Escolar & Canet, 2023).

Internet use can improve efficiency and productivity in different economic sectors. Online communication, remote collaboration and access to digital resources can reduce operational costs and improve work processes in companies and institutions, thus boosting economic development and competitiveness (Adomako & Nguyen, 2023). Internet access can also stimulate innovation and entrepreneurship by facilitating the exchange of ideas, collaboration and access to finance (Felicetti et al., 2024). Online platforms provide a conducive environment for the development and launch of new products and services, thereby supporting economic growth and private sector diversification.

In the current context of the digital society, given that widespread household access to the Internet is not only an opportunity but also a determining factor for sustainable economic development, we can formulate the following hypothesis:

H1: Digitization induced by widespread household access to the Internet has a statistically significant effect on sustainable economic development.

This underlines the importance of policies and initiatives that promote digital connectivity and universal Internet access to support long-term economic and social development.

In the current economic context, questions of sustainability are becoming increasingly important, reflecting a growing awareness of the need to balance development with environmental protection. Discussions focus on how employment growth can be aligned with economic sustainability objectives so that progress is not achieved at the expense of natural resources or environmental quality. This includes exploring ways in which new jobs can be created in sectors that promote green practices, such as renewable energy, recycling or green building.

Economic studies show that higher employment rates can boost productivity and economic growth (Maestas et al., 2023; Saba & Ngepah, 2022). A larger and better skilled workforce can generate more resources and innovation, thus fuelling the economic growth cycle (Hojnik et al., 2023; Kaplinsky & Kraemer-Mbula, 2022).

Higher employment can help reduce poverty and social inequality. By providing employment opportunities, it can ensure incomes and access to resources for a wider range of people, thereby strengthening social cohesion and economic stability (Zintl & Loewe, 2022; Ghouse et al., 2022). An active and engaged workforce can improve the quality of life and overall well-being of the population (Kosec et al., 2022). Engagement in paid work can bring financial, social and psychological benefits, contributing to personal satisfaction and fulfilment.

An economy with a stable and prosperous workforce can be more resilient to economic shocks and better equipped to face future challenges. High employment can provide a solid foundation for long-term growth and development, thus ensuring economic sustainability (Udeagha & Muchapondwa, 2023).

From the perspective of these aspects and the links identified in the literature we can formulate the following hypothesis:

H2: There is a significant direct link between employment growth and economic sustainability.

Promoting employment growth could play a key role in ensuring sustainable economic development and improving the overall well-being of society.

In the modern world, the risk of in-work poverty is increasingly relevant, with profound implications for economic and social development. This problem highlights the situation in which employed people do not earn enough to rise above the poverty line, leading to a low quality of life. The phenomenon of in-work poverty highlights the deficiencies in the labour market and social protection systems which fail to guarantee a decent living for all citizens. In conditions of uncertainty, social protection issues are of paramount importance, requiring support measures for the vulnerable population, which have an impact on social costs. These costs have to be included in the state budget and generate budgetary imbalances that need to be counterbalanced by relevant fiscal policy measures. In the study by Antohi and the collective of authors (Antohi et al., 2023) it was proposed to develop a social security index, based on state budgets and demographic indicators, whose dynamics will reflect the impact of the necessary measures in a period of economic and financial uncertainty. The key indicators used to calculate the social security index were the composite financial risk, quantified by dynamic budget expenditures, the composite labour force risk, using the employment stock and unemployment, and the composite social risk, using the balance between the active and retired labour force. The study analysed the evolution of this index to identify inflection points impacting social security policy. The results of the study identified the financial risk diagram, which, based on the predicted clusters of financial, social and labour market risks, created a useful picture for social policymakers, highlighting the current vulnerabilities of the three clusters from a social perspective. Finally, the presentation of the social security index is a valuable outcome for practitioners in their efforts to optimize social policies and increase socio-economic well-being. The results of this research will allow policymakers to adjust social policies on an informed basis in relation to elements of vulnerability in periods of uncertainty, compared to elements of stability identified in periods of economic growth.

The growth of in-work poverty is often associated with growing inequality, insecure employment contracts and inadequate pay, especially in labour-intensive but low-paid sectors. This puts pressure on social and economic structures, accentuating the need for effective policy interventions to support wage growth, ensure decent working conditions and promote a fair distribution of income.

Measures such as setting a living minimum wage, strengthening collective bargaining and ensuring fair working conditions are key to tackling in-work poverty. There is also a need to invest in education and training to upgrade workers' skills, giving them more opportunities in growing sectors of the economy. These strategies not only help to reduce poverty but also contribute to the long-term sustainability of economic growth and social cohesion.

A number of studies in the field have shown that reducing the risk of in-work poverty can encourage workers' long-term commitment and boost productivity growth (Kose et al., 2024; Hodgetts et al., 2022). Workers who do not face the threat of poverty are more likely to focus their efforts on professional development and contributing to economic growth.

A reduction in the risk of in-work poverty can help reduce social and economic inequalities. Access to secure, adequately paid jobs with development prospects can balance income disparities and enhance social cohesion in a society (Goniewicz et al., 2023; European Commission Proposal, 2022). Workers at risk of in-work poverty are more susceptible to economic instability and insecurity. Reducing this risk can therefore help to strengthen economic stability and increase resilience to economic shocks and challenges. A stable and engaged workforce can serve as a sound basis for investing in human capital and promoting innovation (Zhang & Li, 2023). Reducing the risk of in-work poverty can encourage lifelong learning and training, contributing to skills upgrading and the adoption of advanced technologies (Perkins et al., 2022).

A review of the literature reveals a number of issues and links that suggest the following hypothesis:

H3: Reducing the risk of in-work poverty contributes significantly to long-term economic sustainability.

This hypothesis can be supported by research that highlights the positive impact of reducing the risk of in-work poverty on various aspects of the economy and society. By implementing policies and measures aimed at reducing the risk of in-work poverty, several economic and social benefits can be realized. These policies could contribute to increasing productivity and long-term engagement of workers, reducing social and economic inequalities, strengthening economic stability, and promoting investment in human capital and innovation.

It is therefore proposed that strategies and public policies should be geared towards reducing the risk of in-work poverty in order to promote sustainable and inclusive economic development. These efforts could increase the resilience of the economy and contribute to improving social welfare in a way that is sustainable in the long term.

## Data and Method

The following indicators have been used to develop the econometric model: gross domestic product per capita (SDG8GDPloc), risk of in-work poverty (SDG8RRSAR), employment rate (SDG8ROCFM) and household Internet access (SDG8INTA).

These indicators have been assessed on the basis of descriptive statistics for the period 2010–2021 considering the national developments of each indicator for all EU Member States, the database being organized in a panel data format as presented in Table 9.1. The results of the descriptive analysis are presented in Table 10.1.

The descriptive statistics table shows that the average poverty rate at the European level was 8.12% during the analysed period, assimilated to the median range of evolution of frequencies between the minimum of 2.7% (in 2017 in Finland) and the maximum of 19.8% recorded in 2014 in

**Table 10.1** Descriptive statistics

| *Variable* | *SDG8RRSAR* | *SDG8ROCFM* | *SDG8INTA* | *SDG8PIBloc* |
|---|---|---|---|---|
| Comments | 324 | 324 | 324 | 324 |
| Average | 8.12 | 70.49 | 80.44 | 25,625.12 |
| Standard deviation | 3.2 | 6.48 | 12.12 | 16,493.33 |
| Minim | 2.7 | 52.5 | 41.16 | 5080 |
| Maxim | 19.8 | 81.8 | 99.18 | 84,840 |

Source: Author

Romania. The standard deviation is small (3.2%), confirming a semi-homogeneity in the frequency distributions of the risk of poverty at the level of Member States. The employment rate is at the European average of 70.49% of the total population, with a small standard deviation of 6.48%, which confirms homogeneity in the implementation of social policies for decent work in Europe. The mean value follows the Gaussian distribution between the minimum value of 52.5% in 2013 in Greece and the maximum value of 81.8% in 2018 in Sweden. As for the level of household Internet access it averages 80.44% of all European households, with a standard deviation of 12.12%. In this case there is an accumulation of frequencies to the right, the average value being much closer to the historical maximum of 99.18% (in 2021 in Luxembourg) than to the minimum recorded in 2010 in Bulgaria of 41.16%, which demonstrates that digitization is a quasi-generalized orientation of European citizens, making sustainable development inconsistent in its absence. In terms of GDP per capita there is a leftward deviation of the average (25625.12 euro per capita) from the Gaussian frequency curve with a minimum point of 5080 in 2010 in Bulgaria and a maximum of 84840 in Luxembourg in 2016. The level of disparity of frequencies is significant at 16493.33 euro per capita and testifies to the differences in the economic development of the Member States, which constitutes a limit to the economic sustainability of the EU.

Variable testing was carried out as a preliminary step in the conceptualization of the model, the first tests being the autocorrelation tests presented in Table 10.2.

According to the results in Table 4.11, there is a lack of autocorrelation, the values of the coefficients being lower than the autocorrelation threshold of 0.7, which allows modelling the data.

**Table 10.2** Correlation matrix

| *Variable* | *SDG8RRSAR* | *SDG8ROCFM* | *SDG8INTA* | *SDG8PIBloc* |
|---|---|---|---|---|
| SDG8RRSAR | 1.000 | | | |
| SDG8ROCFM | −0.4652 | 1.000 | | |
| SDG8INTA | −0.3300 | 0.6966 | 1.000 | |
| SDG8PIBloc | −0.3022 | 0.4028 | 0.6544 | 1.000 |

Source: Author

The Levin-Lin-Chin, Breitung, Im-Pesaran-Shin, ADF-Fisher Chi-square, PP-Fisher Chi-square and Hadri stationarity tests were applied. The results are presented centralized in Table 10.3.

Five different two-order (Order 0 and Order 1) stationarity tests were applied for four data series (SDG8PIBloc, SDG8RRSAR, SDG8ROCFM, SDG8INTA). The tests aim to determine the stationarity of the data by rejecting the null hypothesis. The value of the test statistic and the associated p-value confirm the stationarity of the variables of order 0 or 1.

The stationarity of a time series is an important property in time analysis, indicating that the statistical properties of the series (mean and variance) do not change over time.

The Levin Lin-Chin test is used to check for stationarity in panel data. Large negative values of the test statistics (such as −3.437 for SDG8PIBloc at order 0) and small p-values (0.000) suggest rejection of the null hypothesis of non-stationarity, indicating that the series is stationary. The Breitung test results are observed with some large positive statistics (such as 3.003 for SDG8ROCFM at order 0), suggesting non-stationarity (p-value 0.999) and some large negative ones (−4.192 for SDG8PIBloc at order 1) indicating stationarity (p-value 0.000). The Im-Pesaran-Shin test shows that the series is stationary, i.e. −5.461 for SDG8RRSAR at order 1 with p-value 0.000. The ADF-Fisher Chi-square and PP-Fisher Chi-square suggest stationarity and high chi-square score values with p-value close to zero (282.910 for SDG8INTA at order 1).

The results of the Hadri test, respectively 29.352 with p-value 0.000, for SDG8PIBloc at order 0 indicate non-stationarity.

In conclusion, the SDG8PIBloc, SDG8RPCFM and SDG8INTA series are first-order integrated, while the SDG8RRSAR series is 0-order integrated. For this reason, we use an ARDL model.

**Table 10.3** Stationarity tests

| *The stationarity test* | *SDG8PIBloc* | | *SDG8RRSAR* | | *SDG8ROCFM* | | *SDG8INTA* | |
|---|---|---|---|---|---|---|---|---|
| | *Order 0* | *Order 1* | *Order 0* | *Order 1* | *Order 0* | *Order 1* | *Order 0* | *Order 1* |
| Levin-Lin-Chin | −3.437 | NA | −1.807 | NA | −2.020 | NA | −5.407 | NA |
| | (0.000) | | (0.035) | | (0.022) | | (0.000) | |
| Breitung | 0.136 | −4.192 | −1.247 | −2.393 | 1.050 | −2.912 | 3.003 | −2.350 |
| | (0.554) | (0.000) | (0.106) | (0.008) | (0.853) | (0.002) | (0.999) | (0.009) |
| Im-Pesaran-Shin | 0.735 | −1.343 | −0.033 | −5.461 | 3.639 | −2.012 | 1.676 | −4.927 |
| | (0.769) | (0.090) | (0.487) | (0.000) | (0.999) | (0.022) | (0.953) | (0.000) |
| ADF-Fisher | 45.016 | 118.477 | 118.334 | NA | 38.021 | 140.645 | 42.473 | 282.910 |
| Chi-square | (0.803) | (0.000) | (0.000) | | (0.951) | (0.000) | (0.872) | (0.000) |
| PP-Fisher | 45.016 | 118.477 | 118.334 | NA | 38.021 | 140.645 | 42.473 | 282.910 |
| Chi-square | (0.803) | (0.000) | (0.000) | | (0.951) | (0.000) | (0.872) | (0.000) |
| Hadri | 29.352 | 1.634 | 13.830 | −1.779 | 28.725 | 6.430 | 31.808 | 0.144 |
| | (0.000) | (0.051) | (0.000) | (0.962) | (0.000) | (0.000) | (0.000) | (0.443) |

Source: Author

The data were checked for co-integration using the Pedroni co-integration test shown in Table 10.4.

By analysing Table 10.4 we can say that we reject the null hypothesis and accept the alternative hypothesis, i.e. the series are co-integrated.

To determine the type of model (PMG, Pooled Mean Group, or MG, Mean Group) the Hausman test was applied, where the null hypothesis means that the model is MG and the alternative hypothesis PMG model (see Table 10.5).

After applying the Hausman test, it was concluded that the null hypothesis is rejected, and the alternative hypothesis is accepted, and the PMG model will be used. The Pooled Mean Group (PMG) model, developed by Pesaran, Shin and Smith, is an extension of the MG model. This model is used when it is assumed that there is a common long-run relationship between variables in different cross-sections, but short-run behaviour may vary. PMG is efficient for long-run estimates while retaining the flexibility to model group-specific dynamics in the short run. The PMG model is often preferred in situations where there is reason to believe that long-run relationships are stable across groups, but short-run adjustments may differ.

**Table 10.4** Pedroni residual cointegration test

Series: SDG8LPIBLOC, SDG8INTA, SDG8ROCFM, SDG8RRSAR
Sample: 2010–2021
Remarks included: 324
Cross-sections included: 27
Null hypothesis: No cointegration
The trend hypothesis: No deterministic trend
User-specified lag length: 1
Automatic Newey-West and Bartlett Kernel bandwidth selection
Alternative hypothesis: common AR coefficients (within dimension)

| | Statistic | Prob. | Statistics Considered | Prob. |
|---|---|---|---|---|
| Panel v-Statistic | 1.100986 | 0.1355 | 0.885587 | 0.1879 |
| rho-Statistic Panel | 2.983617 | 0.9986 | 2.562638 | 0.9948 |
| Panel PP-Statistic | 1.571637 | 0.9420 | 0.168823 | 0.5670 |
| Panel ADF-Statistic | −0.965024 | 0.1673 | −0.679755 | 0.2483 |

Alternative hypothesis: individual AR coefficients. (between dimensions)

| | Statistic | Prob. |
|---|---|---|
| Group rho-Statistic | 5.218430 | 1.0000 |
| Group PP-Statistic | 0.414367 | 0.6607 |
| Group ADF-Statistic | −0.273609 | 0.3922 |

Source: Author

**Table 10.5** Hausman test

| *Variable* | *Coefficients* | | *Difference* | *Standard error* |
|---|---|---|---|---|
| | *(b)* *Mg* | *(B)* *pmg* | *(b-B)* | |
| SDG8RRSAR | 0.7729646 | −0.0358541 | 0.8,088,187 | 2.922,923 |
| SDG8ROCFM | 0.417,067 | −0.0282283 | 0.3,888,387 | 1.51,399 |
| SDG8INTA | −0.281,673 | −0.0040456 | −0.2,776,297 | 1.056867 |

b = consistent under null and alternative hypothesis; obtained from xtpmg
B = inconsistent under alternative hypothesis, efficient under null hypothesis; obtained from xtpmg
Test: Null hypothesis: The difference in coefficients is not systematic
$Chi^2$ (2) = 1.45, Prob>$chi^2$ = 0.6936

Source: Author

The ARDL model equation is as follows:

$$y_{i,t} = \sum_{i=1}^{p} \delta_i y_{i,t-j} + \sum_{j=0}^{q} \beta_{ij} x_{i,t-j} + \varphi_i + e_{i,t} \quad (10.1)$$

where:

$y_{i,\,t}$ is the dependent variable, gross domestic product per capita (SDG8GDP per capita);
$x_{i,\,t}$ are the integrated I(0) or I(1) or cointegrated independent variables, (risk of in-work poverty (SDG8RRSAR), employment rate (SDG8ROCFM) and household Internet access (SDG8INTA));
$\delta_i$ are the coefficients of the lagged dependent variables;
$\beta_{ij}$ are the coefficients of the independent variables;
$\varphi_i$ is the unit specific to fixed bills;
p,q are the optional delay values;
$e_{i,\,t}$ is the error.

This econometric specification provides a robust framework for estimating causal relationships between variables, allowing both the identification of direct and indirect effects and the testing of research hypotheses in a rigorous and reproducible manner, in line with good methodological practices in the literature.

## Results and Discussions

Econometric model evaluation tests were applied, and the results are presented in Table 10.6.

The dataset was analysed by the Autoregressive Distributed Lag (ARDL) model using the Pooled Mean Group (PMG) method and a selection based on Akaike information criterion (AIC) which provides a detailed analysis of the influence of the independent variables, viz. employment rate (SDG8ROCFM), household Internet access level (SDG8INTA) and risk of in-work poverty (SDG8RRSAR), on gross domestic product per capita (SDG8LPIBloc), for a sample of 27 EU Member States over the period 2010–2021.

In the long run the variable SDG8ROCFM has a negative impact, while the other two variables have a positive impact on the dependent variable. All three independent variables are statistically significant.

The household Internet access level indicator (SDG8INTA) has a coefficient of 0.092555, indicating that an increase in Internet access has a significant positive impact on GDP per capita, with a t-statistic value of 14.55689 and a probability of almost zero, suggesting a statistically significant influence. This demonstrates working hypothesis 1: Digitization induced by widespread household Internet access has a statistically significant effect on sustainable economic development. Increased levels of

**Table 10.6** Summary of the PMG model (2,1,2,2,2)

| *Variable* | *Coefficient* | *Standard error* | *t-statistic* | *Prob.* |
|---|---|---|---|---|
| | Long-term coefficients (grouped) | | | |
| SDG8INTA | 0.092555 | 0.006358 | 14.55689 | 0.0000 |
| SDG8ROCFM | 0.103121 | 0.006113 | 16.86962 | 0.0000 |
| SDG8RRSAR | −0.055535 | 0.007991 | −6.949701 | 0.0000 |
| | Short-term (group-average) coefficients | | | |
| COINTEQ | 0.015907 | 0.003396 | 4.684106 | 0.0000 |
| D(SDG8LPIBLOC(−1)) | −0.011309 | 0.110648 | −0.102211 | 0.9187 |
| D(SDG8INTA) | −0.000140 | 0.000669 | −0.209975 | 0.8339 |
| D(SDG8ROCFM) | 0.009768 | 0.001457 | 6.703927 | 0.0000 |
| D(SDG8ROCFM(−1)) | 0.004517 | 0.002002 | 2.256012 | 0.0249 |
| D(SDG8RRSAR) | −0.000786 | 0.002042 | −0.384713 | 0.7008 |
| D(SDG8RRSAR(−1)) | −0.000200 | 0.002555 | −0.078139 | 0.9378 |
| Log-likelihood: | 1194.113 | | | |

Source: Author

Internet access have shown a positive impact on GDP per capita, suggesting that digitization and information technology drive economic growth. In the European context, where there is a significant trend towards a digital economy, these results underline the importance of investing in telecommunications infrastructure, digital education and cybersecurity. Improved Internet access facilitates innovation, improves service efficiency and expands economic opportunities in less developed regions.

The results obtained in the analysis of the effect of the level of Internet access on GDP per capita are in line with numerous studies in the literature that support the hypothesis that digitization induced by Internet access can have a significant impact on sustainable economic development. Numerous studies have shown that increased Internet access is associated with an increase in GDP and economic productivity (Fernández-Portillo et al., 2020; Edquist et al., 2021). This is in part because the Internet facilitates access to information, promotes innovation, and stimulates the development of online businesses and markets. Digitalization and access to the Internet have been associated with an increase in innovation and creativity in different economic sectors. Through the Internet, entrepreneurs and innovators have access to resources, collaborative networks and global markets, which can lead to the emergence of new products, services and business models (Felicetti et al., 2024; Wang et al., 2023).

Internet access can open up new employment opportunities and stimulate entrepreneurship and self-employment. Through the Internet, people can access online jobs, develop digital skills and participate in the digital economy, thus contributing to economic growth and poverty reduction (Reim et al., 2022; Bresciani et al., 2021). The Internet provides access to educational and informational resources, helping to increase education and skills levels among the population (Li, 2022; Haleem et al., 2022). This leads to a more skilled and adaptable workforce, which can support long-term economic development.

Therefore, the results obtained in the study on the impact of Internet access on GDP per capita confirm the hypothesis that digitization induced by Internet access can have a statistically significant effect on sustainable economic development. These findings underline the importance of investing in telecommunications infrastructure and digital literacy to stimulate economic growth and social inclusion.

The employment rate (SDG8ROCFM) has a positive correlation coefficient (0.103121) on GDP per capita, with a t-statistic value of 16.86962 and a probability of almost zero, being statistically significant. This validates hypothesis 2: There is a significant direct link between employment growth and sustainability. In the long run the employment rate showed a positive effect on GDP per capita; this contributes to economic stability, reducing vulnerabilities to economic shocks.

The relationship between the employment rate and GDP per capita is consistent and there are relevant links with previous research in the literature; therefore the results obtained support the hypothesis that there is a significant direct link between employment growth and economic sustainability. Several studies have shown that an increase in the employment rate can contribute to improved productivity and economic performance (Murshed et al., 2022; Černý et al., 2024). A larger labour force can mean higher production of goods and services, which can lead to higher GDP per capita. Employment can be an important factor in reducing poverty and economic inequality (Bergstrom, 2022; Lakner et al., 2022). By increasing the number of jobs and ensuring adequate incomes, employment can contribute to raising the living standards of the population and to a more equitable distribution of economic resources. A high employment rate can contribute to economic stability and resilience to economic shocks (Rezaei Soufi et al., 2022; Šťastná et al., 2024). By ensuring a high level of employment, the economy can be less vulnerable to market fluctuations and other shocks, thus contributing to long-term sustainability. Government employment policies and measures can have a significant impact on economic performance (Li & Maskin, 2021; Becker et al., 2021). Investing in training and retraining programmes, improving the business environment and tax incentives to create new jobs can help increase employment and support economic development.

The results of the study on the relationship between employment rate and GDP per capita therefore confirm the hypothesis that there is a significant direct link between employment growth and economic sustainability. These findings underline the importance of policies and measures aimed at promoting employment and ensuring a more stable and resilient economy in the face of challenges.

The risk of in-work poverty (SDG8RRSAR) has a negative coefficient of −0.055535 with a t-statistic of −6.949701, suggesting that a decrease in the risk of in-work poverty contributes positively to the growth of GDP per capita, which confirms a positive correlation. These aspects validate working hypothesis 3: Reducing the risk of in-work poverty contributes significantly to long-term economic sustainability. The results show that a reduction in the risk of in-work poverty has a positive impact on GDP per capita, emphasizing the importance of social and economic stability. This underlines the need to develop policies that ensure decent income, fair working conditions and access to resources for all categories of employees. Combating in-work poverty is important to ensure inclusive and sustainable economic growth in the EU.

The results obtained in the analysis of the risk of in-work poverty and its impact on GDP per capita validate hypothesis 3, which argues that reducing this risk contributes significantly to the development of long-term economic sustainability. These findings are consistent with previous research in the literature, which emphasizes the importance of reducing in-work poverty for economic growth and social stability. Several studies have shown that reducing the risk of in-work poverty can contribute to increased productivity and economic performance (Spencer, 2023; Whiteoak et al., 2023). Employees experiencing in-work poverty may find it difficult to realize their full potential and contribute to economic growth. Reducing in-work poverty can therefore stimulate economic growth and overall prosperity in society. Tackling in-work poverty can contribute to reducing social and economic inequalities and enhancing social cohesion (Teles, 2023; Lee, 2022). By ensuring a decent income and fair working conditions for all employees, a fairer and more inclusive society can be promoted, which can support more balanced and sustainable economic development.

The implementation of social policies and protective measures for employees in situations of in-work poverty can be instrumental in alleviating this phenomenon and promoting sustainable economic development (De Stefano et al., 2022; Sompolska-Rzechuła & Kurdyś-Kujawska, 2022). Ensuring decent wages, access to social services and protection against discrimination can help to reduce the risk of in-work poverty and strengthen economic and social stability. Investment in education and training can play a significant role in reducing in-work poverty and increasing skills and employment opportunities (Iwang et al., 2023; Papadakis et al., 2022). A well-educated and skilled workforce can reduce the risk of in-work poverty and contribute to more sustainable economic development.

The study on the relationship between the reduction of the risk of in-work poverty and GDP per capita underlines the importance of adopting appropriate policies and measures to combat in-work poverty and to promote inclusive and sustainable economic development. These aspects confirm the relevance of the hypothesis that reducing the risk of in-work poverty contributes significantly to long-term economic sustainability, emphasizing the need for coordinated political and social action to achieve this objective.

In the short run there is a link between long-run variables at a 5% significance level. Any deviation from long-run equilibrium is corrected at a rate of approximately 1.5%. Thus, all variables except SDG8ROCFM have a negative impact on SDG8PIBLOC, but are statistically insignificant. The variable that has a positive impact on the dependence is the first-order difference of the variable SDG8ROCFM, but also the lagged difference of the same variable, and these are also statistically significant.

These results show that Internet access and the reduction of in-work poverty are important factors for long-term economic growth in the EU. In the short run, adjustments in employment rates and error corrections play a significant role in immediate economic dynamics, indicating the need for continuous monitoring and adjusted interventions to maintain economic stability. At the same time, the results suggest that economic policy at the EU level needs to focus on improving access to technology, increasing the quality and sustainability of jobs, and reducing social inequality. Investments in technology and education, together with labour market reforms, lead to robust economic growth and a better quality of life for the population.

## Conclusions

The chapter's conclusions reveal that the sustainable economic performance of the EU depends on a complex set of interconnected factors, in which investment in human capital, digital infrastructure and innovation act as key drivers of growth and social cohesion. The results obtained by applying the proposed econometric models confirm the hypothesis that digitization and innovation, supported by coherent public policies and a stimulating fiscal framework, can generate significant multiplier effects on GDP per capita, employment and the reduction of regional disparities.

The analysis also highlighted that the persistence of structural problems—such as high rates of NEETs, inequalities in access to education and technology, or excessive dependence on low-productivity sectors—can slow progress towards sustainable development goals, requiring integrated interventions tailored to the specificities of each national economy. At the same time, the positive influence of investment in digital infrastructure on economic performance depends on the ability of Member States to absorb and capitalize on new technologies, highlighting the importance of a unified strategic framework at European level.

Overall, the conclusions confirm that achieving a high level of economic sustainability in the EU requires strategic interconnection between innovation, social inclusion and the green transition, supported by evidence-based public policies that are adaptable to structural and contextual changes. Strengthening economic resilience and reducing identified vulnerabilities are fundamental prerequisites for the European objectives of sustainable growth and decent work to become a reality in the long term.

## References

Adomako, S., & Nguyen, N. P. (2023). Digitalization, inter-organizational collaboration, and technology transfer. *The Journal of Technology Transfer*. https://doi.org/10.1007/s10961-023-10031-z

Anrijs, S., Mariën, I., De Marez, L., & Ponnet, K. (2023). Excluded from essential internet services: Examining associations between digital exclusion, socio-economic resources and internet resources. *Technology in Society, 73*, 102211. https://doi.org/10.1016/j.techsoc.2023.102211

Antohi, V. M., Ionescu, R. V., Dinca, M. S., Zlati, M. L., & Fortea, C. (2023). Dynamics of the social security index in the context of the economic crisis in Romania. *Sustainability, 15*.

Ballerini, J., Herhausen, D., & Ferraris, A. (2023). How commitment and platform adoption drive the E-commerce performance of SMEs: A mixed-method inquiry into e-commerce affordances. *International Journal of Information Management, 72*, 102649. https://doi.org/10.1016/j.ijinfomgt.2023.102649

Ballerini, J., Ključnikov, A., Juárez-Varón, D., & Bresciani, S. (2024). The E-commerce platform conundrum: How manufacturers' leanings affect their internationalization. *Technological Forecasting and Social Change, 202*, 123199. https://doi.org/10.1016/j.techfore.2023.123199

Battisti, S., Agarwal, N., & Brem, A. (2022). Creating new tech entrepreneurs with digital platforms: Meta-organizations for shared value in data-driven retail ecosystems. *Technological Forecasting and Social Change, 175*, 121392. https://doi.org/10.1016/j.techfore.2021.121392

Becker, S. O., Heblich, S., & Sturm, D. M. (2021). The impact of public employment: Evidence from Bonn. *Journal of Urban Economics, 122*, 103291. https://doi.org/10.1016/j.jue.2020.103291

Behera, B., Haldar, A., & Sethi, N. (2024). Investigating the direct and indirect effects of information and communication technology on economic growth in the emerging economies: Role of financial development, foreign direct investment, innovation, and institutional quality. *Information Technology for Development, 30*, 33–56. https://doi.org/10.1080/02681102.2023.2233463

Bergstrom, K. (2022). The role of income inequality for poverty reduction. *World Bank Economic Review, 36*, 583–604. https://doi.org/10.1093/wber/lhab026

Bresciani, S., Huarng, K.-H., Malhotra, A., & Ferraris, A. (2021). Digital transformation as a springboard for product, process and business model innovation. *Journal of Business Research, 128*, 204–210. https://doi.org/10.1016/j.jbusres.2021.02.003

Brodny, J., & Tutak, M. (2022). Analyzing the level of digitalization among the Enterprises of the European Union Member States and their impact on economic growth. *Journal of Open Innovation: Technology, Market, and Complexity, 8*, 70. https://doi.org/10.3390/joitmc8020070

Černý, M., Bruckner, M., Weinzettel, J., Wiebe, K., Kimmich, C., Kerschner, C., & Hubacek, K. (2024). Global employment and skill level requirements for 'Post-Carbon Europe'. *Ecological Economics, 216*, 108014. https://doi.org/10.1016/j.ecolecon.2023.108014

Cheng, C.-Y., Chien, M.-S., & Lee, C.-C. (2021). ICT diffusion, financial development, and economic growth: An international cross-country analysis. *Economic Modelling, 94*, 662–671. https://doi.org/10.1016/j.econmod.2020.02.008

De Stefano, V., Durri, I., Stylogiannis, C., & Wouters, M. (2022). *A research agenda for the gig economy and society*. Edward Elgar Publishing. ISBN 9781800883512.

Edquist, H., Goodridge, P., & Haskel, J. (2021). The internet of things and economic growth in a panel of countries. *Economics of Innovation and New Technology, 30*, 262–283. https://doi.org/10.1080/10438599.2019.1695941

European Commission Proposal for a Joint Employment Report; 2022; ISBN 9789276591276.

Felicetti, A. M., Corvello, V., & Ammirato, S. (2024). Digital innovation in entrepreneurial firms: A systematic literature review. *Review of Managerial Science, 18*, 315–362. https://doi.org/10.1007/s11846-023-00638-9

Fernández-Portillo, A., Almodóvar-González, M., & Hernández-Mogollón, R. (2020). Impact of ICT development on economic growth. A study of OECD European Union countries. *Technology in Society, 63*, 101420. https://doi.org/10.1016/j.techsoc.2020.101420

Ghouse, G., Aslam, A., & Bhatti, M. I. (2022). The impact of the environment, digital–social inclusion, and institutions on inclusive growth: A conceptual and empirical analysis. *Energies, 15*.

Goniewicz, K., Khorram-Manesh, A., Burkle, F. M., Hertelendy, A. J., & Goniewicz, M. (2023). The European Union's post-pandemic strategies for public health, economic recovery, and social resilience. *Global Transitions, 5*, 201–209. https://doi.org/10.1016/j.glt.2023.10.003

Haleem, A., Javaid, M., Qadri, M. A., & Suman, R. (2022). Understanding the role of digital technologies in education: A review. *Sustainable Operations and Computers, 3*, 275–285. https://doi.org/10.1016/j.susoc.2022.05.004

Herman, P. R., & Oliver, S. (2023). Trade, policy, and economic development in the digital economy. *Journal of Development Economics, 164*, 103135. https://doi.org/10.1016/j.jdeveco.2023.103135

Hodgetts, D. J., Young-Hauser, A. M., Arrowsmith, J., Parker, J., Carr, S. C., Haar, J., & Alefaio, S. (2022). Deliberating upon the living wage to alleviate in-work poverty: A rhetorical inquiry into key stakeholder accounts. *Frontiers in Psychology, 13*. https://doi.org/10.3389/fpsyg.2022.810870

Hojnik, J., Ruzzier, M., Konečnik Ruzzier, M., Sučić, B., & Soltwisch, B. (2023). Challenges of demographic changes and digitalization on eco-innovation and the circular economy: Qualitative insights from companies. *Journal of Cleaner Production, 396*, 136439. https://doi.org/10.1016/j.jclepro.2023.136439

Hussain, S., Gul, R., & Ullah, S. (2023). Role of financial inclusion and ICT for sustainable economic development in developing countries. *Technological Forecasting and Social Change, 194*, 122725. https://doi.org/10.1016/j.techfore.2023.122725

Iwang, B., Rizlan, A. N., & T, I. (2023). Poverty in West Sulawesi; analysis of education level and investment through economic growth. *EcceS (Economics Social and Development Studies), 10*, 90–114. https://doi.org/10.24252/ecc.v10i1.37197

Kaplinsky, R., & Kraemer-Mbula, E. (2022). Innovation and uneven development: The challenge for low- and middle-income economies. *Research Policy, 51*, 104394. https://doi.org/10.1016/j.respol.2021.104394

Kose, M. A., Bank, W., & Ohnsorge, F. (2024). *Falling long-term growth prospects: Trends, expectations, and policies.* Chicago Review Press Incorporated DBA Indepe. ISBN 9781464820007.

Kosec, Z., Sekulic, S., Wilson-Gahan, S., Rostohar, K., Tusak, M., & Bon, M. (2022). Correlation between employee performance, well-being, job satisfaction, and life satisfaction in sedentary jobs in Slovenian enterprises. *International Journal of Environmental Research and Public Health, 19.*

Lakner, C., Mahler, D. G., Negre, M., & Prydz, E. B. (2022). How much does reducing inequality matter for global poverty? *The Journal of Economic Inequality, 20*, 559–585. https://doi.org/10.1007/s10888-021-09510-w

Laskar, M. H. (2023). Examining the emergence of digital society and the digital divide in India: A comparative evaluation between urban and rural areas. *Frontiers in Sociology, 8*. https://doi.org/10.3389/fsoc.2023.1145221

Lee, S. (2022). Social inclusion and the role of social workers BT. In P. Liamputtong (Ed.), *Handbook of social inclusion: research and practices in health and social sciences* (pp. 2107–2122). Springer International Publishing. ISBN 978-3-030-89594-5.

Li, L. (2022). Reskilling and upskilling the future-ready workforce for industry 4.0 and beyond. *Information Systems Frontiers*. https://doi.org/10.1007/s10796-022-10308-y

Li, D. D., & Maskin, E. S. (2021). Government and economics: An emerging field of study. *Journal of Government and Economics, 1*, 100005. https://doi.org/10.1016/j.jge.2021.100005

Maestas, N., Mullen, K. J., & Powell, D. (2023). The effect of population aging on economic growth, the labor force, and productivity. *American Economic Journal: Macroeconomics, 15*, 306–332. https://doi.org/10.1257/mac.20190196

Murshed, M., Apergis, N., Alam, M. S., Khan, U., & Mahmud, S. (2022). The impacts of renewable energy, financial inclusivity, globalization, economic growth, and urbanization on carbon productivity: Evidence from net moderation and mediation effects of energy efficiency gains. *Renewable Energy, 196*, 824–838. https://doi.org/10.1016/j.renene.2022.07.012

Papadakis, N., Drakaki, M., Saridaki, S., Amanaki, E., & Dimari, G. (2022). Educational capital/ level and its association with precarious work and social vulnerability among youth, in EU and Greece. *International Journal of Educational Research, 112*, 101921. https://doi.org/10.1016/j.ijer.2021.101921

Pérez-Escolar, M., & Canet, F. (2023). Research on vulnerable people and digital inclusion: Toward a consolidated taxonomical framework. *Universal Access in the Information Society, 22*, 1059–1072. https://doi.org/10.1007/s10209-022-00867-x

Perkins, G., Gilmore, S., Guttormsen, D. S. A., & Taylor, S. (2022). Analysing the impacts of universal basic income in the changing world of work: Challenges to the psychological contract and a future research agenda. *Human Resource Management Journal, 32*, 1–18. https://doi.org/10.1111/1748-8583.12348

Reim, W., Yli-Viitala, P., Arrasvuori, J., & Parida, V. (2022). Tackling business model challenges in SME internationalization through digitalization. *Journal of Innovation and Knowledge, 7*, 100199. https://doi.org/10.1016/j.jik.2022.100199

Rezaei Soufi, H., Esfahanipour, A., & Akbarpour Shirazi, M. (2022). A quantitative approach for analysis of macroeconomic resilience due to socio-economic shocks. *Socio-Economic Planning Sciences, 79*, 101101. https://doi.org/10.1016/j.seps.2021.101101

Saba, C. S., & Ngepah, N. (2022). ICT diffusion, industrialisation and economic growth nexus: An international cross-country analysis. *Journal of the Knowledge Economy, 13*, 2030–2069. https://doi.org/10.1007/s13132-021-00795-w

Sompolska-Rzechuła, A., & Kurdyś-Kujawska, A. (2022). Assessment of the development of poverty in EU countries. *International Journal of Environmental Research and Public Health, 19*.

Spencer, D. A. (2023). Technology and work: Past lessons and future directions. *Technology in Society, 74*, 102294. https://doi.org/10.1016/j.techsoc.2023.102294

Šťastná, S., Ženka, J., & Krtička, L. (2024). Regional economic resilience: Insights from five crises. *European Planning Studies, 32*, 506–533. https://doi.org/10.1080/09654313.2023.2267250

Tan, Y., & Li, X. (2022). The impact of internet on entrepreneurship. *International Review of Economics and Finance, 77*, 135–142. https://doi.org/10.1016/j.iref.2021.09.016

Teles, F. (2023). *Handbook on local and regional governance*. Edward Elgar Publishing. ISBN 9781800371200.

Udeagha, M. C., & Muchapondwa, E. (2023). Environmental sustainability in South Africa: Understanding the criticality of economic policy uncertainty, fiscal decentralization, and green innovation. *Sustainable Development, 31*, 1638–1651. https://doi.org/10.1002/sd.2473

Wang, C., Chen, M., Wang, Q., & Fang, Y. (2023). The study of value network reconstruction and business model innovation driven by entrepreneurial orientation. *The International Entrepreneurship and Management Journal, 19*, 2013–2036. https://doi.org/10.1007/s11365-023-00869-y

Whiteoak, J., Abell, D., & Becker, K. (2023). The leadership challenge of increasing productivity in the workplace without increasing burnout risk. *Leadership & Organization Development Journal, 44*, 260–273. https://doi.org/10.1108/LODJ-07-2021-0330

Zhang, J., & Li, S. (2023). The impact of human capital on green technology innovation—Moderating role of environmental regulations. *International Journal of Environmental Research and Public Health, 20.*

Zintl, T., & Loewe, M. (2022). More than the sum of its parts: Donor-sponsored cash-for-work programmes and social cohesion in Jordanian communities hosting Syrian refugees. *European Journal of Development Research, 34*, 1285–1307. https://doi.org/10.1057/s41287-022-00536-y

CHAPTER 11

# Analysis of Romania's Economic Efficiency Compared to EU Member States Using the DEA Method

## Introduction

In the context of the EU's strategic objectives for sustainable growth, competitiveness, and social cohesion, the evaluation of economic efficiency across Member States has gained increasing relevance. The heterogeneity of resource endowments, institutional capacities and development trajectories within the EU generates significant differences in how countries transform inputs—such as labour, technology and infrastructure—into economic and social outcomes. Against this backdrop, comparative analyses that employ robust quantitative techniques are essential for identifying efficiency gaps, highlighting best practices, and informing policy design aimed at convergence and resilience.

Romania's position within the EU economy presents a complex interplay of strengths, vulnerabilities and untapped potential. While the country has registered notable progress in economic performance over the last decade, persistent disparities relative to more advanced Member States underline the need for evidence-based strategies to enhance competitiveness. The Data Envelopment Analysis (DEA) method offers a rigorous framework for measuring relative efficiency, enabling the identification of benchmark economies and the determination of input–output combinations that yield optimal results. By capturing multidimensional performance indicators linked to Sustainable Development Goal 8 (SDG8) on


C. Fortea, *Sustainable Economic Development and the European Green Deal*, https://doi.org/10.1007/978-3-032-10326-0_11

"Decent Work and Economic Growth", DEA provides valuable insights into both productive capacity and sustainability-oriented outcomes.

This chapter contributes to the literature by delivering a comparative DEA-based assessment of Romania's economic efficiency relative to the EU average and selected Member States over the period 2010–2021. The novelty of the approach lies in its integration of diverse economic, social and technological indicators into a unified efficiency model, allowing for a nuanced diagnosis of structural strengths and constraints. Specifically, the analysis addresses the following research questions:

R1: To what extent does Romania achieve economic efficiency compared to leading EU economies?
R2: Which input and output factors exert the most significant influence on efficiency levels, and how can policy interventions target these dimensions to foster sustainable growth?

By answering these questions, the study not only positions Romania within the European efficiency frontier but also provides actionable recommendations for enhancing resource allocation, supporting digitalization and promoting sectoral diversification, thereby reinforcing the country's long-term resilience and competitiveness in the EU single market.

## Literature Review

The analysis of economic efficiency at the EU level has become a topic of major interest over the past two decades, against the backdrop of heightened competitiveness, sustainability, and economic and social cohesion objectives. In an economic area characterized by structural diversity—ranging from mature, highly digitized economies to countries still undergoing institutional transition—each country's ability to transform available resources into economic and social outcomes is central to convergence processes. Modern evaluation methods, such as Data Envelopment Analysis (DEA), allow not only the measurement of the relative position of countries on an efficiency frontier, but also the identification of the determinants of this performance, including the emerging role of digitalization, specialized human capital and the green transition.

This section aims to summarize recent contributions from the literature, organizing them into four main directions: the conceptual framework of economic efficiency in the European context and its links to SDG8 indicators; methodological developments in DEA and its advantages over other approaches; relevant empirical evidence for EU Member States; and Romania's position in relation to these results and the research gap addressed by this study.

### *The Conceptual Framework of Economic Efficiency in the EU*

Economic efficiency is, broadly speaking, the ratio between results (outputs) and resources used (inputs), calculated under the conditions imposed by technological, institutional and environmental constraints. In theory, it's defined either in terms of factor productivity, which is how well capital, labour and other resources are turned into goods and services (Dell'Anno, 2022; Rehman & Islam, 2023; Wang & Shao, 2024), or in terms of "technical efficiency", relative to a multi-factor production frontier that delimits the maximum possible combinations of outputs for a given set of inputs (Aparicio et al., 2023; Førsund, 2021; Vrabková et al., 2024). This frontier, conceptualized by Farrell (Farrell, 1957) and further developed in DEA models (Charnes et al., 1978), allows the relative position of an economy to be assessed in relation to observable "best practices".

In the EU, recent approaches to measuring economic efficiency explicitly integrate economic social, and sustainability dimensions, as reflected in the indicators of Sustainable Development Goal 8 (SDG8 – Decent Work and Economic Growth). This assessment framework emphasizes that economic performance cannot be separated from job quality, social inclusion, the reduction of inequalities and the ability of economies to adapt to the digital and green transition (Bonnedahl et al., 2022; Chigbu & Nekhwevha, 2023; Monaco, 2024; Shafik, 2025). Thus, efficiency analysis involves not only maximizing production but also optimizing how resources are used to generate sustainable, equitable and resilient growth.

In this context, digitization has become a central structural determinant. According to specialized studies (Bilan et al., 2023; Brodny & Tutak, 2022; Doroiman & Sîrghi, 2024), investments in digital infrastructure, advanced digital skills, and human capital specialized in information and communication technology (ICT) show significant and positive correlations with the innovation rate and GDP per capita growth in EU Member States. Digitalization is not limited to streamlining existing processes, but acts simultaneously as a pure efficiency factor, reducing production costs and times, optimizing resource allocation, and as a vector of technological progress, accelerating the shift of the production frontier through the emergence of new processes, products and business models (Fu & Madni, 2024; Mahmood et al., 2024; Vărzaru & Bocean, 2024). This dual function amplifies the cumulative effects of digital investment and explains the performance differences between economies with similar levels of physical capital but different degrees of digitization.

At the same time, the green transition introduces both constraints and opportunities in defining and measuring efficiency. Eco-efficiency studies (Bergougui & Satrovic, 2025; Georgescu et al., 2025; Sánchez-García et al., 2024) show that countries that integrate clean technologies, harness renewable energy sources and implement circular economy models achieve superior performance not only from an environmental protection perspective, but also in the long term in terms of economic competitiveness. Sustainability-oriented policies stimulate innovation, generate green jobs and reduce dependence on finite resources, creating the conditions for growth that is resilient to external shocks.

Thus, in the contemporary European context, economic efficiency is no longer assessed exclusively in terms of traditional economic returns, but through a multidimensional perspective that reflects structural sustainability, institutional resilience and long-term competitiveness. In this sense, the interdependence between digitalization and the green transition becomes a key element: the ability of an economy to simultaneously integrate digital technologies and sustainable practices will define not only its position on the efficiency frontier, but also its potential for convergence within the EU.

### *Measurement Methods: Developments in DEA and Its Alternatives*

Data Envelopment Analysis (DEA) has established itself in economic and management literature as one of the most versatile non-parametric methods for evaluating the relative efficiency of decision-making units (DMUs), whether they are countries, regions, economic sectors, public institutions or companies. Its introduction by Charnes, Cooper and Rhodes (1978) was a defining moment for comparative performance analysis, as the method allows for the simultaneous comparison of multiple inputs and outputs without imposing a pre-established functional form on the production function. In transnational evaluations, DEA provides a robust framework for constructing efficiency frontiers based on empirical data and for calculating relative efficiency scores, while identifying reference units (peers) for inefficient entities.

Over the last decade, literature has developed a series of methodological extensions that have increased the relevance of DEA in the context of analyses of EU Member States.

The first important direction is represented by non-radial models and the Slack-Based Measure (SBM), introduced by Tone (2011, 2017), which allow the assessment of inefficiencies associated with each input and output. Unlike classical radial models, which adjust all indicators proportionally, these versions identify and quantify exactly the bottlenecks in the production or output process. In the case of EU country assessments, SBM models are particularly useful for isolating the effects of specific factors—such as the shortage of ICT specialists or low high-speed Internet coverage—on overall efficiency.

The second relevant methodological direction is the Malmquist index, used for dynamic efficiency analysis (Amirteimoori et al., 2024; Wang & Tang, 2024; Woo et al., 2015; Zhang et al., 2023b). It breaks down performance changes into two components: pure efficiency change (catching-up effect) and technological progress (frontier shift). In recent studies applied to the digital and green transition, Malmquist has proven capable of highlighting the differences between states that are catching up by optimizing resource use and those that are innovating and shifting the production frontier (Cobbinah et al., 2025; Horváthová & Mokrišová, 2024; Le & Dang, 2024). This approach is highly relevant in times of rapid structural change, such as the acceleration of digitalization or the implementation of Green Deal policies.

A third significant contribution is represented by parallel and network DEA models (Amirteimoori et al., 2025; Koronakos et al., 2022; Moghaddas et al., 2025; Zhang et al., 2023a). These break down the overall production process into interconnected economic, social and environmental sub-processes, allowing for a detailed analysis of efficiency in each area. By avoiding premature aggregations, these models reduce the risk that high performance in one area artificially compensates for major shortcomings in another. In the EU context, where competitiveness objectives must be harmonized with sustainability objectives, Network DEA offers a granular perspective for prioritizing public policies (Trane et al., 2025).

Compared to parametric approaches such as Stochastic Frontier Analysis (SFA), DEA has several major advantages: flexibility in handling heterogeneous indicators, no strict assumptions about error distribution, and the ability to work with relatively small samples while maintaining comparative relevance. In addition, DEA is a powerful tool for benchmarking and the transfer of best practices, explicitly identifying reference units for less efficient entities.

However, the method also has limitations. First, it is sensitive to extreme values and measurement errors, as the efficiency frontier is determined by the best-performing units in the sample. Second, DEA does not intrinsically include a mechanism for dealing with statistical uncertainty, which may affect the robustness of the results. To counteract these limitations, the literature recommends the use of complementary procedures, such as bootstrap DEA (de Oliveira et al., 2025; Gómez-Vega et al., 2021; Ye et al., 2022) for estimating confidence intervals, Tobit models for analysing efficiency determinants, or cluster analysis techniques for identifying performance typologies (Lei & Wei, 2023; Mo & Zeng, 2025; Ölkers et al., 2025).

Overall, recent developments in the DEA have strengthened the method's ability to analyse the structural complexity of European economies, particularly when the research objective is to identify efficiency differences, determining factors, and priority areas for public policy intervention.

### *Recent Empirical Evidence for EU Member States*

The literature published in recent years presents a relatively coherent set of findings on the determinants and patterns of economic efficiency performance in EU Member States. A recurring finding is that countries that have systematically invested in high-speed digital infrastructure and in human capital specialized in information and communication technologies (ICT) tend to consistently rank at the efficiency frontier, even when the assessment includes both socio-economic outcomes (such as employment rates or sectoral value added) and environmental constraints (Aleca & Mihai, 2025; Javaid et al., 2024). Multi-country comparative studies, using both output-oriented DEA models and extensions with the Malmquist index, highlight robust associations between digital intensity, innovation dynamics and aggregate economic performance, with more pronounced effects in regions characterized by high university density and well-established innovation ecosystems (Banjerdpaiboon & Limleamthong, 2023; Guo & Ye, 2025; Jain et al., 2023; Peykani et al., 2025).

A second set of evidence relates to the environmental-economic dimension of efficiency. Recent studies applied at the EU-27 level show significant variations in eco-efficiency, mainly explained by industrial structure, the share of different energy sources and the architecture of public environmental policies (Brodny & Tutak, 2025; Gogu et al., 2025; Mandel et al., 2023). Northern and Western European countries frequently appear in the efficient zone on both the economic and environmental components, while some Southern and Central-Eastern economies show persistent deficits in green performance, even though they achieve results comparable to the EU average in terms of economic indicators (Bănică et al., 2024; Efthymiou et al., 2025; European Investment Bank, 2025). This discrepancy indicates the existence of dual efficiency trajectories, with uneven convergence potential between the two dimensions.

At the sectoral level, empirical evidence for areas such as health and tourism suggests that national efficiency patterns directly reflect the orientation of public policies and the level of investment in organizational capital and infrastructure (European Commission, 2024; Rimidis & Butkus, 2025). Even countries that have recently joined the Union can achieve high levels of technical efficiency, but they face difficulties in maintaining sustained productivity growth in the medium term, which can slow down the convergence process (European Union, 2024; Lopez-Garcia, 2021). Studies on European tourism show that almost half of the countries achieve maximum efficiency scores, while the rest are constrained by unfavourable combinations of physical infrastructure, environmental pressures and the level of workforce skills (Mamatzakis et al., 2022; Stoiljković et al., 2025).

In this context, digitization emerges as a cross-cutting determinant of efficiency. Recent EU-wide analyses (Caravella et al., 2023; Ciacci et al., 2025; Magoutas et al., 2024), including NUTS2 subdivisions, indicate that accelerating digital progress is associated with both GDP growth per capita and improvements in total factor productivity, reflecting network effects and technological diffusion. The adoption of advanced technologies, such as cloud computing, big data analytics and artificial intelligence, shows systematic positive correlations with macroeconomic indicators of growth and competitiveness, which validates the integration of these variables into DEA models focused on economic outcomes (Drago et al., 2025; Haftor et al., 2024; OECD, 2024b).

From a methodological point of view, applications combining DEA with the Malmquist index have identified two distinct patterns of dynamics: catching up through pure efficiency gains in some Central and Eastern European economies and shifting of the technological frontier in Western and Northern economies, driven by intensified innovation and technological modernization. This differentiation suggests that digital and human capital indicators act both as instruments of relative catching up and as drivers of technological advancement—with direct implications for public policy design.

Studies applying parallel models in the European context show that separating sub-processes, for example, economy versus environment, prevents distorted interpretations of aggregate performance. There are countries that score high on the economic component but remain inefficient on the environmental dimension, and vice versa. Parallel SBM models recently applied in the EU provide a granular picture of structural strengths and weaknesses, providing a robust basis for prioritizing policy measures and optimizing resource use.

### *Romania Between Relative Performance and Structural Challenges: Arguments for an Integrated DEA Model*

In the context of recent evidence from European literature on the determinants of economic efficiency, Romania's case illustrates a particular combination of relative performance and persistent structural challenges. The experience of the last decade shows that an economy with more limited resources than the EU average can achieve high levels of efficiency when critical inputs, especially digital and institutional ones, are directed towards outcomes with a direct impact on sectoral value added and employment. Recent studies (Brodny & Tutak, 2024; Constantin et al., 2025) confirm that the effect of digitization on economic growth and of ICT-specialized human capital on competitiveness explicitly supports the inclusion of these variables in efficiency assessment models. In Romania, the rapid expansion of broadband connectivity and the increase in the number of ICT specialists are favourable prerequisites, but the literature points out that the sustainability of these gains depends on strengthening advanced digital skills and reducing territorial gaps in high-speed infrastructure (European Commission, 2025; Noja et al., 2022).

Another key dimension is the link between eco-efficiency and sectoral structure. Comparative results at the EU level suggest that countries with a high share of agriculture in total value added may experience vulnerabilities in sectoral outputs if investments in technology, management and the green transition remain insufficient (Castillo-Díaz et al., 2025; Ronzon et al., 2022). Recent work (Bocean, 2024; Khan & Bounade, 2025; Zeng et al., 2024) shows that technological modernization, digitization of agricultural processes, and the adoption of sustainable practices have the potential to reposition countries on the efficiency frontier. For Romania, where agriculture still makes a significant contribution to the economy, these findings validate the inclusion in the analysis of inputs related to human capital and digital infrastructure, as well as an output that reflects agricultural value added—a potential critical point for national efficiency.

From a methodological perspective, the literature reveals a notable gap: few studies integrate SDG8 indicators, digital variables, and sectoral economic results for all EU Member States into a single framework over long periods of time and with explicit identification of reference units (peers) for bilateral benchmarking (e.g. Romania versus the EU average or countries with a similar profile). Most research focuses either on eco-efficiency and the environment, or on specific areas such as health or tourism, or on statistical correlations between digitization and innovation, without constructing a multi-output matrix conceptually anchored in SDG8.

In addition, contemporary debates on sustainability and efficiency suggest that, in order to fully capture performance dynamics, it is useful to extend the analysis through dynamic methods (the Malmquist index) and/or parallel architectures (Parallel SBM) that allow for the identification of trade-offs and synergies between the economy, the environment and human capital. Although the present study adopts a radial Constant Returns to Scale (CRS) model oriented towards outputs, suitable for static benchmarking and for formulating recommendations on maximizing outputs given existing inputs, it also provides a solid basis for further developments that include these methodological extensions, ensuring a deeper understanding of productivity trajectories and structural shifts between domains. Therefore, Romania's position in the specialized literature and its structural particularities justify the adoption of an integrated DEA model capable of simultaneously capturing economic performance, the digital dimension and sustainability components, thus providing a value-added tool for informing public policy and supporting the convergence process within the EU.

The analysis of the specialized literature reveals a clear convergence towards extending the concept of economic efficiency beyond the traditional input-output ratio towards a multidimensional approach that integrates digital, social and sustainability dimensions, in line with SDG8 objectives. Methodological developments in Data Envelopment Analysis—from classical radial models to non-radial, parallel and dynamic approaches—have allowed for a more accurate capture of the complex realities of economic performance in the EU, while providing more precise tools for diagnosis and benchmarking. Recent empirical evidence for EU Member States confirms the strategic role of digitalization and ICT-specialized human capital in maintaining or reaching the efficiency frontier, as well as the importance of industrial structure and environmental policies in shaping each country's performance profile.

In Romania's case, the literature reveals both opportunities and structural constraints. Although the dynamics of connectivity and the growth of the pool of ICT specialists create favourable conditions for efficiency, the sustainability of these results depends on strengthening advanced skills, reducing territorial disparities, and coherently integrating the green transition into key economic sectors, particularly agriculture. The identified gap—the absence of an integrated framework that simultaneously includes SDG8 indicators, digital variables and sectoral economic outcomes for all EU countries over an extended time horizon—fully justifies the approach proposed in this study.

Thus, the theoretical foundations, methodological advances and empirical evidence analysed in the literature support the need for an output-oriented DEA model capable of assessing Romania's relative position in relation to other EU Member States and providing concrete benchmarks for public policy. The contribution of this research lies in the construction of an analytical framework that not only measures economic efficiency but also contextualizes it within the logic of the structural transformations imposed by digitalization and the green transition, thus ensuring its relevance for both academic research and policymaking.

## Methodology

The DEA (Data Envelopment Analysis) method provides a detailed insight into how each country uses available resources to achieve economic results. This method can identify states that are efficient in their use of resources and provides models for less efficient states. By analysing the economic efficiency of EU Member States, it identifies opportunities to improve economic performance and increase competitiveness in the internal and international market. Thus, EU Member States can use the results of the DEA to implement policies and strategies that improve economic efficiency and lead to better use of available resources. It can also be useful for monitoring progress over time and for comparing economic performance between Member States. DEA of economic efficiency performance contributes to strengthening the European single market and promoting sustainable economic development throughout the EU. In addition, the use of DEA helps to identify weaknesses in national economies and to implement specific strategies to improve them. In this way, greater economic and social cohesion between Member States can be ensured, contributing to an overall increase in competitiveness and prosperity within the EU. Moreover, promoting sustainable economic development can also have a positive impact on the environment through the adoption of environmentally friendly and sustainable practices. These measures can help reduce carbon emissions, conserve natural resources and protect biodiversity. By implementing responsible and sustainable economic policies, Member States can help combat climate change and promote a circular economy that uses resources efficiently and reduces environmental impacts. Sustainable economic development can thus not only bring economic benefits but also have a positive impact on society and the environment. At the same time, adopting responsible production and consumption practices can stimulate innovation and long-term economic growth, thus contributing to improving the quality of life for future generations. Investing in renewable energy and green technologies can also create new jobs and economic opportunities, thus strengthening the long-term competitiveness and sustainability of national economies. It is important that all sectors and economic actors are involved in these joint efforts to ensure a smooth and efficient transition to a sustainable economic development model. Education and public awareness are also important to promote the necessary changes in consumer behaviour and in the way natural resources are managed. It is important to create education and training programmes in the field of green energy to ensure a skilled and specialized workforce in this growing sector.

The analysis of Romania's economic efficiency is important for identifying the weaknesses of the economy and for establishing strategies for sustainable growth and development at national level. The assessment of economic efficiency identifies sectors with growth potential and the measures that should be taken to stimulate them. The analysis of economic efficiency also provides important information for the development of public policies and the attraction of foreign investment in Romania. By monitoring the country's economic efficiency, it is possible to observe the evolution of the performance of the different sectors and identify possible problems or obstacles hindering their development. The DEA of economic efficiency also provides an overview of Romania's international competitiveness and serves as a useful tool for developing export promotion strategies and attracting foreign capital.

We plan to perform the economic efficiency analysis of Romania in the European context, and we will use the DEA method for which the following inputs and outputs have been established according to Table 11.1.

**Table 11.1** Presentation of analysed indicators

| *Symbol* | *Indicator name* | *Unit of measurement* | *Source* | *Tip* |
|---|---|---|---|---|
| SDG8VIMPM | Labour tax revenues | % GDP | OECD (2024a) | Input |
| SDG8TNEET | Young people not in employment, education or training (NEET) | % | Eurostat (2024h) | Input |
| SDG8ROCFM | Employment rate | % | Eurostat (2024) | Input |
| SDG8INTA | Level of Internet access—households | % | Eurostat (2024e) | Input |
| SDG8UTINT | Internet usage by individuals | % | Eurostat (2024d) | Input |
| SDG8ATIC | ICT specialists employed—total | % | Eurostat (2024f) | Input |
| SDG8AINT | High-speed Internet coverage | % | Eurostat (2024b) | Input |
| SDG8VAAG | Value added in agriculture | % | OECD (2024a) | Output |
| SDG8VAIN | Value added in industry | % | OECD (2024a) | Output |
| SDG8VASE | Value added in services | % | OECD (2024a) | Output |
| SDG8PIBloc | GDP per capita | Euro per inhabitant | Eurostat (2024g) | Output |
| SDG8RRSAR | Risk of in-work poverty | % | Eurostat (2024c) | Output |

Source: Author

To demonstrate economic efficiency at the European level, the following working hypotheses are established:

Q1: Most European countries are economically efficient;
I2: The EU picks up the trend of inefficient developing countries being economically inefficient;
Q3: The most efficient countries are Luxembourg, Ireland, Sweden, the Netherlands, Finland, Austria, Germany, Finland and Sweden;
I4: The most economically inefficient countries are Spain, Slovakia and Estonia.

Data Envelopment Analysis (DEA) can be used as a technique based on linear programming and optimization to evaluate the efficiency of each unit. To improve the efficiency of each unit, a benchmark set for an inefficient unit is determined and the efficiency of different units can be compared with the efficiency limit.

## Results and Discussion

We used 28 decision-making units (DMUs) that were investigated with respect to seven inputs and five outputs for the period 2010–2021. The type of DEA used in this study is the radial model based on the CRS (Constant Returns to Scale) model and using the OUT (Output) approach. The economic efficiency value obtained by the defined model is shown in Table 11.2.

Table 11.2 shows that most countries are economically efficient over the period 2010–2021. There are three partially economically inefficient EU Member States whose trend is towards increasing economic efficiency towards the end of the analysis period. These are Spain, Slovakia and Estonia. This proves hypotheses 1 and 4. The European average falls short of the economic efficiency threshold by picking up the economic vulnerabilities of Spain, Slovakia and Estonia. Hypothesis 2 is demonstrated. The most efficient countries highlighted in the Pareto diagram are Luxembourg, Ireland, Sweden, the Netherlands, Finland, Austria and Germany. Hypothesis 3 is demonstrated.

Using the DEA method, the efficiency of the analysed unit is projected to the maximum level, and the process is concluded by equating the efficiency thresholds to 1 for as many compared units as possible. Thus, efficiency benchmarks are obtained for each DMU analysed.

**Table 11.2** The SDG8 efficiency score at EU Member State level and the European average

| DMU | 2010 | 2011 | 2012 | 2013 | 2014 | 2015 | 2016 | 2017 | 2018 | 2019 | 2020 | 2021 |
|---|---|---|---|---|---|---|---|---|---|---|---|---|
| Austria | 1.000 | 1.000 | 1.000 | 1.000 | 1.000 | 1.000 | 1.000 | 1.000 | 1.000 | 1.000 | 1.000 | 1.000 |
| Belgium | 1.000 | 1.000 | 1.000 | 1.000 | 1.000 | 1.000 | 1.000 | 1.000 | 1.000 | 1.000 | 1.000 | 1.000 |
| Bulgaria | 1.000 | 1.000 | 1.000 | 1.000 | 1.000 | 1.000 | 1.000 | 1.000 | 1.000 | 1.000 | 1.000 | 1.000 |
| Czech Republic | 1.000 | 1.000 | 1.000 | 1.000 | 1.000 | 1.000 | 1.000 | 1.000 | 1.000 | 1.000 | 1.000 | 1.000 |
| Cyprus | 1.000 | 1.000 | 1.000 | 1.000 | 1.000 | 1.000 | 1.000 | 1.000 | 1.000 | 1.000 | 1.000 | 0.992 |
| Croatia | 1.000 | 1.000 | 1.000 | 1.000 | 1.000 | 1.000 | 1.000 | 1.000 | 1.000 | 1.000 | 1.000 | 1.000 |
| Denmark | 1.000 | 1.000 | 1.000 | 1.000 | 1.000 | 1.000 | 1.000 | 1.000 | 1.000 | 1.000 | 1.000 | 1.000 |
| Estonia | 0.929 | 1.000 | 0.945 | 0.955 | 1.000 | 0.942 | 0.922 | 0.996 | 0.949 | 1.000 | 1.000 | 0.987 |
| EU27 | 0.948 | 0.955 | 0.962 | 0.959 | 0.961 | 0.959 | 0.955 | 0.955 | 0.963 | 0.966 | 1.000 | 1.000 |
| Finland | 1.000 | 1.000 | 1.000 | 1.000 | 1.000 | 0.974 | 0.985 | 1.000 | 1.000 | 1.000 | 1.000 | 1.000 |
| France | 1.000 | 1.000 | 1.000 | 1.000 | 1.000 | 0.972 | 0.949 | 0.951 | 0.953 | 0.959 | 0.951 | 0.965 |
| Germany | 1.000 | 1.000 | 1.000 | 1.000 | 1.000 | 1.000 | 1.000 | 1.000 | 1.000 | 1.000 | 1.000 | 1.000 |
| Greece | 1.000 | 1.000 | 1.000 | 1.000 | 1.000 | 1.000 | 1.000 | 1.000 | 1.000 | 1.000 | 1.000 | 1.000 |
| Ireland | 1.000 | 1.000 | 1.000 | 1.000 | 1.000 | 1.000 | 1.000 | 1.000 | 1.000 | 1.000 | 1.000 | 1.000 |
| Italy | 1.000 | 1.000 | 1.000 | 1.000 | 1.000 | 1.000 | 1.000 | 1.000 | 1.000 | 1.000 | 1.000 | 1.000 |
| Latvia | 1.000 | 0.995 | 0.991 | 1.000 | 1.000 | 1.000 | 1.000 | 1.000 | 1.000 | 1.000 | 1.000 | 1.000 |
| Lithuania | 1.000 | 1.000 | 1.000 | 1.000 | 1.000 | 1.000 | 1.000 | 1.000 | 1.000 | 1.000 | 1.000 | 1.000 |
| Luxembourg | 1.000 | 1.000 | 1.000 | 1.000 | 1.000 | 1.000 | 1.000 | 1.000 | 1.000 | 1.000 | 1.000 | 1.000 |
| Malta | 1.000 | 1.000 | 1.000 | 1.000 | 1.000 | 1.000 | 1.000 | 1.000 | 1.000 | 1.000 | 1.000 | 1.000 |
| Netherlands | 1.000 | 1.000 | 1.000 | 1.000 | 1.000 | 1.000 | 1.000 | 1.000 | 1.000 | 1.000 | 1.000 | 1.000 |
| Poland | 1.000 | 1.000 | 1.000 | 1.000 | 1.000 | 1.000 | 1.000 | 1.000 | 1.000 | 1.000 | 1.000 | 1.000 |
| Portugal | 1.000 | 1.000 | 1.000 | 1.000 | 1.000 | 1.000 | 1.000 | 1.000 | 1.000 | 1.000 | 1.000 | 1.000 |
| Romania | 1.000 | 1.000 | 1.000 | 1.000 | 1.000 | 1.000 | 1.000 | 1.000 | 1.000 | 1.000 | 1.000 | 1.000 |
| Slovakia | 0.955 | 0.965 | 0.993 | 0.956 | 0.968 | 0.962 | 0.960 | 0.992 | 1.000 | 1.000 | 1.000 | 1.000 |
| Slovenia | 1.000 | 1.000 | 1.000 | 1.000 | 1.000 | 1.000 | 1.000 | 1.000 | 1.000 | 1.000 | 1.000 | 1.000 |
| Spain | 0.967 | 0.975 | 0.988 | 0.991 | 0.993 | 0.984 | 0.967 | 0.987 | 1.000 | 0.994 | 0.980 | 1.000 |
| Sweden | 1.000 | 1.000 | 1.000 | 1.000 | 1.000 | 1.000 | 1.000 | 1.000 | 1.000 | 1.000 | 1.000 | 1.000 |
| Hungary | 1.000 | 1.000 | 1.000 | 1.000 | 1.000 | 1.000 | 1.000 | 1.000 | 1.000 | 1.000 | 1.000 | 1.000 |

Source: Author

Table 11.3 presents Romania's efficiency benchmarks by year compared to the European average and Spain.

It can be seen from Table 11.3 that Romania is an economic reference for the EU only in the period 2010–2011, a period in which the impact of the economic crisis has marked the whole European area by strong economic convulsions, which favoured the outbreak of stock market crashes and the bankruptcy of renowned banks such as Lehman Brothers. Against this backdrop, Member States had to take austerity measures and implement structural reforms to counter the negative effects of the crisis. Several financial assistance programmes for countries in difficulty were adopted and the European Central Bank intervened in the market to maintain

**Table 11.3** Romania's efficiency benchmarks by year

| DMU | An | Peer1 | Peer2 | Peer3 | Peer4 | Peer5 | Peer6 | Peer7 |
|---|---|---|---|---|---|---|---|---|
| EU27 | 2010 | Greece | Luxembourg | Malta | Poland | Romania | Slovenia | |
| | 2011 | Greece | Luxembourg | Malta | Poland | Romania | Slovenia | |
| | 2012 | Belgium | Greece | Luxembourg | Malta | Poland | Portugal | Slovenia |
| | 2013 | Austria | Greece | Luxembourg | Malta | Poland | Portugal | Slovenia |
| | 2014 | Belgium | Greece | Luxembourg | Malta | Poland | Portugal | Slovenia |
| | 2015 | Belgium | Greece | Luxembourg | Malta | Poland | Portugal | Slovenia |
| | 2016 | Greece | Ireland | Luxembourg | Malta | Poland | Portugal | Slovenia |
| | 2017 | Belgium | Greece | Ireland | Luxembourg | Poland | Slovenia | - |
| | 2018 | Greece | Ireland | Luxembourg | Poland | Slovenia | - | - |
| | 2019 | Croatia | Greece | Ireland | Luxembourg | Poland | Portugal | Slovenia |
| | 2020 | EU27 | Greece | Ireland | Luxembourg | - | - | - |
| | 2021 | EU27 | - | - | - | - | - | - |
| Spain | 2010 | Greece | Italy | Luxembourg | Malta | Romania | - | |
| | 2011 | Greece | Italy | Luxembourg | Malta | Romania | - | |
| | 2012 | Croatia | Greece | Luxembourg | Romania | - | - | - |
| | 2013 | Greece | Luxembourg | Romania | Slovenia | - | - | - |
| | 2014 | Greece | Luxembourg | Romania | Slovenia | - | - | - |
| | 2015 | Greece | Luxembourg | Poland | Romania | - | - | - |
| | 2016 | Greece | Luxembourg | Romania | Slovenia | - | - | - |
| | 2017 | Greece | Luxembourg | Romania | Slovenia | - | - | - |
| | 2018 | Spain | - | - | - | - | - | - |
| | 2019 | Greece | Luxembourg | Poland | Romania | - | - | - |
| | 2020 | Greece | Ireland | Luxembourg | Romania | - | - | - |
| | 2021 | Spain | - | - | - | - | - | - |

Source: Author

financial stability. Greater emphasis was also placed on strengthening monetary union and increasing cooperation between Member States to prevent similar situations. The joint efforts of the European authorities have contributed to the economic recovery of the region and restored confidence in financial markets. Compared to the European average, in the case of Spain, Romania is the efficiency benchmark for the whole period under analysis except for the years 2018 and 2021, when it reaches the economic efficiency threshold. Table 11.4 also presents the number of repeated peer units.

Table 11.4 shows that Romania is a benchmark of economic efficiency throughout the period analysed, ranking in the top half of the European efficiency ranking. It ranks 5th out of the 24 economic efficiency models in 2021, ahead of Germany, the Netherlands and Portugal, which recommends it as suitable for the study of efficiency differences for the European average and Spain. We determined λ values (lambdas = weights for equal units) that represent the combination of equal units used to construct each virtual unit. The values of λ are presented in Table 11.5.

**Table 11.4** Frequency ranking of benchmarks by year for economically efficient EU Member States

| | 2010 | 2011 | 2012 | 2013 | 2014 | 2015 | 2016 | 2017 | 2018 | 2019 | 2020 | 2021 |
|---|---|---|---|---|---|---|---|---|---|---|---|---|
| Ranking | EN 4/23 | EN 4/23 | EN 5/22 | EN 8/24 | EN 6/25 | EN 13/21 | EN 12/21 | EN 11/22 | EN 13/24 | EN 9/24 | EN 7/25 | EN 5/24 |
| Peer frequencies | Austria (1) | Austria (1) | Austria (3) | Austria (2) | Austria (1) | Austria (4) | Austria (2) | Austria (2) | Austria (1) | Austria (4) | Austria (2) | Austria (4) |
| | Belgium (1) | Belgium (1) | Belgium (2) | Belgium (1) | Belgium (2) | Belgium (2) | Belgium (1) | Belgium (4) | Belgium (1) | Belgium (1) | Belgium (1) | Belgium (2) |
| | Bulgaria (1) | Bulgaria (1) | Bulgaria (3) | Bulgaria (1) | Bulgaria (1) | Bulgaria (1) | Bulgaria (1) | Bulgaria (1) | Bulgaria (1) | Bulgaria (1) | Bulgaria (1) | Bulgaria (3) |
| | Czech Republic (2) | Czech Republic (3) | Czech Republic (2) | Czech Republic (3) | Czech Republic (2) | Czech Republic (2) | Czech Republic (1) | Czech Republic (1) | Czech Republic (1) | Czech Republic (1) | Czech Republic (2) | Czech Republic (2) |
| | Cyprus (1) | Cyprus (2) | Cyprus (1) | Cyprus (1) | Cyprus (1) | Cyprus (2) | Cyprus (1) | Cyprus (1) | Cyprus (2) | Cyprus (1) | Cyprus (1) | Croatia (2) |
| | Croatia (2) | Croatia (2) | Croatia (3) | Croatia (1) | Croatia (1) | Croatia (1) | Croatia (1) | Croatia (1) | Croatia (1) | Croatia (3) | Croatia (1) | EU27 (1) |
| | Finland (1) | Estonia (1) | Finland (2) | Denmark (1) | Denmark (1) | Germany (2) | Germany (1) | Finland (1) | Finland (1) | Estonia (1) | Estonia (1) | Finland (1) |
| | France (1) | Finland (1) | France (1) | Finland (1) | Estonia (1) | Greece (7) | Greece (6) | Germany (2) | Germany (3) | Finland (1) | EU27 (1) | Germany (2) |
| | Germany (1) | France (1) | Germany (1) | France (1) | Finland (1) | Ireland (3) | Ireland (5) | Greece (5) | Greece (7) | Germany (1) | Finland (1) | Greece (6) |
| | Greece (4) | Germany (1) | Greece (4) | Germany (1) | France (1) | Italy (1) | Italy (1) | Ireland (5) | Ireland (9) | Greece (6) | Germany (1) | Ireland (5) |
| | Ireland (1) | Greece (4) | Ireland (2) | Greece (3) | Germany (1) | Latvia (1) | Latvia (1) | Italy (1) | Italy (1) | Ireland (5) | Greece (9) | Italy (1) |
| | Italy (2) | Ireland (1) | Italy (1) | Ireland (1) | Greece (3) | Lithuania (4) | Lithuania (4) | Latvia (1) | Latvia (1) | Italy (1) | Ireland (6) | Latvia (1) |
| | Latvia (1) | Italy (2) | Lithuania (5) | Italy (1) | Ireland (1) | Luxembourg (8) | Luxembourg (8) | Lithuania (4) | Lithuania (3) | Latvia (3) | Italy (1) | Lithuania (1) |
| | Lithuania (1) | Lithuania (3) | Luxembourg (5) | Latvia (1) | Italy (1) | Malta (5) | Malta (5) | Luxembourg (6) | Luxembourg (8) | Lithuania (1) | Latvia (1) | Luxembourg (4) |
| | Luxembourg (5) | Luxembourg (5) | Malta (3) | Lithuania (3) | Latvia (1) | Netherlands (2) | Netherlands (2) | Malta (2) | Malta (3) | Luxembourg (8) | Lithuania (2) | Malta (4) |
| | Malta (6) | Malta (5) | Netherlands (2) | Luxembourg (4) | Lithuania (2) | Poland (6) | Poland (5) | Netherlands (1) | Netherlands (2) | Malta (1) | Luxembourg (9) | Netherlands (3) |
| | Netherlands (1) | Netherlands (1) | Poland (4) | Malta (4) | Luxembourg (5) | Portugal (2) | Portugal (2) | Poland (3) | Poland (3) | Netherlands (1) | Malta (1) | Poland (1) |
| | Poland (4) | Poland (3) | Portugal (2) | Netherlands (2) | Malta (3) | Romania (3) | Romania (4) | Portugal (2) | Portugal (4) | Poland (3) | Netherlands (1) | Portugal (4) |
| | Portugal (1) | Portugal (1) | Romania (5) | Poland (4) | Netherlands (1) | Slovenia (4) | Slovenia (8) | Romania (3) | Romania (2) | Portugal (5) | Poland (3) | Romania (5) |
| | Romania (6) | Romania (6) | Slovenia (2) | Portugal (2) | Poland (3) | Sweden (1) | Sweden (2) | Slovenia (5) | Slovakia (1) | Romania (4) | Portugal (3) | Slovakia (1) |
| | Slovenia (5) | Slovenia (3) | Sweden (1) | Romania (3) | Portugal (2) | Hungary (3) | Hungary (2) | Sweden (1) | Slovenia (5) | Slovakia (1) | Romania (4) | Slovenia (4) |

Source: Author

**Table 11.4** (continued)

| | 2010 | 2011 | 2012 | 2013 | 2014 | 2015 | 2016 | 2017 | 2018 | 2019 | 2020 | 2021 |
|---|---|---|---|---|---|---|---|---|---|---|---|---|
| | Sweden (1) | Sweden (1) | Hungary (1) | Slovenia (4) | Romania (3) | | | Hungary (2) | Spain (1) | Slovenia (5) | Slovakia (1) | Spain (1) |
| | Hungary (2) | Hungary (1) | | Sweden (1) | Slovenia (4) | | | | Sweden (1) | Sweden (2) | Slovenia (4) | Sweden (2) |
| | | | | Hungary (2) | Sweden (1) | | | | Hungary (6) | Hungary (3) | Sweden (1) | Hungary (2) |
| | | | | () | Hungary (1) | | | | | | Hungary (2) | |

**Table 11.5** Lambda coefficients of the reference unit for Romania

| | Romania | | | | | | | | | | | |
|---|---|---|---|---|---|---|---|---|---|---|---|---|
| **DMU/ An** | **2010** | **2011** | **2012** | **2013** | **2014** | **2015** | **2016** | **2017** | **2018** | **2019** | **2020** | **2021** |
| **Austria** | 0 | 0 | 0 | 0 | 0 | 0 | 0 | 0 | 0 | 0 | 0 | 0 |
| **Belgium** | 0 | 0 | 0 | 0 | 0 | 0 | 0 | 0 | 0 | 0 | 0 | 0 |
| **Bulgaria** | 0 | 0 | 0 | 0 | 0 | 0 | 0 | 0 | 0 | 0 | 0 | 0 |
| **Czech Republic** | 0 | 0 | 0 | 0 | 0 | 0 | 0 | 0 | 0 | 0 | 0 | 0 |
| **Cyprus** | 0 | 0 | 0 | 0 | 0 | 0 | 0 | 0 | 0 | 0 | 0 | 0 |
| **Croatia** | 0 | 0 | 0 | 0 | 0 | 0 | 0 | 0 | 0 | 0 | 0 | 0 |
| **Denmark** | 0 | 0.007 | 0 | 0 | 0 | 0 | 0 | 0 | 0 | 0 | 0 | 0 |
| **Estonia** | 0.095 | 0 | 0.017 | 0 | 0 | 0 | 0.156 | 0 | 0.029 | 0 | 0 | 0.097 |
| **EU27** | 0.126 | 0.041 | 0 | 0 | 0 | 0 | 0 | 0 | 0 | 0 | 0 | 0 |
| **Finland** | 0 | 0 | 0 | 0 | 0 | 0 | 0 | 0 | 0 | 0 | 0 | 0 |
| **France** | 0 | 0 | 0 | 0 | 0 | 0 | 0 | 0 | 0 | 0 | 0 | 0 |
| **Germany** | 0 | 0 | 0 | 0 | 0 | 0 | 0 | 0 | 0 | 0 | 0 | 0 |
| **Greece** | 0 | 0 | 0 | 0 | 0 | 0 | 0 | 0 | 0 | 0 | 0 | 0 |
| **Ireland** | 0 | 0 | 0 | 0 | 0 | 0 | 0 | 0 | 0 | 0 | 0 | 0 |
| **Italy** | 0 | 0 | 0 | 0 | 0 | 0 | 0 | 0 | 0 | 0 | 0 | 0 |
| **Latvia** | 0 | 0.247 | 0.115 | 0 | 0 | 0 | 0 | 0 | 0 | 0 | 0 | 0 |
| **Lithuania** | 0 | 0 | 0 | 0 | 0 | 0 | 0 | 0 | 0 | 0 | 0 | 0 |
| **Luxembourg** | 0 | 0 | 0 | 0 | 0 | 0 | 0 | 0 | 0 | 0 | 0 | 0 |
| **Malta** | 0 | 0 | 0 | 0 | 0 | 0 | 0 | 0 | 0 | 0 | 0 | 0 |
| **Netherlands** | 0 | 0 | 0 | 0 | 0 | 0 | 0 | 0 | 0 | 0 | 0 | 0 |
| **Poland** | 0 | 0 | 0 | 0 | 0 | 0 | 0 | 0 | 0 | 0 | 0 | 0 |
| **Portugal** | 0 | 0 | 0 | 0 | 0 | 0 | 0 | 0 | 0 | 0 | 0 | 0 |
| **Romania** | 1 | 1 | 1 | 1 | 1 | 1 | 1 | 1 | 1 | 1 | 1 | 1 |
| **Slovakia** | 0.435 | 0.374 | 0.23 | 0.332 | 0.334 | 0.095 | 0.197 | 0.312 | 0 | 0 | 0 | 0 |
| **Slovenia** | 0 | 0 | 0 | 0 | 0 | 0 | 0 | 0 | 0 | 0 | 0 | 0 |
| **Spain** | 0.199 | 0.167 | 0.215 | 0.129 | 0.133 | 0.096 | 0.202 | 0.331 | 0 | 0.361 | 0.341 | 0 |
| **Sweden** | 0 | 0 | 0 | 0 | 0 | 0 | 0 | 0 | 0 | 0 | 0 | 0 |
| **Hungary** | 0 | 0 | 0 | 0 | 0 | 0 | 0 | 0 | 0 | 0 | 0 | 0 |

Source: Author

It can be observed that Romania is a model of efficiency for Spain (10 out of 12 years), Slovakia (8 out of 12 years) and Estonia (5 out of 12 years). For the EU, Romania is a model of economic efficiency only in the period 2010–2011 according to Table 11.5. It can be seen from the above that both for the EU and for Spain the non-zero values of the lambda coefficients determined for the DMU recommend Romania as a (partial) efficiency solution.

Tables 11.6 and 11.7 present the values of the variables for the economic efficiency model, showing the weights attributable by the DEA method to the input values (Table 11.6) and output values (Table 11.7) respectively.

Table 11.7 shows that the weights significantly different from 0 of the improvable input variables are for Spain related to professionals employed in the ICT sector. This indicator needs to be improved in order to achieve economic efficiency from an SDG8 perspective for Spain. For Romania and the European average there are no indicators with weights significantly different from 0.

Table 11.7 shows that the significantly different weights of 0 of the improvable output variables are for Romania and Spain for value added in agriculture. Agriculture is an extremely important sector for the two countries, with a significant impact on the economy and employment, which needs to be improved in order to reach the efficiency optimum and contribute to the sustainable development of these two countries.

The input and output vulnerabilities related to each unit are shown in Tables 11.8 and 11.9 respectively.

Table 11.8 shows that unlike the European average and Spain, Romania's economic efficiency model does not generate input vulnerabilities. At the EU level these consist of labour tax revenues, the level of household Internet access, Internet use by individuals, the number of ICT specialists employed, and only for 2018 high-speed Internet coverage. The same vulnerabilities are also found for Spain with the exception that high-speed Internet coverage was a vulnerability throughout the period of the analysis except for 2018 and 2021.

With regard to the exit vulnerabilities (for which no significantly different values have been determined 0 in the case of Romania being economically efficient) they affect Spain more than the EU average, in the sense that for the EU average the vulnerabilities related to the value added in agriculture and the level of risk of poverty are significant up to 2015 inclusive, whereas, in the case of Spain, additional vulnerabilities have been observed from 2014, notably those arising from fluctuations in the realised gross domestic product per capita.

Based on these vulnerabilities, entry and exit efficiency thresholds were projected for Romania, Spain and the European average.

**Table 11.6** Weights for the input variables of the economic efficiency model

| *DMU* | *Romania* | | | | | | | *EU27* | | | | | | |
|---|---|---|---|---|---|---|---|---|---|---|---|---|---|---|
| *An/ Indicator* | *SDG8 VIMPM* | *SDG8 TNEET* | *SDG8 ROCFM* | *SDG8 INTA* | *SDG8 UTINT* | *SDG8 ATIC* | *SDG8 AINT* | *SDG8 VIMPM* | *SDG8 TNEET* | *SDG8 ROCFM* | *SDG8 INTA* | *SDG8 UTINT* | *SDG8 ATIC* | *SDG8 AINT* |
| 2010 | 0 | 0 | 0 | 0 | 0 | 0 | 0 | 0 | 0 | 0 | 0 | 0 | 0 | 0 |
| 2011 | 0 | 0 | 0 | 0 | 0 | 0 | 0 | 0 | 0 | 0 | 0 | 0 | 0 | 0 |
| 2012 | 0 | 0 | 0 | 0 | 0 | 0 | 0 | 0 | 0 | 0 | 0 | 0 | 0 | 0 |
| 2013 | 0 | 0 | 0 | 0 | 0 | 0 | 0 | 0 | 0 | 0 | 0 | 0 | 0 | 0 |
| 2014 | 0 | 0 | 0 | 0 | 0 | 0 | 0 | 0 | 0 | 0 | 0 | 0 | 0 | 0 |
| 2015 | 0 | 0 | 0 | 0 | 0 | 0 | 0 | 0 | 0 | 0 | 0 | 0 | 0 | 0 |
| 2016 | 0 | 0 | 0 | 0 | 0 | 0 | 0 | 0 | 0 | 0 | 0 | 0 | 0 | 0 |
| 2017 | 0 | 0 | 0 | 0 | 0 | 0 | 0 | 0 | 0 | 0 | 0 | 0 | 0 | 0 |
| 2018 | 0 | 0 | 0 | 0 | 0 | 0 | 0 | 0 | 0 | 0 | 0 | 0 | 0 | 0 |
| 2019 | 0 | 0 | 0 | 0 | 0 | 0 | 0 | 0 | 0 | 0 | 0 | 0 | 0 | 0 |
| 2020 | 0 | 0 | 0 | 0 | 0 | 0 | 0 | 0 | 0 | 0 | 0 | 0 | 0 | 0 |
| 2021 | 0 | 0 | 0 | 0 | 0 | 0 | 0 | 0 | 0 | 0 | 0 | 0 | 0 | 0 |
| | Spain | | | | | | | | | | | | | |
| | SDG8 VIMPM | SDG8 TNEET | SDG8 ROCFM | SDG8 INTA | SDG8 UTINT | SDG8 ATIC | SDG8 AINT | | | | | | | |
| 2010 | 0 | 0 | 0 | 0 | 0 | 0.02 | 0 | | | | | | | |
| 2011 | 0 | 0 | 0 | 0 | 0 | 0.02 | 0 | | | | | | | |
| 2012 | 0 | 0 | 0 | 0 | 0 | 0.03 | 0 | | | | | | | |
| 2013 | 0 | 0 | 0 | 0 | 0 | 0.03 | 0 | | | | | | | |
| 2014 | 0 | 0 | 0 | 0 | 0 | 0 | 0 | | | | | | | |
| 2015 | 0 | 0 | 0 | 0 | 0 | 0 | 0 | | | | | | | |
| 2016 | 0 | 0 | 0 | 0 | 0 | 0 | 0 | | | | | | | |
| 2017 | 0 | 0 | 0 | 0 | 0 | 0 | 0 | | | | | | | |
| 2018 | 0 | 0 | 0 | 0 | 0 | 0 | 0 | | | | | | | |
| 2019 | 0 | 0 | 0 | 0 | 0 | 0.01 | 0 | | | | | | | |
| 2020 | 0 | 0 | 0 | 0 | 0 | 0 | 0 | | | | | | | |
| 2021 | 0 | 0 | 0 | 0 | 0 | 0.01 | 0 | | | | | | | |

Source: Author

**Table 11.7** Weights for the values of the output variables of the economic efficiency model

| *DMU* | *Romania* | | | | | *EU27* | | | | | *Spain* | | | | |
|---|---|---|---|---|---|---|---|---|---|---|---|---|---|---|---|
| *An/ Indicator* | *SDG8 VAAG* | *SDG8 VAIN* | *SDG8 VASE* | *SDG8 PIBloc* | *SDG8 RRSAR* | *SDG8 VAAG* | *SDG8 VAIN* | *SDG8 VASE* | *SDG8 PIBloc* | *SDG8 RRSAR* | *SDG8 VAAG* | *SDG8 VAIN* | *SDG8 VASE* | *SDG8 PIBloc* | *SDG8 RRSAR* |
| 2010 | 0.01 | 0 | 0 | 0 | 0 | 0 | 0 | 0 | 0 | 0 | 0 | 0 | 0 | 0 | 0 |
| 2011 | 0.01 | 0 | 0 | 0 | 0 | 0 | 0 | 0 | 0 | 0 | 0 | 0 | 0 | 0 | 0 |
| 2012 | 0 | 0 | 0 | 0 | 0 | 0 | 0 | 0 | 0 | 0 | 0 | 0 | 0 | 0 | 0 |
| 2013 | 0.02 | 0 | 0 | 0 | 0 | 0 | 0 | 0 | 0 | 0 | 0 | 0 | 0 | 0 | 0 |
| 2014 | 0 | 0 | 0 | 0 | 0 | 0 | 0 | 0 | 0 | 0 | 0 | 0 | 0 | 0 | 0 |
| 2015 | 0 | 0 | 0 | 0 | 0 | 0 | 0 | 0 | 0 | 0 | 0 | 0 | 0 | 0 | 0 |
| 2016 | 0 | 0 | 0 | 0 | 0 | 0 | 0 | 0 | 0 | 0 | 0 | 0 | 0 | 0 | 0 |
| 2017 | 0 | 0 | 0 | 0 | 0 | 0 | 0 | 0 | 0 | 0 | 0 | 0 | 0 | 0 | 0 |
| 2018 | 0 | 0 | 0 | 0 | 0 | 0 | 0 | 0 | 0 | 0 | 0.01 | 0 | 0 | 0 | 0 |
| 2019 | 0 | 0 | 0 | 0 | 0 | 0 | 0 | 0 | 0 | 0 | 0 | 0 | 0 | 0 | 0 |
| 2020 | 0.01 | 0 | 0 | 0 | 0 | 0 | 0 | 0 | 0 | 0 | 0 | 0 | 0 | 0 | 0 |
| 2021 | 0.01 | 0 | 0 | 0 | 0 | 0 | 0 | 0 | 0 | 0 | 0 | 0 | 0 | 0 | 0 |

Source: Author

**Table 11.8** Input vulnerabilities hindering economic efficiency in Romania

| *DMU* | *Year* | *SDG8VIMPM* | *SDG8TNEET* | *SDG8ROCFM* | *SDG8INTA* | *SDG8UTINT* | *SDG8ATIC* | *SDG8AINT* |
|---|---|---|---|---|---|---|---|---|
| Romania | 2010 | 0 | 0 | 0 | 0 | 0 | 0 | 0 |
| | 2011 | 0 | 0 | 0 | 0 | 0 | 0 | 0 |
| | 2012 | 0 | 0 | 0 | 0 | 0 | 0 | 0 |
| | 2013 | 0 | 0 | 0 | 0 | 0 | 0 | 0 |
| | 2014 | 0 | 0 | 0 | 0 | 0 | 0 | 0 |
| | 2015 | 0 | 0 | 0 | 0 | 0 | 0 | 0 |
| | 2016 | 0 | 0 | 0 | 0 | 0 | 0 | 0 |
| | 2017 | 0 | 0 | 0 | 0 | 0 | 0 | 0 |
| | 2018 | 0 | 0 | 0 | 0 | 0 | 0 | 0 |
| | 2019 | 0 | 0 | 0 | 0 | 0 | 0 | 0 |
| | 2020 | 0 | 0 | 0 | 0 | 0 | 0 | 0 |
| EU27 | 2021 | 0 | 0 | 0 | 0 | 0 | 0 | 0 |
| | 2010 | 569.282 | 0 | 0 | 0 | 215.397 | 11.85 | 0 |
| | 2011 | 399.039 | 0 | 0 | 0 | 101.36 | 2.825 | 0 |
| | 2012 | 249.843 | 0 | 0 | 0 | 60.364 | 0 | 0 |
| | 2013 | 350.201 | 0 | 0 | 0 | 0 | 11.276 | 0 |
| | 2014 | 235.889 | 0 | 0 | 0 | 0 | 7.93 | 0 |
| | 2015 | 317.849 | 0 | 0 | 0 | 0 | 31.697 | 0 |
| | 2016 | 420.791 | 0 | 0 | 112.908 | 0 | 23.762 | 0 |
| | 2017 | 273.09 | 0 | 0 | 112.509 | 4.954 | 20.232 | 0 |
| | 2018 | 286.976 | 0 | 0 | 12.322 | 95.598 | 18.503 | 98.491 |
| | 2019 | 315.607 | 0 | 0 | 0 | 9.413 | 29.831 | 0 |
| | 2020 | 0 | 0 | 0 | 0 | 0 | 0 | 0 |
| | 2021 | 0 | 0 | 0 | 0 | 0 | 0 | 0 |

(*continued*)

**Table 11.8** (continued)

| *DMU* | *Year* | *SDG8VIMPM* | *SDG8TNEET* | *SDG8ROCFM* | *SDG8INTA* | *SDG8UTINT* | *SDG8ATIC* | *SDG8AINT* |
|---|---|---|---|---|---|---|---|---|
| Spain | 2010 | 44.266 | 0 | 0 | 0 | 943.817 | 75.102 | 438.287 |
| | 2011 | 96.571 | 0 | 0 | 0 | 877.244 | 64.217 | 2547.741 |
| | 2012 | 258.367 | 0 | 0 | 279.609 | 814.405 | 82.782 | 3094.049 |
| | 2013 | 162.35 | 0 | 0 | 467.014 | 626.138 | 77.174 | 432.41 |
| | 2014 | 208.459 | 0 | 0 | 253.266 | 777.253 | 68.753 | 2234.262 |
| | 2015 | 169.934 | 0 | 0 | 241.748 | 598.473 | 69.545 | 3654.366 |
| | 2016 | 105.326 | 0 | 0 | 288.218 | 457.418 | 58.025 | 3200.316 |
| | 2017 | 201.067 | 0 | 0 | 153.778 | 759.857 | 40.064 | 3008.883 |
| | 2018 | 0 | 0 | 0 | 0 | 0 | 0 | 0 |
| | 2019 | 316.676 | 0 | 0 | 429.697 | 826.074 | 18.679 | 2760.332 |
| | 2020 | 801.471 | 0 | 0 | 769.567 | 825.917 | 58.961 | 3744.334 |
| | 2021 | 0 | 0 | 0 | 0 | 0 | 0 | 0 |

Source: Author

**Table 11.9** Output vulnerabilities hampering economic efficiency in Romania

| *DMU* | *Romania* | | | | | *EU27* | | | | | *Spain* | | | | |
|---|---|---|---|---|---|---|---|---|---|---|---|---|---|---|---|
| *A/ Indicator* | *SDG8 VAAG* | *SDG8 VAIN* | *SDG8 VASE* | *SDG8 PIBloc* | *SDG8 RRSAR* | *SDG8 VAAG* | *SDG8 VAIN* | *SDG8 VASE* | *SDG8 PIBloc* | *SDG8 RRSAR* | *SDG8 VAAG* | *SDG8 VAIN* | *SDG8 VASE* | *SDG8 PIBloc* | *SDG8 RRSAR* |
| 2010 | 0 | 0 | 0 | 0 | 0 | 95.438 | 0 | 0 | 0 | 300.078 | 7.599 | 0 | 0 | 0 | 37.452 |
| 2011 | 0 | 0 | 0 | 0 | 0 | 100.075 | 0 | 0 | 0 | 146.664 | 40.087 | 0 | 0 | 0 | 66.508 |
| 2012 | 0 | 0 | 0 | 0 | 0 | 63.616 | 0 | 0 | 0 | 99.867 | 116.32 | 0 | 0 | 0 | 224.109 |
| 2013 | 0 | 0 | 0 | 0 | 0 | 74.917 | 0 | 0 | 0 | 107.621 | 61.876 | 0 | 0 | 0 | 195.858 |
| 2014 | 0 | 0 | 0 | 0 | 0 | 58.712 | 0 | 0 | 0 | 2.739 | 65.883 | 0 | 0 | 127043.1 | 0 |
| 2015 | 0 | 0 | 0 | 0 | 0 | 72.386 | 0 | 0 | 0 | 99.653 | 32.532 | 0 | 0 | 284008.5 | 0 |
| 2016 | 0 | 0 | 0 | 0 | 0 | 74.785 | 0 | 0 | 0 | 0 | 3.918 | 0 | 0 | 399934.9 | 0 |
| 2017 | 0 | 0 | 0 | 0 | 0 | 96.584 | 0 | 0 | 0 | 0 | 14.424 | 0 | 0 | 707094.6 | 0 |
| 2018 | 0 | 0 | 0 | 0 | 0 | 99.729 | 0 | 0 | 0 | 0 | 0 | 0 | 0 | 0 | 0 |
| 2019 | 0 | 0 | 0 | 0 | 0 | 101.391 | 0 | 0 | 0 | 0 | 30.169 | 0 | 0 | 872552.6 | 0 |
| 2020 | 0 | 0 | 0 | 0 | 0 | 0 | 0 | 0 | 0 | 0 | 43.152 | 0 | 0 | 731895.1 | 0 |
| 2021 | 0 | 0 | 0 | 0 | 0 | 0 | 0 | 0 | 0 | 0 | 0 | 0 | 0 | 0 | 0 |

Source: Author

Table 11.10 shows actual values and input efficiency thresholds for Spain and the European average compared to Romania.

Table 11.10 shows that Romania does not differ in inputs relative to the efficiency thresholds determined using the DEA method. In the case of the EU average, the differences (representing the need for efficiency) of the indicators in relation to the determined efficiency thresholds concern income from labour taxation (SDG8VIMPM), the level of household Internet access (SDG8INTA), Internet use by individuals (SDG8UTINT), and ICT specialist employees (SDG8ATIC). In addition to the European average, Spain adds the need for efficiency in high-speed Internet coverage (SDG8AINT) to support the digitalization processes and achieve economic efficiency.

Table 11.11 shows the actual values and efficiency thresholds of the outputs for Romania compared to Spain and the European average.

Table 11.11 highlights that Romania remains within the established efficiency thresholds, which serve as the reference benchmark for comparison with the EU and Spain. With the exception of the period 2020–2021 in the case of the EU, and 2018 and 2021 in the case of Spain, these regions show significant differences with respect to the efficiency thresholds determined for all economic indicators (Value added in agriculture, Value added in industry, Value added in services, GDP per capita) except for the at-risk-of-work poverty rate.

The DEA method has shown that by assuming accelerated growth strategies Romania has become economically efficient, meaning that in Romania the resources utilized generate adequate economic returns in relation to Romania's economic capacity. In contrast to some European countries, Spain, although benefiting from much more significant resources than Romania, is not able to reach the efficiency thresholds to ensure sustainable economic growth, one of the obstacles being the optimal provision of high-speed Internet capacity to support digitalization.

It is important for Romania to focus on the development of human resources, in order to increase the skill level of the workforce and encourage innovation in various fields. The government should also pay more attention to the transport and communications infrastructure to ensure better connectivity and access to international markets. By implementing coherent policies and economic development strategies, Romania could improve its efficiency and become more competitive on the European market. In this way, the country could attract more foreign direct investment and stimulate long-term economic growth. It is also important for

**Table 11.10** Actual values and input efficiency thresholds for Spain and the European average compared to Romania

| *Tip* | | *Input* | *Efficiency threshold* | *Input* | *Efficiency threshold* | *Input* | *Efficiency threshold* | *Input* | *Efficiency threshold* | *Input* | *Efficiency threshold* | *Input* | *Efficiency threshold* | *Input* | *Efficiency threshold* |
|---|---|---|---|---|---|---|---|---|---|---|---|---|---|---|---|
| DMU | Year | SDG8 VIMPM | SDG8 VIMPM | SDG8 TNEET | SDG8 TNEET | SDG8 ROCFM | SDG8 ROCFM | SDG8 INTA | SDG8 INTA | SDG8 UTINT | SDG8 UTINT | SDG8 ATIC | SDG8 ATIC | SDG8 AINT | SDG8 AINT |
| Romania | 2010 | 1196 | 1196 | 2420 | 2420 | 5630 | 5630 | 4246 | 4246 | 3547 | 3547 | 110 | 110 | 5470 | 5470 |
| | 2011 | 1249 | 1249 | 2440 | 2440 | 5600 | 5600 | 4744 | 4744 | 4001 | 4001 | 125 | 125 | 5800 | 5800 |
| | 2012 | 1228 | 1228 | 2430 | 2430 | 5680 | 5680 | 5377 | 5377 | 4588 | 4588 | 140 | 140 | 5820 | 5820 |
| | 2013 | 1208 | 1208 | 2450 | 2450 | 5690 | 5690 | 5807 | 5807 | 4976 | 4976 | 160 | 160 | 5470 | 5470 |
| | 2014 | 1212 | 1212 | 2480 | 2480 | 5800 | 5800 | 6054 | 6054 | 5408 | 5408 | 160 | 160 | 5800 | 5800 |
| | 2015 | 1191 | 1191 | 2580 | 2580 | 5920 | 5920 | 6771 | 6771 | 5576 | 5576 | 190 | 190 | 5820 | 5820 |
| | 2016 | 1169 | 1169 | 2430 | 2430 | 6030 | 6030 | 7240 | 7240 | 5950 | 5950 | 200 | 200 | 5970 | 5970 |
| | 2017 | 1195 | 1195 | 2210 | 2210 | 6270 | 6270 | 7645 | 7645 | 6375 | 6375 | 210 | 210 | 6100 | 6100 |
| | 2018 | 1239 | 1239 | 2130 | 2130 | 6390 | 6390 | 8089 | 8089 | 7068 | 7068 | 220 | 220 | 6270 | 6270 |
| | 2019 | 1212 | 1212 | 2090 | 2090 | 6510 | 6510 | 8361 | 8361 | 7366 | 7366 | 230 | 230 | 6810 | 6810 |
| | 2020 | 1271 | 1271 | 2060 | 2060 | 6520 | 6520 | 8624 | 8624 | 7846 | 7846 | 240 | 240 | 7590 | 7590 |
| | 2021 | 1227 | 1227 | 2030 | 2030 | 6710 | 6710 | 8874 | 8874 | 8359 | 8359 | 260 | 260 | 8710 | 8710 |
| EU27 | 2010 | 2138 | 1568.72 | 1540 | 1540 | 6700 | 6700 | 6880 | 6880 | 6744 | 6528.60 | 300 | 288.15 | 1560 | 1560 |
| | 2011 | 2158 | 1758.96 | 1550 | 1550 | 6710 | 6710 | 7155 | 7155 | 6936 | 6834.64 | 310 | 307.18 | 1950 | 1950 |
| | 2012 | 2221 | 1971.16 | 1600 | 1600 | 6690 | 6690 | 7454 | 7454 | 7155 | 7094.64 | 320 | 320 | 2190 | 2190 |
| | 2013 | 2249 | 1898.80 | 1640 | 1640 | 6680 | 6680 | 7717 | 7717 | 7334 | 7334 | 330 | 318.72 | 1560 | 1560 |
| | 2014 | 2250 | 2014.11 | 1600 | 1600 | 6750 | 6750 | 7961 | 7961 | 7607 | 7607 | 340 | 332.07 | 1950 | 1950 |
| | 2015 | 2236 | 1918.15 | 1550 | 1550 | 6850 | 6850 | 8137 | 8137 | 7775 | 7775 | 350 | 318.30 | 2190 | 2190 |
| | 2016 | 2234 | 1813.21 | 1480 | 1480 | 6960 | 6960 | 8421 | 8308.09 | 8015 | 8015 | 360 | 336.24 | 2520 | 2520 |
| | 2017 | 2243 | 1969.91 | 1400 | 1400 | 7090 | 7090 | 8581 | 8468.49 | 8202 | 8197.05 | 370 | 349.77 | 2920 | 2920 |
| | 2018 | 2260 | 1973.02 | 1330 | 1330 | 7190 | 7190 | 8794 | 8781.68 | 8385 | 8289.40 | 380 | 361.50 | 3330 | 3231.51 |
| | 2019 | 2250 | 1934.39 | 1280 | 1280 | 7270 | 7270 | 8968 | 8968 | 8593 | 8583.59 | 390 | 360.17 | 5010 | 5010 |
| | 2020 | 1124 | 1124 | 1390 | 1390 | 7170 | 7170 | 9130 | 9130 | 8762 | 8762 | 430 | 430 | 5980 | 5980 |
| | 2021 | 1245 | 1245 | 1310 | 1310 | 7310 | 7310 | 9231 | 9231 | 8900 | 8900 | 450 | 450 | 7020 | 7020 |

(*continued*)

**Table 11.10** (continued)

| *Tip* | | *Input* | *Efficiency threshold* | *Input* | *Efficiency threshold* | *Input* | *Efficiency threshold* | *Input* | *Efficiency threshold* | *Input* | *Efficiency threshold* | *Input* | *Efficiency threshold* | *Input* | *Efficiency threshold* |
|---|---|---|---|---|---|---|---|---|---|---|---|---|---|---|---|
| Spain | 2010 | 1877 | 1832.73 | 2000 | 2000 | 6280 | 6280 | 5932 | 5932 | 6403 | 5459.18 | 343 | 267.90 | 2270 | 1831.71 |
| | 2011 | 1901 | 1804.43 | 2060 | 2060 | 6200 | 6200 | 6271 | 6271 | 6647 | 5769.76 | 338 | 273.78 | 4480 | 1932.26 |
| | 2012 | 1915 | 1656.63 | 2220 | 2220 | 5960 | 5960 | 6659 | 6379.39 | 6948 | 6133.60 | 333 | 250.22 | 5280 | 2185.95 |
| | 2013 | 1902 | 1739.65 | 2250 | 2250 | 5860 | 5860 | 6973 | 6505.99 | 7164 | 6537.86 | 330 | 252.83 | 2270 | 1837.59 |
| | 2014 | 1933 | 1724.54 | 2070 | 2070 | 5990 | 5990 | 7435 | 7181.73 | 7619 | 6841.75 | 320 | 251.25 | 4480 | 2245.74 |
| | 2015 | 1871 | 1701.07 | 1940 | 1940 | 6200 | 6200 | 7875 | 7633.25 | 7869 | 7270.53 | 320 | 250.46 | 5280 | 1625.63 |
| | 2016 | 1862 | 1756.67 | 1810 | 1810 | 6390 | 6390 | 8193 | 7904.78 | 8056 | 7598.58 | 340 | 281.98 | 6280 | 3079.68 |
| | 2017 | 1892 | 1690.93 | 1640 | 1640 | 6550 | 6550 | 8339 | 8185.22 | 8460 | 7700.14 | 350 | 309.94 | 7140 | 4131.12 |
| | 2018 | 1941 | 1941 | 1530 | 1530 | 6700 | 6700 | 8636 | 8636 | 8611 | 8611 | 360 | 360 | 7740 | 7740 |
| | 2019 | 2011 | 1694.32 | 1490 | 1490 | 6800 | 6800 | 9144 | 8714.30 | 9072 | 8245.93 | 370 | 351.32 | 8900 | 6139.67 |
| | 2020 | 2249 | 1447.53 | 1730 | 1730 | 6570 | 6570 | 9538 | 8768.43 | 9321 | 8495.08 | 390 | 331.04 | 9170 | 5425.67 |
| | 2021 | 2487 | 2487 | 1410 | 1410 | 6770 | 6770 | 9592 | 9592 | 9390 | 9390 | 410 | 410 | 9380 | 9380 |

Source: Author

**Table 11.11** Actual values and output efficiency thresholds for Spain and EU average compared to Romania

| *Typ* | | *Output* | *Efficiency threshold* | *Output* | *Efficiency threshold* | *Output* | *Efficiency threshold* | *Output* | *Efficiency threshold* | *Output* | *Efficiency threshold* |
|---|---|---|---|---|---|---|---|---|---|---|---|
| *DMU* | *Year* | *SDG8 VAAG* | *SDG8 VAAG* | *SDG8 VAIN* | *SDG8 VAIN* | *SDG8 VASE* | *SDG8 VASE* | *SDG8 PIBloc* | *SDG8 PIBloc* | *SDG8 RRSAR* | *SDG8 RRSAR* |
| Romania | 2010 | 560 | 560 | 4259 | 4259 | 5181 | 5181 | 634,000 | 634,000 | 1790 | 1790 |
| | 2011 | 711 | 711 | 4402 | 4402 | 4887 | 4887 | 665,000 | 665,000 | 1910 | 1910 |
| | 2012 | 533 | 533 | 3731 | 3731 | 5736 | 5736 | 681,000 | 681,000 | 1900 | 1900 |
| | 2013 | 610 | 610 | 3669 | 3669 | 5721 | 5721 | 686,000 | 686,000 | 1840 | 1840 |
| | 2014 | 533 | 533 | 3620 | 3620 | 5847 | 5847 | 716,000 | 716,000 | 1980 | 1980 |
| | 2015 | 477 | 477 | 3427 | 3427 | 6096 | 6096 | 742,000 | 742,000 | 1880 | 1880 |
| | 2016 | 454 | 454 | 3359 | 3359 | 6188 | 6188 | 768,000 | 768,000 | 1890 | 1890 |
| | 2017 | 476 | 476 | 3191 | 3191 | 6332 | 6332 | 836,000 | 836,000 | 1740 | 1740 |
| | 2018 | 479 | 479 | 3119 | 3119 | 6401 | 6401 | 891,000 | 891,000 | 1530 | 1530 |
| | 2019 | 456 | 456 | 2982 | 2982 | 6562 | 6562 | 930,000 | 930,000 | 1570 | 1570 |
| | 2020 | 438 | 438 | 2967 | 2967 | 6596 | 6596 | 900,000 | 900,000 | 1490 | 1490 |
| | 2021 | 482 | 482 | 3076 | 3076 | 6443 | 6443 | 916,000 | 916,000 | 1550 | 1550 |

(*continued*)

**Table 11.11** (continued)

| *Typ* | | *Output* | *Efficiency threshold* | *Output* | *Efficiency threshold* | *Output* | *Efficiency threshold* | *Output* | *Efficiency threshold* | *Output* | *Efficiency threshold* |
|---|---|---|---|---|---|---|---|---|---|---|---|
| *DMU* | *Year* | *SDG8 VAAG* | *SDG8 VAAG* | *SDG8 VAIN* | *SDG8 VAIN* | *SDG8 VASE* | *SDG8 VASE* | *SDG8 PIBloc* | *SDG8 PIBloc* | *SDG8 RRSAR* | *SDG8 RRSAR* |
| EU27 | 2010 | 184 | 289.583 | 2560 | 2701.152 | 7256 | 7656.079 | 2,490,000 | 2,627,293 | 850 | 850 |
| | 2011 | 192 | 301.211 | 2573 | 2695.438 | 7235 | 7579.284 | 2,533,000 | 2,653,535 | 900 | 900 |
| | 2012 | 190 | 261.164 | 2545 | 2646.105 | 7266 | 7554.656 | 2,511,000 | 2,610,754 | 890 | 890 |
| | 2013 | 195 | 278.299 | 2502 | 2609.544 | 7303 | 7616.906 | 2,506,000 | 2,613,716 | 910 | 910 |
| | 2014 | 191 | 257.471 | 2500 | 2601.57 | 7309 | 7605.95 | 2,543,000 | 2,646,317 | 960 | 960 |
| | 2015 | 183 | 263.303 | 2546 | 2656.142 | 7271 | 7585.549 | 2,596,000 | 2,708,305 | 970 | 970 |
| | 2016 | 178 | 261.217 | 2551 | 2671.842 | 7271 | 7615.431 | 2,641,000 | 2,766,106 | 980 | 980 |
| | 2017 | 190 | 295.57 | 2543 | 2663.268 | 7267 | 7610.684 | 2,711,000 | 2,839,214 | 950 | 950 |
| | 2018 | 181 | 287.704 | 2542 | 2639.96 | 7277 | 7557.43 | 2,762,000 | 2,868,438 | 930 | 930 |
| | 2019 | 177 | 284.625 | 2532 | 2621.185 | 7290 | 7546.777 | 2,806,000 | 2,904,836 | 900 | 900 |
| | 2020 | 183 | 183 | 2510 | 2510 | 7307 | 7307 | 2,645,000 | 2,645,000 | 880 | 880 |
| | 2021 | 181 | 181 | 2549 | 2549 | 7270 | 7270 | 2,620,667 | 2,620,667 | 890 | 890 |
| Spain | 2010 | 265 | 281.755 | 2521 | 2608.107 | 7214 | 7463.262 | 2,304,000 | 2,383,609 | 1090 | 1090 |
| | 2011 | 258 | 304.6 | 2396 | 2456.479 | 7346 | 7531.425 | 2,277,000 | 2,334,475 | 1090 | 1090 |
| | 2012 | 262 | 381.6 | 2287 | 2315.632 | 7451 | 7544.284 | 2,208,000 | 2,235,643 | 1080 | 1080 |
| | 2013 | 287 | 351.462 | 2217 | 2236.977 | 7496 | 7563.544 | 2,185,000 | 2,204,688 | 1050 | 1050 |
| | 2014 | 278 | 345.859 | 2203 | 2218.657 | 7519 | 7572.438 | 2,222,000 | 2,364,835 | 1250 | 1250 |
| | 2015 | 301 | 338.486 | 2211 | 2247.385 | 7488 | 7611.224 | 2,309,000 | 2,631,006 | 1310 | 1310 |
| | 2016 | 311 | 325.606 | 2203 | 2278.713 | 7486 | 7743.279 | 2,378,000 | 2,859,662 | 1310 | 1310 |
| | 2017 | 307 | 325.555 | 2211 | 2240.747 | 7481 | 7581.65 | 2,444,000 | 3,183,977 | 1310 | 1310 |
| | 2018 | 305 | 305 | 2195 | 2195 | 7500 | 7500 | 2,489,000 | 2,489,000 | 1290 | 1290 |
| | 2019 | 272 | 303.912 | 2210 | 2224.162 | 7518 | 7566.175 | 2,518,000 | 3,406,688 | 1270 | 1270 |
| | 2020 | 315 | 364.553 | 2206 | 2250.826 | 7479 | 7630.974 | 2,225,000 | 3,002,107 | 1180 | 1180 |
| | 2021 | 289 | 289 | 2252 | 2252 | 7459 | 7459 | 2,146,667 | 2,146,667 | 1270 | 1270 |

Source: Author

Romania to diversify its economy and adapt to the changes in the global economic environment in order to be more resilient in the face of crises. By promoting entrepreneurship and innovation, the country could realize its potential and become an important player on the European market.

## Conclusions

The comparative assessment of Romania's economic efficiency in the EU context, conducted through the Data Envelopment Analysis (DEA) method for the period 2010–2021, highlights several key findings with direct implications for policy design and strategic planning. The results confirm that Romania has maintained a position on the efficiency frontier throughout the analysed period, serving as a benchmark for several EU Member States—most notably Spain, Slovakia and Estonia. This consistent performance underscores the country's capacity to generate proportional economic outcomes from its available resources, despite structural limitations relative to more advanced economies.

At the EU level, the analysis reveals that most Member States achieve high levels of efficiency, although the overall European average is slightly constrained by the underperformance of a limited group of countries. For Romania, the absence of significant input vulnerabilities indicates that its current resource allocation model is relatively balanced in relation to the output structure. However, the persistence of agricultural sector output as an area for potential improvement suggests that targeted investment, innovation, and modernization in agriculture could strengthen both productivity and sustainability outcomes.

From a comparative perspective, Spain's recurrent efficiency gaps, particularly in ICT specialist employment and high-speed Internet coverage, illustrate the importance of digital infrastructure and human capital in sustaining economic performance. The EU average also reflects vulnerabilities linked to digitalization-related inputs, reinforcing the role of technology adoption as a critical determinant of competitiveness.

The findings support the view that Romania's future efficiency gains will depend on advancing structural reforms, fostering human capital development, expanding digital infrastructure and stimulating sectoral diversification. Moreover, the integration of sustainability-oriented practices—such as promoting green technologies, circular economy principles and environmentally responsible innovation—can enhance long-term resilience while aligning with EU strategic objectives. In this regard,

Romania's performance trajectory demonstrates that sustained policy coherence and investment in strategic sectors can consolidate its role as a competitive and efficient economy within the European single market.

*Policy Implications*

The DEA provides several actionable insights that can inform Romania's economic strategy and contribute to the EU's broader objectives of sustainable growth, competitiveness and convergence. First, the identification of Romania as a benchmark for several Member States demonstrates the potential for knowledge transfer and the dissemination of best practices in resource management, particularly in economies facing similar structural challenges. Leveraging this position, Romania could engage more actively in EU platforms dedicated to policy learning and capacity building.

Second, the agricultural sector emerges as a strategic priority for targeted investment and innovation. Policies aimed at modernizing agricultural production, integrating digital technologies and promoting sustainable farming practices can enhance value added in agriculture, thereby reducing the sector's productivity gap relative to leading EU performers. This approach should be coupled with incentives for research and development in agri-tech and rural infrastructure improvement.

Third, given the EU-wide vulnerabilities linked to ICT human capital and high-speed Internet infrastructure, Romania should intensify investments in digital transformation. Expanding broadband coverage, enhancing cybersecurity infrastructure, and increasing the proportion of ICT specialists through education and vocational training programmes would not only improve efficiency scores but also foster resilience in the face of economic disruptions.

Fourth, the diversification of the economic base remains critical to sustaining efficiency in the long term. Supporting high-value-added industries, stimulating innovation ecosystems, and encouraging public–private partnerships can strengthen the country's competitive advantage. Policies should also promote entrepreneurship, especially in technology-intensive sectors, and facilitate access to finance for innovative SMEs.

Finally, aligning efficiency-oriented strategies with the EU's Green Deal and Sustainable Development Goals will ensure that competitiveness gains are compatible with environmental sustainability. Encouraging circular economy models, investing in renewable energy and embedding eco-innovation across industries can yield dual dividends—enhancing productivity while meeting climate and environmental commitments.

By pursuing these policy directions, Romania can consolidate its efficiency performance, support EU-wide cohesion objectives and reinforce its strategic positioning within the single market.

## References

Aleca, O. E., & Mihai, F. (2025). The role of digital infrastructure and skills in enhancing labor productivity: Insights from Industry 4.0 in the European Union. *Systems, 13*(2). https://doi.org/10.3390/systems13020113

Amirteimoori, A., Allahviranloo, T., & Nematizadeh, M. (2024). A firm-specific Malmquist productivity index model for stochastic data envelopment analysis: An application to commercial banks. *Financial Innovation, 10*(1), 66. https://doi.org/10.1186/s40854-023-00583-2

Amirteimoori, A., Allahviranloo, T., & Zadmirzaei, M. (2025). Performance analysis and optimal scale size in the European forest sector: A two-stage data envelopment analysis. *Environment, Development and Sustainability*. https://doi.org/10.1007/s10668-025-06091-w

Aparicio, J., Zofío, J. L., & Pastor, J. T. (2023). Decomposing economic efficiency into technical and allocative components: An essential property. *Journal of Optimization Theory and Applications, 197*(1), 98–129. https://doi.org/10.1007/s10957-023-02188-2

Bănică, A., Ţigănaşu, R., Nijkamp, P., & Kourtit, K. (2024). Institutional quality in green and digital transition of EU Regions—A recovery and resilience analysis. *Global Challenges, 8*(9), 2400031. https://doi.org/10.1002/gch2.202400031

Banjerdpaiboon, A., & Limleamthong, P. (2023). Assessment of national circular economy performance using super-efficiency dual data envelopment analysis and Malmquist productivity index: Case study of 27 European countries. *Heliyon, 9*(6), e16584. https://doi.org/10.1016/j.heliyon.2023.e16584

Bergougui, B., & Satrovic, E. (2025). Towards eco-efficiency of OECD countries: How does environmental governance restrain the destructive ecological effect of the excess use of natural resources? *Ecological Informatics, 87*, 103093. https://doi.org/10.1016/j.ecoinf.2025.103093

Bilan, Y., Oliinyk, O., Mishchuk, H., & Skare, M. (2023). Impact of information and communications technology on the development and use of knowledge. *Technological Forecasting and Social Change, 191*, 122519. https://doi.org/10.1016/j.techfore.2023.122519

Bocean, C. G. (2024). A cross-sectional analysis of the relationship between digital technology use and agricultural productivity in EU countries. *Agriculture, 14*(4). https://doi.org/10.3390/agriculture14040519

Bonnedahl, K. J., Heikkurinen, P., & Paavola, J. (2022). Strongly sustainable development goals: Overcoming distances constraining responsible action. *Environmental Science & Policy, 129*, 150–158. https://doi.org/10.1016/j.envsci.2022.01.004

Brodny, J., & Tutak, M. (2022). Analyzing the level of digitalization among the enterprises of the European Union Member States and their impact on economic growth. *Journal of Open Innovation: Technology, Market, and Complexity, 8*(2), 70. https://doi.org/10.3390/joitmc8020070

Brodny, J., & Tutak, M. (2024). A multi-criteria measurement and assessment of human capital development in EU-27 countries: A 10-year perspective. *Journal of Open Innovation: Technology, Market, and Complexity, 10*(4), 100394. https://doi.org/10.1016/j.joitmc.2024.100394

Brodny, J., & Tutak, M. (2025). Decade of Progress: A multidimensional measurement and assessment of energy sustainability in EU – 27 nations. *Applied Energy, 382*, 125222. https://doi.org/10.1016/j.apenergy.2024.125222

Caravella, S., Valeria, C., Francesco, C., Dario, G., & Menghini, M. (2023). The diffusion of digital skills across EU regions: Structural drivers and polarisation dynamics. *Regional Studies, Regional Science, 10*(1), 820–844. https://doi.org/10.1080/21681376.2023.2265498

Castillo-Díaz, F. J., Belmonte-Ureña, L. J., Gálvez-Sánchez, F. J., & Camacho-Ferre, F. (2025). Sustainable technological innovations in agriculture: Financial challenges and investment priorities under the European Green Deal. *Journal of Environmental Management, 389*, 126150. https://doi.org/10.1016/j.jenvman.2025.126150

Charnes, A., Cooper, W. W., & Rhodes, E. (1978). Measuring the efficiency of decision making units. *European Journal of Operational Research, 2*(6), 429–444. https://doi.org/10.1016/0377-2217(78)90138-8

Chigbu, B. I., & Nekhwevha, F. (2023). Exploring the concepts of decent work through the lens of SDG 8: Addressing challenges and inadequacies. *Frontiers in Sociology, 8*, 2023. https://doi.org/10.3389/fsoc.2023.1266141

Ciacci, A., Ivaldi, E., Penco, L., & Testa, G. (2025). Measuring digital sustainability paying attention to the economic, social, and environmental dimensions: A European perspective. *Social Indicators Research, 177*(1), 1–29. https://doi.org/10.1007/s11205-024-03459-9

Cobbinah, J., Osei, A., & Amoah, J. O. (2025). Innovating for a greener future: Do digital transformation and innovation capacity drive enterprise green total factor productivity in the knowledge economy? *Journal of the Knowledge Economy*. https://doi.org/10.1007/s13132-025-02673-1

Constantin, A., Cetulean, M., Radu, C.-G., Dumitra, E.-C., & Iacob, A. T. (2025). The impact of digitalisation on supply chain competitiveness: A multi-country comparative approach. *Sustainability, 17*(9). https://doi.org/10.3390/su17094038

de Oliveira, L. F. A., Baião, F. A., Oliveira, F. L. C., & Peres, I. T. (2025). Determinants of primary healthcare efficiency in the Brazilian Legal Amazon: A hybrid approach using data envelopment analysis and Tobit regression. *Socio-Economic Planning Sciences, 101*, 102257. https://doi.org/10.1016/j.seps.2025.102257

Dell'Anno, R. (2022). Theories and definitions of the informal economy: A survey. *Journal of Economic Surveys, 36*(5), 1610–1643. https://doi.org/10.1111/joes.12487

Doroiman, M. M., & Sîrghi, N. (2024). An empirical assessment of the impact of EU digital policies on economic growth. In S. Grima, I. Romānova, G. G. Noja, & T. Dorożyński (Eds.), *Economic development and resilience by EU Member States* (Vol. 115, p. 0). Emerald Publishing Limited. https://doi.org/10.1108/S1569-375920240000115005

Drago, C., Costantiello, A., Savorgnan, M., & Leogrande, A. (2025). Macroeconomic and labor market drivers of AI adoption in Europe: A machine learning and panel data approach. *Economies, 13*(8). https://doi.org/10.3390/economies13080226

Efthymiou, L., Tsiamis, N., & Tsagarakis, K. P. (2025). Compliance with the European environmental law: Leaders and Laggards. *Euro-Mediterranean Journal for Environmental Integration*. https://doi.org/10.1007/s41207-025-00781-7

European Commission. (2024). *Ninth report on economic, social and territorial cohesion*. https://ec.europa.eu/regional_policy/sources/reports/cohesion9/9CR_Report_FINAL.pdf

European Commission. (2025). *Romania 2025 Digital Decade Country Report*. https://digital-strategy.ec.europa.eu/en/factpages/romania-2025-digital-decade-country-report

European Investment Bank. (2025). *Investment Report 2024/2025: Innovation, integration and simplification in Europe*. https://www.eib.org/attachments/lucalli/20240354_investment_report_2024_en.pdf

European Union. (2024). *The future of European competitiveness*. https://commission.europa.eu/document/download/ec1409c1-d4b4-4882-8bdd-3519f86bbb92_en?filename=ThefutureofEuropeancompetitiveness_In-depthanalysisandrecommendations_0.pdf

Eurostat. (2024b). *High-speed internet coverage, by type of area*. https://ec.europa.eu/eurostat/databrowser/view/sdg_17_60/default/table?lang=en&category=sdg.sdg_09

Eurostat. (2024c). *In work at-risk-of-poverty rate*. https://ec.europa.eu/eurostat/databrowser/view/sdg_01_41/default/table?lang=en&category=sdg.sdg_08

Eurostat. (2024d). *Internet use by individuals*. https://ec.europa.eu/eurostat/databrowser/view/tin00028/default/table?lang=en&category=t_isoc.t_isoc_i.t_isoc_iiu

Eurostat. (2024e). *Level of internet access - households*. https://ec.europa.eu/eurostat/databrowser/view/tin00134/default/table?lang=en&category=t_isoc.t_isoc_i.t_isoc_ici

Eurostat. (2024f). *Percentage of the ICT personnel on total employment*. Europa.Eu.

Eurostat. (2024g). *Real GDP per capita*. https://ec.europa.eu/eurostat/databrowser/view/sdg_08_10/default/table?lang=en

Eurostat. (2024h). *Young people neither in employment nor in education and training by sex*. https://ec.europa.eu/eurostat/databrowser/view/tesem150/default/table?lang=en

Eurostat. (2024). *Employment rate*. Europa.Eu.

Farrell, M. J. (1957). The measurement of productive efficiency. *Journal of the Royal Statistical Society: Series A (General), 120*(3), 253–281. https://doi.org/10.2307/2343100

Førsund, F. R. (2021). Performance measurement and joint production of intended and unintended outputs. *Journal of Productivity Analysis, 55*(3), 157–175. https://doi.org/10.1007/s11123-021-00599-9

Fu, Z., & Madni, G. R. (2024). Unveiling the affecting mechanism of digital transformation on total factor productivity of Chinese firms. *PLoS One, 19*(2), e0298428. https://doi.org/10.1371/journal.pone.0298428

Georgescu, L. P., Fortea, C., Antohi, V. M., Balsalobre-Lorente, D., Zlati, M. L., & Barbuta–Misu, N. (2025). Economic, technological and environmental drivers of the circular economy in the European Union: A panel data analysis. *Environmental Sciences Europe, 37*(1), 76. https://doi.org/10.1186/s12302-025-01119-4

Gogu, E., Mihai, F., & Aleca, O. E. (2025). The economic impact and the decoupling of economic growth from renewable energy consumption within the European Union in the context of social well-being. *Eastern European Economics*, 1–37. https://doi.org/10.1080/00128775.2025.2533210

Gómez-Vega, M., Herrero-Prieto, L. C., & López, M. V. (2021). Clustering and country destination performance at a global scale: Determining factors of tourism competitiveness. *Tourism Economics, 28*(6), 1605–1625. https://doi.org/10.1177/13548166211007598

Guo, R., & Ye, M. (2025). Input-output efficiency, productivity dynamics, and determinants in western China's higher education: A three-stage DEA, global Malmquist index, and Tobit model approach. *PLoS One, 20*(6), e0325901. https://doi.org/10.1371/journal.pone.0325901

Haftor, D. M., Costa-Climent, R., & Ribeiro-Navarrete, S. (2024). Firms' use of predictive artificial intelligence for economic value creation and appropriation. *International Journal of Information Management, 79*, 102836. https://doi.org/10.1016/j.ijinfomgt.2024.102836

Horváthová, J., & Mokrišová, M. (2024). The use of the data envelopment analysis–Malmquist approach to measure the performance of digital transformation in EU countries. *Economies, 12*(11). https://doi.org/10.3390/economies12110291

Jain, M., Jain, T., & Jain, P. (2023). Revisiting the nexus between economic growth and environment health: An empirical study on 180 nations. *Environmental Science and Pollution Research, 30*(58), 122550–122579. https://doi.org/10.1007/s11356-023-30585-7

Javaid, M., Haleem, A., Singh, R. P., & Sinha, A. K. (2024). Digital economy to improve the culture of industry 4.0: A study on features, implementation and challenges. *Green Technologies and Sustainability, 2*(2), 100083. https://doi.org/10.1016/j.grets.2024.100083

Khan, Y., & Bounade, C. D. (2025). Particulate matter 2.5 air pollution mitigation strategy: The role of green investment, digitalization, and renewable energy in the organization for economic co-operation and development (OECD) countries. *Clean Technologies and Environmental Policy, 27*(3), 1037–1051. https://doi.org/10.1007/s10098-024-02864-5

Koronakos, G., Sotiros, D., Despotis, D. K., & Kritikos, M. N. (2022). Fair efficiency decomposition in network DEA: A compromise programming approach. *Socio-Economic Planning Sciences, 79*, 101100. https://doi.org/10.1016/j.seps.2021.101100

Le, T.-N., & Dang, T.-T. (2024). Performance analysis of Vietnamese Provinces' FDI attractiveness: An application of DEA and Malmquist Indexes. *SAGE Open, 14*(3), 21582440241260504. https://doi.org/10.1177/21582440241260505

Lei, Z., & Wei, J. (2023). Assessing the eco-efficiency of industrial parks recycling transformation: Evidence from data envelopment analysis (DEA) and fuzzy set qualitative comparative analysis (fsQCA). *Frontiers in Environmental Science, 11*, 2023. https://doi.org/10.3389/fenvs.2023.1170688

Lopez-Garcia, P. (2021). Key factors behind productivity. 268.

Magoutas, A. I., Chaideftou, M., Skandali, D., & Chountalas, P. T. (2024). Digital progression and economic growth: Analyzing the impact of ICT advancements on the GDP of European Union Countries. *Economies, 12*(3). https://doi.org/10.3390/economies12030063

Mahmood, M., Chowdhury, P., Yeassin, R., Hasan, M., Ahmad, T., & Chowdhury, N.-U.-R. (2024). Impacts of digitalization on smart grids, renewable energy, and demand response: An updated review of current applications. *Energy Conversion and Management: X, 24*, 100790. https://doi.org/10.1016/j.ecmx.2024.100790

Mamatzakis, E., Pegkas, P., & Staikouras, C. (2022). Labour market regulations and efficiency in tourism industry. *Tourism Economics, 29*(4), 1032–1054. https://doi.org/10.1177/13548166221081522

Mandel, T., Kranzl, L., Popovski, E., Sensfuß, F., Müller, A., & Eichhammer, W. (2023). Investigating pathways to a net-zero emissions building sector in the European Union: What role for the energy efficiency first principle? *Energy Efficiency, 16*(4), 22. https://doi.org/10.1007/s12053-023-10100-0

Mo, M., & Zeng, L. (2025). Analysis of technology innovation efficiency and its impact factors based on DEA-fsQCA method: Evidence from listed seed companies in China. *Heliyon, 11*(4). https://doi.org/10.1016/j.heliyon.2025.e42914

Moghaddas, Z., Hosseinzadeh Lotfi, F., & Yazdani, M. (2025). Inverse network DEA for Industry 4.0: identifying pitfalls and proposing solutions. *International Journal of Quality & Reliability Management*. https://doi.org/10.1108/IJQRM-07-2024-0244

Monaco, S. (2024). SDG 8. Promote sustained, inclusive and sustainable economic growth, full and productive employment, and decent work for all. In S. Monaco (Ed.), *Identity, territories, and sustainability: challenges and opportunities for achieving the UN Sustainable Development Goals* (p. 0). Emerald Publishing Limited. https://doi.org/10.1108/978-1-83797-549-520241009

Noja, G. G., Cristea, M., Sîrghi, N., & Vădăsan, I. (2022). The role of digitalisation in reducing risks and bridging regional economic welfare gaps within a sustainable development framework: The case of Romania. In S. Grima, E. Özen, & I. Romānova (Eds.), *Managing risk and decision making in times of economic distress, Part B* (Vol. 108B, p. 0). Emerald Publishing Limited. https://doi.org/10.1108/S1569-37592022000108B037

OECD. (2024a). *Green growth indicators*. OECD.Stat.

OECD. (2024b). *The impact of Artificial Intelligence on productivity, distribution and growth: Key mechanisms, initial evidence and policy challenges*. https://doi.org/10.1787/8d900037-en

Ölkers, T., Liu, S., Mußhoff, O., & Yu, X. (2025). Patterns and heterogeneity in credit repayment performance: Evidence from Malian farmers. *Applied Economic Perspectives and Policy, 47*(2), 694–722. https://doi.org/10.1002/aepp.13484

Peykani, P., Soltani, R., Tanasescu, C., Shojaie, S. E., & Jandaghian, A. (2025). The Robust Malmquist productivity index: A framework for measuring productivity changes over time under uncertainty. *Mathematics, 13*(11). https://doi.org/10.3390/math13111727

Rehman, F. U., & Islam, M. M. (2023). Financial infrastructure—total factor productivity (TFP) nexus within the purview of FDI outflow, trade openness, innovation, human capital and institutional quality: Evidence from BRICS economies. *Applied Economics, 55*(7), 783–801. https://doi.org/10.1080/00036846.2022.2094333

Rimidis, M., & Butkus, M. (2025). Can regional infrastructure predict its economic resilience? Limited evidence from spatial modelling. *Sustainability, 17*(15). https://doi.org/10.3390/su17157046

Ronzon, T., Iost, S., & Philippidis, G. (2022). Has the European Union entered a bioeconomy transition? Combining an output-based approach with a shift-share analysis. *Environment, Development and Sustainability, 24*(6), 8195–8217. https://doi.org/10.1007/s10668-021-01780-8

Sánchez-García, E., Martínez-Falcó, J., Marco-Lajara, B., & Manresa-Marhuenda, E. (2024). Revolutionizing the circular economy through new technologies: A new era of sustainable progress. *Environmental Technology & Innovation, 33*, 103509. https://doi.org/10.1016/j.eti.2023.103509

Shafik, W. (2025). SDG 8: Decent work and economic growth—technology for employment and economic opportunities. In W. Shafik (Ed.), *Factoring technology in global sustainability: A focus on the sustainable development goals* (pp. 277–301). Springer Nature Singapore. https://doi.org/10.1007/978-981-96-7299-8_10

Stoiljković, A., Marcikić Horvat, A., & Tomić, S. (2025). Assessing the tourism efficiency of European countries using data envelopment analysis: A sustainability approach. *Sustainability, 17*(4). https://doi.org/10.3390/su17041493

Tone, K. (2011). Slacks-based measure of efficiency. In W. W. Cooper, L. M. Seiford, & J. Zhu (Eds.), *Handbook on data envelopment analysis* (pp. 195–209). Springer US. https://doi.org/10.1007/978-1-4419-6151-8_8

Tone, K. (2017). Non-radial DEA models. In *Advances in DEA theory and applications* (pp. 11–19). https://doi.org/10.1002/9781118946688.ch2

Trane, M., Borchardt, S., Marelli, L., Siragusa, A., Pollo, R., & Lombardi, P. (2025). What role for cities in the EU green deal? Analysis of policy framework, interlinkages and contribution to the 2030 agenda. *Sustainable Development, 33*(4), 5949–5967. https://doi.org/10.1002/sd.3423

Vărzaru, A. A., & Bocean, C. G. (2024). Digital transformation and innovation: The influence of digital technologies on turnover from innovation activities and types of innovation. *Systems, 12*(9). https://doi.org/10.3390/systems12090359

Vrabková, I., Vaňková, I., & Lee, S. (2024). Relationship and factors of technical efficiency and quality of hospital care: The federal state system of Germany. *Health Services And Outcomes Research Methodology*. https://doi.org/10.1007/s10742-024-00337-2

Wang, D., & Shao, X. (2024). Research on the impact of digital transformation on the production efficiency of manufacturing enterprises: Institution-based analysis of the threshold effect. *International Review of Economics & Finance, 91*, 883–897. https://doi.org/10.1016/j.iref.2024.01.046

Wang, L., & Tang, T. (2024). Evaluation of innovation efficiency of high-tech enterprise based on DEA and Malmquist index under the background of sustainable development. *Asia Pacific Journal of Innovation and Entrepreneurship, 18*(4), 340–354. https://doi.org/10.1108/APJIE-10-2023-0190

Woo, C., Chung, Y., Chun, D., Seo, H., & Hong, S. (2015). The static and dynamic environmental efficiency of renewable energy: A Malmquist index analysis of OECD countries. *Renewable and Sustainable Energy Reviews, 47*, 367–376. https://doi.org/10.1016/j.rser.2015.03.070

Ye, M., Jin, Y., & Deng, F. (2022). Municipal waste treatment efficiency in 29 OECD countries using three-stage Bootstrap-DEA model. *Environment, Development and Sustainability, 24*(9), 11369–11391. https://doi.org/10.1007/s10668-022-02227-4

Zeng, F., Zhou, Y., & Wei, B. (2024, 2024). Empowering sustainable development: Revolutionizing agricultural green total factor productivity through rural digitalization. *Frontiers in Sustainable Food Systems, 8*. https://doi.org/10.3389/fsufs.2024.1455732

Zhang, X., Xia, Q., & Wei, F. (2023a). Efficiency evaluation of two-stage parallel-series structures with fixed-sum outputs: An approach based on SMAA and DEA. *Expert Systems with Applications, 227*, 120264. https://doi.org/10.1016/j.eswa.2023.120264

Zhang, G., Ye, Y., & Sun, M. (2023b). Assessing the static and dynamic efficiency of digital economy in China: Three stage DEA–Malmquist index based approach. *Sustainability, 15*(6). https://doi.org/10.3390/su15065270

CHAPTER 12

# Proposed Sustainable Development Solutions from the Perspective of Sustainable Development Goal 8

The analysis of the Romanian strategies on sustainable development from the perspective of SDG8 highlighted the three pillars of sustainable development and the areas of interdependence of the three pillars for sustainable development (Ciucu-Durnoi et al., 2023; Milea (Pârvu) et al., 2025). The implementation of the strategic legal framework for sustainable development entailed a historical overview of the main moments of sustainable development in Romania starting with the adoption of the National Environmental Action Plan in 1995 until the adoption of the Romanian Sustainable Development Strategy with Horizon 2030 in November 2018 (Goverment of Romania\United Nations Development Program, 2008). Thus, the strategic directions and objectives for sustainable development in Romania were assessed, which imply the strengthening and expansion of the governance framework, education and training programmes for sustainable development, and the implementation of the National Sustainable Development Strategy for Horizon 2030.

In Chap. 8, economic sustainability in the European context was modelled using the Sustainable Development Goal 8 indicators of decent work and growth (Eurostat, 2025a; Kreinin & Aigner, 2022). Using linear regression, 12 economic sustainability models were obtained that capture the effects of economic development through labour force dynamics, digitization and economic activity expressed in terms of industry, agriculture and services outputs (Kalai et al., 2024; Kálmán et al., 2025). Finally, the



C. Fortea, *Sustainable Economic Development and the European Green Deal*, https://doi.org/10.1007/978-3-032-10326-0_12

impact of economic development in terms of changes in working poverty rates was assessed. The 12 models have proved to be a source of information on the correlation of the various indicators providing a comprehensive picture of the implementation of SDG8 at national and European level (Bieszk-Stolorz & Dmytrów, 2023; Kuc-Czarnecka et al., 2023).

The overall **SDG8.1 model** of European economic sustainability from the perspective of the SDG8GDPloc (Gross Domestic Product per capita) indicator is mainly characterized by the inverse influence of the change in the employment rate, followed by the direct influence of the share of Internet use by individuals and of labour tax revenues. At the European level, the most economically well-represented countries are Denmark, Ireland, Luxembourg and Sweden, followed by Bulgaria, Croatia, Hungary, Latvia, Poland and Romania.

To promote sustainable economic growth at European level and to develop a sustainable gross domestic product (GDP), effective public policies need to be implemented across Europe (Chamusca, 2023; Limosani et al., 2025). These policies must address current economic, social and environmental challenges, balancing growth with sustainability. The main proposals that could contribute to this objective are: expanding investment in renewable energy and energy efficiency; accelerating circular economy practices; promoting digitization and innovation; improving the quality of education and training; increasing social cohesion and reducing inequalities; implementing green fiscal policies; and creating sustainable infrastructure and increasing international cooperation. Promoting renewable energy sources and improving energy efficiency in industry, buildings and transport will reduce fossil fuel dependency and CO2 emissions (European Commission, 2025f; European Environment Agency, 2024). It will also have an effect on stimulating innovation and job creation in green sectors. Implementing the principles of the circular economy is useful in minimizing waste and maximizing the reuse and recycling of resources with the effect of reducing environmental impacts and creating new economic opportunities (Domenech & Bahn-Walkowiak, 2019; Islam et al., 2024). We believe that investment in digital technologies and innovation will contribute to increased productivity and economic efficiency, while facilitating the transition to more sustainable practices across all economic sectors. Raising the quality of education and broadening the coverage of vocational training with a focus on digital skills and skills related to the green economy and innovation will ensure the success of the new sustainable economic orientations (Albertz & Pilz, 2025; OECD,

2023a). Ensuring that the benefits of economic growth are fairly distributed in society, through policies that support social inclusion, reduce inequalities and ensure equal access to opportunities for all citizens, will reduce social disparities by increasing cohesion and improving economic sustainability (Betts-Davies et al., 2024; Hariram et al., 2023). We consider that in the economic field new climate neutrality goals must be supported by the implementation of carbon taxes and other fiscal instruments that discourage unsustainable practices and incentivize investments in sustainable technologies and practices. Investments in sustainable infrastructure, including public transport, green energy grids and energy-efficient buildings, are important to sustain long-term economic growth (Meng et al., 2024; Okunevičiūtė Neverauskienė et al., 2025). They will reduce logistical costs and facilitate labour flows. At the same time, supporting research and development in green and sustainable technologies will have the effect of accelerating innovation and the uptake of energy-efficient green technologies on a large scale that will reduce consumption and the environmental impact of economic activities (Muhammad & Hoffmann, 2024; Shahzad et al., 2022).

The successful implementation of these policies requires the commitment and collaboration of governments, the private sector and civil society and the adaptation of the economic environment to global economic and technological change. Economic competitiveness requires access to new technologies, with digitization and the circular economy being key to this (Möller et al., 2025; Sánchez-García et al., 2024).

The **SDG8.2 model** of European economic sustainability from the perspective of the SDG8AINT indicator (high-speed Internet coverage) is significantly influenced by employment rates, high-speed Internet coverage and the existence of a sufficient number of ICT specialists employed in the digital economy. According to Eurostat and OECD data, Denmark, Latvia, Romania and Sweden are among the top performers in this area. Greece, Cyprus, Austria, Belgium and Croatia are at the bottom of the European ranking in terms of high-speed Internet coverage.

At European level, there are several policies and initiatives aimed at encouraging high-speed Internet coverage in all EU Member States (European Commission, 2024g; Kuś et al., 2025). These policies are coordinated by the European Commission and focus on several aspects, including funding, regulation and cooperation between Member States. Among the policies already in place are: the Digital Agenda for Europe (European Union, 2024a); the European Regional Development Fund

(ERDF) (European Commission, 2024c); the EU's 5G Plan (European Commission, 2024a); the Network Infrastructure Access Directive and the WiFi4EU® programme (European Commission, 2025j). The Digital Agenda for Europe was launched by the European Commission in 2010 and aims to boost growth and competitiveness using digital technologies. Its 2020–2030 horizon (European Commission, 2024d) is to secure digital safe spaces, ensure fair competition in digital markets, and strengthen Europe's digital sovereignty through the use of artificial intelligence. The Agenda also aims to achieve climate neutrality by 2050. The European Regional Development Fund provides funding for infrastructure projects, including projects to extend and upgrade high-speed Internet networks in less developed regions of the EU. Under the 5G Plan, the EU aims to become a global leader in the deployment of 5G technology by ensuring adequate infrastructure and spectrum deployment for 5G. At the same time, the success of this plan means providing incentives for network operators to adopt this technology. The new 2030 target of this plan aims to ensure the wide availability of 5G services, the development of 5G-based lead markets, and the start of deployment of 6G services which should be available by 2030 (Comisia Europeană, 2024).

We believe that in the context of the rapid transition to the digital economy, the provision of high-speed Internet services plays an important role in achieving economic sustainability. This requires the development of well-informed public policies oriented towards innovation, inclusion and efficiency. First and foremost, it is important to promote investment in digital infrastructure, with a focus on the roll-out of fibre networks and 5G technologies (Akcali Gur, 2022; Blind & Niebel, 2022). This approach will not only increase the speed and quality of Internet services but will also facilitate the development of IoT solutions, essential for Industry 5.0 and smart cities, contributing to resource efficiency and reducing the carbon footprint. A second aspect concerns stimulating competition in the Internet service provider sector, thus not only ensuring affordable prices for consumers, but also encouraging innovation in service provision (Ahokangas et al., 2023; Gounari et al., 2024; OECD, 2025a). At the same time, public policies need to place particular emphasis on digital inclusion, ensuring high-speed Internet access in rural areas and for vulnerable groups. Government programmes should be geared towards providing subsidies for the expansion of networks in areas less attractive to the private sector and educational programmes to improve the digital skills of the population (de Clercq et al., 2023; Djatmiko et al., 2025; European

Commission, 2025h). We believe that integrating cybersecurity and data protection considerations into all public policies related to high-speed Internet is a significant element to ensure the smooth functioning of data transfer. Given the increasing cyber threats, governments need to work closely with the private sector to develop robust security standards and protocols, thus protecting critical infrastructure and citizens' personal data

The **SDG8.3 model** of European economic sustainability from the perspective of the SDG8INTA indicator (level of household Internet access) is significantly influenced by the variation of the indicator share of Internet use by individuals, which shows that household Internet access depends significantly on the willingness of individuals to use the Internet. In some countries this limits the sustainable development of the digital economy due to insufficient skills of individuals in using the Internet. In terms of the share of Internet usage by individuals at European level, Denmark, Luxembourg, the Netherlands and Sweden rank first. Bulgaria, Greece, Romania, Lithuania, Portugal, Croatia and Cyprus are at the opposite pole.

At European level, there are several policies and initiatives aimed at improving the level of household Internet access in the EU Member States. These policies aim to ensure that all citizens have access to high-speed Internet, regardless of where they live or their economic situation (European Commission, 2025h; Mack et al., 2023; Pateiro-Rodríguez et al., 2024). The EU's Recovery and Resilience Plan (RRF) (European Commission, 2024e) provides for investment in digital infrastructure to support the transition to a digital economy and to ensure open access to essential digital services, including high-speed Internet, for all European citizens. The EU's Digital Transformation Agenda is known as the "Digital Decade Roadmap" (European Commission, 2025d). It sets out digital goals and tasks to be achieved by 2030. The programme is organized around four sections: skills, business, administration and infrastructure.

The **SDG8.4 model** of European economic sustainability from the perspective of the SDG8ROCFM indicator (employment rate) is significantly influenced by the share of Internet use by individuals driving the change in employment rate, a significant aspect of the digital economy where the focus is on the skills of the workforce to use digital technologies. At European level, the countries with the highest employment rates are Sweden, the Netherlands and Germany. Greece, Romania, Italy, Croatia and Spain rank at the opposite pole.

Public employment rate policy must be geared towards getting young people into work and increasing the digital specialization of the population (International Labour Organization, 2023, 2025; Raileanu Szeles & Simionescu, 2021). At the same time, promoting access to the European labour market through European platforms for job vacancies in the EU helps to reduce unemployment and increase the availability of labour resources in the European area (European Parliament, 2025b). Government programmes to promote retraining help to diversify job opportunities for the European population and are active policies for reducing unemployment by reducing the pressure of labour shortages and migration from East Asia to Europe (Mejía Dorantes & Allen, 2024; OECD, 2024, 2025b). The main policies should be geared towards the implementation of a flexicurity framework combining labour market flexibility with employment security and strong social protection systems and the development of specific programmes for the labour market integration of young people, people with disabilities and marginalized groups. Investments in infrastructure, green technology and digitalization using European funds (Next Generation EU) (European Union, 2024b) and the harmonization of fiscal policies to avoid unfair competition between Member States and to support sustainable investments are also important for reducing unemployment and sustainable economic growth (European Environment Agency, 2023; Li & Wong, 2025).

The **SDG8.5 model** of European economic sustainability from the perspective of the SDG8RRSAR indicator (at-risk-of-work poverty rate) is significantly determined by the variation of value added in services, which demonstrates the orientation towards the consumer economy. Romania, Greece, Luxembourg and Spain rank first in Europe in terms of the at-risk-of-work poverty rate. Finland, the Czech Republic, Belgium, Ireland, the Netherlands and Croatia are at the opposite end of the scale.

The at-risk-of-work poverty rate is a significant problem in many European countries, where working people still live in poverty or economic vulnerability (Devos et al., 2025; Halleröd et al., 2015; OECD, 2023b). Tackling in-work poverty is a concern for the EU, which has already adopted EU legislation on the implementation of European social protection policies, EU minimum wage regulations and working conditions, promoting employment and growth and tackling gender inequality and discrimination (European Parliament, 2025c; Padrón et al., 2023). In the European area in 2022, Directive (EU) 2022/2041 of the European Parliament and of the Council of 19 October 2022 (European Union,

2022) on adequate minimum wages in the EU was enacted, which ensures that European employees are adequately paid and have decent working conditions. One proposal for the development of public policies that would contribute to protecting employees against in-work poverty is the establishment of a European Social Protection Agency to monitor the levels of social insurance provided in the Member States, including their minimum thresholds that would allow a decent subsistence level for people at risk of poverty.

The **SDG8.6 model** of European economic sustainability in terms of the SDG8VIMPM indicator (tax revenues from labour) is mainly influenced by the share of Internet use by individuals, which is characteristic of the digital economy, followed by economic growth as reflected by GDP per capita. Austria, Sweden, France and Belgium are among the European leaders in terms of labour tax revenues. The poorest performers in the indicator are Bulgaria, Malta, Romania, Ireland, Cyprus and Latvia. .

Public policy on tax revenues from taxation on employment at European level aims to ensure the efficient collection of taxes and social contributions from work, to promote tax fairness and to support growth and employment (Athanasios et al., 2022; Balasoiu et al., 2023). EU Member States apply different levels of taxes and social contributions on earned income. These rates can vary according to individual income, family status and other factors. Some countries have progressive taxes, where higher earners pay higher rates of tax, while others apply flatter taxes (Eurostat, 2025b; OECD, 2025c). Governments need to adopt policies that reduce the tax burden on employers to create new jobs and stimulate investment in human capital. Impact measures include tax cuts for employers, subsidies for job creation or providing other financial incentives (OECD, 2022; Rosário et al., 2024). To improve the labour market and increase employability, appropriate policies aim to reduce taxes on earned income, reduce taxes for low- and middle-income workers, and provide tax deductions for work-related expenses or other tax benefits. These measures must be accompanied by combating tax evasion and undeclared work. These policies may include measures to monitor and enforce tax laws, simplify tax procedures and promote transparency in the tax area.

The **SDG8.7 model** of European economic sustainability from the perspective of the SDG8VASE indicator (value added in services) is significantly influenced in an inversely proportional manner by the variation in value added in industry, which is a normal feature of a developed economy. Luxembourg, Cyprus, Malta and Greece rank first in Europe in terms of value added in services. Romania, the Czech Republic, Poland, Slovakia, and Ireland are at the opposite pole.

Public policy on value added in services at European level should be geared towards promoting competitiveness and innovation in the services sector (Di Carlo & Schmitz, 2023; European Commission, 2025a). Member State governments should implement funding and support programmes for research and development in the services sector, which may target the provision of subsidies, grants or other forms of financial assistance to companies investing in innovation and the development of new technologies and business models in the services sector (Foreman-Peck & Zhou, 2022; Moon, 2022). Public policies should facilitate access to finance for service sector companies, for small and medium-sized enterprises (SMEs) and start-ups (credit guarantee programmes, venture capital financing schemes and other financial instruments designed to support business growth and development). At the same time, policies can be implemented that facilitate international trade and investment in the services sector, thereby promoting growth and market expansion for service providers.

The **SDG8.8 model** of European economic sustainability from the perspective of the SDG8VAIN indicator (value added in industry) shows a significant inverse influence for gross value added in services. The Czech Republic, Romania, Ireland and Poland rank first at European level. Luxembourg, Cyprus, Malta, Greece, France, the Netherlands, and Belgium rank last in terms of gross value added.

Public policy on value added in industry at European level aims primarily to promote competitiveness and innovation in the industrial sector (McNamara, 2024; Teixeira & Tavares-Lehmann, 2022; Wigger, 2023). In the EU context, several initiatives and policies aim to support these objectives: research and innovation investment policies; digitization of industry; environmental and sustainability policies; and promotion of skills and skilled workforce (Dell'Agli & Saabeel, 2025; European Parliament, 2025a; Senna et al., 2023). The EU and the Member States aim to support research and innovation in industry through research programmes and funds, such as Horizon 2027 and the EU Framework Program for Research and Innovation (European Commission, 2024d). Promoting digitization in industry is a priority for the EU being supported by European programmes and directives heavily funded through the European Development Funds aimed at the adoption of digital technologies such as the Internet of Things, artificial intelligence and additive manufacturing in order to improve production processes, streamline operations and create new business models (European Commission, 2025c; Kölling & Hernández-Moreno, 2024). The EU promotes policies and initiatives aimed at reducing carbon emissions and promoting industrial sustainability (promoting renewable energies, encouraging energy efficiency and supporting innovation in clean technologies).

The **SDG8.9 model** of European economic sustainability from the perspective of the SDG8VAAG indicator (value added in agriculture) is significantly influenced by labour taxation (direct correlation) and the level of economic development represented by the gross domestic product per capita (indirect correlation). Romania, Bulgaria, Latvia and Hungary rank first in Europe in terms of agricultural value added. Luxembourg, Belgium, Germany, Malta, Ireland and Austria come last.

Public policy on added value in agriculture is important to support the sustainable development and competitiveness of the agricultural sector (Amgai et al., 2025; European Commission, 2025i; Mergoni et al., 2024). In the context of the EU, there are several policies and initiatives that aim to add value in agriculture such as: the Common Agricultural Policy (CAP) (European Commission, 2024b); the Rural Development Program (European Commission, 2024f); Innovation and Research in Agriculture (European Commission, 2023, 2025g) and the Promotion of Sustainable and Organic Farming (European Commission, 2025e; Gamage et al., 2023). The Common Agricultural Policy is one of the EU's main instruments to support agriculture and rural development. CAP objectives include ensuring food security, promoting sustainable development of agriculture and stabilizing agricultural markets. It provides financial support for farmers in the form of direct payments, market measures and funding for rural development.

The Rural Development Program is part of the CAP and provides funding for projects aimed at the sustainable development of rural areas. The programme finances investments in infrastructure, environmental protection, economic diversification, promoting rural tourism, improving the quality of life in rural areas, and supporting sustainable agriculture and organic farming practices. The EU encourages sustainable and organic farming practices through the CAP and other programmes and initiatives (Boix-Fayos & de Vente, 2023; European Commission, 2024h). These policies promote the responsible use of natural resources, the conservation of biodiversity, the improvement of animal welfare and the reduction of environmental impacts of farming activities. The EU also supports agricultural research and innovation through the EU Framework Program for Research and Innovation.

The **SDG8.10 model** of European economic sustainability from the perspective of the SDG8ATIC indicator (number of employed ICT professionals) is characterized by the significant influence of the level of household Internet access and employment rate. At European level the countries with the highest number of employed ICT professionals are Finland, Sweden, the Netherlands and Luxembourg. Romania, Greece, Latvia, Bulgaria, Poland and Cyprus are at the opposite pole. In the context of the EU, promoting employment in information and communication technologies (ICT) and boosting the number of ICT professionals employed are important objectives to ensure competitiveness and innovation in the economy.

We appreciate that investment in ICT education and training stimulates the interest and skills of employees in this field, increasing the attractiveness of working in the digital economy. We believe that it is important to offer scholarships and retraining programmes for adults who wish to develop their ICT skills to meet the objectives of developing the digital economy. Labour mobility policies can facilitate the recruitment of ICT specialists from other EU and non-EU countries to meet the demand for specialized ICT workforce (Aksenova et al., 2025; Kotavaara & Prokkola, 2023). Promoting digital convergence should be undertaken to develop digital infrastructure and digital services across the EU to stimulate economic growth and create ICT job opportunities in less developed regions (Javaid et al., 2024; Magoutas et al., 2024; Obelovska et al., 2025).

The **SDG8.11 model** of European economic sustainability from the perspective of the SDG8TNEET indicator (share of young people neither in employment nor in education or training (NEET) in the total population) is characterized by the inverse influence of the employment rate. At European level, the countries with the highest proportion of young people neither in employment nor in education are Italy, Romania, Greece and Bulgaria. At the bottom are the Netherlands, Sweden, Luxembourg, Slovenia, Denmark and Austria. Promoting the social inclusion and employment of NEET young people is a priority for the EU and several policies and initiatives have been developed at European level (European Commission, 2024i; European Union, 2025). One initiative is the Youth Employment Initiative (European Commission, 2025k). This programme was launched by the EU to support Member States in reducing youth unemployment and integrating young people into the labour market. The initiative includes funding for employment, training and internship programmes for NEET young people. Another Youth Guarantee programme offers NEET young people under 25 the opportunity to benefit from a job, education, training or internship within four months of leaving school or inactivity in the labour market and has as its main objective to reduce the risk of social exclusion and encourage youth employment (European Commission, 2024i). In the medium term, we consider the following public policies to be important: supporting the transition to the labour market, supporting entrepreneurship, and developing social and inclusion policies. These policies should focus on: providing career counselling and guidance services to help young NEETs identify and pursue appropriate career paths; promoting internship and apprenticeship programmes, in partnership with businesses, to facilitate the transition from education to work; launching training and mentoring programmes for young people interested in entrepreneurship, together with access to finance for start-ups; encouraging the involvement of NEET young people in the social economy, through cooperatives and social enterprises, as an alternative pathway to employment and social integration; implementing tailor-made programmes to address the individual cases of NEET young people, taking into account different barriers such as mental health, poverty or caring responsibilities; and promoting the participation of NEET young people in community, sports and cultural activities to combat social isolation and improve psychosocial well-being. These policies and initiatives are important to tackle NEET youth unemployment and social exclusion at European level and to offer them better prospects for integration into the labour market and society.

The **SDG8.12 model** of European economic sustainability in terms of the SDG8UTINT indicator (share of Internet use by individuals) is significantly influenced by the level of household Internet access and employment rate. Denmark, Luxembourg, Sweden and the Netherlands top the European rankings. Romania, Bulgaria, Greece, Italy, Portugal, and Croatia are at the opposite pole.

Promoting individuals' use of the Internet is an important objective for the EU, as access to the Internet and digital competences are considered important for active participation in modern society and integration into the labour market (European Commission, 2025b; Țarcă et al., 2024). These policies and initiatives are important to stimulate Internet use by individuals across the EU and to ensure that all citizens have access to the benefits of digital technology in modern society. Public policies on digitization, i.e. the Digital Agenda for Europe, the EU 5G Plan and the Network Infrastructure Access Directive, have been analysed in the framework of the SDG8.2 and SDG8.3.

The main own contribution in terms of economic sustainability is the regression-based development of the economic sustainability function determined on the basis of the unit weighting of the significance of the economic sustainability models developed, characterized by equation (SED):

$$
\begin{aligned}
SED = {} & 0.104 * \overline{PIBloc}_{ODD8.1} + 0.045 * \overline{AINT}_{ODD8.2} + 0.112 * \overline{INTA}_{ODD8.3} \\
& + 0.101 * \overline{ROCFM}_{ODD8.4} + 0.051 * \overline{RRSAR}_{ODD8.5} \\
& + 0.057 * \overline{VIMPM}_{ODD8.6} + 0.12 * \overline{VASE}_{ODD8.7} \\
& + 0.12 * \overline{VAIN}_{ODD8.8} + 0.087 * \overline{VAAG}_{ODD8.9} \\
& + 0.093 * \overline{ATIC}_{ODD8.10} + 0.096 * \overline{TNEET}_{ODD8.11} \\
& + 0.116 * \overline{UTINT}_{ODD8.12}
\end{aligned}
\tag{12.1}
$$

The economic sustainability function demonstrates that at Member State level there are co-occurrences of sustainability in the economic development segment in correlation with the level of social well-being of certain socio-occupational groups (agricultural workers or young people out of work and out of education), this representing the first component of socio-economic vulnerability (C1—work poverty risk). The second component aims at sustainable economic development at branch level supported by digitization (C2—digital economy), which contributes to the economic well-being of Member States by embedding digitization efforts in economic branches with an effect on employment rates. The third component addresses the disparities between countries in terms of gross domestic product (C3—economic development) and the consumption orientation of the European economy (gross value added in services).

In Chap. 7 we have developed a new model of the impact of economic sustainability by quantifying the evolution of growth and decent work factors, demonstrating the beneficial contribution of digitization to sustainable development in conjunction with employment growth and poverty reduction. In the short run, adjustments in employment rates and error corrections play a significant role in immediate economic dynamics, indicating the need for continuous monitoring and adjusted interventions to maintain economic stability. At the same time, the results suggest that economic policy at the EU level should focus on improving access to technology, increasing the quality and sustainability of jobs, and reducing social inequality. Investments in technology and education, together with labour market reforms, lead to robust economic growth and a better quality of life for people.

We have applied the DEA method to analyse economic efficiency and have demonstrated that most European countries including Romania are economically efficient. The analysis revealed that the Romanian economic model is a benchmark of efficiency for the EU (2010–2011) and for Spain (2010–2020). Romania, although it has an efficient economic strategy, needs to improve some aspects of its human resources development, sustainable growth and labour force qualification. At the same time, the main public policies with an effect on sustainable economic development should be oriented towards improving the communications infrastructure, increasing connectivity and access to international markets, adapting to changes in the global economic environment, and promoting entrepreneurship and digitalization.

To improve its economic performance and achieve its sustainability goals, Romania should continue to implement reforms. To determine how effective they will be in the period 2010–2021, we conducted a hierarchical cluster analysis of the SDG8 indicators for Romania using the statistical program SPSS version 26 based on the Beverage method and the sustainability proximity matrix. We highlighted the multi-year cluster linkages based on the Euclidean distances calculated in the proximity matrix (Table 12.1). The analysis evaluated the Euclidean clustered Euclidean distance of the 11 clusters corresponding to each year of the analysed period.

The proximity matrix presented in Table 12.1 quantifies the distances between the annual achievements of the economic sustainability indicators in Romania (SDG8VAAG, SDG8VAIN, SDG8VASE, SDG8VIMPM, SDG8PIBloc, SDG8TNEET, SDG8ROCFM, SDG8RRSAR, SDG8INTA, SDG8UTINT, SDG8ATIC and SDG8AINT) for the period 2010–2021. It can be observed that the periods of consistency of economic policies are those related to the post-crisis recovery (2011–2014 period) and the periods of economic stability in the pre-pandemic years. More significant variations occurred in the recession periods (2010–2015 years) and in the 2020–2021 pandemic crisis period. Other elements of

**Table 12.1** Economic proximity matrix in Romania (based on real Euclidean distances)

| *Year* | *2010* | *2011* | *2012* | *2013* | *2014* | *2015* | *2016* | *2017* | *2018* | *2019* | *2020* | *2021* |
|---|---|---|---|---|---|---|---|---|---|---|---|---|
| 2010 | 0.00 | 310.11 | 470.33 | 520.49 | 820.47 | 1080.57 | 1340.63 | 2020.57 | 2570.61 | 2960.64 | 2660.88 | 2821.05 |
| 2011 | 310.11 | 0.00 | 160.61 | 210.82 | 510.52 | 770.60 | 1030.64 | 1710.53 | 2260.57 | 2650.59 | 2350.84 | 2511.00 |
| 2012 | 470.33 | 160.61 | 0.00 | 50.47 | 350.17 | 610.26 | 870.33 | 1550.31 | 2100.36 | 2490.40 | 2190.61 | 2350.79 |
| 2013 | 520.49 | 210.82 | 50.47 | 0.00 | 300.07 | 560.15 | 820.23 | 1500.23 | 2050.29 | 2440.33 | 2140.54 | 2300.73 |
| 2014 | 820.47 | 510.52 | 350.17 | 300.07 | 0.00 | 260.13 | 520.19 | 1200.18 | 1750.24 | 2140.28 | 1840.48 | 2000.68 |
| 2015 | 1080.57 | 770.60 | 610.26 | 560.15 | 260.13 | 0.00 | 260.08 | 940.10 | 1490.16 | 1880.21 | 1580.41 | 1740.63 |
| 2016 | 1340.63 | 1030.64 | 870.33 | 820.23 | 520.19 | 260.08 | 0.00 | 680.04 | 1230.10 | 1620.15 | 1320.34 | 1480.57 |
| 2017 | 2020.57 | 1710.53 | 1550.31 | 1500.23 | 1200.18 | 940.10 | 680.04 | 0.00 | 550.07 | 940.12 | 640.44 | 800.78 |
| 2018 | 2570.61 | 2260.57 | 2100.36 | 2050.29 | 1750.24 | 1490.16 | 1230.10 | 550.07 | 0.00 | 390.07 | 91.50 | 251.66 |
| 2019 | 2960.64 | 2650.59 | 2490.40 | 2440.33 | 2140.28 | 1880.21 | 1620.15 | 940.12 | 390.07 | 0.00 | 300.15 | 141.75 |
| 2020 | 2660.88 | 2350.84 | 2190.61 | 2140.54 | 1840.48 | 1580.41 | 1320.34 | 640.44 | 91.50 | 300.15 | 0.00 | 160.52 |
| 2021 | 2821.05 | 2511.00 | 2350.79 | 2300.73 | 2000.68 | 1740.63 | 1480.57 | 800.78 | 251.66 | 141.75 | 160.52 | 0.00 |

Source: Prepared by the author using the statistical program SPSS vs 26

variability associated with the events in the Romanian economy were the period 2017–2020 when the Romanian financial sector was marked by profound transformations amid the increase in credit risk and the crisis in the real estate sector. These are presented in the dendogram in Fig. 12.1.

We propose the Sustainable Development Strategy (SD) for decent work and economic growth for Romania—raising the skill level of the workforce and improving Internet skills, together with increasing access to international markets by boosting the competitiveness of Romanian products, will foster sustainable economic growth of the economy, reduce the risk of in-work poverty, and help guarantee equal opportunities to ensure a prosperous future for Romania.

The projected implementation of the Horizon 2030 strategy will result in multiple beneficial transformations that will lead to more sustainable development. Sustainable economic growth through increased digitization and implementation of technological reforms will boost labour

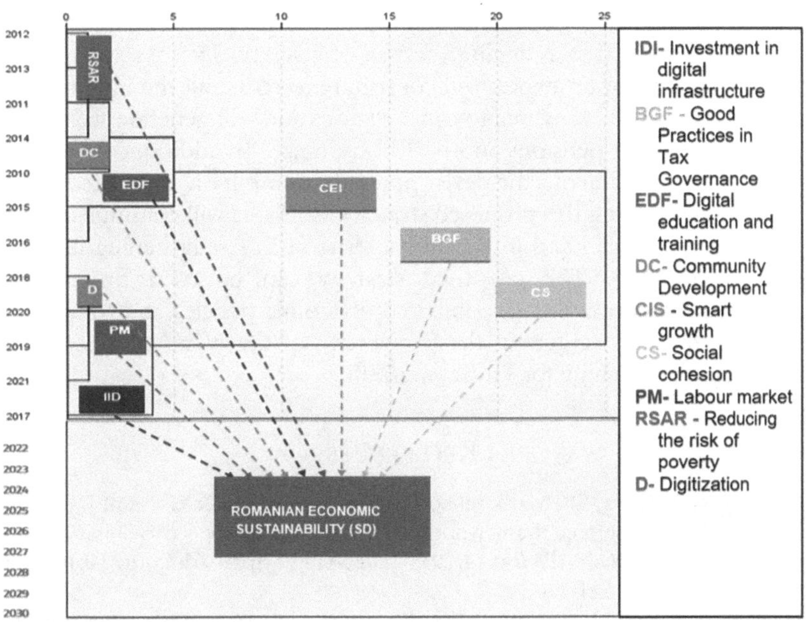


**Fig. 12.1** Cluster dendogram of Romanian economic sustainability from the perspective of the proposed strategy. Source: Author

productivity and create the conditions for sustainable economic growth. Digitalization and digital literacy will play a significant role in transforming public services and the business environment. The implementation of advanced technologies and artificial intelligence solutions is expected to improve operational efficiency and create new opportunities for Romanian products and services to access the international market. Good fiscal governance practices will contribute to the creation of a stable economic climate, increasing the attractiveness for foreign direct investment and fostering sustainable development. Community development will contribute to reducing regional economic disparities and will generate better management of EU funds, while being an important factor for sustainable development. Smart economy development involves adapting and integrating advanced technologies such as artificial intelligence, big data and the Internet of Things (IoT) to improve productivity and economic competitiveness. Smart economic development aims not only to increase GDP but also to improve quality of life, ensuring sustainable and social progress. Social cohesion will improve the welfare parameters of the Romanian economy by increasing solidarity and trust among citizens and minimizing social disparities, thus reducing the risk of poverty. The development of the Romanian labour market will contribute to reducing the migration of skilled labour from Romania to other regions and will generate stability in social budgets for pensions and health insurance. In addition, this necessary direction will favour the development of new jobs in digitalized fields.

By implementing this proposed strategy, Romania will continue to integrate into European and international structures, strengthening its position in the EU. The proposed strategy can be used by national decision-makers to adjust the initiated economic policies and to recalculate the efficiency targets in the perspective of the National Sustainable Development Strategy for Horizon 2030.

## References

Ahokangas, P., Gisca, O., Matinmikko-Blue, M., Yrjölä, S., & Gordon, J. (2023). Toward an integrated framework for developing European 6G innovation. *Telecommunications Policy, 47*(9), 102641. https://doi.org/10.1016/j.telpol.2023.102641

Akcali Gur, B. (2022). Cybersecurity, European digital sovereignty and the 5G rollout crisis. *Computer Law and Security Review, 46*, 105736. https://doi.org/10.1016/j.clsr.2022.105736

Aksenova, Z. A., Yashin, S. N., Markova, O. M., Chudaeva, A. A., & Alieva, P. R. (2025). Assessing the impact of digital economy programs on alleviating skill shortages in the EU labor market for digital professionals. *Journal of the Knowledge Economy, 16*(2), 9072–9094. https://doi.org/10.1007/s13132-024-02202-6

Albertz, A., & Pilz, M. (2025). Green alignment, green vocational education and training, green skills and related subjects: A literature review on actors, contents and regional contexts. *International Journal of Training and Development, 29*(2), 243–254. https://doi.org/10.1111/ijtd.12359

Amgai, S., Komarek, A. M., & Adhikari, R. P. (2025). Understanding the role of policy in enhancing agrifood value chain competitiveness: A systematic literature review. *Journal of Agriculture and Food Research, 22*, 102022. https://doi.org/10.1016/j.jafr.2025.102022

Athanasios, A., Charalampos, K., & Eleni, K. (2022). Assessing the effectiveness of tax administration in macroeconomic stability: Evidence from 26 European Countries. *Economic Change and Restructuring, 55*(4), 2237–2261. https://doi.org/10.1007/s10644-022-09384-6

Balasoiu, N., Chifu, I., & Oancea, M. (2023). Impact of direct taxation on economic growth: Empirical evidence based on panel data regression analysis at the level of Eu countries. *Sustainability, 15*(9). https://doi.org/10.3390/su15097146

Betts-Davies, S., Barrett, J., Brockway, P., & Norman, J. (2024). Is all inequality reduction equal? Understanding motivations and mechanisms for socioeconomic inequality reduction in economic narratives of climate change mitigation. *Energy Research & Social Science, 107*, 103349. https://doi.org/10.1016/j.erss.2023.103349

Bieszk-Stolorz, B., & Dmytrów, K. (2023). Decent work and economic growth in EU countries—Static and dynamic analyses of sustainable development goal 8. *Sustainability, 15*(18). https://doi.org/10.3390/su151813327

Blind, K., & Niebel, C. (2022). 5G roll-out failures addressed by innovation policies in the EU. *Technological Forecasting and Social Change, 180*, 121673. https://doi.org/10.1016/j.techfore.2022.121673

Boix-Fayos, C., & de Vente, J. (2023). Challenges and potential pathways towards sustainable agriculture within the European Green Deal. *Agricultural Systems, 207*, 103634. https://doi.org/10.1016/j.agsy.2023.103634

Chamusca, P. (2023). Public policies for territorial cohesion and sustainability in Europe: An overview. *Sustainability, 15*(8). https://doi.org/10.3390/su15086890

Ciucu-Durnoi, A.-N., Florescu, M. S., & Delcea, C. (2023). Envisioning Romania's path to sustainable development: A prognostic approach. *Sustainability, 15*(17). https://doi.org/10.3390/su151712671

Comisia Europeană. (2024). *Strategia 5G a Europei în deceniul digital.* https://Digital-Strategy.Ec.Europa.Eu/

de Clercq, M., D'Haese, M., & Buysse, J. (2023). Economic growth and broadband access: The European urban-rural digital divide. *Telecommunications Policy, 47*(6), 102579. https://doi.org/10.1016/j.telpol.2023.102579

Dell'Agli, S., & Saabeel, W. (2025). *European digital sustainability skills strategy – Building skills for the twin transition in Europe.*

Devos, L., Lippens, L., Lens, D., Rycx, F., Volral, M., & Baert, S. (2025). Labour market disadvantages of citizens with a migration background in Belgium: A systematic review. *De Economist, 173*(1), 121–175. https://doi.org/10.1007/s10645-024-09443-5

Di Carlo, D., & Schmitz, L. (2023). Europe first? The rise of EU industrial policy promoting and protecting the single market. *Journal of European Public Policy, 30*(10), 2063–2096. https://doi.org/10.1080/13501763.2023.2202684

Djatmiko, G. H., Sinaga, O., & Pawirosumarto, S. (2025). Digital transformation and social inclusion in public services: A qualitative analysis of E-government adoption for marginalized communities in sustainable governance. *Sustainability, 17*(7). https://doi.org/10.3390/su17072908

Domenech, T., & Bahn-Walkowiak, B. (2019). Transition towards a resource efficient circular economy in Europe: Policy lessons from the EU and the member states. *Ecological Economics, 155*, 7–19. https://doi.org/10.1016/j.ecolecon.2017.11.001

European Commission. (2023). *Research and innovation making EU agriculture fit for the future.* https://agriculture.ec.europa.eu/media/news/research-and-innovation-making-eu-agriculture-fit-future-2023-05-30_en

European Commission. (2024a). *5G action plan.* https://digital-strategy.ec.europa.eu/en/policies/5g-action-plan

European Commission. (2024b). *Common agricultural policy funds.* https://agriculture.ec.europa.eu/common-agricultural-policy/financing-cap/cap-funds_en

European Commission. (2024c). *European regional development fund.* https://ec.europa.eu/regional_policy/funding/erdf_en

European Commission. (2024d). *Horizon Europe.* https://research-and-innovation.ec.europa.eu/funding/funding-opportunities/funding-programmes-and-open-calls/horizon-europe_en

European Commission. (2024e). *Recovery and resilience plans.* https://reform-support.ec.europa.eu/what-we-do/recovery-and-resilience-plans_en

European Commission. (2024f). *Rural development.* https://agriculture.ec.europa.eu/common-agricultural-policy/rural-development_en

European Commission. (2024g). *Shaping Europe's digital future.* https://digital-strategy.ec.europa.eu/en

European Commission. (2024h). *Sustainable agricultural practices and methods*. https://agriculture.ec.europa.eu/cap-my-country/sustainability/environmental-sustainability/sustainable-agricultural-practices-and-methods_en

European Commission. (2024i). *The reinforced youth guarantee*. https://employment-social-affairs.ec.europa.eu/policies-and-activities/european-employment-strategy/youth-employment-support/reinforced-youth-guarantee_en

European Commission. (2025a). *A competitiveness compass for the EU*. https://commission.europa.eu/document/download/10017eb1-4722-4333-add2-e0ed18105a34_en

European Commission. (2025b). *Digital skills*. https://digital-strategy.ec.europa.eu/en/policies/digital-skills

European Commission. (2025c). *Funding for digital in the 2021–2027 multiannual financial framework*. https://digital-strategy.ec.europa.eu/en/activities/funding-digital

European Commission. (2025d). *National digital decade strategic roadmaps*. https://digital-strategy.ec.europa.eu/en/policies/national-strategic-roadmaps

European Commission. (2025e). *Organic action plan*. https://agriculture.ec.europa.eu/farming/organic-farming/organic-action-plan_en

European Commission. (2025f). *Renewable energy targets*. https://energy.ec.europa.eu/topics/renewable-energy/renewable-energy-directive-targets-and-rules/renewable-energy-targets_en

European Commission. (2025g). *Research, innovation and knowledge exchange*. https://agriculture.ec.europa.eu/overview-vision-agriculture-food/research-innovation-knowledge-exchange_en

European Commission. (2025h). *Support for digital connectivity*. https://digital-strategy.ec.europa.eu/en/policies/digital-connectivity-support

European Commission. (2025i). *Vision for agriculture and food*. https://agriculture.ec.europa.eu/overview-vision-agriculture-food/vision-agriculture-and-food_en

European Commission. (2025j). *WiFi4EU – Free Wi-Fi in public spaces*. https://digital-strategy.ec.europa.eu/en/policies/wifi4eu

European Commission. (2025k). *Youth employment initiative (YEI)*. https://employment-social-affairs.ec.europa.eu/policies-and-activities/eu-employment-policies/youth-employment-support/youth-employment-initiative-yei_en

European Environment Agency. (2023). *Investments in the sustainability transition: Leveraging green industrial policy against emerging constraints*. https://www.eea.europa.eu/publications/investments-into-the-sustainability-transition

European Environment Agency. (2024). *Energy efficiency*. https://www.eea.europa.eu/en/topics/in-depth/energy-efficiency

European Parliament. (2025a). *Innovation policy*. https://www.europarl.europa.eu/factsheets/en/sheet/67/innovation-policy

European Parliament. (2025b). *Reducing unemployment: Key facts and EU measures explained*. https://www.europarl.europa.eu/topics/en/article/20190612STO54312/reducing-unemployment-key-facts-and-eu-measures-explained

European Parliament. (2025c). *The fight against poverty, social exclusion and discrimination*. https://www.europarl.europa.eu/factsheets/en/sheet/60/the-fight-against-poverty-social-exclusion-and-discrimination

European Union. (2022). *Directive (EU) 2022/2041 of the European Parliament and of the Council of 19 October 2022 on adequate minimum wages in the European Union*. https://eur-lex.europa.eu/eli/dir/2022/2041/oj/eng

European Union. (2024a). *Digital agenda for Europe*. https://www.europarl.europa.eu/factsheets/en/sheet/64/digital-agenda-for-europe

European Union. (2024b). *NextGenerationEU*. https://next-generation-eu.europa.eu/index_en

European Union. (2025). *EU youth strategy*. https://youth.europa.eu/strategy/social-inclusion_en

Eurostat. (2025a). *8. Decent work and economic growth*. https://ec.europa.eu/eurostat/web/sdi/database/decent-work-and-economic-growth

Eurostat. (2025b). *Tax revenue statistics*. https://ec.europa.eu/eurostat/statistics-explained/index.php?title=Tax_revenue_statistics

Foreman-Peck, J., & Zhou, P. (2022). R&D subsidies and productivity in eastern European countries. *Economic Systems, 46*(2), 100978. https://doi.org/10.1016/j.ecosys.2022.100978

Gamage, A., Gangahagedara, R., Gamage, J., Jayasinghe, N., Kodikara, N., Suraweera, P., & Merah, O. (2023). Role of organic farming for achieving sustainability in agriculture. *Farming System, 1*(1), 100005. https://doi.org/10.1016/j.farsys.2023.100005

Gounari, M., Stergiopoulos, G., Pipyros, K., & Gritzalis, D. (2024). Harmonizing open banking in the European Union: An analysis of PSD2 compliance and interrelation with cybersecurity frameworks and standards. *International Cybersecurity Law Review, 5*(1), 79–120. https://doi.org/10.1365/s43439-023-00108-8

Goverment of Romania\United Nations Development Program. (2008). *National sustainable development strategy of Romania 2013-2020-2030*.

Halleröd, B., Ekbrand, H., & Bengtsson, M. (2015). In-work poverty and labour market trajectories: Poverty risks among the working population in 22 European countries. *Journal of European Social Policy, 25*(5), 473–488. https://doi.org/10.1177/0958928715608794

Hariram, N. P., Mekha, K. B., Suganthan, V., & Sudhakar, K. (2023). Sustainalism: An integrated socio-economic-environmental model to address sustainable development and sustainability. *Sustainability, 15*(13). https://doi.org/10.3390/su151310682

International Labour Organization. (2023). *World Employment and Social Outlook Trends 2023.* https://www.ilo.org/sites/default/files/wcmsp5/groups/public/@dgreports/@inst/documents/publication/wcms_865332.pdf

International Labour Organization. (2025). *World employment and social outlook: Trends 2025.* https://www.ilo.org/publications/flagship-reports/world-employment-and-social-outlook-trends-2025

Islam, N. F., Gogoi, B., Saikia, R., Yousaf, B., Narayan, M., & Sarma, H. (2024). Encouraging circular economy and sustainable environmental practices by addressing waste management and biomass energy production. *Regional Sustainability, 5*(4), 100174. https://doi.org/10.1016/j.regsus.2024.100174

Javaid, M., Haleem, A., Singh, R. P., & Sinha, A. K. (2024). Digital economy to improve the culture of industry 4.0: A study on features, implementation and challenges. *Green Technologies and Sustainability, 2*(2), 100083. https://doi.org/10.1016/j.grets.2024.100083

Kalai, M., Becha, H., & Helali, K. (2024). Effect of artificial intelligence on economic growth in European countries: A symmetric and asymmetric cointegration based on linear and non-linear ARDL approach. *Journal of Economic Structures, 13*(1), 22. https://doi.org/10.1186/s40008-024-00345-y

Kálmán, B. G., Zéman, Z., & Malatyinszki, S. (2025). Measuring sustainability in economic output in the member states that joined the European Union in 2004. *Sustainable Futures, 9*, 100724. https://doi.org/10.1016/j.sftr.2025.100724

Kölling, M., & Hernández-Moreno, J. (2024). The multiannual financial framework 2021–2027 and next generation EU – A turning point of EU multi-level governance? *Journal of Contemporary European Studies, 32*(2), 459–473. https://doi.org/10.1080/14782804.2023.2241832

Kotavaara, N., & Prokkola, E.-K. (2023). Employers, the state and highly skilled migration: An employer-based study on ICT sector companies in Finland. *European Planning Studies, 31*(10), 2110–2127. https://doi.org/10.1080/09654313.2022.2095199

Kreinin, H., & Aigner, E. (2022). From "Decent work and economic growth" to "Sustainable work and economic degrowth": A new framework for SDG 8. *Empirica, 49*(2), 281–311. https://doi.org/10.1007/s10663-021-09526-5

Kuc-Czarnecka, M., Markowicz, I., & Sompolska-Rzechuła, A. (2023). SDGs implementation, their synergies, and trade-offs in EU countries – Sensitivity analysis-based approach. *Ecological Indicators, 146*, 109888. https://doi.org/10.1016/j.ecolind.2023.109888

Kuś, A., Kuflewska, W., & Trocewicz, A. (2025). European vision of a gigabit society: Evidence from Poland. *Sustainability, 17*(3). https://doi.org/10.3390/su17031271

Li, X., & Wong, Y. C. (2025). Increasing public investment, fostering digitalization, and supporting the green transition – A difficult challenge. *Selected Issues Papers, 2025*(019), A001. https://doi.org/10.5089/9798229004657.018.A001

Limosani, M., Millemaci, E., & Mustica, P. (2025). Do green policies enhance short-term economic growth? Assessing EU Recovery and Resilience Plans through the lens of Sustainable Development Goals. *Economic Modelling, 147*, 107044. https://doi.org/10.1016/j.econmod.2025.107044

Mack, E. A., Loveridge, S., Keene, T., & Mann, J. (2023). A review of the literature about broadband internet connections and rural development (1995–2022). *International Regional Science Review, 47*(3), 231–292. https://doi.org/10.1177/01600176231202457

Magoutas, A. I., Chaideftou, M., Skandali, D., & Chountalas, P. T. (2024). Digital progression and economic growth: Analyzing the impact of ICT advancements on the GDP of European Union countries. *Economies, 12*(3). https://doi.org/10.3390/economies12030063

McNamara, K. R. (2024). Transforming Europe? The EU's industrial policy and geopolitical turn. *Journal of European Public Policy, 31*(9), 2371–2396. https://doi.org/10.1080/13501763.2023.2230247

Mejía Dorantes, L., & Allen, H. (2024). A review of the future transport labour market: An EU approach. *European Transport Studies, 1*, 100007. https://doi.org/10.1016/j.ets.2024.100007

Meng, J., Ye, Z., & Wang, Y. (2024). Financing and investing in sustainable infrastructure: A review and research agenda. *Sustainable Futures, 8*, 100312. https://doi.org/10.1016/j.sftr.2024.100312

Mergoni, A., Dipierro, A. R., & Colamartino, C. (2024). European agricultural sector: The tortuous path across efficiency, sustainability and environmental risk. *Socio-Economic Planning Sciences, 92*, 101848. https://doi.org/10.1016/j.seps.2024.101848

Milea (Pârvu), A., Moraru, R.-I., & Cioca, L.-I. (2025). Occupational risk management through the lens of the sustainable development goals (SDGs): An integrated approach to promoting sustainability in the workplace. *Sustainability, 17*(5). https://doi.org/10.3390/su17051864

Möller, D. P. F., Wang, Q., Huang, L., Xiong, B., Guo, Y., Shi, T., & Zhang, R. (2025). Impact of digital transformation for sustainable circular economic environments. *Carbon Neutral Systems, 1*(1), 7. https://doi.org/10.1007/s44438-025-00001-3

Moon, B. (2022). Unleash liquidity constraints or competitiveness potential: The impact of R&D grant on external financing on innovation. *European Research on Management and Business Economics, 28*(3), 100195. https://doi.org/10.1016/j.iedeen.2022.100195

Muhammad, S., & Hoffmann, C. (2024). From investment to impact: The role of green finance and technological innovation on German energy transition. *Renewable Energy, 237*, 121665. https://doi.org/10.1016/j.renene.2024.121665

Obelovska, K., Abziatov, A., Doroshenko, A., Dronyuk, I., Liskevych, O., & Liskevych, R. (2025). Analysis of digital skills and infrastructure in EU countries based on DESI 2024 data. *Future Internet, 17*(6). https://doi.org/10.3390/fi17060228

OECD. (2022). *Good practices in Europe for supporting employers to promote skills development.* https://www.oecd.org/skills/Good-practices-in-Europe-for-supporting-employers-to-promote-skills-development.pdf

OECD. (2023a). *Building future-ready vocational education and training systems.* https://doi.org/10.1787/28551a79-en

OECD. (2023b). *On shaky ground? Income instability and economic insecurity in Europe.* https://doi.org/10.1787/9bffeba6-en

OECD. (2024). *Addressing labour and skills shortages in a fast-changing economy.* https://doi.org/10.1787/757311cb-en

OECD. (2025a). *Closing broadband connectivity divides for all.* https://doi.org/10.1787/d5ea99b2-en

OECD. (2025b). *Place-based policies for displaced workers: Lessons from past economic disruptions.* https://www.oecd.org/en/publications/place-based-policies-for-displaced-workers_69b86784-en.html

OECD. (2025c). *Taxing wages 2025: Decomposition of personal income taxes and the role of tax reliefs.* https://doi.org/10.1787/b3a95829-en

Okunevičiūtė Neverauskienė, L., Dirma, V., Tvaronavičienė, M., & Danilevičienė, I. (2025). Assessing the role of renewable energy in the sustainable economic growth of the European Union. *Energies, 18*(4). https://doi.org/10.3390/en18040760

Padrón, T. G., Kovačević, L., & Moreno, M. I. R. (2023). In D. Vujadinović, M. Fröhlich, & T. Giegerich (Eds.), *Labour law and gender BT – Gender-competent legal education* (pp. 583–630). Springer International Publishing. https://doi.org/10.1007/978-3-031-14360-1_17

Pateiro-Rodríguez, C., Martín-Bermúdez, F., Pateiro-López, C., & Escourido-Calvo, M. (2024). Universal service regulation and network effects in services of general economic interest in the European Union. *Economies, 12*(10). https://doi.org/10.3390/economies12100280

Raileanu Szeles, M., & Simionescu, M. (2021). Improving the school-to-work transition for young people by closing the digital divide: Evidence from the EU regions. *International Journal of Manpower, 43*(7), 1540–1555. https://doi.org/10.1108/IJM-03-2021-0190

Rosário, C., Varum, C., & Botelho, A. (2024). The role of public incentives in promoting innovation: An analysis of recurrently supported companies. *Economies, 12*(6). https://doi.org/10.3390/economies12060148

Sánchez-García, E., Martínez-Falcó, J., Marco-Lajara, B., & Manresa-Marhuenda, E. (2024). Revolutionizing the circular economy through new technologies: A new era of sustainable progress. *Environmental Technology & Innovation, 33*, 103509. https://doi.org/10.1016/j.eti.2023.103509

Senna, P. P., Bonnin Roca, J., & Barros, A. C. (2023). Overcoming barriers to manufacturing digitalization: Policies across EU countries. *Technological Forecasting and Social Change, 196*, 122822. https://doi.org/10.1016/j.techfore.2023.122822

Shahzad, M., Qu, Y., Rehman, S. U., & Zafar, A. U. (2022). Adoption of green innovation technology to accelerate sustainable development among manufacturing industry. *Journal of Innovation & Knowledge, 7*(4), 100231. https://doi.org/10.1016/j.jik.2022.100231

Ţarcă, V., Luca, F.-A., & Ţarcă, E. (2024). The digital edge: Skills that matter in the European labour market after COVID-19. *Economies, 12*(10). https://doi.org/10.3390/economies12100273

Teixeira, J. E., & Tavares-Lehmann, A. T. C. P. (2022). Industry 4.0 in the European Union: Policies and national strategies. *Technological Forecasting and Social Change, 180*, 121664. https://doi.org/10.1016/j.techfore.2022.121664

Wigger, A. (2023). The new EU industrial policy and deepening structural asymmetries: Smart specialisation not so smart. *JCMS: Journal of Common Market Studies, 61*(1), 20–37. https://doi.org/10.1111/jcms.13366

CHAPTER 13

# Analysis of the Romanian Economy's Strategies for Achieving Sustainable Development Goal 9

## Introduction

The Industrial Strategy at European level is based on the Commission's 2020 vision of the dual transition to a green and digital economy. The objectives of competitiveness and strategic autonomy are in line with the European Agenda and are adapted to the new requirements imposed by the downgrading of the pandemic and geopolitical conflict. The resilient and competitive development of European industry requires financial efforts and the active promotion of innovation. European small and medium-sized enterprises are targeted in an inclusive context, and their actions must be geared towards reducing dependencies in supply chains and accelerating the transition to the green and digital economy. From the financial point of view, the industrial strategy promotes combating late payments and increasing solvency with the effect of increasing the resilience of economic entities. In the context of the multiple crises, the role of the single integrated global market has been emphasized, and from this perspective the European Commission (2021) has established new tasks for regulators, proposing the single market as an emergency instrument as a structural solution to guarantee the free movement of goods and services, the harmonization of standards for essential services, and the digitalization of the market.



C. Fortea, *Sustainable Economic Development and the European Green Deal*, https://doi.org/10.1007/978-3-032-10326-0_13

In terms of monitoring these markets, the industrial ecosystems in Fig. 13.1 are followed.

Other proposals to make strategic autonomy more flexible are the establishment of diversified international partnerships, industrial alignments, including the Processors and Semiconductor Technologies Alliance and the Industrial Data, High-Tech and Cloud Technologies Alignment. The next two alignments prepared by the committee are the Space Launch Vehicle Alignment and the Zero Emission Aviation Alignment.

According to the new Industrial Strategy 2020 Update: Building a stronger single market to support Europe's recovery (European Commission, 2020), the EU's industrial sector is addressing opportunities and challenges for a double transformation, requiring real economic foresight, coherent and stable regulation, access to capacity and infrastructure, financing for innovation, raw materials and clean energy, and adequate skills for competitive transformation.

The EU pushes to support the implementation of the green and digital economy through the Green Deal and NextGenerationEU (European Union, 2023). These policies aim to accelerate the redeployment of resources and investment in Europe and strengthen the EU's commitment to green and digital transformation. The EU encourages Member

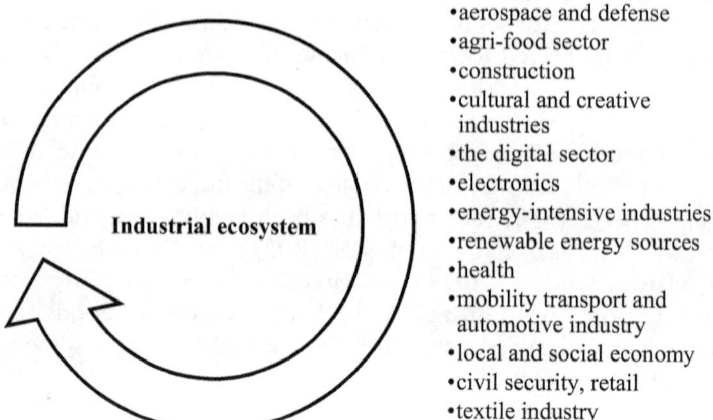


**Fig. 13.1** Industrial ecosystems. Source: Prepared by the author according to the Industrial Strategy for Europe (European Commission, 2021)

States to include green and digital investments in their national plans, ensuring that at least 37% of funding is dedicated to green investments and 20% is dedicated to digitization. The EU's commitment to promote multinational projects offers a unique opportunity to join forces in projects that build digital and green capacity. According to the New Industrial Strategy 2020 Update: Building a stronger single market to support Europe's recovery (European Commission, 2020), a number of Member States have signalled their intention to include multinational projects in their projects, potentially accelerating investments in the areas of hydrocarbons, 5G networks, infrastructure, data exchange, sustainable transport, blockchain technology and European Digital Innovation Hubs. In the field of environment and energy, the EU, through the new Industrial Strategy and Green Plan, will enable Member States to support transnational companies in decarbonizing their production processes and adopting greener technologies.

New EU environmental and energy standards will allow Member States to support transnational companies in decarbonizing production processes and adopting greener technologies. The EU is also preparing a new strategy on sustainable financing and a legislative initiative on corporate governance to reduce the risks associated with global carbon emissions.

The main objective of the Horizon Europe programme (European Commission, 2023) is to support the pan-European next-generation innovation ecosystem for the green and digital transition. The Innovation Fund will continue to provide essential support for the commercial demonstration of innovative low-carbon technologies in several sectors. According to the update of the new Industrial Strategy 2020: Building a stronger single market to support Europe's recovery (European Commission, 2020), current investment in renewables, energy storage, networks, interconnections and industrial transformation in the EU is too slow. For the green transition to bring truly sustainable competitiveness, industry needs access to abundant, affordable and decarbonized electricity and additional efforts are needed. The European Commission is working with Member States to raise the level of ambition for renewable energy and streamline permitting procedures. The Energy and Industrial Geography Lab, a tool being developed by the Commission's Joint Research Center in collaboration with industry stakeholders, provides geospatial information for companies and energy infrastructure planners. Industrial consumers, SMEs and communities can work together to ensure long-term price security for renewable energy projects and improve their environmental footprint.

Through sustainable development strategies developed by Romanian government representatives (Ionel-Valentin Vlad, 2017), the industrial strategy is focused on economic transformation with accelerated technological influx, emphasizing economic integration into international chains and the transition to the digital economy. In this context, investments in human capital are becoming necessary, as it is recognized that currently the specialization of personnel is not adequate for the new directions of sustainable development, promoting the circular economy to valorize unusable resources, i.e. by-products of production and consumption processes (Ionel-Valentin Vlad, 2017). Also, at the national level it is necessary to implement new technologies to increase the efficiency of energy resources and develop the green economy.

The accelerated trend of demographic reduction of the skilled labour force has had as an effect a vulnerability of the national economy that has materialized in the modest increase in labour productivity, which currently places Romania at the bottom in Europe in terms of the use of economic and financial potential to produce sustainable growth. To this has been added the low productivity of material resources, with a downward trend inversely compared to the EU average, which has recorded significant productivity increases in this area in recent decades. Innovation capacity and competitiveness are other vulnerable aspects of the Romanian economy, which has led to the share of Romanian-owned firms becoming a minority compared to the share of foreign-owned firms. Sustainable development on the economic pillar is seen from the perspective of increasing economic efficiency, economic completeness, and the Romanian economy being assimilated to an emerging economy that requires infusions of technology to increase productivity. From a strategic point of view, the Romanian economy is projected to be transformed by 2028 into an efficiency-driven economy and by 2038 into a creativity and innovation-driven economy. The scenarios developed in the Strategy for Romania's Sustainable Development are based on the evolution of favourable phenomena and processes with the overcoming of uncertainty events generated by crises, recessions, inflation or geopolitical conflicts promoting economic-financial balance as a feature of the national economy's efficiency and the reduction of economic and technological gaps.

Figure 13.2 shows the links with the other national strategies and plans for the implementation of the 5G Strategy for Romania, as well as the sectors identified because of the interactions with the national strategies.

The aim of the 2022–2027 strategy called the National Strategy for Research, Innovation (Government of Romania, 2022) is to support and reward basic and applied research and to develop public–private collaboration. According to the Strategy (Government of Romania, 2022), Romania aims to provide a welcoming environment for experienced researchers who can sustain performance. The proposed targets of the strategy are (Government of Romania, 2022): to increase the number of PhD graduates to more than 10% of the total number of tertiary graduates; to increase the number of researchers by 0.12 per thousand employed; to increase the number of researchers working at national level by 2030; and to increase the quality of knowledge processes expressed by increasing the proportions of articles published in recognized journals and patents. In terms of innovation enterprises for Horizon 2030, it is proposed to change Romania's emerging innovator status to moderate innovator status, these

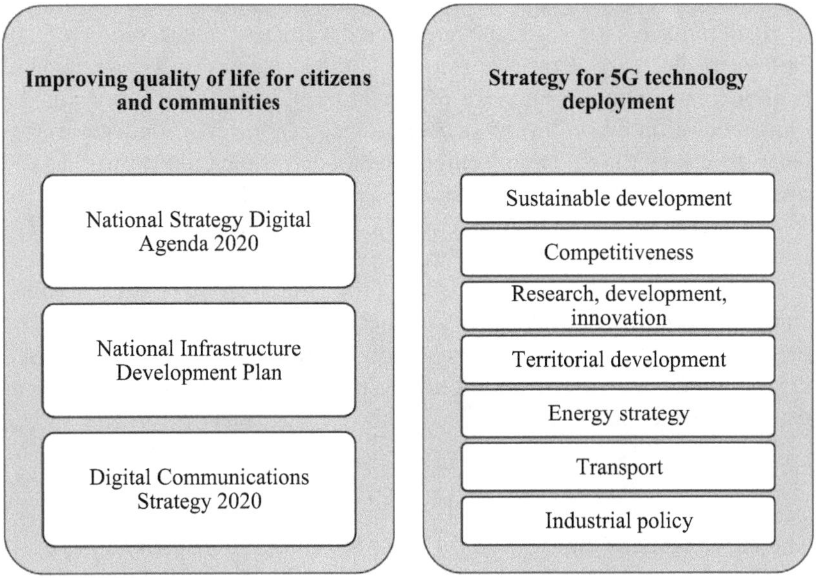


**Fig. 13.2** National strategies to implement the 5G Strategy. Source: Prepared by the author according to the 5G Strategy for Romania (ANCOM, 2019)

aspects being analysed from the perspective of the European Innovation Scoreboard criteria. At the same time, concrete measures will promote enterprises introducing new innovative products and collaboration with research organizations. An important target is to increase employment in innovative enterprises from 2.5% to 6%. As regards smart specializations, the focus is on innovation ecosystems associated with smart specializations, the national smart specialization priorities being synergistic with the smart specializations of the regions. In terms of public priorities and changes, structural changes are sought in the research, development and innovation (RDI) system to increase the efficiency of governance, develop public–private partnerships as key elements of innovation, and internationalize the international research, development and innovation system in the European Research Area.

The National Authority for Administration and Regulation in Communications (ANCOM) has developed and implemented the Digitization Strategy, also called the 5G Strategy, for Romania (ANCOM, 2019) which proposes some specific measures for the development of digitalization by creating mechanisms for the implementation of user fee measures, identification of cross-border corridors for the use of 5G technologies in road transport of road and connected vehicles, transposition of the European Electronic Communications Code into a national code, facilitation of construction permits for 5G facilitation, incentive funding for the implementation of 5G infrastructure projects, creation of the legal framework necessary for the interconnection of communication networks, and operationalization of the Alliance for 5G.

In general, the opportunities that support the development of SDG9 in Romania are represented by the massive growth of the Internet of Data, the rise of the Internet of Things (IoT), the digitalization of the economy, and the accelerated development of the ICT and software industry. The risks for the national economy are mainly manifested in the lack of legislation adapted to the digitization of the economy and the risks of data security and protection.

## Literature Review

The importance of digitization for sustainable economic growth lies in its potential to accelerate the achievement of the 17 Sustainable Development Goals, such as reducing child and maternal mortality, eradicating extreme poverty, promoting sustainable agriculture, decent work and universal literacy. However, digital technology also poses risks and problems, such as data theft, terrorism and the spread of crime, due to its international character and relative anonymity. The complexity of digital devices is also a challenge, as the global population is not specialized for new jobs due to digitization. Understanding the role of digitization in sustainable development is essential to understanding its role in state development.

There are numerous impact studies on sustainable development in the field of digitization in the literature. We used the Web of Science database to search for the phrase "sustainable development industry" used in the titles, abstracts and keywords of the publications included in this database and performed the bibliometric analysis using the VOSviewer program (Fig. 13.3).

In the year 2022, the total number of papers identified on the Web of Science platform was 9746 articles recognized in 35,970 papers that cited them (without self-citations) with a citation rate of 4.64 times per article and a Hirsch index of 52 points.

These publications address various research issues, including the impact of fiscal policy on sustainable development in the field of digitization, the impact of sustainable development in the dimension of the technological revolution Industry 4.0, the influence of financial performance on sustainable development in the industrial sector, and the assessment of digital technology and cultural industries.

The review of the literature on the correlation of SD indicators through the lens of the transition to SDG9 is presented below.

- **Spending on Research, Development and Innovation**

In an interesting approach, Gajdzik and Wolniak (2022) propose to analyse the development of the metallurgical industry in Poland on the basis of R&D and innovation expenditures with impact on sustainable development according to Fig. 13.4. The analysed indicators consist of R&D expenditures in metallurgy and research added value, expenditures on innovative processes at the branch level, and outputs in the field of environmental protection. The authors conclude based on the hypotheses that the increase in R&D has had a positive impact on the metallurgical industry, these expenditures have been steadily increasing, and their effects have led to an increase in innovative processes at the branch level with an impact on productivity. At the same time, environmental protection innovations

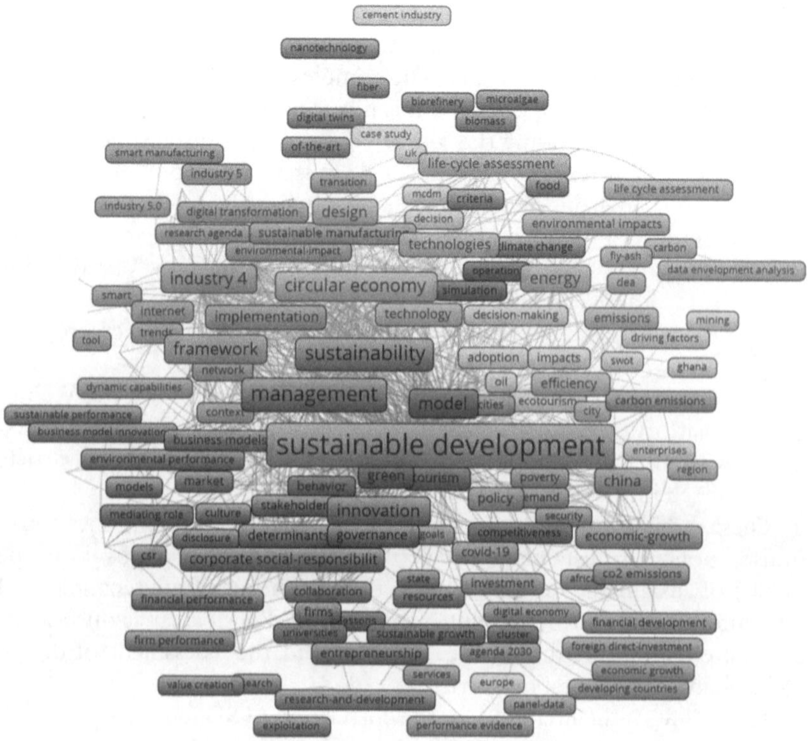


**Fig. 13.3** Bibliometric analysis on sustainable development in industry. Source: Author using VOSviewer software

have had a significant impact on the decarbonization of the branch in Poland.

A study on the digitization of small and medium enterprises with impact on economic growth by Brodny and Tutak (2022) determined the level of digital maturity of SMEs in the EU27 and the relationship between the digital maturity index and basic economic parameters. The results revealed that the digitization strategy has created significant regional disparities remaining a priority for the development of a competitive and innovative economy. The main results showed that the most developed digital technologies in the EU are data traffic, cloud services and cybersecurity, with heterogeneous development of technologies across two groups of

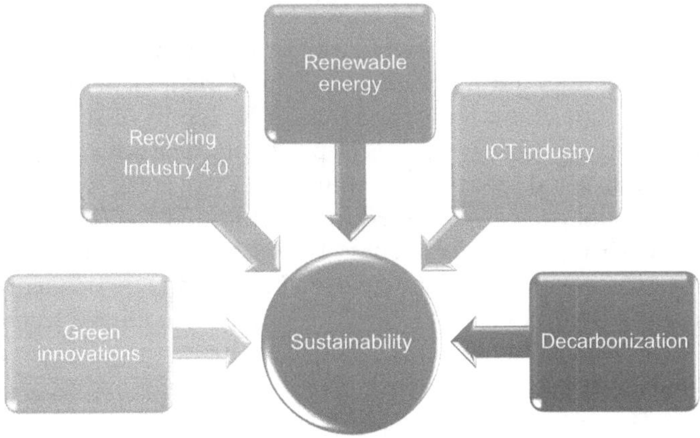


**Fig. 13.4** The pillars of sustainable development in metallurgical R&D and innovation. Source: Prepared by the author according to the article "Framework for R&D&I Activities in the Steel Industry in Popularizing the Idea of Industry 4.0" (Gajdzik & Wolniak, 2022)

countries, namely developed and developing countries. The authors also found a statistically significant relationship between economic development as represented by GDP per capita and SMEs' research and development expenditure, these parameters being important for SMEs' digitalization. Innovative development in the context of industrial security is analysed by Kuzior et al. (2022) who quantify the qualitative and normative consistency of dynamics and directions of technological processes based on a 3R model. The authors show that the main influencing factors of the circular economy from the point of view of industrial security are resource stocks and stock management with impact on performance.

- **R&D Staff**

In another approach, staff training for the development of digital skills allowed a team of authors, Espina-Romero et al. (2023), to identify the most sensitive areas in terms of the need for qualified personnel to implement digital technologies. According to the authors, these are engineering, communications, engineering education, software design and project management.

Also from the personnel perspective, Hu et al. (2019) show that in a competitive global economy, the critical factors affecting the development of economic entities are innovation and the development of employees' capabilities to utilize innovative products. The results of the study show that the innovative capacity of R&D personnel depends on continuous learning, practice and variation over time, and there are flows between the two classes of innovators presented in the study. The authors also show that in order to improve completeness it is necessary to constantly improve the innovativeness skills of staff employed in the R&D department and to interest new employees in the innovative process. Additional studies (Hu et al., 2019; Meyer-Krahmer et al., 1983) emphasise the influence of government facilities on the development of the innovation industry.

- **Economic Development Through Digitization**

An interesting approach to the achievements in the field of European digitization is by Cave (2023) who analyses European digital economy issues from the perspective of assumed and unimplemented strategic goals (universal access to the Internet, universal digital education and improving people's digital skills, protecting the environment through digital systems, accessible and digital public services, and ethical principles in the digital economy). At the same time, by presenting the case studies the authors show that the digitization strategy is implemented in an incipient way and has not yet achieved the main goal of improving universal digital connectivity and 5G coverage for all citizens. Although costly the process can bring benefits for economic progress, increased productivity and resilience. In the same research direction Blind and Niebel (2022) analyse the 5G ecosystems and their taxonomy to ensure the implementation of connectivity policies. The results are oriented towards substantiating European 5G policies as future action directions for European decision-makers (direct support of R&D firms, entrepreneurial policies, cluster policies, development of innovative networks, development of innovation-based research, public cybersecurity policies).

Analysing the European Gigabit Society objective in the 2025 connectivity strategy, Ferrandis et al. (2021) identify the need for new measures to attract investment in the field and to reduce the rural–urban environment connectivity gap. The estimation models used allow the creation of a policy framework for action at local and regional level to increase connectivity in Europe.

De Clercq et al. (2023) analyse economic development through connectivity and show that increased connectivity and investment in communication technologies contribute to sustainable economic growth and operationalization of network access in rural areas, resulting in economic growth through the impact of government investment and spending, increased employment and improved economic marginal effects. The authors point out that the reduction of urban–rural disparities will contribute to increased welfare and will have an effect of increasing the returns on investment through the industrialization of rural areas.

Also in terms of connectivity, Martins and Wernick (2021) in their analysis demonstrate that the demand for connectivity services is higher in households with a higher density of people and the user profiles depend on the regional structure of the population. The authors develop some public policy proposals on the implementation of telework with effects on reducing pollution and increasing flexibility, creating digital networks in health and public services, and achieving the goal of developing the digital society by increasing the digital activities of the population and ensuring good connectivity to enable digital applications to operate in optimal parameters.

The literature shows that researchers' approaches to SDG9 capture varied aspects of modern issues aimed at capitalizing on technological progress, improving labour productivity, adapting staff skills to the demands of new jobs in the digital and green economy, managing resource stocks, and advancing digital connectivity. The results show that Romania is at the bottom of the European ranking and that reforms need to be accelerated in order to implement SDG9.

## Analysis of the Main Sustainable Development Goal Indicators 9

As shown in the previous section, from the official statistics there are signs of Romania's significant development gap with the European average. Research, development, innovation, sustainable industries and infrastructure are important for the realization of SDG9 in the context of the EU. The monitoring of SDG9 focuses mainly on R&D, R&D personnel, patent applications and industry.

R&D funding is a beneficial component for sustainable and smart growth. Bringing new ideas to the market encourages job creation, worker productivity and resource efficiency. Maintaining the EU's capacity for research and innovation, competitiveness, support for digital and environmental initiatives, and human resource skills is key to finding solutions to today's challenges of climate change, clean energy and public security.

We aim to analyse, through the main indicators reported by Eurostat, the evolution trend of the implementation of SDG9 in Romania compared to the European average between 2010 and 2021. The indicators used are as follows (Eurostat, 2023):

- **CDI** – Gross domestic expenditure on research and development indicates gross domestic expenditure on research and development as a percentage of gross domestic product.
- **PERCD** – Research and Development Personnel indicates the share of R&D personnel in the institutional sectors: business, government, higher education and private non-profit organizations. Individuals working in research and development are directly involved in the process and focus on innovative and methodical efforts to advance knowledge, including understanding about people, culture and society, and to develop new applications for existing knowledge.
- **BRV** – Patent applications at the European Patent Office indicate the number of applications for protection of an invention submitted to the European Patent Office, irrespective of whether an inventor's application for protection is approved or rejected.
- **AINT** – High-speed Internet coverage indicates the higher Internet speed and other technical features that enable access or delivery of new content, applications and services.

The analysis of the indicator Gross Domestic Expenditure on Research and Development (% of GDP) at EU level (EUGDI27) shows that over the period 2010–2021 it has had a dynamic of 16.75%, i.e. from a minimum of 1.97% in 2010 to 2.3% in 2020 (Fig. 13.5).

On trend, the indicator showed an overall upward trend of 0.29%, the calculated overall average of the indicator being 2.137%, with a standard error estimated by descriptive statistics of 0.027% (as shown in Table 13.1)

The analysis of the indicator Gross Domestic Expenditure on Research and Development (% of GDP) in Romania (CDIROM) shows that in the period 2010–2021 it had a dynamic of 31.58%, respectively from a minimum value of 0.38% in 2014 to 0.5% in 2017 AND 2018 (Fig. 13.6).

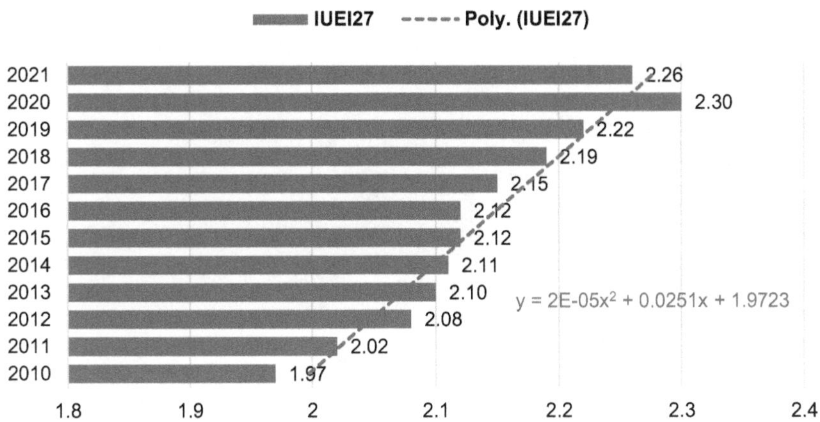


**Fig. 13.5** Dynamics of the Gross Domestic Expenditure on Research and Development indicator over the period 2010–2021. Source: Author based on Eurostat data

**Table 13.1** Comparative descriptive statistics of the indicator Gross Domestic Expenditure on Research and Development at European and national level over the period 2010–2021

| *Gross domestic expenditure on research and development (% of GDP)* | *European Union—27 countries* | *Romania* |
|---|---|---|
| Minim | 1.97 | 0.38 |
| Maxim | 2.30 | 0.50 |
| Average | 2.1370 | 0.4620 |
| Standard error of the mean | 0.02700 | 0.01100 |
| Standard deviation | 0.09500 | 0.03900 |
| Variance | 0.009 | 0.002 |
| Asymmetry | 0.062 | −1.428 |
| Asymmetry error | 0.637 | 0.637 |
| Flattening | −0.208 | 1.252 |
| Standard error of flattening | 1.232 | 1.232 |

Source: Author based on Eurostat data

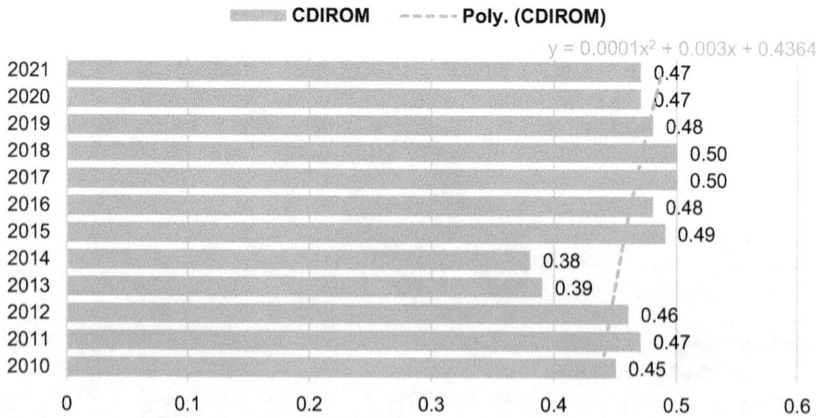


**Fig. 13.6** Dynamics of the indicator Gross Domestic Expenditure on Research and Development at national level in the period 2010–2021. Source: Author based on Eurostat data

On trend, the indicator showed an overall upward trend of 0.02%, the calculated overall average of the indicator being 0.462%, with a standard error estimated by descriptive statistics of 0.011% (as shown in Table 13.1).

The analysis of the dynamic variations of the indicator in Romania compared to the European average shows that for our country, the overall average of seasonal variations was lower than the European average, as shown in Fig. 13.7

The EU economy faces global competition and can maintain its competitiveness by strengthening its science and technology base. Encouraging greater investment in research and development has been one of the main objectives of EU policies in recent decades. Analyses of R&D intensity and gross domestic product (GDP) are used to track this. EU R&D intensity has increased only slightly over the last 20 years, despite a three-year target. The EU's moderate intention to increase R&D intensity to 3% by 2030 has fallen by 0.74% (Eurostat, 2023).

An analysis of the Gross Domestic Expenditure on R&D indicator at EU level shows that business (66%) and higher education (21.6%) are the two largest spending sectors in 2021 (Eurostat, 2023). At the same time government expenditure accounted for 11.8% of total expenditure.

The analysis of the indicator Research and Development Personnel by sector (% of population in the workforce, full time) at EU level

(PERCDUE27) shows that in the period 2010–2021 it had a dynamic of 39.26%, i.e. from a minimum of 1.08% in 2010 to 1.5% in 2021 (Fig. 13.8).

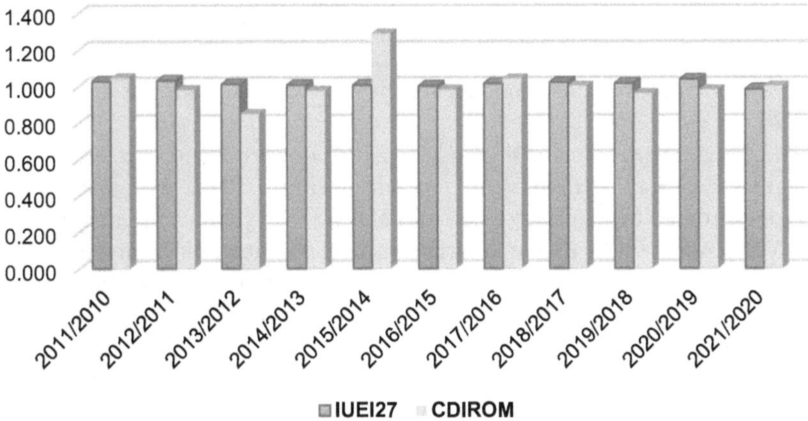


**Fig. 13.7** Analysis of the dynamic variations of the indicator Gross Domestic Expenditure on Research and Development in Romania compared to the European average. Source: Author based on Eurostat data

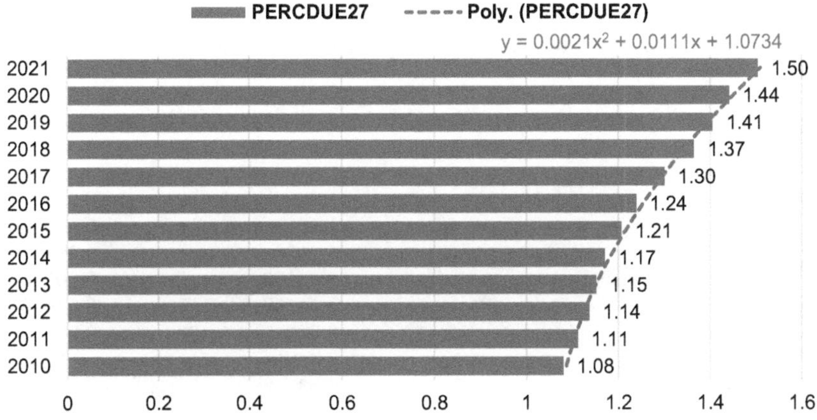


**Fig. 13.8** Dynamics of the indicator Research and Development Personnel at European level over the period 2010–2021. Source: Author based on Eurostat data

On trend, the indicator showed an overall upward trend of 0.424%, the calculated overall average of the indicator being 1.26%, with a standard error estimated by descriptive statistics of 0.041% (see Table 13.2).

The analysis of the indicator Research and Development Personnel (% of population in the labour force, full time) at the level of Romania (PERCDROM) shows that in the period 2010–2021 it had a dynamic of 27.49%, respectively from the minimum value of 0.331% in 2010 to 0.4% in 2021 (Fig. 13.9).

On trend, the indicator showed an overall upward trend of 0.091%, the calculated overall average of the indicator being 0.394%, with a standard error estimated by descriptive statistics of 0.007% (as shown in Table 13.2).

The analysis of the dynamic variations of the indicator in Romania compared to the European average shows that for our country, the overall average of seasonal variations was lower than the European average, as shown in Fig. 13.10.

Human capital is becoming increasingly important due to the focus on the EU economy and society, as well as labour market changes and demographic trends. Ambitious investment in research, development and innovation, including further investment in skills development and lifelong learning, is needed to achieve the sustainable development goals. At EU level, the R&D workforce has been growing steadily from 1.08% in 2010

**Table 13.2** Comparative descriptive statistics of the indicator Research and Development Personnel by sector at European and national level over the period 2010–2021

| *R&D personnel by sector (% of population in full-time workforce)* | *European Union—27 countries* | *Romania* |
|---|---|---|
| Minim | 1.08 | 0.33 |
| Maxim | 1.50 | 0.42 |
| Average | 1.2600 | 0.3940 |
| Standard error of the mean | 0.04100 | 0.00700 |
| Standard deviation | 0.14100 | 0.02300 |
| Variance | 0.020 | 0.001 |
| Asymmetry | 0.469 | −2.016 |
| Asymmetry error | 0.637 | 0.637 |
| Flattening | −1.163 | 5.560 |
| Standard error of flattening | 1.232 | 1.232 |

Source: Author based on Eurostat data

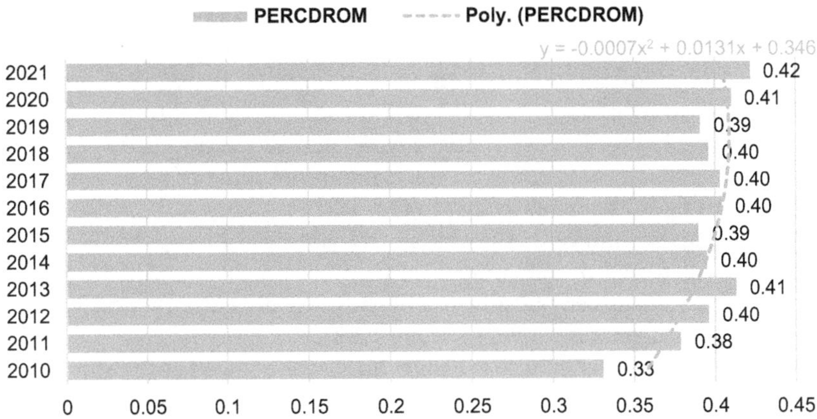


**Fig. 13.9** Dynamics of the indicator Research and Development Personnel at national level in the period 2010–2021. Source: Author based on Eurostat data

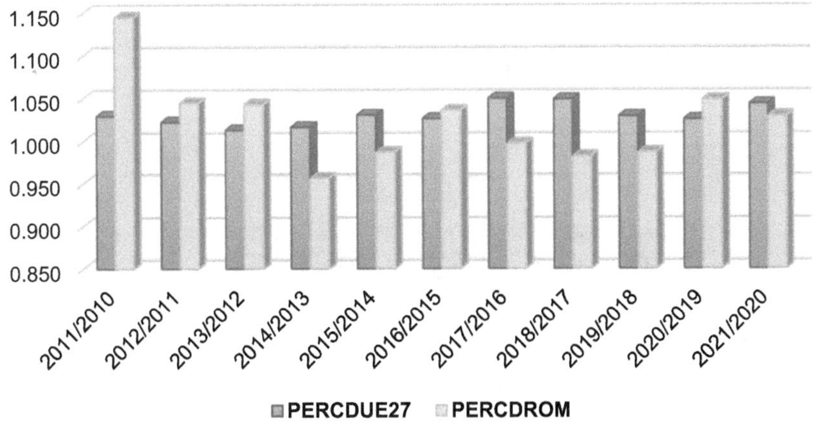


**Fig. 13.10** Analysis of the dynamic variations of the indicator Research and Development Personnel in Romania compared to the European average. Source: Author based on Eurostat data

to 1.50% in 2021, mainly driven by the business sector, which employed around 60% of the R&D workforce in 2021 (Eurostat, 2023).

The analysis of the indicator Patent Applications Filed at the European Patent Office by country of residence of the applicants/inventors at the EU level (BRVUE27) reveals that in the analysed period 2010–2021 it had a dynamic of 13.74%, i.e. from the minimum value of 59,626 patents in 2011 to 67,820 patents in 2021 (Fig. 13.11).

On trend, the indicator showed an overall upward trend of 6585 patents, the calculated overall average of the indicator being 63,330.75 patents, with a standard error estimated by the descriptive statistics calculation of 777.375 patents (as shown in Table 13.3).

The analysis of the indicator Patent Applications Filed at the European Patent Office by country of residence of the applicants/inventors in Romania (BRVROM) shows that in the analysed period 2010–2021 it had a dynamic of 292.86%, respectively from the minimum value of 14 patents in 2010 to 55 patents in 2020 (Fig. 13.12).

On trend, the indicator showed an overall upward trend of 17 patents, the calculated overall average of the indicator being 34,917 patents, with a standard error estimated by calculating descriptive statistics of 3604 patents, as shown in Table 13.3.

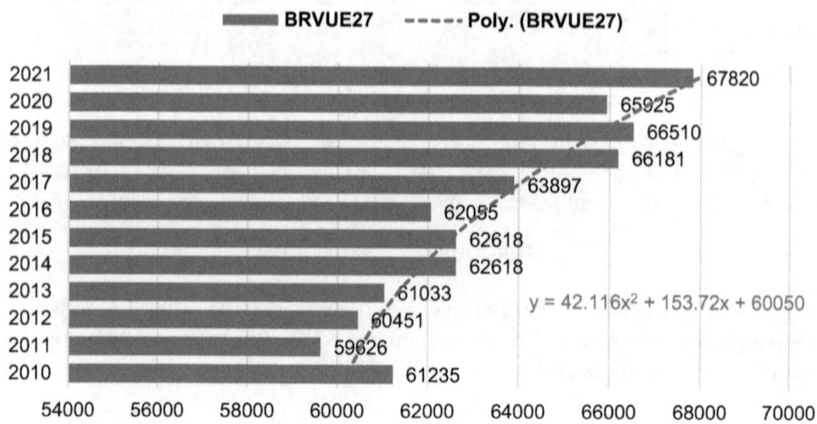


**Fig. 13.11** Dynamics of the indicator Patent Applications Filed at the European Patent Office at European level in the period 2010–2021. Source: Author based on Eurostat data

**Table 13.3** Comparative descriptive statistics of the indicator Patent Applications Filed at the European Patent Office at European and national level in the period 2010–2021

| *Patent applications filed at the European Patent Office* | *European Union—27 countries* | *Romania* |
|---|---|---|
| Minim | 59626.00 | 14.00 |
| Maxim | 67820.00 | 55.00 |
| Average | 63330.7500 | 34.9170 |
| Standard error of the mean | 777.37500 | 3.60400 |
| Standard deviation | 2692.90700 | 12.48600 |
| Variance | 7251746.568 | 155.902 |
| Asymmetry | 0.361 | 0.202 |
| Asymmetry error | 0.637 | 0.637 |
| Flattening | −1.255 | −0.503 |
| Standard error of flattening | 1.232 | 1.232 |

Source: Author based on Eurostat data

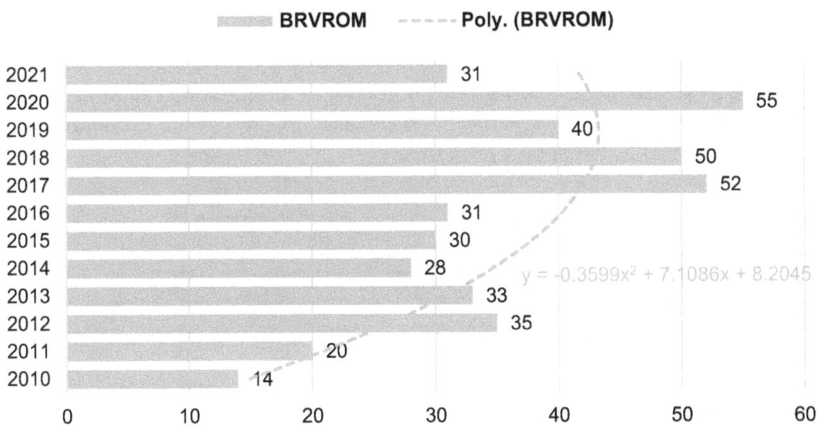


**Fig. 13.12** Dynamics of the indicator Patent Applications Filed at the European Patent Office at national level in the period 2010–2021. Source: Author based on Eurostat data

The analysis of the dynamic variations of the indicator in Romania compared to the European average shows that for our country, the general average of seasonal variations was higher than the European average, as shown in Fig. 13.13.

The analysis of the indicator High-speed Internet Coverage in the EU (AINTUE27) shows that in the period 2010–2021 it had a dynamic of 996.88%, i.e. from a minimum of 6.4% in 2020 to 70.2% in 2021 (as shown in Fig. 13.14).

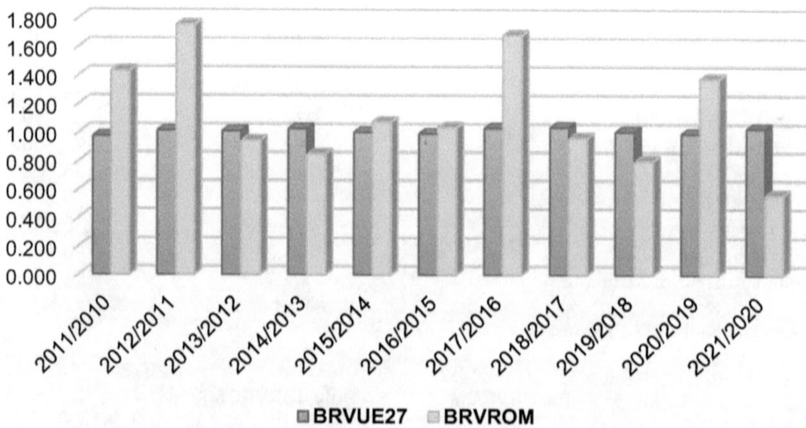


**Fig. 13.13** Analysis of dynamic variations of the indicator Patent Applications Filed at the European Patent Office in Romania compared to the European average. Source: Author based on Eurostat data

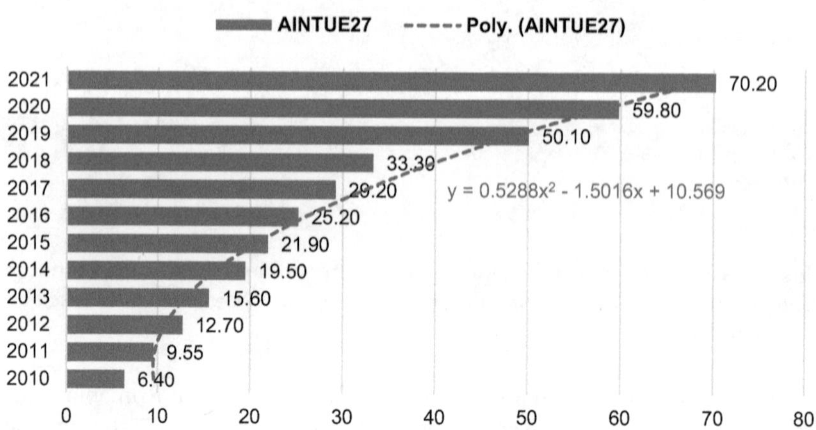


**Fig. 13.14** High-speed Internet Coverage at European level in the period 2010–2021. Source: Author based on Eurostat data

**Table 13.4** Comparative descriptive statistics of the indicator High-speed Internet Coverage at European and national level in the period 2010–2021

| *High-speed Internet coverage by type of area* | *European Union—27 countries* | *Romania* |
|---|---|---|
| Minim | 6.40 | 49.96 |
| Maxim | 70.20 | 87.10 |
| Average | 29.4540 | 61.7100 |
| Standard error of the mean | 5.90100 | 3.10700 |
| Standard deviation | 20.44200 | 10.76200 |
| Variance | 417.887 | 115.810 |
| Asymmetry | 0.964 | 1.388 |
| Asymmetry error | 0.637 | 0.637 |
| Flattening | −0.104 | 1.774 |
| Standard error of flattening | 1.232 | 1.232 |

Source: Author based on Eurostat data

On trend, the indicator showed an overall upward trend of 63.8%, the calculated overall average of the indicator being 29.454%, with a standard error estimated by descriptive statistics of 5.901% (see Table 13.4)

The analysis of the indicator High-speed Internet Coverage in Romania (AINTROM) shows that in the analysed period 2010–2021 it had a dynamic of 74.34%, respectively from the minimum value of 49.96% in 2010 to 87.1% in 2021 (Fig. 13.15).

On trend, the indicator showed an overall upward trend of 37.14%, the calculated overall average of the indicator being 61.71%, with a standard error estimated by descriptive statistics of 3.107% (as shown in Table 13.4).

The analysis of the dynamic variations of the indicator in Romania compared to the European average shows that for our country, the general average of seasonal variations was lower than the European average, as shown in Fig. 13.16.

## Conclusions

An analysis of Romania's strategies for achieving Sustainable Development Goal 9 (SDG9) highlights a significant gap compared to the EU average in terms of the performance of key indicators: expenditure on research and development, the share of personnel engaged in RDI activities, the number of patent applications, and high-speed Internet coverage. Although

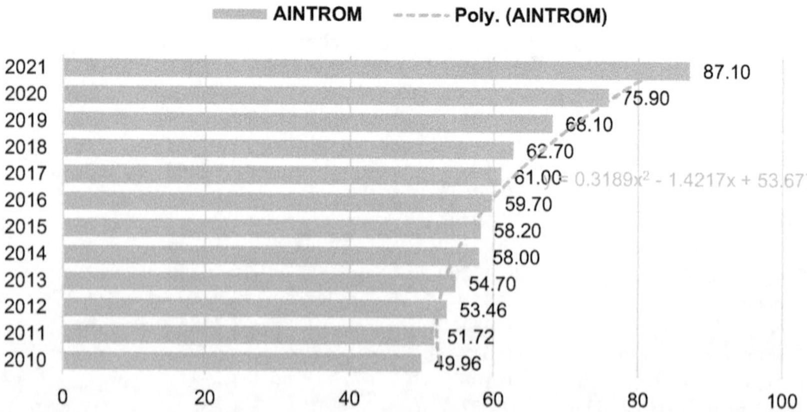


**Fig. 13.15** High-speed Internet Coverage at national level in the period 2010–2021. Source: Author based on Eurostat data

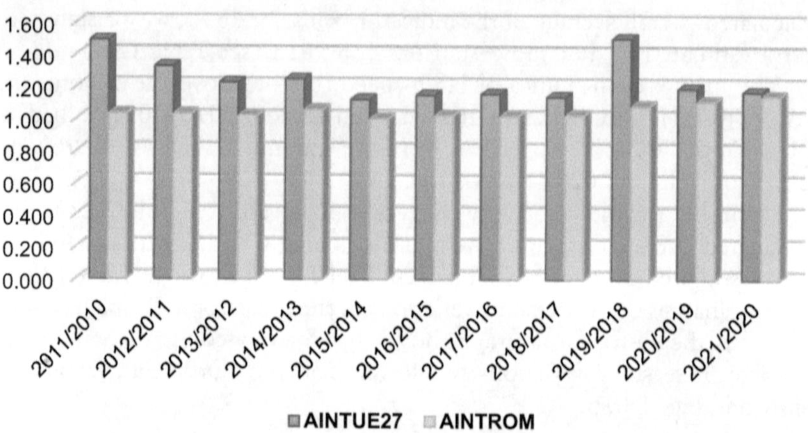


**Fig. 13.16** Analysis of dynamic variations of the indicator high-speed Internet Coverage in Romania compared to the European average. Source: Author based on Eurostat data

overall trends point to positive long-term developments, the pace of progress remains insufficient to ensure rapid convergence with European standards. Investment in R&D and skilled human resources is still low, limiting the national economy's capacity to generate innovation and seize the opportunities offered by the green and digital transition.

The results suggest that industrial policies, the digitalization strategy and initiatives on smart specialization need to be integrated into a coherent framework that combines investment in digital and energy infrastructure with incentives for innovation and public–private partnerships. The increase in the number of patents and the expansion of high-speed Internet infrastructure demonstrate the potential for progress, but this advance must be supported by tailored legislative measures, sustainable financing and continuous training of human capital.

Looking ahead, accelerating the implementation of SDG9 in Romania requires a medium- and long-term strategic approach focused on increasing economic efficiency, reducing technological gaps and strengthening innovation ecosystems. Only by combining investments in technology, infrastructure and skills with proactive public policies can Romania transform the green and digital transition into a real driver of competitiveness and sustainable development.

## References

ANCOM. (2019). *The 5G strategy for Romania*. Ancom.Ro. https://www.ancom.ro/uploads/articles/Strategia5G_rev10_06_2019-finalnotrack.pdf

Blind, K., & Niebel, C. (2022). 5G roll-out failures addressed by innovation policies in the EU. *Technological Forecasting and Social Change, 180*, 121673. https://doi.org/10.1016/j.techfore.2022.121673

Brodny, J., & Tutak, M. (2022). Digitalization of small and medium-sized enterprises and economic growth: Evidence for the EU-27 countries. *Journal of Open Innovation: Technology, Market, and Complexity, 8*(2), 67. https://doi.org/10.3390/joitmc8020067

Cave, M. (2023). The achievement of digitalisation in the EU and its reliance on gigabit connectivity. *Telecommunications Policy*, 102592. https://doi.org/10.1016/j.telpol.2023.102592

De Clercq, M., D'Haese, M., & Buysse, J. (2023). Economic growth and broadband access: The European urban-rural digital divide. *Telecommunications Policy, 47*(6), 102579. https://doi.org/10.1016/j.telpol.2023.102579

Espina-Romero, L. C., Aguirre Franco, S. L., Dworaczek Conde, H. O., Guerrero-Alcedo, J. M., Ríos Parra, D. E., & Rave Ramírez, J. C. (2023). Soft skills in personnel training: Report of publications in scopus, topics explored and future research agenda. *Heliyon, 9*(4), e15468. https://doi.org/10.1016/j.heliyon.2023.e15468

European Commission. (2020). *Updating the 2020 new industrial strategy: Building a stronger single market for Europe's recovery*. Europa.Eu. https://eur-lex.europa.eu/legal-content/EN/TXT/PDF/?uri=CELEX:52021DC0350

European Commission. (2021). *European industrial strategy*. Europa.Eu. https://single-market-economy.ec.europa.eu/industry/strategy_en

European Commission. (2023). *Horizon Europe*. Europa.Eu. https://research-and-innovation.ec.europa.eu/funding/funding-opportunities/funding-programmes-and-open-calls/horizon-europe_en

European Union. (2023). *NextGenerationEU*. https://Next-Generation-Eu.Europa.Eu. https://next-generation-eu.europa.eu/index_en

Eurostat. (2023). *SDG 9 – Industry, innovation and infrastructure*. Europa.Eu. https://ec.europa.eu/eurostat/statistics-explained/index.php?title=SDG_9_-_Industry,_innovation_and_infrastructure#Industry.2C_innovation_and_infrastructure_in_the_EU:_overview_and_key_trends

Ferrandis, J., Ramos, S., & Feijóo, C. (2021). An assessment of estimation models and investment gaps for the deployment of high-speed broadband networks in NUTS3 regions to meet the objectives of the European Gigabit Society. *Telecommunications Policy, 45*(7), 102170. https://doi.org/10.1016/j.telpol.2021.102170

Gajdzik, B., & Wolniak, R. (2022). Framework for R&D&I activities in the steel industry in popularizing the idea of industry 4.0. *Journal of Open Innovation: Technology, Market, and Complexity, 8*(3), 133. https://doi.org/10.3390/joitmc8030133

Government of Romania. (2022). *National strategy for research, innovation, and smart specialization 2022–2027*. Ministry of Research, Innovation, and Digitalization. https://www.mcid.gov.ro/wp-content/uploads/2022/12/strategia-na-ional-de-cercetare-inovare-i-specializare-inteligent-2022-2027.pdf

Hu, Y., Liu, H., Zhao, J., & Tu, L. (2019). Dynamic analysis of dissemination model of innovation ability of enterprise R&D personnel. *Physica A: Statistical Mechanics and its Applications, 531*, 121743. https://doi.org/10.1016/j.physa.2019.121743

Ionel-Valentin Vlad. (2017). *Strategia de dezvoltare a României în următorii 20 de ani: sinteză (EDITURA AC)*. https://acad.ro/bdar/strategiaAR/doc14/Strategia-Sinteza.pdf

Kuzior, A., Arefieva, O., Vovk, O., & Brożek, P. (2022). Innovative development of circular systems while ensuring economic security in the industry. *Journal of Open Innovation: Technology, Market, and Complexity, 8*(3), 139. https://doi.org/10.3390/joitmc8030139

Meyer-Krahmer, F., Gilelow, G., & Kuntze, U. (1983). Impacts of government incentives towards industrial innovation: An analysis of the federal programme funding R&D personnel in the Federal Republic of Germany. *Research Policy, 12*(3), 153–169. https://doi.org/10.1016/0048-7333(83)90016-1

Strube Martins, S., & Wernick, C. (2021). Regional differences in residential demand for very high bandwidth broadband internet in 2025. *Telecommunications Policy, 45*(1), 102043. https://doi.org/10.1016/j.telpol.2020.102043

CHAPTER 14

# Modelling European Industrial Sustainability Based on Economic Indicators Related to Sustainable Development Goal 9

## Introduction

In the contemporary global economy, the pursuit of sustainable industrial development has emerged as a cornerstone of long-term competitiveness, social cohesion and environmental stewardship. Within the EU, these objectives are crystallized in Sustainable Development Goal 9 (SDG9), which calls for the construction of resilient infrastructure, the promotion of inclusive and sustainable industrialization, and the fostering of innovation. Achieving these targets is not only a matter of technological advancement, but also of aligning economic, environmental and social policies to address intertwined challenges such as climate change, resource scarcity and economic inequality.

The European industrial sector operates within a complex policy landscape shaped by the European Green Deal, the Circular Economy Action Plan, and a range of sectoral strategies aimed at accelerating the green and digital transitions. In this context, robust analytical tools are essential to measure progress, identify structural vulnerabilities and guide policy interventions. Modelling European industrial sustainability based on a multidimensional set of economic and innovation-related indicators provides a rigorous framework for monitoring performance and benchmarking progress across Member States.


C. Fortea, *Sustainable Economic Development and the European Green Deal*, https://doi.org/10.1007/978-3-032-10326-0_14

This chapter develops an integrated econometric modelling approach grounded in the Backward Feature Selection (BFS) method, applied to a set of indicators sourced from Eurostat and the OECD. These indicators capture key dimensions of industrial sustainability—ranging from environmental taxation and resource consumption to innovation capacity, R&D investment, and technology development. By normalizing data distributions and reducing heteroscedasticity effects, the modelling process ensures statistical robustness and enables meaningful cross-country comparisons.

The novelty of this study lies in its systematic examination of interdependencies between economic performance, environmental policies and innovation dynamics within the European industrial sector. The proposed models not only identify the most significant predictors of industrial sustainability but also reveal potential vulnerabilities, thereby offering valuable insights for policymakers, industry stakeholders and researchers. Ultimately, the findings contribute to the broader discourse on how the EU can reconcile competitiveness with sustainability in an era defined by rapid technological change, geopolitical uncertainty and pressing environmental imperatives.

## Literature Review

In recent decades, the issue of industrial sustainability has become increasingly central to economic literature, against a backdrop of pressures from climate change, natural resource constraints, and structural transformations driven by globalization and digitalization. At the European level, this concern is framed by Sustainable Development Goal 9 (SDG9), which promotes the building of resilient infrastructure, inclusive and sustainable industrialization, and the promotion of innovation. Recent studies (Brodny & Tutak, 2023; Hariram et al., 2023; Klimczuk et al., 2024) show that these dimensions cannot be addressed in isolation, but require an integrated vision that links economic efficiency, environmental responsibility and social cohesion.

Empirical research (Hung, 2023; Kovacic et al., 2024; Kwilinski et al., 2025) shows that sustainable industrialization is not limited to technological modernization, but also requires the adaptation of fiscal, investment and institutional policies to support the green and digital transition. Within the EU, theoretical and applied debate revolves around the fundamental question: How can the global competitiveness of European industry be maintained when decarbonization and circularity objectives are becoming imperative? Specialist studies (Lella et al., 2024; Troitiño et al., 2024) argue that the answer depends on the Union's ability to integrate monitoring tools through harmonized indicators that allow comparisons between states and the identification of structural vulnerabilities.

From a public policy perspective, the literature highlights the role of the European strategic framework, in particular the Green Deal (European Commission, 2023a) and the Circular Economy Action Plan (European Commission, 2023b), but also the importance of national implementation mechanisms. Uneven results across Member States show that the success of the transition depends both on the capacity for innovation and absorption of European funds and on the quality of internal governance. Therefore, shaping industrial sustainability at the European level becomes an indispensable endeavour, providing an empirical basis for evidence-based policies.

### *The Conceptual Framework of Industrial Sustainability*

Industrial sustainability is an extension of the sustainable development paradigm established by the Brundtland Report (United Nations, 1987), which set out the principle of meeting current needs without compromising the ability of future generations to meet their own needs. At the industrial level, this concept translates into the integration of economic, environmental and social objectives into a coherent system in which competitiveness is combined with environmental protection and social inclusion. Specialized studies (H. Islam, 2025; Musetsho et al., 2024; OECD, 2023a) emphasize that these three pillars cannot be addressed in isolation, as their interdependencies define the essence of industrial sustainability.

Sustainable Development Goal 9 (SDG9) embodies this vision by focusing on resilient infrastructure, inclusive and sustainable industrialization, and promoting innovation. Research (Kuś et al., 2025; Shafik, 2025; Sharifi et al., 2024) shows that SDG9 is cross-cutting in nature: it supports the achievement of other goals, such as SDG7 (clean energy), SDG8 (decent work and economic growth) and SDG12 (responsible consumption and production). In the EU, this framework is articulated through the concept of the "double transition"—ecological and digital—which is becoming the basis for future global competitiveness (Bianchi et al., 2024; Pulignano et al., 2023).

Recent theoretical developments have strengthened the conceptual foundations of industrial sustainability by integrating the concepts of industrial ecology and circular economy. Recent research (N. F. Islam et al., 2024; Kouser et al., 2025; Sánchez-García et al., 2024) argues that industrial sustainability requires reducing dependence on non-renewable resources, expanding reuse and recycling practices, and adopting eco-innovation as a central principle in industrial process design. Furthermore, the current literature highlights the interconnection between industrial sustainability and the global resilience of value chains, particularly in the context of disruptions caused by crises such as the COVID-19 pandemic or the conflict in Ukraine (Kareem et al., 2025; McDougall & Davis, 2024; Tsang et al., 2024).

Recent research (Ahlström et al., 2025; Elegbede et al., 2025; Nuutinen et al., 2025) indicates that industrial sustainability should be viewed as a systemic dynamic in which economic actors, institutions and communities interact in a complex ecosystem. For this reason, assessing progress requires composite sets of indicators, integrated into econometric and computational models that can capture the causal and non-linear relationships between variables. Thus, the literature converges towards the idea that industrial sustainability is not a point in time outcome, but an adaptive and multidimensional process, dependent on innovation, human capital and coherent public policies.

### *European Policies and Initiatives*

The EU has built a comprehensive regulatory and strategic framework to guide the transition to a sustainable industry, in line with SDG9. The European Green Deal is the fundamental document, setting the goal of climate neutrality by 2050 and placing industry at the heart of the decarbonization process. This is complemented by the Circular Economy Action Plan, which promotes resource efficiency, waste reduction and innovation in product design, and by the Horizon Europe framework programme (European Commission, 2024b), which mobilizes substantial funds for research and technological development.

However, recent literature confirms that the impact of these policies is mixed. Empirical studies (Banga & Gaile-Sarkane, 2025; Belanová et al., 2025; Commission, 2025) show that Western European countries, with well-established innovation ecosystems and strong institutional capacities, are able to leverage European policies to enhance their competitiveness. In contrast, countries in Central and Eastern Europe face constraints related to low R&D investment, poor infrastructure and governance challenges (Brodny & Tutak, 2024; European Investment Bank, 2025).

The introduction of the Fit for 55 Package (European Council, 2023) has increased pressure on industries to reduce emissions by 55% by 2030. Various studies (OECD, 2023b; Szymczyk & Włodarczyk, 2025; Yan & Lin, 2025) point out that, although these measures stimulate the development of clean technology markets, they may accentuate economic polarization between countries with robust institutional and financial resources and those with more fragile economies. In this context, cohesion mechanisms, such as structural funds and the Recovery and Resilience Facility (European Commission, 2024c), become essential to avoid a "two-speed" transition.

However, recent research (Economidou et al., 2023; Fernández-Pasarín & Lanaia, 2025; Polverari, 2025; Reimer et al., 2025) highlights that the effectiveness of these instruments depends on the capacity of Member States to implement structural reforms and mobilize complementary private investment. The literature also shows that European policies need to be sufficiently flexible to take into account the structural diversity of national economies and their vulnerabilities to external shocks, such as the energy crisis or geopolitical volatility. Thus, the EU has the strategic framework and financial resources, but turning these into real progress depends on a mix of effective governance, innovation and cooperation between Member States.

### *Economic and Industrial Indicators of Sustainability*

The literature has developed a wide range of indicators used to measure industrial sustainability, as it is a multidimensional phenomenon involving economic, technological and environmental dimensions. Among the most commonly used are environmental taxes, resource consumption, GDP per capita, patent applications, research and development (R&D) personnel, and gross R&D expenditure (Bashir et al., 2022; Dahmani, 2024; Khan et al., 2025). These indicators allow for monitoring progress and comparability between countries, as well as identifying structural vulnerabilities.

Environmental taxes play a central role in sustainability analysis because they reflect governments' efforts to internalize the external costs generated by pollution and excessive resource consumption. Recent studies (Ebaidalla, 2024; Li et al., 2024; Sen et al., 2025) show that, although they may affect companies' profitability in the short term, in the long term they stimulate the adoption of clean technologies and innovation. Resource consumption is another fundamental indicator, with various studies (OECD, 2024b; Potkány et al., 2025; Sardianou et al., 2024) showing that low material intensity is associated with more competitive and resilient economies.

In terms of innovation, the number of patents and R&D expenditure are proxies for technological capacity. Various analyses (European Council, 2024; Eurostat, 2024c; Fabrizi et al., 2024) show that countries with high research spending perform better not only in terms of competitiveness but also in terms of environmental protection. At the same time, the number of patents in green technologies is considered a direct indicator of progress in sustainable innovation (Esmaeilpour Moghadam & Karami, 2024; Kharb et al., 2024; Rainville et al., 2025).

Per capita GDP remains an essential benchmark for capturing the level of economic development, but recent literature suggests a non-linear relationship between prosperity and sustainability. Various authors (Becha et al., 2025; Liang et al., 2024; Yeboah et al., 2024) show that although GDP growth favours investment in research, it does not automatically guarantee the adoption of environmentally friendly practices. This highlights the importance of public policies and the institutional framework.

Therefore, the literature confirms that the use of a diverse set of indicators is indispensable for capturing the complexity of industrial sustainability. One-dimensional analyses are insufficient, and multidimensional models, which integrate economic, environmental and innovation variables, are becoming increasingly common in recent assessments.

### *Innovation and Human Capital as Factors of Sustainability*

The emerging consensus in the literature is that innovation and human capital are the fundamental drivers of industrial sustainability. In a global context marked by the green and digital transition, an economy's ability to generate and absorb innovation becomes decisive for competitiveness and resilience.

The "triple helix" model (university–industry–government), developed by Etzkowitz and Zhou (Etzkowitz & Zhou, 2017), is frequently invoked to explain the dynamics of innovative ecosystems. Recent research confirms that regions with a high density of highly skilled labour and a well-established network of research centres are quicker to adopt green technologies and generate sustainable solutions (Basilico & Grashof, 2024; European Commission, 2025b; Radulescu et al., 2024).

Patenting activity is a tangible indicator of innovation. Multiple studies (Alexiou & Petreski, 2025; Cutcu et al., 2024; Pata et al., 2024) have shown that countries with a high number of patents in environmental technologies experience faster growth in green sectors. R&D expenditure is also an essential predictor of sustainable industrial performance, but its impact depends on the efficiency of resource allocation. A number of studies (Audretsch et al., 2024; Huynh, 2025; Yström et al., 2025) point out that investment in research must be linked to policies that support knowledge transfer and cross-sectoral collaboration in order to generate significant results.

Human capital is not limited to research personnel, but also includes a workforce trained for emerging sectors. Empirical studies (Mishra et al., 2024; Pugno, 2024; Umair et al., 2024) demonstrate that investments in education and health amplify the positive relationship between labour force participation and economic growth, creating a virtuous circle between well-being, innovation and productivity. At the same time, recent literature highlights the importance of social inclusion and equal access to education to ensure a fair industrial transition (Bianchi et al., 2024; Djatmiko et al., 2025; OECD, 2023c).

Thus, innovation and human capital are considered both direct determinants of industrial sustainability and factors that amplify the effects of other policies—from environmental taxation to public investment. Without a robust education system and incentives for innovation, SDG9 targets remain difficult to achieve.

### *The Fiscal Dimension: The Role of Environmental Taxes*

Environmental taxes are a basic fiscal instrument in the transition to industrial sustainability, serving to internalize the external costs generated by pollution and excessive resource use. The "double dividend" hypothesis (Bovenberg & de Mooij, 1994) continues to inspire the literature, arguing that environmental taxes can simultaneously contribute to environmental protection and tax efficiency by reducing other distortionary taxes. Recent research (Alola & Nwulu, 2022; Yang et al., 2024) confirms the validity of this hypothesis in certain contexts, but also highlights its limitations.

The experience of the Nordic countries shows that high environmental taxes, combined with recycling policies and subsidies for innovation, can boost competitiveness and social equity (Benito & Meyer, 2024; Kalaš et al., 2025; Stameski et al., 2024). In contrast, in Central and Eastern Europe, the lack of effective redistribution mechanisms makes high environmental taxes a burden on businesses and consumers, affecting industrial competitiveness (European Commission, 2024a; Gajdosikova & Vojtekova, 2024; Muth et al., 2024).

The current literature insists that the impact of environmental taxation depends on institutional design. The destination of the revenues raised, the progressivity of taxes, and complementarity with public investment in green infrastructure are essential factors for the success of these policies (Martínez Córdoba et al., 2025; Noubissi Domguia, 2023; Pranita & Sarjana, 2025). More recent research (Boostani et al., 2024; Hedegaard & Kongshøj, n.d.; Muth, 2025) shows that the social acceptability of environmental taxes is closely linked to how revenues are used: subsidies for renewable energy or compensation for vulnerable households increases fiscal legitimacy and public support.

In addition, recent literature explores the interaction between environmental taxes and innovation objectives. The European Commission report (European Commission, 2025a) emphasizes that revenues from environmental taxation can be directed towards supporting research and technological development, thereby creating a multiplier effect on industrial sustainability. Therefore, environmental taxes are not only a tool to discourage polluting behaviour, but also a potential mechanism for financing innovation and the green transition.

### *Econometric and Analytical Approaches in Literature*

The study of industrial sustainability has undergone significant methodological diversification in recent years, due to the complexity of the phenomenon and the increasing availability of data. Classic econometric methods, such as panel regressions and vector autoregression (VAR) models, continue to be used to capture the dynamic relationships between sustainability indicators (Bilgili et al., 2025; Leitão & Ferreira, 2021; Muneer et al., 2025). These allow for the identification of short- and long-term effects and comparability between states.

However, the limitations of traditional models have led to the adoption of innovative approaches. Feature selection techniques, such as Backward Feature Selection (BFS), also applied in the present study, are used to identify significant predictors and reduce multicollinearity (Gholami et al.,

2024). Other research uses structural equation modelling (SEM) to analyse latent constructs such as "innovation capacity" or "resource efficiency" (Adiguzel & Sonmez Cakir, 2025; Latip et al., 2025).

At the same time, methods based on big data and artificial intelligence are gaining ground. Various studies (Ajala et al., 2025; J. Yao, 2024; X. Yao et al., 2024) have demonstrated that neural networks and machine learning algorithms can predict industrial $CO_2$ emissions with greater accuracy than traditional econometric models. Recent studies are also exploring hybrid combinations of machine learning and econometrics to capture non-linear relationships and interaction effects between indicators (Fozap, 2025; Kristjanpoller, 2024; Martyushev et al., 2025).

This methodological diversification reflects the recognition that industrial sustainability is a complex phenomenon with multiple interdependencies. Modern models are not limited to explaining relationships, but also have a predictive role, supporting decision-makers in formulating data-based policies. Therefore, contemporary literature promotes convergence between advanced econometrics and data science as a major research direction.

The literature reviewed confirms the multidimensional and interdependent nature of European industrial sustainability. Conceptually, it is based on the integration of economic competitiveness, environmental responsibility and social inclusion under the umbrella of SDG9. European policies such as the Green Deal, the Circular Economy Action Plan and the Horizon Europe programme provide strategic direction, but their implementation reveals asymmetries between Member States.

Empirical indicators such as environmental taxes, resource consumption, GDP per capita, patents and R&D investment are recognized as relevant proxies for industrial sustainability, but their effects are contextual. Innovation and human capital consistently emerge as key determinants of progress, while environmental taxes can generate both positive incentives and constraints, depending on the fiscal architecture.

Methodologically, the field is moving from classical econometrics towards hybrid models combining panel data, machine learning algorithms and structural modelling. However, gaps remain, particularly regarding the long-term causal relationships between fiscal policies, innovative ecosystems and industrial performance.

This synthesis highlights the need for integrated, evidence-based public policy frameworks that balance economic growth, environmental responsibility and social cohesion. In this context, the present research contributes to the existing literature by modelling European industrial sustainability using SDG9 indicators and provides a solid basis for further empirical analysis.

## Methodology

Modelling European industrial sustainability involves a multidimensional approach, incorporating economic, social and environmental indicators that reflect both current performance and future directions for industry, innovation and infrastructure. Sustainable Development Goal 9 (SDG9) emphasizes the importance of building resilient infrastructure, promoting inclusive and sustainable industrialization, and encouraging innovation. In the European context, this is manifested through a range of initiatives and strategies aimed at strengthening the industrial base while addressing global challenges such as climate change and economic inequality.

By integrating and analysing these indicators, decision-makers can assess progress towards achieving SDG9 and identify areas where further efforts are needed. Public policies, accompanied by private sector commitments and international cooperation, are important elements to improve industrial performance in a sustainable way. Modelling European industrial sustainability based on economic and industrial indicators provides an important framework for monitoring European progress. With limited resources and growing environmental challenges, a balanced and innovative approach is imperative to ensure a competitive, inclusive and sustainable European industry.

The Backward Feature Selection (BFS) feature selection method was applied to determine the European industrial sustainability model.

The indicators presented in Table 14.1 were used to determine the model.

Data were collected from Eurostat and OECD and then modelled using the statistical program Python.

Previously the set of indicators presented above was subjected to the log normalization procedure using Logit linear regression analysis. In this way the normalization of the data was obtained by transforming them to a Gaussian normal distribution, reducing the effects of heteroscedasticity and reducing the influences of extreme values (increasing the robustness of the model).

**Table 14.1** Presentation of analysed indicators

| *Symbol* | *Indicator name* | *Unit of measurement* | *Source* |
|---|---|---|---|
| SDG9TAXM | Environmental taxes | % GDP | OECD (2024a) |
| SDG9VTAXT | Revenue from charges related to road transport | % of total environmental tax revenues | OECD (2024a) |
| SDG9CMPR | Consumption of raw materials | Thousand tons | Eurostat (2024e) |
| SDG9CBV | Patent applications filed at the European Patent Office by country of residence of applicants/inventors | Number | Eurostat (2024b) |
| SDG9PCDI | Research and development staff | % | Eurostat (2024d) |
| SDG9CHCDI | Gross domestic expenditure on research and development | % GDP | Eurostat (2024a) |
| SDG9PIBloc | GDP per capita | Euro per inhabitant | Eurostat (2024f) |
| SDG9DTHM | Developing environmental technologies | % inventions per capita | OECD (2024a) |
| SDG9AOF | Official Development Assistance | % GNI | OECD (2024a) |

Source: Author

Linear regression used the dependent variable $Y$ or its logarithm, which is modelled as a linear function of one or more independent variables. The equation can be formulated as follows:

$$\ln(Y) = \beta_1 \ln(X_1) + \beta_2 \ln(X_2) + \ldots + \beta_n \ln(X_n) + \varepsilon \tag{14.1}$$

where

$\ln(Y)$ is the natural logarithm of the dependent variable, representing an indicator of Sustainable Development Goal 9;
$\beta_1$, $\beta_2$, $\beta_n$ are the coefficients reflecting the sensitivity of the logarithm of variable $Y$ to a percentage change in each indicator $X_i$;
$\ln(X_1)$, $\ln(X_2)$, $\ln(X_n)$ are the natural logarithms of the selected indicators;
$\varepsilon$ is the constant.

The application of the BFS method involves the gradual elimination of variables $X_i$ that contribute least to the model, based on criteria such as $P$-value, adjusted coefficient of determination (adjusted $R^2$) or variance inflation factor (VIF). This process continues until every remaining variable in the model is significant, and the elimination of any additional variable would lead to a significant deterioration in model performance. The BFS method was applied until a valid solution was obtained, i.e. until the variance inflation factors of the indicators fell within the 10-point significance threshold, excluding multicollinearity. This ensured the performance of the models by monitoring the correlation coefficient and the mean squared error. This improved the prediction and increased the stability of the nine proposed models.

## Results and Discussions

The SDG9.1 model of European industrial sustainability from the perspective of the SDG9PIBloc indicator has the selected dependent variable gross domestic product per capita. The independent variables are: SDG9DTHM representing development of environment-related technologies, SDG9AOF representing Official Development Assistance (ODA), SDG9TAXM representing environment-related taxes as a percentage of GDP, SDG9VTAXT representing revenues from road transport-related taxes as a percentage of total environmental tax revenues, SDG9CMPR representing consumption of raw materials, SDG9CBV representing number of patent applications filed at the European Patent Office, SDG9PCDI representing percentage of personnel employed in R&D, and SDG9CHCDI representing gross domestic expenditure on R&D. A linear regression model is constructed with the independent variables defined above for which regression coefficients have been calculated according to equation number 14.2.

$$\begin{aligned} \text{SDG9PIBloc} = {} & 0.03 * \text{SDG9DTHM} + 0.13 * \text{SDG9AOF} \\ & - 0.23 * \text{SDG9TAXM} + 0.06 * \text{SDG9VTAXT} \\ & - 0.22 * \text{SDG9CMPR} + 0.21 * \text{SDG9CBV} \\ & + 0.33 * \text{SDG9PCDI} - 0.19 * \text{SDG9CHCDI} + 5.78 \end{aligned} \tag{14.2}$$

For Model SDG9.1 we can observe that for the influence of the independent variables on the dependent variable in the case of the variable SDG9DTHM representing the development of environmental technologies, a positive influence on the dependent variable is observed, i.e. a 1% increase in the development of environmental technologies leads to a 0.03% increase in GDP per capita. This suggests that investments and advances in environmental technologies have a positive impact on the economy, contributing to an increase in GDP per capita. The development of more resource-efficient and environmentally friendly technologies can boost innovation, competitiveness and productivity, with beneficial effects on people's economic well-being. Regarding the variable SDG9AOF, Official Development Assistance, a positive influence on the dependent variable is observed, i.e. a 1% increase in Official Development Assistance leads to a 0.13% increase in GDP per capita. This suggests that foreign investment for development can significantly contribute to the growth of the economy and the welfare of the population. Official Development Assistance can be used to finance projects and programmes that stimulate economic growth and reduce poverty in developing countries, with a positive impact on GDP per capita. According to the variable SDG9TAXM, environmental taxes as a percentage of GDP, an inverse influence on the dependent variable is revealed, i.e. a 1% increase in environmental taxes as a percentage of GDP leads to a 0.23% decrease in GDP per capita. This influence of an increase in the share of environmental taxes in GDP may negatively affect GDP per capita. Higher environmental taxes can negatively influence economic activities, reduce the profitability of firms and reduce the income available for consumption. Thus, higher taxation leads to a reduction in economic activity and hence in GDP. In the case of the variable SDG9VTAXT representing road transport-related tax revenues as a percentage of total environmental tax revenues, a positive influence on the dependent variable is found, i.e. a 1% increase in road transport-related tax revenues as a percentage of total environmental tax revenues leads to a 0.06% increase in GDP per capita. Regarding the variable SDG9CMPR representing the consumption of raw materials, there is an inverse influence on the dependent variable, i.e. a 1% increase in the consumption of raw materials leads to a 0.22% decrease in GDP per capita. This may indicate that an economy that is more dependent on raw materials may be less efficient or have a less value-added productive sector. In the case of the variable SDG9CBV, the number of patent applications filed at the European Patent Office, there is a positive influence on the dependent variable, i.e. a 1% increase in the number of patent applications filed at the European Patent Office leads to a 0.21% increase in GDP per capita. This suggests that innovation and intellectual property protection can stimulate economic growth. This underlines the importance of R&D investment for economic growth. In the case of the variable SDG9PCDI representing the percentage of personnel engaged in R&D, there is a positive influence on the dependent variable, i.e. a 1% increase in the percentage of personnel engaged in R&D leads to a 0.33% increase in GDP per capita. According to the variable SDG9CHCDI representing gross domestic expenditure on R&D, there is an inverse influence on the dependent variable, i.e. a 1% increase in gross domestic expenditure on R&D leads to a 0.19% decrease in GDP per capita. Stimulating innovation and patenting, together with efficient investment in R&D, can be beneficial for economic growth, while over-reliance on raw materials or inefficient R&D spending could have adverse effects. Particular attention should also be paid to the development of skilled human resources, ensuring that the workforce is ready for the economy of the future. In addition, promoting collaboration between the public, private and academic sectors can play an important role in stimulating innovation and knowledge transfer. It is also important to develop the necessary infrastructure to support economic growth and facilitate access to international markets. Labour is a key factor in the conduct of economic activities, especially in countries with labour surpluses. In a study by Umair and a group of authors (Umair et al., 2024) the impact of labour force participation on economic growth is explored, focusing on how this impact depends on the levels of spending on health and education, using Autoregressive Distributed Lag (ARDL), the Error Correction Model (ECM) and Granger causality techniques for empirical analysis. The ARDL results indicate that labour force participation significantly boosts economic growth in both the short and long run. The estimates reveal that better health and education facilities reinforce the positive effects of labour force participation on economic growth, suggesting a complementary relationship between health, education and labour force in boosting economic growth.

Figure 14.1 shows the ranking of the importance of the predictors related to the influence on the dependent variable SDG9PIBloc.

Figure 14.1 shows that the most significant influence on the dependent variable is the percentage of personnel employed in R&D, suggesting that investment in human capital, especially R&D, is strongly correlated with higher GDP per capita. The number of patent applications filed at the

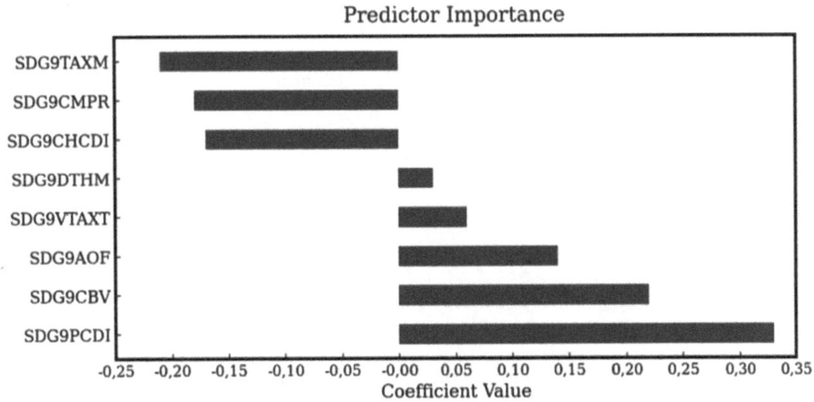


**Fig. 14.1** Importance of predictors related to the influence on the variable SDG9PIBloc. Source: Developed by the author using Python

European Patent Office also has a significant influence, indicating that innovation as measured by patent filings contributes to GDP growth. Likewise, revenues from road transportation-related taxes as a percentage of total revenues from environmental taxes and consumption of raw materials do not show significant influences on economic growth. Thus, factors related to R&D, innovation and technology have a positive influence on GDP, while a higher reliance on environmental taxes and consumption of raw materials do not have a significant effect.

The variable that represents a vulnerability of European industrial sustainability in terms of economic growth is the development of environmental technologies.

Figure 14.2 was produced based on the vulnerability indicator rankings of the SDG9.1 Gross Domestic Product model for the reference year 2021. This model is influenced by the low realization of industrial development as reflected by the indicator of environmental technology development. Thus, in terms of gross domestic product the countries with a deficient policy are Bulgaria, Romania, Croatia, Estonia, Latvia, Hungary, and Slovakia.

The SDG9.2 model of European industrial sustainability from the perspective of the SDG9CHCDI indicator has the selected dependent variable gross domestic expenditure on research and development. The independent variables are SDG9GDPloc as gross domestic product per

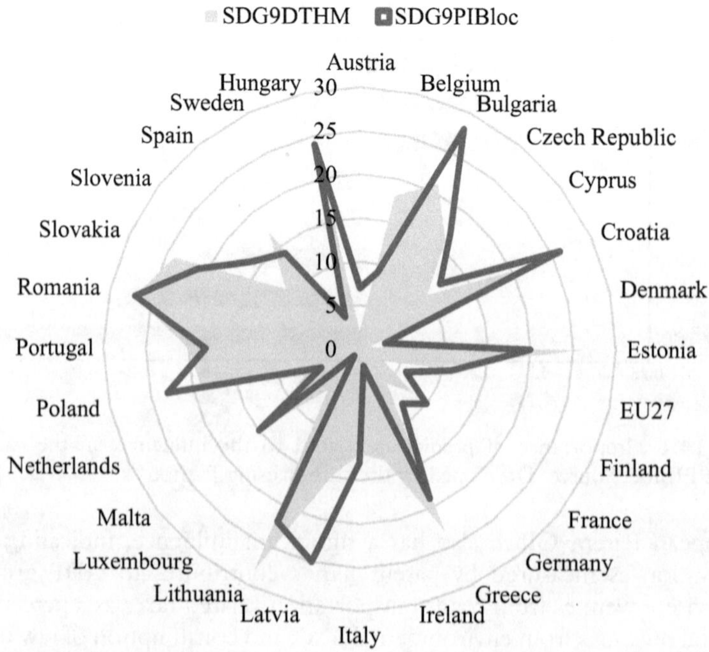


**Fig. 14.2** Vulnerability diagram of the variable SDG9PIBloc. Source: Author

capita, SDG9DTHM as the development of environmental technologies, SDG9TAXM as environmental taxes as a percentage of GDP, SDG9CBV as the number of patent applications filed at the European Patent Office, and SDG9PCDI as the percentage of personnel employed in R&D. A linear regression model is constructed with the independent variables defined above for which regression coefficients have been calculated according to Eq. 14.3.

$$\begin{aligned} SDG9CHCDI = & -0.24 * SDG9PIBloc + 0.09 * SDG9DTHM \\ & + 0.08 * SDG9TAXM + 0.06 * SDG9CBV \\ & + 0.90 * SDG9PCDI + 1.07 \end{aligned} \quad (14.3)$$

For Model SDG9.2 it is observed that for the influence of the independent variables on the dependent variable according to the variable SDG9GDP per capita, there is an inverse influence on the dependent variable, i.e. a 1% increase in GDP per capita leads to a 0.24% decrease in gross domestic expenditure on research and development. This finding suggests that in economies with a higher GDP per capita, a smaller proportion of income is allocated to R&D, due to higher efficiency or different priorities in resource allocation. As for the variable SDG9DTHM representing the development of environmental technologies, there is a positive influence on the dependent variable, i.e. a 1% increase in the development of environmental technologies leads to a 0.09% increase in gross domestic expenditure on R&D. This highlights the importance of investing in sustainable and environmentally friendly technologies. According to the variable SDG9TAXM representing environmental taxes as a percentage of GDP, a positive influence on the dependent variable is observed, i.e. a 1% increase in environmental taxes leads to a 0.08% increase in gross domestic expenditure on R&D. This reflects the fact that environmental taxes can be reinvested in innovative research to develop sustainable solutions. In the case of the variable SDG9CBV representing the number of patent applications filed at the European Patent Office, a positive influence on the dependent variable is found, i.e. a 1% increase in the number of patent applications filed at the European Patent Office leads to a 0.06% increase in gross domestic expenditure on R&D. This highlights the link between innovation, intellectual property protection and investment in research and innovation. As for the variable SDG9PCDI representing the percentage of personnel engaged in R&D, there is a positive influence on the dependent variable, i.e. a 1% increase in the percentage of personnel engaged in R&D leads to a 0.9% increase in gross domestic expenditure on R&D. This influence emphasizes the crucial role of human capital in stimulating research and innovation. These results emphasize the importance of various factors such as gross domestic product per capita, innovation and sustainability in determining the level of R&D investment. They provide valuable insights for policymakers and business managers in stimulating sustainable growth and innovation.

Figure 14.3 shows the ranking of the importance of predictors related to the influence on the dependent variable SDG9CHCDI.

Figure 14.3 shows that the most significant predictor is the percentage of personnel employed in R&D, suggesting that the availability of R&D labour is closely related to R&D spending growth. Gross domestic

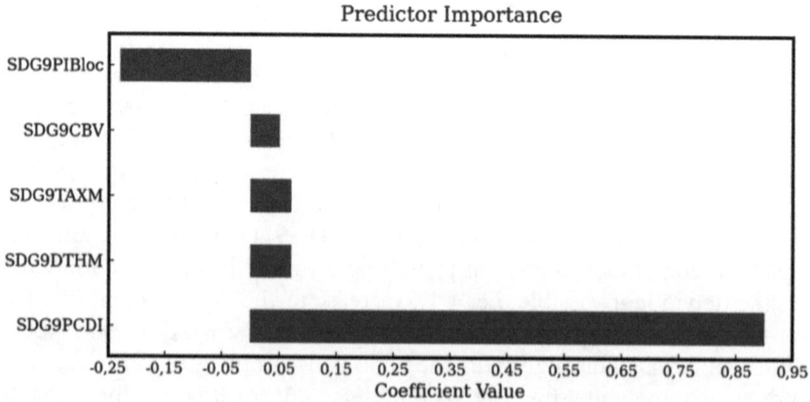


**Fig. 14.3** Importance of predictors related to the influence on the variable SDG9CHCDI. Source: Developed by the author using Python

product does not show a significant influence on R&D spending, indicating that as GDP increases, more resources are available for R&D investment.

The SDG9.3 model of European industrial sustainability from the perspective of the SDG9PCDI indicator has the percentage of personnel engaged in R&D as the selected dependent variable. The independent variables are SDG9GDPloc as gross domestic product per capita, SDG9AOF as Official Development Assistance, SDG9CBV as the number of patent applications filed at the European Patent Office, and SDG9CHCDI as gross domestic expenditure on R&D. A linear regression model is constructed with the independent variables defined above for which regression coefficients have been calculated according to equation number 14.4.

$$\begin{aligned} \text{SDG9PCDI} = {} & 0.17 * \text{SDG9PIBloc} + 0.10 * \text{SDG9AOF} \\ & - 0.02 * \text{SDG9CBV} + 0.62 * \text{SDG9CHCDI} \\ & - 0.77 \end{aligned} \tag{14.4}$$

For Model SDG9.3 it can be observed that for the influence of the independent variables on the dependent variable in the case of the variable SDG9PIBloc representing GDP per capita, a positive influence on the

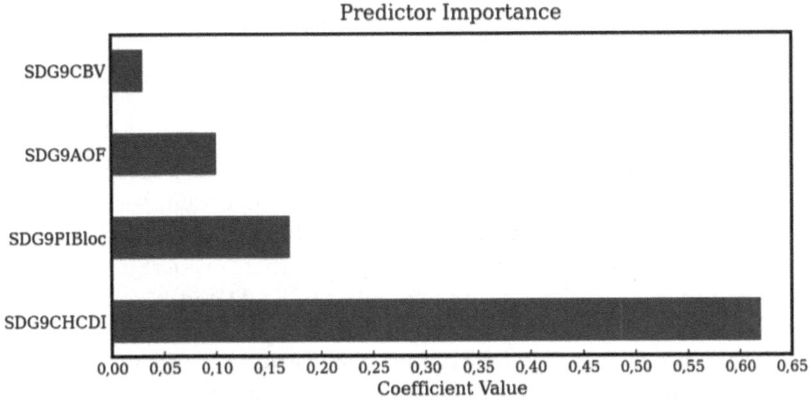


**Fig. 14.4** Importance of predictors related to the influence on the variable SDG9PCDI. Source: Developed by the author using Python

dependent variable is found, i.e. a 1% increase in GDP per capita leads to a 0.17% increase in the percentage of personnel employed in research and development. This indicates that developed economies have more resources to invest in R&D, which may lead to additional innovation and productivity growth. Regarding the variable SDG9AOF representing Official Development Assistance, there is a positive influence on the dependent variable, i.e. a 1% increase in Official Development Assistance leads to a 0.1% increase in the percentage of personnel engaged in R&D. This influence indicates that international aid can support R&D in recipient countries by funding research projects or building the necessary infrastructure. In the case of the variable SDG9CBV representing the number of patent applications filed at the European Patent Office, there is an inverse influence on the dependent variable, i.e. a 1% increase in the number of patent applications filed at the European Patent Office leads to a 0.02% decrease in the percentage of personnel employed in R&D. As for the variable SDG9CHCDI representing gross domestic expenditure on R&D, a positive influence on the dependent variable is found, i.e. a 1% increase in gross domestic expenditure on R&D leads to a 0.62% increase in the percentage of personnel employed in R&D. This shows a positive impact of research funding on the innovation capacity of an economy. These results highlight the complexity of the relationships between economic growth, R&D investment and innovation. It is important for public policies to balance R&D investment with stimulating the demand for innovation and protecting intellectual property to maximize the impact on economic growth and global competitiveness.

Figure 14.4 shows the ranking of the importance of the predictors related to the influence on the dependent variable SDG9PCDI.

Figure 14.4 shows a strong influence on the dependent variable gross domestic expenditure on R&D. This variable has the largest influence on the percentage of R&D personnel, implying that an increase in R&D expenditure leads to changes in the number of R&D personnel.

The SDG9.4 model of European industrial sustainability from the perspective of the SDG9CBV indicator has the selected dependent variable as the number of patent applications filed at the European Patent Office. The independent variables are SDG9GDPloc representing gross domestic product per capita, SDG9DTHM representing the development of environmental technologies, SDG9AOF representing Official Development Assistance, SDG9TAXM representing environmental taxes as a percentage of GDP, SDG9CMPR representing raw material consumption, SDG9PCDI representing the percentage of personnel engaged in R&D, and SDG9CHCDI representing gross domestic expenditure on R&D. A linear regression model is constructed with the independent variables defined above for which regression coefficients have been calculated according to equation number 14.5.

$$\begin{aligned} SDG9CBV = {} & 1.81 * SDG9PIBloc + 0.27 * SDG9DTHM \\ & + 0.21 * SDG9AOF + 0.34 * SDG9TAXM \\ & + 0.92 * SDG9CMPR - 0.45 * SDG9PCDI \\ & + 0.42 * SDG9CHCDI - 11.84 \end{aligned} \tag{14.5}$$

As evidenced by the regression equation for Model SDG9.4, the variable GDP per capita (SDG9PIBloc) exerts a strong positive influence on the dependent variable: a 1% increase in GDP per capita corresponds to a 1.81% growth in the number of patent applications filed with the European Patent Office. This indicates a significant link between economic welfare and innovative activity, highlighting that more prosperous economies are often sources of increased innovation. Regarding the variable SDG9DTHM representing the development of environmental technologies, a positive

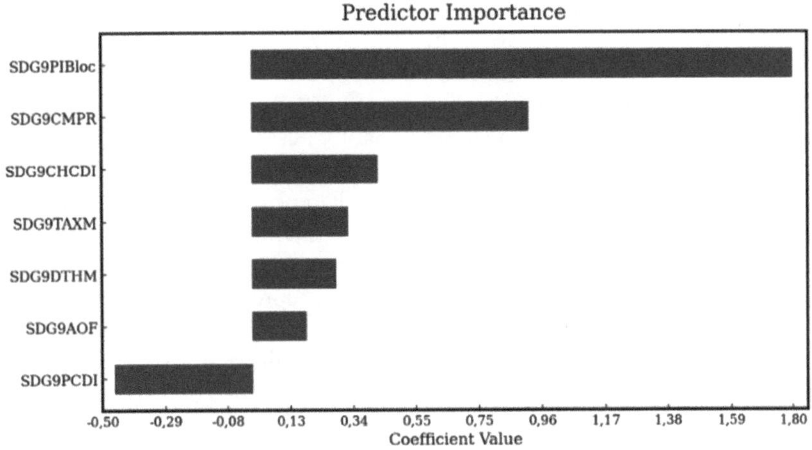


**Fig. 14.5** Importance of predictors related to influence on the variable SDG9CBV. Source: Developed by the author using Python

influence on the dependent variable is found, i.e. a 1% increase in the development of environmental technologies leads to a 0.27% increase in the number of patent applications filed at the European Patent Office. This suggests that innovation in sustainable technologies is a priority in green growth and that these technologies are being actively developed and patented. According to the variable SDG9AOF representing Official Development Assistance, there is a positive influence on the dependent variable, i.e. a 1% increase in Official Development Assistance leads to a 0.21% increase in the number of patent applications filed at the European Patent Office. This indicates that development funds help stimulate innovation, possibly by improving R&D infrastructure. In the case of the variable SDG9TAXM representing environmental fees as a percentage of GDP, there is a positive influence on the dependent variable, i.e. a 1% increase in environmental fees as a percentage of GDP leads to a 0.34% increase in the number of patent applications filed at the European Patent Office. This influence may reflect the fact that sustainability pressures and environmental regulations stimulate innovation in green technologies. According to the variable SDG9CMPR representing raw material consumption, a positive influence on the dependent variable is observed, i.e. a 1% increase in raw material consumption leads to a 0.92% increase in the number of patent applications filed at the European Patent Office, suggesting that resource-intensive industries may seek to innovate to improve efficiency and reduce environmental impact. In the case of the variable SDG9PCDI representing the percentage of R&D personnel, there is an inverse influence on the dependent variable, i.e. a 1% increase in the percentage of R&D personnel leads to a 0.45% decrease in the number of patent applications filed at the European Patent Office. This could indicate that there is a saturation point at which the increase in the number of researchers is no longer directly reflected in an increase in innovative output. In the case of the variable SDG9CHCDI representing gross domestic expenditure on R&D, there is a positive influence on the dependent variable, i.e. a 1% increase in gross domestic expenditure on R&D leads to a 0.42% increase in the number of patent applications filed at the European Patent Office. This highlights the importance of financial investment in R&D to stimulate innovative activities.

The results presented above highlight the complex interconnections between economic, R&D, environmental and innovation activity, providing insights for the formulation of policies and strategies to stimulate innovation and technological development.

Figure 14.5 shows the hierarchy of importance of the predictors related to the influence on the dependent variable SDG9CBV.

Figure 14.5 shows that the strongest predictor is SDG9GDP per capita, suggesting that gross domestic product per capita is the strongest predictor of the number of patents filed, indicating that a stronger economy per capita is associated with more patenting activity. A high GDP per capita is positively associated with the number of patent applications filed. This suggests that countries with greater financial resources can invest more in R&D, which may lead to more innovations and hence more patents being filed.

The variable that represents a vulnerability of sustainable European industrial development in terms of the number of patent applications filed at the European Patent Office is Official Development Assistance.

Figure 14.6 is based on the ranking of vulnerability indicators of the SDG9.4 model in 2021. The figure shows that the countries with the weakest distribution of the dependent variable, Cyprus, Bulgaria, Croatia, Latvia and Romania, are at the top of the European countries ranking.

The SDG9.5 model of European industrial sustainability from the perspective of the SDG9CMPR indicator has the selected dependent variable raw material consumption. The independent variables are SDG9GDPloc as gross domestic product per capita, SDG9DTHM as the development of environmental technologies, SDG9TAXM as environmental taxes as a percentage of GDP, and SDG9CBV as the number of patent applications filed at the European Patent Office. A linear regression model is constructed with the independent variables defined above for which regression coefficients have been calculated according to equation number 14.6.

$$\begin{aligned} SDG9CMPR = & -1.77 * SDG9PIBloc - 0.16 * SDG9DTHM \\ & -0.52 * SDG9TAXM + 0.83 * SDG9CBV + 12.66 \end{aligned} \tag{14.6}$$

According to the regression equation for the SDG9.5 model, the influence of the independent variables on the dependent variable is, in the case of the SDG9PIBloc variable representing GDP per capita, an inverse

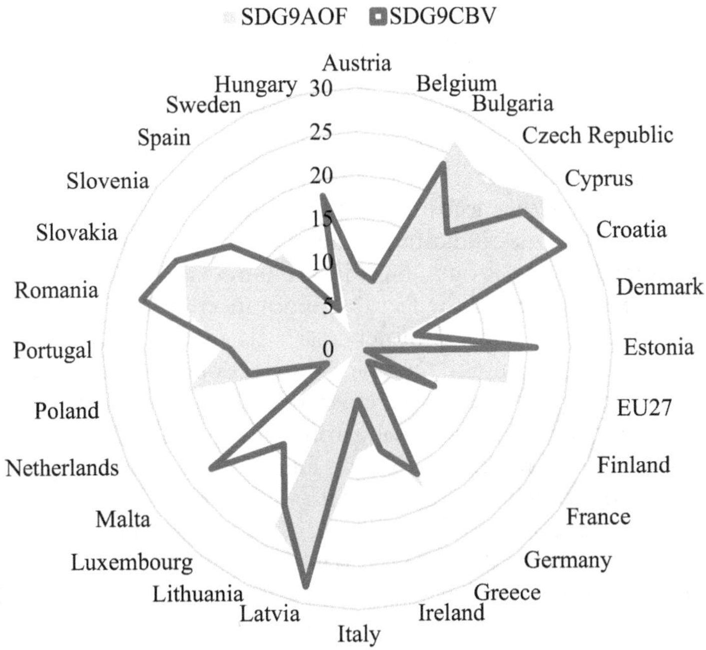


**Fig. 14.6** Vulnerabilities diagram of the variable SDG9CBV. Source: Author

influence on the dependent variable, i.e. a 1% increase in GDP per capita leads to a 1.77% decrease in the consumption of raw materials. This suggests that more advanced economies tend to be more resource-efficient due to the adoption of more advanced technologies or an economic mix that favours services over resource-intensive industrial production. Regarding the variable SDG9DTHM representing the development of environmental technologies, there is an inverse influence on the dependent variable, i.e. a 1% increase in the development of environmental technologies leads to a 0.16% decrease in the consumption of raw materials. This influence indicates that progress in environmental technologies can lead to more efficient use of resources and reduced dependence on raw materials through innovations that improve efficiency or by substituting traditional materials with more sustainable alternatives. In the case of the variable SDG9TAXM representing environmental taxes as a percentage of GDP, there is an inverse influence on the dependent variable, i.e. a 1% increase in environmental taxes as a percentage of GDP leads to a 0.52% decrease in raw material consumption. This shows that environmental tax policies can have a significant effect in discouraging resource-intensive use and promoting sustainability by increasing the costs associated with extracting and processing natural resources. In the case of the variable SDG9CBV representing the number of patent applications filed at the European Patent Office, there is a positive influence on the dependent variable, i.e. a 1% increase in the number of patent applications filed at the European Patent Office leads to a 0.83% increase in the consumption of raw materials. This may indicate that intensive R&D activity, as measured by patent applications, is often linked to resource-intensive industrial sectors. This may also reflect the fact that innovation in some areas requires intensive exploration and use of new materials and resources. The above observations highlight the complex interactions between economic growth, technological innovation, environmental policy and resource use. While technological progress and environmental policies can contribute to resource efficiency, increased research and development, particularly in certain sectors, can increase demand for raw materials.

Figure 14.7 shows the ranking of the importance of predictors related to the influence on the dependent variable SDG9CMPR.

Figure 14.7 shows that gross domestic product does not show a significant influence in the prediction model of raw material consumption, suggesting the lack of a pattern between GDP per capita and raw material consumption. Increases in GDP per capita may be associated with an

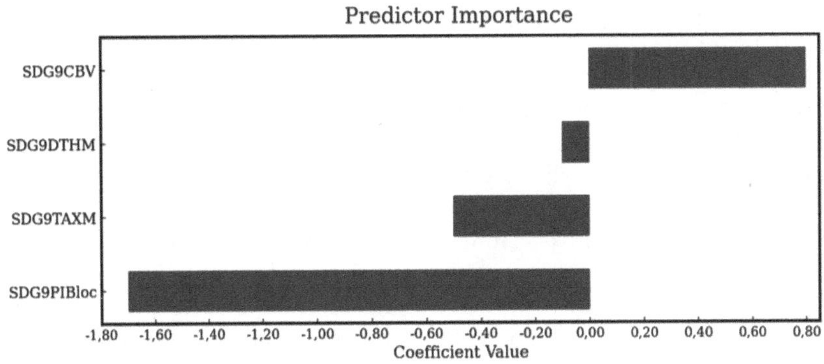


**Fig. 14.7** Importance of predictors related to the influence on the variable SDG9CMPR. Source: Developed by the author using Python

improvement in resource use efficiency due to technological innovation or shifts towards less resource-intensive economic sectors.

The SDG9.6 model of European industrial sustainability from the perspective of the SDG9DTHM indicator has the selected dependent variable development of environmental technologies. The independent variables are SDG9GDPloc as gross domestic product per capita, SDG9AOF as Official Development Assistance, SDG9CMPR as consumption of raw materials, SDG9CBV as number of patent applications filed at the European Patent Office, and SDG9CHCDI as gross domestic expenditure on research and development. We construct a linear regression model with the independent variables defined above for which regression coefficients have been calculated according to equation number 14.7.

$$\begin{aligned} \text{SDG9DTHM} = {} & 0.25 * \text{SDG9PIBloc} + 0.19 * \text{SDG9AOF} \\ & - 0.27 * \text{SDG9CMPR} + 0.34 * \text{SDG9CBV} \\ & + 0.77 * \text{SDG9CHCDI} + 0.60 \end{aligned} \tag{14.7}$$

As indicated by the regression equation for Model SDG9.6, GDP per capita exerts a positive and statistically significant influence on the dependent variable: a 1% increase in GDP per capita corresponds to a 0.25% improvement in environmental technology development. This indicates that more advanced economies have more financial and technical resources to invest in sustainable technologies and green innovations. In the case of the variable SDG9AOF representing Official Development Assistance, there is a positive influence on the dependent variable, i.e. a 1% increase in Official Development Assistance leads to a 0.19% increase in the development of environmental technologies. This indicates that international funds can help promote environmental technologies, especially in developing countries, by facilitating technology and knowledge transfer. With respect to the variable SDG9CMPR representing the consumption of raw materials, there is an inverse influence on the dependent variable, i.e. a 1% increase in the consumption of raw materials leads to a 0.27% decrease in the development of environmental technologies. This could emphasize that a high dependence on natural resources is often linked to less sustainable practices and may inhibit investments in green technologies. In the case of the variable SDG9CBV representing the number of patent applications filed at the European Patent Office, a positive influence on the dependent variable is found, i.e. a 1% increase in the number of patent applications filed at the European Patent Office leads to a 0.34% increase in the development of environmental technologies. This influence emphasizes the role of innovation and intellectual property protection in promoting sustainable technological development. According to the SDG9CHCDI variable representing gross domestic expenditure on R&D, a positive influence on the dependent variable is found, i.e. a 1% increase in gross domestic expenditure on R&D leads to a 0.77% increase in the development of environmental technologies, highlighting the importance of R&D investment for innovation in environmental technologies. The results presented underline the complexity and multidimensionality of the factors contributing to the development of environmental technologies, suggesting that an integrated approach, combining economic growth, international support, resource efficiency, innovation and R&D investment, is important to promote sustainability and green technologies.

Figure 14.8 shows the ranking of the importance of predictors related to the influence on the dependent variable SDG9DTHM.

Figure 14.8 analyses the importance of different independent variables in influencing the development of environmental technologies, represented by the dependent variable SDG9DTHM. R&D expenditure is the most important predictor of the development of environmental technologies, showing that R&D investment is important for innovation in environmental technologies. Consumption of raw materials does not have a significant impact on the development of environmental technologies, which supports that a raw materials-based economy is less conducive to

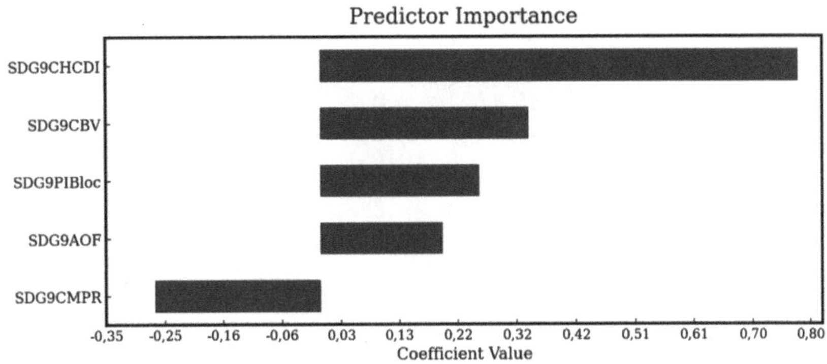


**Fig. 14.8** Importance of predictors related to influence on the variable SDG9DTHM. Source: Developed by the author using Python

innovation in environmental technologies as well as that high consumption of raw materials is associated with less need for innovation in those technologies.

The one variable that represents a vulnerability of European industrial sustainability in the development of environmental technologies is Official Development Assistance.

Figure 14.9 has been produced based on the vulnerability indicator ranking of the SDG9.6 model on the development of environment-related technologies for the reference year 2021. This model is influenced by the poor fruition of sustainable development reflected using the Official Development Assistance indicator. Thus, in terms of the development of environmental technologies, the countries with a deficient policy are Bulgaria, Croatia, Lithuania, Romania and Slovakia.

The SDG9.7 model of European industrial sustainability from the perspective of the SDG9TAXM indicator has the selected dependent variable denoting environmental taxes as a percentage of GDP. The independent variables are SDG9GDPloc as gross domestic product per capita, SDG9AOF as Official Development Assistance, SDG9VTAXT as revenues from road transport-related taxes as a percentage of total revenues from environmental taxes, SDG9CMPR as consumption of raw materials, SDG9CBV as number of patent applications filed at the European Patent Office, and SDG9CHCDI as gross domestic expenditure on research and development. We construct a linear regression model with the

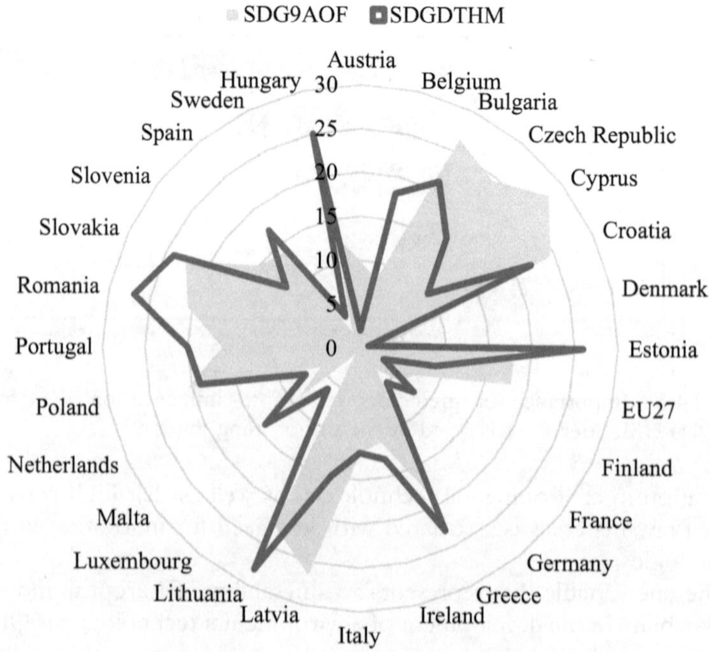


**Fig. 14.9** Diagram of vulnerabilities of variable SDG9DTHM. Source: Author

independent variables defined above for which regression coefficients have been calculated according to Eq. 14.8.

$$\begin{aligned} SDG9TAXM = & -0.28 * SDG9PIBloc - 0.08 * SDG9AOF \\ & + 0.08 * SDG9VTAXT - 0.10 * SDG9CMPR \\ & + 0.05 * SDG9CBV + 0.20 * SDG9CHCDI + 2.13 \end{aligned} \tag{14.8}$$

For Model SDG9.7 we find a significant inverse influence of the variable SDG9PIBloc representing GDP per capita, i.e. a 1% increase in GDP per capita leads to a 0.28% decrease in environmental taxes as a percentage of GDP. This indicates that in more advanced economies, the share of environmental taxes in GDP may be relatively lower, possibly due to higher economic efficiency or a different tax structure. In the case of the variable SDG9AOF representing Official Development Assistance, there is an inverse influence on the dependent variable, i.e. a 1% increase in Official

Development Assistance leads to a 0.08% decrease in environmental taxes as a percentage of GDP. This influence could indicate that countries receiving more development assistance rely less on environmental taxes for revenue or that external assistance may reduce the need for such taxes by directly financing environmental initiatives. In the case of the variable SDG9VTAXT representing road transport-related tax revenues as a percentage of total environmental tax revenues, there is a positive influence on the dependent variable, i.e. a 1% increase in road transport-related tax revenues as a percentage of total environmental tax revenues leads to a 0.08% increase in environmental taxes as a percentage of GDP. This underlines the importance of transport taxes in the overall environmental tax structure and may reflect efforts to combat pollution and promote sustainable transport. According to the variable SDG9CMPR representing the consumption of raw materials, there is an inverse influence on the dependent variable, i.e. a 1% increase in the consumption of raw materials leads to a 0.1% decrease in environmental taxes as a percentage of GDP. This influence could suggest that a higher dependence on natural resources leads to fiscal policies that encourage their extraction and use, possibly at levels that do not reflect the associated external costs. As for the variable SDG9CBV representing the number of patent applications filed at the European Patent Office, there is a positive influence on the dependent variable, i.e. a 1% increase in the number of patent applications filed at the European Patent Office leads to a 0.05% increase in environmental fees as a percentage of GDP. This may indicate that innovation and intensive patenting activity are associated with higher environmental standards and the adoption of fiscal policies that support sustainability. In the case of the variable SDG9CHCDI representing gross domestic expenditure on R&D, there is a positive influence on the dependent variable, i.e. a 1% increase in gross domestic expenditure on R&D leads to a 0.2% increase in environmental taxes as a percentage of GDP. This influence suggests that significant R&D investment may be linked to greater awareness and action on environmental policies, including through the implementation of environmentally targeted taxes.

These results underline the complex relationships between economic development, resource management, innovation and environmental fiscal policies, highlighting the need to balance economic growth with environmental responsibility and the promotion of sustainable technologies and research.

Figure 14.10 shows the ranking of the importance of predictors related to the influence on the dependent variable SDG9TAXM.

Figure 14.10 shows that the most significant predictor for the prediction of SDG9TAXM is R&D expenditure, which may imply that an increase in R&D expenditure is associated with a higher proportion of environmental taxes in GDP. Gross domestic product per capita has a weakly significant influence on the dependent variable, suggesting that in countries with higher GDP per capita, the proportion of environmental taxes in GDP is lower, reflecting a broader tax base that reduces the need for specific environmental taxes. This points to a complex relationship between spending on research and development, innovation, development assistance, resource use and the level of economic development with environmental policy in Europe.

The SDG9.8 model of European industrial sustainability from the perspective of the SDG9VTAXT indicator has the selected dependent variable as road transport-related tax revenues as a percentage of total environmental tax revenues. The independent variables are SDG9GDPloc representing GDP per capita, SDG9AOF representing Official Development Assistance, and SDG9TAXM representing environmental taxes as a percentage of GDP. A linear regression model is constructed with the independent variables defined above for which regression coefficients have been calculated according to equation number 14.9 presented.

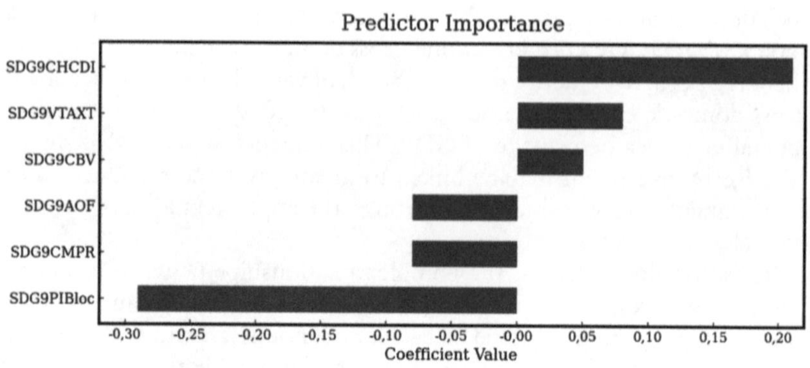


**Fig. 14.10** Importance of predictors related to influence on the variable SDG9TAXM. Source: Developed by the author using Python

$$SDG9VTAXT = 0.47 * SDG9PIBloc + 0.10 * SDG9AOF + 0.49 * SDG9TAXM - 2.33 \quad (14.9)$$

According to the regression equation for Model SDG9.8, there is a significant influence of the variable SDG9PIBloc representing GDP per capita, i.e. a 1% increase in GDP per capita leads to a 0.47% increase in road transport-related tax revenues as a percentage of total environmental tax revenues. This suggests that in more advanced economies, a higher proportion of environmental revenues comes from transport taxation due to more developed infrastructure and greater awareness of the environmental impacts of transport. As for the variable SDG9AOF representing Official Development Assistance, there is a positive influence on the dependent variable, i.e. a 1% increase in Official Development Assistance leads to a 0.1% increase in road transport-related tax revenues as a percentage of total environmental tax revenues. This indicates that development funds can indirectly contribute to the increase in transport-related tax revenues by improving infrastructure or promoting sustainable transport policies. According to the variable SDG9TAXM representing environmental taxes as a percentage of GDP, there is a positive influence on the dependent variable, i.e. a 1% increase in environmental taxes as a percentage of GDP leads to a 0.49% increase in road transport tax revenues as a percentage of total environmental tax revenues. This reflects efforts to internalize the external costs of transport, such as pollution and infrastructure wear and tear, by taxing transport activities more. These results emphasize the importance of the interaction between economic, development and environmental policies in shaping the structure of environmental and transport-related tax revenue. They highlight the key role of transport in environmental policy and how economic growth and external support can influence countries' approach to transport taxation in the broader context of sustainability and environmental finance.

Figure 14.11 shows the ranking of the importance of the predictors related to the influence on the dependent variable SDG9VTAXT.

Figure 14.11 shows that the most important predictor is environmental taxes and gross domestic product. Gross domestic product per capita is the most important predictor of transportation tax revenues as a percentage of total environmental tax revenues. This could be explained by the fact that countries with higher GDP per capita have more vehicles, which leads to higher revenues from transportation-related taxes. Official

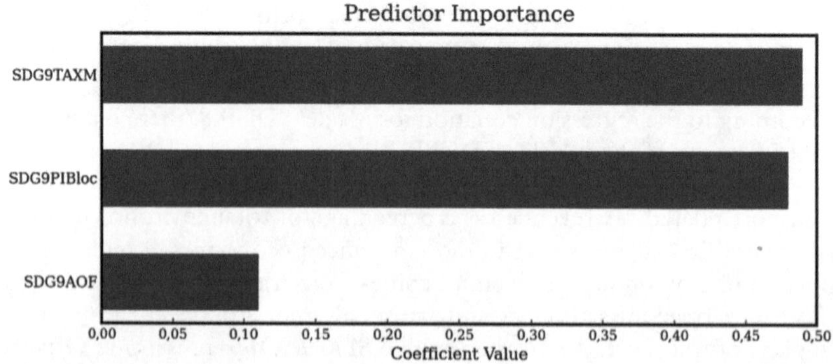


**Fig. 14.11** Importance of predictors related to the influence on the variable SDG9VTAXT. Source: Developed by the author using Python

Development Assistance also has a positive impact, indicating that foreign financial aid can help to improve transport infrastructure and increase government revenues from these taxes.

The SDG9.9 model of European industrial sustainability from the perspective of the SDG9AOF indicator has the selected dependent variable Official Development Assistance. The independent variables are: SDG9GDPloc representing gross domestic product per capita, SDG9DTHM representing the development of environment-related technologies, SDG9TAXM representing environment-related taxes as a percentage of GDP, SDG9VTAXT representing revenues from road transport-related taxes as a percentage of total revenues from environment-related taxes, SDG9CBV representing the number of patent applications filed at the European Patent Office, and SDG9PCDI representing the percentage of personnel employed in research and development. A linear regression model is constructed with the independent variables defined above for which regression coefficients have been calculated according to equation number 14.10.

$$\begin{aligned}\text{SDG9AOF} = {} & 0.56 * \text{SDG9PIBloc} + 0.08 * \text{SDG9DTHM} \\ & - 0.20 * \text{SDG9TAXM} + 0.08 * \text{SDG9VTAXT} \\ & + 0.01 * \text{SDG9CBV} + 0.45 * \text{SDG9PCDI} - 3.69 \end{aligned} \quad (14.10)$$

For Model SDG9.9 it can be observed that the greatest influence on the dependent variable is SDG9GDP per capita, and a positive influence on the dependent variable is found, i.e. a 1% increase in GDP per capita leads to a 0.56% increase in Official Development Assistance. This influence indicates that countries with larger economies tend to provide more development assistance due to larger financial resources. Regarding the variable SDG9DTHM representing the development of environmental technologies, there is a positive influence on the dependent variable, i.e. a 1% increase in the development of environmental technologies leads to a 0.08% increase in Official Development Assistance. This indicates that progress in environmental technologies can contribute to an increase in ODA, reflecting countries' commitment to sustainability. In the case of the variable SDG9TAXM representing environmental taxes as a percentage of GDP, there is an inverse influence on the dependent variable, i.e. a 1% increase in environmental taxes as a percentage of GDP leads to a 0.2% decrease in Official Development Assistance. This reveals that countries with stricter environmental fiscal policies are unable to allocate many resources to foreign development assistance due to the prioritization of domestic environmental issues. According to the variable SDG9VTAXT representing road transport-related tax revenues as a percentage of total environmental tax revenues, there is a positive influence on the dependent variable, i.e. a 1% increase in road transport-related tax revenues as a percentage of total environmental tax revenues leads to a 0.08% increase in Official Development Assistance, suggesting that higher transport tax revenues may contribute to a country's ability to provide development assistance by generating additional funds available for foreign aid. In the case of the variable SDG9CBV representing the number of patent applications filed at the European Patent Office, we find a positive influence on the dependent variable, i.e. a 1% increase in the number of patent applications filed at the European Patent Office leads to a 0.01% increase in Official Development Assistance, showing that innovation and patenting activity at the national level are weakly correlated with the level of development assistance provided, due to the fact that these activities reflect more the domestic dynamics of innovation than the commitment to international assistance. In the case of the variable SDG9PCDI representing the percentage of personnel engaged in R&D, there is a positive influence on the dependent variable, i.e. a 1% increase in the percentage of personnel engaged in R&D leads to a 0.45% increase in Official Development Assistance. This influence indicates a strong link between a country's commitment to R&D and its ability to provide Official Development Assistance, emphasizing the importance of investments in knowledge and innovation to support global development. These results highlight the complex relationships between economic, environmental and innovation factors and countries' commitment to Official Development Assistance, emphasizing the importance of an integrated approach when examining the factors influencing international aid flows.

Figure 14.12 shows the ranking of the importance of predictors related to the influence on the dependent variable SDG9AOF.

Figure 14.12 shows that the most important predictors are gross domestic product and the percentage of staff engaged in R&D, highlighting the importance of R&D in promoting sustainability. These suggest that initiatives to develop sustainable technologies are important for achieving sustainable development goals. A less significant influence on the dependent variable is exerted by environmental taxes as a percentage of GDP.

The regression functions were tested on the significance level and residual standard deviation of residuals (RMSE) data, as presented in Table 14.2.

It is observed that the standard deviation falls in the range 0.1743–0.6580. Maximizing the statistical significance of the model indicates the models SDG9.4, SDG9.1, SDG9.5, SDG9.2, SDG9.3 and SDG9.6 as statistically relevant with a significance greater than 70% and a standard deviation of the residuals up to 0.6580 (which confirms that for the prediction right-hand side there are deviations of the normal distribution on the mean).

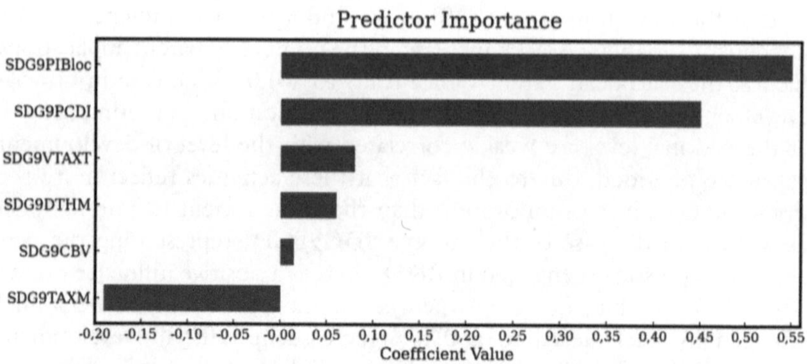


**Fig. 14.12** Importance of predictors related to influence on the variable SDG9AOF. Source: Developed by the author using Python

**Table 14.2** Validation of industrial sustainability models

| *Model* | *Dependent variable* | *Coefficient of determination* | *Residue standard deviation (RMSE)* |
|---|---|---|---|
| SDG9.1 | SDG9PIBloc | 0.8803 | 0.2078 |
| SDG9.2 | SDG9CHCDI | 0.8708 | 0.2081 |
| SDG9.3 | SDG9PCDI | 0.8710 | 0.1743 |
| SDG9.4 | SDG9CBV | 0.9278 | 0.6040 |
| SDG9.5 | SDG9CMPR | 0.8230 | 0.5763 |
| SDG9.6 | SDG9DTHM | 0.7778 | 0.6580 |
| SDG9.7 | SDG9TAXM | 0.1916 | 0.2367 |
| SDG9.8 | SDG9VTAXT | 0.2319 | 0.6490 |
| SDG9.9 | SDG9AOF | 0.7807 | 0.3641 |

Source: Developed by the author using Python

The variance inflation factor (VIF) analysis was used to test for multicollinearities among the independent variables of the proposed regression models and is presented in Table 14.3.

Table 14.3 shows that the homogeneity of the proposed models is significant, with the largest deviations from the trend line being recorded for SDG9.7 and SDG9.8. However, the models have a range of error representation that tends to 0 in almost all cases, being well statistically determined and relevant for the proposed purpose. The multicollinearity of the models has been tested, the inflation factors being below the threshold of multicollinearity representation (VIF<10), which demonstrates that the evaluated models are appropriate for determining the causal relationships of economic sustainability on composite factors.

## Conclusions

The empirical modelling of European industrial sustainability based on Sustainable Development Goal 9 (SDG9) indicators highlights the multidimensional nature of the relationship between economic performance, innovation capacity, environmental policy and resource efficiency. The nine econometric models developed through the Backward Feature Selection (BFS) method demonstrate that variables related to research and development—particularly the share of R&D personnel, gross domestic expenditure on R&D and the number of patent applications—are consistently among the most significant predictors of industrial sustainability

**Table 14.3** The homogeneity table of industrial sustainable development models

| *Model* | *Dependent variable* | *Independent variables* | *P* | *VIF* |
|---|---|---|---|---|
| SDG9.1 | SDG9PIBloc 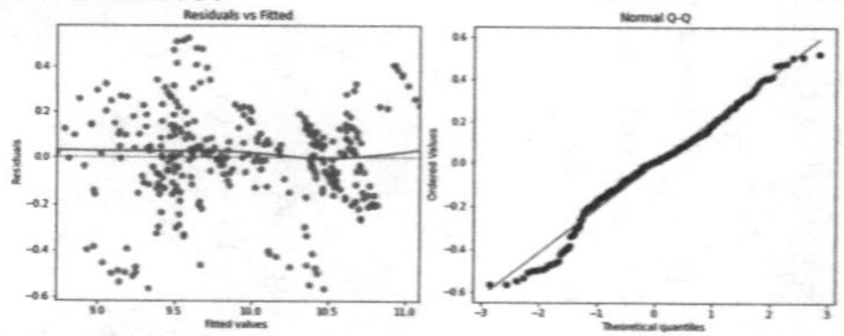 | SDG9DTHM | 0.03068 | 4.5562 |
| | | SDG9AOF | 1.197e-05 | 4.4287 |
| | | SDG9TAXM | 9.375e-07 | 1.1771 |
| | | SDG9VTAXT | 0.001012 | 1.3338 |
| | | SDG9CMPR | 5.254e-34 | 3.6673 |
| | | SDG9CBV | 4.755e-35 | 8.7102 |
| | | SDG9PCDI | 5.443e-07 | 7.3797 |
| | | SDG9CHCDI | 0.0004173 | 7.6077 |
| SDG9.2 | SDG9CHCDI 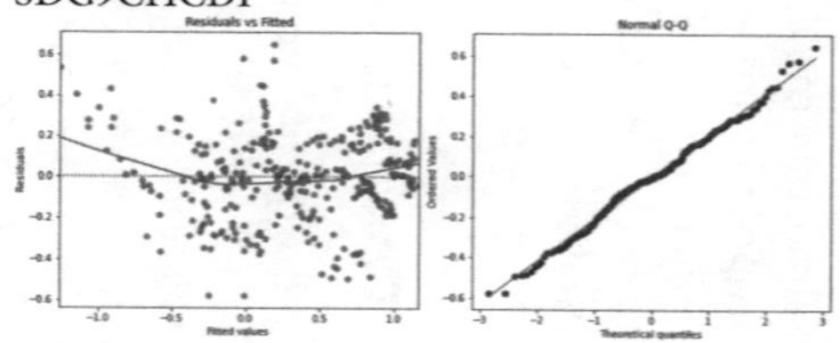 | SDG9PIBloc | 1.516e-11 | 3.4510 |
| | | SDG9DTHM | 7.505e-08 | 3.9119 |
| | | SDG9TAXM | 0.05821 | 1.1051 |
| | | SDG9CBV | 1.148e-11 | 2.9534 |
| | | SDG9PCDI | 2.275e-66 | 2.9395 |
| SDG9.3 | SDG9PCDI 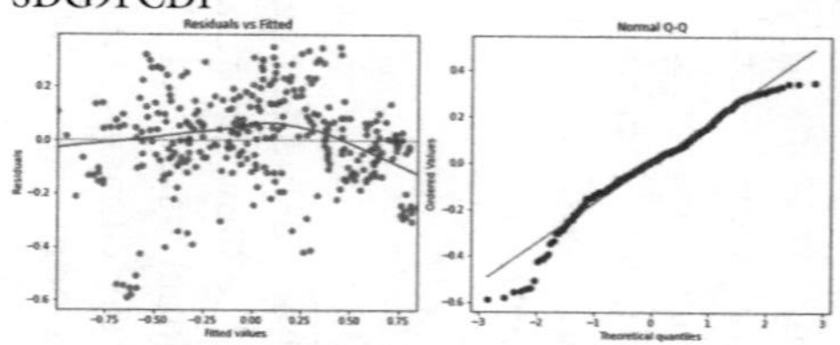 | SDG9PIBloc | 1.908e-07 | 4.0548 |
| | | SDG9AOF | 6.285e-05 | 4.1776 |
| | | SDG9CBV | 0.0002436 | 3.0584 |
| | | SDG9CHCDI | 2.693e-69 | 2.6483 |

| | | | | | |
|---|---|---|---|---|---|
| SDG9.4 | SDG9CBV | 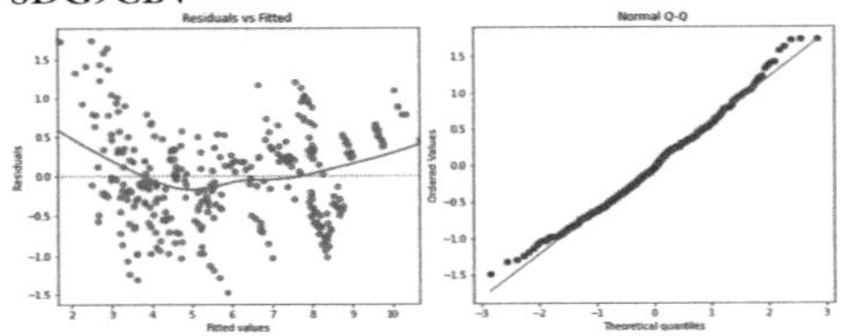  | SDG9PIBloc | 3.438e-37 | 4.9403 |
| | | | SDG9DTHM | 8.505e-08 | 4.2199 |
| | | | SDG9AOF | 0.01852 | 4.5235 |
| | | | SDG9TAXM | 0.01407 | 1.1844 |
| | | | SDG9CMPR | 5.634e-99 | 1.4230 |
| | | | SDG9PCDI | 0.01918 | 7.8169 |
| | | | SDG9CHCDI | 0.00986 | 7.7287 |
| SDG9.5 | SDG9CMPR | 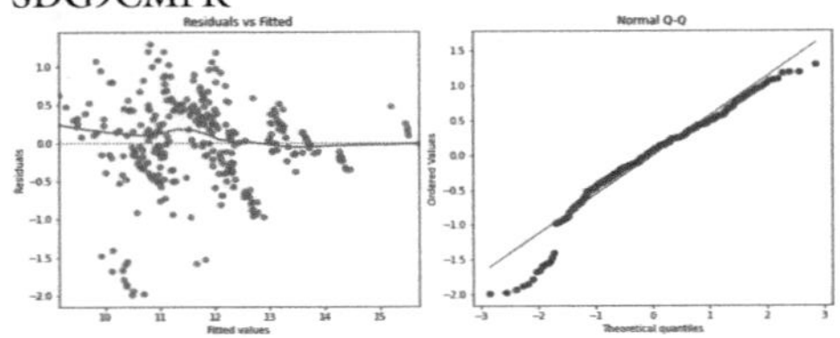  | SDG9PIBloc | 4.021e-54 | 3.0981 |
| | | | SDG9DTHM | 0.0001253 | 3.6088 |
| | | | SDG9TAXM | 4.432e-05 | 1.0790 |
| | | | SDG9CBV | 4.053e-111 | 2.8101 |
| SDG9.6 | SDG9DTHM | 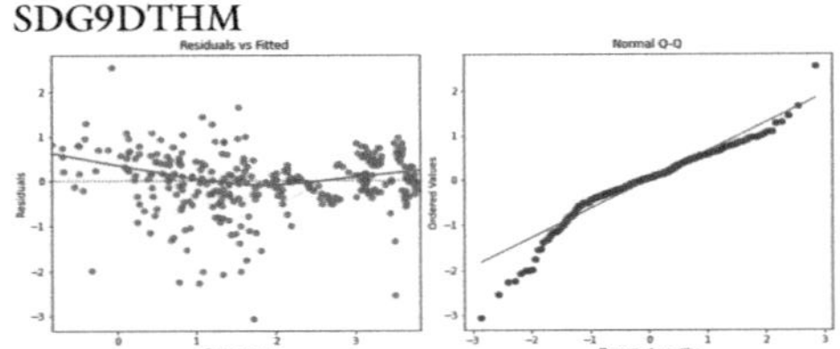  | SDG9PIBloc | 0.1128 | 7.1904 |
| | | | SDG9AOF | 0.04772 | 4.2267 |
| | | | SDG9CMPR | 7.41e-06 | 5.1457 |
| | | | SDG9CBV | 3.862e-09 | 12.2558 |
| | | | SDG9CHCDI | 4.244e-13 | 2.6494 |

*(continued)*

**Table 14.3** (continued)

| *Model* | *Dependent variable* | *Independent variables* | *P* | *VIF* |
|---|---|---|---|---|
| SDG9.7 | SDG9TAXM 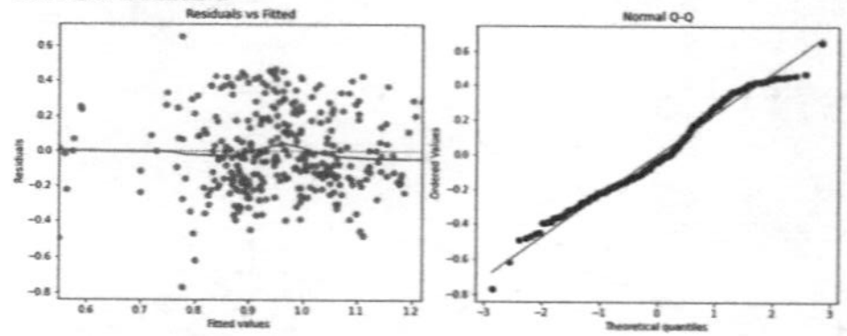  | SDG9PIBloc | 2.545e-06 | 7.2969 |
| | | SDG9AOF | 0.01405 | 4.2769 |
| | | SDG9VTAXT | 7.623e-05 | 1.3069 |
| | | SDG9CMPR | 2.279e-06 | 5.1856 |
| | | SDG9CBV | 0.006908 | 12.3004 |
| | | SDG9CHCDI | 6.61e-08 | 2.6899 |
| SDG9.8 | SDG9VTAXT 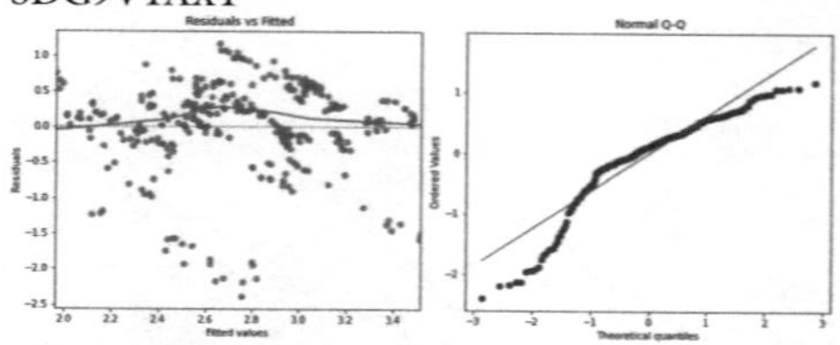  | SDG9PIBloc | 3.1e-05 | 3.6133 |
| | | SDG9AOF | 0.2421 | 3.5884 |
| | | SDG9TAXM | 0.0004436 | 1.0313 |
| SDG9.9 | SDG9AOF 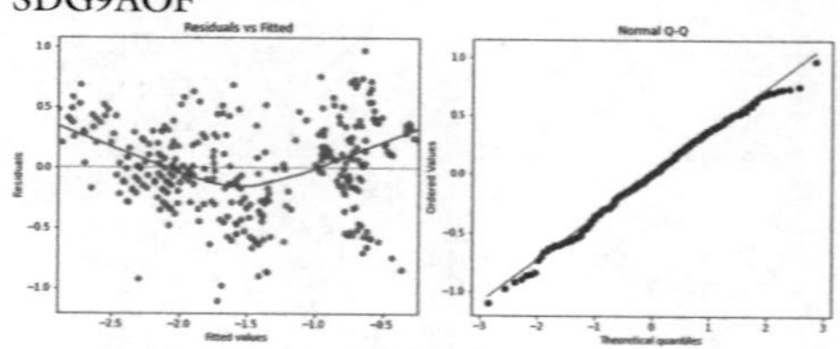  | SDG9PIBloc | 3.535e-15 | 4.0449 |
| | | SDG9DTHM | 0.00411 | 3.9121 |
| | | SDG9TAXM | 0.01349 | 1.1590 |
| | | SDG9VTAXT | 0.005832 | 1.3431 |
| | | SDG9CBV | 0.2863 | 2.9543 |
| | | SDG9PCDI | 1.276e-09 | 2.9920 |

Source: Developed by the author using Python

across Member States. These findings underline the central role of innovation and human capital in driving both competitiveness and environmental performance.

At the same time, the results reveal structural vulnerabilities, such as the uneven development of environmental technologies, the over-reliance on raw material consumption in certain economies, and the limited effectiveness of environmental taxation in stimulating sustainable industrial transformation. The identification of these weaknesses offers a valuable basis for targeted policy interventions, especially in countries where industrial modernization and technological upgrading remain constrained.

The modelling exercise confirms that the interplay between economic growth and sustainability outcomes is complex and, in some cases, counterintuitive. For example, higher GDP per capita does not automatically translate into increased R&D spending or reduced resource consumption, while environmental taxes may have both stimulating and constraining effects depending on the sectoral and national context. This calls for integrated policy frameworks that combine fiscal incentives, innovation support and resource efficiency measures, tailored to the specific structural characteristics of each Member State.

From a policy perspective, the chapter's results suggest that the EU's ambitions under SDG9 and the European Green Deal can only be achieved through a coordinated approach that fosters technological innovation, strengthens industrial resilience, and reduces disparities among Member States. Investing in human capital, enhancing cross-sectoral collaboration, and aligning fiscal and innovation policies emerge as strategic priorities for ensuring that European industry remains competitive, inclusive, and environmentally sustainable in the decades to come.

## References

Adiguzel, Z., & Sonmez Cakir, F. (2025). Leveraging green information systems and big data analytics infrastructure flexibility for sustainable performance: The mediating role of green technological turbulence in energy companies. *Industrial Management & Data Systems*. https://doi.org/10.1108/IMDS-10-2024-1040

Ahlström, H., Williams, A., Wassénius, E., & Downing, A. S. (2025). Deepening the conversation on systemic sustainability risks: A social-ecological systems approach. *Journal of Business Ethics, 199*(3), 495–506. https://doi.org/10.1007/s10551-024-05860-3

Ajala, A. A., Adeoye, O. L., Salami, O. M., & Jimoh, A. Y. (2025). An examination of daily CO2 emissions prediction through a comparative analysis of machine learning, deep learning, and statistical models. *Environmental Science and Pollution Research, 32*(5), 2510–2535. https://doi.org/10.1007/s11356-024-35764-8

Alexiou, C., & Petreski, M. (2025). Patent strength, innovation, and CO2 emissions: Evidence of non-linear environmental impacts across economies. *Business Strategy & Development, 8*(3), e70178. https://doi.org/10.1002/bsd2.70178

Alola, A. A., & Nwulu, N. (2022). Do energy-pollution-resource-transport taxes yield double dividend for Nordic economies? *Energy, 254*, 124275. https://doi.org/10.1016/j.energy.2022.124275

Audretsch, D. B., Belitski, M., & Chowdhury, F. (2024). Knowledge investment and search for innovation: Evidence from the UK firms. *The Journal of Technology Transfer, 49*(4), 1387–1410. https://doi.org/10.1007/s10961-023-10045-7

Banga, K., & Gaile-Sarkane, E. (2025). Methods for measuring open innovation's impact on innovation ecosystems in the context of the European innovation scoreboard. *Business, 5*(3). https://doi.org/10.3390/businesses5030029

Bashir, M. F., Bashir, M. A., Radulescu, M., & Shahzad, U. (2022). Investigating the role of environmental taxes and regulations for renewable energy consumption: Evidence from developed economies. *Economic Research-Ekonomska Istraživanja, 35*(1), 1262–1284. https://doi.org/10.1080/1331677X.2021.1962383

Basilico, S., & Grashof, N. (2024). Accelerating the sustainability transition of brown regions: Unlocking the speed factor. *Environmental Innovation and Societal Transitions, 51*, 100840. https://doi.org/10.1016/j.eist.2024.100840

Becha, H., Kalai, M., Houidi, S., & Helali, K. (2025). Digital financial inclusion, environmental sustainability and regional economic growth in China: Insights from a panel threshold model. *Journal of Economic Structures, 14*(1), 4. https://doi.org/10.1186/s40008-025-00347-4

Belanová, K., Ochotnický, P., & Sivák, R. (2025). Innovation performance of EU countries in context of R&D: R&D trap risk in Slovakia? *Journal of Innovation and Entrepreneurship, 14*(1), 59. https://doi.org/10.1186/s13731-025-00533-5

Benito, G. R. G., & Meyer, K. E. (2024). Industrial policy, green challenges, and international business. *Journal of International Business Studies, 55*(9), 1093–1107. https://doi.org/10.1057/s41267-024-00722-6

Bianchi, P., Lisa, D. P., & Labory, S. (2024). People-centred policies for a just transition (digital, green and skills). *Contemporary Social Science, 19*(1–3), 262–282. https://doi.org/10.1080/21582041.2024.2351479

Bilgili, F., Önderol, S., Kuşkaya, S., Alnour, M., Hoque, M. E., & Balsalobre-Lorente, D. (2025). Renewable energy and technology adoption: Mitigating CO2 emissions through implementation strategies. *Natural Resources Forum, 49*(2), 1478–1535. https://doi.org/10.1111/1477-8947.12441

Boostani, P., Pellegrini-Masini, G., & Klein, J. (2024). The role of community energy schemes in reducing energy poverty and promoting social inclusion: A systematic literature review. *Energies, 17*(13). https://doi.org/10.3390/en17133232

Bovenberg, A. L., & de Mooij, R. A. (1994). Environmental levies and distortionary taxation. *The American Economic Review, 84*(4), 1085–1089. http://www.jstor.org/stable/2118046

Brodny, J., & Tutak, M. (2023). Assessing regional implementation of Sustainable Development Goal 9 "Build resilient infrastructure, promote sustainable industrialization and foster innovation" in Poland. *Technological Forecasting and Social Change, 195*, 122773. https://doi.org/10.1016/j.techfore.2023.122773

Brodny, J., & Tutak, M. (2024). Disparities of Central and Eastern European countries of European Union in innovation potential: A multi-criteria assessment. *Journal of Open Innovation: Technology, Market, and Complexity, 10*(2), 100282. https://doi.org/10.1016/j.joitmc.2024.100282

Commission, E. (2025). *European innovation scoreboard 2025 – Exploratory study on the linkages between innovation and resilience*. Publications Office of the European Union. https://doi.org/10.2777/0663803

Cutcu, I., Cil, D., Karis, C., & Kocak, S. (2024). Determining the green technology innovation accelator and natural resources towards decarbonization for the EU countries: Evidence from MMQR. *Environmental Science and Pollution Research, 31*(12), 19002–19021. https://doi.org/10.1007/s11356-024-32302-4

Dahmani, M. (2024). Environmental quality and sustainability: Exploring the role of environmental taxes, environment-related technologies, and R&D expenditure. *Environmental Economics and Policy Studies, 26*(2), 449–477. https://doi.org/10.1007/s10018-023-00387-9

Djatmiko, G. H., Sinaga, O., & Pawirosumarto, S. (2025). Digital transformation and social inclusion in public services: A qualitative analysis of E-government adoption for marginalized communities in sustainable governance. *Sustainability, 17*(7). https://doi.org/10.3390/su17072908

Ebaidalla, E. M. (2024). The impact of taxation, technological innovation and trade openness on renewable energy investment: Evidence from the top renewable energy producing countries. *Energy, 306*, 132539. https://doi.org/10.1016/j.energy.2024.132539

Economidou, M., Della Valle, N., Melica, G., & Bertoldi, P. (2023). The role of European municipalities and regions in financing energy upgrades in buildings.

*Environmental Economics and Policy Studies.* https://doi.org/10.1007/s10018-023-00363-3

Elegbede, I. O., Fakoya, K. A., Adewolu, M. A., Jolaosho, T. L., Adebayo, J. A., Oshodi, E., Hungevu, R. F., Oladosu, A. O., & Abikoye, O. (2025). Understanding the social–ecological systems of non-state seafood sustainability scheme in the blue economy. *Environment, Development and Sustainability, 27*(2), 2721–2752. https://doi.org/10.1007/s10668-023-04004-3

Esmaeilpour Moghadam, H., & Karami, A. (2024). Green innovation: Exploring the impact of environmental patents on the adoption and advancement of renewable energy. *Management of Environmental Quality: An International Journal, 35*(8), 1815–1835. https://doi.org/10.1108/MEQ-10-2023-0360

Etzkowitz, H., & Zhou, C. (2017). *The triple helix: University–industry–government innovation and entrepreneurship.* Routledge. https://doi.org/10.4324/9781315620183

European Commission. (2023a). *A European green deal.* https://commission.europa.eu/strategy-and-policy/priorities-2019-2024/european-green-deal_en

European Commission. (2023b). *Circular economy action plan.* https://environment.ec.europa.eu/strategy/circular-economy-action-plan_en

European Commission. (2024a). *Annual report on taxation 2024.* https://taxation-customs.ec.europa.eu/taxation/economic-analysis/annual-report-taxation_en

European Commission. (2024b). *Horizon Europe.* https://single-market-economy.ec.europa.eu/industry/strategy/hydrogen/funding-guide/eu-programmes-funds/horizon-europe_en

European Commission. (2024c). *The recovery and resilience facility.* https://commission.europa.eu/business-economy-euro/economic-recovery/recovery-and-resilience-facility_en

European Commission. (2025a). *Green taxation – In support of a more sustainable future.* https://taxation-customs.ec.europa.eu/archives/other-taxe/green-taxation_en

European Commission. (2025b). *Horizon Europe work programme 2025-7.* Digital, Industry and Space.

European Council. (2023). *Fit for 55.* https://www.consilium.europa.eu/en/policies/green-deal/fit-for-55-the-eu-plan-for-a-green-transition/

European Council. (2024). *Competitiveness of the European economy – Statement of the Eurogroup in inclusive format.* https://www.consilium.europa.eu/en/press/press-releases/2024/11/04/competitiveness-of-the-european-economy-statement-of-the-eurogroup-in-inclusive-format/

European Investment Bank. (2025). *Growth and competitiveness in Central, Eastern and South-Eastern Europe: The role of innovation.* https://www.eib.

org/attachments/lucalli/20240356_economics_working_paper_2025_01_en.pdf
Eurostat. (2024a). *Gross domestic expenditure on R&D by sector*. https://ec.europa.eu/eurostat/databrowser/view/sdg_09_10/default/table?lang=en
Eurostat. (2024b). *Patent applications to the European Patent Office by applicants' / inventors' country of residence*. https://ec.europa.eu/eurostat/databrowser/view/sdg_09_40/default/table?lang=en
Eurostat. (2024c). *R&D expenditure*. https://ec.europa.eu/eurostat/statistics-explained/index.php?title=R%26D_expenditure
Eurostat. (2024d). *R&D personnel by sector*. https://ec.europa.eu/eurostat/databrowser/view/sdg_09_30/default/table?lang=en&category=sdg.sdg_09
Eurostat. (2024e). *Raw material consumption (RMC)*. https://ec.europa.eu/eurostat/databrowser/product/view/sdg_12_21?lang=en
Eurostat. (2024f). *Real GDP per capita*. https://ec.europa.eu/eurostat/databrowser/view/sdg_08_10/default/table?lang=en&category=sdg.sdg_08
Fabrizi, A., Gentile, M., Guarini, G., & Meliciani, V. (2024). The impact of environmental regulation on innovation and international competitiveness. *Journal of Evolutionary Economics, 34*(1), 169–204. https://doi.org/10.1007/s00191-024-00852-y
Fernández-Pasarín, A. M., & Lanaia, A. (2025). The governance of the recovery and resilience facility. The incremental innovation of standard conditionality regime. *European Policy Analysis, 11*(1), 75–93. https://doi.org/10.1002/epa2.1230
Fozap, F. M. (2025). Hybrid machine learning models for long-term stock market forecasting: Integrating technical indicators. *Journal of Risk and Financial Management, 18*(4). https://doi.org/10.3390/jrfm18040201
Gajdosikova, D., & Vojtekova, S. (2024). Comparative analysis of business environment dynamics in Central and Eastern Europe: A multi-criteria approach. *Economies, 12*(12). https://doi.org/10.3390/economies12120320
Gholami, H., Darvishi, E., Moradi, N., Mohammadifar, A., Song, Y., Li, Y., Niu, B., Kaskaoutis, D., & Pradhan, B. (2024). An interpretable (explainable) model based on machine learning and SHAP interpretation technique for mapping wind erosion hazard. *Environmental Science and Pollution Research, 31*(56), 64628–64643. https://doi.org/10.1007/s11356-024-35521-x
Hariram, N. P., Mekha, K. B., Suganthan, V., & Sudhakar, K. (2023). Sustainalism: An integrated socio-economic-environmental model to address sustainable development and sustainability. *Sustainability, 15*(13). https://doi.org/10.3390/su151310682
Hedegaard, T. F., & Kongshøj, K. (n.d.). How redistribution can make carbon taxes more acceptable to the public. *The Social Science Journal*, 1–14. https://doi.org/10.1080/03623319.2024.2416774

Hung, N. T. (2023). Green investment, financial development, digitalization and economic sustainability in Vietnam: Evidence from a quantile-on-quantile regression and wavelet coherence. *Technological Forecasting and Social Change, 186*, 122185. https://doi.org/10.1016/j.techfore.2022.122185

Huynh, T. (2025). Collaborative research in healthcare: Uncovering the impact of industry collaboration on the service innovativeness of university hospitals. *The Journal of Technology Transfer, 50*(1), 1–28. https://doi.org/10.1007/s10961-024-10083-9

Islam, H. (2025). Nexus of economic, social, and environmental factors on sustainable development goals: The moderating role of technological advancement and green innovation. *Innovation and Green Development, 4*(1), 100183. https://doi.org/10.1016/j.igd.2024.100183

Islam, N. F., Gogoi, B., Saikia, R., Yousaf, B., Narayan, M., & Sarma, H. (2024). Encouraging circular economy and sustainable environmental practices by addressing waste management and biomass energy production. *Regional Sustainability, 5*(4), 100174. https://doi.org/10.1016/j.regsus.2024.100174

Kalaš, B., Mirović, V., Bolesnikov, D., Akadiri, S. S., & Radulescu, M. (2025). Environmental taxes and sustainable development in the EU: A decade of data-driven insights. *Systems, 13*(7). https://doi.org/10.3390/systems13070503

Kareem, S., Fehrer, J. A., Shalpegin, T., & Stringer, C. (2025). Navigating tensions of sustainable supply chains in times of multiple crises: A systematic literature review. *Business Strategy and the Environment, 34*(1), 316–337. https://doi.org/10.1002/bse.3990

Khan, A., Sattar, A., Alnafisah, H., & Fatima, N. (2025). Do environmental taxes and green technological innovation represent the crux of environmental sustainability? Insights from OECD region with MMQR approach. *Frontiers in Environmental Science, 13*. https://doi.org/10.3389/fenvs.2025.1537535

Kharb, R., Saini, N., & Kumar, D. (2024). Driving environmental sustainability in emerging economies: The nexus of green finance, foreign direct investment, financial development, and green technology innovation. *Business Strategy & Development, 7*(4), e70008. https://doi.org/10.1002/bsd2.70008

Klimczuk, A., Gawron, G. P., Klimczuk-Kochańska, M., & Toczyski, P. (2024). Editorial: towards 2030: Sustainable development goal 9: Industry, innovation and infrastructure. A sociological perspective. *Frontiers in Sociology, 9*. https://doi.org/10.3389/fsoc.2024.1491091

Kouser, R., Mahmood, G., Watto, W. A., Fahlevi, M., & Aziz, A. L. (2025). Assessing the impact of green manufacturing and green technology innovation on sustainable green practices: Unveiling the mediating role of eco-design. *International Journal of Sustainable Engineering, 18*(1), 2538868. https://doi.org/10.1080/19397038.2025.2538868

Kovacic, Z., Casañas, G., Cristina, A., Lucía, Y. S., Paloma, R.-F., Ramon, P., & Louisa, & March, Hug. (2024). The twin green and digital transition: High-level policy or science fiction? *Environment and Planning E: Nature and Space, 7*(6), 2251–2278. https://doi.org/10.1177/25148486241258046

Kristjanpoller, W. (2024). A hybrid econometrics and machine learning based modeling of realized volatility of natural gas. *Financial Innovation, 10*(1), 45. https://doi.org/10.1186/s40854-023-00577-0

Kuś, A., Kuflewska, W., & Trocewicz, A. (2025). European vision of a gigabit society: Evidence from Poland. *Sustainability, 17*(3). https://doi.org/10.3390/su17031271

Kwilinski, A., Dacko-Pikiewicz, Z., Szczepanska-Woszczyna, K., Lyulyov, O., & Pimonenko, T. (2025). The role of innovation in the transition to a green economy: A path to sustainable growth. *Journal of Open Innovation: Technology, Market, and Complexity, 11*(2), 100530. https://doi.org/10.1016/j.joitmc.2025.100530

Latip, M., Sharkawi, I., & Mohamed, Z. (2025). Enhancing sustainability practices in Malaysian food manufacturing SMEs: The mediating effect of innovation capability. *Corporate Social Responsibility and Environmental Management, 32*(3), 4035–4052. https://doi.org/10.1002/csr.3170

Leitão, J., & Ferreira, J. (2021). Dynamic effects of material production and environmental sustainability on economic vitality indicators: A panel VAR approach. *Journal of Risk and Financial Management, 14*(2). https://doi.org/10.3390/jrfm14020074

Lella, L., Oses-Eraso, N., & Stamos, I. (2024). Pioneering a sustainable development goals monitoring framework for European regions. *Ecological Indicators, 166*, 112248. https://doi.org/10.1016/j.ecolind.2024.112248

Li, C., Teng, Y., Zhou, Y., & Feng, X. (2024). Can environmental protection tax force enterprises to improve green technology innovation? *Environmental Science and Pollution Research, 31*(6), 9371–9391. https://doi.org/10.1007/s11356-023-31736-6

Liang, Y., Ur Rahman, S., Shafaqat, A., Ali, A., Ali, M. S. E., & Khan, H. (2024). Assessing sustainable development in E-7 countries: Technology innovation, and energy consumption drivers of green growth and environment. *Scientific Reports, 14*(1), 28636. https://doi.org/10.1038/s41598-024-79908-9

Martínez Córdoba, P. J., Ramos, V. C., Gómez, E. Z., & Gómez, J. L. Z. (2025). Efficiency of public spending on environmental protection: The role of renewable energy, governance and fossil fuel subsidies. *Sustainable Development, n/a*(n/a). https://doi.org/10.1002/sd.70008

Martyushev, N. V., Spitsin, V., Klyuev, R. V., Spitsina, L., Konyukhov, V. Y., Oparina, T. A., & Boltrushevich, A. E. (2025). Predicting firm's performance based on panel data: Using hybrid methods to improve forecast accuracy. *Mathematics, 13*(8). https://doi.org/10.3390/math13081247

McDougall, N., & Davis, A. (2024). The local supply chain during disruption: Establishing resilient networks for the future. *Journal of Cleaner Production, 462*, 142743. https://doi.org/10.1016/j.jclepro.2024.142743

Mishra, N., Grima, S., & Ozen, E. (2024). Unpacking the black box: Investigating the role of social protection programmes in promoting decent work and economic growth in low-income countries. *Sustainable Development, 32*(5), 5825–5835. https://doi.org/10.1002/sd.3008

Muneer, S., Singh, A., & Tripathi, A. (2025). Economic evolution in the digital age: Assessing the influence of digital transformation and energy consumption on sustainable development. *Frontiers in Human Dynamics, 7*. https://doi.org/10.3389/fhumd.2025.1523887

Musetsho, K. D., Mwendera, E., Madzivhandila, T., Makungo, R., Volenzo, T. E., Mamphweli, N. S., & Nephawe, K. A. (2024). Assessing and mapping water-energy-food nexus smart innovations and practices in Vhembe District Municipality, Limpopo Province, South Africa. *Frontiers in Water, 6*. https://doi.org/10.3389/frwa.2024.1253921

Muth, D. (2025). Investigating the mechanisms linking revenue recycling to increased political acceptability of carbon pricing. *Review of Policy Research, 42*(4), 1050–1075. https://doi.org/10.1111/ropr.12625

Muth, D., Weiner, C., & Lakócai, C. (2024). Public support and willingness to pay for a carbon tax in Hungary: Can revenue recycling make a difference? *Energy, Sustainability and Society, 14*(1), 30. https://doi.org/10.1186/s13705-024-00463-2

Noubissi Domguia, E. (2023). Taxing for a better life? The impact of environmental taxes on income distribution and inclusive education. *Heliyon, 9*(11). https://doi.org/10.1016/j.heliyon.2023.e21443

Nuutinen, M., Valkokari, K., & Jurmu, M. (2025). Critical features of ecosystem practice empowering industrial sustainability transformation. *Creativity and Innovation Management, 34*(1), 111–124. https://doi.org/10.1111/caim.12630

OECD. (2023a). *Driving policy coherence for sustainable development: Accelerating progress on the SDGs*. https://doi.org/10.1787/a6cb4aa1-en

OECD. (2023b). *Economic effects of the EU's 'Fit for 55' climate mitigation policies: A computable general equilibrium analysis*. https://doi.org/10.1787/f1a8cfa2-en

OECD. (2023c). *Equity and inclusion in education*. https://doi.org/10.1787/e9072e21-en

OECD. (2024a). *Green growth indicators*. OECD.Stat.

OECD. (2024b). *Monitoring progress towards a resource-efficient and circular economy*. https://doi.org/10.1787/3b644b83-en

Pata, U. K., Kartal, M. T., & Erdogan, S. (2024). Ecological effects of distinct patents on reducing waste-related greenhouse gas emissions in BRIC countries: Evidence from novel quantile methods. *International Journal of Sustainable Development and World Ecology, 31*(5), 554–566. https://doi.org/10.1080/13504509.2023.2301375

Polverari, L. (2025). Coordinative Europeanization as a response to crisis: What lessons from the RRF for future EU cohesion policy? *Comparative European Politics, 23*(1), 76–96. https://doi.org/10.1057/s41295-024-00388-2

Potkány, M., Lesníková, P., Schmidtová, J., Musová, Z., & Neykov, N. (2025). Indicators of circular economy and their link to performance and competitiveness: Multi-criteria analysis in the EU countries. *Discover Sustainability, 6*(1), 825. https://doi.org/10.1007/s43621-025-01774-w

Pranita, D., & Sarjana, S. (2025). A conceptual approach to defining a carbon tax in the transport sector in Indonesia: Economic, social, and environmental aspects. *Energies, 18*(13). https://doi.org/10.3390/en18133493

Pugno, M. (2024). Creativity, well-being, and economic development: An evolutionary approach. *Journal of Evolutionary Economics, 34*(1), 205–225. https://doi.org/10.1007/s00191-024-00858-6

Pulignano, V., Hauptmeier, M., & Frans, D. (2023). Determinants of union strategies towards the twin digital and green transitions in the German and Belgian automotive industry. *Transfer: European Review of Labour and Research, 29*(1), 121–138. https://doi.org/10.1177/10242589231158066

Radulescu, M., Hossain, M. R., Alofaysan, H., & Si Mohammed, K. (2024). Do emission trading systems, green technology, and environmental governance matter for environmental quality? Evidence from the European Union. *International Journal of Environmental Research, 19*(1), 6. https://doi.org/10.1007/s41742-024-00667-6

Rainville, A., Dikker, I., & Buggenhagen, M. (2025). Tracking innovation via green patent classification systems: Are we truly capturing circular economy progress? *Journal of Cleaner Production, 486*, 144385. https://doi.org/10.1016/j.jclepro.2024.144385

Reimer, F., Guter-Sandu, A., Haas, A., & Murau, S. (2025). Schrödinger's off-balance-sheet fiscal agency: The Recovery and Resilience Facility and the limits to incremental fiscal integration in Europe. *Journal of European Integration*, 1–22. https://doi.org/10.1080/07036337.2025.2491618

Sánchez-García, E., Martínez-Falcó, J., Marco-Lajara, B., & Manresa-Marhuenda, E. (2024). Revolutionizing the circular economy through new technologies: A new era of sustainable progress. *Environmental Technology & Innovation, 33*, 103509. https://doi.org/10.1016/j.eti.2023.103509

Sardianou, E., Nikou, V., Evangelinos, K., & Nikolaou, I. (2024). What are the key dimensions that CE emphasizes on? A systematic analysis of circular economy definitions. *Environment Systems and Decisions, 44*(3), 547–562. https://doi.org/10.1007/s10669-023-09956-5

Sen, K. K., Hosan, S., Karmaker, S. C., Chapman, A. J., & Saha, B. B. (2025). Environmental taxes and renewable energy consumption nexus: Role of environmental governance and technological innovation. *Sustainable Futures, 9*, 100825. https://doi.org/10.1016/j.sftr.2025.100825

Shafik, W. (2025). SDG 9: Industry, innovation, and infrastructure—Smart technologies for sustainable industry. In W. Shafik (Ed.), *Factoring technology in global sustainability: A focus on the sustainable development goals* (pp. 305–331). SpringerNatureSingapore.https://doi.org/10.1007/978-981-96-7299-8_11

Sharifi, A., Allam, Z., Bibri, S. E., & Khavarian-Garmsir, A. R. (2024). Smart cities and sustainable development goals (SDGs): A systematic literature review of co-benefits and trade-offs. *Cities, 146*, 104659. https://doi.org/10.1016/j.cities.2023.104659

Stameski, N., Radulescu, M., Zelenović, V., Mirović, V., Kalaš, B., & Pavlović, N. (2024). Investigating the effects of environmental tax revenues on economic development: The case of Nordic countries. *Sustainability, 16*(18). https://doi.org/10.3390/su16187957

Szymczyk, K., & Włodarczyk, A. (2025). How to be green in highly turbulent business conditions? Evidence from family firms in Poland. *Journal of Family Business Management*. https://doi.org/10.1108/JFBM-12-2024-0289

Troitiño, D. R., Mazur, V., & Kerikmäe, T. (2024). E-governance and integration in the European union. *Internet of Things, 27*, 101321. https://doi.org/10.1016/j.iot.2024.101321

Tsang, Y. P., Fan, Y., Feng, Z. P., & Li, Y. (2024). Examining supply chain vulnerability via an analysis of ESG-Prioritized firms amid the Russian-Ukrainian conflict. *Journal of Cleaner Production, 434*, 139754. https://doi.org/10.1016/j.jclepro.2023.139754

Umair, M., Ahmad, W., Hussain, B., Fortea, C., Zlati, M. L., & Antohi, V. M. (2024). Empowering Pakistan's economy: The role of health and education in shaping labor force participation and economic growth. *Economies, 12*(5). https://doi.org/10.3390/economies12050113

United Nations. (1987). *Report of the world commission on environment and development – Our common future*. https://gat04-live-1517c8a4486c41609369c68f30c8-aa81074.divio-media.org/filer_public/6f/85/6f854236-56ab-4b42-810f-606d215c0499/cd_9127_extract_from_our_common_future_brundtland_report_1987_foreword_chpt_2.pdf

Yan, K., & Lin, B. (2025). How climate policy shapes global utility markets: Dynamic evidence from the EU carbon market. *Sustainable Development, n/a*(n/a). https://doi.org/10.1002/sd.3486

Yang, S., Jahanger, A., Hu, J., & Awan, A. (2024). Impact of China's carbon emissions trading scheme on firm-level pollution abatement and employment: Evidence from a national panel dataset. *Energy Economics, 136*, 107744. https://doi.org/10.1016/j.eneco.2024.107744

Yao, J. (2024). A fusion method integrated econometrics and deep learning to improve the interpretability of prediction: Evidence from Chinese carbon emissions forecast based on OLS-CNN model. *Computational Economics*. https://doi.org/10.1007/s10614-024-10793-0

Yao, X., Zhang, H., Wang, X., Jiang, Y., Zhang, Y., & Na, X. (2024). Which model is more efficient in carbon emission prediction research? A comparative study of deep learning models, machine learning models, and econometric models. *Environmental Science and Pollution Research, 31*(13), 19500–19515. https://doi.org/10.1007/s11356-024-32083-w

Yeboah, S. D., Gatsi, J. G., Appiah, M. O., & Fumey, M. P. (2024). Examining the drivers of inclusive growth: A study of economic performance, environmental sustainability, and life expectancy in BRICS economies. *Research in Globalization, 9*, 100267. https://doi.org/10.1016/j.resglo.2024.100267

Yström, A., Plantec, Q., Ferrary, M., Miller, K., Rennings, M., & Sarpong, D. (2025). From science management to innovation management: New forms of science-industry relations and knowledge transfer. *Technovation, 145*, 103257. https://doi.org/10.1016/j.technovation.2025.103257

CHAPTER 15

# New Impact Model of European Industrial Sustainability from the Perspective of the Evolution of R&D Expenditures in the Industry Using Panel Data Analysis

## Introduction

In the contemporary global context, marked by profound structural transformations, climate change challenges and intensifying competitive pressures, the concept of industrial sustainability has become a strategic imperative for the EU. The dual pursuit of economic growth and environmental protection is central to the EU's long-term vision, as reflected in the European Green Deal, the Digital Compass and the Sustainable Development Goals (SDGs). Industry, as a cornerstone of economic productivity, innovation capacity and job creation, faces the necessity to adapt to accelerating technological change, digitalization and environmental regulations that redefine production processes, supply chains and market structures.

Within this framework, research and development (R&D) plays a pivotal role in enabling the transition towards sustainable industrial models. R&D investment not only fosters technological innovation but also underpins the shift towards cleaner production, resource efficiency and the integration of advanced digital solutions in industrial processes. However, the capacity of R&D to drive sustainable industrial transformation depends on several interlinked factors, including the continuity of funding, the adaptation to evolving industrial strategies, the maturity of innovation outputs, and the strategic management of human capital.



C. Fortea, *Sustainable Economic Development and the European Green Deal*, https://doi.org/10.1007/978-3-032-10326-0_15

Although previous studies have addressed the relationship between R&D, industrial competitiveness and sustainability, there is still a scarcity of empirical research that captures these dynamics in an integrated econometric framework at the level of the EU. Existing literature often focuses on isolated relationships, short-term policy impacts or specific industrial sectors, without fully accounting for the structural interplay between technological change, fiscal instruments and innovation capacity across all Member States over time.

This chapter aims to fill this gap by proposing and testing a new impact model of European industrial sustainability from the perspective of the evolution of R&D expenditures in the industry. Using panel data covering the period 2010–2021 for all EU Member States, the analysis investigates the extent to which industrial strategies, environmental taxation, economic growth and R&D personnel influence the capacity of industry to achieve sustainability objectives. The novelty of this approach lies in integrating the temporal sensitivity of R&D effects, the life-cycle dimension of innovation, and the role of human resources into a unified econometric specification.

## Study of Literature and Hypotheses

In the current context, characterized by global challenges such as climate change and economic pressures, industrial sustainability is becoming a central pillar for the sustainable development of the EU. The recognition of the impact that industry has on the environment and society has motivated extensive research in the field of effective industrial sustainability strategies. By applying advanced statistical analysis methodologies on longitudinal datasets, the chapter aims to identify emerging trends and assess the effectiveness of current sustainability policies.

In the context of technological evolution and strategic change in industry, changes in industrial development strategies and technological change, including digitization, induce a high sensitivity of the continuity of R&D efforts, with significant effects on industrial sustainability. This hypothesis is based on the premise that technological innovations and changes in industrial development strategies can significantly influence industry's ability to adapt to change and ensure long-term sustainability.

Expert studies highlight the significant impact of digitization on industrial processes and the way they are managed and carried out (Borowski, 2021; Felsberger et al., 2022). Digitalization brings radical changes in production, management and trade patterns, generating an increased need for adaptation and innovation within industry. Previous research emphasizes that industry is increasingly sensitive to technological change and shifts in development strategies, requiring increased adaptability and flexibility to remain competitive in the marketplace (Napoleone et al., 2023; Atkinson et al., 2022). This is essential to ensure the long-term sustainability of the industry.

Various studies point to the need for significant investment in research and development to meet the demands of a constantly changing industry (Ma et al., 2022; Fang et al., 2022). Improving the capacity to innovate and adapt is essential to ensure the long-term competitiveness and sustainability of industry. Studies (Shet & Pereira, 2021; Yuan & Cao, 2022) show that an industry's ability to remain relevant and competitive in the face of technological and strategic change can have a significant impact on economic and social sustainability. An adaptable and innovative industry can contribute to economic growth and sustainable job creation.

To emphasize the importance of adaptability and innovation within the industry to ensure sustainable development and long-term competitiveness, the following hypothesis can be formulated:

H1: Changes in industrial development strategies or technological impact changes such as digitization induce a high sensitivity of the continuity of R&D efforts with effects on industrial sustainability.

A focus on industrial sustainability, particularly in the context of environmental policy changes such as industrial decarbonization, requires a longer period of continuity to produce significant effects. The short-term sensitivity of industrial development capacity (IDC) is affected by the life-cycle length of innovation products, and environmental objectives require a long-term approach to be effective and sustainable. Numerous studies highlight the importance of industrial decarbonization in the context of combating climate change and reducing greenhouse gas emissions (Nagaj et al., 2024; AbdulRafiu et al., 2022). This implies significant changes in environmental policy and industrial development strategies to promote clean technologies and reduce dependence on fossil fuels. Other studies (Song et al., 2020; Hao et al., 2023) have shown that the life cycle of innovation products, from conception and development to production and disposal, can influence the short-term sensitivity of industrial development capacity to environmental policy changes. Products with longer or more complex life cycles may require more significant adjustments to comply with new environmental regulations. Other studies in the literature (Nilsson et al., 2021; Hainsch et al., 2022) emphasize that transition periods towards industrial sustainability require continuity and long-term commitment from industry actors and policymakers. Sudden changes or lack of continuity can affect the effectiveness and efficiency of environmental protection measures. Some authors consider that moving towards industrial sustainability can have significant effects on long-term industrial and economic development (Fang et al., 2022; Li et al., 2023). Investments in clean technologies and sustainable production practices can bring economic benefits and contribute to increased competitiveness in international markets.

To emphasize the importance of the short-term sensitivity of industrial development capacity to the life-cycle length of innovation products and the need for a long-term approach to achieve environmental and industrial sustainability goals, the following hypothesis can be formulated:

H2: The orientation towards industrial sustainability in the context of changing environmental policies such as industrial decarbonization requires a longer period of continuity, as the short-term sensitivity of RDI is affected by the life-cycle length of innovation products.

R&D investment is one of the main drivers of innovation and economic progress in a society. Sustainable economic growth benefits from the continued contribution of R&D, especially after the completion of initial research projects, are supported by several aspects and links to the literature.

Previous studies (Hai et al., 2022; Hojnik et al., 2022) highlight that R&D investment plays a crucial role in the process of innovation and bringing new products and technologies to the market. R&D investment can boost industrial competitiveness and contribute to economic growth by generating innovations that respond to market needs and bring social and economic benefits. Other studies (Wernicke et al., 2023; Gómez-Marín et al., 2022) emphasize the importance of maturity of research projects in the context of long-term economic benefits. Even after the completion of a research project, the results and knowledge gained can continue to generate value through subsequent innovations and practical applications in various industrial and economic fields. Research (Al-Qudah et al., 2022; Wahab et al., 2022) shows that innovation is a key factor in promoting sustainable development and sustainable economic growth. Continued investment in research and development can contribute to the development of clean, energy-efficient and environmentally friendly technologies that support the transition to a green economy and reduce negative impacts on natural resources and the environment. Investing in R&D can have long-term economic benefits, including increasing competitiveness, boosting job creation, improving quality of life and promoting sustainable economic growth overall (Vîrjan et al., 2023; European Investment Bank Investment Barriers in the European Union, 2023).

The transition to a green economy is on the European agenda as a main objective, alongside climate neutrality, which is scheduled to be implemented by 2050. To achieve this significant goal, the EU is promoting a regulatory framework based on directives, actions and plans aimed at linking the economy to sustainable development objectives and projects to protect the environment and combat climate change. In this context, Fortea and colleagues (Fortea et al., 2024) conducted a study on the economic-energy impact of the transition to a green economy, selecting six countries according to the criteria for action against climate change and greenhouse gas emission reduction targets for 2020. The six Member States were Belgium, France, Italy, Germany, Luxembourg, the Netherlands. The research developed an econometric model of the economic-energy impact of the transition to the green economy, based on a methodology that included econometric modelling of databases using the multiple linear regression method and the use of the generalized linear mixed model to quantify the effort of transition to the green economy in the countries under study. The results of the study assessed the level of impact of renewable energy use on financial development and economic growth and quantified the effects of the implementation of the transition to the green economy in terms of costs and benefits of implementation.

Investments in R&D generate innovations and advanced technologies that support the transition to a green economy and contribute to increased competitiveness and long-term economic sustainability. These aspects help to formulate the following:

H3: Sustainable economic growth benefits from R&D input once research projects reach maturity.

In an economy increasingly oriented towards innovation and technological progress, investment in R&D is becoming more and more relevant to sustain economic growth and market competitiveness. There is a significant link between R&D personnel and gross domestic expenditure on R&D. Studies in the literature have highlighted the importance of human resources in the innovation process and their impact on the effectiveness of financial investment in R&D (Anagnostopoulou & Avgoustaki, 2023; Perez-Alaniz et al., 2023).

Much research has captured the importance of R&D personnel in the innovation process (Engelsberger et al., 2022; Yin et al., 2023). The experience, skills and creativity of employees in R&D departments can significantly influence an organization's ability to generate new ideas, develop innovative products and remain competitive in the marketplace. Financial investment in R&D is a measure of an organization's commitment to innovation and development (Rodrigo et al., 2022; Doni, 2024). These expenditures include salary costs of R&D personnel, purchase of equipment and materials, and other resources needed for R&D activities. Multiple studies (Li-Ying et al., 2022; Adomako & Ahsan, 2022) highlight the close interdependence between R&D personnel and the availability of financial resources for R&D. Well-trained and motivated staff can contribute to the efficient use of financial resources and maximize the impact of R&D investments. A well-coordinated and motivated R&D team can generate synergies and better results than the sum of individual contributions. Thus, a positive relationship between R&D personnel and gross domestic expenditure on R&D may indicate greater efficiency in the use of resources and greater innovativeness of the organization (Erdin & Çağlar, 2023; Zhang & Huang, 2022).

Investment in skilled human resources in R&D can influence the level and effectiveness of financial investment in R&D, thereby helping to stimulate innovation and economic progress. In view of the above to support the importance of strategic management of human and financial resources in R&D to achieve innovation and economic growth objectives, the following can be hypothesized:

H4: There is a significant relationship between R&D personnel and gross domestic expenditure on R&D.

## Data and Method

The following indicators were used to develop the econometric model: gross domestic expenditure on research and development (SDG9CHCDI), environmental taxes (SDG9TAXM), gross domestic product per capita (SDG9GDP per capita) and R&D personnel (SDG9PCDI).

These indicators have been assessed on the basis of descriptive statistics for the period 2010–2021 taking into account the national developments of each indicator for all EU Member States, the database being organized in panel data as presented in Table 15.1. The results of the descriptive analysis are presented in Table 15.1.

The descriptive statistics table shows that the European average of R&D expenditure as a percentage of GDP is 1.61%, being aligned under the Gaussian distribution curve between the minimum point of 0.38% of GDP (recorded in Romania in 2014) and the maximum point of 3.71% of GDP (in Finland in 2010). The standard deviation is about 50% of the mean value, confirming the tendency of frequency clustering below the Gaussian curve. The share of environment-related taxes is on average 2.65% of GDP at the European level, showing a significant difference with the share of R&D expenditures, the variation being positive in favour of the environmental tax by more than 1%, an unfavourable aspect for the implementation of industrial sustainability. The distribution of frequencies falls also in this case in the Gaussian curve with a minimum point of 1.01% of GDP (recorded in 2021 in Ireland) and a maximum point of 4.64% of GDP (in Slovenia in 2016).

In terms of gross domestic product per capita there is a leftward deviation of the average (25625.12 euro per capita) from the Gaussian frequency curve with a minimum of 5080 in 2010 in Bulgaria and a maximum of 84840 in Luxembourg in 2016. The level of frequency disparity is

**Table 15.1** Descriptive statistics

| *Variable* | *SDG9CHCDI* | *SDG9TAXM* | *SDG9PIBloc* | *SDG9PCDI* |
|---|---|---|---|---|
| Comments | 324 | 324 | 324 | 324 |
| Average | 1.61 | 2.65 | 25625.12 | 1.17 |
| Standard deviation | 0.88 | 0.71 | 16820.57 | 0.52 |
| Minim | 0.38 | 1.01 | 5080 | 0 |
| Maxim | 3.71 | 4.64 | 84840 | 2.32 |

Source: Author

significant at 16493.33 euro per capita and testifies to the differences in the economic development of the Member States, which constitutes a limit to the economic sustainability of the EU. The number of R&D personnel is also low, the European average being 1.17% of the employed population, which confirms the poor results of industrial reform from the R&D perspective.

Variable testing was carried out as a preliminary step in the conceptualization of the model, the first tests being the autocorrelation tests presented in Table 15.2.

According to the results in Table 15.2 the lack of autocorrelation is observed, the values of the coefficients being lower than the autocorrelation threshold of 0.7, which allows modelling the data.

The Levin-Lin-Chin, Breitung, Im-Pesaran-Shin, ADF-Fisher Chi-square, PP-Fisher Chi-square and Hadri stationarity tests were applied. The results are presented centralized in Table 15.3.

Five different two-order (Order 0 and Order 1) stationarity tests were applied for four data series (SDG9CHCI, SDG9TAXM, SDG9PIBloc, SDG9PCDI). The tests aim to determine the stationarity of the data by rejecting the null hypothesis. The value of the statistical test and the associated *p*-value confirm the stationarity of 0 or 1 order of the variables.

The stationarity of a time series is an important property in time analysis, indicating that the statistical properties of the series (mean and variance) do not change over time.

According to the Levin-Lin-Chin test, it follows that smaller and significantly negative values ($p < 0.05$) indicate stationarity. Another test for stationarity is Breitung, with similar results to Levin-Lin-Chin. Negative values indicate stationarity, and positive values indicate non-stationarity. Thus, for SDG9CHCI at Order 1, the test value is −2.260 indicating stationarity ($p = 0.012$). In the case of the Im-Pesaran-Shin test significant

**Table 15.2** Correlation matrix

| *Variable* | *SDG9CHCDI* | *SDG9TAXM* | *SDG9PIBloc* | *SDG9PCDI* |
|---|---|---|---|---|
| SDG9CHCDI | 1.000 | | | |
| SDG9TAXM | 0.0330 | 1.000 | | |
| SDG9PIBloc | 0.4667 | −0.2205 | 1.000 | |
| SDG9PCDI | 0.6500 | 0.0119 | 0.6476 | 1.000 |

Source: Author

**Table 15.3** Stationarity tests

| *Stationarity test* | *SDG9CHCI* | | *SDG9TAXM* | | *SDG9PIBloc* | | *SDG9PCDI* | |
|---|---|---|---|---|---|---|---|---|
| | *Order 0* | *Order 1* | *Order 0* | *Order 1* | *Order 0* | *Order 1* | *Order 0* | *Order 1* |
| Levin-Lin-Chin | −2.884 | NA | −4.336 | NA | −3.437 | NA | −3.408 | NA |
| | (0.002) | | (0.000) | | (0.000) | | (0.000) | |
| Breitung | 3.860 | −2.260 | −0.393 | −3.275 | 0.136 | −4.192 | 3.814 | 0.259 |
| | (0.999) | (0.012) | (0.347) | (0.001) | (0.554) | (0.000) | (0.999) | (0.602) |
| Im-Pesaran-Shin | 1.284 | −2.636 | 0.214 | −2.731 | 0.735 | −1.343 | 1.029 | −0.790 |
| | (0.901) | (0.004) | (0.585) | (0.003) | (0.769) | (0.090) | (0.848) | (0.215) |
| ADF-Fisher | 49.113 | 94.161 | 88.940 | NA | 45.016 | 118.477 | 52.329 | 72.898 |
| Chi-square | (0.663) | (0.001) | (0.002) | | (0.803) | (0.000) | (0.539) | (0.044) |
| PP-Fisher | 42.053 | 238.456 | 47.682 | 182.331 | 45.016 | 118.477 | 105.660 | 171.617 |
| Chi-square | (0.663) | (0.000) | (0.715) | (0.000) | (0.803) | (0.000) | (0.000) | (0.000) |
| Hadri | 8.166 | 10.265 | 17.584 | 4.311 | 29.352 | 1.634 | 8.604 | 8.190 |
| | (0.000) | (0.000) | (0.000) | (0.000) | (0.000) | (0.051) | (0.000) | (0.000) |

Source: Author

negative values indicate stationarity (SDG9TAXM at Order 1 has a value of −2.731 ($p$ = 0.003), indicating stationarity). The ADF-Fisher Chi-square test was applied, with results indicating stationarity values (SDG9PCDI at Order 1 has a $p$-value of 0.000 in PP-Fisher, indicating stationarity). The last Hadri test indicates non-stationarity (for SDG9LPIB at Order 0, the value is 29.352 ($p$ = 0.000), suggesting that the series is non-stationary at this level).

Thus, it follows that all the series are integrations of Order 1 and we will proceed to check for cointegration to determine whether there is a long-run relationship. Following the application of the cointegration test, the null hypothesis that the series are not cointegrated is accepted and the vector autoregression (VAR) model is chosen for the estimation, which means that we are dealing with a short-run model. In a VAR system, all variables are endogenous.

The model equation is as follows:

$$Y_{it} = \sum_{j=1}^{p} \lambda_{ij} Y_{i,t-j} + \sum_{j=0}^{q} \delta_{ij} X_{i,t-j} + \mu_i + \xi_{it} \tag{15.1}$$

where

$Y_{it}$ = dependent variable for group $i$
$X_{it}$ = vector of exogenous variables for group $i$
$\lambda_{ij}$ and $\delta_{ij}$ = the vector of coefficients, the groups are denoted by $i$, while $t$ is the time period
$\mu_i$ = fixed effects
$\xi_{it}$ = random variable

The dependent variable is represented by its lagged values and the lagged values of the other variables.

The regression order of the independent variables was set to two, so the model that will estimate the relationship between the variables is of the form:

$$\begin{aligned} \text{SDG9CHCDI}_{it} = {} & \beta_{0i} + \delta_1 \text{SDG9CHCDI}_{it-1} + \delta_2 \text{SDG9CHCDI}_{it-2} \\ & + \beta_1 \text{SDG9LPIBloc}_{it-1} + \beta_2 \text{SDG9LPIBloc}_{it-2} \\ & + \beta_3 \text{SDG9TAXM}_{it-1} + \beta_4 \text{SDG9TAXM}_{it-2} \\ & + \beta_5 \text{SDG9PCDI}_{it-1} + \beta_6 \text{SDG9PCDI}_{it-2} + \vartheta_{it} \end{aligned} \tag{15.2}$$

Applying the Hausman test, the fixed-effects model was established. The results of the Chi-square test indicate the rejection of the null hypothesis, and the small value of the probability (Prob > Chi2 = 0.0000) shows that the differences between these coefficients are significant at the level of the whole model.

## Results and Discussions

The fixed-effects model analyses the dependence of gross domestic expenditure on R&D (SDG9CHCDI) using a panel of data covering the 27 EU Member States over a 10-year period (2012–2021), recording a total of 270 observations. The methodology adopted is Panel Least Squares with fixed-effects specification (Table 15.4).

The values of the statistical determinants of representativeness, $R$-squared (0.991) and adjusted $R$-squared (0.990), are high, indicating

**Table 15.4** Fixed-effects model

| *Variable* | *Coefficients* | *Standard error* | *t-Statistic* | *Probability* |
|---|---|---|---|---|
| SDG9CHCDI(−1) | 0.864 | 0.061 | 14.164 | 0.000 |
| SDG9CHCDI(−2) | −0.186 | 0.057 | −3.259 | 0.001 |
| SDG9TAXM(−1) | 0.018 | 0.039 | 0.465 | 0.642 |
| SDG9TAXM(−2) | 0.050 | 0.039 | 1.253 | 0.211 |
| SDG9LPIBLOC(1) | 0.172 | 0.437 | 0.394 | 0.693 |
| SDG9LPIBLOC(2) | 0.140 | 0.433 | 0.323 | 0.746 |
| SDG9PCDI(−1) | 0.182 | 0.101 | 1.810 | 0.071 |
| SDG9PCDI(−2) | −0.007 | 0.083 | −0.087 | 0.930 |
| C | −1.207 | 0.867 | −1.392 | 0.165 |
| | *Effects specification* | | | |
| *Fixed cross-section (dummy variables)* | | | | |
| $R$-square | 0.991 | Average dep. | | 1.633 |
| Adjusted $R$-squared | 0.990 | Standard deviation dep. | | 0.884 |
| Standard error | 0.087 | Akaike info criteria | | −1.912 |
| Residual square | 1.801 | Schwarz criterion | | −1.446 |
| Probability log | 293.217 | The Hannan-Quinn criterion. | | −1.725 |
| F-statistic | 800.806 | Durbin-Watson | | 2.214 |
| Prob (F-statistic) | 0.000 | | | |

Source: Author

that the model explains almost all the variation in R&D expenditure based on the included variables (SDG9TAXM, SDG9LPIBLOC and SDG9PCDI). The Durbin-Watson coefficient statistic has a value of 2.214, suggesting that there is no significant residual autocorrelation between terms and there is good independence between observations. The F-function value and significance coefficient indicate that the model is overall statistically significant. The analysis suggests that gross domestic R&D expenditures are influenced by their past values, while the impact of environmental taxes, GDP per capita and R&D personnel is limited and requires a prudent policy approach to limit external vulnerabilities induced by economic shocks, industrial changes under the impact of environmental requirements and fluctuations in R&D personnel.

SDG9CHCDI(−1) and SDG9CHCDI(−2) are the coefficients of the lag of gross domestic expenditure on R&D, indicating the influence of the previous values of the same variables on the current values. The coefficient for SDG9CHCDI(−1) is positive and significant (0.864), suggesting a positive and strong relationship between the previous value of R&D expenditure and the current value. In contrast, the coefficient for SDG9CHCDI(−2) is negative (−0.186) and statistically significant, indicating a negative influence of the values two periods ago on current value. This demonstrates working hypothesis 1: Changes in industrial development strategies or technological impact changes such as digitization induce a high sensitivity of the continuity of R&D efforts with effects on industrial sustainability. This evolution of the coefficients (SDG9CHCDI(−1) and SDG9CHCDI(−2)) is in line with the significant changes of industrial revolutions under the impact of Industry 5.0 and digitalization, which have altered approaches in industrial research by transferring research efforts from the area of conventional industry to the area of digital technologies research and advanced automation. This shift reflects global trends to modernize and optimize industrial processes to meet increasingly complex market requirements and to capitalize on the advantages of emerging technologies.

The main challenge for researchers was the short-term changes to projects that had to be adapted on the fly to the new industrial reality.

Hypothesis 1 suggests that changes in industrial development strategies or technological changes, including those related to digitization, induce an increased sensitivity of the continuity of R&D efforts, with effects on industrial sustainability. The results obtained from the analysis of SDG9CHCDI(−1) and SDG9CHCDI(−2) coefficients support this hypothesis, highlighting the importance of continuing R&D investments and constantly adapting to new industrial paradigms.

Compared to the literature, these results are in line with perspectives in the field of economic and industrial studies. Much research has emphasized the importance of continuous innovation and adaptation to technological change for maintaining industrial competitiveness and sustainability (Teixeira & Tavares-Lehmann, 2022; Brodny & Tutak, 2023; Hajighasemi et al., 2022). Moreover, digitization and new technologies are recognized as key factors in shaping the industrial future, with the potential to revolutionize R&D processes and improve industrial efficiency and sustainability (Mondejar et al., 2021; Alojail & Khan, 2023; Commission, E, et al., 2022).

SDG9TAXM(−1) and SDG9TAXM(−2) represent the effect of the delay in environmental taxes on gross domestic expenditure on R&D. Both coefficients are positive (0.018 and 0.050), but not statistically significant, implying that the orientation towards industrial sustainability in the context of environmental policy changes such as industrial decarbonization requires a longer period of continuity, the short-run sensitivity of RDI being affected by the life-cycle length of innovation products, thus demonstrating working hypothesis 2. This reflects the need to implement policies that incentivize R&D investments through green taxation and to accelerate the transition to green industry as a European objective committed by the European Green Pact.

The SDG9TAXM(−1) and SDG9TAXM(−2) coefficients are used to assess the effect of the delay in environmental taxes on gross domestic expenditure on research and development. In this case, both coefficients are positive, indicating a positive correlation between environmental taxes and R&D expenditure. However, these coefficients are not statistically significant, meaning that the observed relationship is not strong enough to be considered statistically different from zero.

These results support Hypothesis 2, according to which moving towards industrial sustainability in the context of changing environmental policies requires a longer period of continuity. It is argued that the short-run sensitivity of R&D expenditures is affected by the life-cycle length of innovation products. In other words, changes in environmental policies, such as industrial decarbonization, may take time to show their impact on R&D investments, and this influence may be influenced by the length of time it takes for new technologies and innovations to be developed and widely adopted.

Compared with the literature, these results are in line with insights from economics and public policy. Much research has shown that the implementation of environmental policies can have varied and often lagged effects on firms' behaviour and investment in innovation (Flachenecker et al., 2022; Süsser et al., 2022; Rodríguez-Antón et al., 2022). It is also recognized that the transition to a greener economy requires a holistic and continuous approach, addressing regulatory, technology, financing and other relevant factors (Chatzistamoulou & Tyllianakis, 2022; Cheba et al., 2022; Vezzoni, 2023).

The results thus provide support for the need for coherent and long-term environmental policies to stimulate R&D investment towards a more sustainable and resilient economy.

SDG9LLPIBLOC(−1) and SDG9LPIBLOC(−2) represent the influence of the lag of GDP per capita on R&D expenditure, and have positive but weakly statistically significant coefficients, which demonstrates the third working hypothesis, i.e. sustainable economic growth benefits from R&D input after the maturity of research projects. Under the impact of new transformations in European industry, sustainable economic growth has not benefited from the full contribution of RDI, with some projects requiring additional time to reach maturity, which has affected the effectiveness of RDI in transition periods.

Both coefficients are positive, indicating a positive correlation between the previous level of GDP and current R&D expenditure. However, the coefficients are not statistically significant, meaning that the observed relationship is not statistically strong enough.

These results support Hypothesis 3 that sustainable economic growth benefits from R&D input after the maturity of research projects. As R&D projects may take time to reach their full potential and have a significant impact on the economy, their influence may not be immediately visible. This delay in the manifestation of R&D&I effects can be explained by the complexity of the innovation process and the time needed for the adoption and adaptation of new technologies and practices in industry.

Compared to the literature, these results reflect the common understanding that R&D investment is often a vital component of a sustainable and innovative economy (Bórawski et al., 2022; Sarpong et al., 2023; Michalak & Wolniak, 2023). Many studies have shown that innovations and new technologies can drive long-term economic growth, but it may take considerable time for these benefits to become evident (Blind et al., 2022; Acheampong et al., 2022). It is also recognized that the innovation process may be influenced by external factors such as government policies, regulations and market conditions, which may explain the delay in the manifestation of the effects of R&D&I (Alegre et al., 2024; Anzola-Román et al., 2024).

The results therefore underline the importance of sustaining continued R&D efforts, even in times of economic transition, to ensure sustainable and resilient economic growth in the EU and other regions.

SDG9PCDI(−1) and SDG9PCDI(−2) illustrate the effect of R&D personnel on gross domestic expenditure on R&D. The coefficient for SDG9PCDI(−1) is positive (0.182) and significant at the 10% confidence level ($p = 0.071$), suggesting a positive relationship, which demonstrates working hypothesis 4, that is, there is a significant relationship between R&D personnel and gross domestic expenditure on R&D. This indicates that a higher number of researchers and developers is associated with higher R&D expenditure.

The new model of industrial sustainability confirms the urgent need to improve the quantity of R&D allocations supported by an effective training programme leading to an increase in the number of R&D personnel and the development of innovative solutions to accelerate the transition to Industry 5.0 and green industry. These results support Hypothesis 4 that there is a significant relationship between R&D personnel and gross domestic R&D expenditure. This is in line with the common understanding that investment in human capital, including R&D, can be a key factor in boosting innovation and economic growth.

In terms of comparisons with the literature, our results are in line with the findings of several studies that have shown a positive association between the number of researchers and developers and R&D expenditure in different sectors and countries (Grafström et al., 2023; Zastempowski, 2023; Abbas et al., 2023). Previous research has also emphasized the importance of investing in skilled human resources and innovation capacity building to support the transition to more sustainable and innovation-oriented economies (Yadav et al., 2023; Diodato et al., 2023; Wigger, 2023).

Our findings therefore underline the need to promote investment in R&D personnel and to develop effective training programmes to support the transition to a greener and more innovative industry. These efforts could be significant for accelerating the transition to Industry 5.0 and promoting sustainable development in the current context of accelerated technological and industrial change.

## Conclusions

The econometric analysis conducted in this chapter confirms the decisive role of research and development (R&D) in shaping the trajectory of European industrial sustainability, especially in the context of accelerated technological transformations, digitalization and the twin green–digital transition. The results obtained through the fixed-effects panel model for EU Member States over the period 2012–2021 provide robust empirical evidence in support of the four research hypotheses formulated.

First, the strong and statistically significant influence of lagged R&D expenditures validates the premise that changes in industrial strategies and technological paradigms—particularly those induced by Industry 5.0 and advanced digitalization—generate heightened sensitivity in the continuity of R&D efforts, with direct implications for industrial sustainability. This underlines the necessity for stable, predictable and well-targeted R&D policies capable of ensuring adaptability to industrial paradigm shifts.

Second, although environmental taxation shows a positive but statistically weak correlation with R&D expenditure, the results support the idea that environmental policy instruments, such as decarbonization measures, require long-term continuity to produce substantial effects on industrial innovation capacity. The time lag inherent in the life cycle of innovation products calls for policy frameworks that integrate fiscal incentives with sustained R&D support to accelerate the transition towards a green economy.

Third, the delayed but positive relationship between GDP per capita and R&D expenditure reinforces the view that sustainable economic growth benefits significantly from R&D outputs once research projects reach maturity. The findings highlight the strategic importance of maintaining R&D funding throughout transitional economic phases to secure long-term competitiveness and resilience.

Fourth, the significant association between the number of R&D personnel and the volume of R&D expenditure demonstrates the critical role of human capital in leveraging financial resources for innovation. Strengthening the skills base and expanding the pool of qualified researchers emerges as a cornerstone for advancing industrial sustainability and ensuring a smooth transition to Industry 5.0.

Overall, the proposed new model of industrial sustainability suggests that the EU's industrial policy must combine consistent financial commitments to R&D with human capital development, coherent environmental taxation and strategic planning for technological transitions. Such an integrated approach can enhance the capacity of European industry to innovate, decarbonize, and remain competitive in an increasingly complex and environmentally constrained global economy.

## References

Abbas, K., Butt, K. M., Xu, D., Baz, K., Sheraz, M., & Kharl, S. H. (2023). Dynamic prognostic interaction between social development and energy consumption optimization: Evidence from European Union member countries. *Energy, 278*, 127791. https://doi.org/10.1016/j.energy.2023.127791

AbdulRafiu, A., Sovacool, B. K., & Daniels, C. (2022). The dynamics of global public research funding on climate change, energy, transport, and industrial decarbonisation. *Renewable and Sustainable Energy Reviews, 162*, 112420. https://doi.org/10.1016/j.rser.2022.112420

Acheampong, A. O., Dzator, J., Dzator, M., & Salim, R. (2022). Unveiling the effect of transport infrastructure and technological innovation on economic growth, energy consumption and CO2 emissions. *Technological Forecasting and Social Change, 182*, 121843. https://doi.org/10.1016/j.techfore.2022.121843

Adomako, S., & Ahsan, M. (2022). Entrepreneurial passion and SMEs' performance: Moderating effects of financial resource availability and resource flexibility. *Journal of Business Research, 144*, 122–135. https://doi.org/10.1016/j.jbusres.2022.02.002

Alegre, I., Berbegal-Mirabent, J., & Martin-Sanchez, V. (2024). The role of experience and diversity on research consortia' performance: An exploratory approach. *Small Business Economics*. https://doi.org/10.1007/s11187-024-00894-3

Alojail, M., & Khan, S. B. (2023). Impact of digital transformation toward sustainable development. *Sustainability*, 15.

Al-Qudah, A. A., Al-Okaily, M., & Alqudah, H. (2022). The relationship between social entrepreneurship and sustainable development from economic growth perspective: 15 "RCEP" countries. *Journal of Sustainable Finance & Investment, 12*, 44–61. https://doi.org/10.1080/20430795.2021.1880219

Anagnostopoulou, S. C., & Avgoustaki, A. (2023). The impact of human resource practices on corporate investment efficiency. *International Review of Financial Analysis, 87*, 102609. https://doi.org/10.1016/j.irfa.2023.102609

Anzola-Román, P., Garcia-Marco, T., & Zouaghi, F. (2024). The influence of CSR orientation on innovative performance: Is the effect conditioned to the implementation of organizational practices? *Journal of Business Ethics, 190*, 261–278. https://doi.org/10.1007/s10551-023-05406-z

Atkinson, P., Hizaji, M., Nazarian, A., & Abasi, A. (2022). Attaining organisational agility through competitive intelligence: The roles of strategic flexibility and organisational innovation. *Total Quality Management and Business Excellence, 33*, 297–317. https://doi.org/10.1080/14783363.2020.1842188

Blind, K., Ramel, F., & Rochell, C. (2022). The influence of standards and patents on long-term economic growth. *The Journal of Technology Transfer, 47*, 979–999. https://doi.org/10.1007/s10961-021-09864-3

Bórawski, P., Wyszomierski, R., Bełdycka-Bórawska, A., Mickiewicz, B., Kalinowska, B., Dunn, J. W., & Rokicki, T. (2022). Development of renewable energy sources in the European Union in the context of sustainable development policy. *Energies*, 15.

Borowski, P. F. (2021). Digitization, digital twins, blockchain, and industry 4.0 as elements of management process in enterprises in the energy sector. *Energies*, 14.

Brodny, J., & Tutak, M. (2023). The level of implementing sustainable development goal "Industry, Innovation and Infrastructure" of agenda 2030 in the European Union countries: Application of MCDM methods. *Oeconomia Copernicana, 14*, 47–102. https://doi.org/10.24136/oc.2023.002

Chatzistamoulou, N., & Tyllianakis, E. (2022). Green growth & sustainability transition through information. Are the greener better informed? Evidence from European SMEs. *Journal of Environmental Management, 306*, 114457. https://doi.org/10.1016/j.jenvman.2022.114457

Cheba, K., Bąk, I., Szopik-Depczyńska, K., & Ioppolo, G. (2022). Directions of green transformation of the European Union countries. *Ecological Indicators, 136*, 108601. https://doi.org/10.1016/j.ecolind.2022.108601

Commission, E, Centre, J. R., Muench, S., Stoermer, E., Jensen, K., Asikainen, T., Salvi, M., & Scapolo, F. (2022). *Towards a green & digital future – Key requirements for successful twin transitions in the European Union*. Publications Office of the European Union.

Diodato, D., Huergo, E., Moncada-Paternò-Castello, P., Rentocchini, F., & Timmermans, B. (2023). Introduction to the special issue on "the Twin (Digital and Green) Transition": Handling the economic and social challenges. *Industry and Innovation, 30*, 755–765. https://doi.org/10.1080/13662716.2023.2254272

Doni, F.; Fiameni, M. Can innovation affect the relationship between environmental, social, and governance issues and financial performance? Empirical evidence from the STOXX200 index. Business Strategy and the Environment 2024, 33, 546–574, https://doi.org/10.1002/bse.3500.

Engelsberger, A., Halvorsen, B., Cavanagh, J., & Bartram, T. (2022). Human resources management and open innovation: The role of open innovation mindset. *Asia-Pacific Journal of Human Resources, 60*, 194–215. https://doi.org/10.1111/1744-7941.12281

Erdin, C., & Çağlar, M. (2023). National innovation efficiency: A DEA-based measurement of OECD countries. *International Journal of Innovation Science, 15*, 427–456. https://doi.org/10.1108/IJIS-07-2021-0118

European Investment Bank Investment Barriers in the European Union. (2023). Luxembourg, 2023.

Fang, W., Liu, Z., & Surya Putra, A. R. (2022). Role of research and development in green economic growth through renewable energy development: Empirical evidence from South Asia. *Renewable Energy, 194*, 1142–1152. https://doi.org/10.1016/j.renene.2022.04.125

Felsberger, A., Qaiser, F. H., Choudhary, A., & Reiner, G. (2022). The impact of industry 4.0 on the reconciliation of dynamic capabilities: Evidence from the European manufacturing industries. *Production Planning and Control, 33*, 277–300. https://doi.org/10.1080/09537287.2020.1810765

Flachenecker, F., Kornejew, M., & Janiri, M. L. (2022). The effects of publicly supported environmental innovations on firm growth in the European Union. *Journal of Cleaner Production, 372*, 133429. https://doi.org/10.1016/j.jclepro.2022.133429

Fortea, C., Dinca, M. S., Ionescu, R. V., Zlati, M. L., & Antohi, V.-M. (2024). Analyzing the socio-economic and energy implications of green economy transition across six EU member states. *European Research Studies Journal, XXVII*, 288–301. https://doi.org/10.35808/ersj/3361

Gómez-Marín, N., Cara-Jiménez, J., Bernardo-Sánchez, A., Álvarez-de-Prado, L., & Ortega-Fernández, F. (2022). Sustainable knowledge management in academia and research organizations in the innovation context. *International Journal of Management Education, 20*, 100601. https://doi.org/10.1016/j.ijme.2022.100601

Grafström, J., Söderholm, P., Gawel, E., Lehmann, P., & Strunz, S. (2023). Government support to renewable energy R&D: Drivers and strategic interactions among EU member states. *Economics of Innovation and New Technology, 32*, 1–24. https://doi.org/10.1080/10438599.2020.1857499

Hai, B., Yin, X., Xiong, J., & Chen, J. (2022). Could more innovation output bring better financial performance? The role of financial constraints. *Financial Innovation, 8*, 6. https://doi.org/10.1186/s40854-021-00309-2

Hainsch, K., Löffler, K., Burandt, T., Auer, H., Crespo del Granado, P., Pisciella, P., & Zwickl-Bernhard, S. (2022). Energy transition scenarios: What policies, societal attitudes, and technology developments will realize the EU green deal? *Energy, 239*, 122067. https://doi.org/10.1016/j.energy.2021.122067

Hajighasemi, A., Oghazi, P., Aliyari, S., & Pashkevich, N. (2022). The impact of welfare state systems on innovation performance and competitiveness: European Country clusters. *Journal of Innovation and Knowledge, 7*, 100236. https://doi.org/10.1016/j.jik.2022.100236

Hao, X., Wen, S., Sun, Q., Irfan, M., Wu, H., & Hao, Y. (2023). How does the target of green innovation for cleaner production change in management process? Quality targeting and link targeting. *Journal of Environmental Management, 345*, 118832. https://doi.org/10.1016/j.jenvman.2023.118832

Hojnik, J., Prokop, V., & Stejskal, J. (2022). R&D as bridge to sustainable development? Case of Czech Republic and Slovenia. *Corporate Social Responsibility and Environmental Management, 29*, 146–160. https://doi.org/10.1002/csr.2190

Li, Z., Wu, Y., Rasoulinezhad, E., Sheng, Y., & Bi, C. (2023). Green economic recovery in Central Asia by utilizing natural resources. *Resources Policy, 83*, 103621. https://doi.org/10.1016/j.resourpol.2023.103621

Li-Ying, J., Sofka, W., & Tuertscher, P. (2022). Managing innovation ecosystems around big science organizations. *Technovation, 116*, 102523. https://doi.org/10.1016/j.technovation.2022.102523

Ma, Q., Tariq, M., Mahmood, H., & Khan, Z. (2022). The Nexus between digital economy and carbon dioxide emissions in China: The moderating role of investments in research and development. *Technology in Society, 68*, 101910. https://doi.org/10.1016/j.techsoc.2022.101910

Michalak, A., & Wolniak, R. (2023). The innovativeness of the country and the renewables and non-renewables in the energy mix on the example of European Union. *Journal of Open Innovation: Technology, Market, and Complexity, 9*, 100061. https://doi.org/10.1016/j.joitmc.2023.100061

Mondejar, M. E., Avtar, R., Diaz, H. L. B., Dubey, R. K., Esteban, J., Gómez-Morales, A., Hallam, B., Mbungu, N. T., Okolo, C. C., Prasad, K. A., et al. (2021). Digitalization to achieve sustainable development goals: Steps towards a smart green planet. *Science of the Total Environment, 794*, 148539. https://doi.org/10.1016/j.scitotenv.2021.148539

Nagaj, R., Gajdzik, B., Wolniak, R., & Grebski, W. W. (2024). The impact of deep decarbonization policy on the level of greenhouse gas emissions in the European Union. *Energies*, 17.

Napoleone, A., Pozzetti, A., Macchi, M., & Andersen, R. (2023). Time to be responsive in the process industry: A literature-based analysis of trends of change, solutions and challenges. *Production Planning and Control, 34*, 572–586. https://doi.org/10.1080/09537287.2021.1942282

Nilsson, L. J., Bauer, F., Åhman, M., Andersson, F. N. G., Bataille, C., de la Rue du Can, S., Ericsson, K., Hansen, T., Johansson, B., Lechtenböhmer, S., et al. (2021). An industrial policy framework for transforming energy and emissions intensive industries towards zero emissions. *Climate Policy, 21*, 1053–1065. https://doi.org/10.1080/14693062.2021.1957665

Perez-Alaniz, M., Lenihan, H., Doran, J., & Hewitt-Dundas, N. (2023). Financial resources for research and innovation in small and larger firms: Is it a case of the more you have, the more you do? *Industry and Innovation, 30*, 189–232. https://doi.org/10.1080/13662716.2022.2036597

Rodrigo, L., Ortiz-Marcos, I., Palacios, M., & Romero, J. (2022). Success of organisations developing digital social innovation: Analysis of motivational key drivers. *Journal of Business Research, 144*, 854–862. https://doi.org/10.1016/j.jbusres.2022.02.029

Rodríguez-Antón, J. M., Rubio-Andrada, L., Celemín-Pedroche, M. S., & Ruíz-Peñalver, S. M. (2022). From the circular economy to the sustainable development goals in the European Union: An empirical comparison. *International Environmental Agreements: Politics, Law and Economics, 22*, 67–95. https://doi.org/10.1007/s10784-021-09553-4

Sarpong, D., Boakye, D., Ofosu, G., & Botchie, D. (2023). The three pointers of research and development (R&D) for growth-boosting sustainable innovation system. *Technovation, 122*, 102581. https://doi.org/10.1016/j.technovation.2022.102581

Shet, S. V., & Pereira, V. (2021). Proposed managerial competencies for industry 4.0 – Implications for social sustainability. *Technological Forecasting and Social Change, 173*, 121080. https://doi.org/10.1016/j.techfore.2021.121080

Song, M., Wang, S., & Zhang, H. (2020). Could environmental regulation and R&D tax incentives affect green product innovation? *Journal of Cleaner Production, 258*, 120849. https://doi.org/10.1016/j.jclepro.2020.120849

Süsser, D., Martin, N., Stavrakas, V., Gaschnig, H., Talens-Peiró, L., Flamos, A., Madrid-López, C., & Lilliestam, J. (2022). Why energy models should integrate social and environmental factors: Assessing user needs, omission impacts, and real-word accuracy in the European Union. *Energy Research and Social Science, 92*, 102775. https://doi.org/10.1016/j.erss.2022.102775

Teixeira, J. E., & Tavares-Lehmann, A. T. C. P. (2022). Industry 4.0 in the European Union: Policies and national strategies. *Technological Forecasting and Social Change, 180*, 121664. https://doi.org/10.1016/j.techfore.2022.121664

Vezzoni, R. (2023). Green growth for whom, how and why? The REPowerEU plan and the inconsistencies of European Union energy policy. *Energy Research and Social Science, 101*, 103134. https://doi.org/10.1016/j.erss.2023.103134

Vîrjan, D., Manole, A. M., Stanef-Puică, M. R., Chenic, A. S., Papuc, C. M., Huru, D., & Bănacu, C. S. (2023). Competitiveness—The engine that boosts economic growth and revives the economy. *Frontiers in Environmental Science*, 11.

Wahab, S., Imran, M., Safi, A., Wahab, Z., & Kirikkaleli, D. (2022). Role of financial stability, technological innovation, and renewable energy in achieving sustainable development goals in BRICS countries. *Environmental Science and Pollution Research, 29*, 48827–48838. https://doi.org/10.1007/s11356-022-18810-1

Wernicke, B., Stehn, L., Sezer, A. A., & Thunberg, M. (2023). Introduction of a digital maturity assessment framework for construction site operations. *International Journal of Construction Management, 23*, 898–908. https://doi.org/10.1080/15623599.2021.1943629

Wigger, A. (2023). The new EU industrial policy and deepening structural asymmetries: Smart specialisation not so smart. *JCMS: Journal of Common Market Studies, 61*, 20–37. https://doi.org/10.1111/jcms.13366

Yadav, S., Samadhiya, A., Kumar, A., Majumdar, A., Garza-Reyes, J. A., & Luthra, S. (2023). Achieving the sustainable development goals through net zero emissions: Innovation-driven strategies for transitioning from incremental to radical lean, green and digital technologies. *Resources, Conservation and Recycling, 197*, 107094. https://doi.org/10.1016/j.resconrec.2023.107094

Yin, X., Qi, L., Ji, J., & Zhou, J. (2023). How does innovation spirit affect R&D investment and innovation performance? The moderating role of business environment. *Journal of Innovation and Knowledge, 8*, 100398. https://doi.org/10.1016/j.jik.2023.100398

Yuan, B., & Cao, X. (2022). Do corporate social responsibility practices contribute to green innovation? The mediating role of green dynamic capability. *Technology in Society, 68*, 101868. https://doi.org/10.1016/j.techsoc.2022.101868

Zastempowski, M. (2023). Analysis and modeling of innovation factors to replace fossil fuels with renewable energy sources – Evidence from European Union enterprises. *Renewable and Sustainable Energy Reviews, 178*. https://doi.org/10.1016/j.rser.2023.113262

Zhang, L., & Huang, S. (2022). Social capital and regional innovation efficiency: The moderating effect of governance quality. *Structural Change and Economic Dynamics, 62*, 343–359. https://doi.org/10.1016/j.strueco.2022.05.013

CHAPTER 16

# Analysis of Romania's Industrial Efficiency Compared to EU Member States Using the DEA Method

## Introduction

In the context of the profound changes brought about by the transition to a green and digital economy, industrial efficiency has become central to economic competitiveness in the EU. European strategies, including the European Green Deal and the 2030 Agenda for Sustainable Development, emphasize the importance of integrating innovation, research and development, and the sustainable use of resources into industrial processes to achieve emission reduction and sustainable economic growth targets. In this context, Romania faces major structural challenges, caused by both a low level of technological development and innovation and a high dependence on resource- and emission-intensive industrial sectors.

A comparative analysis of the industrial performance of EU Member States allows the identification of determinants of efficiency and gaps between developed and transition economies. The Data Envelopment Analysis (DEA) method provides a robust framework for assessing relative performance by simultaneously integrating input and output variables associated with Sustainable Development Goal 9 (SDG9, Industry, Innovation and Infrastructure). This approach allows not only the quantification of efficiency levels, but also the identification of vulnerabilities and optimal thresholds that can be achieved through public policies and strategic investments.



C. Fortea, *Sustainable Economic Development and the European Green Deal*, https://doi.org/10.1007/978-3-032-10326-0_16

The novelty of this study lies in the application of the DEA method to an extensive set of relevant indicators for the period 2010–2021, covering both the fiscal dimension (environmental taxes, road transport revenues) and the technological and economic dimensions (R&D personnel and expenditure, patents, GDP per capita, development of environmental technologies). Through this approach, the research provides an integrated perspective on how Romania ranks in relation to the European average and to benchmark countries in terms of industrial efficiency, such as Luxembourg, Germany and Sweden.

The purpose of this chapter is to assess Romania's industrial efficiency in the European context and to identify concrete directions for improvement by benchmarking against successful models. The main objectives are:

- to determine Romania's level of industrial efficiency and compare it with that of EU Member States;
- to identify input and output factors that generate vulnerabilities and opportunities for improvement;
- to formulate strategic recommendations for convergence towards European industrial efficiency standards.

Through its results, the analysis contributes to strengthening the empirical basis necessary for the development of industrial and innovation policies, while supporting sustainable development objectives and the transition to a competitive, resilient and green economy.

## Study of Literature

Industrial efficiency analysis has become a central topic in the literature, in the context of the transition to a green and digital economy, where sustainability and competitiveness intersect with European policy requirements. Over the past two decades, studies have focused on identifying the structural factors that condition industrial performance, from innovation and research and development (R&D) to the integration of green technologies and adaptation to the requirements of the European Green Deal (European Commission, 2023b) and the 2030 Agenda for Sustainable Development (European Commission, 2022). Methodologically, the application of non-parametric techniques, such as Data Envelopment Analysis (DEA), has provided a robust framework for measuring relative efficiency between countries or regions in a way that allows for multidimensional comparison of inputs and outputs.

Recent literature suggests that industrial efficiency cannot be analysed in isolation, but must be placed at the intersection of public policies, fiscal factors, technological infrastructure and specialized human resources (Khan et al., 2025; Schmitz et al., 2025; Wenjuan & Zhao, 2023). Comparative studies also highlight persistent gaps between developed EU countries and those in transition, such as Romania, which are driven by both structural differences and uneven public policies (Gogu et al., 2025; Prigoreanu et al., 2025; Sotiriou et al., 2025). The objective of this analysis is to systematize recent theoretical and empirical contributions, identifying the main directions of research on the role of innovation, fiscal policies and evaluation methodologies in shaping European industrial strategies.

### *Industrial Efficiency in the Context of the European Green and Digital Transition*

In the literature, the green and digital transition is seen as the driving force behind the redefinition of the industrial efficiency paradigm. Recent European studies show that the European Green Deal and policies associated with climate neutrality by 2050 have imposed new performance standards, where efficiency is no longer assessed solely in terms of economic productivity, but also in terms of reducing emissions intensity and natural resource consumption (Mikropoulos et al., 2025; Neil Makaroff, 2023; Talenti, 2025). According to the European Commission report (European Commission, 2023c) and other studies (Javaid et al., 2024; Khan et al., 2025; Vărzaru & Bocean, 2024), industrial efficiency is becoming inextricably linked to progress in digitalization, which enables process optimization and reduced operating costs through automation and smart technologies.

Numerous authors (Bianchini et al., 2023; Diodato et al., 2023; L. P. Georgescu et al., 2025; Khan et al., 2025) highlight the dual nature of this transition: on the one hand, opportunities for innovation and global competitiveness, and on the other hand, challenges related to the high costs of adapting industrial infrastructure and the resistance of traditional sectors. In recent research (Bigerna et al., 2022; P.-L. Georgescu et al., 2025; Khalique et al., 2025), European industrial performance is described as a balance between environmental pressures and market demands, which calls for coherent integration between sustainability and economic innovation policies.

For Central and Eastern European countries, including Romania, the literature highlights the difficulties caused by structural dependence on energy-intensive and high-emission industries. Studies (European Commission, 2024; Fedajev et al., 2023; László, 2025) confirm that these economies are less aligned with green objectives than the EU average, mainly due to low levels of investment in digital infrastructure and research. At the same time, other analyses (Agrawal et al., 2024; Drago & Gatto, 2022; European Environment Agency, 2023) highlight that, in order to achieve convergence objectives, lower-performing countries need to implement green reindustrialization policies that combine investments in energy efficiency, the development of environmental technologies, and the stimulation of human capital in digital fields.

Thus, specialized studies converge on the idea that industrial efficiency, in the current context, is no longer just a technical indicator, but an expression of states' ability to simultaneously manage the ecological and digital transitions.

### *The Contribution of Innovation and Research and Development to Industrial Performance*

There is broad consensus in international literature that innovation and investment in research and development are key determinants of industrial efficiency. According to empirical research (Bathelt & Storper, 2023; Boix-Domènech et al., 2024; Chen et al., 2023), periods of radical technological change have always been associated with major structural transformations of industries, implying that economic performance is inextricably linked to the dynamics of innovation.

Recent studies (European Commission, 2025; Nicolescu et al., 2024; Żółtaszek & Olejnik, 2024) classify EU Member States into four categories: innovation leaders, strong innovators, moderate innovators and emerging innovators. Romania is consistently ranked in the last category, with low performance on indicators such as the number of patents, R&D expenditure intensity and the share of specialized personnel. This ranking confirms the structural gaps and justifies the low levels of industrial efficiency highlighted by DEA applications.

At the same time, literature (Aristovnik et al., 2023; Bloch et al., 2023; Moncada-Paternò-Castello, 2022) shows that countries with sustained investment in R&D, such as Germany, Sweden, Finland and the Netherlands, manage to maintain a constant level of industrial efficiency, even during periods of economic crisis. This is attributed to the ability of these economies to transform invested resources into tangible results: patents, green technologies and growth in GDP per capita. According to various studies (Bärnthaler et al., 2025; Schneider, 2023; Veugelers et al., 2024), national innovation systems constitute the invisible infrastructure that supports long-term industrial competitiveness.

Recent literature also explores the correlation between green innovation and industrial performance. Empirical studies (Altuzarra Artola, 2024; Hojnik et al., 2024; Vasconcelos-Garcia & Carrilho-Nunes, 2024) show that investments in eco-innovations not only reduce environmental impact but also increase productivity and open up new international markets. Thus, innovation becomes a dual driver: it stimulates technical efficiency and contributes to the achievement of sustainability goals.

For Romania, the conclusions of this research indicate the need for a coherent strategy that combines investment in digital infrastructure with human capital development and an increase in the number of patents. Without such integration, convergence with the EU average remains unlikely.

### *The Role of Public Policies and the Fiscal Framework in Stimulating Industrial Efficiency*

Specialized literature emphasizes that industrial efficiency cannot be achieved exclusively through market mechanisms, but requires consistent support from public policies and the fiscal framework. Specialized studies (European Enviromental Agency, 2023; Flachenecker et al., 2022; Lu et al., 2025) show that fiscal instruments, such as environmental taxes or innovation support schemes, have a direct impact on the behaviour of industrial enterprises, steering them towards more sustainable and efficient models.

Empirical analyses (Behera et al., 2025; Kafeel et al., 2024; Owusu Atuahene et al., 2025) show that environmental taxes, if well calibrated, stimulate the adoption of green technologies, but at the same time can be a burden on emerging industries in low-income countries. In this regard, the literature (Juhász et al., 2024; Kovacs & Domonkos, 2024; Özçelik & Özmen, 2023) emphasizes the importance of balancing fiscal incentives and constraints in order to avoid premature deindustrialization.

Several comparative studies (Knapp et al., 2025; Wang et al., 2024; Yunxia & Yuqing, 2025) show that effective public policies are those that combine strict emissions regulations with support schemes for investment in research infrastructure and digitization. These policies not only reduce environmental impact but also increase industrial resilience and competitiveness.

In the case of Romania, the literature (Doran et al., 2023; European Commission, 2023a) shows that fiscal policies have often been reactive and fragmented, leading to overtaxation of some sectors (such as road transport) and underfunding of critical areas (R&D, green technologies). According to a number of studies (Afshan et al., 2023; D'Orazio, 2025; Edmondson et al., 2025), the lack of a predictable framework and a coherent policy mix reduces the ability of businesses to make long-term investments. Thus, the literature converges on the idea that the success of the transition to industrial efficiency depends on the coherence of public policies, which must create an environment conducive to innovation, reduce unjustified fiscal barriers, and stimulate private capital to invest in the structural transformation of the economy.

### *Methodological Applications of Data Envelopment Analysis (DEA) in Performance Evaluation*

The DEA method has become a central tool in industrial efficiency assessment, being widely applied in international literature to compare performances between countries, regions or industrial sectors. The introduction of this method by Charnes, Cooper and Rhodes (Charnes et al., 1978) marked a paradigm shift, allowing multi-input and multi-output evaluation without requiring the specification of a pre-established production function.

Recent literature (Campoli et al., 2024; Charles & Emrouznejad, 2024; Zakari et al., 2022) shows that DEA is used not only to measure economic efficiency but also to assess performance against sustainable development indicators (SDGs). According to empirical research (Alves & Meza, 2023; Huang et al., 2024; Mergoni et al., 2025; Tone & Tsutsui, 2014), methodological extensions such as the slacks-based measure (SBM) or network DEA allow for a more accurate capture of complex industrial realities.

The application of DEA in the European context has demonstrated persistent differences between Western European countries, which consistently achieve efficiency scores close to unity, and Eastern European countries, which remain below the efficiency threshold. Studies (European Investment Bank, 2025b; OECD, 2025b; Simeonovski et al., 2021) confirm that the key factors differentiating performance are investment in research, the number of patents and the tax structure applied to industry.

With regard to Romania, existing literature highlights that DEA scores remain consistently below the European average, suggesting structural vulnerabilities (Prigoreanu et al., 2025). Studies show that although Romania has made moderate progress in digitization and reducing energy intensity, the lack of systematic investment in R&D limits convergence towards the efficiency frontier (Burciu et al., 2025; Noja et al., 2022; OECD, 2024a).

Thus, the literature recognizes DEA as an indispensable tool in comparative analysis, capable of providing detailed information for informing public policy and identifying good practices for transfer from efficient states to those in transition.

### *Comparative Studies on Romania and Convergence Towards the EU Average*

A growing body of literature has focused on analysing Romania's position relative to the EU average, highlighting structural gaps and barriers to achieving industrial efficiency. According to the Eurostat report (Eurostat, 2024), Romania ranks among the lowest-performing countries in terms of patents, R&D expenditure and industrial productivity. These findings are confirmed by multiple analyses (Bruno et al., 2022; European Investment Bank, 2025a; Grafström & Alm, 2025; Kijek et al., 2022), which show that the gaps between Eastern European countries and the EU average remain despite overall economic convergence.

Comparative studies (European Investment Bank, 2025b; Ibinceanu et al., 2021; Nichifor et al., 2025) highlight that the critical factors behind Romania's gap are: low public and private spending on research, fragmented industrial strategies, underdeveloped logistics infrastructure, and unbalanced fiscal policies. In contrast, the models of Luxembourg and Germany demonstrate that continuous investment in R&D and digitalization, combined with smart fiscal policies, generates a consistent level of industrial efficiency (Manta et al., 2025; Teixeira & Tavares-Lehmann, 2022; Wigger, 2023).

The literature (Joița et al., 2023; Niță et al., 2025; Panton, 2023) also draws attention to the fact that Romania is highly dependent on polluting industries, which amplifies its vulnerability to green transition objectives. According to empirical analyses (Aprile, 2025; Bircan & Salah, 2024; Ding et al., 2025), the lack of coherent investment in eco-innovation and environmental technologies limits the capacity to reduce emissions intensity, keeping the economy in a zone of structural inefficiency.

However, some recent research (OECD, 2022, 2024b) suggests that Romania has significant potential for recovery if public policies are reoriented towards stimulating innovation and reducing the tax burden on strategic sectors. Proximity to European markets, natural resources and a relatively competitive labour force can be comparative advantages, but these need to be turned into competitive advantages through investment in technology and infrastructure.

The literature reviewed paints a clear picture: industrial efficiency in Europe is a multidimensional phenomenon driven by the interaction between innovation, public policy, digitalization and the green transition. Developed countries with well-established innovation systems and coherent fiscal policies consistently achieve high industrial efficiency scores, confirming the validity of DEA models. In contrast, countries such as Romania, Greece and Bulgaria remain inefficient, reflecting structural gaps and incomplete public policies.

A point of convergence in the literature is the importance of innovation as a driver of industrial performance. Investment in R&D, human capital and patents are indispensable factors for achieving efficiency. At the same time, public policies play an essential role, as they can accelerate or slow down the transition to a green and digital industry. Methodologically, the application of DEA remains one of the most robust approaches, capable of providing detailed comparative results and informing policy recommendations.

For Romania, the literature points to both significant limitations and opportunities for convergence. Closing the gap requires an integrated strategy that includes sustained investment in research, digitization and environmental technologies, as well as tax reforms that stimulate competitiveness. Only through such an approach can Romania advance towards the EU's industrial efficiency standards and actively contribute to global sustainability and competitiveness goals.

## Methodology

The analysis of industrial efficiency using the DEA (Data Envelopment Analysis) method provides a detailed insight into Romania's industrial performance compared to other EU Member States. By identifying the key factors contributing to industrial efficiency, the Romanian authorities can take measures to improve the competitiveness of the industrial sector and stimulate economic growth. The use of the DEA method also provides a clear picture of the weaknesses of the Romanian industry, allowing the authorities to prioritize investments and develop effective strategies to overcome these problems. Thus, DEA is an important tool for the development of long-term economic and industrial policies that contribute to a sustainable and balanced growth of the Romanian economy in the context of globalization.

We propose to perform the industrial efficiency analysis of Romania in the European context, and we will use the DEA method for which the following inputs and outputs have been established according to Table 16.1.

The following working hypotheses are made to demonstrate industrial efficiency:

H1: The majority of European countries are industrially inefficient and lack adequate support for research and innovation.
H2: The EU is industrially efficient thanks to the massive input of research and innovation from developed countries.
H3: The most efficient countries are Germany, Luxembourg, Malta, the Netherlands, Sweden and Estonia; additionally, the EU average also displays a high level of industrial efficiency.
H4: The most industrially inefficient countries are Romania, Cyprus and Greece.

Data Envelopment Analysis (DEA) can be used as a technique based on linear programming and optimization to evaluate the efficiency of each unit. To improve the efficiency of each unit, a benchmark set for an inefficient unit is determined and the efficiency of different units can be compared with the efficiency limit.

In this study, 28 decision-making units (DMUs) were used which were investigated with respect to three inputs and six outputs. The type of DEA

**Table 16.1** Presentation of analysed indicators

| *Symbol* | *Indicator name* | *Unit of measurement* | *Source* | *Tip* |
|---|---|---|---|---|
| SDG9TAXM | Environmental taxes | % GDP | OECD (2025a) | Input |
| SDG9VTAXT | Revenue from charges related to road transport | % of total environmental tax revenues | OECD (2025c) | Input |
| SDG9CMPR | Consumption of raw materials | Thousand tons | Eurostat (2025d) | Input |
| SDG9CBV | Patent applications filed at the European Patent Office by country of residence of applicants/inventors | Number | Eurostat (2025b) | Output |
| SDG9PCDI | R&D personnel | % | Eurostat (2025c) | Output |
| SDG9CHCDI | Gross domestic expenditure on research and development | % | Eurostat (2025a) | Output |
| SDG9PIBloc | GDP per capita | Euro per inhabitant | Eurostat (2025e) | Output |
| SDG9DTHM | Developing environmental technologies | % inventions per capita | OECD (2025c) | Output |
| SDG9AOF | Official Development Assistance | % GNI | OECD (2025c) | Output |

Source: Author

used in this study is the radial model based on constant returns to scale (CRS) model and using the IN (input) approach.

## Results and Discussions

The efficiency value obtained by the defined model is shown in Table 16.2.

Table 16.2 shows that the countries that are industrially efficient over the whole period of analysis 2010–2021 are Germany, Luxembourg, Malta, the Netherlands, Sweden and Estonia. This demonstrates working hypothesis 3. As for the European average, it benefits from the innovation input of the developed countries, with the EU level proving that industrial efficiency is appropriate over the whole period analysed. Working hypothesis 2 is demonstrated. Some states have reached industrial efficiency only over a certain period of time; thus Austria, Belgium and Slovenia manage

**Table 16.2** EU Member States and the European average performance of Sustainable Development Goal 9

| DMU | 2010 | 2011 | 2012 | 2013 | 2014 | 2015 | 2016 | 2017 | 2018 | 2019 | 2020 | 2021 |
|---|---|---|---|---|---|---|---|---|---|---|---|---|
| Austria | 1.000 | 0.965 | 1.000 | 0.996 | 0.975 | 0.953 | 0.998 | 0.917 | 0.989 | 1.000 | 1.000 | 1.000 |
| Belgium | 0.879 | 0.806 | 0.910 | 0.999 | 0.931 | 0.920 | 0.971 | 0.981 | 1.000 | 1.000 | 1.000 | 1.000 |
| Bulgaria | 0.282 | 0.262 | 0.288 | 0.293 | 0.364 | 0.433 | 0.368 | 0.353 | 0.357 | 0.395 | 0.372 | 0.314 |
| Czech Republic | 0.512 | 0.537 | 0.654 | 0.711 | 0.704 | 0.655 | 0.587 | 0.594 | 0.687 | 0.709 | 0.718 | 0.708 |
| Cyprus | 0.249 | 0.254 | 0.295 | 0.372 | 0.407 | 0.383 | 0.381 | 0.383 | 0.422 | 0.462 | 0.567 | 0.638 |
| Croatia | 0.297 | 0.290 | 0.324 | 0.351 | 0.302 | 0.288 | 0.270 | 0.270 | 0.323 | 0.364 | 0.425 | 0.440 |
| Denmark | 1.000 | 1.000 | 1.000 | 1.000 | 1.000 | 1.000 | 1.000 | 1.000 | 1.000 | 1.000 | 1.000 | 0.891 |
| Estonia | 1.000 | 1.000 | 1.000 | 1.000 | 1.000 | 1.000 | 1.000 | 1.000 | 1.000 | 1.000 | 1.000 | 1.000 |
| EU27 | 1.000 | 1.000 | 1.000 | 1.000 | 1.000 | 1.000 | 1.000 | 1.000 | 1.000 | 1.000 | 1.000 | 1.000 |
| Finland | 1.000 | 1.000 | 1.000 | 0.958 | 0.842 | 0.787 | 0.721 | 0.760 | 0.736 | 0.773 | 0.755 | 0.783 |
| France | 0.865 | 0.840 | 0.845 | 0.780 | 0.772 | 0.839 | 0.858 | 0.823 | 0.808 | 0.905 | 0.897 | 0.825 |
| Germany | 1.000 | 1.000 | 1.000 | 1.000 | 1.000 | 1.000 | 1.000 | 1.000 | 1.000 | 1.000 | 1.000 | 1.000 |
| Greece | 0.260 | 0.288 | 0.286 | 0.271 | 0.261 | 0.290 | 0.294 | 0.327 | 0.365 | 0.378 | 0.430 | 0.385 |
| Ireland | 0.889 | 0.845 | 0.887 | 0.843 | 0.832 | 0.739 | 0.729 | 0.802 | 0.845 | 1.000 | 1.000 | 0.973 |
| Italy | 0.417 | 0.388 | 0.376 | 0.374 | 0.386 | 0.389 | 0.404 | 0.406 | 0.420 | 0.448 | 0.471 | 0.445 |
| Latvia | 0.312 | 0.325 | 0.334 | 0.303 | 0.314 | 0.290 | 0.289 | 0.244 | 0.282 | 0.283 | 0.324 | 0.373 |
| Lithuania | 1.000 | 0.888 | 0.849 | 0.729 | 0.791 | 0.823 | 0.747 | 0.793 | 0.812 | 0.872 | 0.808 | 0.670 |
| Luxembourg | 1.000 | 1.000 | 1.000 | 1.000 | 1.000 | 1.000 | 1.000 | 1.000 | 1.000 | 1.000 | 1.000 | 1.000 |
| Malta | 1.000 | 1.000 | 1.000 | 1.000 | 1.000 | 1.000 | 1.000 | 1.000 | 1.000 | 1.000 | 1.000 | 1.000 |
| Netherlands | 1.000 | 1.000 | 1.000 | 1.000 | 1.000 | 1.000 | 1.000 | 1.000 | 1.000 | 1.000 | 1.000 | 1.000 |
| Poland | 0.367 | 0.348 | 0.404 | 0.375 | 0.413 | 0.423 | 0.414 | 0.431 | 0.508 | 0.633 | 0.699 | 0.683 |
| Portugal | 0.498 | 0.554 | 0.577 | 0.554 | 0.486 | 0.450 | 0.449 | 0.435 | 0.471 | 0.501 | 0.525 | 0.569 |
| Romania | 0.200 | 0.241 | 0.256 | 0.229 | 0.179 | 0.214 | 0.222 | 0.285 | 0.284 | 0.292 | 0.282 | 0.272 |
| Slovakia | 0.374 | 0.380 | 0.480 | 0.470 | 0.503 | 0.691 | 0.485 | 0.530 | 0.517 | 0.502 | 0.491 | 0.458 |
| Slovenia | 0.906 | 0.912 | 1.000 | 1.000 | 1.000 | 1.000 | 1.000 | 1.000 | 1.000 | 0.984 | 1.000 | 1.000 |
| Spain | 0.752 | 0.749 | 0.754 | 0.575 | 0.547 | 0.524 | 0.523 | 0.529 | 0.554 | 0.568 | 0.610 | 0.604 |
| Sweden | 1.000 | 1.000 | 1.000 | 1.000 | 1.000 | 1.000 | 1.000 | 1.000 | 1.000 | 1.000 | 1.000 | 1.000 |
| Hungary | 0.472 | 0.474 | 0.525 | 0.623 | 0.572 | 0.538 | 0.503 | 0.537 | 0.645 | 0.640 | 0.672 | 0.639 |

Source: Author

to maximize their efficiency in dynamics by improving their R&D policy, and Ireland follows the same trend with the caveat that in 2021 the efficiency score falls below the efficiency threshold, Ireland becoming industrially inefficient due to Brexit. Denmark is another country that, with the exception of 2021, falls within the efficiency parameters. For Denmark the year 2021 marked strong social demonstrations against the restrictions imposed during the pandemic which affected the economy of the country, also reflected in the decrease of the industrial efficiency score.

It is found that 15 European countries, including Romania, are industrially inefficient, which proves Hypothesis 1.

The most industrially efficient countries are Austria, Denmark, Estonia, Finland, Lithuania, Luxembourg, Malta, the Netherlands and Sweden. The European average is similarly in the range of efficient regions benefiting from the innovation input of developed countries. At the opposite pole, the most inefficient countries are Romania, Cyprus, Greece, Bulgaria, Croatia and Latvia. This demonstrates Hypothesis 4.

The DEA method is used to project the efficiency of the analysed unit at the maximum level, and the process is completed by equating the efficiency thresholds to 1 for as many compared units as possible. This yields the industrial efficiency benchmarks for each analysed DMU.

Table 16.3 presents Romania's industrial efficiency benchmarks by year.

It can be seen from Table 16.3 that in the case of Romania, Luxembourg is the efficiency benchmark for each year, and this comparison will be further analysed to determine the vulnerabilities in terms of Romania's industrial efficiency. Another comparison could be made with Sweden, but it is found that Sweden is not an efficiency benchmark for each year of the period analysed.

Table 16.4 shows the ranking of the frequency of references by year for industrially efficient EU Member States.

Table 16.4 shows that Luxembourg represents for the whole period under analysis the industrial efficiency model with the highest peer frequencies among all industrially efficient European countries, which recommends it as suitable for the study.

**Table 16.3** Romania's efficiency benchmarks by year

| *DMU* | *Years* | *Peer1* | *Peer2* | *Peer3* | *Peer4* |
|---|---|---|---|---|---|
| Romania | 2010 | Finland | Germany | Luxembourg | Sweden |
| | 2011 | Luxembourg | Sweden | – | – |
| | 2012 | Luxembourg | Sweden | – | – |
| | 2013 | EU27 | Luxembourg | Sweden | – |
| | 2014 | Estonia | EU27 | Luxembourg | Sweden |
| | 2015 | Estonia | EU27 | Luxembourg | Sweden |
| | 2016 | Estonia | EU27 | Luxembourg | Sweden |
| | 2017 | Estonia | EU27 | Luxembourg | Sweden |
| | 2018 | Estonia | EU27 | Luxembourg | Sweden |
| | 2019 | Estonia | Germany | Luxembourg | – |
| | 2020 | Estonia | Germany | Luxembourg | – |
| | 2021 | Estonia | EU27 | Germany | Luxembourg |

Source: Author

**Table 16.4** Frequency ranking of benchmarks by year for industrially efficient Member States

| Year | 2010 | 2011 | 2012 | 2013 | 2014 | 2015 | 2016 | 2017 | 2018 | 2019 | 2020 | 2021 |
|---|---|---|---|---|---|---|---|---|---|---|---|---|
| Ranking | Lux 1/11 | Lux 1/9 | Lux 1/11 | Lux 1/9 | Lux 1/9 | Lux 1/9 | Lux 1/9 | Lux 1/9 | Lux 1/10 | Lux 1/11 | Lux 1/12 | Lux 1/10 |
| Peer frequencies | Austria (1) | Denmark (2) | Austria (1) | Denmark (3) | Denmark (1) | Denmark (2) | Denmark (1) | Denmark (3) | Belgium (4) | Austria (1) | Austria (2) | Austria (2) |
| | Denmark (1) | Estonia (12) | Denmark (1) | Estonia (13) | Estonia (10) | Estonia (11) | Estonia (11) | Estonia (11) | Denmark (2) | Belgium (4) | Belgium (5) | Belgium (7) |
| | Estonia (6) | EU27 (2) | Estonia (13) | EU27 (9) | EU27 (10) | EU27 (9) | EU27 (8) | EU27 (9) | Estonia (9) | Denmark (2) | Denmark (2) | Estonia (15) |
| | EU27 (4) | Finland (2) | EU27 (5) | Germany (3) | Germany (3) | Germany (6) | Germany (5) | Germany (6) | EU27 (11) | Estonia (11) | Estonia (13) | EU27 (7) |
| | Finland (12) | Germany (5) | Finland (1) | Luxembourg (20) | Luxembourg (20) | Luxembourg (22) | Luxembourg (21) | Luxembourg (22) | Germany (7) | EU27 (1) | EU27 (1) | Germany (9) |
| | Germany (7) | Luxembourg (20) | Germany (5) | Malta (2) | Malta (2) | Malta (3) | Malta (3) | Malta (3) | Luxembourg (20) | Germany (13) | Germany (12) | Luxembourg (19) |
| | Lithuania (1) | Malta (1) | Luxembourg (19) | Netherlands (1) | Netherlands (1) | Netherlands (1) | Netherlands (1) | Netherlands (1) | Malta (2) | Ireland (1) | Ireland (1) | Malta (3) |
| | Luxembourg (19) | Netherlands (2) | Malta (1) | Slovenia (2) | Slovenia (2) | Slovenia (3) | Slovenia (1) | Slovenia (1) | Netherlands (1) | Luxembourg (18) | Luxembourg (17) | Netherlands (1) |
| | Malta (1) | Sweden (17) | Netherlands (1) | Sweden (18) | Sweden (18) | Sweden (18) | Sweden (18) | Sweden (18) | Slovenia (2) | Malta (2) | Malta (2) | Slovenia (4) |
| | Netherlands (2) | | Slovenia (3) | | | | | | Sweden (17) | Netherlands (1) | Netherlands (1) | Sweden (8) |
| | Sweden (14) | | Sweden (17) | | | | | | | Sweden (12) | Slovenia (2) | |
| | | | | | | | | | | | Sweden (11) | |

Source: Author

The values of $\lambda$ (lambdas = weights for equal units) were determined which represent the combination of equal units used to construct each virtual unit. The values of $\lambda$ are shown in Table 16.5.

It can be observed that for Romania the values of lambda coefficients determined for the Luxembourg DMU are non-zero throughout the analysed period, which confirms the efficiency solution of the Luxembourg model in terms of sustainable development based on the SDG9 indicators for Romania.

Tables 16.6 and 16.7 present the values of the variables for the industrial efficiency model, showing the weights attributable by the DEA method to the input values (Table 16.6) and output values (Table 16.7) respectively.

As shown in Table 16.6, the improvable input variables that exhibit statistically significant weights (i.e., weights different from zero) for

**Table 16.5** Lambda coefficients of the reference unit Luxembourg

| DMU | 2010 | 2011 | 2012 | 2013 | 2014 | 2015 | 2016 | 2017 | 2018 | 2019 | 2020 | 2021 |
|---|---|---|---|---|---|---|---|---|---|---|---|---|
| Austria | 0 | 0.134 | 0 | 0.29 | 0.285 | 0.319 | 0.423 | 0.396 | 0.434 | 0 | 0 | 0 |
| Belgium | 0.269 | 0.146 | 0.166 | 0.145 | 0.281 | 0.306 | 0.5 | 0.597 | 0 | 0 | 0 | 0 |
| Bulgaria | 0.142 | 0.183 | 0.166 | 0.153 | 0.102 | 0.134 | 0.261 | 0.225 | 0.317 | 0.28 | 0.279 | 0.274 |
| Czech Republic | 0.229 | 0.198 | 0.209 | 0.173 | 0.282 | 0.224 | 0.284 | 0.317 | 0.318 | 0.392 | 0.395 | 0.318 |
| Cyprus | 0.293 | 0.273 | 0.256 | 0.298 | 0.326 | 0.208 | 0.354 | 0.385 | 0.462 | 0.568 | 0.681 | 0.405 |
| Croatia | 0.42 | 0.172 | 0.177 | 0.124 | 0.568 | 0.624 | 0.637 | 0.656 | 0.746 | 0.789 | 0.793 | 0.543 |
| Denmark | 0 | 0 | 0 | 0 | 0 | 0 | 0 | 0 | 0 | 0 | 0 | 2.466 |
| Estonia | 0 | 0 | 0 | 0 | 0 | 0 | 0 | 0 | 0 | 0 | 0 | 0 |
| EU27 | 0 | 0 | 0 | 0 | 0 | 0 | 0 | 0 | 0 | 0 | 0 | 0 |
| Finland | 0 | 0 | 0 | 0.101 | 0.248 | 0.363 | 0.447 | 0.266 | 0.325 | 0.36 | 0.382 | 0.61 |
| France | 0.169 | 0.181 | 0.199 | 0.203 | 0.164 | 0.2 | 0.17 | 0.216 | 0.25 | 0.273 | 0.267 | 0.324 |
| Germany | 0 | 0 | 0 | 0 | 0 | 0 | 0 | 0 | 0 | 0 | 0 | 0 |
| Greece | 0.206 | 0.278 | 0.317 | 0.342 | 0.335 | 0.428 | 0.426 | 0.445 | 0.631 | 0.653 | 0.388 | 0.405 |
| Ireland | 0.796 | 0.392 | 0.464 | 0.479 | 0.875 | 0.664 | 0.696 | 0.643 | 0.632 | 0 | 0 | 0.766 |
| Italy | 0.202 | 0.226 | 0.253 | 0.256 | 0.2 | 0.266 | 0.309 | 0.412 | 0.501 | 0.501 | 0.468 | 0.455 |
| Latvia | 0.419 | 0.266 | 0.176 | 0.375 | 0.514 | 0.312 | 0.472 | 0.41 | 0.492 | 0.53 | 0.408 | 0.192 |
| Lithuania | 0 | 0.183 | 0.206 | 0.209 | 0.166 | 0.125 | 0.184 | 0.2 | 0.234 | 0.288 | 0.3 | 0.339 |
| Luxembourg | 1 | 1 | 1 | 1 | 1 | 1 | 1 | 1 | 1 | 1 | 1 | 1 |
| Malta | 0 | 0 | 0 | 0 | 0 | 0 | 0 | 0 | 0 | 0 | 0 | 0 |
| Netherlands | 0 | 0 | 0 | 0 | 0 | 0 | 0 | 0 | 0 | 0 | 0 | 0 |
| Poland | 0.088 | 0.12 | 0.087 | 0.077 | 0.063 | 0.088 | 0.086 | 0.231 | 0.253 | 0.197 | 0.225 | 0.215 |
| Portugal | 0.056 | 0.166 | 0.189 | 0.211 | 0.193 | 0.273 | 0.356 | 0.338 | 0.375 | 0.4 | 0.387 | 0.302 |
| Romania | 0.063 | 0.091 | 0.124 | 0.156 | 0.136 | 0.102 | 0.097 | 0.091 | 0.097 | 0.097 | 0.116 | 0.124 |
| Slovakia | 0.24 | 0.221 | 0.192 | 0.149 | 0.229 | 0.296 | 0.223 | 0.223 | 0.209 | 0.252 | 0.263 | 0.217 |
| Slovenia | 0.944 | 0.8 | 0 | 0 | 0 | 0 | 0 | 0 | 0 | 1.313 | 0 | 0 |
| Spain | 0.16 | 0.164 | 0.175 | 0.169 | 0.154 | 0.192 | 0.205 | 0.251 | 0.269 | 0.265 | 0.204 | 0.2 |
| Sweden | 0 | 0 | 0 | 0 | 0 | 0 | 0 | 0 | 0 | 0 | 0 | 0 |
| Hungary | 0.414 | 0.166 | 0.175 | 0.113 | 0.388 | 0.222 | 0.263 | 0.169 | 0.263 | 0.329 | 0.322 | 0.251 |

Source: Author

Romania are the contribution of environment-related taxes to GDP and the share of road-transport-related tax revenues in total environmental tax revenues. In terms of raw material consumption there are no significantly different weights of 0 (improvable for Romania). At the European and Luxembourg level the only improvable variable is road transport-related tax revenues as a share of total environmental tax revenues. Thus, it is estimated that industrial development overtaxes the logistics sector, as road transport is excessively taxed due to the polluting logistics infrastructure owned by Member States.

Table 16.7 shows that for Romania, the significantly different weights of the improvable input variables from 0 refer to insufficient R&D personnel in relation to the needs of the sector, but also to inadequately budgeted gross domestic expenditure on R&D, which affects the efficiency of

**Table 16.6** Weights for the input variable values of the industrial efficiency model

| *DMU* | *Romania* | | | *EU27* | | | *Luxembourg* | | |
|---|---|---|---|---|---|---|---|---|---|
| *An* | *SDG9 TAXM* | *SDG9 VTAXT* | *SDG9 CMPR* | *SDG9 TAXM* | *SDG9 VTAXT* | *SDG9 CMPR* | *SDG9 TAXM* | *SDG9 VTAXT* | *SDG9 CMPR* |
| 2010 | 0.376 | 0.013 | 0 | 0 | 0.017 | 0 | 0 | 0 | 0 |
| 2011 | 0.513 | 0 | 0 | 0 | 0.015 | 0 | 0 | 0 | 0 |
| 2012 | 0.505 | 0 | 0 | 0 | 0.016 | 0 | 0 | 0 | 0 |
| 2013 | 0.493 | 0 | 0 | 0 | 0.01 | 0 | 0 | 0 | 0 |
| 2014 | 0.181 | 0.041 | 0 | 0 | 0.009 | 0 | 0 | 0.011 | 0 |
| 2015 | 0.174 | 0.042 | 0 | 0 | 0.008 | 0 | 0 | 0.123 | 0 |
| 2016 | 0.14 | 0.05 | 0 | 0 | 0.008 | 0 | 0 | 0 | 0 |
| 2017 | 0.185 | 0.062 | 0 | 0 | 0.007 | 0 | 0 | 0 | 0 |
| 2018 | 0.198 | 0.059 | 0 | 0 | 0.008 | 0 | 0 | 0.028 | 0 |
| 2019 | 0.212 | 0.079 | 0 | 0 | 0.014 | 0 | 0 | 0 | 0 |
| 2020 | 0.257 | 0.067 | 0 | 0 | 0.021 | 0 | 0 | 0 | 0 |
| 2021 | 0.331 | 0.052 | 0 | 0 | 0.011 | 0 | 0 | 0.099 | 0 |

Source: Author

**Table 16.7** Weights for the output variable values of the industrial efficiency model

| *DMU* | *1Romania* | | | | | | *EU27* | | | | | | *Luxembourg* | | | | | |
|---|---|---|---|---|---|---|---|---|---|---|---|---|---|---|---|---|---|---|
| *Year* | *SDG9 CBV* | *SDG9 PCDI* | *SDG9 CHCDI* | *SDG9 PIBloc* | *SDG9 DTHM* | *SDG9 AOF* | *SDG9 CBV* | *SDG9 PCDI* | *SDG9 CHCDI* | *SDG9 PIBloc* | *SDG9 DTHM* | *SDG9 AOF* | *SDG9 CBV* | *SDG9 PCDI* | *SDG9 CHCDI* | *SDG9 PIBloc* | *SDG9 DTHM* | *SDG9 AOF* |
| 2010 | 0 | 0.29 | 0.233 | 0 | 0 | 0 | 0 | 0 | 0 | 0 | 0 | 0 | 0 | 0 | 0 | 0 | 0 | 0 |
| 2011 | 0 | 0.433 | 0.159 | 0 | 0 | 0 | 0 | 0 | 0 | 0 | 0 | 0 | 0 | 0 | 0 | 0 | 0 | 0 |
| 2012 | 0 | 0.527 | 0.098 | 0 | 0 | 0 | 0 | 0 | 0 | 0 | 0 | 0 | 0 | 0 | 0 | 0 | 0 | 0 |
| 2013 | 0 | 0.428 | 0.138 | 0 | 0 | 0 | 0 | 0 | 0 | 0 | 0 | 0 | 0 | 0 | 0 | 0 | 0 | 0 |
| 2014 | 0 | 0.134 | 0.334 | 0 | 0 | 0 | 0 | 0 | 0 | 0 | 0 | 0 | 0 | 0 | 0 | 0 | 0 | 0 |
| 2015 | 0 | 0.117 | 0.343 | 0 | 0 | 0 | 0 | 0 | 0 | 0 | 0 | 0 | 0 | 0 | 0 | 0 | 0 | 0 |
| 2016 | 0 | 0.076 | 0.391 | 0 | 0 | 0 | 0 | 0 | 0 | 0 | 0 | 0 | 0 | 0 | 0 | 0 | 0 | 0 |
| 2017 | 0 | 0.12 | 0.465 | 0 | 0 | 0 | 0 | 0 | 0 | 0 | 0 | 0 | 0 | 0 | 0 | 0 | 0 | 0 |
| 2018 | 0 | 0.133 | 0.461 | 0 | 0 | 0 | 0 | 0 | 0 | 0 | 0 | 0 | 0 | 0 | 0 | 0 | 0 | 0 |
| 2019 | 0 | 0.228 | 0.422 | 0 | 0 | 0 | 0 | 0 | 0 | 0 | 0 | 0 | 0 | 0 | 0 | 0 | 0.023 | 0 |
| 2020 | 0 | 0.311 | 0.328 | 0 | 0 | 0 | 0 | 0 | 0 | 0 | 0 | 0 | 0 | 0 | 0.123 | 0 | 0 | 0 |
| 2021 | 0 | 0.326 | 0.289 | 0 | 0 | 0 | 0 | 0 | 0 | 0 | 0 | 0 | 0 | 0 | 0 | 0 | 0 | 0 |

Source: Author

**Table 16.8** Input vulnerabilities hindering industrial efficiency in Romania

| *DMU* | *Romania* | | | *EU27* | | | *Luxembourg* | | |
|---|---|---|---|---|---|---|---|---|---|
| *Indicator/ year* | *SDG9 TAXM* | *SDG9 VTAXT* | *SDG9 CMPR* | *SDG9 TAXM* | *SDG9 VTAXT* | *SDG9 CMPR* | *SDG9 TAXM* | *SDG9 VTAXT* | *SDG9 CMPR* |
| 2010 | 0 | 0 | 0 | 0 | 0 | 0 | 0 | 0 | 0 |
| 2011 | 0 | 0.349 | 65898.07 | 0 | 0 | 0 | 0 | 0 | 0 |
| 2012 | 0 | 0.904 | 67824.45 | 0 | 0 | 0 | 0 | 0 | 0 |
| 2013 | 0 | 1.29 | 0 | 0 | 0 | 0 | 0 | 0 | 0 |
| 2014 | 0 | 0 | 0 | 0 | 0 | 0 | 0 | 0 | 0 |
| 2015 | 0 | 0 | 0 | 0 | 0 | 0 | 0 | 0 | 0 |
| 2016 | 0 | 0 | 0 | 0 | 0 | 0 | 0 | 0 | 0 |
| 2017 | 0 | 0 | 0 | 0 | 0 | 0 | 0 | 0 | 0 |
| 2018 | 0 | 0 | 0 | 0 | 0 | 0 | 0 | 0 | 0 |
| 2019 | 0 | 0 | 38122.87 | 0 | 0 | 0 | 0 | 0 | 0 |
| 2020 | 0 | 0 | 57289.39 | 0 | 0 | 0 | 0 | 0 | 0 |
| 2021 | 0 | 0 | 0 | 0 | 0 | 0 | 0 | 0 | 0 |

Source: Author

**Table 16.9** Output vulnerabilities hampering industrial efficiency in Romania

| *DMU* | *Romania* | | | | | | *EU27* | | | | | | *Luxembourg* | | | | | |
|---|---|---|---|---|---|---|---|---|---|---|---|---|---|---|---|---|---|---|
| *Year/ Indicator* | *SDG9 CBV* | *SDG9 PCDI* | *SDG9 CHCDI* | *SDG9 PIBloc* | *SDG9 DTHM* | *SDG9 AOF* | *SDG9 CBV* | *SDG9 PCDI* | *SDG9 CHCDI* | *SDG9 PIBloc* | *SDG9 DTHM* | *SDG9 AOF* | *SDG9 CBV* | *SDG9 PCDI* | *SDG9 CHCDI* | *SDG9 PIBloc* | *SDG9 DTHM* | *SDG9 AOF* |
| 2010 | 977.88 | 0 | 0 | 2959.03 | 6.10 | 0.07 | 0 | 0 | 0 | 0 | 0 | 0 | 0 | 0 | 0 | 0 | 0 | 0 |
| 2011 | 414.52 | 0 | 0 | 5373.10 | 7.49 | 0.11 | 0 | 0 | 0 | 0 | 0 | 0 | 0 | 0 | 0 | 0 | 0 | 0 |
| 2012 | 357.99 | 0 | 0 | 7258.35 | 5.87 | 0.13 | 0 | 0 | 0 | 0 | 0 | 0 | 0 | 0 | 0 | 0 | 0 | 0 |
| 2013 | 878.35 | 0 | 0 | 8488.29 | 3.94 | 0.15 | 0 | 0 | 0 | 0 | 0 | 0 | 0 | 0 | 0 | 0 | 0 | 0 |
| 2014 | 780.17 | 0 | 0 | 6907.29 | 5.82 | 0.11 | 0 | 0 | 0 | 0 | 0 | 0 | 0 | 0 | 0 | 0 | 0 | 0 |
| 2015 | 1058.97 | 0 | 0 | 5503.81 | 5.68 | 0.12 | 0 | 0 | 0 | 0 | 0 | 0 | 0 | 0 | 0 | 0 | 0 | 0 |
| 2016 | 1084.97 | 0 | 0 | 5269.29 | 6.22 | 0.08 | 0 | 0 | 0 | 0 | 0 | 0 | 0 | 0 | 0 | 0 | 0 | 0 |
| 2017 | 1280.38 | 0 | 0 | 4293.99 | 4.37 | 0.08 | 0 | 0 | 0 | 0 | 0 | 0 | 0 | 0 | 0 | 0 | 0 | 0 |
| 2018 | 1381.64 | 0 | 0 | 4029.24 | 5.17 | 0.07 | 0 | 0 | 0 | 0 | 0 | 0 | 0 | 0 | 0 | 0 | 0 | 0 |
| 2019 | 2353.64 | 0 | 0 | 2847.05 | 6.07 | 0.06 | 0 | 0 | 0 | 0 | 0 | 0 | 0 | 0 | 0 | 0 | 0 | 0 |
| 2020 | 2145.63 | 0 | 0 | 4129.66 | 5.97 | 0.06 | 0 | 0 | 0 | 0 | 0 | 0 | 0 | 0 | 0 | 0 | 0 | 0 |
| 2021 | 2645.23 | 0 | 0 | 4586.45 | 5.78 | 0.04 | 0 | 0 | 0 | 0 | 0 | 0 | 0 | 0 | 0 | 0 | 0 | 0 |

Source: Author

the Romanian industrial model. At EU and Luxembourg level no improvable output variables are identified.

The input and output vulnerabilities related to each unit are shown in Tables 16.8 and 16.9 respectively.

In contrast to Luxembourg, which achieves industrial efficiency, Romania shows vulnerabilities related to the following inputs: revenues from road transportation taxes and consumption of raw materials. Neither the European nor the Luxembourg model registers input efficiency vulnerabilities (as shown in Table 16.9).

Unlike Luxembourg, which achieves industrial efficiency, Romania has vulnerabilities related to the following outputs: patent applications filed at the European Patent Office by country of residence of applicants/inventors; GDP per capita and development of environmental technologies and Official Development Assistance.

On the basis of these vulnerabilities, input and output efficiency thresholds were projected for Romania. Table 16.10 shows the actual values and input efficiency thresholds for Romania compared to the European average and Luxembourg.

Table 16.10 shows that Romania needs to improve the inputs of the variables related to SDG9 in order to reduce environmental taxes, revenues from taxes related to road transport and the consumption of raw materials so that they do not exceed the recommended values for 2021, namely 0.38% of GDP for the value of environmental taxes, 2.7% of environmental taxes for road transport taxation and a significant reduction in the consumption of raw materials through innovation and industrial re-engineering. At EU and Luxembourg level the efficiency thresholds are met, the models are efficient.

Table 16.11 shows the actual values and output efficiency thresholds for Romania compared to Luxembourg and the European average.

Table 16.11 shows that in order to achieve the industrial efficiency targets, Romania needs to improve its R&D activity by increasing the number of patents filed at the European Patent Office according to the country of residence of the applicants/inventors. In addition, economic growth needs to be accelerated, as there is currently a shortfall of at least 50% of GDP per capita, which needs to increase from €9160 per capita to over €13,700 to ensure efficiency in terms of the MDG9. Other inefficiencies in industrial development are the development of environmental technologies and Official Development Assistance, which are real impediments to achieving industrial efficiency. The development of environmental

**Table 16.10** Actual values and input efficiency thresholds for Romania compared to the European average and Luxembourg

| *Input type* | | *Input* | *Efficiency threshold* | *Input* | *Efficiency threshold* | *Input* | *Efficiency threshold* |
|---|---|---|---|---|---|---|---|
| *DMU* | *Year* | *SDG9TAXM* | | *SDG9VTAXT* | | *SDG9CMPR* | |
| Romania | 2010 | 2.11 | 0.423 | 15.09 | 3.023 | 277980.5 | 55689.73 |
| | 2011 | 1.95 | 0.47 | 12.21 | 2.595 | 386418.9 | 27281.21 |
| | 2012 | 1.98 | 0.507 | 13.36 | 2.516 | 358436.5 | 23933.97 |
| | 2013 | 2.01 | 0.461 | 13.76 | 1.864 | 354146.9 | 81164.93 |
| | 2014 | 2.32 | 0.416 | 11.27 | 2.02 | 370641.2 | 66447.69 |
| | 2015 | 2.43 | 0.519 | 10.36 | 2.214 | 442153.7 | 94484.78 |
| | 2016 | 2.33 | 0.517 | 10.11 | 2.242 | 451342.7 | 100111.9 |
| | 2017 | 1.96 | 0.558 | 7.03 | 2.003 | 420506.5 | 119813.1 |
| | 2018 | 2.07 | 0.587 | 6.63 | 1.882 | 454586.5 | 129015.7 |
| | 2019 | 1.8 | 0.525 | 7.8 | 2.274 | 540032.3 | 119305.5 |
| | 2020 | 1.59 | 0.448 | 8.85 | 2.495 | 585683.8 | 107794.4 |
| | 2021 | 1.38 | 0.376 | 9.9 | 2.697 | 601411.6 | 163818.2 |
| EU27 | 2010 | 2.94 | 2.94 | 2 | 2 | 6511694 | 6511694 |
| | 2011 | 2.74 | 2.74 | 2.36 | 2.36 | 6813451 | 6813451 |
| | 2012 | 2.75 | 2.75 | 2.45 | 2.45 | 6289683 | 6289683 |
| | 2013 | 1.29 | 1.29 | −28.99 | −28.99 | 6158612 | 6158612 |
| | 2014 | 1.41 | 1.41 | −31.96 | −31.96 | 6203694 | 6203694 |
| | 2015 | 1.69 | 1.69 | −33.98 | −33.98 | 6224029 | 6224029 |
| | 2016 | 2.27 | 2.27 | −35.21 | −35.21 | 6238260 | 6238260 |
| | 2017 | 2.42 | 2.42 | −36.9 | −36.9 | 6343007 | 6343007 |
| | 2018 | 2.98 | 2.98 | −37.74 | −37.74 | 6464016 | 6464016 |
| | 2019 | 4.17 | 4.17 | 12.49 | 12.49 | 6469454 | 6469454 |
| | 2020 | 2.81 | 2.81 | 39.23 | 39.23 | 6108243 | 6108243 |
| | 2021 | 2.25 | 2.25 | 1.79 | 1.79 | 6543391 | 6543391 |
| Luxembourg | 2010 | 2.28 | 2.28 | 7.56 | 7.56 | 17480.56 | 17480.56 |
| | 2011 | 2.32 | 2.32 | 6.98 | 6.98 | 17868.59 | 17868.59 |
| | 2012 | 2.25 | 2.25 | 6.66 | 6.66 | 15456.83 | 15456.83 |
| | 2013 | 2.06 | 2.06 | 7.51 | 7.51 | 16203.27 | 16203.27 |
| | 2014 | 1.91 | 1.91 | 7.91 | 7.91 | 16302.43 | 16302.43 |
| | 2015 | 1.78 | 1.78 | 8.04 | 8.04 | 18566.45 | 18566.45 |
| | 2016 | 1.68 | 1.68 | 8.08 | 8.08 | 17129.53 | 17129.53 |
| | 2017 | 1.65 | 1.65 | 7.94 | 7.94 | 18634.69 | 18634.69 |
| | 2018 | 1.72 | 1.72 | 7.41 | 7.41 | 17072.34 | 17072.34 |
| | 2019 | 1.76 | 1.76 | 7.04 | 7.04 | 16853.22 | 16853.22 |
| | 2020 | 1.41 | 1.41 | 8.59 | 8.59 | 15573.19 | 15573.19 |
| | 2021 | 1.06 | 1.06 | 10.14 | 10.14 | 19895.36 | 19895.36 |

Source: Author

**Table 16.11** Actual values and output efficiency thresholds for Romania compared to the European average and Luxembourg

| *Output type* | *Year* | *Output* | *Efficiency threshold* | *Output* | *Efficiency threshold* | *Output* | *Efficiency threshold* | *Output* | *Efficiency threshold* | *Output* | *Efficiency threshold* | *Output* | *Efficiency threshold* |
|---|---|---|---|---|---|---|---|---|---|---|---|---|---|
| *DMU* | *Year* | *SDG9CBV* | | *SDG9PCDI* | | *SDG9CHCDI* | | *SDG9PIBloc* | | *SDG9DTHM* | | *SDG9AOF* | |
| Romania | 2010 | 14 | 991.88 | 0.33 | 0.33 | 0.45 | 0.45 | 6340 | 9299.028 | 0.99 | 7.087 | 0.07 | 0.143 |
| | 2011 | 20 | 434.517 | 0.38 | 0.38 | 0.48 | 0.48 | 6650 | 12023.1 | 0.87 | 8.361 | 0.09 | 0.2 |
| | 2012 | 35 | 392.992 | 0.4 | 0.4 | 0.46 | 0.46 | 6810 | 14068.35 | 1.38 | 7.248 | 0.09 | 0.217 |
| | 2013 | 33 | 911.351 | 0.41 | 0.41 | 0.39 | 0.39 | 6860 | 15348.29 | 1.05 | 4.992 | 0.07 | 0.217 |
| | 2014 | 28 | 808.168 | 0.39 | 0.39 | 0.38 | 0.38 | 7160 | 14067.29 | 0.63 | 6.448 | 0.11 | 0.217 |
| | 2015 | 30 | 1088.974 | 0.39 | 0.39 | 0.49 | 0.49 | 7420 | 12923.81 | 0.52 | 6.197 | 0.09 | 0.214 |
| | 2016 | 31 | 1115.968 | 0.4 | 0.4 | 0.49 | 0.49 | 7680 | 12949.29 | 0.74 | 6.955 | 0.11 | 0.193 |
| | 2017 | 52 | 1332.383 | 0.4 | 0.4 | 0.51 | 0.51 | 8360 | 12653.99 | 1.6 | 5.974 | 0.11 | 0.194 |
| | 2018 | 50 | 1431.642 | 0.4 | 0.4 | 0.5 | 0.5 | 8910 | 12939.24 | 0.96 | 6.131 | 0.11 | 0.183 |
| | 2019 | 40 | 2393.636 | 0.39 | 0.39 | 0.48 | 0.48 | 9300 | 12147.05 | 0.53 | 6.599 | 0.1 | 0.162 |
| | 2020 | 55 | 2200.625 | 0.41 | 0.41 | 0.47 | 0.47 | 9000 | 13129.66 | 0.1 | 6.072 | 0.13 | 0.188 |
| | 2021 | 31 | 2676.231 | 0.42 | 0.42 | 0.47 | 0.47 | 9160 | 13746.45 | −0.33 | 5.445 | 0.15 | 0.191 |
| EU27 | 2010 | 61235 | 61235 | 1.08 | 1.08 | 1.97 | 1.97 | 24900 | 24900 | 22.56 | 22.56 | 0.1 | 0.1 |
| | 2011 | 59626 | 59626 | 1.11 | 1.11 | 2.02 | 2.02 | 25330 | 25330 | 24 | 24 | 0.11 | 0.11 |
| | 2012 | 60451 | 60451 | 1.14 | 1.14 | 2.08 | 2.08 | 25110 | 25110 | 23.51 | 23.51 | 0.11 | 0.11 |
| | 2013 | 61033 | 61033 | 1.15 | 1.15 | 2.1 | 2.1 | 25060 | 25060 | 21.54 | 21.54 | 0.59 | 0.59 |
| | 2014 | 62618 | 62618 | 1.17 | 1.17 | 2.11 | 2.11 | 25430 | 25430 | 21.19 | 21.19 | 0.58 | 0.58 |
| | 2015 | 62618 | 62618 | 1.21 | 1.21 | 2.12 | 2.12 | 25960 | 25960 | 20.75 | 20.75 | −0.55 | −0.55 |
| | 2016 | 62055 | 62055 | 1.24 | 1.24 | 2.12 | 2.12 | 26410 | 26410 | 20.65 | 20.65 | 0.37 | 0.37 |
| | 2017 | 63897 | 63897 | 1.3 | 1.3 | 2.15 | 2.15 | 27110 | 27110 | 21.57 | 21.57 | 0.42 | 0.42 |
| | 2018 | 66181 | 66181 | 1.37 | 1.37 | 2.18 | 2.18 | 27620 | 27620 | 21.36 | 21.36 | −0.4 | −0.4 |
| | 2019 | 66510 | 66510 | 1.4 | 1.4 | 2.23 | 2.23 | 28060 | 28060 | 19.04 | 19.04 | 0.4 | 0.4 |
| | 2020 | 65925 | 65925 | 1.44 | 1.44 | 2.3 | 2.3 | 26450 | 26450 | 16.72 | 16.72 | 0.38 | 0.38 |
| | 2021 | 67820 | 67820 | 1.49 | 1.49 | 2.27 | 2.27 | 26206.67 | 26206.67 | 14.4 | 14.4 | 0.16 | 0.16 |

(*continued*)

**Table 16.11** (continued)

| *Output type* | *Year* | *Output* | *Efficiency threshold* | *Output* | *Efficiency threshold* | *Output* | *Efficiency threshold* | *Output* | *Efficiency threshold* | *Output* | *Efficiency threshold* | *Output* | *Efficiency threshold* |
|---|---|---|---|---|---|---|---|---|---|---|---|---|---|
| *DMU* | *Year* | *SDG9CBV* | | *SDG9PCDI* | | *SDG9CHCDI* | | *SDG9PIBloc* | | *SDG9DTHM* | | *SDG9AOF* | |
| Luxem-bourg | 2010 | 420 | 420 | 2.17 | 2.17 | 1.42 | 1.42 | 83650 | 83650 | 28.27 | 28.27 | 1.05 | 1.05 |
| | 2011 | 393 | 393 | 2.22 | 2.22 | 1.43 | 1.43 | 82660 | 82660 | 45.82 | 45.82 | 0.97 | 0.97 |
| | 2012 | 449 | 449 | 1.93 | 1.93 | 1.21 | 1.21 | 82030 | 82030 | 27.16 | 27.16 | 1 | 1 |
| | 2013 | 429 | 429 | 1.98 | 1.98 | 1.23 | 1.23 | 82700 | 82700 | 16.1 | 16.1 | 1 | 1 |
| | 2014 | 454 | 454 | 2.01 | 2.01 | 1.22 | 1.22 | 82880 | 82880 | 26.06 | 26.06 | 1.06 | 1.06 |
| | 2015 | 425 | 425 | 1.92 | 1.92 | 1.25 | 1.25 | 82810 | 82810 | 21.37 | 21.37 | 0.95 | 0.95 |
| | 2016 | 556 | 556 | 1.95 | 1.95 | 1.27 | 1.27 | 84840 | 84840 | 24.85 | 24.85 | 1 | 1 |
| | 2017 | 533 | 533 | 1.94 | 1.94 | 1.24 | 1.24 | 84090 | 84090 | 16.13 | 16.13 | 1 | 1 |
| | 2018 | 431 | 431 | 1.85 | 1.85 | 1.17 | 1.17 | 83510 | 83510 | 24.18 | 24.18 | 0.98 | 0.98 |
| | 2019 | 415 | 415 | 1.9 | 1.9 | 1.18 | 1.18 | 84280 | 84280 | 23.66 | 23.66 | 1.03 | 1.03 |
| | 2020 | 402 | 402 | 1.86 | 1.86 | 1.09 | 1.09 | 82130 | 82130 | 23.14 | 23.14 | 1.03 | 1.03 |
| | 2021 | 433 | 433 | 1.78 | 1.78 | 1.04 | 1.04 | 81926.67 | 81926.67 | 22.62 | 22.62 | 0.99 | 0.99 |

Source: Author

technologies is important for reducing the negative environmental impact of industrial activities. Official Development Assistance should also be directed towards projects that promote innovation and sustainability in industries, thereby contributing to increased efficiency and reduced carbon emissions. It is important that policymakers recognize the importance of these issues and act accordingly to ensure a sustainable future for global industry. Investment in research and development of green technologies must be a priority to accelerate the transition to a more sustainable industrial environment.

## Conclusions

A comparative analysis of Romania's industrial efficiency in relation to EU Member States, carried out using the DEA method, highlights significant structural gaps that limit the performance of the national industrial sector. The results confirm the hypotheses formulated, demonstrating that Romania consistently ranks among the least efficient industrial countries, alongside other economies with low levels of innovation and productivity, while Luxembourg, Germany, Sweden, Malta, the Netherlands and Estonia are benchmarks of efficiency throughout the period analysed.

Domestically, major vulnerabilities are linked to high environmental taxes and road transport taxes, as well as excessive consumption of raw materials, which indicates a structural dependence on resource-intensive technologies and industrial processes. On the output side, critical barriers include insufficient research and development personnel, inadequate budget allocations for R&D, a low number of patents, and a substantial gap in GDP per capita relative to the efficiency threshold.

A comparison with the Luxembourg model points to the need for an integrated strategy to reduce the tax burden on logistics, optimize resource consumption through technological innovation and industrial reengineering, and stimulate the development and diffusion of green technologies. In addition, targeting Official Development Assistance towards sustainable industrial projects and sustained investment in low-carbon technologies are essential for the transition to a competitive and resilient model.

Thus, to converge towards EU industrial efficiency standards, Romania needs to adopt proactive industrial policies based on stimulating innovation, increasing R&D capacity, and aligning productive infrastructure with the requirements of the green transition, while ensuring long-term economic and environmental sustainability.

## References


Afshan, S., Razi, U., Leong, K. Y., Lelchumanan, B., & Cheong, C. W. H. (2023). Navigating the interconnected risks in currency valuation: unveiling the role of climate policy uncertainty. *Environmental Science and Pollution Research, 30*(58), 122580–122600. https://doi.org/10.1007/s11356-023-30687-2

Agrawal, R., Agrawal, S., Samadhiya, A., Kumar, A., Luthra, S., & Jain, V. (2024). Adoption of green finance and green innovation for achieving circularity: An exploratory review and future directions. *Geoscience Frontiers, 15*(4), 101669. https://doi.org/10.1016/j.gsf.2023.101669

Altuzarra Artola, A. (2024). Does eco-innovation lead to company growth? *Innovation & Management Review, 21*(4), 230–243. https://doi.org/10.1108/INMR-04-2023-0052

Alves, C. G. M. d. F., & Meza, L. A. (2023). A review of network DEA models based on slacks-based measure: Evolution of literature, applications, and further research direction. *International Transactions in Operational Research, 30*(6), 2729–2760. https://doi.org/10.1111/itor.13284

Aprile, M. C. (2025). Innovation and environment: Definition and adoption of eco-innovation. In L. Aldieri (Ed.), *Technological evolution: How innovations are changing our future* (pp. 1–26). Springer Nature Switzerland. https://doi.org/10.1007/978-3-031-85814-7_1

Aristovnik, A., Yang, G., Song, Y., & Ravšelj, D. (2023). Industrial performance of the top R&D enterprises in world-leading economies: A metafrontier approach. *Socio-Economic Planning Sciences, 89*, 101698. https://doi.org/10.1016/j.seps.2023.101698

Bärnthaler, R., Mang, S., & Hickel, J. (2025). Toward a post-growth industrial policy for Europe: Navigating emerging tensions and long-term goals. *Globalizations*, 1–25. https://doi.org/10.1080/14747731.2025.2501821

Bathelt, H., & Storper, M. (2023). Related variety and regional development: A critique. *Economic Geography, 99*(5), 441–470. https://doi.org/10.1080/00130095.2023.2235050

Behera, D. K., Rahut, D. B., Sahoo, B., & Mohanty, R. K. (2025). Air pollution and environmental tax: Exploring the dynamics in developed nations. *Environmental and Sustainability Indicators, 27*, 100805. https://doi.org/10.1016/j.indic.2025.100805

Bianchini, S., Damioli, G., & Ghisetti, C. (2023). The environmental effects of the "twin" green and digital transition in European regions. *Environmental and Resource Economics, 84*(4), 877–918. https://doi.org/10.1007/s10640-022-00741-7

Bigerna, S., D'Errico, M. C., & Polinori, P. (2022). Sustainable power generation in Europe: A panel data analysis of the effects of market and environmental regulations. *Environmental and Resource Economics, 83*(2), 445–479. https://doi.org/10.1007/s10640-021-00631-4

Bircan, T., & Salah, A. A. (2024). *Emerging big data sources for studying migration* (pp. 83–103). Edward Elgar Publishing. https://doi.org/10.4337/9781800378032.00015

Bloch, C., Eklund, C., & Piekkola, H. (2023). Innovative competences, the financial crisis and firm-level productivity in Denmark and Finland. *Economics of Innovation and New Technology, 32*(2), 198–212. https://doi.org/10.1080/10438599.2021.1895496

Boix-Domènech, R., Sforzi, F., Galletto, V., & Capone, F. (2024). Born to innovate, not to produce: Three decades of compared change, evolution and innovation in the dynamic Marshallian Industrial Districts of Spain and Italy. *European Planning Studies*, 1–18. https://doi.org/10.1080/09654313.2025.2525492

Bruno, R. L., Douarin, E., Korosteleva, J., & Radosevic, S. (2022). The two disjointed faces of R&D and the productivity gap in Europe. *JCMS: Journal of Common Market Studies, 60*(3), 580–603. https://doi.org/10.1111/jcms.13260

Burciu, A., Bostan, I., Kicsi, R., Buta, S., Zoltan, R., & Condratov, I. (2025). Towards a sustainable approach of energy policy in the EU: Empirical evidence for Romania vs. the Visegrad Group based on the relationship among disruptive technology, knowledge and final energy consumption. *Frontiers in Energy Research, 13*. https://doi.org/10.3389/fenrg.2025.1515788

Campoli, J. S., Alves Junior, P. N., Kodama, T. K., Nagano, M. S., & Burnquist, H. L. (2024). G20 countries' progress on the 7th SDG under circular economy DEA model. *Environmental Science & Policy, 160*, 103839. https://doi.org/10.1016/j.envsci.2024.103839

Charles, V., & Emrouznejad, A. (2024). DEA-based index systems for addressing the United Nations' SDGs. *Environmental Science & Policy, 162*, 103950. https://doi.org/10.1016/j.envsci.2024.103950

Charnes, A., Cooper, W. W., & Rhodes, E. (1978). Measuring the efficiency of decision making units. *European Journal of Operational Research, 2*(6), 429–444. https://doi.org/10.1016/0377-2217(78)90138-8

Chen, X., Zhou, P., & Hu, D. (2023). Influences of the ongoing digital transformation of the Chinese Economy on innovation of sustainable green technologies. *Science of the Total Environment, 875*, 162708. https://doi.org/10.1016/j.scitotenv.2023.162708

D'Orazio, P. (2025). Addressing climate risks through fiscal policy in emerging and developing economies: What do we know and what lies ahead? *Energy Research & Social Science, 119*, 103852. https://doi.org/10.1016/j.erss.2024.103852

Ding, Y., Bi, C., & Sun, P. (2025). Low carbon constraints, innovation driven and carbon neutral technological innovation: Empirical evidence based on multiple policy combinations. *Scientific Reports, 15*(1), 22912. https://doi.org/10.1038/s41598-025-06207-2

Diodato, D., Huergo, E., Moncada-Paternò-Castello, P., Rentocchini, F., & Timmermans, B. (2023). Introduction to the special issue on "the twin (digital and green) transition: Handling the economic and social challenges". *Industry and Innovation, 30*(7), 755–765. https://doi.org/10.1080/13662716.2023.2254272

Doran, M. D., Poenaru, M. M., Zaharia, A. L., Vatavu, S., & Lobont, O. R. (2023). Fiscal policy, growth, financial development and renewable energy in Romania: An autoregressive distributed lag model with evidence for growth hypothesis. *Energies, 16*(1). https://doi.org/10.3390/en16010070. WE - Science Citation Index Expanded (SCI-EXPANDED).

Drago, C., & Gatto, A. (2022). Policy, regulation effectiveness, and sustainability in the energy sector: A worldwide interval-based composite indicator. *Energy Policy, 167*, 112889. https://doi.org/10.1016/j.enpol.2022.112889

Edmondson, D., Flachsland, C., aus dem Moore, N., Koch, N., Koller, F., Gruhl, H., & Brehm, J. (2025). Anticipatory climate policy mix pathways: A framework for ex-ante construction and assessment applied to the road transport sector. *Climate Policy, 25*(3), 438–467. https://doi.org/10.1080/14693062.2024.2397440

European Commission. (2022). *The 2030 agenda for sustainable development and the SDGs.* https://ec.europa.eu/environment/sustainable-development/SDGs/index_en.htm

European Commission. (2023a). *2023 country report Romania.* https://doi.org/10.2765/34357

European Commission. (2023b). *A European green deal.* https://commission.europa.eu/strategy-and-policy/priorities-2019-2024/european-green-deal_en

European Commission. (2023c). *Report on the state of the digital decade 2023.* https://eur-lex.europa.eu/legal-content/EN/TXT/HTML/?uri=CELEX:52023DC0570

European Commission. (2024). *2024 country report – Romania.* https://economy-finance.ec.europa.eu/document/download/dcac26a0-120e-4233-88b6-8c7b0d919257_en?filename=SWD_2024_623_1_EN_Romania.pdf

European Commission. (2025). *European innovation scoreboard 2025 – Exploratory study on the linkages between innovation and resilience.* Publications Office of the European Union. https://doi.org/10.2777/0663803

European Enviromental Agency. (2023). *The role of (environmental) taxation in supporting sustainability transitions.* https://www.eea.europa.eu/publications/the-role-of-environmental-taxation

European Environment Agency. (2023). *Investments in the sustainability transition: Leveraging green industrial policy against emerging constraints.* https://www.eea.europa.eu/publications/investments-into-the-sustainability-transition

European Investment Bank. (2025a). *Growth and competitiveness in Central, Eastern and South-Eastern Europe: The role of innovation.* https://www.eib.org/attachments/lucalli/20240356_economics_working_paper_2025_01_en.pdf

European Investment Bank. (2025b). *Innovation, integration and simplification in Europe.* https://www.eib.org/en/publications/20240354-investment-report-2024

Eurostat. (2024). *R&D expenditure.* https://ec.europa.eu/eurostat/statistics-explained/index.php?title=R%26D_expenditure&oldid=650859

Eurostat. (2025a). *Gross domestic expenditure on research and development (R&D).* https://ec.europa.eu/eurostat/databrowser/view/tipsst10/default/table?lang=en

Eurostat. (2025b). *Patent applications to the European Patent Office by applicants' / inventors' country of residence.* https://ec.europa.eu/eurostat/databrowser/view/sdg_09_40/default/table?lang=en&category=sdg.sdg_09

Eurostat. (2025c). *R&D personnel by sector.* https://ec.europa.eu/eurostat/databrowser/view/sdg_09_30/default/table?lang=en&category=sdg.sdg_09

Eurostat. (2025d). *Raw material consumption (RMC).* https://ec.europa.eu/eurostat/databrowser/view/sdg_12_21/default/table?lang=en

Eurostat. (2025e). *Real GDP per capita.* https://ec.europa.eu/eurostat/databrowser/view/sdg_08_10/default/table

Fedajev, A., Mitić, P., Kojić, M., & Radulescu, M. (2023). Driving industrial and economic growth in Central and Eastern Europe: The role of electricity infrastructure and renewable energy. *Utilities Policy, 85*, 101683. https://doi.org/10.1016/j.jup.2023.101683

Flachenecker, F., Kornejew, M., & Janiri, M. L. (2022). The effects of publicly supported environmental innovations on firm growth in the European Union. *Journal of Cleaner Production, 372*, 133429. https://doi.org/10.1016/j.jclepro.2022.133429

Georgescu, P.-L., Barbuta-Misu, N., Zlati, M. L., Fortea, C., & Antohi, V. M. (2025). Quantifying the performance of European agriculture through the new European sustainability model. *Agriculture, 15*(2). https://doi.org/10.3390/agriculture15020210

Georgescu, L. P., Fortea, C., Antohi, V. M., Balsalobre-Lorente, D., Zlati, M. L., & Barbuta-Misu, N. (2025). Economic, technological and environmental drivers of the circular economy in the European Union: A panel data analysis. *Environmental Sciences Europe, 37*(1), 76. https://doi.org/10.1186/s12302-025-01119-4

Gogu, E., Mihai, F., & Aleca, O. E. (2025). The economic impact and the decoupling of economic growth from renewable energy consumption within the European Union in the context of social well-being. *Eastern European Economics*, 1–37. https://doi.org/10.1080/00128775.2025.2533210

Grafström, J., & Alm, C. (2025). Diverging or converging technology capabilities in the European Union? *The Journal of Technology Transfer, 50*(2), 728–751. https://doi.org/10.1007/s10961-024-10070-0

Hojnik, J., Ruzzier, M., Konečnik Ruzzier, M., Sučić, B., Soltwisch, B., & Rus, M. (2024). Review of EU projects with a focus on environmental quality: Innovation, eco-innovation, and circular-economy elements. *International Journal of Innovation Studies, 8*(1), 1–12. https://doi.org/10.1016/j.ijis.2023.10.001

Huang, T., Li, S., Liu, F., & Diao, H. (2024). A slacks-based measure model for computing game cross-efficiency. *System, 12*(3). https://doi.org/10.3390/systems12030078

Ibinceanu, C., Cristache, N., Dobrea, R. C., & Florescu, M. (2021). Regional development in Romania: Empirical evidence regarding the factors for measuring a prosperous and sustainable economy. *Sustainability, 13*(7). https://doi.org/10.3390/su13073942

Javaid, M., Haleem, A., Singh, R. P., & Sinha, A. K. (2024). Digital economy to improve the culture of industry 4.0: A study on features, implementation and challenges. *Green Technologies and Sustainability, 2*(2), 100083. https://doi.org/10.1016/j.grets.2024.100083

Joița, D., Panait, M., Dobrotă, C. E., Diniță, A., Neacșa, A., & Naghi, L. E. (2023). The European dilemma—Energy security or green transition. *Energies, 16*(9). https://doi.org/10.3390/en16093849

Juhász, R., Lane, N., & Rodrik, D. (2024). The new economics of industrial policy. Annual review of economics, *16*, 213–242. https://doi.org/10.1146/annurev-economics-081023-024638

Kafeel, K., Zhou, J., Phetkhammai, M., Heyan, L., & Khan, S. (2024). Green innovation and environmental quality in OECD countries: The mediating role of renewable energy and carbon taxes. *Environmental Science and Pollution Research, 31*(2), 2214–2227. https://doi.org/10.1007/s11356-023-31111-5

Khalique, A., Wang, Y., & Ahmed, K. (2025). Europe's environmental dichotomy: The impact of regulations, climate investments, and renewable energy on carbon mitigation in the EU-22. *Energy Policy, 198*, 114498. https://doi.org/10.1016/j.enpol.2025.114498

Khan, M. I., Yasmeen, T., Khan, M., Hadi, N. U., Asif, M., Farooq, M., & Al-Ghamdi, S. G. (2025). Integrating industry 4.0 for enhanced sustainability: Pathways and prospects. *Sustainable Production and Consumption, 54*, 149–189. https://doi.org/10.1016/j.spc.2024.12.012

Kijek, T., Kijek, A., & Matras-Bolibok, A. (2022). Club convergence in R&D expenditure across European regions. *Sustainability, 14*(2). https://doi.org/10.3390/su14020832

Knapp, D., Bayrle-Kelso, N., Nigg-Stock, A., & Brecht, L. (2025). The impact of governmental regulations and environmental activities on innovation efficiency. *Sustainability, 17*(2). https://doi.org/10.3390/su17020467

Kovacs, O., & Domonkos, E. (2024). Deindustrialisation and reindustrialisation patterns in V4 countries – Industry 4.0 as a way forward? *Post-Communist Economies, 36*(4), 432–463. https://doi.org/10.1080/14631377.2024.2323834

László, T. (2025). Economic convergence of Central and Eastern European countries in the European Union. *Political Research Exchange, 7*(1), 2507633. https://doi.org/10.1080/2474736X.2025.2507633

Lu, Z., Gou, D., Yang, L., Wu, Z., & Feng, H. (2025). The impact of environmental tax reform on industrial green development: Evidence from China. *Frontiers in Environmental Science, 13.* https://doi.org/10.3389/fenvs.2025.1593549

Manta, L. F., Manta, A. G., & Gherțescu, C. (2025). Decoding digital synergies: How mechatronic systems and artificial intelligence shape banking performance through quantile-driven method of moments. *Applied Sciences, 15*(10). https://doi.org/10.3390/app15105282

Mergoni, A., Emrouznejad, A., & De Witte, K. (2025). Fifty years of data envelopment analysis. *European Journal of Operational Research, 326*(3), 389–412. https://doi.org/10.1016/j.ejor.2024.12.049

Mikropoulos, E., Roelfsema, M., Chen, H.-H., Staffell, I., Oreggioni, G., Hdidouan, D., Thellufsen, J. Z., Chang, M. A., Fragkos, P., Giannousakis, A., Chatterjee, S., Ürge-Vorsatz, D., Pfenninger, S., Pickering, B., Victoria, M., Brown, T., & van Vuuren, D. P. (2025). Examining pathways for a climate neutral Europe by 2050; a model comparison analysis including integrated assessment models and energy system models. *Energy, 319*, 134809. https://doi.org/10.1016/j.energy.2025.134809

Moncada-Paternò-Castello, P. (2022). Top R&D investors, structural change and the R&D growth performance of young and old firms. *Eurasian Business Review, 12*(1), 1–33. https://doi.org/10.1007/s40821-022-00206-3

Neil Makaroff. (2023). *Turning the European green deal into reality.* https://doi.org/10.56043/reveco-2024-0023

Nichifor, B., Zait, L., & Turcu, O. (2025). Renewable investments, environmental spending, and emissions in Eastern Europe: A spatial-economic analysis of management and policy decisions efficiency. *Sustainability, 17*(7). https://doi.org/10.3390/su17073010

Nicolescu, A.-C., Lobonţ, O.-R., Vătavu, S., & Bozga, E. (2024). Entrepreneurship and digitalisation in EU: Twinning insights through a panel threshold regression. *Journal of Business Economics and Management, 25*(2), 315–336. https://doi.org/10.3846/jbem.2024.21206

Niţă, D., Stoicuţa, N., Niţescu, A., Isac, C., & Dobre-Baron, O. (2025). The impact of the transition to a green economy on Romania's economic growth. *Energy, Sustainability and Society, 15*(1), 19. https://doi.org/10.1186/s13705-025-00520-4

Noja, G. G., Cristea, M., Panait, M., Trif, S. M., & Ponea, C. Ş. (2022). The impact of energy innovations and environmental performance on the sustainable development of the EU countries in a globalized digital economy. *Frontiers in Environmental Science, 10.* https://doi.org/10.3389/fenvs.2022.934404

OECD. (2022). *OECD Journal on Budgeting, 2022*(3). https://doi.org/10.1787/dedebeca-en

OECD. (2024a). *OECD economic surveys: Romania 2024.* https://www.oecd.org/content/dam/oecd/en/publications/reports/2024/03/oecd-economic-surveys-romania-2024_12c283a2/106b32c4-en.pdf

OECD. (2024b). *OECD economic surveys: Romania 2024.* https://doi.org/10.1787/106b32c4-en

OECD. (2025a). *OECD data explorer.*

OECD. (2025b). *OECD economic surveys: European Union and Euro area 2025.* https://doi.org/10.1787/5ec8dcc2-en

OECD. (2025c). *Sustainable development goal 09 – Industry, innovation, and infrastructure.* https://data-explorer.oecd.org/vis?tm=SustainableDevelopmentGoal09&pg=0&snb=1&hc[SDG target]=&hc[SDGseries]=&vw=tb&df[ds]=dsDisseminateFinalDMZ&df[id]=DSD_SDG%40DF_SDG_G_9&df[ag]=OECD.WISE.RSB&df[vs]=1.0&dq=....._T._T._T._T._T.&lom=LASTNPERIODS&lo=5&to[TIME_PERIOD]=false

Owusu Atuahene, S. O., Owusu, G. M. Y., & Agyenim-Boateng, C. (2025). The effect of environmental taxes on sustainable energy transition prospects. *Sustainability Accounting, Management and Policy Journal.* https://doi.org/10.1108/SAMPJ-12-2024-1453

Özçelik, E., & Özmen, E. (2023). Premature deindustrialisation: The international evidence. *Cambridge Journal of Economics, 47*(4), 725–746. https://doi.org/10.1093/cje/bead023

Panton, A. J. (2023). Making Romania fit and resilient for the net-zero transition. *Selected Issues Papers, 2023*(063), A001. https://doi.org/10.5089/9798400263736.018.A001

Prigoreanu, I., Radu, G., Grigore-Sava, A., Costuleanu, C. L., Ungureanu, G., & Ignat, G. (2025). Assessing the economic sustainability of the EU and Romanian farming sectors. *Sustainability, 17*(10). https://doi.org/10.3390/su17104440

Schmitz, L., Seidl, T., & Wuttke, T. (2025). The costs of conditionality. IPCEIs and the constrained politics of EU industrial policy. *Competition and Change*, 10245294251320676. https://doi.org/10.1177/10245294251320675

Schneider, E. (2023). Germany's industrial strategy 2030, EU competition policy and the crisis of new constitutionalism. (Geo-)political economy of a contested paradigm shift. *New Political Economy, 28*(2), 241–258. https://doi.org/10.1080/13563467.2022.2091535

Simeonovski, K., Kaftandzieva, T., & Brock, G. (2021). Energy efficiency management across EU countries: A DEA approach. *Energies, 14*, 2619. https://doi.org/10.3390/en14092619

Sotiriou, A., Petrakos, G., & Alexiou, S. (2025). The drivers of regional discontent in the EU. *Global Challenges & Regional Science, 1*, 100002. https://doi.org/10.1016/j.gcrs.2024.100002

Talenti, R. (2025). Climate neutrality through green growth? Addressing possible tensions between the European green deal and the precautionary principle. *International Environmental Agreements: Politics, Law and Economics*. https://doi.org/10.1007/s10784-025-09675-z

Teixeira, J. E., & Tavares-Lehmann, A. T. C. P. (2022). Industry 4.0 in the European Union: Policies and national strategies. *Technological Forecasting and Social Change, 180*, 121664. https://doi.org/10.1016/j.techfore.2022.121664

Tone, K., & Tsutsui, M. (2014). Dynamic DEA with network structure: A slacks-based measure approach. *Omega, 42*(1), 124–131. https://doi.org/10.1016/j.omega.2013.04.002

Vărzaru, A. A., & Bocean, C. G. (2024). Digital transformation and innovation: The influence of digital technologies on turnover from innovation activities and types of innovation. *System, 12*(9). https://doi.org/10.3390/systems12090359

Vasconcelos-Garcia, M., & Carrilho-Nunes, I. (2024). Internationalisation and digitalisation as drivers for eco-innovation in the European Union. *Structural Change and Economic Dynamics, 70*, 245–256. https://doi.org/10.1016/j.strueco.2024.02.010

Veugelers, R., Tagliapietra, S., & Trasi, C. (2024). Green industrial policy in Europe: Past, present, and prospects. *Journal of Industry, Competition and Trade, 24*(1), 4. https://doi.org/10.1007/s10842-024-00418-5

Wang, Y., Umair, M., Oskenbayev, Y., & Saparova, A. (2024). Digital government initiatives for sustainable innovations, digitalization, and emission reduction policies to balance conservation impact. *Natural Resources Forum, n/a*(n/a). https://doi.org/10.1111/1477-8947.12570

Wenjuan, S., & Zhao, K. (2023). Balancing fiscal expenditure competition and long-term innovation investment: Exploring trade-offs and policy implications for local governments. *PLoS One, 18*(11), e0293158. https://doi.org/10.1371/journal.pone.0293158

Wigger, A. (2023). The new EU industrial policy and deepening structural asymmetries: Smart specialisation not so smart. *JCMS: Journal of Common Market Studies, 61*(1), 20–37. https://doi.org/10.1111/jcms.13366

Yunxia, X., & Yuqing, N. (2025). The technological advancement environmental regulations and their impact on energy efficiency and CO2 emissions. *Scientific Reports, 15*(1), 2781. https://doi.org/10.1038/s41598-025-86581-z

Zakari, A., Khan, I., Tan, D., Alvarado, R., & Dagar, V. (2022). Energy efficiency and sustainable development goals (SDGs). *Energy, 239*, 122365. https://doi.org/10.1016/j.energy.2021.122365

Żółtaszek, A., & Olejnik, A. (2024). Regional effectiveness of innovation: leaders and followers of the EU NUTS 0 and NUTS 2 regions. *Innovation: The European Journal of Social Science Research, 37*(2), 399–420. https://doi.org/10.1080/13511610.2020.1870440

CHAPTER 17

# Proposed Sustainable Development Solutions for Romania from the Perspective of Sustainable Development Goal 9

The Romanian economy's strategies for Sustainable Development Goal 9 are based on the dual transition towards a green and digital economy. The national plans aim at implementing the 5G Strategy for Romania which will result in sustainable development, competitiveness, innovation and improved industrial policies (European Commission, 2025a). Romania has adopted for the period 2022–2027 the National Strategy for Research and Innovation (Ministry of Investments and European Projects, 2022) which emphasizes fundamental applied research and improved public–private collaboration. The main lines of action in implementing the national strategy for research, innovation and smart specialization consist in developing the research, development and innovation system, supporting innovation ecosystems associated with smart specializations, mobilizing towards innovation, and increasing European and international collaboration.

We have analysed the main indicators for Sustainable Development Goal 9, which at the Romanian level showed the stationarity of gross domestic expenditure for R&D as a percentage of GDP, the favourable dynamics of the number of staff employed in R&D (increasing by 9% in the period 2010–2021), the favourable dynamics of patent applications filed at the European Patent Office (with a decrease during the pandemic period), and the favourable dynamics of the indicator on high-speed



C. Fortea, *Sustainable Economic Development and the European Green Deal*, https://doi.org/10.1007/978-3-032-10326-0_17

Internet coverage, which increased by more than 37% in the period analysed.

Modelled European industrial sustainability based on SDG9 indicators and evaluated 9 econometric linear regression models.

The **SDG9.1 model** of European industrial sustainability in terms of the SDG9GDPloc (gross domestic product per capita) indicator is characterized by the positive influence of the percentage of personnel engaged in R&D, suggesting that investment in human capital, especially R&D, is strongly correlated with GDP per capita. Luxembourg, Ireland, Denmark and Sweden top the European rankings. Bulgaria, Romania, Hungary, Latvia, Croatia and Poland rank last in terms of GDP per capita.

Public policies on European industrial sustainability from a gross domestic product (GDP) per capita perspective contain a range of strategies and initiatives aimed at ensuring that Europe's economic development is in line with the principles of environmental, social and economic sustainability (Bădîrcea et al., 2025; García-Velasco Garzás & Ruiz-Fuensanta, 2025). Understanding and promoting sustainable industry is important to ensure balanced economic growth and access to resources for future generations. Public policies must take into account energy and climate change, the promotion of innovation research and the circular economy, as well as social inclusion and employment (OECD, 2025b; Paleari, 2024; Rodríguez-Antón et al., 2022). The EU has implemented policies such as the European Green Pact (European Commission, 2023a) and the Paris Agreement (United Nations, 2023) to ensure energy security and the development of green industry. These policies encourage innovation and investment in sustainable technologies such as renewable energy and energy efficiency. The EU's Framework Program for Research and Innovation (Horizon Europe) (European Commission, 2024b) supports the development of innovative technologies and solutions that promote industrial sustainability by providing funding for research projects aimed at improving industrial processes, reducing waste and increasing resource efficiency. The circular economy policies and directives encourage recycling, reuse and regeneration of materials and resources in the economy to reduce waste and promote more efficient use of natural resources, thus contributing to increased industrial sustainability (European Commission, 2023c; Nowak-Marchewka et al., 2025; Pinyol Alberich et al., 2023).

Social inclusion and employment are important directions that ensure the transition to a sustainable industry without affecting jobs or communities (Crespy & Munta, 2023; OECD, 2023; Rinaldi et al., 2022).

These policies and initiatives are important to ensure that European industry moves forward in a sustainable way, balancing economic growth with environmental protection and the social well-being of communities.

The **SDG9.2 model** of European industrial sustainability from the perspective of the SDG9CHCDI indicator (gross domestic expenditure on R&D) is positively influenced by the percentage of R&D personnel, suggesting that the availability of R&D workforce is closely linked to increased R&D expenditure. Sweden, Austria, Denmark and Finland rank first in Europe in terms of gross domestic expenditure on R&D. Romania, Cyprus, Latvia, Malta, Bulgaria, Slovakia and Croatia rank at the bottom.

Public policy at European level on gross domestic expenditure on research and development is essential to boost innovation and competitiveness within the EU (Beltran et al., 2025; Eurostat, 2024; Hajighasemi et al., 2022). The EU and the Member States have adopted several policies and initiatives to increase investment in research and development, such as: the Framework Program for Research and Innovation (European Commission, 2024b), the European Regional Development Fund (ERDF) (European Commission, 2024a) and the European Research Area Strategy (European Commission, 2025c). The Framework Program for Research and Innovation provides funding for research and development projects in various fields, including information and communication technologies, health, energy and environment. The European Regional Development Fund (ERDF) provides funding for infrastructure and economic development projects, including research and innovation projects, in European regions by supporting investment in research infrastructure and innovation centres, thus contributing to increased spending on research and development. The European Research Area Strategy is an EU initiative aimed at integrating and coordinating research and innovation efforts across Europe. Its aim is to improve the efficiency and impact of investment in research and development by promoting transnational collaboration and the exchange of knowledge and resources. The adoption and implementation of new policies to stimulate gross R&D spending, such as increasing public funding for R&D, stimulating private investment in R&D and improving research and innovation infrastructure, can significantly contribute to the development of the R&D sector in the European area, stimulating innovation and strengthening the global competitiveness of the EU (Belanová et al., 2025; Benoit et al., 2025; Iacob et al., 2023).

The **SDG9.3 model** of European industrial sustainability from the perspective of the SDG9PCDI indicator (percentage of personnel engaged in R&D) is characterized by the significant influence of gross domestic expenditure on R&D. Denmark, Finland, Luxembourg and Sweden rank first in Europe in terms of R&D personnel. At the bottom are Cyprus, Romania, Latvia and Croatia.

Public policy at European level on the percentage of staff engaged in research and development is aimed at stimulating growth and innovation throughout the EU and is common with that for SDG9.2 (Eurostat, 2023; Hu & Jernej, 2025). In addition, we consider that promoting the mobility of researchers and academic exchanges and developing public–private partnerships for research and innovation would be useful for the development of the indicator under analysis. The EU has already supported programmes that facilitate the mobility of researchers and academic exchanges between EU Member States and which have proved to be effective (such as Erasmus) (European Commission, 2025b; Kosztyán et al., 2023). We believe that in the future there will be a need to promote new programmes aimed at improving the transfer of knowledge and experience in the field of research and development. These policies and initiatives will help to stimulate an increase in the percentage of people engaged in research and development across the EU, thereby supporting innovation and long-term competitiveness.

The **SDG9.4 model** of European industrial sustainability from the perspective of the SDG9CBV indicator (number of patent applications filed at the European Patent Office) is significantly influenced by per capita gross domestic product, indicating that a stronger economy per capita is associated with higher patenting activity. Germany, France and the Netherlands rank first in Europe in terms of the number of patent applications filed at the European Patent Office. Croatia, Latvia, Lithuania, Bulgaria, Romania, Estonia and Slovakia, are at the opposite end of the scale.

European public policy on the number of patent applications filed at the European Patent Office may vary depending on a number of factors, including the strategic objectives of the EU in the field of innovation and research (Angori et al., 2024; Orlando et al., 2025). At European level, we believe that promoting innovation and research is a driver of economic and social growth. To this end, policies must be adopted to encourage companies and research institutions to file patent applications to protect their innovations and inventions. The EU must become more actively involved in funding programmes and initiatives that facilitate research and development activities. These programmes can include research grants, funding for start-ups and SMEs, as well as technical assistance and advisory programmes for innovators. European public policies should encourage collaboration between research organizations, universities and companies from different countries, as well as technology and knowledge transfer between the public and private sectors. Harmonization of intellectual property legislation is important to achieve this. The EU has set out to harmonize intellectual property legislation between Member States in order to facilitate the process of filing and protecting patents throughout the EU (Lamping et al., 2023; Ullrich, 2023). However, more needs to be done to finalize the legislative framework conducive to patenting. We appreciate that the proposed public policies can stimulate innovation and contribute to increased competitiveness and value creation in the European economy.

The **SDG9.5 model** of European industrial sustainability from the perspective of the SDG9CMPR indicator (consumption of raw materials) is characterized by the significant inverse influence of gross domestic product. Germany, France and Italy rank first in Europe in terms of raw material consumption. Malta, Luxembourg, Cyprus, Latvia Slovenia, Estonia and Lithuania rank last.

European public policy on raw material consumption is geared towards promoting more efficient and sustainable use of natural resources and reducing negative environmental impacts (Distefano et al., 2024; Firoiu et al., 2025). Appropriate public policies in this area cover: the circular economy, the transition to the green economy and the promotion of responsible resource consumption. The EU promotes the transition to a circular economy, where resources are used efficiently, recycled and reused continuously. Public policies to this end aim to stimulate the recycling of materials and products, reduce waste, and promote sustainable product design (Burinskienė et al., 2025; Dragomir & Dumitru, 2024). European public policies should encourage measures to increase resource efficiency in different economic sectors, including through environmental performance standards, eco-design measures and supply chain management tools. Green technology projects and the development of the renewable energy sector contribute to achieving sustainability on the basis of reduced resource consumption (Caglar & Yavuz, 2023; Oyebanji & Kirikkaleli,

2023). In addition, sustainable mobility and smart energy infrastructure can contribute to improving industrial sustainability metrics by reducing raw material dependency and promoting more sustainable consumption patterns (Al-lami et al., 2025; Munonye, 2025). The EU has adopted a strategy for critical raw materials, which aims to diversify and secure the supply of key raw materials for the European economy, such as rare metals, minerals and other strategic resources (Baldassarre & Carrara, 2025; Hool et al., 2024). It includes incentives for the responsible exploration and exploitation of these resources, as well as support for related research and innovation.

The proposed EU public policies will help protect the environment and ensure the sustainable use of natural resources for future generations.

The **SDG9.6 model** of European industrial sustainability from the perspective of the SDG9DTHM indicator (development of environmental technologies) is characterized by the direct influence of R&D expenditure, showing that R&D investments are important for innovation in environmental technologies. Denmark, Germany, Austria and Sweden rank first at the European level in the development of environmental technologies. Romania, Bulgaria, Croatia, Cyprus, Poland and Greece are at the opposite end of the scale.

European public policy on environmental technology development is geared towards promoting innovation and sustainable technological solutions to protect the environment and combat climate change (Chivot, 2023; Cifuentes-Faura, 2022; Erdoğdu et al., 2025). The policies on the European Green Deal, the Strategic Innovation Fund and Horizon Europe are recognized in this respect. The European Green Pact is the EU's key strategy for combating climate change and transforming Europe into a low-carbon economy. It includes ambitious targets such as reducing greenhouse gas emissions, promoting renewable energy and improving energy efficiency, all underpinned by significant investment in research and innovation to develop and deploy green technologies. Horizon Europe is the EU's framework programme for research and innovation, which supports research projects in a wide range of areas, including environmental technologies. It provides funding for projects aimed at the development and deployment of sustainable technologies, as well as for basic research in the field of environmental protection and climate change. The Strategic Innovation Fund is an EU initiative to stimulate investment in innovation, including environmental technologies. It provides funding for research and development projects that have the potential to bring about significant changes in terms of sustainability and environmental protection.

We believe that these European public policies are important for stimulating innovation and the development of sustainable technologies, thus contributing to protecting the environment and combating climate change.

The **SDG9.7 model** of European industrial sustainability from the perspective of the SDG9TAXM indicator (environmental taxes as a percentage of GDP) is significantly influenced by R&D expenditure, showing that an increase in R&D expenditure is associated with a higher proportion of environmental taxes in GDP. At the European level, the top performers are Slovenia, Denmark, Croatia and Greece. At the bottom are Luxembourg, Spain, Germany, Ireland, Lithuania, Romania and Slovakia.

European policy on environmental taxes is designed to promote the sustainable use of resources and to internalize the external costs of activities that affect the environment (Dogan et al., 2023; European Commission, 2025d; Kalaš et al., 2025). To this end, the Energy Taxation Directive (European Commission, 2021), which sets requirements for the taxation of energy products and electricity in the EU, has already been implemented at European level with the aim of promoting energy efficiency and reducing greenhouse gas emissions. At the same time, the Emissions Trading System (European Commission, 2023b) is the largest greenhouse gas emissions trading scheme in the world and operates in all EU Member States as well as other countries. It imposes limits on greenhouse gas emissions for the industrial and energy sectors and allows companies to buy and sell emission permits, putting a price on pollution and stimulating investment in clean technologies. The EU Energy Taxation Directive (European Commission, 2021) provides guidance for Member States on the introduction of environmental excise duties on certain products and services that have a significant impact on the environment. Other legislative initiatives with an impact on industrial sustainability in the environmental protection segment are car taxation and waste taxes.

We appreciate that the steps taken by the EU have set out significant courses of action on reducing industrial environmental impacts, with the effect of internalizing the external costs of activities that affect the environment and stimulating more environmentally sustainable behaviour within the EU.

The **SDG9.8 model** of European industrial sustainability from the perspective of the SDG9VTAXT indicator (road transport-related tax revenues as a percentage of total environmental tax revenues) is characterized by the significant influence of environmental taxes and gross domestic product. Gross domestic product per capita is the most important factor in determining transport tax revenues as a percentage of total environmental tax revenues. Malta, Denmark, Austria and Ireland rank first in Europe. Estonia, Lithuania, Luxembourg, Poland, Slovakia and Slovenia are at the bottom of the European ranking in terms of road transport-related tax revenues.

European public policy on revenues from road transport-related charges aims both to generate funds to finance transport infrastructure and services and to promote sustainable and resource-efficient mobility (Anthony Jnr, 2023; European Investment Bank, 2022; Feldman, 2023; Pata et al., 2024). To this end the EU has implemented Eurovignette, tolls, transit charges, pollution charges and congestion charges (Takman & Gonzalez-Aregall, 2024). The EU is also pursuing an active policy for the use of environmentally friendly vehicles by applying exemptions from taxes and charges for non-polluting vehicles. Another strategic direction is the harmonization of road taxes and charges between countries in order to ensure non-discriminatory treatment of hauliers. The Eurovignette Directive (European Union, 2022) establishes the framework for road infrastructure charging in the EU. Member States may levy road user charges for heavy goods vehicles on the basis of distance travelled, pollution emissions or other relevant criteria. Member States may also introduce tolls and transit charges for motor vehicles using their road network. Another category used to reduce negative environmental impacts and manage congestion in cities is additional charges for vehicles emitting high levels of pollution or for access to areas with traffic restrictions. The EU and Member States offer tax incentives or other advantages for low- or zero-emission vehicles, such as electric or hydrogen-powered cars (exemptions from road tolls or tax rebates for owners of green vehicles) (Gil Ribeiro & Silveira, 2024; Pfaffenbichler et al., 2024). The EU encourages the harmonization of road transport taxes and charges between Member States to ensure fair and non-discriminatory treatment for hauliers across Europe.

We appreciate that in the area of pollution taxation, public policies are coherent in ensuring adequate financing of road transport infrastructure and promoting sustainable and efficient mobility within the EU.

The **SDG9.9 model** of European industrial sustainability in terms of the SDG9AOF (Official Development Assistance) indicator is significantly influenced by gross domestic product and the percentage of personnel engaged in R&D, highlighting the importance of R&D in promoting sustainability. Sweden, Luxembourg, Denmark and the Netherlands rank first in Europe in terms of Official Development Assistance. At the bottom are Cyprus, Croatia, Latvia, Romania, Bulgaria, Slovakia and Poland.

Official Development Assistance (ODA) (OECD, 2025a) is the financial and technical contributions provided by developed countries to promote economic development and poverty reduction in developing countries. The EU and its Member States have specific public policies on ODA that are consistent with their international development objectives and global commitments (European Council, 2024; Hoekman & Shingal, 2024). The EU and its Member States are committed to supporting the implementation of the United Nations 2030 Agenda for Sustainable Development and the 17 SDGs (Krasodomska et al., 2023; Megyesiova et al., 2023; Ricciolini et al., 2024). This commitment is reflected in their ODA policy, which is geared towards achieving these goals in partner countries. European public policies in the field of ODA promote alignment with the priorities and needs of recipient countries, respecting the principles of national ownership and development cooperation (Hoekman & Shingal, 2024; Smolaga & Zajaczkowski, 2025). This includes supporting national development plans, addressing specific poverty and development problems, and promoting human rights and social welfare. The European authorities aim to improve the effectiveness and coherence of ODA, ensuring that resources are used optimally and that development programmes are coherent with each other and with other relevant policies and initiatives such as trade, migration or climate change. We consider that in terms of Official Development Assistance, European policies adequately cover the case studies addressed contributing to better sustainable development in Europe.

The principal original contribution to the field of industrial sustainability consists in the development, through linear regression techniques, of an industrial sustainability function derived from the equal weighting of the significance levels of the constructed models; this function is formally presented in equation (SEI).

$$\begin{aligned} SEI = {} & 0.139 * \widehat{PIBloc_{ODD9.1}} + 0.137 * \widehat{CHCDI_{ODD9.2}} + 0.137 * \widehat{PCDI_{ODD9.3}} \\ & + 0.146 * \widehat{CBV_{ODD9.4}} + 0.13 * \widehat{CMPR_{ODD9.5}} + 0.122 * \widehat{DTHM_{ODD9.6}} \\ & + 0.03 * \widehat{TAXM_{ODD9.7}} + 0.036 * \widehat{VTAXT_{ODD9.8}} + 0.123 * \widehat{AOF_{ODD9.9}} \end{aligned} \quad (17.1)$$

The industrial sustainability function demonstrates that at Member State level there are co-occurrences of sustainability in the industrial development segment in correlation with the policy of reducing the environmental impact of industry (C1, promoting green industry). Within this component the indicators development of environmental technologies and environmental taxes as percentage of GDP are important. The second component is aimed at innovation in industry (C2, research-development-innovation) and has as included variables R&D personnel, patent applications filed at the European Patent Office, and gross domestic expenditure on research and innovation. The third component is oriented towards sustainable economic development; in this category are included GDP per capita indicators, road transportation taxes and Official Development Assistance as percentage of GNI (C3, sustainable industrial development).

Europe's economic and social development will be influenced by digitalization and technologies. The industrial revolution will lead to the integration of different technologies with an impact on the workforce. Rapid economic concentration and new technical solutions around the world are creating "innovation" economies. Public authorities and policymakers need to invest in long-term planning and engage in dialogue with stakeholders to prepare for transitions and shape policies effectively.

We designed the new European industrial sustainability impact model from the perspective of the evolution of R&D expenditure in the industry with the help of panel data analysis, highlighting the need to promote investment in R&D personnel and to develop effective training programmes to support the transition towards a greener and more innovative industry.

The analysis of Romania's industrial efficiency was carried out using the DEA method, which revealed that Romania ranks last among European countries in terms of industrial efficiency. At the same time, because of the analysis, proposals were made to improve the industrial efficiency objectives in terms of promoting research and development, stimulating the increase in the number of patents filed at the European Patent Office, and accelerating economic growth by at least 50% of GDP per capita based on viable industrial development strategies. Other inefficiencies identified from an industrial development perspective are the development of environmental technologies and the improvement of Official Development Assistance, which should be directed towards projects to promote innovation and sustainability in industry.

The analysis in this chapter allowed the formulation of the strategy for industrial sustainability in Romania based on the hierarchical cluster analysis of the SDG9 indicators by the Baverage method using the proximity matrix of industrial sustainability for Romania for the period 2010–2021 and the multi-annual cluster links based on the real Euclidean distances calculated in the proximity matrix (Table 17.1), thus determining 11 clusters for the analysed period.

The matrix reflects the actual distances between the annual values for the industrial sustainability indicators (SDG8PIBloc, SDG9DTHM, SDG9AOF, SDG9TAXM, SDG9VTAXT, SDG9CMPR, SDG9CBV, SDG9PCDI and SDG9CHCDI) for the period 2010–2021. In this context, the differences in the values of the indicators by year suggest annual differences in the industrial policies adopted in Romania. It can be observed that the largest differences are in the period 2014–2021, this period corresponding to the transition to Industry 5.0. Another significant period is the period 2010–2012, in which the Romanian economy went through a deep economic crisis reflected in the industrial sector through multiple bankruptcies and reorganizations of industrial production companies. Based on the matrix we observe the distinct influence of the pandemic that although it has quantified a smaller Euclidean distance between 2019 and 2021 nevertheless it seems significant in terms of industrial effects. The dendogram of industrial sustainability in Romania has been realized and is presented in Fig. 17.1.

We propose the Industrial Sustainability Strategy for Romania from the perspective of the transition to green industry. Increasing R&D spending on green technologies and improving the conditions of social responsibility of industry personnel will contribute to increasing industrial sustainability by accelerating the use of the circular economy and by streamlining the work of the Official Development Assistance offices. The forecasts for the implementation of the industrial strategy for Horizon 2030 argue for the following effects of its implementation: industrial decarbonization, circular economy, research and development, corporate social responsibility, development of environmental technologies, Official Development Assistance, patents, and transportation infrastructure.

Romania will continue to adopt low-carbon production technologies with a significant transition to renewable energy sources. Increased investment in carbon capture and storage and modernization of industrial infrastructure to reduce energy consumption and emissions will have the

**Table 17.1** Industrial proximity matrix in Romania (based on real Euclidean distances)

| *Years* | *2010* | *2011* | *2012* | *2013* | *2014* | *2015* | *2016* | *2017* | *2018* | *2019* | *2020* | *2021* |
|---|---|---|---|---|---|---|---|---|---|---|---|---|
| 2010 | 0 | 108439 | 80457 | 76168 | 92664 | 164177 | 173367 | 142540 | 176625 | 262069 | 307715 | 323443 |
| 2011 | 108439 | 0 | 27983 | 32273 | 15786 | 55740 | 64932 | 34130 | 68205 | 153636 | 199279 | 215007 |
| 2012 | 80457 | 27983 | 0 | 4290 | 12210 | 83719 | 92910 | 62089 | 96173 | 181613 | 227258 | 242986 |
| 2013 | 76168 | 32273 | 4290 | 0 | 16497 | 88009 | 97199 | 66376 | 100461 | 185901 | 231547 | 247275 |
| 2014 | 92664 | 15786 | 12210 | 16497 | 0 | 71513 | 80703 | 49880 | 83964 | 169405 | 215050 | 230779 |
| 2015 | 164177 | 55740 | 83719 | 88009 | 71513 | 0 | 9193 | 21668 | 12522 | 97897 | 143539 | 159267 |
| 2016 | 173367 | 64932 | 92910 | 97199 | 80703 | 9193 | 0 | 30844 | 3469 | 88704 | 134348 | 150076 |
| 2017 | 142540 | 34130 | 62089 | 66376 | 49880 | 21668 | 30844 | 0 | 34085 | 119530 | 165179 | 180907 |
| 2018 | 176625 | 68205 | 96173 | 100461 | 83964 | 12522 | 3469 | 34085 | 0 | 85447 | 131097 | 146825 |
| 2019 | 262069 | 153636 | 181613 | 185901 | 169405 | 97897 | 88704 | 119530 | 85447 | 0 | 45652 | 61379 |
| 2020 | 307715 | 199279 | 227258 | 231547 | 215050 | 143539 | 134348 | 165179 | 131097 | 45652 | 0 | 15729 |
| 2021 | 323443 | 215007 | 242986 | 247275 | 230779 | 159267 | 150076 | 180907 | 146825 | 61379 | 15729 | 0 |

Source: Author

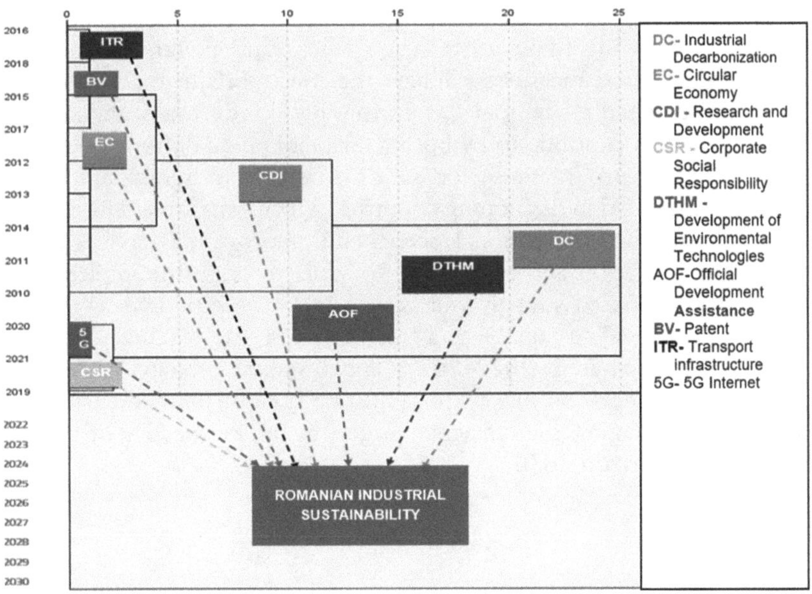


**Fig. 17.1** Cluster dendogram of Romanian industrial sustainability from the perspective of the proposed strategy. Source: Author

impact of reducing industry's carbon footprint, improving air quality and aligning with the objectives of the Paris Agreement on climate change.

The focus on resource reuse will increase recycling and streamline business models based on the circular economy, with an impact on minimizing industrial waste, increasing resource efficiency, and supporting innovation in the creation of sustainable materials and processes.

Increased budget allocations for R&D will allow the development of sustainable and innovative technologies. This will improve Romania's innovation capabilities, increase the number of patents, and boost the competitiveness of Romanian products and services on international markets.

Companies will increasingly integrate corporate social responsibility practices, particularly in areas related to the environment and ethics, which will have the effect of improving the relationship between corporations and local communities, contributing to sustainable social and economic development.

Increased investment in technologies will minimize negative environmental impacts, including waste management and pollution reduction technologies. These measures will have the effect of reducing dependence on fossil fuel-based technologies, contributing to industrial sustainability.

Romania will continue to be both a recipient and a donor in development assistance programmes, focusing on improving infrastructure and industrial capacities in developing countries, which will increase Romania's influence on the international scene and improve bilateral relations through cooperation and assistance. Romania through the implementation of this proposed strategy will get closer to the proposed targets for ensuring industrial sustainability as forecasted by the National Research and Innovation Strategy 2022–2027. The proposed strategy can be used by the national decision-makers for adjusting the initiated industrial policies and recalculating the efficiency targets in the perspective of the 5G Strategy for Horizon 2030.

## Conclusions

The analysis carried out in this chapter confirms that Romania faces major structural challenges in achieving the sustainable industrial development goals set out in SDG9, requiring a strategic recalibration to converge towards average European performance. The econometric models developed highlighted the decisive role of investment in research and development, specialized human capital and technological innovation in industrial sustainability, emphasizing that the high performance of the reference countries (Luxembourg, Germany, Sweden, Denmark) is associated with a positive correlation between R&D and economic, technological and environmental indicators.

The results show that Romania consistently ranks low in European rankings for key indicators such as GDP per capita, gross expenditure on research and development, number of patents, development of environmental technologies, and Official Development Assistance, which indicates a lack of industrial competitiveness and insufficient use of resources for innovation. Furthermore, high consumption of raw materials and low environmental taxes relative to GDP confirm the need for an accelerated transition to resource- and emission-intensive production models.

The proposed industrial sustainability strategy for Romania—based on cluster analysis and the industrial proximity matrix—recommends increasing investment in green technologies, strengthening research and development capacities, stimulating patenting, and widely adopting the circular economy. Its implementation by 2030 would have tangible positive effects: decarbonization of industry, increased resource efficiency, enhanced competitiveness of Romanian products, strengthened corporate social responsibility, and improved position of Romania in international cooperation and development assistance networks.

In conclusion, achieving a high level of industrial sustainability requires not only technical and investment measures, but also a coherent public policy vision, aligned with European strategies, and capable of integrating the economic, technological, social and environmental dimensions into a competitive and resilient industrial model in the long term.

## References

Al-lami, A., Török, A., Alatawneh, A., & Alrubaye, M. (2025). Future energy consumption and economic implications of transport policies: A scenario-based analysis for 2030 and 2050. *Energies, 18*(12). https://doi.org/10.3390/en18123012

Angori, G., Marzocchi, C., Ramaciotti, L., & Rizzo, U. (2024). A patent-based analysis of the evolution of basic, mission-oriented, and applied research in European universities. *The Journal of Technology Transfer, 49*(2), 609–641. https://doi.org/10.1007/s10961-023-10001-5

Anthony Jnr, B. (2023). Sustainable mobility governance in smart cities for urban policy development – A scoping review and conceptual model. *Smart and Sustainable Built Environment, 14*(3), 649–671. https://doi.org/10.1108/SASBE-05-2023-0109

Bădîrcea, R. M., Doran, N. M., Manta, A. G., Cercel Zamfirache, C., Jianu, E., & Gheorghe, A. (2025). Bridging regional development and sustainability: The contribution of the European Regional development fund to sustainable development goals progress in the EU. *Sustainability, 17*(8). https://doi.org/10.3390/su17083665

Baldassarre, B., & Carrara, S. (2025). Critical raw materials, circular economy, sustainable development: EU policy reflections for future research and innovation. *Resources, Conservation and Recycling, 215*, 108060. https://doi.org/10.1016/j.resconrec.2024.108060

Belanová, K., Ochotnický, P., & Sivák, R. (2025). Innovation performance of EU countries in context of R&D: R&D trap risk in Slovakia? *Journal of Innovation and Entrepreneurship, 14*(1), 59. https://doi.org/10.1186/s13731-025-00533-5

Beltran, L. D., Delgado, M. C., Campoy-Muñoz, P., & Rodero-Cosano, M. L. (2025). Competitiveness in structurally similar regions: Why do they perform differently?

*Journal of the Knowledge Economy, 16*(1), 1183–1203. https://doi.org/10.1007/s13132-024-01855-7

Benoit, F., Karvounaraki, A., & Stevenson, A. (2025). *Shaping the future EU R & D investments explained.* https://doi.org/10.2777/3117336

Burinskienė, A., Lingaitienė, O., & Byčenkaitė, G. (2025). Dynamics of trade of recycled raw materials and the connection with the circular economy. *Discover Sustainability, 6*(1), 680. https://doi.org/10.1007/s43621-025-01502-4

Caglar, A. E., & Yavuz, E. (2023). The role of environmental protection expenditures and renewable energy consumption in the context of ecological challenges: Insights from the European Union with the novel panel econometric approach. *Journal of Environmental Management, 331*, 117317. https://doi.org/10.1016/j.jenvman.2023.117317

Chivot, E. (2023). Enhancing Europe's sustainability through innovation and technology. *European View, 22*(2), 243–254. https://doi.org/10.1177/17816858231204730

Cifuentes-Faura, J. (2022). European Union policies and their role in combating climate change over the years. *Air Quality, Atmosphere and Health, 15*(8), 1333–1340. https://doi.org/10.1007/s11869-022-01156-5

Crespy, A., & Munta, M. (2023). Lost in transition? Social justice and the politics of the EU green transition. *Transfer: European Review of Labour and Research, 29*(2), 235–251. https://doi.org/10.1177/10242589231173072

Distefano, T., Lodi, L., & Biggeri, M. (2024). Material footprint and import dependency in EU27: Past trends and future challenges. *Journal of Cleaner Production, 472*, 143384. https://doi.org/10.1016/j.jclepro.2024.143384

Dogan, E., Hodžić, S., & Šikić, T. F. (2023). Do energy and environmental taxes stimulate or inhibit renewable energy deployment in the European Union? *Renewable Energy, 202*, 1138–1145. https://doi.org/10.1016/j.renene.2022.11.107

Dragomir, V. D., & Dumitru, M. (2024). The state of the research on circular economy in the European Union: A bibliometric review. *Cleaner Waste Systems, 7*, 100127. https://doi.org/10.1016/j.clwas.2023.100127

Erdoğdu, A., Dayi, F., Yanik, A., Yildiz, F., & Ganji, F. (2025). Innovative solutions for combating climate change: Advancing sustainable energy and consumption practices for a greener future. *Sustainability, 17*(6). https://doi.org/10.3390/su17062697

European Commission. (2021). *Revision of the energy taxation directive.* https://taxation-customs.ec.europa.eu/taxation/excise-taxes/revision-energy-taxation-directive_en

European Commission. (2023a). *A European green deal.* https://commission.europa.eu/strategy-and-policy/priorities-2019-2024/european-green-deal_en

European Commission. (2023b). *About the EU ETS*. https://climate.ec.europa.eu/eu-action/eu-emissions-trading-system-eu-ets/about-eu-ets_en

European Commission. (2023c). *Circular economy action plan*. https://environment.ec.europa.eu/strategy/circular-economy-action-plan_en

European Commission. (2024a). *European regional development fund*. https://ec.europa.eu/regional_policy/funding/erdf_en

European Commission. (2024b). *Horizon Europe*. https://research-and-innovation.ec.europa.eu/funding/funding-opportunities/funding-programmes-and-open-calls/horizon-europe_en

European Commission. (2025a). *Digital connectivity in Romania*. https://digital-strategy.ec.europa.eu/en/policies/digital-connectivity-romania

European Commission. (2025b). *Erasmus+ programme guide*. https://erasmus-plus.ec.europa.eu/programme-guide/part-b/key-action-2/partnerships-cooperation

European Commission. (2025c). *European research area*. https://research-and-innovation.ec.europa.eu/strategy/strategy-research-and-innovation/our-digital-future/european-research-area_en

European Commission. (2025d). *Green taxation – In support of a more sustainable future*. https://taxation-customs.ec.europa.eu/archives/other-taxe/green-taxation_en

European Council. (2024). *Official development assistance: The EU and its member states remain the biggest global provider*. https://www.consilium.europa.eu/en/press/press-releases/2024/06/24/official-development-assistance-the-eu-and-its-member-states-remain-the-biggest-global-provider/

European Investment Bank. (2022). *Transport lending policy 2022 – The way forward*. https://www.eib.org/en/publications/eib-transport-lending-policy-2022

European Union. (2022). *Directive (EU) 2022/362 of the European Parliament and of the Council of 24 February 2022 amending Directives 1999/62/EC, 1999/37/EC and (EU) 2019/520, as regards the charging of vehicles for the use of certain infrastructures*. https://eur-lex.europa.eu/eli/dir/2022/362/oj/eng

Eurostat. (2023). *Sustainable development in the European Union Monitoring report on progress towards the SDGs in an EU context 2023 edition*.

Eurostat. (2024). *Gross domestic expenditure on R&D by sector*. https://ec.europa.eu/eurostat/databrowser/view/sdg_09_10/default/table?lang=en

Feldman, O. (2023). Innovative ways for financing transport infrastructure. In A. Woodcock, J. Saunders, K. Fadden-Hopper, & E. O'Connell (Eds.), *Capacity building in local authorities for sustainable transport planning* (pp. 253–278). Springer Nature Singapore. https://doi.org/10.1007/978-981-19-6962-1_14

Firoiu, D., Ionescu, G. H., Cismaş, C. M., Costin, M. P., Cismaş, L. M., & Ciobanu, Ş. C. (2025). Sustainable production and consumption in EU member states: Achieving the 2030 sustainable development goals (SDG 12). *Sustainability, 17*(4). https://doi.org/10.3390/su17041537

García-Velasco Garzás, M., & Ruiz-Fuensanta, M. J. (2025). Analysing the expansion of the circular economy in the European Union: How important is the regional context? *Ecological Economics, 231*, 108560. https://doi.org/10.1016/j.ecolecon.2025.108560

Gil Ribeiro, C., & Silveira, S. (2024). The impact of financial incentives on the total cost of ownership of electric light commercial vehicles in EU countries. *Transportation Research Part A: Policy and Practice, 179*, 103936. https://doi.org/10.1016/j.tra.2023.103936

Hajighasemi, A., Oghazi, P., Aliyari, S., & Pashkevich, N. (2022). The impact of welfare state systems on innovation performance and competitiveness: European country clusters. *Journal of Innovation & Knowledge, 7*(4), 100236. https://doi.org/10.1016/j.jik.2022.100236

Hoekman, B., & Shingal, A. (2024). Development goals, commercial interest and EU aid-for-trade. *World Development, 173*, 106389. https://doi.org/10.1016/j.worlddev.2023.106389

Hool, A., Helbig, C., & Wierink, G. (2024). Challenges and opportunities of the European Critical Raw Materials Act. *Mineral Economics, 37*(3), 661–668. https://doi.org/10.1007/s13563-023-00394-y

Hu, H., & Jernej, P. (2025). Exploring the impact of the belt and road initiative on sustainable development goals 8 and 9: Insights from four European Union countries. *Sustainable Development, n/a*(n/a). https://doi.org/10.1002/sd.70077

Iacob, O. C., Chiotan, R. A., Ganea, O., & Ciobanu, G. (2023). Research funding policies and opportunities in EU countries in the context of new development opportunities. *European Journal of Sustainable Development, 12*(3), 265. https://doi.org/10.14207/ejsd.2023.v12n3p265

Kalaš, B., Mirović, V., Bolesnikov, D., Akadiri, S. S., & Radulescu, M. (2025). Environmental taxes and sustainable development in the EU: A decade of data-driven insights. *System, 13*(7). https://doi.org/10.3390/systems13070503

Kosztyán, Z. T., Kiss, D., & Obermayer, N. (2023). Investigating Erasmus mobility exchange networks with gravity models. *Cogent Social Science, 9*(2), 2253612. https://doi.org/10.1080/23311886.2023.2253612

Krasodomska, J., Zieniuk, P., & Kostrzewska, J. (2023). Reporting on sustainable development goals in the European Union: What drives companies' decisions? *Competitiveness Review: An International Business Journal, 33*(1), 120–146. https://doi.org/10.1108/CR-12-2021-0179

Lamping, M., Batista, P. H. D., Correa, J. I., Hilty, R. M., Kim, D., Slowinski, P. R., & Steinhart, M. (2023). Revisiting the framework for compulsory licensing of patents in the European Union – Reflections on the European Commission's initiative. *GRUR International, 72*(5), 471–482. https://doi.org/10.1093/grurint/ikad029

Megyesiova, S., Dul'ová Spišáková, E., & Gontkovičová, B. (2023). European Union and its progress towards affordable and clean energy in context of the Agenda 2030. *PLoS One, 18*(12), e0291933. https://doi.org/10.1371/journal.pone.0291933

Ministry of Investments and European Projects. (2022). *National research development and innovation plan 2022–2027*. https://oportunitati-ue.gov.ro/en/program/planul-national-de-cercetare-dezvoltare-si-inovare-2022-2027-pncdi-iv/

Munonye, W. C. (2025). Circular economy meets smart energy grids: Designing systems for resource optimization and carbon reduction. *Frontiers in Sustainability, 6*. https://doi.org/10.3389/frsus.2025.1568254

Nowak-Marchewka, K., Osmólska, E., & Stoma, M. (2025). Progress and challenges of circular economy in selected EU countries. *Sustainability, 17*(1). https://doi.org/10.3390/su17010320

OECD. (2023). *Labour and social policies for the green transition: A conceptual framework*. https://doi.org/10.1787/028ffbeb-en

OECD. (2025a). *Official development assistance (ODA)*. https://www.oecd.org/en/topics/official-development-assistance-oda.html

OECD. (2025b). *The circular economy in cities and regions of the European Union*. https://doi.org/10.1787/e09c21e2-en

Orlando, B., Scuotto, V., Cillo, V., & Del Giudice, M. (2025). University-business R&D collaborations and innovation in light of Artificial Intelligence: A new AI-based open innovation paradigm. *The Journal of Technology Transfer*. https://doi.org/10.1007/s10961-025-10231-9

Oyebanji, M. O., & Kirikkaleli, D. (2023). Green technology, green electricity, and environmental sustainability in Western European countries. *Environmental Science and Pollution Research, 30*(13), 38525–38534. https://doi.org/10.1007/s11356-022-24793-w

Paleari, S. (2024). The EU policy on climate change, biodiversity and circular economy: Moving towards a Nexus approach. *Environmental Science & Policy, 151*, 103603. https://doi.org/10.1016/j.envsci.2023.103603

Pata, U. K., Erdogan, S., Karlilar Pata, S., & Kartal, M. T. (2024). Do patents, renewable energies and energy taxes in the transport sector reduce transportation carbon emissions in the European Union? *International Journal of Sustainable Development and World Ecology, 31*(7), 977–988. https://doi.org/10.1080/13504509.2024.2365696

Pfaffenbichler, P., Fearnley, N., Figenbaum, E., & Emberger, G. (2024). Simulating the effects of tax exemptions for plug-in electric vehicles in Norway. *European Transport Research Review, 16*(1), 26. https://doi.org/10.1186/s12544-024-00648-y

Pinyol Alberich, J., Pansera, M., & Hartley, S. (2023). Understanding the EU's circular economy policies through futures of circularity. *Journal of Cleaner Production, 385*, 135723. https://doi.org/10.1016/j.jclepro.2022.135723

Ricciolini, E., Tiralti, A., Paolotti, L., Rocchi, L., & Boggia, A. (2024). Sustainable development according to 2030 agenda in European Union countries: Evidence of the enlargement policy. *Sustainable Development, 32*(3), 1894–1912. https://doi.org/10.1002/sd.2758

Rinaldi, C., Cavicchi, A., & Robinson, R. N. S. (2022). University contributions to co-creating sustainable tourism destinations. *Journal of Sustainable Tourism, 30*(9, SI), 2144–2166. https://doi.org/10.1080/09669582.2020.1797056

Rodríguez-Antón, J. M., Rubio-Andrada, L., Celemín-Pedroche, M. S., & Ruíz-Peñalver, S. M. (2022). From the circular economy to the sustainable development goals in the European Union: An empirical comparison. *International Environmental Agreements: Politics, Law and Economics, 22*(1), 67–95. https://doi.org/10.1007/s10784-021-09553-4

Smolaga, M., & Zajaczkowski, M. (2025). The targeting of ODA by Central and Eastern European EU donors. *Journal of Contemporary European Studies, 33*(2), 653–671. https://doi.org/10.1080/14782804.2024.2385979

Takman, J., & Gonzalez-Aregall, M. (2024). Public policy instruments to promote freight modal shift in Europe: Evidence from evaluations. *Transport Reviews, 44*(3), 612–633. https://doi.org/10.1080/01441647.2023.2279219

Ullrich, H. (2023). Patent dependency under European and European Union patent law – A regulatory gap. *GRUR International, 72*(12), 1107–1124. https://doi.org/10.1093/grurint/ikad109

United Nations. (2023). *The Paris agreement.* https://unfccc.int/process-and-meetings/the-paris-agreement

# Conclusions: Limits of the Scientific Approach and Future Research Directions

## General Conclusions

The book is framed in a broad context of global uncertainty amid the onset of multiple economic, health, environmental, energy and political crises. Our research has shown that this is a hotly debated topic in the literature, particularly in terms of sustainable development models. The research aimed to develop and improve current concepts of sustainable development by adding summarizing components resulting from the process of objective assessment of the phenomenon.

The aim of the research was to model the main Sustainable Development Goals (SDG7, Affordable Clean Energy, SDG8, Decent Work and Growth and SDG9, Industry, Innovation and Infrastructure) in a European context to identify new strategies for Romania's sustainable development. To achieve the research goal, we used an investigative-analytical methodology based on the analysis of descriptive statistics of sustainable development indicators and procedures of hierarchization of the mean distributions by years. In addition, econometric modelling techniques were employed using linear regression and regression statistical significance tests, stationarity and autocorrelation tests. Panel data analysis was analysed to design new models for the impact of energy, economic and industrial sustainability in the European context. We applied the DEA method to analyse the



C. Fortea, *Sustainable Economic Development and the European Green Deal*, https://doi.org/10.1007/978-3-032-10326-0

efficiency of Romania's sustainable development compared to other European Member States.

The objectives were achieved as follows:

O1. Identification of the main stages of sustainable development by global SDGs highlighting the main areas of interest for each goal: From the economic perspective, we found that Goal 1 (No Poverty), Goal 2 (Zero Hunger) and Goal 3 (Health and Well-being) respond to the sustainable improvement of the quality of life, by structuring the SD targets in this area. The mapping of vulnerabilities at the global level revealed that the main global economic problems concern continents such as Africa, Southeast Asia, South America and Oceania. From a technological perspective, we found that Goal 8 (Decent Work and Decent Growth) and Goal 9 (Industry, Innovation and Infrastructure) aim to provide the prerequisites for sustainable economic development. The dynamic analysis of the development targets on Goal 8 revealed that global economic security plays a significant role in sustainable development. In the absence of economic security and under conditions of uncertainty, the situation of the global economy tends to be affected because of interconnection mechanisms and international trade, the case of the 2008 global crisis and the pandemic crisis of 2020–2021 influencing the hypothesis of global vulnerability of the global economy. In the case of Objective 9, it was observed that labour flows and research and development directly influence good sustainable development, with global migration being a by-product of this process. Sustainable social development has been analysed from the perspective of Goals 11, 16 and 17; on this occasion the social problem has been analysed from the demographic and urbanization perspective while social security has been analysed from the perspective of global efforts to ensure these social security limits. As threats under Objective 17, consumer price inflation was analysed as a phenomenon that has the effect of decelerating the global economy. The observations summarized with reference to the social dimension show that today the need for security is widespread in most of the world's population, except for some centralized countries where political security generates social security, but in these countries problems of social injustice are frequently observed. From the perspective of the development of sustainable social equality we analysed Goal 4 (Quality education), Goal 5 (Gender equality) and Goal 10 (Reduced inequalities), finding that the main vulnerabilities of the 163 signatory states of the Paris Agreement stem from the non-uniform approach to education systems and the failure to allocate sufficient funds for education in less developed and underdeveloped countries. From the perspective of sustainable consumption of resources, Goal 6 (Clean water and sanitation), Goal 7 (Clean and affordable energy) and Goal 12 (Responsible consumption and production) were analysed, showing that the issue of clean water is a highly topical one, with more than one third of the global population suffering from poor sanitation due to the quality of drinking water consumed. Another significant issue is the unsustainable consumption of freshwater resources, as observed in Egypt in 2017. Clean energy is also a highly topical issue, both from the perspective of rising consumer prices and the population's access to energy resources in the current geopolitical context. Efforts to promote energy sustainability are complementary to other programmes, such as the Green Deal. The last aspect of the study of sustainability concerns environmental issues, namely Goal 13 (Climate action), Goal 14 (Aquatic life) and Goal 15 (Terrestrial life). Ecosystem degradation and climate change are a major concern for supranational bodies, so achieving environmental sustainability goals is one of the zero priorities of the sustainable development plan.

O2. Identification through literature review of the economic models of sustainable development by chapters of interest on Clean Energy, Decent Work and Growth, and Industry, Innovation and Infrastructure: We presented the synthesis of the economic models of sustainable development on Clean Energy, Decent Work and Growth, and Industry, Innovation and Infrastructure, and thus we found that the general trend is to intensify research efforts when there are triggers of opportunity or vulnerability that could affect the outcome targets proposed by the 2030 Agenda. The patterns identified in the literature are extremely varied and generally capture correlations of sustainable development indicators. Most of the models studied are multiplicative and seasonal models in the case of SDG7, panel or regression multiplicative and forecasting models in the case of SDG8, and neural models, dynamic models and regression models in the case of SDG9. The results obtained by studying the economic models showed that there are some vulnerabilities in their construction, vulnerabilities represented by the partial absence of data, differences in statistical homogeneity between databases, and the frequency of changing uncertainty conditions that affected the quality of the predictions of the proposed models.

O3. Analysis of the sustainable development of the Romanian economy in the European context through the prism of the transition to the sustainability objective Clean Energy and Affordable Energy: The analysis highlighted the fact that Romania is well developed in terms of energy, an aspect highlighted by both the energy sustainability modelling and the energy efficiency analysis of Romania. The main competitive aspects of Romania's energy development are the energy production capacity and the development of renewable energy, which has allowed the reduction of energy prices since 2023.

O4. Determination of energy sustainability models based on the linear regression method. This objective was achieved by designing nine sustainability models based on linear regression functions, the value of the coefficient of determination being significant for the proposed models. The importance plots of the predictors related to the influence exerted on the dependent variable of the nine models were realized and vulnerability plots were designed within the influence models. The results highlight direct and indirect correlations of the dependence with the predictors demonstrating the complexity and interconnections between different aspects of energy sustainability. The models demonstrate that energy sustainability is based on improving Member States' energy independence, reducing the sector's environmental impact (decreasing greenhouse emissions) and increasing the use of renewable energy sources.

O5. Design of two impact models of European energy sustainability using panel data analysis: We have developed two impact models, the energy sustainability impact model by quantifying the correlation balance of energy efficiency on greenhouse gas emissions, and the energy sustainability impact model by quantifying the sectoral sensitivity of energy efficiency on the intensity of air emissions from industry. To determine the type of applicable model, stationarity and co-integration tests were developed and the ARDL model based on the PMG method was selected. The model results showed the complex interconnections between energy policies, economic behaviour and environmental impacts. The first model suggests the need for sustainable energy development through further investments in green technologies and by optimizing fiscal and import policies to encourage greener behaviour for a friendlier and sustainable environment. The impact model of energy sustainability by quantifying the sectoral sensitivity of energy efficiency on the intensity of atmospheric emissions in industry has highlighted the sensitivity of the energy sector on the industrial branch, demonstrating that there are vulnerabilities induced by the development of this sector on the quality of the environment, which turns the sustainability objectives into challenges for the fastest possible implementation of new green technological innovations and ensuring environmental protection against pollution.

O6. Analysis of Romania's energy efficiency compared to European Member States using the DEA method: In terms of energy efficiency using the Pareto energy efficiency diagram, we have shown that Romania is one of the 14 energy-efficient European countries, being the energy efficiency benchmark for the EU and Slovakia. The energy efficiency analysis revealed that there are still significant opportunities to improve energy efficiency in the country. The implementation of appropriate policies and measures could contribute to reducing energy consumption and optimizing the use of energy resources, which would have a positive impact on the environment and the national economy. At the same time, the Romanian government should provide financial and fiscal support for investments in renewable energy and the modernization of buildings, so that these measures become accessible to all citizens. Close cooperation is needed between the public and private sectors to develop and implement advanced energy technologies. By promoting a favourable environment for innovation and investment in the energy sector, Romania can create a competitive and sustainable market which will bring long-term benefits for both the environment and the economy.

O7. Definition of the energy sustainability function: First, the methodology of unit weighting of energy sustainability models was used and the SEN – Energy Sustainability energy sustainability function was developed which demonstrates that at Member State level there are co-occurrences of sustainability in the renewable energy sector development segment in relation to primary energy supply and industrial energy consumption, which means that the achievement of clean energy targets is closely dependent on energy security and sustainable economic development policies. Second, the sustainability of energy sources is correlated with import dependence, the level of income taxation and total primary energy supply. This correlation means that energy security objectives can be achieved if relevant policies are implemented both in terms of energy supply and energy taxation. Third, the energy sustainability function involves the transition to a green economy and the monitoring of emissions at European level, with effects on protecting the environment and combating global warming.

O8. Identification of the main public policies for sustainable energy development: The main public policies identified are policies to promote investments in innovative technologies, facilitate the integration of renewable sources into existing grids, and encourage sustainable consumption. At the same time, we have proposed to stimulate the adoption of energy saving technologies, and to offer energy auditing and policies to improve energy efficiency. On a general level, we believe that the implementation of policies to reduce carbon emissions and the development of the renewable energy sector are timely. As far as energy security is concerned, we believe that efforts to maintain an integrated energy market and reduce dependence on energy imports must continue. Some instruments such as the EU Energy Strategy 2030, the Energy Union, the Energy and Climate Action Plan and the Interconnecting Europe Facility have already produced energy sustainability effects and contribute to the definition of medium-term objectives necessary to achieve integrated energy sustainability.

O9. Designing energy sustainability strategies at Romanian level: At the end of Chap. 3 we identified sustainable development solutions for Romania from the perspective of SDG7. These solutions have been synthesized through the cluster dendogram of Romanian energy sustainability and support the two proposed sustainable development strategies (Energy Sustainable Development Strategy from a climate-neutral perspective and Energy Sustainable Development Strategy through the normalization of energy consumption in agriculture and industry). Implementation of the proposed strategic mix for Horizon 2030 will have the effect of accelerating the transition to a green economy, energy decarbonization, increased renewable energy production, energy efficiency, reduced import dependency, reduced greenhouse gas emissions, and the adoption of green, high-performance technologies.

O10. Analysis of the sustainable development of the Romanian economy in the European context through the prism of the transition to the sustainability objective Economic Growth and Decent Work: We have highlighted the fact that from an economic point of view, based on Romania's accelerated economic growth rate, our country is well positioned in terms of economic sustainability. In terms of Romania's sustainable development, the main positive aspects are good value added in agriculture and services, a gradual reduction in poverty rates, and an increase in GDP per capita.

O11. Determination of economic sustainability models based on the linear regression method: We designed 12 economic sustainability models highlighting the main vulnerabilities of sustainable development based on the weak correlations of the indicators integrated in the 12 linear regressions. We have shown that youth unemployment and in-work poverty rates are elements that should be of concern to the authorities to eliminate the negative medium- and long-term effects induced by these two vulnerabilities. We have also shown that at the economic level, digitalization will have a perpetual effect on economic development, but to achieve an optimal level of sustainable development in the digital economy, it is necessary to improve the population's skills and abilities to use digital technologies. At the same time, it is necessary to promote the attraction of ICT specialists to support the process of technologization and digitalization. The proposed models demonstrate that economic sustainability is based on a combination of factors, of which the efficient use of labour and digital resources together with the development of the circular economy are key drivers of sustainability.

O12. Designing the economic sustainability impact model by quantifying the evolution of growth and decent work factors: Using panel data analysis we have constructed an economic sustainability impact model showing that Internet access and working poverty reduction are important factors for long-term economic growth in the EU. In the short run, adjustments in employment rates and error corrections play a significant role in immediate economic dynamics, indicating the need for continuous monitoring and adjusted interventions to maintain economic stability. At the same time, the results suggest that economic policy at the EU level needs to focus on improving access to technology, increasing the quality and sustainability of jobs, and reducing social inequality. Investments in technology and education, together with labour market reforms, lead to robust economic growth and a better quality of life for the population.

O13. Analysis of Romania's economic efficiency compared to European Member States using the DEA method: Using the DEA method we determined the economic efficiency of Romania, which ranks 20th out of 22 economically efficient Member States. The analysis revealed that Romania is a benchmark of efficiency for the EU and Spain, and the main policy for economic improvement and growth is the development of human resources, to increase the skill level of the labour force and encourage innovation in different fields. The government should also pay more attention to transport and communication infrastructure to ensure better connectivity and access to international markets. By implementing coherent policies and economic development strategies, Romania could improve its efficiency and become more competitive on the European market. In this way, the country could attract more foreign direct investment and stimulate long-term economic growth. It is also important for Romania to diversify its economy and adapt to changes in the global economic environment in order to be more resilient in the face of crises. By promoting entrepreneurship and innovation, the country could realize its potential and become an important player on the European market.

O14. Definition of the economic sustainability function: The economic sustainability function was defined on the basis of the method of unit weighting the significance of economic sustainability models, which demonstrates that at Member State level there are co-occurrences of sustainability in the economic development segment in correlation with the level of social well-being of certain socio-occupational categories (agricultural workers or young people without jobs and without education), this representing the socio-economic vulnerability component 1. The second component aims at sustainable economic development at branch level underpinned by digitization contributing to the economic well-being of Member States by embedding digitization efforts in economic branches with an effect on employment rates. The third component addresses the disparities between countries in terms of gross domestic product and the consumption orientation of the European economy (gross value added in services).

O15. Identification of the main public policies for sustainable economic development: The main public policies for sustainable development have focused on tackling social, environmental and economic challenges in order to achieve appropriate sustainable development. As a result we have formulated public policies on expanding investments in renewable energy and energy efficiency; accelerating circular economy practices; promoting digitization and innovation; improving the quality of education and training; increasing social cohesion and reducing inequalities; implementing green fiscal policies; creating sustainable infrastructure and increasing international cooperation; promoting investments in digital infrastructure, with a focus on the expansion of fibre optic networks and 5G technologies; youth inclusion; and increasing the digital specialization of the population.

O16. The design of the economic sustainability strategy at the Romanian level —realized at the end of Chap. 4—was based on the Beverage method and the economic proximity matrix built on the basis of Euclidean distances between the SDG8 sustainable development indicators over an 11-year period. The economic sustainability cluster dendogram was designed based on a policy mix of investments in digital infrastructure; good fiscal governance practices; digital education and training; community development; smart growth; social cohesion; labour market; poverty risk reduction; and digitization. The economic sustainability for Horizon 2030 is expected to be improved by the implementation of the proposed sustainable development strategy from the perspective of decent work and economic growth for Romania. We believe that by implementing this proposed strategy, Romania will continue to integrate into European and international structures, strengthening its position in the EU. The proposed strategy can be used by national decision-makers to adjust the economic policies initiated and to recalculate the efficiency targets in the light of the National Sustainable Development Strategy for Horizon 2030.

O17. The analysis of the sustainable development of the Romanian economy in the European context through the prism of the transition to the sustainability objective Industry, Innovation and Infrastructure: The analysis in of the sustainable industrial development has revealed that Romania is in last place at European level in chapter 9. The motivations behind this finding are related to the characteristics of Romanian industry, which is insufficiently technologized and energy inefficient and depends to a significant extent on the infusion of imported technology. In this area we have not identified competitive aspects that characterize Romania with other European countries.

O18. Determination of industrial sustainability models based on the linear regression method: Nine industrial sustainability models were developed based on linear regression functions, and the value of the coefficient of determination was significant for the proposed models. The importance plots of the predictors related to the influence exerted on the dependent variable of the nine models were realized and vulnerability plots were designed within the influence models. The results highlight direct and indirect correlations of the dependence, with the predictors demonstrating the complexity and interconnections between different aspects of industrial sustainability. The models demonstrate that industrial sustainability is based on improving innovation and research, reducing the environmental impact of the sector (reducing greenhouse emissions in industry) and promoting responsible resource consumption.

O19. Design of the new European industrial sustainability impact model from the perspective of the evolution of R&D expenditures in the branch with the help of panel data analysis: Using statistical procedures we have developed an industrial sustainability impact model that confirms the urgent need to improve the quantity of R&D allocations supported by an effective training programme, leading to an increase in the number of R&D personnel and the development of innovative solutions to accelerate the transition to Industry 5.0 and green industry.

O20. Analysis of Romania's industrial efficiency compared to European Member States using the DEA method: The analysis of Romania's industrial efficiency compared to European Member States has shown that Romania ranks last in industrial efficiency in Europe. The analysis allowed the formulation of conclusions and policies to reach the threshold of industrial sustainability of Romania, which needs to improve its R&D activity by increasing the number of patents filed at the European Patent Office depending on the country of residence of the applicants/inventors. In addition, economic growth needs to be accelerated as there is currently a shortfall of at least 50% of GDP per capita which needs to increase from €9160 per capita to over €13,700 to ensure efficiency in terms of MDG9. Other inefficiencies in industrial development are the development of environmental technologies and Official Development Assistance, which are real impediments to achieving industrial efficiency. The development of environmental technologies is important for reducing the negative environmental impact of industrial activities. Official Development Assistance should also be directed towards projects that promote innovation and sustainability in industries, thereby contributing to increased efficiency and reduced carbon emissions. It is important that policymakers recognize the importance of these issues and act accordingly to ensure a sustainable future for global industry. Investment in research and development of green technologies must be a priority to accelerate the transition to a more sustainable industrial environment.

O21. Definition of the industrial sustainability function: The methodology of unit weighting the significance values of the models was used and the SEI sustainability function was developed, which demonstrates that at Member State level there are co-occurrences of sustainability in the industrial development segment in correlation with the policy of reducing the environmental impact of industry. Within this component, the indicators of environmental technology development and environmental taxes as a percentage of GDP are important. The second component targets innovation in industry and has as included variables R&D personnel, patent applications filed at the European Patent Office, and gross domestic expenditure on research and innovation. The third component is geared towards sustainable economic development; in this category are included GDP per capita indicators, road transportation taxes and Official Development Assistance as a percentage of GNI.

O22. Identification of the main public policies for sustainable industrial development: Public policies for industrial development have been formulated which consist in promoting investment in human capital capable of ensuring balanced economic growth and access to resources for future generations. Public policies must consider energy and climate change, the promotion of innovation research and the circular economy, as well as social inclusion and employment, the promotion of a more efficient and sustainable use of natural resources, and the reduction of negative environmental impacts. Research has shown that sustainable development has an integrated character such that progress in one sector is necessary for the development of the other sectors and progress in the other two objectives is necessary for the achievement of one objective. In general, sustainable development is the inter-regional prerogative of the EU area, being sensitive to spatiotemporal changes induced by vulnerabilities common to EU Member States. However, if some vulnerabilities are regional in nature, they manifest a regional contagion effect spreading in the time interval $t + 1$, $t + 2$ to other European regions at least neighbouring the base region. In Romania, the contagion effect was generally positive, with an improvement in economic and energy sustainability parameters under the impact of European regulations and European funding. In industry, the lack of reforms and weak, non-visionary management did not allow the contagion effect to manifest its beneficial contribution, Romania remaining the most inefficient industry in Europe.

O23. Designing Romania's industrial sustainability strategy: In summarizing Chap. 5 we have identified sustainable development solutions from the perspective of SDG9. These focused on a mix of policies on industrial decarbonization; scaling up the circular economy; intensifying R&D; corporate social responsibility; developing environmental technologies; providing Official Development Assistance; accelerating patenting; improving transport infrastructure; and transitioning to Industry 5.0. The Industrial Sustainability Cluster Dendrogram highlighted the effects of the proposed new sustainability strategy for Horizon 2030.

## Research Limitations

The limitations of the research are the relatively recent period for which consolidated European-level data on sustainable development indicators are available, the fact that analysis could not be carried out before 2010 due to lack of sufficient data for all Member States, and the fact that for 2022 there is still no complete reporting from all Member States on sustainable development indicators for Sustainable Development Goal 7, Sustainable Development Goal 8 and Sustainable Development Goal 9, so that the results for 2022 in the development of strategies have been predicted. Another limitation of the research is that for new impact models based on panel data analysis, there is a risk of omitting variables that influence outcomes but are not available or not measured in the dataset, which may lead to inconsistent estimates.

## Future Research Directions

Future research directions consist in further adjusting the proposed strategies following the monitoring of the evolution of sustainability indicators for Sustainable Development Goal 7, Sustainable Development Goal 8 and Sustainable Development Goal 9 and extending the framework of the analysis by including a wider range of indicators in the correlative modelling of sustainability functions. Another research direction consists in making extended forecasts for the 2050 horizon of the evolution of the development of Romanian economic sustainability in the European context.

# Index





C. Fortea, *Sustainable Economic Development and the European Green Deal*, https://doi.org/10.1007/978-3-032-10326-0